KARL MARX
FREDERICK ENGELS

Volume
39

MARX AND ENGELS: 1852-55

INTERNATIONAL PUBLISHERS

NEW YORK

This volume has been prepared jointly by Lawrence & Wishart Ltd., London, International Publishers Co. Inc., New York, and Progress Publishers, Moscow, in collaboration with the Institute of Marxism-Leninism, Moscow.

Editorial commissions:
GREAT BRITAIN: E. J. Hobsbawm, Nicholas Jacobs, Martin Milligan, Ernst Wangermann.
USA: James E. Jackson, Louis Diskin, Betty Smith, Philip S. Foner, Leonard B. Levenson, William W. Weinstone.
USSR: for Progress Publishers—N. P. Karmanova, V. N. Sedikh, M. K. Shcheglova; for the Institute of Marxism-Leninism—P. N. Fedoseyev, L. I. Golman, A. I. Malysh, M. P. Mchedlov, A. G. Yegorov.

Library of Congress Cataloging in Publication Data

Marx, Karl, 1818-1883.
    Karl Marx, Frederick Engels: collected works.

    1. Socialism—Collected works. 2. Economics—Collected works. I. Engels, Friedrich, 1820-1895. Works. English. 1975. II. Title.
HX. 39.5 A16 1975   335.4   73-84671
ISBN 0-7178-0539-5 (v. 39)

Printed in the Union of Soviet Socialist Republics in 1982

Contents

KARL MARX AND FREDERICK ENGELS
LETTERS
January 1852-December 1855

1852

1853

1855

APPENDICES

NOTES AND INDEXES

Contents

ILLUSTRATIONS

Translated by

PETER and BETTY ROSS

Preface

Volume 39 of the *Collected Works* of Marx and Engels contains their letters to each other and to third persons from 1852 to 1855.

The letters in this volume give us a glimpse of the creative methods of Marx and Engels, the background to their theoretical writings from 1852 to 1855, and of the genesis of many of their theories. These letters cover the period of political reaction that descended on Europe with the defeat of the 1848-49 revolution. From 1852 to 1855 fairly substantial changes took place in the world's economic and political life. The economic boom that had begun at the end of the 1840s in Europe proved unstable. There were already signs, in 1853, of another economic crisis that came to a head in 1857 and reached world dimensions for the first time. The Crimean War broke out in 1853, and this substantially changed the distribution of political forces on the Continent and influenced the internal development of a number of leading European powers.

The economic and political processes that took place in this period did much to determine the nature of the scientific and practical activities undertaken by Marx and Engels. From 1851 their main objectives were the further development of economic theory and research. Marx's scientific studies in this field were temporarily interrupted in 1852, when he and Engels concentrated on the theoretical generalisation of the results of the revolution, on the struggle against police persecution of members of the Communist League, and on the unmasking of the divisive activities of the sectarian elements in the League and the pseudo-revolutionary pronouncements of various petty-bourgeois refugee groups. From 1853 to 1855, Marx and Engels followed with intense and unflagging interest the development of the conflict over the so-called Eastern Question and the course of the Crimean War. Throughout all these years, as in the previous period, they were both still principally concerned with the struggle for the proletarian party, for the organisational and ideological unity and education of the proletarian revolutionaries, and for the preservation and development of the proletariat's international connections.

In the personal lives of Marx and Engels, these years were among the most difficult. The harsh privations of life in emigration cost Marx and his wife Jenny the lives of two of their children, the one-year-old Franziska and the eight-year-old Edgar. Extremely difficult conditions constantly undermined Marx's health. Engels at this period was forced to give much of his time to commerce, which compelled him to renounce many research plans; however, this work provided a living not only for himself, but for the Marx family. In addition, as we see from many of their letters, Marx and Engels were preoccupied throughout these years with their comrades and sympathisers living in poverty in emigration or languishing in German prisons.

The letters in this volume, as in Volume 38, reflect the enormous amount of work done by Marx and Engels on the theoretical analysis of the experience of the 1848-49 revolution. During the first months of 1852, Marx wrote one of his outstanding works, *The Eighteenth Brumaire of Louis Bonaparte* (see present edition, Vol. 11). The material in this volume makes it possible to trace clearly the story of the publication as well as of the writing of this work, set down immediately after the counter-revolutionary coup in France on 2 December 1851. In addition, the letters contain an analysis of the processes at work after *The Eighteenth Brumaire* was written, at a time when Louis Bonaparte had consolidated his regime and was preparing to proclaim the Empire (see Engels to Weydemeyer on 30 January, Engels to Marx on 18 March, and Marx to Engels on 23 September 1852).

Marx's letter to Weydemeyer of 5 March 1852 is a very important document that seems directly to continue the theoretical generalisation of *The Eighteenth Brumaire of Louis Bonaparte*. In it, Marx briefly outlined the substance of his revolutionary deductions about the world historical role of the proletariat, the innovation that he introduced into the theory of the classes and the class struggle. 'Now as for myself, I do not claim to have discovered either the existence of classes in modern society or the struggle between them. Long before me, bourgeois historians had described the historical development of this struggle between the classes, as had bourgeois economists their economic anatomy. My own contribution was 1. to show that the *existence of classes* is merely bound up with *certain historical phases in the development of production*; 2. that the class struggle necessarily leads to the *dictatorship of the proletariat*; 3. that this dictatorship itself constitutes no more than a transition to the *abolition of all classes* and to a *classless society*' (see this volume, pp. 62-65). Noting the enormous theoretical value of this letter, Lenin wrote: 'In these words, Marx succeeded in expressing with striking clarity, first, the chief and radical difference between his theory and that of the foremost and most profound thinkers of the bourgeoisie; and, secondly, the essence of his theory of the state' (V. I. Lenin, *Collected Works*, Vol. 25, p. 411).

The correspondence contains much interesting information about the writing of Engels' work, *Revolution and Counter-Revolution in Germany* (see present edition, Vol. 11), in which Engels examines the prerequisites, nature and motive forces of the 1848-49 revolution in the German states from the standpoint of historical materialism. The letters in this volume show clearly how much creative contact there was between Marx and Engels in the composition of this work (see, for instance, Engels' letters to Marx of 29 January and 29 April, and Marx's letter to Engels of 18 February 1852).

A large part in the life of Marx and Engels in 1852 and the first half of 1853 was taken up by practical revolutionary activity. In an atmosphere reflecting the general decline of the revolutionary movement, Marx and Engels had to wage an intensive struggle against ideas alien to the working class and against revolutionary adventurism; they also had to overcome the pusillanimity, apathy and ignorance of certain members of the movement.

Of particular interest in this connection is the correspondence with Weydemeyer and Cluss, Communist League members who had emigrated to the USA. Marx and Engels supported in every way the aspirations of these two men to organise the publication in the USA of a German-language weekly, *Die Revolution*. Marx's *The Eighteenth Brumaire of Louis Bonaparte* and Engels' article 'England' (see present edition, Vol. 11) were specially written for it. Seeing contributions to the magazine as an important party task, Marx, as his wife Jenny wrote to Weydemeyer on 13 February 1852, had 'commandeered on your behalf pretty well all available communist quills', that is to say, Wilhelm Wolff, Georg Weerth, Ferdinand Wolff, Ernest Jones, Wilhelm Pieper, Johann Eccarius and Ferdinand Freiligrath (p. 35).

For nearly three years, Cluss and Weydemeyer drew on letters from Marx and Engels when writing their own articles, which were printed in the American and German-American democratic press, and especially in the newspaper *Die Reform,* published in New York (see Marx's letters to Cluss of 17 April, about 14 June, 18 October, mid-November 1853, and others).

In England, Marx and Engels actively assisted and supported the proletarian publications being brought out by Ernest Jones, leader of the Left-wing Chartists. In Ernest Jones's *Notes to the People,* Marx wrote, 'you will find all the day-to-day history of the English proletariat' (see this volume, p. 42). They contributed to *The People's Paper* themselves and induced others to contribute likewise (Eccarius, Pieper, Cluss and their associates), and took part in the actual editorial work (see Marx's letters to Engels of 2 September and 23 September 1852 and 23 November 1853).

The advanced development of capitalist industry in England and its huge working class, together with the revolutionary traditions of Chartism, gave Marx and Engels grounds to assume that conditions existed there for the creation of a mass proletarian party. As their letters show, Marx and Engels helped Jones and other Left-wing Chartist leaders during these years to reorganise the National Charter Association, believing that the struggle for the rebirth of the Chartist movement was vital for the political unification of the proletariat in England. It was only natural that they constantly followed the progress of the strike movement of the English working class (see, for example, Marx's letter to Engels of 30 September 1853).

The struggle for the independence of the working-class movement and its freedom from other class influences was a matter of constant concern to Marx and Engels. They condemned in the strongest terms the shift towards bourgeois radicalism on the part of George Julian Harney, the former Chartist leader, and had a high opinion of the revolutionary firmness of Ernest Jones, who opposed the efforts of the reformists. 'Jones is moving in quite the right direction,' wrote Engels to Marx on 18 March 1852, 'and we may well say that, without our doctrine, he would not have taken the right path' (see this volume, p. 68). When Jones later began vacillating and seemed inclined to make concessions to the petty-bourgeois democrats, Marx reacted with much disapproval (see Marx's letter to Engels of 13 February 1855).

The correspondence reflects the fierce ideological battle fought by Marx and Engels against the bourgeois and petty-bourgeois democrats who were trying to divert the proletarian revolutionaries from the real objectives of the class struggle. Mazzini, Kossuth, Ledru-Rollin and Louis Blanc were all criticised for ignoring the objective economic laws and for their subjectivist approach to crucial decisions, as well as for their extremely limited social programmes and their Bonapartist illusions. Moreover, Marx and Engels firmly rejected the conspiratorial tactics of Mazzini and his adherents (see, in particular, Engels' letter to Marx of 11 February and Marx's letter to Engels of 23 February 1853).

Marx and Engels were implacably hostile to the internal squabbles of the various petty-bourgeois refugee organisations which were turning political activity into careerism and intrigue and were threatening to discredit the revolutionary movement. The letters reveal the background to their joint authorship of the richly comic satirical pamphlet, *The Great Men of the Exile* (see present edition, Vol. 11) in which they denounced the fatuous self-importance and the futile activities of the leaders of the German petty-bourgeois emigration (Kinkel, Ruge, Heinzen, Struve and others).

The founders of Marxism saw a particular danger at this time in the activities of the Willich-Schapper separatist group which had caused a split in the Communist League in 1850. Its pseudo-revolutionary catch-phrases and adventurism brought down police repression on many League members, especially the German workers. Marx wrote angrily to Engels on 30 August 1852: '...from a secure hiding-place, they are playing into the hands of the German governments, especially the Prussian, for the purpose of pseudo-agitation and self-aggrandisement' (p. 169).

The adventurism of the Willich-Schapper group took a particularly dangerous turn, since in 1852 there began in Cologne a trial trumped up by the Prussian police against the communists. This volume (and Volume 38) illustrates Marx's and Engels' struggle, from the very start of the investigation (in May 1851), against the provocatory nature of its preparation and conduct, and against the inhuman treatment of the detainees. Through press agitation and publicity they did all they could to protect the communists from slander and treachery and to unmask the forgeries and irregularities of the Prussian police and court authorities (see, for example, the letters of Marx to Engels of 24 January, Engels to Marx of 28 January, and Marx to Cluss of 7 and about 15 May 1852).

Marx and Engels were particularly active during the trial itself in October and November 1852, when they virtually handled the defence of the accused, supplying the lawyers with the necessary material. A picture of the tremendous work done at the time by Marx, Engels and their comrades in the Communist League is given by a letter from Jenny Marx to Cluss of 30 October 1852, published in the Appendices to this volume. The outstanding contribution to the struggle to expose the Cologne communist trial was Marx's pamphlet, *Revelations Concerning the Communist Trial in Cologne* (see present edition, Vol. 11), the background to which can be traced in the letters in this volume. Attributing great importance to the publication and distribution of this work, which denounced the entire Prussian governmental system, Marx wrote to Cluss on 25 March 1853: '...at the present moment, we could deal our beloved Prussians no more telling blow' (p. 299).

After sentence had been passed in Cologne on the Communist League members, Marx organised, through Cluss, the collection in the USA of money for assistance to the condemned men and their families. On 7 December 1852, sending Cluss a written appeal for the collection of money, Marx wrote: 'Here it is a matter of ... a *definite* party aim whose fulfilment is demanded by the honour of the workers' party' (p. 260).

After the Cologne trial, it became clear that it would be inadvisable to continue, under conditions of reaction, the activities of the Communist League as a relatively narrow illegal organisation. On 19 November 1852, Marx informed Engels that, at his suggestion, a resolution had been passed by the London District of the Communist League on the disbanding of the organisation. After the League had been dissolved, Marx, Engels and their associates continued, in other forms, their activities in welding together the ranks of the proletariat so that the best revolutionary and internationalist traditions of the Communist League should be absorbed and spread by successive generations of participants in the proletarian struggle. Their correspondence, in particular, shows that even during the years after the Communist League ceased to exist, Marx and Engels maintained contact with representatives of the proletarian movement in various countries.

As if summing up what had been achieved, and setting up the targets for the proletarian revolutionaries in the period of reaction and the movement's temporary decline, Engels wrote to

Weydemeyer on 12 April 1853: '...German communism ... has passed its matriculation' (see this volume, p. 308). Engels noted the heightened ideological level of Marx's adherents and their preparedness for new revolutionary battles: '...the Marx party does do a good deal of swotting, and one only has to look at the way the other émigré jackasses snap up this or that new catchword, thereby becoming more bemused than ever, to realise that our party's superiority has increased both absolutely and relatively. As indeed it must, for *la besogne sera rude* [it will be a tough business]' (p. 309). Engels' letter, marking out the line of conduct for the proletarian revolutionaries under the conditions of an expected upsurge in the movement, was an extremely important example of how to decide the tactics of the proletarian party in the bourgeois-democratic revolution.

After the close of the Cologne trial and the publication of *Revelations Concerning the Communist Trial in Cologne,* Marx and Engels once again concentrated their main efforts on theoretical research. Their letters from 1853 to 1855 testify to the scope and variety of their scientific interests. Apart from the works and articles published during these years, several dozen of Marx's notebooks have been preserved with plans, copied passages and notes concerned primarily with economic problems and also with the history of Europe, the Orient and Ancient Rome, the problems of the colonial policy pursued by England and other capitalist states, and so on. Engels began studying the theory of war more intensively, and also world history, philology and other sciences.

The urgent theoretical elaboration of the problems of economics and the criticism of bourgeois political economy were not dictated by scientific interest alone, as Marx had already shown by the mid-40s, but also by the objective demands of arming the revolutionary proletariat ideologically. Economic theory was to introduce the maximum clarity into the understanding of the relationship between labour and capital. Consequently, Engels regarded the completion of Marx's economic research as most urgent. 'You ought to finish your Economy,' he wrote to Marx on 11 March 1853, 'later on, as soon as we have a newspaper, we could bring it out in WEEKLY NUMBERS... This would provide all our by then restored associations with a basis for debate' (p. 293).

In the first half of the 1850s, Marx made important progress in preparing the ground for a revolution in the science of economics—the discovery of the tendencies underlying the capitalist mode of production. However, as is shown by the above-quoted letter from Engels, and also by Marx's letter to Cluss of 15 September 1853 (p. 367), neither Engels nor Marx himself yet realised how much ground had to be covered before the appearance of the first volume of *Capital*.

Meanwhile, the letters in this volume are convincing testimony that certain propositions of Marx's political economy had become known even before the appearance of the first part of *A Contribution to the Critique of Political Economy* and *Capital*. Marx frequently expounded his economic views in his letters to Engels, Lassalle, and also Cluss and Weydemeyer. He endeavoured in this way to arm his associates for the battle of ideas with the petty-bourgeois democrats and their ideologues. For example, in his letter to Weydemeyer of 5 March 1852, already quoted above, in his letter to Engels of 14 June 1853 and in the letters to Cluss of 5 and 18 October 1853, Marx severely criticised the vulgar bourgeois economist Henry Charles Carey, whose views on the 'harmony of classes' in the USA had become fairly widespread by this time. Marx dwelt on certain peculiarities in the development of capitalism in the USA, on its place in the general system of capitalist relations, and on its competitive struggle with English capital and the resulting specific nature of development of American economic thought. Carey's views, wrote Marx, show that 'in the United States bourgeois society is still far too immature for the class struggle to be made perceptible and comprehensible' (p. 62).

Marx notes in his letters the decline of bourgeois political economy, and the marked tendency among the epigones of the English classical school of economists to distort and vulgarise the teachings of Adam Smith and David Ricardo. Comparing the views of Ricardo and Carey on rent and wages, Marx stressed that Carey's attacks on English political economy in the person of Ricardo expressed only Carey's desire to gloss over the contradictions of capitalist production or to prove the possibility of abolishing those contradictions while preserving the foundations of bourgeois society.

Revealing the groundlessness of Carey's claims about the harmony and co-operation of the classes in American society, Marx wrote: 'It is *par trop* [altogether too] naive to suggest that, if the *total product of labour* rises, the three classes among whom it is to be shared will share *equally* in that growth. If profit were to rise by 20%, the workers would have to strike to obtain a 2% rise in WAGES' (p. 384).

Marx's critique of Carey's views in his letters was published by Cluss as an article ('The "Best Paper in the Union" and Its "Best Men" and Political Economists') in the newspaper *Die Reform* (see present edition, Vol. 12, pp. 623-32). It thus became available to a certain section of the American readership. This material of 1852-53 subsequently served Marx as the basis for a more substantial critique of Carey's views and vulgar bourgeois political economy in the *Economic Manuscripts of 1857-1858* and in *Capital.*

Marx invariably passed on to Engels the results of his economic research. Their letters show how closely they followed the economic development of the European countries and America, and how carefully they analysed the statistical material confirming the antagonistic and cyclic nature of capitalist production's development. The elaboration of the problem of crises was of special interest to them, since they associated a new revolutionary upsurge with the end of the prosperous phase and with an inevitable economic decline (see Engels' letter to Marx about this on 24 August 1852 and Marx's letter to Lassalle of 23 January 1855).

From the analysis mainly of English trade and industry, they detected the symptoms of an imminent and inevitable economic crisis which could, under prevailing conditions, serve as a powerful stimulus to the revolutionary movement in Europe (see Engels to Weydemeyer on 27 February 1852, Marx to Engels on 29 January 1853, Engels to Weydemeyer on 12 April 1853, Marx to Cluss on 15 September 1853, and Engels to Marx on 29 September 1853).

Marx and Engels paid great attention to the problems of history. They were stimulated to take up historical research by the desire for a deeper understanding of the processes of social development, especially during the capitalist period, and in order to comprehend the historical factors behind the events and phenomena of their own times. This was important for the development of the correct revolutionary tactics. The letters in the present volume give an idea not only of the range of historical subjects in which Marx and Engels were interested, but of their conclusions and generalisations.

The study of world history enabled Marx and Engels to elucidate certain characteristics in the development of capitalism and also of precapitalist social-economic formations. Thus, dealing with the history of Ancient Rome, Marx disclosed the material causes of the class struggle in ancient society. In his letter to Engels of 8 March 1855, he wrote: 'Internal history resolves itself

PLAINLY into the struggle between small and large landed property, specifically modified, of course, by slavery relations' (p. 527). In his letter to Engels of 27 July 1854, analysing the distinguished French historian Thierry's *Essai sur l'histoire de la formation et du progrès du tiers état* he traces how the elements of the future capitalist system emerged and developed in the bowels of feudalism, and he notes the part played by the struggle of the Third Estate against the feudal aristocracy during the period of transition from feudalism to capitalism. While acknowledging Thierry's merits, Marx points out the limitations of his views, and his inability to understand the material roots of class contradictions or the nature and character of class antagonisms under capitalism. 'Had Mr Thierry read our stuff, he would know that the decisive opposition between bourgeoisie and *peuple* does not, of course, crystallise until the former ceases, as *tiers-état*, to oppose the *clergé* and the *noblesse'* (p. 474). This letter of Marx's is of fundamental importance for pinpointing the general methodological shortcomings in the views common to French bourgeois historians during the Restoration and to bourgeois historiographers in general.

The letter also contains an important formulation on the decisive significance of the alliance between the bourgeoisie and the peasantry in the struggle against feudalism. Lenin laid special emphasis on this idea of Marx's: 'The French bourgeoisie won *when it decided* to go with the peasants' ('Conspectus of "The Correspondence of K. Marx and F. Engels. 1844-1883"', Moscow, 1968, Russian edition, p. 7).

In connection with the revolutionary events in Spain in 1854, Marx studied the history of the revolutionary movement of the Spanish people in order to 'discover exactly the springs behind developments' (p. 480).

On the eve of the Crimean War, when inter-state contradictions became suddenly prominent in Asia Minor and the Balkans, Marx and Engels devoted special attention to analysing the history of Turkey, Persia and the countries of the Arabian peninsula, especially their social and political development, the role of communal landownership, their way of life, culture and religious trends (see Engels to Marx on about 26 May, Marx to Engels on 2 and 14 June, and Engels to Marx on 6 June 1853). These letters illustrate the formation of Marx's and Engels' materialist interpretation of religious movements in the East, showing their connection with the material conditions of life as a result of the transition from the nomadic to the settled life, the changes in trade routes, and so on. The letters in this volume also show the special attention Marx devoted at this time to India, then Great Britain's most important imperial possession.

Studying the history of these countries enabled Marx and Engels to bring out the salient characteristics of their social development. 'The absence of landed property is indeed the key to the whole of the East. Therein lies its political and religious history,' remarked Engels in a letter to Marx of 6 June 1853 (p. 339). In the same letter, he disclosed the reasons for the weak development of private landownership in all the Eastern countries, especially during the Middle Ages: the natural conditions in these countries necessitated the building and maintenance of irrigation works, and this was only possible within the scope of the central authority. 'In the East, the government has always consisted of 3 departments only: Finance (pillage at home), War (pillage at home and abroad), and *travaux publics* [public works], provision for reproduction' (p. 339). Marx used this idea and developed it in his article 'The British Rule in India' (see present edition, Vol. 12). The concentration of considerable means of production in the hands of despotic governments, the closed and isolated position of the village commune, the chief economic and social unit of Asiatic societies— these, concluded Marx and Engels, were behind the more retarded historical development of the Eastern countries when the transition from feudalism to capitalism was being accomplished in the West.

Marx and Engels sharply denounced England's system of colonial domination in India, underlining its destructive consequences. By preserving the worst features of Eastern despotism in the conquered countries, the English had ceased to worry about maintaining irrigation, as a result of which, Engels pointed out, 'Indian agriculture is going to wrack and ruin' (p. 340).

The process by which the colonial and dependent countries were drawn into the orbit of world capitalism led Marx and Engels to the conclusion that there was a deep mutual relationship and mutual dependence between the destiny of the capitalist countries and that of the colonial world. They became increasingly convinced that the proletarian movement in the metropolitan countries could find its own natural ally in the maturing national liberation movement.

During these years, Engels' gifts as military theoretician of the proletarian party came to the fore. He gave great attention to the history of the revolutionary wars of 1848-49, intending to write a book on the subject. 'I should like to have time before the next revolution,' he wrote to Weydemeyer on 12 April 1853, 'to study and describe thoroughly at least the campaigns of 1848 and 1849 in Italy and Hungary' (p. 309). He did not carry out this intention, and this gives all the more significance to his letters to Marx of 6 July 1852, 10 June 1854, and a number of others in which he gives a critical analysis of the military operations of the revolutionary armies in 1848 and 1849. A number of letters contain fundamental observations by Engels on military and military-historical science and its theoreticians, Clausewitz, Napier, Jomini, Willisen, and about the generalship of Napoleon, Wellington and others. Engels outlined his approach to the analysis of military operations and military science in a letter to the editor of *The Daily News*, 30 March 1854. His extensive knowledge of military history and his use of dialectical materialist methodology were demonstrated in his articles for the *New-York Daily Tribune* during the Crimean War. 'Your military articles,' wrote Marx to Engels on 5 January 1854, 'have created a great stir. A rumour is circulating in New York that they were written by General Scott' (p. 407).

Philological studies were always among the scientific interests pursued by Marx and Engels. During these years Marx studied Spanish, reading Calderon and Cervantes in the original. Engels studied the Slavonic (including Russian) and Oriental languages, especially Persian, showing outstanding linguistic abilities. Of considerable interest is Engels' outline of the principles of translation when he was analysing a translation of the first chapter of Marx's *Eighteenth Brumaire of Louis Bonaparte* done from German into English by Wilhelm Pieper (see Engels' letter to Marx of 23 September 1852).

The period from 1852 to 1855 was one of intensive political journalism on the part of Marx and Engels. Their articles provide rich and often witty insights into and valuable analyses of the capitalist world of their times. Their journalistic activity was closely bound up with their theoretical studies. Research helped them to understand the underlying causes of current events, and important theoretical generalisations frequently emerged from articles on specific subjects. This mutual interaction of the various sides of their work is clearly reflected in their correspondence.

A recurrent idea in the letters of Marx and Engels is that of the necessity for using any opportunity during the years of reaction to promote the revolutionary point of view on the most important political questions in order to influence public opinion in the interests of the working class. 'We are not doing our enemies a favour by writting for them. *Tout au contraire* [Quite the contrary].

We could hardly play them a worse trick..." wrote Marx to Cluss on 14 June 1853 (p. 350).

Marx and Engels, who began contributing to the *New-York Daily Tribune* in 1851, continued writing for it in 1852-55. Marx was the official correspondent for the newspaper, but many articles were written at Marx's request by Engels. At first, as can be seen from the letters in this volume, Marx wrote his articles in German and sent them to Engels in Manchester for translation. In January 1853, Marx himself began writing in English. This enabled him to keep his work as correspondent very much up-to-date. From 1853 to 1855, Marx sent to New York nearly every week or twice weekly his own or Engels' articles, devoted to the most topical and varied problems of the time.

The articles by Marx and Engels for this bourgeois newspaper are a model combination of sober analysis and high principles. Frequently, Marx and Engels even managed to publicise ideas opposed to the views of the newspaper's editors (see Marx's letters to Engels about this on 14 June 1853 and 3 May 1854). The articles aroused great interest among the reading public and Marx's services were frequently acknowledged by the newspaper itself (see, for example, Marx's letter to Engels of 26 April 1853).

However, writing for this newspaper, for all its progressiveness, was not easy. The editors treated the articles with scant ceremony, arbitrary interpolations were frequently allowed, and many articles were printed as unsigned leaders. Marx wrote to Engels on 14 December 1853: 'Needless to say, the *Tribune* is making a great splash with your articles, POOR Dana, no doubt, being regarded as their author. At the same time they have appropriated "Palmerston" [Marx's work 'Lord Palmerston'], which means that, for 8 weeks past, Marx-Engels have virtually constituted the EDITORIAL STAFF of the *Tribune*' (see this volume, p. 404). Marx frequently protested against these irregularities (see Marx to Engels on 2 November 1853, 5 January, and 22 April 1854).

From the end of December 1854, a great deal of Marx's journalistic writing went on contributions to the German *Neue Oder-Zeitung*, one of the few German opposition papers to continue appearing during the years of the reaction. The invitation to contribute to this newspaper gave Marx and Engels the chance of direct contact with the German public, including the proletarian readership. A description of the *Neue Oder-Zeitung* is contained in Marx's letter to Moritz Elsner, the editor, on 11 September 1855: 'Considering the difficult circumstances and the limited space at your disposal, your paper is, in my opinion, edited with great skill and tact, and in such a way that the intelligent reader may read between the lines' (p. 553).

The letters show the extent of Marx's and Engels' creative rapport and day-to-day collaboration. For instance, the details on the activities of the Aberdeen coalition cabinet as given in Marx's letter to Engels of 31 January 1855, were used by Engels for his article 'The Late British Government' (see present edition, Vol. 13). They often edited each other's articles. Engels frequently wrote dispatches instead of Marx, who was busy with urgent party matters (for instance, during the period of the Cologne trial) or was unable to work owing to illness or domestic problems.

In their letters, Marx and Engels paid much attention to England's economic and political position, to describing the various classes of English society and to the struggle of the political parties. Acknowledging that the English political system was at that time more progressive than those of other European countries, Marx nevertheless unmasked the myth of England as a bulwark of constitutional freedoms and civic equality. He tried to show the real class nature of the English constitutional monarchy—the oligarchic domination, tricked out in parliamentary forms, of the landed aristocracy and the bourgeoisie. In a series of letters, Marx stressed the anti-democratic nature of the English electoral system, which deprived the majority of the people of voting rights (see, for example, Marx's letter to Cluss of 20 July 1852).

As far back as 1852, Marx had detected signs of crisis in the English oligarchic system of government—a system which helped the ruling classes give their domination the semblance of free rivalry between two political parties, the Whigs and the Tories. From the formation of the Aberdeen coalition government at the end of 1852 until its fall in 1855, Marx and Engels observed the disintegration of these old bourgeois-aristocratic parties of the ruling oligarchy. Marx's letter to Cluss on 20 July 1852 and one from Engels to Weydemeyer on 12 April 1853 developed the idea that the reform of the state system had become urgently necessary and that the crisis of the existing political parties could be overcome only 'from without by the pressure of the masses' and that it would 'no longer be possible to govern England without considerably extending the *pays légal* [franchise]' (pp. 136 and 306-07). In this way, Marx and Engels drew attention to the fact that the English working class, despite the decline of its political activities in the first half of the 1850s in comparison with the period of Chartism at its height, was stepping into the arena of the country's political life as a force without whose participation no progressive changes would be possible.

Marx and Engels showed great interest in the economic and political development of France because they set great store by the revolutionary traditions of the French people and the French working class and did not lose their faith in its vigour and heroism. They foresaw the dangerous consequences for the French and for the whole European proletariat in the consolidation of the Bonapartist dictatorship. The letters disclose the essence of the anti-popular regime of the Second Empire and note the most characteristic feature of Bonapartism—the combination of the traditional policy of crude police and military terror towards the oppressed classes with broad demagogy in social and national questions both in home and foreign policy. The correspondence gives a vivid picture of the stock exchange machinations and speculative ventures of the bourgeoisie during the Second Empire, the corruption and adventurism in the country's economic life as well as in government circles. In 1853, Marx and Engels had already predicted a short life for French industrial 'prosperity', stressing that the government's policy would inevitably plunge the French economy into chaos. They noted with delight the awakening dissatisfaction with the Bonapartist regime on the part of the broad masses and forecast the inevitable collapse of Napoleon III's empire (see Engels to Weydemeyer on 12 April and to Marx on 26 April 1853; Marx to Engels on 12 October 1853 and to Elsner on 8 November 1855).

The main power which was destined to play a decisive role in the struggle with the Bonapartist regime was, in the opinion of Marx and Engels, the French proletariat. 'So you can see,' wrote Marx to Cluss on 25 March 1853, 'that the proletarian lion isn't dead'—thus drawing attention to the mass anti-Bonapartist demonstration at the funeral of Madame Raspail, wife of the famous revolutionary (this volume, p. 300). At the same time, they also bore in mind the demoralising influence on the workers of Bonapartism's social demagogy. 'They will have to be severely chastened by crises if they are to be good for anything again *soon*,' wrote Engels to Marx on 24 September 1852 (pp. 196-97).

As a result of the preparations for and outbreak of the Crimean War, there was a considerable widening of the range of questions with which Marx and Engels were concerned. Above all, they became aware of the need to study seriously the foreign policy of the ruling classes. Marx wrote to Engels on 2 November 1853: 'I am glad that chance should have led me to take a closer look at the foreign policy—diplomatic—of the past 20 years. We had very much neglected this aspect, and one ought to know with whom one is dealing' (p. 395).

The desire to fathom the mysteries of European diplomacy induced Marx to study it in retrospect. Hence his interest in Chateaubriand's book on the Holy Alliance's Congress of Verona, in the actions of the English and French diplomats during the period of the Seven Years' War and in English diplomacy during the Greek people's war for independence.

In the letters of this period, Marx and Engels gave great attention to the outbreak of hostilities in 1853 between Russia and Turkey which led, in 1854, to England, France and Turkey making war on Russia. It was from the standpoint of the revolutionary proletariat that Marx and Engels analysed the foreign policy adopted by the European powers during the Crimean War period, the diplomatic negotiations in Vienna, and the actual progress of military operations.

Disclosing the cause behind the exacerbation of the '*détestable question orientale* [wretched Eastern Question]', Marx stressed that it was a clash of the predatory ambitions of the ruling classes of the warring countries (see Marx to Engels on 10 March 1853 and 17 October 1854).

Marx and Engels gave special attention to unmasking the diplomacy of the English oligarchy and, above all, the invariable chief of the Foreign Office and head of the Cabinet, Palmerston. There are certain shortcomings in Marx's criticism of Palmerston, notably a biased evaluation of his policy as a direct indulgence towards Russian Tsarism (see this volume, p. 395). However, Marx correctly noted what was most important—that England and France had the same counter-revolutionary ambitions in their diplomacy as Tsarist Russia and a fear of revolution that brought them together. From this point of view, as the founders of Marxism noted, the European powers, although rivals of Tsarist Russia in the Middle East and the Balkans, were not interested in weakening Tsarism as a bulwark of reaction. Proceeding from this premise, as early as in the spring of 1854 Marx and Engels expressed the idea that the Western powers would endeavour to localise the war, transfer the theatre of operations to the border regions, and obstruct the development of popular movements (see, for instance, this volume, p. 424). This idea was then substantiated by them in a number of articles for the *New-York Daily Tribune* in 1854 and 1855.

Marx and Engels believed that the conflict between the great powers over the Eastern Question and the approaching economic crisis would lead to an upsurge of the democratic and national liberation movements and to a European revolutionary war against Tsarism and other counter-revolutionary forces. Only as a result of a new revolutionary upsurge in Europe, they believed, would the oppressed nationalities of the Austrian and Ottoman empires obtain the opportunity of freely deciding their own destinies. Marx and Engels saw the granting of independence to the Slavonic and other peoples of the Balkan peninsula as a way to the positive settlement of the Eastern Question (see, for instance, this volume, pp. 288-89).

The letters refute the unfounded judgment that Marx's views on foreign policy questions coincided with those of David Urquhart, the English Conservative journalist and Turkophile. Marx and Engels constantly ridiculed Urquhart's idealisation of the Sultan's Turkey, stressing the reactionary nature of his views (see Engels' letter to Marx of 10 March 1853). They regarded the feudal basis of the empire as the greatest brake on the development of its subject peoples. Marx formulated his attitude to Urquhart's views in a letter to Cluss which the latter used as material for an item in the newspaper *Die Reform* in December 1853 (see present edition, Vol. 12).

Marx and Engels passionately denounced Russian Tsarism as one of the main bulwarks of the European counter-revolution at that time. The letters exposed Tsarism's foreign policy of conquest and the intrigues of Tsarist diplomacy. They show up the reactionary essence of pan-Slavist ideas and the attempts by the Tsarist autocracy to use for its own purposes the sympathies of the Slavonic and other peoples of the Balkan peninsula for Russia and the Russian army, whose victories in the war with Turkey objectively promoted the national liberation of these peoples from the Ottoman yoke.

During this period, the ideas of Marx and Engels about Russia broadened considerably, and there was an increase in the number of sources from which they drew their knowledge not only of Tsarist foreign policy, but of the state of affairs within the country. This was helped by Engels' studies of the Slavonic languages, especially Russian. The letters in this volume show that Marx and Engels were keen students of Russian revolutionary literature, above all the writings of Alexander Herzen. Marx especially drew Engels' attention to the foundation by Herzen in London of the 'Free Russian Press' in 1853 and to the publication of a collection, *Pole Star* (see letters from Marx to Engels of 14 June

1853 and 18 May 1855). It was very much under the influence of Herzen's books that Marx and Engels arrived at the opinion that internal contradictions in Russia were growing and resistance to the Tsarist regime was stiffening in that country. On 12 April 1853, Engels wrote to Weydemeyer that should a European revolutionary war break out against Tsarism, 'an aristocratic-bourgeois revolution in Petersburg with a resulting civil war in the interior is a possibility' (pp. 305-06). The letters also contain a number of critical comments on Herzen's conception of 'Russian socialism', which was based on the Utopian idea of the 'rejuvenation' of Europe by means of the Russian peasant commune (see, for instance, this volume, p. 523).

At the same time, Marx and Engels clarified their position concerning the plans of certain circles of the Polish emigration to wrest Byelorussian and Ukrainian lands from Russia. The above-mentioned letter by Engels to Weydemeyer contains the following: 'As to the former Polish provinces on this side of the Dvina and Dnieper, I want to hear nothing more of them, knowing as I do that the peasants there are all Ukrainians, only the aristocracy and some of the people in the towns being Polish, and that to the peasant there ... the restoration of Poland is synonymous with the restoration of the old ruling aristocracy, its powers unimpaired' (p. 306).

The period 1852-55 was one of the most difficult in the lives of Marx and Engels, and their letters to each other clearly show how they were helped to survive their tribulations by the friendship which they maintained throughout their lives. This was expressed very touchingly by Marx at a moment of great personal loss: 'Amid all the fearful torments I have recently had to endure, the thought of you and your friendship has always sustained me, as has the hope that there is still something sensible for us to do together in the world' (p. 533).

* * *

Volume 39 contains, printed in chronological order, 293 letters written by Marx and Engels from 1852 to 1855. By no means all their letters have been preserved, in particular, Engels' letters for 1855, of which only one survives. The letters were written mainly in German, apart from three in English. Twelve were written in two languages—German and English, German and French, and German and Italian. The overwhelming majority are being published in English for the first time. Only 43 letters (of which 39 in incomplete form) have been published before in English. All these publications are indicated in the notes. The text of former English publications has been checked and improved where necessary.

The Appendices contain letters written by Jenny Marx on her husband's instructions, and also extracts from the letters of Cluss to Weydemeyer giving the contents of a number of letters from Marx to Cluss which have not come down to us. Most of the material in the Appendices is also being published in English for the first time.

In the course of work on this volume, the earlier dating of certain letters has been corrected. The letter from Marx to Cluss of 3 September 1852, previously published as a single document, has been divided in this volume into two, dated 3 September and [after 5 September] 1852.

Study of the correspondence for 1852-55 has made it possible to attribute certain articles to Marx and Engels, and also to date the writing of certain already known articles of that period more accurately. All such attributions and details of dates are mentioned in the notes.

The authors' own contraction of proper and geographical names and of certain words have been reproduced in full. Obvious errors and inaccuracies have been corrected. Defects in the manuscripts, when the text is missing or illegible, are indicated by three dots in square brackets. If the context allows a presumable reconstruction to be made of the missing or illegible words, these words are also in square brackets. Passages struck out by the authors have, as a rule, not been reproduced, except where they represent variant readings which are given in the footnotes.

Foreign words and expressions have been retained in the original language and are given in italics; if they were underlined by the authors they are set in spaced italics.

In the letters written in German, words used by Marx and Engels in English are printed in small caps. Longer passages written in English in the original are placed in asterisks. If a fact or event is referred to in several letters, the same note number is used every time.

The volume was compiled, the texts of the letters and appendices for 1852-53 prepared, and the preface and the relevant notes written by Velta Pospelova; the texts of the letters and appendices for 1854-55 were prepared and the relevant notes written by Irina Shikanyan; the volume was edited by Valentina Smirnova. The index of quoted and mentioned literature was prepared by Irina Shikanyan, the name index and index of periodicals by Nina Loiko; Vassily Kuznetsov assisted with the references and in compiling a glossary of geographical names. The subject index was prepared by Vassily Kuznetsov (Institute of Marxism-Leninism of the CC CPSU).

The translations were done by Peter and Betty Ross and edited by E. J. Hobsbawm (Lawrence and Wishart), Richard Dixon, Natalia Karmanova and Margarita Lopukhina (Progress Publishers) and Norire Ter-Akopyan, scientific editor (USSR Academy of Sciences).

The volume was prepared for the press by the editors Anna Vladimirova and Svetlana Gerasimenko (Progress Publishers).

KARL MARX
and
FREDERICK ENGELS

LETTERS
January 1852-December 1855

1852

1

MARX TO JOSEPH WEYDEMEYER[1]

IN NEW YORK

[London,] 1 January 1852

Dear Weiwi,

A happy New Year to you, and greetings to your wife[a] from myself and wife.

I have not been able to send you the article until now,[2] having been interrupted not only by events coming one on top of another but to an even greater extent by private affairs. Henceforward, I shall be regularity itself.

Lupus[b] has fallen seriously ill and hence has not yet been able to send anything. Red Wolff's[c] article seemed to me unusable, hence I did not send it off.[3]

If, *which I hope will not happen,* your undertaking[d] has to be postponed for any length of time on financial grounds, *let* Dana *have* the article so that he may translate it into English for his paper.[4] However, I hope this will not be necessary.

Give Dana my regards. Tell him I have received his newspapers and his letter and shall be sending him a new WORK next week.[5]

As for the *Revues,*[e] since they are not ready to hand but have to be obtained at some expense and trouble from Hamburg, please let me know roughly how many sales you think I can count on in America.[6]

I shall be sending you from here *Notes to the People* by our friend Ernest Jones, the most important leader of the English party; you should find them a veritable mine when it comes to filling the gaps in your paper.

---

[a] Louise - [b] Wilhelm Wolff - [c] Ferdinand Wolff - [d] the publication of *Die Revolution* - [e] *Neue Rheinische Zeitung. Politisch-ökonomische Revue.*

Send me at once (and in future regularly) a few copies of your weekly.

Greeting and fraternity.

Your

K. Marx

Yesterday I hammered away at Freiligrath for all I was worth and he promised me to concoct a poem for you on the most recent occurrences.[a]

First published in: Marx and Engels, *Works*, First Russian Edition, Vol. XXV, Moscow, 1934

Printed according to the original

Published in English in full for the first time

2

ENGELS TO MARX

IN LONDON

[Manchester,] 6 January 1852

Dear Marx,

BY THIS TIME, you will, I trust, have completely recovered from your afflictions; I also hope that your wife will no longer be angry with me about the coup d'état which plunged you for two days into such depths of melancholy.[7] At any rate, please give her and your children my kindest regards.

I shall get an article done for Weydemeyer in time for next Friday's steamer and hope you will let me have something topical for the *Tribune*, which I shall at once translate. It's really not a paper that calls for any serious exertion. Barnum stalks its columns large as life, and the English is ghastly—but this apart, it has some good qualities which, however, have nothing at all to do with our LINE. If you can see that it reaches me by Thursday—even by the 2nd post—you shall have the translation back in London in time for Saturday's steamer, i.e. by the 2nd post arriving there on Friday. Then, next week, I shall set to work on the articles on Germany and shall soon be done with them.[b]

---

[a] See this volume, p. 8. - [b] This presumably refers to Article VII of *Revolution and Counter-Revolution in Germany*.

The lack of originality with which the Austrians have aped Louis Napoleon and promptly abolished their constitution is certainly deplorable. Now there'll be a fine how-d'ye-do in Prussia— there's no doubt that Prussia has been betrayed and sold by Austria and, if it does not likewise abolish its constitution,[8] may very well be crushed by a Russian-Austrian-French alliance.

In 1851 the English cotton industry consumed 32,000 bales a week as against 29,000 bales in 1850.[a] The entire surplus, and a good deal more, went to the East Indies and China; at present Manchester is almost wholly dependent on deliveries to these two markets and to the HOME TRADE, since very little is going to the Continent. This *cannot* last much longer. They are sailing very near the wind here, and the fact that, e.g., cotton prices are soaring, despite an exceptionally heavy crop, merely in the expectation of even heavier demand, is of itself significant enough.

Weerth dropped me a few lines today from Bradford inquiring about the insufferable Lüders who has written to him. If you can tell me whether and to what extent this old jackass has been involved in the intrigues there, I should be grateful and it might come in handy. Otherwise, nothing else to report, BUSINESS WITH US SLACK, fog and smoke in abundance.

Your
F. E.

First published in *Der Briefwechsel zwischen F. Engels und K. Marx*, Bd. 1, Stuttgart, 1913

Printed according to the original

Published in English for the first time

3

ENGELS TO JENNY MARX

IN LONDON

Manchester, 14 January 1852

Dear Mrs Marx,

I would have answered your kind letter[b] long ago had I not been totally prevented from doing so by a whole mass of things—in particular the presence of my brother-in-law[c] whom I

---

[a] 'State of Trade. Manchester, Jan. 3', *The Times*, No. 21003, 5 January 1852. - [b] See this volume, pp. 567-69. - [c] Emil Blank

had to keep amused for a whole week, certainly no light task here in Manchester. There could, of course, be no question of work during that time, and only now can I turn my mind to what may be done before next Friday's STEAMER. At all events, either this evening or tomorrow evening something will be ready for the *Tribune*, nor will Father Weydemeyer go empty-handed. In the meantime I have heard and seen nothing from the latter—I hope that today will have brought you a letter from him telling us about the prospects for the New Year, since the letters that arrived by yesterday's STEAMER were dated up to 1 January.

I trust that in the meantime the paterfamilias[a] will have arisen from his bed of pain and penance, and only hope that the Library[b] will not entirely drive the *Tribune* from his mind. The information about the honourable Lüders was conveyed forthwith to Weerth, likewise as much as was necessary concerning the worthy Kinkel.

The lambastings received by the great Willich are most pleasing so far as we are concerned, while for him there would appear to be an excellent prospect of repeated applications. Once the spell of inviolability and invincibility cast around himself by the great warrior has been broken by a *bonne volée*,[c] not one blackguard of an émigré, right down to the last Conrad,[9] will rest until he has repeated the experiment and wreaked upon the noble fellow tangible vengeance for his private GRIEVANCES. The great man's *courage malheureux*[d] may then console itself with the thought that those who did the thrashing were all of them 'men of principle'. Thrashings he may have had, but they were 'principled thrashings'.

I return Cluss' letter herewith.[e] As an agent, the fellow's beyond compare. When the business of Willich's mystification[10] comes out, there'll be a fine how-d'ye-do! The philistines will no longer dare to write letters for fear of their falling into our hands. How scurrilously hypocritical it was on Kinkel's part to maintain that he had written to London, telling them to get in touch with us! This fact only goes to show that he has been constantly and most disagreeably 'challenged' on our account in America and that, among the democratic rabble there, we too have a SET of adherents who swear by us, as do the others by Kinkel or Heinzen or Hecker, heaven knows why; these must be adherents *à la* Magnus Gross, Wilhelmi, etc., people who would only have to spend a short time in our company to be better informed both about us and themselves, and to return to the common fold where they belong.

---

[a] Karl Marx - [b] of the British Museum - [c] sound thrashing - [d] discomfited courage - [e] See this volume, pp. 568-69.

I must say, Louis Napoleon grows daily more amusing. While not a single one of those great measures for the abolition of pauperism, etc., has yet managed to see the light of day, the little fellow contrives to provoke all philistines in the world by measures which are merely intended to ensure a temporary consolidation of his authority.[11] No longer does any non-French paper dare speak up for him, even the *Sun* and the *Kölnische* remain silent, and only the good-for-nothing correspondent of the *Globe* continues to deposit his daily scurrilities in the corner allotted to him for the purpose. On top of that, Louis Napoleon has aroused universal suspicion, the whole of Europe resounds with war and rumours of war,[a] and even the peaceable *Daily News* has *nolens volens*[b] to join in the call for NATIONAL DEFENCES. Along with the side of his character which has been most in evidence since 2 December—the GAMBLER—the fellow is gradually beginning to develop another, that of the mad pretender who regards himself as a predestined world redeemer and who swears by his star. And when the time was come, God sent the nephew that he might redeem the world from the bondage of the devil and from the hell of socialism. Luckily parliament will be meeting shortly, which always introduces a little variety into the humbug of politics.

Warm regards to Marx and the little ones from your

F. Engels

First published abridged in *Der Briefwechsel zwischen F. Engels und K. Marx*, Bd. 1, Stuttgart, 1913 and in full in *MEGA*, Abt. III, Bd.1, Berlin, 1929

Printed according to the original

Published in English for the first time

4

MARX TO JOSEPH WEYDEMEYER[12]

IN NEW YORK

London, 16 January 1852
28 Dean Street, Soho

Dear Weydemeyer,

Today I got up for the first time in a fortnight. From this you will see that my indisposition—not yet wholly overcome—was a

---

[a] Matthew 24:6. - [b] willy-nilly

serious one. Hence, even with the best will in the world, I could not send you No. III of my article on Bonaparte[a] this week. Instead, you will find enclosed a poem [13] and a personal letter from Freiligrath. I beseech you now to: 1. See that the poem is carefully printed, with adequate intervals between the verses and allowing plenty of space for the whole. A great deal is lost if poems are too closely printed and over-compressed. 2. Write Freiligrath a friendly letter. Nor need you be over-fearful of paying him compliments, for poets, even the best of them, are all *plus au moins des courtisanes*[b] and *il faut les cajoler, pour les faire chanter.*[c] In private life our Freiligrath is the most amiable, least pretentious of men who conceals beneath a genuine *bonhomie un esprit très fin et très railleur*[d] and whose passion is 'authentic', yet does not render him either 'uncritical' or 'superstitious'. He is a true revolutionary and a man of honour to the marrow, a compliment I would pay to only a very few. Nevertheless a poet, whatever he may be as an *homme,*[e] needs applause and ADMIRATION. This is, I believe, peculiar to the genre as such. I am only telling you all this to remind you not to lose sight, when corresponding with Freiligrath, of the distinction between the 'poet' and the 'critic'. It is, by the by, very nice of him to address his poetical letter directly to you. I think that this will be helpful to you in New York.

I do not know whether I shall manage to send you another article today. Pieper had promised me to write an article for you. Up till this moment he has not yet turned up and when he does, the article will have to be put to the test—i.e. whether it is consigned to the flames, or is considered worthy of crossing the ocean. I am *trop faible encore*[f] to go on writing. More today week. Regards from my family to yours.

Lupus is still not fully recovered and hence has not yet sent anything.

Your
K. Marx

Apropos. Enclosed is yet another 'statement' from a member [14] of our League [15] which you should insert in your paper in small print among the advertisements or below the line.

---

[a] K. Marx, *The Eighteenth Brumaire of Louis Bonaparte,* III. - [b] more or less courtesans - [c] they have to be cajoled to get them to sing - [d] a wit very subtle and very mocking - [e] man - [f] still too weak

Daniels, Becker and Co. have again not been brought up before the January Assizes on the pretext that the investigation was so difficult that it must be begun all over again.[16] They have now been in jug for 9 months.

First published much abridged in *Die Neue Zeit*, Bd. 2, No: 29, Stuttgart, 1906-07 and in full in: Marx and Engels, *Works*, First Russian Edition, Vol. XXV, Moscow, 1934

Printed according to the original

Published in English in full for the first time

5

MARX TO ENGELS

IN MANCHESTER

[London,] 20 January 1852
28 Dean Street, Soho

Dear Engels,

Only since yesterday have I been up and about again and it was not until today that I again took up my pen.

Since I was unable to go out and visit Chapman as I had planned, Pieper, with the enthusiasm he habitually displays in the first ten minutes, offered to discount the bill for me. The other evening he brought me the money, only to declare that he would send you the bill so that you could have it discounted in Manchester. I, as well as my wife, told him that we knew you couldn't do so. But he had already written his letter and, since he made it pretty clear that I appeared, for reasons of my own, to be putting obstacles in his way, I gave him his head and be damned to it, feeling sure that you would return the stuff to him. Now, when he informs me of this *fait*,[a] it turns out that he was not in such a hurry after all, but was merely seeking to give himself airs. For me, it was a nasty business, since you might have thought I had been guilty of an indiscretion.

In France *les choses vont à merveille*.[b] And I hope *la belle France* will not pass through this school too casually but will have to spend a longer time in class. War, whether it comes a few MONTHS

---

[a] fact - [b] things are going splendidly

sooner or later, seems to me inevitable. *Nous avons eu le Napoléon de la paix.*[a] Louis[b] can BY NO MEANS emulate Louis Philippe. *Et alors?*[c]

As you know, our people in Cologne have not been brought before the Assizes under the pretext that the case is so difficult that the investigation must be begun all over again.

Madier has just been here. He proved to me *de la manière la plus crapaude*[d] that the FRENCHMEN are capable of taking London by breakfast time and assaulting all of England's coasts within five hours. One has too much *pitie*[e] for the poor devils not to hold one's tongue *quand ils déraisonnent.*[f]

Write soon.

Your

K. M.

How is *le commerce?*

First published abridged in *Der Briefwechsel zwischen F. Engels und K. Marx,* Bd. 1, Stuttgart, 1913 and in full in *MEGA,* Abt. III, Bd. 1, Berlin, 1929

Printed according to the original

Published in English for the first time

6

ENGELS TO MARX

IN LONDON

[Manchester,] 22 January 1852

Dear Marx,

Herewith the 7th article for the *Tribune.* The eighth, etc., will be done tomorrow evening, and today I shall get something ready for Weydemeyer. In his case, I am for a start restricting myself to England,[17] being unable to bring myself to read German newspapers and do something on Germany. Could you not perhaps persuade Lupus, who, I hope, is fit as a fiddle again, to send off something 'From the German Empire'[18]?—Weerth will produce something for Weydemeyer next week; this week he cannot. I hope to see him here the day after tomorrow and he

---

[a] We have had the Napoleon of peace (Louis Philippe's nickname) - [b] Louis Bonaparte - [c] What then? - [d] in the most philistine manner - [e] pity - [f] when they talk nonsense

may come up to London in a week or a fortnight's time since, out of sheer impatience, he is once again champing at the bit.

The *Pacific* having arrived from New York yesterday, there's a chance that tomorrow might bring the numbers[a] promised me by Weydemeyer—but I am not counting on this since he may have waited for the regular English MAIL STEAMER. By the way, he should not send so many, 50 copies is too much and will probably cost a mint of money, and who are they all to be sent to? I will find out what the charges are and if needs be—that is, if he can't arrange the business more cheaply through parcels consignment agencies—10 copies would be quite sufficient; for he cannot after all count on *subscribers* in Europe. A few in London, perhaps; otherwise maybe only in Hamburg. And that would also call for an agency, which would not pay for itself.

I trust you'll soon be sending me an article to translate for the *Tribune*.

Jones has written to me asking for contributions. I shall do my best and have given him my word.[19] All this means that any spare time I might have for swotting is frittered away piecemeal, and that's bad. I must see how I can arrange things and diddle the office. Jones mentions a dirty trick Harney played on him[20] and says he was cheated out of £15, concerning which you would be able to tell me more—what is all this? He was, of course, VERY BUSY and his letter consists largely of unfinished sentences and exclamation marks.

As to Pieper's DODGE in the matter of the bill, the whole stratagem was, of course, perfectly plain to me, and *Monsieur le bel homme*[b] will have realised that he needs rather more cunning to conjure eight pounds out of my pocket. Being well aware how he stood financially on 2 January, I chaffed him about his supposed shortage of money, warned him against dishonest and unsound bill-brokers in London, declared that the bill must be dispatched as quickly as possible, and finally advised him to have it cashed through Weydemeyer—in which case, it would again pass through your hands and, upon the arrival of the notification of payment, which would, of course, come to you or me, it would quite spontaneously give rise to a further discounting transaction with this youthful trading house. I owe him 2 pounds, for which he also asked; this I also promised to repay, but not before the beginning of February.

That the good Louis Napoleon must go to war is clear as day and, if he can come to an understanding with Russia, he will

---

[a] of *Die Revolution* - [b] Mr Handsome

probably pick a quarrel with England. This would have its good and its bad aspects. The French notion that they could conquer London and England in 5 hours is a very harmless one. But what they *can* do now, is carry out sudden raids with 20, or at the most 30 thousand men, which, however, would nowhere be very effective. Brighton is the one town seriously threatened; Southampton, etc., are safeguarded, not so much by fortifications as by their situation on deep inlets navigable only at high tide and with the help of local pilots. The greatest EFEECT a French landing could hope to achieve would be the destruction of Woolwich, but even then they would have to take damned good care not to advance on London. In the case of any serious invasion, the combined forces of the Continent would inevitably give the English at least A YEAR'S NOTICE, whereas 6 months would suffice to place England in a state of readiness against any attack. The present alarums are being deliberately exaggerated—with the greatest help from the Whigs. All the English have to do to safeguard themselves for the time being is to recall a dozen ships of the line and STEAMERS, fit out another dozen of both kinds which are lying in port half completed, recruit 25,000 more troops, organise volunteer rifle battalions equipped with Minié rifles and, in addition, some militia and some training for the YEOMANRY. But the alarums serve a very good purpose; the government had really excelled itself in allowing things to go to wrack and ruin and this will cease. And then, if it comes to the point, they will be so well armed that they will be able to repulse any attempt at a landing and at once retaliate.

Otherwise, so far as I can see, there are only 2 prospects open to Louis Napoleon if he wants to start a war: 1. against Austria, i.e. against the entire Holy Alliance, or 2. against Prussia, if the latter is dropped by Russia and Austria. However, the second is very doubtful and, as for his picking a quarrel with the Holy Alliance, this is most questionable. Neither England nor the Holy Alliance will abandon Piedmont, Switzerland and Belgium to him. The business is becoming so prettily entangled that in the end pure chance must decide.

And *à l'intérieur*, what splendid goings-on! Attempted assassinations almost a daily occurrence and the measures taken ever prettier. If only Mr de Morny, who still to some degree plays a virtuous hero, were at last thrown out, and if only the noble one[a] were to confiscate the property of the Orleans.[21]

---

[a] Louis Bonaparte

It would hardly be possible to pave the way for a Blanqui government more surely than does this jackass.

Your

F. E.

First published abridged in *Der Briefwech-sel zwischen F. Engels und K. Marx*, Bd. 1, Stuttgart, 1913 and in full in *MEGA*, Abt. III, Bd. 1, Berlin, 1929

Printed according to the original

Published in English for the first time

7

MARX TO JOSEPH WEYDEMEYER

IN NEW YORK

[London,] 23 January 1852
28 Dean Street, Soho

Dear Weydemeyer,

Unfortunately my indisposition has up till now prevented me from writing to you this week, i.e. for your paper.[a] *With much effort* I concocted an article for Dana,[b] who had received nothing from me for six weeks or more. For years, nothing has so pulled me down as this damned haemorrhoidal complaint, not even the last French fiasco.[c] *Enfin*,[d] I shall be all the better for having been forcibly kept away from the library[e] for 4 weeks, hard though this was.

You will be getting two more articles about the 18th Brumaire,[f] of which the first will be dispatched, come what may, on Friday next and the other immediately afterwards, if not at the same time.

Enclosed Pieper's article.[22]

As for Lupus, I have been chivvying him a great deal and he seems to have made up his mind to take a retrospective look at Kossuth's Hungarian *carrière*[g] for your paper. You have made two mistakes, first in failing to name Lupus along with ourselves in your announcement,[23] and secondly in *not approaching* him *direct*. Make good the *second* with a letter which you may enclose in one

---

[a] *Die Revolution* - [b] F. Engels, *Revolution and Counter-Revolution*, VII. - [c] An allusion to Louis Bonaparte's coup d'état of 2 December 1851. - [d] Well - [e] of the British Museum - [f] K. Marx, *The Eighteenth Brumaire of Louis Bonaparte*, III and IV. - [g] career

to myself and in which you urge him to write. No one else among us all has his popular style. He is *extrêmement modeste*. All the more must one avoid giving the impression that his cooperation is regarded as superfluous.

Because I live some distance from Freiligrath and because I received Pieper's article only just before the post left, we have today been compelled to send you *two* letters instead of *one*.[a] This will be avoided next time.

Enclosed another statement from my friend *Pfänder* (Bauer no longer belongs to our League). You will have to publish it, since the Windmill Streeters' statement against him appeared in both the *American* and the European papers.[24] It would be a good idea if, beneath this statement, you were to print the comment that it contains *only* what could be published under *present police conditions* (the accounts between Bauer and Pfänder on the one hand and the former League on the other, further, the control exercised by the *Central Authority* over the administration of those monies, we being in the majority on the C.A.—none of these things can, of course, be published *yet*); that, counting on the political precautions we, for our part, have to take in Germany, Arnold Winkelried Ruge,[b] that old gossip and 'Confusius'[c] of European democracy, made an allusion to those matters (i.e. those of Pfänder and Bauer) about which he himself knew only from hearsay at 3rd or 4th hand, in the hope of incriminating *myself* and *Engels* in the eyes of the public, although the business was no concern of ours,[d] in just the same way as the jackass suggested that it was the Windmill Streeters who threw *us* out when it was *we* who had broken with that society,[e] as Pfänder's letter also implies.

You might also announce that a *new workers' society* has been formed in London under *Stechan's* chairmanship,[25] which will keep aloof from 'Emigration', 'Agitation'[26] and Great Windmill Street alike, and pursue a serious line.

Tu comprends, mon cher,[f] that this society belongs to us, although we only send our younger people there; I refer to our '*heducated*[g] people' not to our workers. They all go there.

---

[a] See next letter. - [b] Arnold Ruge is ironically compared with Arnold Winkelried—a semi-legendary hero of the Swiss war of liberation against the Austrian yoke in the fourteenth century. - [c] A play on the resemblance between *Confusius* (confusion) and Confucius, the name of the Chinese philosopher. - [d] K. Marx and F. Engels, 'Statement' (present edition, Vol. 10, pp. 535-36). - [e] See K. Marx and F. Engels, 'Statement on Resignation from the German Workers' Educational Society in London' (present edition, Vol. 10). - [f] You will understand, my dear fellow - [g] Marx uses Berlin dialect: *jebildeten*.

Stechan has about him something of the solidity of a guild brother and the fickleness of a small master-artisan, but he is educatable and has considerable influence in Northern Germany. That is why I have also called on him to provide contributions for you.[a] We have BY AND BY pushed him into the foreground, which he likes to shun, and into contradiction, which he likes to gloss over. Willich had asked him to guarantee Kinkel's loan[27] but he refused. At first enthusiastically welcomed by Schapper and Willich, and set against us by them, he was soon enabled by his better nature to see through the shabbiness and hollowness of these fellows and their following. And so (with a little help from Lochner and other assistants with whom we had provided him incognito) he openly broke with the rabble.

Is A. Hentze our Hentze from Hamm? If so, I would write to him, for as it is Willich has done everything to blacken me in his eyes. *L'infâme!*[b]

Warmest regards from my family to yours.

Your
K. Marx

I am sending material for pamphlets, etc., all in *one batch*, likewise Jones' *Notes.*[c] Sent piecemeal, they cost too much. *The Northern Star* is no longer in O'Connor's hands but in those of a Chartist faction which is secretly in touch with the Financial and Parliamentary Reformers.[28]

First published in: Marx and Engels, *Works,* First Russian Edition, Vol. XXV, Moscow, 1934

Printed according to the original

Published in English for the first time

8

ENGELS TO JOSEPH WEYDEMEYER[12]

IN NEW YORK

Manchester, 23 January 1852

Dear Weydemeyer,

I hope that in the meantime you will have received my first letter, which I posted on 18 or 19 December in time for the STEAMER *Africa.*[d] It contained an article written in haste and a letter,

---

[a] See this volume, pp. 19-20. - [b] The scoundrel! - [c] *Notes to the People* - [d] This letter has not been found.

likewise written in haste. You should have had it long before the 5th, but it may have only gone with the next STEAMER. Meanwhile, last week I sent you by the *Niagara* an article unaccompanied by a letter,[29] but doubt whether I posted it in time; if it was too late, it will arrive with this one, by the *Europa*, in which case you will have some material in hand. You'll have already had several things from Marx, an anti-Kinkel poem from Freiligrath[a] and also, perhaps, something from Lupus and Pieper. Weerth is very busy just now and has not really settled down in Bradford (Yorkshire); however, he has promised me he will send something by the next STEAMER. I shall probably see him here tomorrow and prod him yet again to make him keep his promise. Unfortunately Marx has been seriously ill for the past fortnight as a result of an almighty binge when I was in London over the New Year, and I was prevented from working until last week, partly because of the fortnight spent in London and partly because of various snags that subsequently cropped up. However, I think I shall be able to send you something regularly each week now, and shortly, perhaps, something for a feuilleton by way of a change.

I am settled here in Manchester for the present, luckily in a position which, besides much independence, affords me various advantages; Marx and other friends occasionally come up from London to see me and, so long as Weerth is in Bradford, we arrange a regular shuttle-service between here and there, as the railway journey only takes $2\,^1/_2$ hours. But now he will probably leave; he cannot abide that beastly hole, Bradford, and he's never happy anywhere if he has to spend more than a year sitting on his backside in the same place. I am considering a trip to the STATES, either next summer or, if there are no political changes in the meantime, the summer after that; to the STATES, New York, and particularly New Orleans. But this depends on my old man,[b] not me, and also on how things go in the cotton market.

Fifty copies of the *Revolution* is too much and the cost will probably be enormous, i.e. four shillings or more each time. In view of the wholesale arrests, dispersion, etc., and the German press laws, we can count on only a few subscribers here and, in Germany, only one or two at most in Hamburg, hence specimen numbers will be of no use to us. Newspapers, one or more to a wrapper, open at the sides, cost 1d (2 cents) per sheet. So send 4 to me and 6-8 direct to London, for otherwise I have to restamp

---

[a] F. Freiligrath, 'An Joseph Weydemeyer', I. - [b] Friedrich Engels senior, Engels' father

them from here to London and I can hardly saddle the business with these massive postal charges. Ten to twelve copies will suffice for us and, if there seems to be any prospect of subscribers here, we can organise a regular agency in London to which the back numbers can be sent all at one time and under the same cover to complete the series. I shall discuss the matter with the people in London and see what can be done.

In France, things are going splendidly. Yesterday evening the *Patrie* reported that the creation of a Police Ministry for de Maupas would be announced in today's *Moniteur*.[a] De Morny who, along with Fould and a few others, represents the material interests of the bourgeoisie (but not their participation in political power) in the Cabinet, will be thrown out, and the reign of those died-in-the-wool adventurers Maupas, Persigny and Co. will begin. That will be the start of imperial true socialism[30]; the first socialist measure will be the confiscation of Louis Philippe's property,[b] for the Act of 6 August 1830, by which he left his property to his children instead of to the State as ancient custom demanded, is invalid. The portion of the Condé estates inherited by Aumale is also to be seized. The news might even arrive by next Saturday's STEAMER if things develop quickly enough. In the southern *départements*, the insurgents are still being hunted like game.[31]

The English Press is now the only reliable one for French news, and occasionally too, the Augsburg *Allgemeine Zeitung*. The paper in which you will find the best news about France is the London *Daily News*, which I therefore specially commend to you. The *Tribune* takes it, and you will certainly also be able to lay hands on it elsewhere, it being far too expensive to take. You will, I am sure, have no difficulty in finding it in the coffee houses of the CITY's commercial quarter.

Dronke may soon be paying you a visit; I hear that anyone who has to leave Switzerland is sent via France only to America, not to England. But now he will be compelled to leave; as we have heard nothing whatever from him he must be in hiding.

Gnam, a former Baden artilleryman and brewer, who went over on the same ship as Heinzen, is a sterling fellow. With them went

---

[a] The decree of 22 January 1852 on the creation of a Police Ministry under de Maupas and the decree of 22 January on the resignation of the Minister of the Interior de Morny and appointment of Persigny were printed in *Le Moniteur universel*, No. 23, 23 January 1852. - [b] The decree of 22 January 1852 on the confiscation of Louis Philippe's property was printed in *Le Moniteur universel*, No. 23, 23 January 1852.

Rothacker, a student from Upper Baden; he used to be a good chap but he may have changed and is, moreover, dangerous on account of his versifying. Little Schickel of Mainz, whose address you can get from Cluss (away in the Alleghenies), will exert himself on behalf of the *Revolution*. Please send him my kind regards, which may be done through Cluss.

Below, a few supplementary notes on my remarks concerning the prospects for an invasion of England,[32] which will explain things to you:

1. Any landing west of Portsmouth runs the risk of being forced into the wedge formed by Cornwall—hence impracticable.

2. Any landing too far north of, or too close to, Dover faces the same hazard between Thames and sea.

3. London and Woolwich—the first *buts d'opération*.[a] Detachments to be sent against Portsmouth and Sheerness (Chatham). Strong occupation force in London, strong guard posts between the coast and London. Out of a landing force 150,000 strong, at least 60,000 needed for this purpose (and that not enough). Thus continuation of operations could proceed with *90,000 men*.

4. Birmingham the second objective (on account of the arms factories). Secure the area south of the Bristol Channel and the Wash, i.e. a line from Gloucester to King's Lynn; in addition, a strong spearhead aimed at Birmingham. However weak and broken the opposing army might be, I consider this impossible with the 90,000 men available. But assuming it succeeds, no tenable defence position will have been won, particularly if the English Navy bestirs itself. The line will be too long and too weak. Hence it will be necessary to resume the advance.

5. Manchester the third objective; all country south of Mersey (or Ribble) and Aire (Humber) to be secured and this line to be held. It is shorter and more tenable, but here again the forces greatly weakened by the need to detach troops. Hence, since the defenders still have room and resources enough to reorganise, either the advance must continue, or else there must be an early retreat.

6. The first tenable line in the relatively narrow part of northern England, either the Tees or even better the Tyne (the line of the Roman wall against the Picts[33]) from Carlisle to Newcastle. But then the agricultural, industrial and commercial resources of the Scottish Lowlands still remain in the hands of the defenders.

---

[a] objectives

7. The conquest of *England proper* can be regarded as complete, and *then only for a time*, only after the capture of Glasgow and Edinburgh, the retreat of the defenders into the Highlands, and the occupation of the admirably short strong line between Clyde and Firth of Forth, having an extensive railway system to the rear.

Only after the conquest, however, would the difficulty, and an *unavoidable* one, be felt—that of consolidating once communications with France have been cut.

In such circumstances, how many men are needed to conquer and hold the entire country from Dover to the Clyde, and to present a decent front on the Clyde?

To my mind, 400,000 would not be too many.

These CONSIDERATIONS are much too detailed for your paper and I lay them before you as a PROFESSIONAL MAN. Take a look at a map of England and tell me what you think. It is an aspect of the matter that is totally neglected by the English.

The letters are going off to the post. I must close. Kindest regards to your wife.[a]

Your

F. E.

First published in part in *Die Neue Zeit,* Bd. 2, No. 29, Stuttgart, 1906-07 and in full in: Marx and Engels, *Works,* First Russian Edition, Vol. XXV, Moscow, 1934

Printed according to the original

Published in English in full for the first time

9

MARX TO JOSEPH WEYDEMEYER[34]

IN NEW YORK

London [between 23 January and 2 February 1852]

Dear Weydemeyer,

Stechan sends you the following notes, but do not mention his name. Later he will send the original article over his signature.

Your

K. M.

---

[a] Louise

Dear Weydemeyer,

Do not print this stuff *word for word,* only make use of it. It is written in a very philistine style.

First published in: Marx and Engels, *Works,* Second Russian Edition, Vol. 50, Moscow, 1981

Printed according to the original

Published in English for the first time

10

MARX TO ENGELS

IN MANCHESTER

[London,] 24 January 1852
28 Dean Street, Soho

Dear Frederic,

No more than a few lines, since a letter has just arrived from Bermbach in Cologne which I would like to be in your hands tomorrow. It is essential that you 1. send me a letter TO THE EDITOR OF THE TIMES on the Cologne affair, together with a few lines which I shall send in advance of the *corpus delicti*[a]; 2. that you do the same in your own name to *The Daily News* although, of course, the actual *corpus delicti,* i.e. the insertion itself, will be signed 'A PRUSSIAN' or some such. I think that for *The Times* 'Doctor' and for *The Daily News* 'Manchester MERCHANT' would do better, i.e. have more chance of being accepted. Refer to people by their titles. Dr Becker, Dr (!) Bürgers, Dr Daniels, Dr Klein, Dr Jacobi, Otto (a chemist well known in German scientific circles), Röser and Nothjung. The Board of indicting magistrates at Cologne is the *nec plus ultra*[b] of cowardice. By the way, under the terms of the new disciplinary law, judges are, at least nominally, no longer 'irremovable'.

Your article for Dana[c] is splendid.

Of course I have only been able to send POOR Weydemeyer one more article[d] since you were here. This time my piles have afflicted me more grievously than the French Revolution. I shall

---

[a] K. Marx and F. Engels, 'To the Editor of *The Times*' (see present edition, Vol. 11, pp. 210-11). - [b] the extreme - [c] F. Engels, *Revolution and Counter-Revolution in Germany,* VII. - [d] K. Marx, *The Eighteenth Brumaire of Louis Bonaparte,* II.

see what I can do next week. The state of my posterior does not permit me to go to the Library yet.

Confiscation of the estates begged or stolen by the Orléans! Resignation of Fould! Persigny![35] Bravo! *Ça marche!*[a]

It is strange how ARMY, NAVY, COLONIES, FORTIFICATIONS AND THE WHOLE ADMINISTRATION have gone rotten under the rule of this curious regime of an aristocratic clique which the English bourgeois have by tradition lugged along with them at the head of the Executive power ever since 1688.[36] After all that English presumption and liberal outcry inspired by Kossuth, after the cosmopolitan-philanthropic-commercial hymns of peace during the EXHIBITION,[37] in short, after this period of bourgeois megalomania, it is refreshing when the canaille now come to discover that not something, but everything, is rotten in the State of Denmark.[b] And then, too, these gents take an altogether too complacent view of the struggles on the Continent.

Salut.

Your

K. M.

Send back the two enclosed letters by return, Cluss', at any rate.

First published in *Der Briefwechsel zwischen F. Engels and K. Marx*, Bd. 1, Stuttgart, 1913

Printed according to the original

Published in English for the first time

11

MARX TO FERDINAND FREILIGRATH

IN LONDON

[London,] 26 January 1852
28 Dean Street, Soho

Dear Freiligrath,

The verse you sent me to have a look at is delicious and expresses the *corpus delicti* in a masterly manner, but I believe it impairs the effect of the whole.[38] *D'abord,*[c] is Kinkel a 'German

---

[a] Things are moving. - [b] Shakespeare, *Hamlet*, Act I, Scene 4. - [c] Firstly

poet'? I and a great many other *bons gens*[a] venture modestly to express some doubt upon this point. Then: will it not detract from the significant contrast between the 'German poet' and the 'commercial' Babylon to deal yet again with the contrast between the 'free' and the 'servile' poet? The more so as the relationship of the puffed-up *man of letters* to the world that confronts the 'poet' is already depicted exhaustively in *Andersen*.[39] Since, as I see it, there is no intrinsic need to bring in Kinkel at this point, your verse would only provide our opponents with the opportunity of coming down on it as the expression of personal pique or rivalry. But as it is so felicitous and ought not to be wasted, you will—if you agree with my view in other respects—certainly have a chance of using it in a different context, in one of the later poetical letters. For the sketch is delicious.

Since Engels-Weerth have not returned the copy of your first poem[b] which I sent them, all I had to offer red Wolff[c] yesterday were the few bits I knew by heart which, however, sufficed to bring on one of his fits of enthusiasm.

Quant à notre ami[d] Ebner,[40] he has undoubtedly had letters from Pieper, the best proof being that Pieper possesses a reply from him. Besides, he wrote him another long letter quite recently, excusing my silence on the grounds of my indisposition.

I have had a letter from Bermbach consisting of some 30 lines. He asks why he has not heard from me for so long. The answer is quite simple. I send about half a sheet to Cologne and, after a very long delay, receive in return a few lines, none of which ever answers my questions. For instance, never a word about Daniels' state of health and the like. You will get this letter as soon as it comes back from Manchester. Engels is going to use it for articles for the English papers.[e] There is nothing of importance in the scrawl save the following: The Board of indicting magistrates, *remarquez le bien*,[f] in view of the fact 'that there was no actual evidence of an indictable offence', rules that the investigation must start *all over again*.[41] First then, on the basis of some stupid presumption, you have to spend 9 months in jug. Next, it transpires that there are no legal grounds for your being in jug. Conclusion: You must remain in jug until the examining magistrate finds himself *à même*[g] to present 'actual evidence of an indictable offence' and, if the 'actual evidence' is not forthcoming, in gaol you remain until you rot.

---

[a] good people - [b] F. Freiligrath, 'An Joseph Weydemeyer', I. - [c] Ferdinand Wolff - [d] As for our friend - [e] See this volume, p. 20. - [f] note it well - [g] in a position

Such shameless poltroonery is unbelievable. The main fault lies with the wretched 'Press' which utters not a word. A few articles in the *Kölnische Zeitung*, the *National-Zeitung* and the *Breslauer Zeitung*—and the Cologne Board of indicting magistrates would never have dared do anything of the sort. But the liberals and democrats, like the curs they are, rejoice at the removal of their communist rivals. Did we not stand up for the Temmes and every imaginable variety of democratic riff-raff whenever they found themselves in conflict with the police and the courts?[a] Not once does Kinkel, for whom Becker was a hearth and Bürgers a haven,[b] render them any thanks in the *Lithographische Korrespondenz* which he sustains with American funds. *Les canailles!*

If I knew of a safe bourgeois address in Cologne, I would write to Mrs Daniels and endeavour to reassure her to some extent about political conditions. From what Pieper tells me, it would seem that every counter-revolutionary advance is exploited by the 'worthy citizens' to alarm and vex her.

Enclosed a note from Miss Jenny to Master Wolfgang.[c]

Kind regards,

Your

K. M.

First published in part in *Die Neue Zeit*, Ergänzungshefte, No. 12, 12 April, Stuttgart, 1912 and in full in: Marx and Engels, *Works*, First Russian Edition, Vol. XXV, Moscow, 1934

Printed according to the original

Published in English for the first time

---

[a] Marx refers, in particular, to his article written for the *Neue Rheinische Zeitung*, 'The Prussian Counter-Revolution and the Prussian Judiciary'. - [b] Pun in the original on the name of Becker and 'hat gebacken' (has baked—figuratively, set up in the world) and the name of Bürgers and 'hat geborgen' (went security for). During the legal proceedings in May 1850 the *Westdeutsche Zeitung*, whose editor was Hermann Becker, came out in defence of Kinkel by publishing Bürgers' articles 'Die Logik in dem Prozesse Kinkels und Genossen' and 'Die Freisprechung Kinkels', Nos. 102-104, 107, 30 April, 1, 2 and 5 May 1850. See also this volume, pp. 34 and 570. - [c] Marx's daughter to Freiligrath's son

12

ENGELS TO MARX

IN LONDON

Manchester, 28 January 1852

Dear Marx,

Enclosed the thing for *The Times*.[a] All you have to write is:* Sir, I believe the publication of the scandalous facts contained in the annexed letter will contribute to throw some light upon the state of things on the Continent. The correctness of these facts I guarantee,* etc. Name and address.

Mine to *The Daily News* will be going off this evening by the second post; if you arrange matters similarly, both letters will arrive at the respective OFFICES at almost the same time and thus may appear in Friday's issue.[42] But post the letter *in Charing Cross*; there is too much delay at the branch OFFICES.

I return herewith the two letters from Cluss and Bermbach. The seal on your Saturday's letter[b] was once again in a sorry state; I enclose it herewith. What can be afoot?

In *The Daily News* I shall simply sign myself A GERMAN MERCHANT. Write soon.

Your
F. E.

First published in *Der Briefwechsel zwischen F. Engels und K. Marx*, Bd. 1, Stuttgart, 1913

Printed according to the original

Published in English for the first time

---

[a] K. Marx and F. Engels, 'To the Editor of *The Times*'. - [b] See this volume, pp. 20-21.

13

ENGELS TO MARX

IN LONDON

Manchester, 29 January 1852

Dear Marx,

How annoying that one cannot rely on anything being done unless one does it oneself. Owing to our messenger's stupidity, my letter to *The Daily News* did not go off yesterday; now it's too late. So all I can do is to keep it in abeyance until I see whether yours is in tomorrow's or Saturday's *Times*. If not, it will go off at once. In the meantime there's one thing to consider: whether *Freiligrath* is not the right man for *The D. News*. Were he to write to them, I could try *The Weekly Press* and *The Sun*. We 2 have been cold-shouldered by *The D. N.* once already.[42]

Enclosed another article for Dana.[a] It might, perhaps, be divided into two at the point where the Polish business ends—though it would be better to keep it entire. If you split it up, you can send both halves by the same STEAMER, since there is not another sailing before tomorrow week. I will now see that I get on fairly quickly, SAY, 2 articles a week, so as to have done with the SUBJECT. There will be 15-16 articles in all.[43]

No copies[b] received from Weydemeyer. No letter either. This surprises me. I shall finish another article[c] for him this evening.

The French are real jackasses. Madier approached me about an industrial matter and, since my brother-in-law,[d] who knows the DODGE, happened to be here, I gave him some very useful hints and advice. Now the dolt writes to say that, as a result of silly chatter by some *crapaud*[e] who knows nothing of this matter, he intends to go about it in a different and MOST UNBUSINESSLIKE way, and I am to obtain, not for him, but for his associate, a man whom I have never seen, letters of introduction from my brother-in-law (who, fortunately, is on the Continent)! You will recall that Madier introduced us to a calico printer who was bound for Manchester. The fellow calls on me, I go to immense pains to be helpful, do

---

[a] F. Engels, *Revolution and Counter-Revolution in Germany*, VIII and IX. - [b] of *Die Revolution* - [c] F. Engels, 'England', II. - [d] Emil Blank - [e] philistine (literally: toad)

what I can, treat him with the utmost consideration, and in return for all this the dolt suddenly vanishes without my being able to learn what has become of him. A fine race!

Your

F. E.

First published much abridged in *Der Briefwechsel zwischen F. Engels und K. Marx*, Bd. 1, Stuttgart, 1913 and in full in *MEGA*, Abt. III, Bd. 1, Berlin, 1929

Printed according to the original

Published in English for the first time

14

MARX TO JOSEPH WEYDEMEYER

IN NEW YORK

[London,] 30 January 1852
28 Dean Street, Soho

Dear Weydemeyer,

Enclosed you will find:

1. A further instalment of my article.[a]
2. A piece by Eccarius,[44] whose grammatical mistakes, punctuation and so forth you yourself will have to correct, since he brought me the thing too late for me to attend to this myself.
3. Translation of an interesting article in *The Times* by Lupus[b] who, however, does not wish his name to appear, the thing being merely a translation.

How goes it with the German book-trade in America? Might I find a publisher there for my Economy,[45] now that things have miscarried in Germany?

Salut.

Your

K. Marx

First published in: Marx and Engels, *Works*, First Russian Edition, Vol. XXV, Moscow, 1934

Printed according to the original

Published in English for the first time

---

[a] K. Marx, *The Eighteenth Brumaire of Louis Bonaparte*, III - [b] Presumably K. Batthyány's article 'The Hungarian Revolution. To the Editor of *The Times*', *The Times*, No. 20998, 30 December 1851.

15

ENGELS TO JOSEPH WEYDEMEYER[1]

IN NEW YORK

[Manchester,] Friday, 30 January 1852

Dear Weydemeyer,

I sent you by last Saturday's STEAMER (the *Europa*, I think) an article together with a letter.[a] Herewith a few more lines.[b] The issues of the *Revolution* you promised have not yet turned up, although your last letter of 5 Jan. gave good reason to believe that they would come by the next STEAMER, and since then 1 Southampton and 3 Liverpool STEAMERS have arrived here with mails from New York dated up to 17 Jan. I hope no snags have arisen to prevent publication. At all events, I expect to hear from you by the next STEAMER, the *Cambria* (out of Boston 21 Jan.), which is due here on Monday 2 Feb.

My anticipations regarding the confiscation of Louis Philippe's fortune and a Persigny Ministry[c] have been confirmed sooner than I could have hoped; given a reasonably well-organised service, news of it must have arrived in New York by way of the Liverpool newspapers at the same time as my letter; hardly was my letter in the post when the telegraphic dispatch about it likewise arrived here. So much the better. The thing's going splendidly and there's better still to come.

Weerth is on his travels again, will be visiting Holland, France, Switzerland, etc., and must at this moment be in London. I have written and told Marx that he should again chivvy him a little about sending you a few things, although he will hardly have the peace and quiet to do so. When one has spent the whole day tramping round calling on Dutch Jews with samples of wool and linen yarn, one feels small inclination to spend the evening at the hotel in writing that sort of thing. However, if anything is to be extracted from him, Marx is the man to do it.

The sudden lull in the émigrés' tittle-tattle brought about by the new turn of events in France is truly comical. Not a whisper do I hear about the whole caboodle.

The prisoners in Cologne are in a serious position. Since there is

---

a F. Engels, 'England', I (see also this volume, pp. 15-19). - b F. Engels, 'England', II. - c See this volume, p. 17.

no charge whatever against them, the Board of indicting magistrates has neither released them nor brought them before the Court of Assizes but—has referred the matter back to the first examining magistrate for a fresh investigation! In other words, they will remain provisionally in clink without books, without letters, without being able to communicate either with one another or with the outside world, until the new state tribunal is ready.[a] Just now we are trying to denounce this outrage in the English bourgeois Press.[b]

Many regards.

Your
F. E.

[On the back of the letter]

Per LIVERPOOL STEAMER *Mr. J. Weydemeyer*, 7 Chambers' Street, New York (City)

First published in: Marx and Engels, *Works*, First Russian Edition, Vol. XXV, Moscow, 1934

Printed according to the original

Published in English in full for the first time

16

ENGELS TO MARX

IN LONDON

[Manchester,] 2 February 1852

Dear Marx,

Do you recall a refugee by the name of *Richter* from Torgau (Prussian Saxony), a saddler and upholsterer—who used to be in London? This man, whom I recall having seen in London—tall, fair, the manners of a refugee—suddenly calls on me here, ostensibly having returned from Barmen where, he maintains, he worked for a time without papers; he brings greetings from Hühnerbein, etc. I can call to mind absolutely nothing about him except that I have seen him before. At all events, our register of refugees and Pfänder's or Rings' good memory should be able to

---

[a] See this volume, p. 22. - [b] ibid., pp. 20, 24, 25, 29 and 30.

tell us more particulars about him. I rather suspect the fellow is a member of Willich's clique [46]—in which case I shall chuck him out at once. The man has already found work here.

So far, I've been able to discover nothing in *The Times* about the business of our people in Cologne.[a] I am only awaiting your reply to write immediately, *s'il y a lieu*,[b] to *The Daily News*. The American STEAMER is in but, much to my surprise, no letter from Weydemeyer, or any copies of the paper,[c] at least up till now. However, it's still possible that these may arrive tomorrow.

Your
F. E.

Tell Pieper I shall shortly be sending him his £2, now the new month has begun.

First published in *Der Briefwechsel zwischen F. Engels und K. Marx*, Bd. 1, Stuttgart, 1913

Printed according to the original

Published in English for the first time

17

MARX TO ENGELS

IN MANCHESTER

[London,] 4 February 1852[d]
28 Dean Street, Soho

Dear Engels,

Weerth left this morning for Holland. Where will he go from there? I do not know and neither does Weerth himself perhaps. He was as always very much disgruntled at his lot and, as for ours, the only disagreeable thing about it seemed to him our being forced to remain here in London instead of Cadiz, Saragossa, or some other confounded place in Spain. Indeed, since he's been living in Yorkshire again, Weerth has been saying that the time spent in Spain was the best in his life. He maintains that he can't stand the English climate and may therefore find that of Holland very COMFORTABLE. Let us wish him *le bon voyage* and wait and see whether he keeps his word and remembers about Weydemeyer.

---

[a] See this volume, p. 24. - [b] if necessary - [c] *Die Revolution* - [d] The original has 1851.

My 'LETTER TO THE EDITOR' was sent to *The Times* last Thursday,[a] *il y a donc presque une semaine.*[b] It would seem that this paper, now that it makes a métier of polemicising against Bonaparte, deems it necessary to spare Prussia. So you must approach *The Daily News.* If that, too, misfires, which I doubt, there still remains *The Spectator. Il est presque sûr.*[c]

Yesterday G. J. Harney sent me the first issue of his resuscitated and somewhat enlarged *Friend of the People.*[47] If that's what he withdrew from the world for 8 months and buried himself in melancholy Scotland for...! But *un seul passage suffira pour te faire goûter ce fruit délicieux*[d]:

Justice—Immutable, Universal, Eternal*—proclaims the sublime principle which will be, at once, our guiding star, the rule of our conduct, and the test, etc.'[e]

En voilà assez![f] Bonaparte, however, he has adequately chastised by calling him 'Louis THE BASE'.

I do not know whether our EXDEAR sent me his little paper in order to wring our hearts or whether, out of spite towards us, he has become even more tritely democratic than we would have believed possible. By the by, alongside the platitudes and the 'JUSTICE IMMUTABLE' there are barefaced tricks played by the TRADING DEMAGOGUE. Against Jones—via the 'SPIRIT OF FREEDOM',[g] via that SPOUTER Massey, secretary of the Tailors' Association of Castle Street, lickspittle to the clerics who keep this SHOP. Herald, *à tort et à travers* of the *petits grands hommes*[h] whom the Continent has spewed out, calumniator of Jones, married to a *saltimbanque*[i] who has duped him into believing that she is clairvoyant—he gets this Massey to have an apologia published for the associations in general and the AMALGAMATED SOCIETY in particular, a piece which threatens to extend over numerous issues.[48] And Rhadamanthus Harney had told Jones in person that *au fond*[j] he shared his views on the Associations. At the same time he announces: 'KOSSUTH'S RECEPTION AND PROGRESS IN AMERICA',[k] although in a letter to Jones he described Kossuth as a HUMBUG. That is what the gentlemen of 'SUBLIME PRINCIPLE' are like. *Je ne sais que c'est que des principes, sinon des règles qu'on*

---

[a] See this volume, p. 24. - [b] i.e. nearly a week ago - [c] It is almost a certainty. - [d] But a single passage will suffice to give you the flavour of this delicious fruit - [e] [G. J. Harney,] 'Prologue', *The Friend of the People*, No. 1, 7 February 1852. - [f] That's enough! - [g] An allusion to the journal *Spirit of Freedom* edited by Massey. - [h] without rhyme or reason; petty panjandrums - [i] a charlatan - [j] basically - [k] A. Bell's article 'Reception and Progress of Kossuth in the United States', *The Friend of the People*, No. 2, 14 February 1852.

prescrit aux autres pour soi.[a] Harney retired for a while, allowing Jones, with his *tempérament fougueux*,[b] to spoil the broth of popularity and then drink it himself. But even though he may harm Jones, he himself will achieve nothing. The fellow's completely done for as a writer and also, according to Lupus who heard him SPEECH-making in Jones Street,[49] as a speaker, but above all as a man. May the devil take these popular movements, more especially when they are *pacifiques*. In the course of this Chartist agitation O'Connor has gone *mad* (have you read about his latest scene in court?),[50] Harney has gone stale and Jones bankrupt. *Voilà le dernier but de la vie dans tous les mouvements populaires.*[c]

Yesterday 'Colonel Bangya' came to see me. Amongst other things he said: 'Kossuth made the following speech to the Hungarian refugees who had foregathered with him in London: "I will take care of you all but I demand that you all remain loyal, devoted and attached to me. I am not such a fool as to sustain people who intrigue with my opponents. I demand that everyone declare himself unconditionally."' Thus the HUMBLE Kossuth behind the scenes. I further learned from Bangya that Szemere, Kasimir Batthyány and Perczel (*le général*) are coming to London and will set up an anti-Kossuth committee. Lastly, the master mind behind the whole DODGE is Signore Mazzini. He is using Kossuth as a mouthpiece and, in his cabinet, regards himself as something of a Machiavelli. It is he who pulls the strings. But this gentleman is unaware that the puppets he causes to dance are heroes only in his own eyes and in no one else's. Thus he wrote and told Kossuth to get on intimate terms with Kinkel, saying that he personally had been unable to do so because he already had the other lot of German bigwigs *sur le bras*[d]; Kossuth must now really make friends with Kinkel and Kinkel must write in all his letters about his worthy, his eminent friend and "equal", Kossuth. As for Kossuth, however, his idea is to lean on Germany's dictator, Kinkel, on the one hand, and on Italy's dictator, Mazzini, on the other, and to secure his rear with his ally, the dictator of France, Ledru-Rollin. The poor devil has sunk low.

A Frenchman, Massol by name, has paid me a visit. For a short spell he was on the *Réforme* under Lamennais. Formerly one of the *civilisateurs*[e] whom Mohammed Ali had summoned from Gaul,[51] he is also one of the few *hommes d'esprit*[f] still to be found

---

[a] I don't know what principles are unless rules which one prescribes for others for one's own benefit. - [b] fiery temperament - [c] That is the ultimate end of life in all popular movements. - [d] on his hands - [e] civilisers - [f] men of wit

among the French. According to him, Sasonow's stay in Paris (which, by the way he must now leave) is wholly attributable to his possession of a very reliable false passport and to his connections with a few *femmes galantes*[a] who have INFLUENCE in the top circles. You will like Massol.

In addition I have seen *les citoyens*[b] Vallières (former Barbèsiste and officer at the barricades), Bianchi and Sabatier. Though very refined, the latter is *en général* not above the usual run.

Dronke, I hear, is in Savoy.

Bangya has suggested that Szemere and Perczel should write for Weydemeyer. What are the main points in the Hungarian business (military or otherwise) upon which elucidation should be sought from these gentlemen? It goes without saying that they must not write under their own names, for we do not want to identify ourselves with *any* coterie. But Perczel is *du moins bon républicain,*[c] and very knowledgeable.

Be so good—and mind you don't forget—as to send me the *Tribunes.* Johnson—Freiligrath's friend—wants to read the articles on Germany.[d] Lupus wants to write an anti-Kossuth piece for Weydemeyer.

As for the commercial business, I can no longer make head or tail of it. At one moment crisis seems imminent and the CITY prostrated, the next everything is set fair. I know that none of this will have any impact on the catastrophe. But at the present moment London is not the place in which to observe the current tendency.

Salut.

Your

K. M.

The matter of the seal is highly suspect.[e] Send *this one* back to me; I have examined it minutely.

First published much abridged in *Der Briefwechsel zwischen F. Engels und K. Marx*, Bd. 1, Stuttgart, 1913 and in full in *MEGA*, Abt. III, Bd. 1, Berlin, 1929

Printed according to the original

Published in English for the first time

---

[a] women of easy virtue - [b] the citizens - [c] at least a good republican - [d] F. Engels, *Revolution and Counter-Revolution in Germany.* - [e] See this volume, p. 24.

18

MARX TO ENGELS

IN MANCHESTER

[London,] Friday, 6 February 1852
28 Dean Street, Soho

Dear Engels,

I have just received your article.[a]

I am writing no more than a line or two, being short of time because of the departure of the mail for America and thus unable to go out to inquire about 'Richter'[b] until later.

I would, by the way, be glad if in the meantime you could send *me* the £2 by postal order. I shall be receiving SOME MONEY next week and shall then deliver the £2 to Pieper in your name. But it is important for me to have it at the *beginning* of the week whereas to him it can only be a matter of indifference, since he is well provided for just now.

Your

K. M.

First published in *Der Briefwechsel zwischen F. Engels und K. Marx*, Bd. 1, Stuttgart, 1913

Printed according to the original

Published in English for the first time

19

MARX TO JOSEPH WEYDEMEYER[52]

IN NEW YORK

[London,] 13 February 1852
28 Dean Street, Soho

Dear Weydemeyer,

Herewith the continuation of my article.[c] The thing seems to grow of its own accord, and you will be getting two more articles about it. In addition I shall be sending you by the next post something on

---

[a] F. Engels, *Revolution and Counter-Revolution in Germany*, X. - [b] See this volume, p. 28. - [c] K. Marx, *The Eighteenth Brumaire of Louis Bonaparte*, IV.

Signore Mazzini. But it is high time that we had some copies of your paper.[a] After all, to be able to write for a journal one needs to see it, and the zeal of my colleagues is stimulated by seeing their things in print.

Herewith a note, which you should turn into an article, about the position of our imprisoned friends in Cologne.[53]

These people have now been in jug getting on for ten months.

In November the case went through the Ratskammer, and was referred to the Court of Assizes. Next the case came up before the Board of indicting magistrates which, before Christmas, delivered a verdict, which was motivated as follows: 'In consideration of the fact that there is no actual evidence of an indictable offence and hence no grounds for sustaining the charge...' (but that, in view of the importance attached to the matter by the government, we fear for our posts if we drop the case against these people) 'we accordingly refer the case back to the first magistrate for instruction on various points.' The chief reason for this procrastination is the government's conviction that, before a jury, it would fail ignominiously. Meanwhile it hopes to see the creation of a High Court for high treason, or at least the withdrawal of JURIES in all cases of political offences, to which end a petition has already been laid before the First Prussian Chamber. Our friends are locked up in cells, cut off from one another and from the world, may receive neither letters nor visits nor even books—things that are never denied common criminals in Prussia.

The Board could never have pronounced such an outrageous verdict had the Press evinced the least concern for the case. But liberal papers such as the *Kölnische* remained silent out of cowardice and 'democratic' ones (including the *Lithographische Korrespondenz*, published by Kinkel with the help of American money) out of hatred for the communists, out of fear of forfeiting some of their own importance, out of rivalry towards 'new' martyrs.[54] Such is the gratitude shown by these curs to the *N.Rh.Z.*, which always stood up for the democratic rabble whenever they clashed with the government (e.g. Temme *et al*). Such is the gratitude shown by Mr Kinkel to the *Westdeutsche Zeitung*, in which Becker was his hearth and Bürgers his haven.[b] *Les canailles! Il faut les attaquer à mort.*[c]

Greetings from my family to yours.

Your
K. M.

---

[a] *Die Revolution* - [b] See this volume, p. 23. - [c] The scoundrels! They must be fought to the death.

[From Jenny Marx]

We all of us long to hear from you, dear Mr Weydemeyer, but alas, one ship after another comes in without bringing news of you, your dear wife,[a] your children, your paper, etc., etc. I trust you have safely received all the help sent from London. My husband has commandeered on your behalf pretty well all available communist quills (and has also turned to Germany), and some of these pieces, for instance Freiligrath's poem,[b] will assuredly secure circulation for your paper. If you could somehow contrive to publish pamphlets, I would beg you to think it over. We are in a very sad plight here, there being no more hope for us in Europe. My husband believes that his articles on France, which will run to two more,[c] are of the greatest topical interest and would thus provide the most suitable material for a small pamphlet, if only as a sequel to his *Revue* articles.[d] If a New York bookseller were able to establish contact with Germany, he could count on not inconsiderable sales there. In any case the thing is written for Europe rather than America. However, we shall, of course, leave this to your own discretion. My husband further asks that you urge Dana to give us the name of a business house here in London where we can collect the fees with the minimum of delay. At this distance, Karl could not possibly give Dana any real idea of our circumstances or the urgency of the matter, since the situation was quite different when Dana knew us in Cologne and such a comfortably situated American has no idea how everything hangs in the balance here, and how ten shillings, coming at the right moment, can often rescue one from a horrifying situation. Sometime or other you may, perhaps, find an opportunity of telling him this personally. With kindest regards and warm greetings to your wife

from Jenny Marx

First published in: Marx and Engels, *Works,* First Russian Edition, Vol. XXV, Moscow, 1934

Marx's letter is printed according to the original, Jenny Marx's note according to a copy in unknown hand

Published in English in full for the first time

20

ENGELS TO MARX

IN LONDON

[Manchester,] 17 February 1852

Dear Marx,

You will be furious with me for being so cursory, but I'll be damned if I know whether I'm coming or going, what with all this

---

[a] Louise - [b] F. Freiligrath, 'An Joseph Weydemeyer', I and II. - [c] K. Marx, *The Eighteenth Brumaire of Louis Bonaparte.* See also this volume, p. 40. - [d] K. Marx, *The Class Struggles in France, 1848 to 1850.*

work and COMMERCE. *Voici les faits*[a]: 1. Charles[b] has gone to Germany and has left me not only with all his own work, but also with a nice little residue of tasks left undone at the year's end; 2. Last year's balance sheet shows a *definite loss* for my old man which may be a good lesson for him, but means that I am inundated with an unholy mass of vexations, calculations, and jobs of various kinds; 3. One of the Ermens[c] has given notice of termination and you can imagine the intrigues and correspondence which that brings in its train. Enough: this evening I shall be stuck in the office until 8 and, instead of being able to write to you at greater length, still have to write a letter to my old man and take it to the POST OFFICE before twelve o'clock tonight; tomorrow evening I must do something for Jones[d] and the day after tomorrow I shall see to it that I finish an article for the *Tribune*.[e] For the present there can be no thought of spare time before 7 or 8 in the evening, and the worst of it is that, for some time to come, I shall have to devote my whole attention to filthy commerce, otherwise everything will go wrong here and my old man will cut off my SUPPLIES.

You will have received the £2. I hope to hear from you soon, even if I don't have sufficient leizure to answer your last letter at length.

According to today's *Daily News* Louis Napoleon is certain to exhume Kaspar Hauser and to claim succession to the throne of Baden through his Aunt Stéphanie. *Voilà de grandes nouvelles pour le citoyen Seiler dont l'étoile va se lever incessamment.*[f] Could you not persuade Kaspar Hauser's great historian[g] to write to Louis Napoleon and offer him his important sources on this matter? *Il y a là de quoi faire un grand coup.*[h]

Your
F. E.

How is it that Weydemeyer sends no word? If a letter doesn't arrive by the *Arctic* tomorrow morning, I shall despair; something

---

[a] Here are the facts. - [b] Roesgen - [c] Gottfried - [d] F. Engels, 'Real Causes Why the French Proletarians Remained Comparatively Inactive in December Last', I. - [e] for the series *Revolution and Counter-Revolution in Germany* - [f] That's great news for Citizen Seiler, whose star will be constantly in the ascendant - [g] An allusion to Sebastian Seiler's work *Kaspar Hauser, der Thronerbe von Badens*. - [h] A great deal could be made of that.

must have gone wrong. So far as I know, he has not written since 5 January, or at least I have heard nothing.

First published in *Der Briefwechsel zwischen F. Engels und K. Marx*, Bd. 1, Stuttgart, 1913

Printed according to the original

Published in English for the first time

21

MARX TO ENGELS

IN MANCHESTER

[London,] 18 February [1852]
28 Dean Street, Soho

I shall write to you at length on *Saturday*. Only a few lines today.

I have not yet received the money that was promised me from home and so have not yet been able to hand over your £2 to Pieper, but have told him I have had a few lines from you in which you informed me that I should be receiving money for him from you. I hope I shall be able to pay him before the week is out.

If your time is very much taken up, you would certainly do better to write for Dana than for Jones. The enclosed letter from Weydemeyer[55] will show you even more plainly how essential it is not to interrupt these articles.[a] What must be done now is to redouble our attacks in the *Tribune* on the Frankfurt Left,[56] especially when you come to the 'March Association'.[57] To help you, I am today sending you Bauer's book,[b] in which at least a few facts are to be found.

I again pray you to send me the issues of the 'Tribune' by return, since Johnson is the only Englishman to whom I can turn when *in extremis*[c] — and I hover constantly on the brink. Don't forget it this time!

---

[a] F. Engels, *Revolution and Counter-Revolution in Germany.* - [b] B. Bauer, *Der Untergang des Frankfurter Parlaments.* - [c] in extreme need

How is it that Weydemeyer has not received a *single one* of your articles[a]? You must set an inquiry on foot.

Your
K. M.

First published in *Der Briefwechsel zwischen F. Engels und K. Marx*, Bd. 1, Stuttgart, 1913

Printed according to the original

Published in English for the first time

22

ENGELS TO MARX

IN LONDON

Manchester, 19 February 1852

Dear Marx,

Despite tremendous efforts—your letter only arrived this morning—I have still not finished the article for Dana[b] and it is now 11 o'clock at night. I have received the Bauer[c]—it is coming in very useful. In return, and whatever happens, you will receive 2 articles for Dana for next Tuesday's STEAMER. Since your letters reach Weydemeyer and mine don't, I'd be glad if you would forthwith dispatch the enclosed note to W.[d] in one of your own. It's an altogether curious business. It seems that two or three of my letters to my old man have also failed to reach him. *Cela n'est pas clair.*[e]

Tell Jones he will be getting something from me next week, or write him a note to that effect. God knows why so many snags should crop up all at once and prevent me from getting down to anything. But on Saturday and Sunday I shall shut myself away, and then I hope to get something done.[19]

---

[a] F. Engels, 'England'. - [b] for the series *Revolution and Counter-Revolution in Germany.*- [c] B. Bauer, *Der Untergang des Frankfurter Parlaments.* - [d] See this volume, pp. 39-40. - [e] It's not clear (Beaumarchais, *La folle journée, ou le mariage de Figaro,* Act. V, Scene 16).

Why doesn't that accursed Weydemeyer enclose Simon's article[a] so·that we can attend to it ourselves? A stinging counter-article would soon show Dana that nothing is to be gained by accepting articles that attack us.

Your
F. E.

Write some time giving me the exact address under which *you* have written to Weydemeyer.

First published in *Der Briefwechsel zwischen F. Engels und K. Marx*, Bd. 1, Stuttgart, 1913

Printed according to the original

Published in English for the first time

23

ENGELS TO JOSEPH WEYDEMEYER

IN NEW YORK

Manchester, 19 February 1852

Dear Weydemeyer,

To my intense surprise I see from your letter of 6 Feb. per the *Arctic* that not one of my letters to you has arrived. I have sent you 4, if not 5, articles on England[17] and only desisted a fortnight ago because I had heard absolutely nothing from you: my last article went by the STEAMER which left on Saturday 31 Jan. from Liverpool, and concerned the REFORM BILL to be anticipated from little Russell. The first 2 letters were addressed to Mr J. Weydemeyer, Deutsche Vereinsbuchhandlung, William Street, New York; the others to Mr J. W., 7 Chambers' Street, New York (City). Since this matter requires investigation, I am sending you this through Marx whose letters, it seems, are reaching you; I would ask you, 1. to go to the above places and see whether the letters were presented there; 2. if not, to go and inquire at the N. Y. CITY POST OFFICE. If they are not to be found there, advise me by the first Liverpool STEAMER and I shall see what further steps can be taken here; I can easily get the thing into the newspapers over here if the local postmaster fails to give me a satisfactory answer. I posted several of the letters myself, the rest went with the business mail, and that proves that they were

---

[a] L. Simon's 'Movements of the German Political Exiles', *New-York Daily Tribune*, No. 3369, 4 February 1852. See also this volume, p. 37.

properly attended to, since all our business letters have arrived. Take these steps, I beg you, without delay, for otherwise there is little point in my sending you any more articles when the *Revolution* comes to life again.

Make sure you send us L. Simon's *Tribune* article,[a] either a cutting—giving the date of the issue—or the whole issue in a wrapper, since that sort of thing is always good reading.

My address is still the same.

Your

F. E.

First published in: Marx and Engels, *Works,* First Russian Edition, Vol. XXV, Moscow, 1934

Printed according to the original

Published in English for the first time

24

MARX TO JOSEPH WEYDEMEYER [12]

IN NEW YORK

[London,] 20 February 1852

Dear Weydemeyer,

I can send you nothing this week for the simple reason that for a week or more I have been so beset by money troubles that I have not even been able to pursue my studies at the Library,[b] let alone write articles.

However, I think that by Tuesday (the 24th) and Friday (the 27th) I shall be able to send you Nos. 5 and 6 of my article,[c] which are the concluding ones.

I received your letter, along with Cluss' concluding remarks on 18 February. You have been particularly unfortunate in two respects: 1. unemployment in New York; 2. the raging westerlies, which have driven vessels bound from London to America off course. For, with the exception of the early days, contributions have been sent you from England (by me, Engels, Freiligrath,

---

a See this volume, p. 39. - b of the British Museum - c K. Marx, *The Eighteenth Brumaire of Louis Bonaparte.*

Eccarius, etc.) as *regularly* as any newspaper could hope for. However, the people here have begun to flag because no news has arrived from America, albeit a multitude of ships. I did not think fit to inform anyone other than Engels and Lupus of the suspension of your paper.[a] It would only make people more dilatory.

If, by the by, you wish to receive regular support from here, you will have to fulfil the following conditions:

1. Write *every* week and give the date of the letters you have received from us.

2. Keep us fully *au courant* with everything over there and regularly supplied with relevant documents, etc., newspaper cuttings, etc.

You will realise, *mon cher*,[b] how difficult it is to contribute to a paper on the other side of the ocean without any knowledge of its readers, etc. But if you fulfil the above conditions I can guarantee you the necessary contributions. I am here at their backs, WHIP in hand, and shall have no difficulty in keeping their noses to the grindstone. From Germany, too, I have received promises on your behalf of contributions and collaboration. If I only knew that the paper would survive, I would have someone *in Paris* who is READY to send you a *weekly contribution gratis.* I shall write to the man,[c] who is one of my best and most intelligent friends. The worst of it is that no one likes to work *pour le roi de Prusse*,[d] and daily reports lose all value if not published immediately on arrival. Since, then, you are unable to make any payment, it is all the more necessary to convince people that they are doing *real* party work and that their letters are not being pigeonholed.

It seems to me that you are making a mistake in having your letters delivered instead of doing what every newspaper must do, that is, advise the Post Office that you will have them collected regularly on the arrival of a vessel. In this way misunderstandings and delays are more easily avoided.

Apropos. Do not print Hirsch's statement[14] if you have not already done so.

A mass of blackguards is leaving here for New York (amongst them tailor Lehmann and tailor Joseph Meyer). Some of them will approach you in my name. But don't trust anyone who does not bring with him a few lines in my *writing*. The fellows will serve

---

[a] *Die Revolution* - [b] my dear fellow - [c] R. Reinhardt - [d] for the king of Prussia, i.e. for nothing

well enough to answer questions about Willich, etc. Lehmann and Meyer are devotees of Jesus Willich.

As for Dana, I think it was foolish of him to accept articles from Simon.^a If my money-box allowed, I should immediately refuse to send him any further contributions. Let him publish attacks on myself and Engels but not by such an impertinent nincompoop. It's sheer stupidity to permit Agitation and Emigration,[26] those twin fictions which exist only on newspaper pages, to be presented to the American public as historical realities by a vain fellow who has imposed upon Germany the Prussian Emperor,[58] the March Associations[57] and the Imperial Regent, Vogt,[59] and now, with his bankrupt accomplices, would like to impose *himself* afresh upon the people, along with Parliament and a somewhat modified Imperial constitution. *Rien de plus ridicule que ce gredin-là qui du haut des Alpes laisse tomber des paroles d'homme d'état.*^b I should have credited Dana with more tact. Ludwig Simon—*von* Trier! When will this fellow drop his patent of parliamentary nobility?

Here in London, you know, all these fellows have completely drifted apart. The only thing that keeps them in any way together is the prospect of being *redeemed* by Gottfried Christ Kinkel's money. On the other hand we have that idiot Ruge, together with Ronge and two or 3 other jackasses, who conceal their lazy still-life by calling it 'agitation', just as a stagnant swamp might be dubbed 'open sea'.

Europe, of course, is now busying itself with other troubles than these. Ledru-Rollin himself has collapsed here like a punctured balloon since 2 December^c and the arrival of new revolutionary elements from France. Mazzini is making ultra-reactionary speeches, one of which I shall shortly analyse for you.

As regards Ernest Jones' *Notes to the People,* in which you will find all the day-to-day history of the English proletariat, I shall send you it as soon as my financial circumstances permit. I have to pay 8 shillings every time I send a parcel to America.

Give Cluss my warm regards. We are eagerly awaiting his letters. Why haven't you sent us his statement[60]?

I, together with my wife, Freiligrath and wife,^d and Lupus, all send our heart-felt greetings to your wife, whom please assure of

---

^a In particular L. Simon's 'Movements of the German Political Exiles', *New-York Daily Tribune,* No. 3369, 4 February 1852. - ^b There's nothing more ridiculous than this scoundrel who, from Alpine heights, lets fall these statesmanlike pronouncements. - ^c coup d'état in France on 2 December 1851 - ^d Ida

our sincere regard. We hope that the new world citizen will make his appearance cheerfully in the New World.

Farewell.

Your

K. Marx

If it does not work out with your newspaper, could you not bring out my pamphlet,[a] sheet by sheet or, if possible, in sections as sent to you? Otherwise it will take too long.

First published in: Marx and Engels, *Works*, First Russian Edition, Vol. XXV, Moscow, 1934

Printed according to the original

Published in English in full for the first time

25

MARX TO ENGELS

IN MANCHESTER

[London,] 23 February [1852]

DEAR Frederic,

I must again chivvy you about the *Tribune* since I am myself being chivvied daily by Johnson.[b] I would also ask you to send me such documents as you may have received from Weydemeyer. The address you gave for Weydemeyer was perfectly correct.

Apropos. By Pfänder's account the Straubinger[61] Richter is a creature of Willich's.

E. Jones has been puffing your article for all he is worth without, of course, mentioning your name.[c] He has been compelled thus to cry his wares by competition from Harney who has got hold of some money, the devil knows where from, and has large *advertising waggons* driving round the City, with the legend 'READ THE *FRIEND OF THE PEOPLE*', the paper being displayed and on sale in all socialist SHOPS.

---

[a] K. Marx, *The Eighteenth Brumaire of Louis Bonaparte.* - [b] See this volume, pp. 32 and 37. - [c] F. Engels, 'Real Causes Why the French Proletarians Remained Comparatively Inactive in December Last'. See also [E. Jones,] 'Continental Notes', *Notes to the People*, No. 43, 21 February 1852.

I shall search out and send you the issue of the *Tribune* in which Mr Simon blows his own trumpet.[55] The incompetent nincompoop! He still goes on signing himself 'Simon von Trier'. The fellow can't make up his mind to dispense with his parliamentary nobility title. Seiler has read the translation of the crap in the *Staatszeitung*. You know how garbled his accounts always are. So far as I could gather it went something like this: Ludwig Simon von Trier, speaking on behalf of the Swiss émigrés, treats the great controversy between 'Agitation' (the name used by Ruge and Co. to conceal the dullness of their still-life) and 'Emigration',[26] with the most prodigious pomposity, as Europe's *question brûlante*[a] from his 'Alpine height'. At this juncture—and here Willich is also cited as a man of the utmost importance, all manner of diffuse reflections being proffered concerning the acquisition of this hero—he comes to the third of the dangerous parties in London, 'the *party of imposition*', the leaders of which are Engels and Marx. For we seek to impose 'liberty' on the peoples by force. We are worse tyrants than the Emperor of Russia. We were the first to treat 'universal franchise', etc., with 'scorn and contumely'. And even before that, we ruined everything with our 'lust for imposition'. *Le pauvre garçon!*[b] Did we impose the Prussian Emperor,[58] the 'March Associations'[57] or the Imperial Regent Vogt, on the Germans[59]? On him we shall impose a *coup de pied*.[c] So far as these jackasses are concerned, Bonaparte has lived in vain. They still go on believing in 'universal franchise', and are solely preoccupied with paltry calculations as to how they can again impose their rotten personalities on the German people. One can hardly believe one's ears when one hears the fellows indefatigably bawling out the same old tune again. They are proper blockheads, incorrigible blockheads. As to how the vain little rogue found his way into the *Tribune*, I am in no doubt. *Le citoyen Fröbel aura été l'homme intermédiaire.*[d] He has long been connected with Dana.

Enclosed a letter from Reinhardt, which contains some pretty *cancans*.[e]

Russell has been overthrown in the drollest possible manner.[62] I can ask nothing more than that Derby should take the helm. During this short session you will have seen how pitiable the Manchester men[63] can be when not driven by *la force des choses*.[f] I don't hold it against these fellows. Each successive democratic

---

[a] burning question - [b] Poor chap! - [c] a kick - [d] Citizen Fröbel will have acted as intermediary. - [e] gossip. Excerpts from Reinhardt's letter see on pp. 47-49 of this volume. - [f] force of circumstances

Ferdinand Freiligrath

28 Dean Street, Soho, London, where Marx lived from 1850 to 1856

victory, e.g. the BALLOT,[64] is a concession which, of course, they make to the workers only *en cas d'urgence*.[a]

Yesterday I was talking to a French MERCHANT just come from Paris. Business wretched. And do you know what the jackass said? Bonaparte *fait pire que la république. Les affaires allaient mieux.*[b] It is truly fortunate that the French bourgeois should always hold their government responsible for commercial crises. No doubt Bonaparte is also to blame for the unemployment in New York and the bankruptcies in London.

Another very interesting piece of information (*tu sens ici l'influence de l'illustre Seiler*[c]) about Bonaparte. Bangya, as I have already told you, is connected with Szemere and Batthyány.[d] He is an agent of the latter's. He confided to me that Batthyány and Czartoryski are in collusion with Bonaparte and see him nearly every day. He wants to secure allies behind the backs of Russia and Austria amongst the *aristocratic* émigrés and those streaming in from Poland and Hungary and has, moreover, definitely told them that, in spite of Nicholas and all the rest, he is going to invade Belgium and perhaps Baden as well, and this in the near future.

Ewerbeck has sent me 12 copies of his bulky work, *L'Allemagne et les Allemands*. One for you. Nothing quite like it has ever been seen or heard of before. The historical part, which begins *ab ovo*,[e] is copied from out-dated primers. You may judge how competent he is as regards more recent history from the following particulars: *F. List* introduced the doctrine of Free Trade, and Ruge that of social science, into Germany. Hegel has immortalised himself by (literally) enlightening the Germans on the categories of quality, quantity, etc., and Feuerbach has proved that men cannot extend their knowledge beyond the range of human understanding. Pedro Düsar (brother of the Struve woman) is one of the greatest German men of liberty, and Freiligrath made his name as a *collaborateur* on the *Neue Rheinische Zeitung*. On top of that a style *à pouffer de rire*,[f] e.g. how Jason's warriors grew from dragon's teeth, which is why the German tribes are perpetually at odds with one another. Romulus Augustulus *était un jeune homme doux et agréable*,[g] and for three hundred years Germans have been

---

[a] in case of need - [b] is doing worse than the Republic. Business used to be better. - [c] here you may descry the influence of the illustrious Seiler - [d] See this volume, p. 31. - [e] from the egg—from the very beginning - [f] to make one split one's sides - [g] was a nice, gentle young man

used to hearing themselves referred to by their neighbours as *des bêtes.*[a]

Have you read Mazzini's simple-minded infamous speech?

Your

K. M.

First published much abridged in *Der Briefwechsel zwischen F. Engels und K. Marx*, Bd. 1, Stuttgart, 1913 and in full in *MEGA*, Abt. III, Bd. 1, Berlin, 1929

Printed according to the original

Published in English for the first time

26

MARX TO FERDINAND LASSALLE

IN DÜSSELDORF

London, 23 February 1852
28 Dean Street, Soho

Dear Lassalle,

I should greatly like to know whether my second letter[65] similarly failed to arrive. Knowing how punctilious you are about answering, I can only attribute the delay in hearing from you to some accident.

Since I last wrote my state of health has again improved, although I am still having much trouble with my eyes. My social circumstances, on the other hand, have deteriorated. I have had a definite *refus*[b] from the publisher in respect of my Economy[45]; my anti-Proudhon manuscript,[c] which for the past year has been wandering around Germany, has likewise failed to find a berth; the financial crisis has finally reached a level comparable only to the commercial crisis now making itself felt in New York and London. Unlike the gentlemen of commerce, I cannot, alas, even have recourse to bankruptcy. Mr Bonaparte was in similar straits when he chanced his *coup d'état*.

---

[a] beasts - [b] rejection - [c] K. Marx, *The Poverty of Philosophy.*

As to this Mr Bonaparte, I feel I can do no better than give you extracts from a letter conveyed to me by a friend in Paris,[a] *un ami qui est très sceptique et qui ne partage pas les opinions les plus favorables sur le peuple. Maintenant, écoutez*[b]:

'All in all, the mood of the Parisian public has experienced a noticeable change and, even though it has as yet not gone beyond resignation, this last is felt all the more genuinely and grimly, and far more generally. The main reason for this, among the middle and lower classes, is that trade and hence employment, despite initial favourable appearances, simply cannot be got going, whereas those same classes had sacrificed all other considerations to the hope that these things would improve. And then the slow-witted majority of the less advanced workers — which places more hope in the Republic than in the monarchies of long and bitter memory — has, as a result of Napoleon's decrees, gradually come to realise that the President is in no way concerned with the preservation of the Republic; and he has done himself great harm in the eyes of property owners by confiscating the Orleans' estates, a measure which, after all, sets a dangerous official example. Chaps such as Fould, de Morny and Dupin — for reasons of private interest of course — have even refused to subscribe to this measure, a fact all the more striking on account of their spotless antecedents, which are more or less common knowledge. As for Dupin, the President of the defunct National Assembly, it has since been learnt that his last pretty move was to suppress, on the morning of 2 December and with the connivance of Bonaparte, a letter from the Archbishop of Paris inviting the representatives to assemble in the church of Notre Dame while he himself intended to stand in the porch to protect them, in their capacity as the representatives of popular sovereignty, against the soldiers of the usurper. This might have given quite a different turn to the whole thing, the more so since the *haute cour de justice*[c] had assembled at the same time and had already begun to register a protest against the *coup d'état.*

'As for de Morny, the minister who resigned with Dupin, he was known as the *escroc*[d] of his mistress' (Countess Lehon's) husband, a circumstance which caused Émile de Girardin's wife to say that while it was not unprecedented for governments to be in the hands of men who were governed by their wives, none had ever been known to be in the hands of *hommes entretenus.*[e] Well, at present this same Countess Lehon holds a salon where she is one of Bonaparte's most vociferous opponents and it was she who, on the occasion of the confiscation of the Orleans' estates, let fall the well-known witticism: "*C'est le premier vol de l'aigle.*"[f] Because of this remark of his wife's, Émile de Girardin was expelled. Rémusat's expulsion is attributed to a similar cause. The latter is said to have arrived one morning at the Ministry of the Interior where Morny had installed young Lehon as *Chef de Bureau*; upon catching sight of Rémusat, Lehon rudely asked him his name, whereat R. replied: "*Monsieur, dans ma famille on porte le nom de son père, c'est pourquoi je me nomme de Rémusat.*"[g] At much the same time Lehon is said to have

---

a Reinhardt - b a friend who is very sceptical and does not have the highest opinion of the people. Now, listen: - c High Court of Justice - d swindler - e kept men - f 'It is the first flight (theft) of the eagle.' (This witticism and Madame de Girardin's remark cited above are used by Marx in *The Eighteenth Brumaire of Louis Bonaparte,* see present edition, Vol. 11, pp. 196 97.) - g 'In my family, sir, we bear our father's name. That's why I am called de Rémusat.'

had another row, on this occasion in Ham. When he gave General Le Flô official notification of expulsion, the general threw him out, shouting: *"Comment, c'est vous, gredin, qui osez venir m'annoncer mon exil?"* [a] In such circumstances, it is not difficult to assess how much respect a fledgling government will continue to command, even from the most mediocre of *honnêtes gens*.[b] A lady known to me personally, a ward of Napoleon's, who had been in close contact with him ever since she was a child, told him on 2 December that she would have nothing more to do with him, adding that he and his associates were a *gouvernement de voleurs et d'assassins*.[c] True, the real plutocrats continue to adhere to Napoleon as being the only possible expression of authority just now and the last bulwark of existing society, but their faith in the possible durability of his régime has been much undermined by his measures, with the result that, after a brief interval, they have again begun to hug their money, as is evident from the stagnant Bourse and the check to the revival of trade. Thus the President's only real following consists of those who are bound to him by the most blatant self-interest, along with the privileged clerical clique and the army, although considerable dissatisfaction and a feeling of uncertainty and irresolution has crept into the latter as a result of the many dismissals of Orleanist officers, a state of affairs which enormously impairs its power. Moreover, personally and in private, the President is said to be most anxious and downcast. Indeed, in this changed climate of opinion, all that is needed is the removal of his sorry person and everything would be thrown into chaos again without any effort. Little or no attempt would be made at resistance. In this connection the remark by the experienced Guizot, on learning of the successful *coup d'état*, is worthy of note: *"C'est le triomphe complet et définitif du socialisme!"* [d]

'Having both before and after fallen out with every party without exception, Bonaparte is seeking a counterbalance by means of this or that popular measure—vast expansion of public works, prospects of a general amnesty for the participants of 2 December, etc.—just as he will soon attempt something similar by means of this or that measure in favour of this or that class, and all without consistency of purpose. And what matters most of all is his failure to win back the masses, since he is unable to give them bread, i.e. any source of labour for their livelihood, and has actually deprived them of their favourite pastime, the innocent consolation they derived from the trees of liberty and the republican inscriptions in the streets; similarly they can no longer while away an hour in the wine and coffee shops, since all political discourse is strictly prohibited there. The peaceable bourgeois are angered by the loss of their hobby-horse, the National Guard... Nor do they fancy those aristocratic routs, the state balls, from which they stay away; thus, apart from foreigners and two or three Parisian exceptions, the only people to attend the last, splendide, Tuileries ball were ladies of doubtful virtue. The reckless squandering that goes on is a source of disquiet to the thrifty citizens, who look ahead to the day when the Orleans funds will be exhausted.

'What particularly offends all who have a modicum of intelligence is the destruction of the Press.

'Again, the organisation of the resuscitated Police Ministry and the spy system associated with it generates bad blood throughout the *départements*. The Parisian salons are again full of distinguished, unsuspected informers, just as in the days of the Empire.

'And all the time much *tripotage*[e] on the Bourse on the part of those who, in

---

[a] 'What, it's you, you scoundrel, who dares to come and tell me of my expulsion?' - [b] respectable people - [c] government of thieves and murderers - [d] 'It is the total and definitive victory of socialism!' - [e] sharp practice

one way or another, arbitrarily grant or withdraw concessions for railways, etc., the instructions about which they alone had knowledge of, and upon which they speculate the previous day. It was believed that a secret college of Jesuits, headed by Montalembert, who had always been on terms of some intimacy with the President, exerted direct and immediate influence on his decisions; but as for Montalembert, it soon emerged that, after availing himself of his advice, Bonaparte suddenly dismissed him from his presence never to receive him again, so that ever since they have been the bitterest of enemies, and M., personally no less *misérable*, used the Orleans decree merely as a pretext for dissociating himself officially with honour. Now there is talk of nothing but B.'s craving for conquest. It will be his complete undoing.'

So much for my *ami.*

The important news from here is that the Tories have replaced the Whigs, and formed a ministry headed by the Earl of Derby (Lord Stanley).[62] This *événement*[a] is splendid. In England our movement can progress only under the Tories. The Whigs conciliate all over the place and lull everyone to sleep. On top of that there is the commercial crisis, which is looming ever closer and whose early symptoms are erupting on every hand. *Les choses marchent.*[b] If only we can manage *tant bien que mal*[c] through the interim period! It is nearly time for the post. I must close.
Salut.

K. Marx

First published in *F. Lassalle. Nachgelassene Briefe und Schriften,* Bd. III, Stuttgart-Berlin, 1922

Printed according to the original

Published in English for the first time

27

MARX TO ENGELS

IN MANCHESTER

[London,] 27 February 1852
28 Dean Street, Soho

Dear Engels,

I see that last time I forgot Reinhardt's letter.[d] The article has gone off to Dana,[e] who has not yet replied to my request that he advise me of a business house here in London. Despite her

---

[a] event - [b] Things are moving. - [c] somehow - [d] See this volume, pp. 47-49. - [e] F. Engels, *Revolution and Counter-Revolution in Germany,* XI.

promise, I have still heard nothing from my mater.[a] Nor has there as yet been any reply to my letters to acquaintances in Germany. A week ago I reached the pleasant point where I am unable to go out for want of the coats I have in pawn, and can no longer eat meat for want of credit. Piffling it all may be, but I'm afraid that one day it might blow up into a scandal. The only good news comes from my ministerial sister-in-law,[b] namely the news that my wife's indestructible uncle[c] is ill. If the cur dies now I shall be out of this pickle.

I shall not be writing at length today, being busy with the dictation of an article for Weydemeyer[d] and the dispatch and correction of the other contributions for him.

I see from the Augsburg paper (through the humble offices of Seiler) that Mr Stirner has produced a 'history of the counter-revolution'.[e] He tries to prove that the revolution collapsed because it was 'sacrosanct' whereas the counter-revolution prevailed because of its 'egoistical' stance.

On 25 February the French held a February banquet, or rather a dry MEETING accompanied by tea and sandwiches. I and wife were invited. The rest of the public had to pay 1 franc to go in. Since I neither could nor wished to attend, I sent my wife there with a FRENCHMAN. Ledru, Pyat, Thoré, Martin Bernard, etc., in short the whole Rollinist clique by whom the affair had been mooted, failed to appear because they considered the entrée,[f] for the benefit of the refugees, to be beneath their dignity. L. Blanc had also cried off. Only the lowest dregs of the emigration were there, most of whom style themselves Blanquists. But the little pseudo-Corsican[g] was waiting in some near-by parlour; after being assured by his spies of the absence of Ledru and Co., he appeared and, in view of the total lack of talent and authority, his natty, steel-blue tail-coat was received with RAPTUROUS APPLAUSE. His speech, after which he immediately departed, sent his enemies into transports. Enchanted them. Vanquished them. And what did THAT LITTLE MAN say, that Johnny Russell of socialism? That here abroad, people were wondering at the strange events in France, that he believed more firmly than ever in the star de la patrie.[h] And why? Je veux, said he, vous expliquer le mouvement historique,[i] etc. Namely, that in

---

[a] Henriette Marx - [b] Louise von Westphalen - [c] Heinrich Georg von Westphalen - [d] K. Marx, The Eighteenth Brumaire of Louis Bonaparte, V. - [e] An anonymous review of M. Stirner's Geschichte der Reaction in Allgemeine Zeitung, No. 56, 25 February 1852, supplement: 'Buchmacherei' - [f] entrance fee - [g] Louis Blanc - [h] of the fatherland - [i] I wish, said he, to explain historical tendencies to you.

the lives of all great soldiers, e.g. of *Frédéric le Grand,* of *Napoléon le grand,* there are *des grandes victoires et des grands revers. Eh bien! La France est une nation militaire.*[a] She has her *élans* and her catastrophes. *Quod erat demonstrandum.* What she wanted she has always achieved, feudalism banished in 1789, the monarchy in 1830. Whom did she wish to overthrow in 1848? The bourgeoisie, do you suppose? Certainly not. *La misère, la hideuse misère.*[b] There follows a flood of socialist tears over *la misère. La misère, ce n'est pas quelque chose de fixe, quelque chose de saisissable,*[c]—nevertheless, the French nation will overcome *la misère* in the new revolution and then *la mère ne détruira plus de ses propres mains le fruit de ses entrailles, la petite fille de sept ans ne se 'groupera' plus sous la machine*[d] and more inanities of the same kind. Such was his prodigality that his speech contained three whole jokes. He called Bonaparte 1. *un aventurier,* 2. *un bâtard* and 3. *le singe de son oncle.*[e] This last novelty threw those present into a veritable St. Vitus' dance. *Qu'en dis-tu?*[f] It's enough to make one despair of the *crapauds.*[g] Seen as a whole, their story is epigrammatic, a genuine dramatic work of art, but the fellows themselves! *Mon dieu!* Mr Blanc's sally reminds me of a joke I was told by Massol. By midnight Bonaparte is invariably befuddled, in the company of the *mâles* and *femelettes*[h] he collects around him for his orgies. Then he begins to curse and swear. *'Mais c'est un militaire!',*[i] says one of his lady acquaintants in exoneration.

Addio.

Your
K. Marx

First published slightly abridged in *Der Briefwechsel zwischen F. Engels und K. Marx,* Bd. 1, Stuttgart, 1913 and in full in *MEGA,* Abt. III, Bd. 1, Berlin, 1929

Printed according to the original

Published in English for the first time

---

[a] Frederick the Great, Napoleon the great, there are great victories and great reverses. Well, France is a *military nation.* - [b] Poverty, hideous poverty. - [c] Poverty is not something permanent, something tangible - [d] the mother will no longer destroy with her own hands the fruit of her womb, the little seven-year-old girl will no longer 'huddle' beneath the machine - [e] 1. an adventurer, 2. a bastard and 3. his uncle's (i.e. Napoleon I's) pantograph - [f] What do you say to that? - [g] philistines - [h] males and little females - [i] 'But he's a soldier.'

28

ENGELS TO JOSEPH WEYDEMEYER[12]

IN NEW YORK

Manchester, 27 Feb. 1852

Dear Weydemeyer,

I am glad to see that some of my letters have at last arrived and hence that no further obstacles stand in the way of our correspondence.[66] The first two were addressed to J. W., Deutsche Vereinsbuchhandlung, William Str., New York. The copies of the *Revolution* and the *Demokrat* have arrived safely and are being forwarded to London today. Mr Heinzen will be delighted by your riposte.[a] You summed him up very neatly. Send all further consignments of printed matter in the same way, open at both ends; the postage costs very little.

Of my articles, you could *at very most* include only the one on the invasion[67] in any future miscellany. The others are unsuitable and have already been overtaken by events.

As for *confrère* Standau, the fellow's an erstwhile conspirator who fits exactly into the category we depicted in the *Revue,* in the critique of Chenu[b]—very useful in certain respects, very prone to idleness, not always reliable and something of a Rodomonte. Anyhow, give him my regards.

Schmidt of Löwenberg is conducting a crusade against the Jesuits in the neighbourhood of St. Louis and has for chief ally the ex-trickster and agent of Duchâtel, Mr Börnstein of Parisian fame. What else he is up to I do not know. That Dr Maas is a supporter of the Marx clique is news to me. I know him only as an ex-Palatinate ranter. Fischer, the editor of the New Orleans *Deutsche Zeitung,* is an acquaintance of mine and was a member of my bodyguard in Kaiserslautern,[68] but this day-dreamer has since become infernally corrupted and Kinkelified, and if Kinkel himself has been in New Orleans, he will have done a great deal of mischief since he will have met with no opposition.

---

[a] An allusion to Weydemeyer's article against Heinzen, *New-Yorker Demokrat,* No. 311, 29 January 1852. - [b] K. Marx and F. Engels, Reviews from the *Neue Rheinische Zeitung. Politisch-ökonomische Revue,* No. 4: '*Les Conspirateurs,* par A. Chenu', '*La naissance de la République en février 1848,* par Lucien de la Hodde'.

So far as the question of a war against England is concerned,[a] just now it interests me primarily as a military problem which one tries to elucidate and solve in just the same way as an exercise in geometry. But I do not regard a coalition war of this kind as out of the question although for the time being, so long as Derby remains at the helm, it will certainly be deferred. The gentlemen of the Holy Alliance[69] assess their forces today no less incorrectly than was done in the various coalitions from 1792 to 1807. And as for Russia's dependence on England, 1. one cannot expect the Tsar[b] to be sensible of it, and secondly, a suspension of trade, while it would result in stagnation, poverty and the spoiling of produce, could, after all, be endured for 2-3 years just as could a commercial crisis of the same duration. Bear in mind that in Russia virtually no money circulates in the country among the peasantry, the vast majority, and that these barbarians' every household necessity can be produced in any village. True, the cities and the aristocracy would suffer, but the Russian Empire is founded on peasants and on petty country gentry. An uprising on the Continent instigated by England presents great difficulties; Spain was helped by her terrain, her great size and sparse population, and the lack of provisions, and also the fact of being surrounded on nearly all sides by the sea. But Hungary and Poland are land-locked countries while Italy, save for the islands, could hardly be held by the English and the insurgents against the superior forces of the coalition. Furthermore, England is not now in a position, and will not be so a year after the outbreak of war, to muster an army like the one sent to Wellington in Spain.[70] But ships without a landing force can never gain a foothold.

It's a real stroke of luck that the Tories should have taken the helm. As a result of the continual victories in the field of commercial policy and the long era of prosperity, the manufacturers had grown thoroughly indolent. Parliamentary reform, even when more far-reaching than Russell's paltry Bill,[71] failed to arouse the *slightest interest*. Now, with the devil hard on their heels, they are already scared out of their wits, the more so since *every one* of the new ministers represents, and most brazenly, some aspect or other of protectionism. The Anti-Corn Law League[72] is being revived here. Parliamentary reform, the extension of the franchise, the equalisation of constituencies, secret ballot, have all become *questions of vital moment to the industrial bourgeoisie*, whereas before

---

[a] See this volume, pp. 18-19. - [b] Nicholas I

they were of immediate interest only to the philistines. Derby must announce a dissolution and will probably do so as soon as the Army Act and the taxes for the coming year have been voted. In May we shall doubtless have another election. The Protectionists will gain a few votes and in exchange throw out a few Peelites.[73] But they are still in the minority and, should Derby dare to propose the immediate introduction of protective tariffs, he will unquestionably take a tumble. But he may be cunning enough to defer this. At any rate the movement is now FAIRLY under way in England. With Palmerston's dismissal[74] the fun began, as it was bound to do after the endless ministerial defeats of the previous session. Derby is the second act. Dissolution will be the third. As for England's foreign policy under Derby it too, of course, will be reactionary; but little that is decisive will happen; maybe a few prosecutions of refugees, in which the government will fail, attempts to introduce Aliens Bills,[75] which will likewise fail, perhaps support for attempts to form an anti-Louis Napoleon coalition, which will also come to nothing. The Tories are frightfully circumscribed in England and, unless they attempt to restore the Sidmouth-Castlereagh despotism of 1815-21, whereby they could burn their fingers devilish badly for, within the law and on behalf of FREE TRADE, your English bourgeois fights like a tiger—the conservative gentlemen will make sorry fools of themselves. But Derby (formerly, in his father's lifetime, Lord Stanley) is a hot-head and may well have recourse to extreme, if not illegal, measures.

All that is lacking now is a commercial crisis and, with Derby up, I rather suspect that it will soon be upon us. The rapid succession of English FREE TRADE measures, followed by the opening up of the Dutch colonies, the lowering of tariffs in Spain, Sardinia, etc., etc., and the fall in cotton prices (since Sept. 1850 down to half their former value), are keeping prosperity going longer than might have been expected. But, given the state of the Indian and to some extent the American markets (appreciably fewer manufactures were exported to the United States last month than in the same period last year), the thing cannot be expected to last much longer. If, as seems hardly probable, the crisis comes as early as May, then the fun will begin. But it will hardly be here before September or October.

My regards to your wife.

Your

F. E.

Shortly an article on the position of the English industrial bourgeoisie and on commercial matters[76]—I shall be very busy for the next fortnight or so.

First published in: Marx and Engels, *Works,* First Russian Edition, Vol. XXV, Moscow, 1934

Printed according to the original

Published in English in full for the first time

29

ENGELS TO MARX

IN LONDON

Manchester, 2 March 1852

Dear Marx,

By now you will have received the £5 I sent off yesterday, half of it direct to you and half under cover to Lupus. My congratulations on the news of the illness of the old Brunswick inheritance-thwarter[a]; I trust the catastrophe will at last come to pass.

According to the Augsburg *Allgemeine Zeitung,* Stirner's *Geschichte der Reaktion* is a wretched compilation, or rather a patchwork of gleanings from what he has read and from his own published and unpublished newspaper articles—'rejected leaves and blossoms' on everything in the world and somewhat more—2 volumes which conclude with the threat that the third will contain 'the groundwork and the system'.[b] Far from aspiring to sacrosanctity, his own glosses seem rather to be destined for higher schools for young ladies.

Little Simon von Trier must inevitably make an absolute ass of himself in Dana's eyes by attributing such ludicrous nonsense to us, when Dana can see for himself that our articles contain ANYTHING BUT THAT.[c] It is preposterous of Dana not to send us the *Tribune* or you the money; I think the best plan would be to set Weydemeyer onto him, he at least would be able to send us the *Tribune* and at the same time settle the money question by word

a Heinrich Georg von Westphalen - b *Allgemeine Zeitung,* No. 56, 25 February 1852, supplement: 'Buchmacherei'. - c See this volume, pp. 37 and 43-44.

of mouth. Whether he advises you of a business house in London or sends a bill of exchange is immaterial. My article, which was to have gone by the Southampton STEAMER, missed it since I had miscalculated its departure by one day. Now you will be getting it on Friday, along with another which will bring the thing up to the end of 1848.[a] These will be followed by the Prussian Chambers, the campaign for the Imperial Constitution[77] and, finally, the Prusso-Austrian squabbles of 1850/51, lastly the conclusion— altogether the whole may, perhaps, run to another six-8 articles, *summa summarum* 17-20 articles.

Charles[b] will be back here in a fortnight, when I shall have more time. Until then Jones will have to be patient.

So Mr Derby declares outright that, *à la* Sir James Graham, he will again help the Austrians and Co. to lay their hands on any likely bandieras.[78] Hence once again letters will be broken open *en masse*. The main sufferers will be Mazzini and the Hungarians. We ourselves will be little inconvenienced.

But what effrontery on Derby's part! 'I hereby declare that given a suitable opportunity, I shall impose a tax on corn. Just when that will be is for me alone to decide. But if you, the majority in the House of Commons, do not wish to be *des factieux*,[c] you must leave me in peace until I have so far consolidated my position and so far toryfied the land that I can undo unperturbed all that has been accomplished during the past twenty years.'[d] Poor HOUSE OF COMMONS! In place of a ministry that found itself in a relative minority, they now have one that is in absolute and permanent minority; and they are not even permitted to oppose it. But those milksops, the FREE TRADERS, have got no more than their deserts. The fellows won a battle, captured a new strategic line, and failed to occupy and fortify it, failed, indeed, to profit by their victory and even merely to pursue the enemy. Now they must again join battle on the same ground. The Tory *avènement*,[e] however, has suddenly made these questions abundantly plain to the fellows. Parliamentary reform, taken to the point at which Tories and Whigs, at least in their unadulterated form, are for ever precluded from power and a majority of industrialists in the Cabinet and in Parliament is assured, has now become a vital question to the manufacturers. Here these GENTLEMEN are again very active. At this moment the Anti-Corn Law League[72] is meeting and discussing whether to reorganise itself. Cobden, Bright,

---

[a] F. Engels, *Revolution and Counter-Revolution in Germany*, XII and XIII. - [b] Roesgen - [c] sedition-mongers - [d] Engels ridicules Derby's speech in the House of Lords on 27 February published in *The Times*, No. 21050, 28 February 1852. - [e] accession

Milner Gibson, etc., are here. No doubt they will at least piece together again the bare bones of the organisation. But not until the dissolution will the real fun begin. The dissolution, however, cannot be long in coming for, despite Derby's honied words and his pacific and conciliatory intentions, clashes are unavoidable.

Unfortunately there is little prospect of the commercial crisis coinciding with the dissolution. Business here continues splendid. The news from America is exceedingly favourable. What is staving off the crisis, and may continue to stave it off for a little while longer, is 1. California, both the TRADE it provides and the masses of gold coming into circulation, as well as emigration thither, in short, all the stimulus that California exerts upon the whole of the United States; 2. the curb imposed by the high cotton prices of 1849 and 1850 upon the cotton industry which did not experience brisk progress until the spring of 1851; 3. the enormous fall in cotton prices—almost 50%—during the past eighteen months. In New Orleans the price of cotton (MIDDLING—the average kind) on 1 Sept. 1850 was $13\,^1/_2$ cents$=7\,^3/_4$d in Liverpool; today the price of MIDDLING in New Orleans is $7\,^5/_8$ cents$=4\,^7/_8$d in Liverpool, and for a time it stood at .7 cents. Obviously this is bound to bring about a considerable increase in consumption. Last year—Jan. and Feb.—here in the cotton district, 29,000 bales were consumed weekly, this year 33,000 and that solely American; in addition there is Surat, Egyptian, etc.[a]—If things continue thus, England will consume 800-850 million pounds of cotton this year; 4. the general timidity to speculate and to launch with any persistent enthusiasm even into gold mines and steamships. From everything I see I should say that another 6 months of such intensive production as at present would suffice to inundate the whole world; if another 4 months or so be allowed for the goods to reach their destination and positive news of over-supply to come back, as also for an interim period of reflection before people are seized by panic,—then the most likely time for the onset of the crisis will be somewhere between Nov. 1852 and Feb. 1853. But all this is GUESS-WORK and we could just as well have it in September. It should, though, be a fine how-d'ye-do, for never before has such a mass of goods of all descriptions been pushed onto the market, nor have there ever been such colossal means of production. The foolish ENGINEERS' strike[79] will hold it up for at least a month; virtually no machines are being made now and they are

---

[a] Engels takes statistical data from 'The Spirit of the Annual Trade Circulars. The Year That Is Past', *The Economist*, No. 437, 10 January 1852.

very much in demand. Hibbert, Platt and Sons have hundreds of orders from both here and abroad, not one of which they can, of course, execute. And when this commercial thunderstorm moreover breaks over Mr Derby's head, it will be bad for him!

The last balance sheet made my old man really hopping mad for it shows him as having lost money, despite the general prosperity, and he is likely to give notice of termination (i.e. of his corporate contract with the Ermens). In which case this business will probably shut down as early as next year. The chaos arising out of all these goings-on has now reached a peak, and is partly why I have such a mass of things to do.

Don't bother to send me Ewerbeck's book. It's not worth the 6d the postage would cost.

My warm regards to your wife and children.

Your
F. E.

First published slightly abridged in *Der Briefwechsel zwischen F. Engels und K. Marx*, Bd. 1, Stuttgart, 1913 and in full in *MEGA*, Abt. III, Bd. 1, Berlin, 1929

Printed according to the original

Published in English for the first time

30

MARX TO ENGELS

IN MANCHESTER

London, 5 March [1852]
28 Dean Street, Soho

Dear Engels,

I received the £5 on Monday, although Lupus lives at 3, not 4, Broad Street. Also today your very felicitous article for Dana.[a]

Your package containing the *Revolution* and the *Tribune* had been opened. They had not even taken the trouble to do it up again.

From the enclosed letter you will see how we stand with the police.[80] The facts are wrong, save that Lupus took the chair

---

[a] F. Engels, *Revolution and Counter-Revolution in Germany*, XII.

instead of myself on 5 February and that the denouncer mistook our letter to *The Times*[a] for a reply to Mrs Daniels.[81] The spy is 'Hirsch' of Hamburg whom we had already thrown out of the League[b] a fortnight before. He became a member in Germany and, since I never really trusted him, I never mentioned anything in the least compromising in his presence.

With regard to Weydemeyer's anti-Heinzen article,[c] Jones has sent him by today's post an official letter in which he treats Heinzen *avec un dédain suprême*[d] and enlightens him on the 'WAR OF CLASSES'.[82] The day before yesterday the National Reform League[83] held a big meeting with an audience of at least 2,000. Jones subjected Messrs Hume, Walmsley and Co. to some rough treatment and scored a real triumph. London and Manchester now seem to divide the work between them in such a way that the bourgeois there tend to launch political attacks, and those here commercial ones.

A few days ago a manifesto by Signore Mazzini written in *Italian* fell into my hands. He is the *holy* bourgeois *quand même*[e] and fumes at the 'profane' French bourgeois. He shifts the initiative from Paris to Rome. '*Il materialismo*' and '*il egoismo*' have ruined France. The workers have inherited both vices from the bourgeoisie. Since 1815 France has no longer been the country of initiative. Italy and Hungary are now the chosen countries.

While 'signore Mazzini', as Peter the Hermit, castigates the wicked French, he licks the boots of the English FREE TRADERS who doubtless personify '*le dévouement*' and '*la foi*'. *L'imbécile!*[f]

Please return the enclosed letter. Only very little today because what with getting things off to America my hands are full.

Your
K. Marx

First published slightly abridged in *Der Briefwechsel zwischen F. Engels und K. Marx*, Bd. 1, Stuttgart, 1913 and in full in *MEGA*, Abt. III, Bd. 1, Berlin, 1929

Printed according to the original

Published in English for the first time

---

[a] K. Marx and F. Engels, 'To the Editor of *The Times*' - [b] the Communist League - [c] See this volume, p. 52. - [d] with supreme disdain - [e] all the same - [f] 'devotion' and 'faith'. The idiot!

31

MARX TO JOSEPH WEYDEMEYER [84]

IN NEW YORK

London, 5 March 1852
28 Dean Street, Soho

Dear Weywy,

I am afraid there has been a bit of a muddle because, HAVING MISUNDERSTOOD THY LAST LETTER, I addressed the last 2 packages to: Office of the *Revolution*, 7 Chambers' Street, Box 1817. What caused the confusion was that damned 'Box 1817', since you had written telling me to append this to the 'old address' without drawing any distinction between the first address and the second. But I hope the matter will have resolved itself before this letter arrives, the more so since last Friday's letter[a] contained the very detailed fifth instalment of my article. This week I was prevented from finishing the sixth, which is also the last one.[85] If your paper is appearing again, this delay will not prove an obstacle since you have an ample supply of material.

Your article against Heinzen, unfortunately sent to me too late by Engels, is very good, at once coarse and *fine*, and this is the right combination for any polemic worthy of the name. I have shown this article to Ernest Jones and enclosed you will find a letter from him addressed to you, intended for publication.[82] Since Jones writes very illegibly and with abbreviations, and since I assume that you are not yet an OUT-AND-OUT Englishman, I am sending you, along with the original, a copy made by my wife, together with the German translation; you should print them both, the original and the translation, side by side. Below Jones' letter you might add the following comment: As to *George Julian Harney*, likewise one of Mr Heinzen's authorities, he published our *Communist Manifesto* in English in his *Red Republican* with a marginal note describing it as 'THE MOST REVOLUTIONARY DOCUMENT EVER GIVEN TO THE WORLD',[b] and in his *Democratic Review* he translated the

---

[a] Jenny Marx's letter to Joseph Weydemeyer of 27 February 1852. See this volume, pp. 572-73. - [b] *The Communist Manifesto* was published in English in *The Red Republican*, Nos. 21, 22, 23, 24 of 9, 16, 23 and 30 November 1850. It was on this occasion that Marx and Engels were first named as its authors. In this letter Marx gives the quotations in English followed by the German translation.

words of 'wisdom brushed aside' by Heinzen, namely my articles on
the French Revolution from the *Revue der N. Rh. Z.*,[a] and in a
paper on Louis Blanc he refers his readers to these articles as
being the 'true critical examination' of the French affair.[b] By the
way, in England there is no need to have recourse only to
'extremists'. If, in England, a Member of Parliament becomes a
minister, he must have himself re-elected. Thus *Disraeli*, the new
Chancellor, LORD OF THE EXCHEQUER, writes to his constituents on
1 March:

* 'We shall endeavour to terminate that *strife of classes* which, of late years, has
exercised so pernicious an influence over the welfare of this kingdom.*[c]

Whereupon *The Times* of 2 March comments:

* 'If anything would ever divide classes in this country beyond reconciliation,
and leave no chance of a just and honourable peace, it would be a tax on foreign
corn.'*

And lest some ignorant 'man of character'[d] like Heinzen should
suppose that the aristocrats are *for* and the bourgeois *against* the
Corn Laws[72] because the former want '*monopoly*' and the latter
'*freedom*'—your worthy citizen sees opposites only in this ideological form—we shall content ourselves with saying that, in England,
in the eighteenth century, the aristocrats were for 'freedom' (of
trade) and the bourgeois for 'monopoly',—precisely the same
attitude as is adopted by the two classes in present-day 'Prussia'
towards the 'Corn Laws'.[86] There is no more rabid FREE TRADER than
the *Neue Pr. Z.*

Finally, if I were you, I should tell the democratic gents *en
général* that they would do better to acquaint themselves with
bourgeois literature before they venture to yap at its opponents.
For instance they should study the historical works of Thierry,
Guizot, John Wade and so forth, in order to enlighten themselves
as to the past 'history of the classes'. They should acquaint

---

[a] K. Marx, *The Class Struggles in France, 1848 to 1850.* Published in the *Neue
Rheinische Zeitung. Politisch-ökonomische Revue.* By the English translation of this
work Marx means Engels' review of the first chapter published under the title 'Two
Years of a Revolution; 1848 and 1849' in *The Democratic Review,* April-June
1850. - [b] [G. J. Harney,] Review of Louis Blanc's *Historic Pages from the French
Revolution of February 1848* in *The Democratic Review,* May 1850, pp. 465-
66. - [c] Here and below Marx quotes from Disraeli's 'Address to His Constituents'
published under the date-line: 'London, Tuesday, 2 March 1852', *The Times,*
No. 21052, 2 March 1852. - [d] Presumably an allusion to Heine's satirical poem
Atta Troll, Chap. XXIV—'kein Talent, doch ein Charakter' (Talent none, but
character).

themselves with the fundamentals of political economy before attempting to criticise the critique of political economy. For example, one need only open Ricardo's magnum opus to find, on the first page, the words with which he begins his preface:

* 'The produce of the earth—all that is derived from its surface by the united application of labour, machinery, and capital, is divided among *three classes* of the community; namely the proprietor of the land, the owner of the stock or capital necessary for its cultivation, and the labourers by whose industry it is cultivated.' * [a]

Now, in the United States bourgeois society is still far too immature for the class struggle to be made perceptible and comprehensible; striking proof of this is provided by *C. H. Carey* (of Philadelphia),[b] the only North American economist of any note. He attacks *Ricardo*, the most classic representative[c] of the bourgeoisie and the most stoical opponent of the proletariat, as a man whose works are an arsenal for anarchists and socialists, for all enemies of the bourgeois order.[d] He accuses not only him, but also Malthus, Mill, Say, Torrens, Wakefield, MacCulloch, Senior, Whately, R. Jones, etc.—those who lead the economic dance in Europe—of tearing society apart, and of paving the way for civil war by showing that the economic bases of the various classes are such that they will inevitably give rise to a necessary and ever-growing antagonism between the latter. He tries to refute them, not, it is true, like the fatuous Heinzen, by relating the existence of classes to the existence of *political* privileges and *monopolies,* but by seeking to demonstrate that *economic* conditions: rent (landed property), *profit* (capital) and wages (wage labour),[e] rather than being conditions of struggle and antagonism, are conditions of association and harmony.[87] All he proves, of course, is that the 'undeveloped' relations in the United States are, to him, 'normal relations'.

Now as for myself, I do not claim to have discovered either the existence of classes in modern society or the struggle between them. Long before me, bourgeois historians had described the historical development of this struggle between the classes, as had bourgeois economists their economic anatomy. My own contribution was 1. to show that the *existence of classes* is merely bound up with *certain historical phases in the development of production;* 2. that the class struggle necessarily leads to the *dictatorship of the*

---

[a] D. Ricardo, *On the Principles of Political Economy, and Taxation,* Third Edition, London, 1821, p. V. - [b] See H. Ch. Carey, *Essay on the Rate of Wages...* - [c] Above 'representative' Marx wrote 'interpreter'. - [d] See also this volume, pp. 345-46. - [e] ibid., pp. 378-84 and 392.

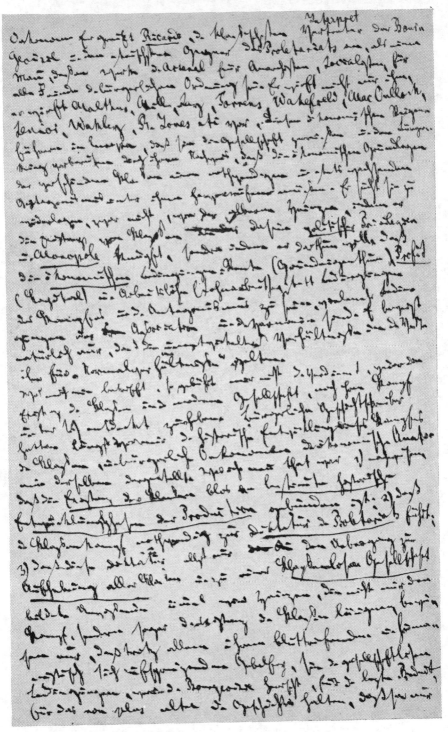

Third page of Marx's letter to Weydemeyer of 5 March 1852

proletariat; 3. that this dictatorship itself constitutes no more than a transition to the *abolition of all classes* and to a *classless society.* Ignorant louts such as Heinzen, who deny not only the struggle but the very existence of classes, only demonstrate that, for all their bloodthirsty, mock-humanist yelping, they regard the social conditions in which the bourgeoisie is dominant as the final product, the *non plus ultra*[a] of history, and that they themselves are simply the servants of the bourgeoisie, a servitude which is the more revolting, the less capable are the louts of grasping the very greatness and transient necessity of the bourgeois regime itself.

Select from the above notes whatever you think fit.[88] By the way, Heinzen has adopted our 'centralisation' in place of his 'federative republic', etc.[89] When the views on classes we are now disseminating have become familiar objects of 'sound common sense',[b] then the scoundrel will proclaim them aloud as the latest product of his 'own sagacity' and yap his opposition to our onward progress. Thus, in the light of his 'own sagacity', he yapped at Hegelian philosophy[c] so long as it was progressive. Now he feeds on its stale scraps, spat out undigested by Ruge.

Herewith also the end of the Hungarian article.[d] It is all the more essential that you should try to make some use of this—assuming your paper exists—because *Szemere,* the erstwhile prime minister of Hungary, now in Paris, has promised me to write a long article for you, *signed with his own name.*

If your paper has come into being, send *more* copies so that it can be distributed more widely.

Your

K. Marx

Kind regards to you and your wife from all your friends here, especially my wife.

Apropos. I am sending you the *Notes*[e] and a few copies of my Assizes speech[f] (this last for Cluss, to whom I promised it) by the

---

[a] the uttermost point - [b] An allusion to Heinzen's expression 'sound common sense' (der gesunde Menschenverstand). See K. Marx, 'Moralising Criticism and Critical Morality', present edition, Vol. 6, pp. 317, 330 and 337. - [c] An allusion to Heinzen's comedy *Doktor Nebel, oder: Gelehrsamkeit und Leben*, Cologne, 1841. See K. Marx and F. Engels, *The Great Men of the Exile*, present edition, Vol. 11, p. 277. - [d] See this volume, p. 32. - [e] *Notes to the People* - [f] K. Marx, 'The First Trial of the *Neue Rheinische Zeitung*' and 'The Trial of the Rhenish District Committee of Democrats' in *Zwei politische Prozesse*, Cologne, 1849.

hand of the ex-Montagnard Hochstuhl (an Alsatian).[90] There's nothing to the fellow.

Herewith the Rules.[91] I would advise you to arrange them in more logical order. *London* is designated as the district responsible for the United States. Hitherto we have been able to exercise our authority only *in partibus.*

If you have not already done so, do not accept 'Hirsch's' statement.[14] He's an unsavoury individual, although in the right where Schapper and Willich are concerned.

First published in part in *Die Neue Zeit,* Bd. 2, No. 31, Stuttgart, 1906-07 and in full in *Jungsozialistische Blätter,* 1930

Printed according to the original

Published in English in full for the first time

32

ENGELS TO MARX[92]

IN LONDON

[Manchester,] 18 March 1852

Dear Marx,

I return herewith Pixie's[a] letter. I am *pour le moment entièrement dépourvu*[b] and would not be able to raise the £2—at least this month; moreover, his letter is dated the 5th and there is absolutely no knowing whether the money would still reach him. And then it's always a ticklish business sending money to Ewerbeck; the fellow is capable of making superannuated claims for God only knows what old postal expenses, and of pocketing the whole amount or the best part of it. For all these reasons I am unable just now to help the little sprite,[a] doubtful though I am that he will be able to extract more than five sous at one go from Monsieur Ewerbeck. Meanwhile, the *piccolo*[a] has left Geneva for Paris and thus will no doubt also come to London, if at the cost of some 'toil and trouble'; and then we shall know just how much his dunning letters mean.

---

[a] Ernst Dronke - [b] At the moment I am completely penniless

If the little man[a] does come, you will have some difficulty in restraining his pugnacious temperament, surely much exacerbated by prolonged 'toil and trouble'; in this country fisticuffs and brawls cost too much money for him to be permitted to indulge in them.[93] It would be best if you entrusted him to Pieper so that the latter could instruct him in political economy. What you told me about Massol[b] is very interesting, and if he stays over there I should very much like to meet him.

I am delighted by what you tell me about Jones[c]—just now I have damnably little time, otherwise I would send him more articles. But Charles[d] is not yet back from Germany and then, after toiling all day in the office, it would really be too much to write a regular weekly article for him and/or Weydemeyer on top of the article for the *Tribune* and the weekly report for my old man. Moreover, I must at long last get to grips with the Slav business.[94] In my previous dilettante fashion, I achieved nothing for a whole year and, having at least made a start and got too far to abandon the thing, I must now regularly devote some time to it. For the past fortnight I have been swotting hard at Russian and have now got the grammar pretty well licked; in another 2-3 months I shall have acquired the necessary vocabulary, and then I shall be able to tackle something else. I must be done with the Slavonic languages this year and *au fond*[e] they are not so very difficult. Apart from the linguistic interest I derive from the thing, there is the further consideration that, come the next big political drama, at least one of us should be familiar with the languages, history, literature and the minutiae of the social institutions of those particular nations with which we shall immediately find ourselves in conflict. In effect, Bakunin only came to anything because no one knew Russian. And a great deal is going to be made of the old pan-Slavic DODGE of transmogrifying the old Slav system of communal property into communism and depicting the Russian peasants as born communists.

Now that old O'Connor has definitely gone mad, Jones is perfectly right to crowd on all sail. This is his chance and if, in addition, CITIZEN Hip-hip-hurrah[f] gives up, his cause is won. From all that I see, the Chartists are in such a state of complete dissolution and disintegration, and at the same time are so lacking in able people, that either they must disband altogether and break up into cliques, i.e. in effect become a mere appendage of the

---

[a] Ernst Dronke - [b] See this volume, pp. 31-32. - [c] ibid., p. 59. - [d] Roesgen - [e] at bottom - [f] Harney

FINANCIALS,[28] or else be reconstructed on a new basis by some
competent fellow. Jones is moving in quite the right direction and
we may well say that, without our doctrine, he would not have
taken the right path and would never have discovered how, on the
one hand, one can not only maintain the only possible basis for
the reconstruction of the Chartist party—the instinctive class
hatred of the workers for the industrial bourgeoisie—but also
enlarge and develop it, so laying the foundations for enlightening
propaganda, and how, on the other, one can still be progressive
and resist the workers' reactionary appetites and their prejudices.
MASTER Harney, by the way, is in for a surprise if he continues as
he is; the group of enthusiasts which supports him will very soon
kick him out, and not even the portraits of Kościuszko and other
'patriots'[95] that adorn his bumf will save him.

Quoad Napoleonem,[a] did the man not tell L. Blanc when he went
to France: 'Quand je serai président, je mettrai en pratique vos idées'[b]?
And now we see how a financial predicament may drive even a
true socialist like L. N. to financial measures of an impeccably
bourgeois kind, such as the conversion of bonds.[96] Your
SHOPKEEPER and small industrialist is prepared to overlook twenty
socialist capers in return for this one saving of 18 millions, and
The Daily News admires the measure. Anything more stupid or
more abject than the Débats' comments on this topic would be
hard to imagine.[c] The same old story: postal reform=socialism!
Conversion of bonds=socialism! FREE TRADE=socialism! My only fear
is that Mynheer Napoleon who, for all that he proceeds very
diffidently when it comes to his genuinely socialist undertakings and
goes no further in the matter of mortgages than the bourgeois
Prussian credit institutions, may, in the end, be compelled, by force
of circumstances, to transform all his socialist inclinations into simple
bourgeois reforms, and then nothing can deliver us but the
inevitable financial predicament. The Daily News is right, conversion
of bonds is a mesure éminemment pacifique[d] as well as being a most
ominous indication that L. N. is tending to fall into the ways of
bourgeois COMMON SENSE. But when, I ask you, has it ever been possible
to rule France with COMMON SENSE, and what a hotch-potch of
circumstances would be required to bring together a L. N. and
COMMON SENSE! At all events the climate on the Continent does not seem

---

a As regards Napoleon - b When I am President, I shall put your ideas into
practice. - c This refers to the article by Armand Bertin 'Paris, 14 mars', Journal des
Débats politiques et littéraires, 15 March 1852. - d eminently peaceable measure

very revolutionary to me, although the little sprite will bring quite different news.

I do not think that Derby will obtain a majority although this place, where unanimity reigns when it comes to the Corn Laws,[72] is a poor *point d'observation*. However, I should like him to obtain one, for then things must come about as you say. He is, by the way, a fool for not dissolving Parliament at once. The longer he procrastinates, the greater the risk of the election coinciding with a commercial crisis, and then he'll get fanatical Tories in Parliament who are too rabid even for him, and determined, rapacious MANCHESTER MEN[63] under threat of bankruptcy, these latter probably in the majority and hence the determining element.

Our CONCERN here seems likely to collapse within the year. In which case, while the liquidation is under way, I shall at first enjoy far more liberty and be less tied down by the regular routine of the office. Later, my old man writes, he might be able to find me a *better* position—I suspect that he will fall in with my old plan to remove to Liverpool and buy cotton for him there. That would be splendid and, if it comes off and you have completed your preliminary work on economics,[45] you and your whole family must come up for 6 months—we would live by the sea at New Brighton, and you would, besides, save money. At all events, I shall get myself a rise—there's no doubt about that.

Today, unfortunately, I shall not have a quiet moment in which to do the *Tribune* article, but an American STEAMER sails next Wednesday, so you shall have it by Monday or Tuesday, and then I'll do another one for Friday's STEAMER.

Many regards.

Your
F. E.

This is the first time the seal on your letter has been intact and undamaged.

First published abridged in *Der Briefwechsel zwischen F. Engels und K. Marx*, Bd. 1, Stuttgart, 1913 and in full in *MEGA*, Abt. III, Bd. 1, Berlin, 1929

Printed according to the original

Published in English in full for the first time

33

MARX TO JOSEPH WEYDEMEYER[12]

IN NEW YORK

London, 25 March 1852
28 Dean Street, Soho

Dear Weydemeyer,

Good luck to the new world citizen! There is no more splendid time to enter this world than the present. Come the day when people can travel from London to Calcutta in a week, both our heads will long since have rolled or started to loll. And Australia and California and the Pacific Ocean! The new world citizens will be unable to comprehend how small our world once was.

If you did not receive the final instalment[a] enclosed herewith a week ago, your total silence is to blame.

Now in the pamphlet,[97] too, I would like my article to be divided up as it was sent to you, under headings I, II, III, IV, V, VI, VII. These figures serve as sign-posts for the reader. They take the place of titles. At the end of V, add the following words: 'But Bonaparte answered the Party of Order as Agesilaus did King Agis: "*I seem to thee an ant, but one day I shall be a lion.*"'[98] But the thing must, of course, be brought out now all at once in its entirety.

Where my wife has failed to leave space enough to indicate the paragraphs, I have marked them with a Γ.

Cluss' statement[60] is splendid.

Why not—it strikes me as a good idea—*include Ernest Jones' letter in your first issue?*[82] A couple of introductory words would suffice to explain it.

Maintenant[b]: Cluss will already have told you about the Szemere business.[99] First a publisher will have to be contacted through me and arrangements made for his pamphlet—some 10 sheets—on Kossuth, L. Batthyány and Görgey—to be brought out in German and later in English. You might, if it can be managed, publish the German original as your second instalment without, of course, any other additions. But the publisher must pay for the thing if you don't publish it yourself.

---

[a] of *The Eighteenth Brumaire of Louis Bonaparte*, VII - [b] Now

When this has been arranged—and perhaps even before that—the *Revolution* will receive 500 dollars from this source, on condition that Bangya comes in as co-editor, i.e. only in the sense that part of the paper is allotted to the *Hungarians* and run by Bangya, Szemere's agent. But you'll have no difficulty in getting on with him, *car il est bon homme.*[a]

I am very glad to hear that you have found employment as a surveyor. You will be able to operate with greater confidence and peace of mind.

One of these days I shall be starting on Mazzini. Whereas Mr Kinkel, whose wisdom, by his own admission, derives from nursery tales, now chooses to see nothing but unity among the 'great men', he finds on his return the battle raging *optima forma.*[b] For Ledru and Mazzini have bought the Brussels daily *La Nation* for 10,000 fr. drawn from the Italian loan. *Mais voilà que*[c] *il Signore Mazzini* looses off an opening article, in which he vents all his infamous anti-French, anti-socialist inanities about the initiative lost by France,[d] and this so wildly that Ledru now feels compelled—and has, it seems, made up his mind—to take issue with him personally. On the other hand, the socialists L. Blanc, Pierre Leroux, Cabet, Mallarmet, etc., have joined forces and published a venomous retort composed by dear little L. Blanc. At the same time the majority of the French émigrés are violently incensed against Ledru, whom they rightly hold responsible for Mazzini's stupidities. Fire has broken out in the very midst of their camp.

Should you happen to get hold of *Der Tag ist angebrochen*, a book by that miserable cleric, Dulon, who fancies himself as a Lamennais, mind you give the cur a good dusting.

Dronke has been arrested in Paris where he lingered too long on his way here from Switzerland instead of hurrying through.

I like your selection very much. Pieper's article[e] might do well enough for a newspaper. For a pamphlet it was dashed off too hastily and perfunctorily.

Can you not get news of Edgar[f] from Braunfels? We have heard nothing from the lazybones and this is causing his mother[g] great anxiety. A crazy lad!

Cluss' protest[h] was greeted with general applause at the League[i]

---

[a] for he's a good fellow - [b] for all it's worth - [c] But now - [d] See this volume, p. 59. - [e] W. Pieper, 'Die Arbeiter Assoziation in England'. - [f] Edgar von Westphalen - [g] Caroline von Westphalen - [h] A. Cluss, 'An den Garanten-Congress des deutschen Anleihens in Cincinnati'. - [i] the Communist League

meeting here, and both we and Stechan's society[25] found your
Revolution to our liking.

Warm regards from my family to yours.

Your
K. M.

In case the infamous reply from Willich's society to Pfänder's
statement[100] should appear in some paper or other (e.g. Weitling's[a]), I am sending you Pfänder's 2nd statement.

What can red Becker[b] be doing? Has he, too, become a
Kinkelian?

Apropos. Some of the engineering workers have come to their
senses and sent apologies to Jones. By now the English workers
have collected sufficient money for Jones to bring out a big STAMPED
weekly[101] in addition to his *Notes*.[c] The jackass who is to convey
these to you has still not left.[d]

First published in: Marx and Engels,
Works, First Russian Edition, Vol. XXV,
Moscow, 1934

Printed according to the original

Published in English in full for the
first time

34

MARX TO ENGELS

IN MANCHESTER

London, 30 March 1852
28 Dean Street, Soho

Dear Frederic,

Just received your article.[e] Enclosed you will find a whole
bundle of new stuff from America which would have reached you
sooner, had it not been necessary to make copies of some of it for
communication to League[f] members.

---

[a] *Republik der Arbeiter* - [b] Presumably Max Joseph Becker. - [c] *Notes to the People* -
[d] Hochstuhl - [e] Presumably, XIII for the series *Revolution and Counter-Revolution in
Germany*. - [f] the Communist League, see also this volume, pp. 71-72

All sorts of things have been happening here. Gottfried Christ Kinkel is dispatching, or rather has dispatched, the student Schurz and Schimmelpfennig to drum together people from Switzerland, Paris, Germany and Belgium for a congress to be held in London in mid-April, the purpose being to guarantee the revolutionary loan[27] and to lay down definitive regulations for the administration of this exchequer and of the democratic government *in partibus*. But you must let me have the trash back by Saturday.

Kossuth, exposed in America by Szemere[102] and completely at odds with the committee he left behind him in London,[103] will be surprised to learn by what schisms the democratic clerics has meanwhile been rent.

For Mr Mazzini, who for the past 2 years has been pope of the democratic church *in partibus*, thought the time at last ripe to discharge his venom in the French tongue against socialism and France, to wit in the Brussels *Nation* which, with Ledru's connivance, he had acquired for 10,000 fr. drawn from the Italian fund. In it he blamed the socialists for the 2nd December, the capture of Rome,[104] in short for the counter-revolution generally and, in his high-flown Dominican style, thundered against heretics, sects, materialism, scepticism, the Romance Babylon, with the same single-mindedness he displays when licking the arse of the English liberal bourgeoisie. France, he said, had lost the revolutionary initiative. The *peuple-roi*[a] no longer existed. Now it was the turn of other nations, etc. In short a veritable bull of excommunication which was done the honour of being taken up by the *Patrie* and the *Constitutionnel*. This was altogether too much for the French. Little L. Blanc, who further saw in it an opportunity to rehabilitate himself and thrust himself to the fore, drummed up Cabet, Pierre Leroux, Bianchi, Nadaud and Vasbenter (Proudhonian). In *The Morning Advertiser* they attacked Mr Mazzini in crudest fashion. The theoretical part of their retort is almost as weak as Mazzini's attack. The personal part, for which Massol gave Leroux the material, annihilates the arrogant *theopompos*.[b]

Ledru, for his part, felt it incumbent upon him to *resign* from the European Central Committee in order not to lose all influence. He too has replied in the *Nation* to the attacks on France. Pitiful. An article with neither head nor tail. Upholds 'France's revolutionary initiative', but in what fashion! *C'est pour faire pitié!*[c] Ledru, it is said, now intends to go to the United States.

Thus, on the one hand, the idiot Ruge forfeits his European

---

[a] regal nation - [b] divine envoy - [c] It's pitiful.

Central Committee. On the other, Kinkel—who, in America, fawned like a dog on his rival Kossuth—sees the general 'confusion', i.e. fusion of all democratic pretenders under the banner of the now stale catchwords of 1848, e.g. 'democratic republic', 'universal franchise', etc., dissipating. Thus the worthy Willich is drawn into the conflict as a 'communist'.

Meanwhile each week the English government is shipping the French émigré mob in crowds out to America at public expense. The wretched LITTLE Blanc proposes to exploit a quite fortuitous general demonstration against Mazzini to set himself up as the visible head of the *ecclesia pressa*.[a] In order to thwart his little intrigues, I shall get Massol to egg on Pierre Leroux. Finally, to complete the confusion, Proudhon is coming here.

How low the official bigwigs sink, you may see from the fact that the delectable Félix Pyat, *cet homme artiste*[b]—an expression used by the French to gloss over an individual's every weakness, his lack of character and intelligence—has written a melodrama on the December days. He has found an English impresario and together they will put on the trash in New York, etc., the murder scenes, expulsions, deportations, etc., etc. Could anyone seek to profit by the misfortunes of his country in a more despicable manner? And the jackass regards this prostitution of France's misfortune as a patriotic act.

Tripotage[c] is the secret key to the historical drama staged by émigré politicians here; thus Siegwart[d]-Kinkel has acted as procurer between the student Schurz and Mrs Ronge's sister, who is said to be rich.

The only misfortune is that by their boastful intrigues these jackasses provide the police with a continuous supply of fresh material and make things worse for our friends in Germany.

Your
K. M.

First published much abridged in *Der Briefwechsel zwischen F. Engels und K. Marx*, Bd. 1, Stuttgart, 1913 and in full in *MEGA*, Abt. III, Bd. 1, Berlin, 1929

Printed according to the original

Published in English for the first time

---

[a] church oppressed - [b] that artistic man - [c] Intrigue - [d] Title character from J. M. Miller's book *Siegwart. Eine Klostergeschichte*.

35

ENGELS TO MARX

IN LONDON

[Manchester,] 1 April 1852

Dear Marx,

Got your letter this morning, actually intact. The new address seems to do some good.

The mirth-provoking émigré documents will be returned to you tomorrow. I shall extract some notes from them.

Little Dronke seems to have got himself properly caught in Paris, otherwise we should probably have heard from him. Do you suppose that some people belonging to 'the Marxian sect' really foregathered at the Café D.,[a] as the *Kölnische Zeitung* alleges?[b] I don't know where these remnants could have come from. In any case it would have been unpardonable of Dronke to have gone to the café and associated *publiquement*[c] with these people. But if he is still at liberty and there is any possibility of corresponding with him, we must certainly do everything we can now to bring him over to London—he is under an expulsion order and the fellows are quite capable of sending him to Algiers for *rupture de ban.*[d] So if we can find out more particulars, I shall see to it that I get hold of the £2, for we must certainly bring the little chap to safety. Write and tell me if you hear anything about him.

I am going home now to finish another article for Dana which, if it is ready, will go off to you by the second post. Last week I had a terrible cold and still have it, so that for several evenings I have been capable of absolutely nothing. Otherwise, more would have been done.

Tell Jones that he will be getting something from me next week,[e]—all my articles for him have, alas, been wretched, since the brevity of each and the negligible room available make me regularly forget what I wrote the week before—in addition, I have to write quickly and cursorily, and have no time whatever to collect and arrange material on the latest happenings in France. This constant improvisation becomes demoralising.

---

[a] du Danemark - [b] '* *Paris, 24. März*' and '⁺*Paris, 24. März*', *Kölnische Zeitung*, No. 74, 26 March 1852. - [c] publicly - [d] violation of the ban - [e] 'Real Causes Why the French Proletarians Remained Comparatively Inactive in December Last', III.

Should I not finish the article for Dana this evening, it will be chiefly because I still have to go through the better part of the *Neue Rheinische Zeitung* for April and March 1849,[a] for on this occasion the Frankfurters[b] must be given a *thorough* lambasting. The Bauer[c] is not adequate for the purpose.

Your
F. E.

First published in *Der Briefwechsel zwischen F. Engels und K. Marx*, Bd. 1, Stuttgart, 1913

Printed according to the original

Published in English for the first time

36

MARX TO ENGELS

IN MANCHESTER

London, 5 April 1852
28 Dean Street, Soho

Dear Frederic,

Enclosed a further consignment from Cluss[105] which I must have back by Wednesday (the day of the League[d] meeting).

The other day, just after you returned his first letter, Dronke wrote to Freiligrath from prison; I had forgotten to tell you. Freiligrath at once sent the letter to Lassalle for the latter to send some money to Paris for him, which could doubtless be done with all the more dispatch since Lassalle could use the letter to touch all the liberal bourgeois of Düsseldorf. Unfortunately, according to the *Patrie*, compromising letters were found on Dronke. Can he have been stupid enough to carry around *testimonia* of his fatuous *Lyonnais*[e] and other connections?

As I foresaw, Louis Blanc is trying to exploit the joint statement against Mazzini to create a new '*réseau d'action*'[f] and to thrust

---

[a] A reference to the material for *Revolution and Counter-Revolution in Germany*, XIII - [b] former deputies to the Frankfurt National Assembly of 1848-49 - [c] B. Bauer, *Der Untergang des Frankfurter Parlaments.* - [d] the Communist League - [e] Guillermain - [f] action network

himself to the fore as head of the revolutionary party. He has even sought to draw me into his fusion of all 'French' socialists and sent me an invitation to meet him. I did not, of course, even deign to answer and instead conveyed to his *intermédiaire* my amazement at such importunity. Since Proudhon is coming here, an alliance with me just now would have been very convenient for the little man.

Dana has written at last and paid £9 according to the number of articles *published*.[a] As the presidential elections will for the present be taking up every column in the paper, he asks me at the same time to condense the remainder into 5-6 articles and, more especially, to discuss in the last one the PROSPECTS OF REVOLUTIONARY GERMANY. This will provide a splendid chance to castigate the émigrés and in a later letter I shall write to you at length about my views on the matter.

Szemere is sending me, in 3-4 batches, his (German) manuscript on 'Kossuth, Görgey and Louis Batthyány'. Weydemeyer is to publish it in America,[99] which means excellent business for him, the more so since he will, in addition, probably receive 500 dollars for his paper[b] from that quarter.

But before the thing goes off to America in German, it must be translated into English here so that, after it has appeared in German in America, it can be brought out as a pamphlet for readers over here. You will hardly have the time for this task, even if you neglect Dana for a while. In which case I shall have to give it to Jones. The payment for translation is £1 per sheet.

Here I have made the acquaintance of Colonel Szerelmey, who is a very cultivated man. In Hungary he took part in 17 battles. Since he is also a first-rate painter, he is now bringing out a magnificent work, with battle reports in the text, and battle illustrations. He himself did the sketches, which were finished off by leading French painters. He has promised me a copy. Each will cost £10. So you will receive an addition to your military library.

Your
K. M.

As you see, Kinkel has been a good deal more arbitrary than Louis Bonaparte. First he nominates the members of his chamber of deputies, the Guarantors' Congress.[c] Next he takes fright at his

---

own creation, keeps neither to the appointed day nor place, but convenes the assembly at a time and place at which only 7 people can attend. Six of those 7 give him a vote of confidence. With these he drafts his constitution. By these he gets himself nominated representative of America, and he makes the committee he has created responsible to them.

First published abridged in *Die Briefwechsel zwischen F. Engels und K. Marx*, Bd. 1, Stuttgart, 1913 and in full in *MEGA*, Abt. III, Bd. 1, 1929

Printed according to the original

Published in English for the first time

37

MARX TO ENGELS

IN MANCHESTER

London, 14 April 1852
28 Dean Street, Soho

Dear Frederic,

Only a couple of lines to let you know that our little child[a] died this morning at a quarter past one.

Your
K. M.

First published in *MEGA*, Abt. III, Bd. 1, 1929

Printed according to the original

Published in English for the first time

---

[a] Franziska

38

ENGELS TO JOSEPH WEYDEMEYER[12]

IN NEW YORK

Manchester, 16 April 1852

Dear Weydemeyer,

Yesterday received your letter of 30 (?) March, together with the account of the revolutionary assembly.[106] I note that you have begun to stamp your letters, which is nonsensical; this CONCERN, *id est* Messieurs Ermen & Engels, can pay the postage. The things have been sent on to Marx.

The day before yesterday I arrived back here from London, where I had spent Easter. Marx's youngest child[a] was very ill and, as I now learn from him,[b] has since died—the second already in London. As you can imagine, his wife is greatly afflicted by it. There has also been some illness in Freiligrath's family, but things are going better there.

Dronke, as you will know, was arrested on his way through Paris. It was partly his own fault for, despite his earlier expulsion, the little man had lingered there for 3 weeks. Now he writes to say that he has been removed from the Mazas prison and taken back to the Préfecture de Police, to be sent to Boulogne and England on Good Friday evening. But up till now we have heard nothing more of him. The little man shows a remarkable talent for constantly getting INTO MISCHIEF, but no doubt he will turn up one of these days. Then the whole of the *N. Rh. Z.* will be in England, for Weerth, though he is in Hamburg again just now, still has connection with Bradford and, no matter how he struggles, will always find himself cast up there again.

It seems probable that our Cologne friends[c] will appear before the Court of Assizes in May, since the Board of indicting magistrates was expected to have decided their case by Monday, 5 April, and will certainly not have discharged them. This is just as well; the public prosecutor would immediately have appealed against an acquittal. If a certain Hansen of Cologne, a working man, should arrive in New York, treat him according to his deserts. The fellow, a member of the League since 1848,

---

[a] Franziska - [b] See this volume, p. 78. - [c] the Communist League members arrested and detained under investigation

administered, i.e. drank, the monies collected for the prisoners before absconding to America.

In the camp of the National Loaners there is considerable dissatisfaction with Reichenbach, the treasurer, for keeping so tight a hold on the purse-strings, since in any case more money has already been spent than can decently be accounted for and, as a well-to-do and respectable citizen, he is faced with the ominous prospect of the forthcoming audit. Hence Kinkel and Willich are furious, but to no effect: Kinkel must return to his tutoring and now, as in the past, Willich is begging and borrowing with an impudence hitherto found only among Polish patriots. Thus, throughout the noble émigré alliance, the most glorious confusion reigns and, if the Guarantors' Congress takes place, or has already taken place, things will come to a very pretty pass. Löwe of Calbe and the rest of the Frankfurters[a] are now also at daggers drawn with Kinkel, 'a chap with whom one can but compromise oneself'.

Has Tellering got his statement into any of the papers?[107] *Voilà ce qu'il nous importe de savoir*[b] for, if so, Marx can attack it. We would, by the way, be very glad if Dana would send us copies of Marx's articles[c]; we have only had the first 6 and should be glad to have the following ones. If Dana pleads too much work, the best thing would be for you to get hold of them yourself and send them here. Marx has long been meaning to write to you about this, but just now is probably not in a state to turn his thoughts to it. See what you can do, for we must have a complete set here; later on that sort of thing will also be important as a document.

My strategical article[d] is no longer any good and is all the less suitable for a collection[108] as the essentials were not really in it, but in my letter to you.[e] So do not hesitate to file it away. As soon as I have time to work undisturbed and some prospect of publication, I shall send you articles on the development of commerce and on the present state of the English industrial bourgeoisie.[17] For the present I must spend the next fortnight or 3 weeks exclusively on the study of Russian and Sanscrit, in which I am now engaged[f]; later, when my material arrives from Germany, I shall turn to

---

[a] former deputies to the Frankfurt National Assembly of 1848-49 - [b] That is what it is important for us to know - [c] Engels is referring to his series of articles, *Revolution and Counter-Revolution in Germany*. - [d] F. Engels, 'England', I. - [e] See this volume, pp. 18-19. - [f] ibid., p. 67.

military matters, but there is plenty of time for that and as a task it is less arduous.

The post is about to go—many regards to your wife and to Cluss.

Your
F. E.

First published in *New Yorker Volks-zeitung*, No. 12, 14 January 1931

Printed according to the original

Published in English in full for the first time

39

ENGELS TO MARX

IN LONDON

[Manchester,] 20 April 1852

Dear Marx,

I was grieved to see that my fears concerning your little daughter have been all too soon confirmed. If only there were some means by which you and your family could move into a more salubrious district and more spacious lodgings!

I would gladly have sent you some money, but while in London [109] I spent so much more than I had anticipated that I shall be pretty short myself until the end of the month, and next month I shall have to pay out at once £12 in bills and for books ordered from Germany. But I shall see if I can get hold of something for you by the beginning of May. I wish I had known beforehand how things stood in London, for in that case I should have foregone what was *au fond*[a] a quite superfluous trip there, and my hands would not have been quite so tied.

Pindar is here, having failed to find employment in Liverpool. He is looking for a position or for private lessons and I shall, of course, do what I can for him. As a token that I am well disposed towards him I have been taking Russian lessons from him. But if I am to recommend him here, I must know something more about him, and since such intelligence can only be dragged out of him with the utmost difficulty, I should be glad if you would write and tell me what you know about him and his circumstances, how you

---

[a] at bottom

became acquainted with him, etc., etc. With his taciturn manner, by the way, it doesn't seem to me as though he'll be lucky here.

In considering the present state of commerce, particularly as regards India, there is one point that should not be overlooked.[a] Despite 3 years of colossal and ever-increasing imports of English industrial goods into India, the news from there has for some time been moderately good again, stocks are gradually being sold and are fetching higher prices. The reason for this can only be that, in the provinces most lately conquered by the English, Sind, the Punjab, etc., etc., where native handicrafts have hitherto almost exclusively predominated, these are now finally being crushed by English competition, either because the manufacturers here have only recently come round to producing materials suitable for these markets, or because the NATIVES have finally sacrificed their preference for local cloths in favour of the cheaper price of the English materials usually exported to India. The last Indian crisis of 1847 and the concomitant sharp DEPRECIATION of English products in India may have contributed greatly to this; and it is already clear from old Gülich that even the parts of India occupied by the English in his day had not for a long time completely abandoned their traditional domestic manufactures.[b] This is the only explanation for the fact that the 1847 affair has not long since recurred in more acute form in Calcutta and Bombay. But all this will be changed once the 3,000,000 bales of cotton from the last crop have come onto the market, been processed and consigned as finished goods, predominantly to India. The cotton industry is now so flourishing that, despite this season's crop, which is 300,000 bales more than that of 1848/49, cotton prices are rising both here and in America, that American manufacturers have already bought 250,000 bales more than last year (when they used in all only 418,000 bales), and that manufacturers here are already beginning to maintain that even a crop of 3 million bales would be insufficient for their needs. Up till now, America has exported 174,000 bales more to England, 56,000 more to France and 27,000 more to the rest of the Continent than she did last year. (Each season runs from 1 Sept. to 7 April.)[c] And, given prosperity of this order, it is of course easy to explain how Louis Napoleon can prepare at leisure for his *bas-empire*[110]; the surplus

---

[a] See also this volume, pp. 83-84. - [b] G. Gülich, *Geschichtliche Darstellung des Handels, der Gewerbe und des Ackerbaus der bedeutendsten handeltreibenden Staaten unserer Zeit*, Bd. 3, S. 263-64. - [c] Engels may have used the article 'Commercial Intelligence. New York, 7 April' in *The Times*, No. 21094, 20 April 1852, but the figures given by him somewhat differ from those in the newspaper.

of direct cotton imports into France between 1850 and 1852 now amounts to 110,000 bales (302,000 against 192,000), i.e. more than 33%.

According to all the rules the crisis should come this year and will, indeed, probably do so; but if one takes into consideration the present quite unexpected resilience of the Indian market, the confusion created by California and Australia, the cheapness of most raw materials, which also means cheap industrial manufactures, and the absence of any heavy speculation, one is almost tempted to forecast that the present period of prosperity will be of exceptionally long duration. At any rate it may well be that the thing will last until the spring. But WITHIN SIX MONTHS MORE OR LESS it is, after all, safest to stick to the old rule.

Many regards to your wife, and write soon.

Your
F. E.

First published abridged in *Der Briefwechsel zwischen F. Engels und K. Marx*, Bd. 1, Stuttgart, 1913 and in full in *MEGA*, Abt. III, Bd. 1, 1929

Printed according to the original

Published in English for the first time

40

MARX TO ADOLF CLUSS[111]

IN WASHINGTON

London, 22 April 1852

... The chief industry, the cotton industry, is doing more splendidly than ever.[a] Despite the fact that the present cotton crop exceeds that of 1848/49 by 300,000 bales, cotton prices are rising both here and in America, so that American manufacturers have already bought 250,000 more bales than last year and manufacturers here are already beginning to maintain that even a crop of 3 million bales would be insufficient for their needs. Up till now America has exported 174,000 bales more to England, 56,000 more to France and 27,000 more to the rest of the Continent than she did last year (each season runs from 1 Sept. to 7 Apr.). On the

---

[a] Cf. this volume, pp. 82-83.

one hand this prosperity explains how Louis Bonaparte can prepare at leisure for his *bas-empire*. The surplus of direct cotton imports into France between 1850 and 1852 now amounts to 110,000 bales—302,000 against 192,000, i.e. more than 33%. On the other hand, it explains the flaccid condition of politics in this country. Given such prosperity, the Tories cannot, for their part, compete with the 'blessings of FREE TRADE', even though they are at the helm, while the FREE TRADERS for their part refrain from provoking political agitation because, so long as business is flourishing, the manufacturers do not want political upheavals and disturbances. The thriving state of the cotton industry is due chiefly to the Indian market, whence there has been good news for some time past—despite continuing colossal imports from England. This may be explained by the fact that in the territories most lately conquered by the English, Sind, the Punjab, etc., where native handicrafts have hitherto almost exclusively predominated, these are now finally being crushed by English competition. The last Indian crisis of 1847 and the concomitant sharp DEPRECIATION of English products in India may have contributed to this. This unexpected resilience of the Indian market, California, Australia, as well as the cheapness of most raw materials in the absence of any heavy speculation, give reason to suppose that the period of prosperity will be of exceptionally long duration. It may well be that the thing will last until the spring, etc., etc., etc....

First published in: Marx and Engels, *Works*, Second Russian Edition, Vol. 28, Moscow, 1962

Printed according to a letter from Cluss to Weydemeyer of 6 June 1852

Published in English for the first time

41

MARX TO ADOLF CLUSS [112]

IN WASHINGTON

[London, 23 April 1852]

... You will realise that Weydemeyer's letter[a] made a very unpleasant impression here, particularly on my wife, since it arrived on the day of my youngest child's[b] funeral; for two years

---

[a] See this volume, p. 85. - [b] Franziska

now she has seen all my enterprises regularly come to grief. The prospect held out by your letter (arrived 19th Apr.) of receiving the 'Bonaparte'[a] in print was therefore all the more welcome to me, for by nature she is very resilient and your letter set her up again...

First published in: Marx and Engels, *Works,* Second Russian Edition, Vol. 28, Moscow, 1962

Printed according to a letter from Cluss to Weydemeyer of 8 May 1852

Published in English for the first time

42

MARX TO ENGELS

IN MANCHESTER

London, 24 April 1852
28 Dean Street, Soho

Dear Frederic,

You cannot imagine what a wretched time I had last week. On the day of the funeral, the money I had been promised from various quarters failed to arrive, so that I was finally compelled to go to some French neighbours in order to pay the English vultures. And on top of this, alas, a letter arrived from Weydemeyer giving reason to suppose that in America, too, all our hopes have been dashed. Cluss, whose letter you will be getting next week, now holds out better prospects. *Quoique de dure complexion,*[b] I was, on this occasion, very hard hit by the wretched business.

Enclosed a letter from that cur Ewerbeck, who never uses a stamp and consistently robs one of one's last 10d. Then an article by B. Bauer from the *Daily New-York Tribune,*[c] to whose pages your article[d] has attracted all the rag-tag and bobtail. Bauer's

---

[a] K. Marx, *The Eighteenth Brumaire of Louis Bonaparte.* - [b] Although by nature tough - [c] B. Bauer, 'The Present Impossibility of War', *New-York Daily Tribune,* No. 3417, 31 March 1852. - [d] F. Engels, *Revolution and Counter-Revolution in Germany.*

revelations about 'the armies' will make you laugh. If you are going to send me articles for Dana now, wait until you have several so that I can send them all off at once.

Mr Tellering is publishing a monthly or weekly in New York; the cur himself sent me the first issue—unadulterated third-form drivel.

Heise (of the *Hornisse*) is now an intimate of Willich's. They are as thick as thieves. What can he see in the fellow? Once again they are bragging about a proposed coup in Germany.

Dronke is a real *imbécile*. His appetite whetted by the £4 we got for him from the Rhineland, he went to Coblenz in the hopes of extorting some more. It never occurred to the jackass that he would be providing fresh ammunition for use against the people in Cologne.[a] The fellow's behaviour is really too disgraceful.

Apropos. Do not forget to send *immédiatement* two notes to London as follows: 1. for *Liebknecht*, empowering him to obtain the £1 from *Hain*. 2. Write a brief note yourself to Hain, telling your 'good friend' in a couple of lines that, having heard he was doing well, you had referred Liebknecht to him *re* the £1. We must be careful not to make an enemy of him.

The fact is that one of our acquaintances, who has hitherto found shelter for the night at Liebknecht's lodgings, was thrown out by the latter's landlords, and not one of us has been able to raise a penny for the poor devil. Accordingly I yesterday sent Liebknecht a note in which I told him you had referred him to Hain *re* the £1. Mr Hain appeared somewhat incredulous and told Liebknecht he must first see it in your handwriting.

Let me have a few STAMPS, for I have a mass of stuff to send you.

Your
K. M.

First published abridged in *Der Briefwechsel zwischen F. Engels und K. Marx*, Bd. 1, Stuttgart, 1913 and in full in *MEGA*, Abt. III, Bd. 1, 1929

Printed according to the original

Published in English for the first time

---

[a] the Communist League members arrested and detained under investigation

43

ENGELS TO MARX

IN LONDON

Manchester, 25 April 1852

Dear Marx,

Yesterday evening I received a note from Hain which I sent you together with my reply to it. After this, I think, Mr Hain will pay.

Herewith the STAMPS, more to follow shortly. Also returning the other stuff. Ewerbeck's letter is a worthy pendant to his book.[a] 'Pray help me oppose Ribbentrop! I shall denounce him to Democracy as a hypocrite and *débaucheur*.'[b] The man must be in his dotage.

Nor has friend Bruno increased in wisdom or divine knowledge.[c] *Il valait bien la peine*[d] to set the American press in motion from Berlin thus, by this most roundabout route, proclaiming to an astonished world that the continental armies are there to maintain internal peace. Mr Bruno still represents the Hegelian dialectic in its deepest stagnation. At this stage of development, his concept of history goes no deeper than providing circumstantial proof of the most banal platitudes by an ample display of solemnity and pseudo-logical development, and then dishing them up as the brand-new findings of zealous research. All this is tolerable in the case of the distant past, but to be thus bamboozled about the immediate present is really too much and any fool should be able to see that there's nothing at all at the bottom of it. And as for the profound truth that governments are right vis-à-vis revolutions because the latter are still immature, but revolutions are also right vis-à-vis governments because they represent the ideas of the future, admittedly in embryonic and immature form, but nevertheless [...] to a substantial degree—that is an old Hegelian joke whose novelty has certainly worn off even in America! And then the eternal 'ill-temper', 'peevishness', 'fundamental indifference' of the 'bourgeois'. 'In some countries, classes war against classes, in others nations against nations.' Strictly speaking, this prodigiously clever sentence is all that Bruno has learnt from the revolution.

Mr Tellering has apparently been chased out of France as being

---

[a] H. Ewerbeck, *L'Allemagne et les Allemands*. - [b] Ewerbeck to Marx, 21 April 1852. - [c] See previous letter. - [d] It was well worth while

a homeless, vagrant member of the *lumpenproletariat* and of no use even to the Société du 10 Décembre.[113]

Unless you know positively that Dronke went to Germany of his own free will, I would think it more probable that, having been already once expelled from France, he was this time transported not to any frontier but to the *German* frontier. But once safely in Nassau, why did the silly fool go to Coblenz when he'd have done far better to go to Hamburg, where no one knows him and he would have found Weerth and Strohn, hence also cash, and from there to England! But Coblenz being so close, he was obviously drawn there from Nassau by the prospect of money, and if he had managed to get through safely, would certainly have gone on to Cologne. At all events, it is fortunate for the Cologne people that they have already been dealt with by the Board of indicting magistrates, otherwise Dronke's arrest would have provided occasion for another six months' examination. But very soon they'll take him to Cologne and maybe attempt to produce him as a witness before the Court of Assizes. This time it serves him perfectly right. He could certainly have found such money as he needed in Frankfurt, or have got Lassalle to send it to him somewhere, but no, the little chap must needs go to Coblenz where he's known to every gendarme and every dog in town. *En attendant il est sûrement logé.*[a]

Your
F. E.

First published abridged in *Der Briefwechsel zwischen F. Engels und K. Marx*, Bd. 1, Stuttgart, 1913 and in full in *MEGA*, Abt. III, Bd. 1, 1929	Printed according to the original Published in English for the first time

44

ENGELS TO MARX

IN LONDON

Manchester, 27 April 1852

Dear Marx,

Herewith Weydemeyer's latest, which sounds rather more hopeful. For the time being I am keeping your article[114] here 1. so as to read it, and 2. so as to translate it into English at some later

---

[a] Meanwhile he is out of harm's way.

date, which will be easily done, omitting such figures of speech as are comprehensible only to Germans.

Voilà donc[a] Moses Hess, in the *Kölnische Zeitung*, with a warrant out against him for high treason.[b] I'll be hanged if this hasn't happened because Father Dronke was found carrying those idiotic papers concerning their important business in Geneva. *Cela valait bien la peine!*[c] In the meantime Moses again becomes a martyr, which will greatly enhance his *otium cum dignitate*[d]; maybe he will shortly be dispatched to London—*est-ce que nous n'échapperons jamais à cet imbécile?*[e] At any rate, all this can make things extremely awkward again for the poor devils in Cologne and provide new grounds for dragging out their trial; had they already been referred to the Court of Assizes, we should surely have heard about it.

Freiligrath has written asking for an introduction to my brother-in-law[f]—I am sending it to him today; evidently he is determined to look round for a post.

Warm greetings to your wife and children.

Your
F. E.

Splendid division on the Militia Bill last night.[115] If the Almighty vouchsafes a few more like it, the new election will be postponed until September or October. SERVES THE WHIGS RIGHT AND THE FINAN-CIALS[28] TOO! I see that Jones intends after all to bring out his PAPER straight away—it was a mean trick Harney played him over the *Star*, but it was lucky that Jones did not acquire that doomed, discredited, wretched old paper.[116] Let Harney dig its grave and his own at the same time.

First published abridged in *Der Briefwech-sel zwischen F. Engels und K. Marx*, Bd. 1, Stuttgart, 1913 and in full in *MEGA*, Abt. III, Bd. 1, 1929

Printed according to the original

Published in English for the first time

---

[a] Here we have - [b] 'Amtliche Bekanntmachungen', *Kölnische Zeitung*, No. 99, 24 April 1852. - [c] It was well worth while! - [d] dignified leisure (Cicero, *Oratio pro Sextio*, 45) - [e] shall we never escape this imbecile? - [f] Emil Blank

45

ENGELS TO MARX [117]

IN LONDON

Manchester, 29 April 1852

D. M.,

Herewith another letter from Weydemeyer. I have not received the newspapers; but the *Atlantic* was reported by telegraph this morning, and they will probably arrive tomorrow morning. Weydemeyer appears to have misunderstood one or two practical hints I gave him on how to pack and dispatch his things in such a way as not to pay unnecessarily high postal charges; however, I have already pointed out his mistake.[a]

So the Coblenz story about the *piccolo*[b] was a pure fabrication and, if the *Kölner Zeitung* is to be believed, Father Dronke must already be in London, his adventures have achieved a purpose. *Tant mieux pour lui.*[c] But this makes the business of Moses'[d] warrant even more inexplicable. Anyhow, it would seem to imply further vexations for the Cologne people. God knows what sort of scrawl the police have picked up this time. *Pauvre*[e] Moses, fancy becoming SO EGREGIOUSLY and *post festum*[f] a martyr *in partibus infidelium*!

Next week I shall write several articles in succession for Dana,[118] and make sure that I take the thing up to the end of the Imperial Constitutional campaign. In order that we may be able to conclude directly, it would be a good idea if you could provide me with a short memorandum for the final articles—THE REVOLUTIONARY PROSPECTS OF GERMANY, and our party's situation during and after the revolution. It is precisely these concluding pieces which are important, and moreover a memorandum of this kind would enable me to write these articles not only better but far more quickly. In this way I could, if I tried hard enough, finish all the 5-6 outstanding articles within a fortnight and meanwhile you could get in touch with Dana about a new series on a subject of greater *actualité, soit la France, soit l'Angleterre.*[g] Since Weydemeyer's pamphlet will probably be coming out soon, it will no longer be

---

[a] See this volume, p. 79. - [b] the little one (Ernst Dronke) - [c] So much the better for him. - [d] Hess. See this volume, p. 89. - [e] Poor - [f] after the event - [g] topicality, either France or England

possible to sell Dana the *18th Brumaire,* even in a different guise; for he will then be able to have it FOR NOTHING and translate it himself. But you could still ask Dana whether he would like to have a modified version in translation, one suitable for the Anglo-American public. In this case the events leading up to 2 December '51 would for the most part be excised and the thing finally brought right up to date, so that successive weekly or fortnightly reports on France would follow straight on.

Your
F. E.

First published abridged in *Der Briefwechsel zwischen F. Engels und K. Marx,* Bd. 1, Stuttgart, 1913 and in full in *MEGA,* Abt. III, Bd. 1, 1929

Printed according to the original

Published in English for the first time

46

MARX TO ENGELS

IN MANCHESTER

London, 30 April 1852
28 Dean Street, Soho

Dear Frederic,

You will receive at the same time as this letter a colossal parcel from America. Today I have also had a letter from Cluss, of which I give excerpts below, as I shall be needing it until next week.

Dronke has arrived here *sain et sauf.*[a] I like him better than I had feared. He has grown taller and has broadened out as well. This has also made him more self-possessed. For the present he hob-nobs with Anschütz, who welcomed him with open arms. He is going to start up a small business, having contracted in Paris to sell cigar cases and purses over here. 10% commission. And, through Anschütz, he will at once acquire the necessary connections for this TRADE.

He tells me that the 'worthy' Techow has sent character sketches of us to Switzerland in which he roundly inveighs against us and

---

[a] safe and sound

you in particular. You have aroused the professional jealousy of the military, *et je pense*[a] that one day you will justify *leurs pressentiments.*[b] Further: from Geneva, Schily demanded that the gentlemen come to terms with us. This elicited an authoritative statement signed by Willich, Techow, Schapper and Schimmelpfennig in which, *inter alia,* it was pointed out that 1. there had been a complete break with this wholly impotent party; 2. there are police spies in our midst who have been reporting everything to the Prussian government.

I don't know whether I have already told you, or whether you heard during your stay here,[119] that Messrs Kinkel *et* Co. possess a *mere* 3,000 dollars in cash *all told,* that all respectable people such as Löwe of Calbe have all withdrawn, that relations between Willich on the one hand and Kinkel and Reichenbach on the other are very strained, and that the whole dungheap is in process of disintegration.

You will receive the memorandum on Germany.[c]

Yesterday the curs held a meeting of guarantors here and elected a definitive committee. Mr Ruge wrote a letter of protest. Willich was not present. From the start Reichenbach refused to have anything more to do with the filthy business. The committee will be paid. Those elected are Kinkel, Willich (doubtful that he'll accept), Löwe of Calbe (will in any case refuse), Fickler, Ronge, Schütz of Mainz and one other. They will make up the total from out of their own midst. In his letter, Ruge attacks Kinkel as an agent of the Prince of Prussia[d] and a freemason.

Here is a passage from Cluss' letter:

Huzel (not to be confused with Huzzelwitt), Cluss' friend, [present as a guarantor] at Kinkel's Cincinnati congress[60] writes and tells Cluss *inter alia:*

'Kinkel tried to floor me with *vulgar invective* against Marx and Engels. I succeeded in doing what I wanted, namely in cornering him so effectively that I shall have him at my mercy for some time to come. He tried to cover himself by obtaining my word of honour not to say anything about the incident or to write anything that would get him "into a stink"... In a letter to Anneke a certain Tellering scolds like a fishwife at Marx...'.

Cluss himself goes on:

'In New York, at the inimitable meeting which I reported in my last letter, the numerous gymnastic clubs[120] constituted themselves a separate body and declared

---

[a] and I think - [b] their presentiments - [c] See this volume, p. 90. - [d] Cf. this volume, p. 573.

their support for my protest[a] and for Weydemeyer's article[b] against Kinkel's memorandum.'[121]

Apropos. I gave Bangya a few pen-sketches of the great German men in London for him to pass on to Szemere.[122] This letter, I know not how, has been read to a German publisher without my name being mentioned. He is now asking for 'character sketches' of these gentlemen and, according to Bangya, is prepared to pay £25 for a few sheets. Anonymous or pseudonymous, of course. Well, *qu'en penses-tu?*[c] We would really have to do a humorous piece of this kind together. I have some doubts. If you think I should take this crap on, you will have to make a compilation from my letters and anything else you have which may contain fragments on the peculiarities of these curs. At all events you would have to send me a few notes about Willich 'in action'[123] and 'in Switzerland'.

Among the things I am sending you, you will find the draft of an advertisement for an illustrated book of battle reports by old Szerelmey. He wants it gingered up a little and done into English as an advertisement, in return for which he promises each of us a copy of his work. *Je crois que ça vaut la peine de faire un petit puff.*[d]

As soon as I set eyes on Mr Carey's first work in print[e] I foresaw that he would bring out an economic work on the 'harmony of interests'.[f]

Mais que dis-tu, mon cher,[g] to the fact that, in the *Janus* we sent you, Ruge seeks—and *how* he seeks, *mon Dieu!*—to appropriate communism as the latest product of his 'humanist thought'.

Have you read the cock-fight between Harney and Jones?[116] If not, I shall send you their mutual philippics.[h] Both of them, the one voluntarily, the other involuntarily, descend to the level of German émigré polemics.

Your
K. M.

---

[a] A. Cluss, 'An den Garanten-Congress des deutschen Anleihens in Cincinnati. Washington, Jan. 23', *Turn-Zeitung*, No. 6, 1 March 1852. - [b] J. Weydemeyer, 'Die revolutionäre Agitation unter der Emigration', *Turn-Zeitung*, No. 6, 1 March 1852. - [c] what do you think of it? - [d] I think it warrants the trouble of a little puff. - [e] H. Ch. Carey, *Essay on the Rate of Wages...* - [f] H. Ch. Carey, *The Harmony of Interests...* In a letter of 15 April 1852 Cluss wrote Marx about the second edition of this book. - [g] But what, my dear fellow, do you say - [h] G. J. Harney, 'To the Readers of *The Star,* and the Democrats of Great Britain and Ireland', *The Star,* No. 753, 17 April 1852 and E. Jones, 'An Appeal for the Judgment of the People', *Notes to the People,* No. 52, 24 April 1852.

Have you ever read more egregious nonsense than B. Bauer's article in the *Tribune*: 'The Decline of England'? The passage most characteristic of the incorrigible old theologian runs as follows:

'While the English Parliament has hitherto persecuted the Romish policy, and availed itself of the popular impulses for the establishment of its sovereignty—while, in the old Romish spirit, it has taken advantage of *internal domestic differences*, as for example, the *differences of High Church, of Scotch Presbyterianism*, and *of Irish Catholicism*, for the formation and development of its aristocratic art of Government, [...] it has now become a party to the Continental struggle between the peoples and the Governments, and it appears as the advocate for Constitutionalism at the very moment when that is approaching its undeniable downfall.'

If that's not champion drivel, I don't know what is.

First published much abridged in *Der Briefwechsel zwischen F. Engels und K. Marx*, Bd. 1, Stuttgart, 1913 and in full in *MEGA*, Abt. III, Bd. 1, 1929

Printed according to the original

Published in English for the first time

47

MARX TO JOSEPH WEYDEMEYER [12]

IN NEW YORK

London, 30 April 1852
28 Dean Street, Soho

Dear Weydemeyer,

The news of the printing is very welcome.[124] You must not take Lupus' letter [125] so much *au sérieux*.[a] In our very straitened circumstances there is, you know, inevitably a surplus of irritation which must always be 'discounted' if one is to strike a right balance.

Neither I nor Engels has received your anti-Kinkel article in the *Turn-Zeitung*.[b] I await it with keen interest since your anti-Heinzen polemic was a model of its kind.[c]

I am *horrified* to learn that Pfänder's statements are appearing in the pamphlet.[126] That sort of thing is all very well for a weekly where what crops up today is submerged tomorrow in the welter of time. In a pamphlet, on the other hand, it acquires altogether

---

[a] seriously - [b] J. Weydemeyer, 'Die revolutionäre Agitation unter der Emigration', *Turn-Zeitung*, No. 6, 1 March 1852. - [c] Weydemeyer's article in the *New-Yorker Demokrat*, No. 311, 29 January 1852.

too much permanence, looks too much like a party manifesto and, if we want to attack the swine, there are, of course, better and different ways of doing so than in Pfänder's statement. Unfortunately this will arrive too late.— Just now I am negotiating with a bookseller here who is to get your *Revolution* sent to Germany. More about this next week.

As regards the newly invented lacquer varnish about which I and Bangya wrote to you,[127] you must not let the thing out of your own hands. It might set you up in funds at one stroke. Write and tell me *when the Exhibition opens* in New York,[128] and all you know about it. You can make use of the opportunity both to strike up acquaintances and to establish all the connections with foreign businessmen necessary to a forwarding agency. Write to me at once, giving full details of the expenses you thereby incur. We must, of course, let you have these *en avance*. In the first place you will need a fellow to keep a constant eye on the stuff at the Exhibition, since you yourself cannot spend the whole day in the building for the sake of it. Secondly, you will need money for advertisements and announcements in the newspapers. So let us have a detailed estimate of expenses.

As to Szemere, his pamphlet[a] will soon be READY. But since I cannot, as he asks, send him a 'bundle' of copies of the *Revolution*, and since our enemies may have whispered in his ear that your paper has appeared only twice before submerging again, I cannot just now get any money from that quarter, for the confidence of these people has been shaken. But he is coming here *in person* and I shall then straighten everything out.

It would be a pity if your anti-Kinkel polemic were not to appear in the very first number. The fellow is going utterly to pot. A Dane by the name of Goldschmidt lampooned him splendidly in the feuilleton of the *Kölner Zeitung*, recounting his meeting with him and Schurz in London.[b] Dronke, finally released from custody in Paris, has arrived here and is saying that in private friend Schurz declares Kinkel a jackass whom he only intends to exploit. This man, Kinkel's 'modest liberator', has smuggled an article into the Augsburg *Allgemeine Zeitung*[c] in which he proclaims himself

---

a The pamphlet was published later, in 1853, under the title: B. Szemere, *Graf Ludwig Batthyány, Arthur Görgei, Ludwig Kossuth. Politische Charakterskizzen aus dem Ungarischen Freiheitskriege*. - b M. Goldschmidt, ['Einige Skizzen aus seiner Reise nach England während der Zeit der großen Ausstellung,'] *Kölnische Zeitung*, No. 100, 25 April 1852. - c An anonymous article ['Hansestädte. Hamburg, 13 April'] in *Allgemeine Zeitung*, No. 108, 17 April 1852.

'the only important man among the London émigrés', declares Kinkel and Ruge to be 'out-moded' and, in proof of his own greatness, cites the fact that he is marrying a 'rich' girl, Ronge's sister-in-law, and that, after completion of the nuptials, he will remove to America. *Quel grand homme! Quant à Tellering,*[a] keep me *au fait* about this individual. As soon as I think *fit*, I can destroy him, not only in the eyes of *our* party, but in the eyes of *all* parties.[b]

Yesterday, then, Mr Kinkel held his Guarantors' Congress.[c] Mr Willich did not appear; he is very embittered with Kinkel as a result of the news which we conveyed to him by a roundabout route (we had had it from Cluss). Mr Ruge sent a letter in which he declared Kinkel to be an agent of the 'King of Prussia',[d] and gave himself superior airs. Mr Reichenbach declared that he wanted to have nothing more to do with the filthy business. Thus a definitive committee was elected, seven in number—of the alleged communists only Willich, who is unlikely to accept. In addition, Löwe of Calbe, who has already refused. Next, Kinkel, Schütz of Mainz, Fickler. I do not know who the other two are. According to some reports, the curs have 3,000 dollars in cash and, according to others, 9,000. They immediately resolved that *the 7 members of the provisional government* should receive **payment**, a fact you must report in the *Turn-Zeitung.*[129] For the rest, the whole dungheap is disintegrating.

Keep at least some of the copies of the *Revolution* READY for *Germany* until you receive my order.

I have forwarded your letter to Jones. He cannot *possibly* pay anything. He is as *dépourvu*[e] as ourselves, and we all write for him gratis. Cluss will have told you about the battle between Jones and Harney. I have sent him details of it.[130] However, the things must be kept from the American Press for as long as possible.

Big business and industry are now doing better than ever in England and hence on the Continent. As a result of the exceptional circumstances—California, Australia, England's commercial penetration of the Punjab, Sind and other only recently conquered parts of India, it may well be that the crisis will be postponed until 1853. But then its eruption will be appalling. And until that time there can be no thought of revolutionary convulsions.

The trial of the Cologne people has again been deferred, this

_____

[a] What a great man! As for Tellering - [b] See this volume, p. 105. - [c] ibid., p. 92. - [d] ibid., pp. 92 and 573. - [e] penniless

time until the July Assizes. By then the Assizes, i.e. the JURIES, will probably have been abolished in Prussia.

Philistine Lüning, so Dronke tells me, has been here with his spouse in order to unify Agitation and Emigration [26]—fruitlessly, of course.

Farewell. Warmest regards to your wife from my wife and myself.

Your

K. M.

Hardly ever have I seen anything more stupid than Bruno Bauer's article on 'the decline of England'.[a]

How did the fellow manage to get in with Dana?

First published in: Marx and Engels, *Works*, First Russian Edition, Vol. XXV, Moscow, 1934

Printed according to the original

Published in English in full for the first time

48

ENGELS TO MARX

IN LONDON

Manchester, 1 May 1852

Dear Marx,

Enclosed a 30/- POST OFFICE ORDER, which is all I can spare for the moment. True, you will not be able to cash the thing tomorrow, on account of its being Sunday, but at least you know that you've got it. Should I find myself able to send off more of the same later on this month, you can be sure you'll get it come what may, but just now I cannot say.

It's very nice to hear that the little man[b] has turned up and is getting on well, and it is all to the good that he has, for the time being, found A FRIEND IN NEED, A FRIEND INDEED in Anschütz. He must visit me some time this summer, once I have seen the back of my old man.

As to the question of the biographical sketches of the great men,[c] I have, oddly enough, long been turning over in my mind a similar

---

a See this volume, pp. 85 and 87. - b Ernst Dronke - c See this volume, p. 93.

idea for an alphabetically arranged collection of such biographies, which could continually be added to and kept in readiness for the great moment 'when it all starts', and then they could all at once be precipitated into the world. As for the publisher's offer, £25 is not to be sneezed at, but we must not forget that, however great the ano- and pseudonymity, everyone will realise *de quel côté ces flèches viennent,*[a] and the responsibility would be laid at both our doors. If published in Germany under the present regime, the thing would seem to be supporting the reactionaries, and not even prefaces expressing the most irreproachable views in the world would make it seem otherwise. And that is always fatal. If the affair were restricted to a few—say, a dozen—of the more noteworthy jackasses, Kinkel, Hecker, Struve, Willich, Vogt and so forth, it might be more feasible, for the omission of our own names would not then matter very much and the things could be taken as issuing direct from the reactionaries. At any rate we ought, if possible, to write it together.[131] So decide what you think is best and *nous verrons. £25 valent bien un peu de scandale.*[b]

Cluss' letter will be returned next week. I'll do the thing for Szerelmey.[c] By midday today the Americans had not yet arrived, maybe they are waiting for me now at home.

Your
F. E.

First published in part in *Der Briefwechsel zwischen F. Engels und K. Marx,* Bd. 1, Stuttgart, 1913 and in full in *MEGA,* Abt. III, Bd. 1, 1929

Printed according to the original

Published in English for the first time

49

ENGELS TO MARX

IN LONDON

Manchester, 4 May 1852

Dear Marx,

Your fat American parcel has not yet arrived.[d] I have made inquiries at Pickford's, since the houses in my street have been renumbered, which gives rise to confusion. But at Pickford's there

---

[a] which direction these barbs are coming from - [b] we shall see. £25 is well worth a bit of a row. - [c] See this volume, p. 93. - [d] See this volume, pp. 91 and 100.

is no parcel for me. Either you didn't send the thing off or, if by post, perhaps not in the prescribed manner, or else something has happened to it. So try and find out what has become of the thing.

I shall be having a visit from my respected pater here this week, when the whole bloody matter of the firm will be settled and my position, too, will be further regulated. Either the contract will be renewed and the firm will continue as it is, which is not very probable, or I shall try so to arrange matters that my old man quits by the end of the year at the latest, and perhaps even by the end of June. Then there'll be the hellish liquidation which, however, should be more or less completed in 6 to 8 months, after which I shall turn my hand to something else, either go to Liverpool or God knows what. This will probably be decided within the next fortnight. I am glad that my old man will soon be here so that the inevitable mess is over as soon as possible and I know where I am.

I return Cluss' letter herewith. I have Jones' articles here, but not those of Harney, which you might send me some time so that I can acquaint myself with both sides and observe Father Harney in his new role. The industrious Jones will soon drive this indolent cur from the field if only he can hang on for a while. And he will certainly be able to raise the circulation[a] to 4,000 a week, which alone means a profit (3,600 covers costs).

The arrival of my old man will, of course, put back my Dana plans[b] by a week or a fortnight. On the other hand you could meanwhile continue, through Szemere, to negotiate with the publisher over the sketches, to look through your correspondence and the *N. Rh. Z.* (especially votes and speeches in the National Assembly) apropos the heroes to be depicted and, if the matter reaches a favourable conclusion, you could come up here for a week and we'd have a go at the thing.[c] I really think it could be done in such a way that no one will discover its *paternité*,[d] and even if they did, little harm would be done.

According to a letter from Ebner, he is still negotiating over your Economy[45] with Löwenthal, who wants to establish himself in Brussels and in the meantime remains a partner in the Frankfurt business.

How is Freiligrath progressing with my brother-in-law?[e] Don't

---

[a] of *The People's Paper* - [b] i.e. work on the series *Revolution and Counter-Revolution in Germany*. - [c] K. Marx and F. Engels, *The Great Men of the Exile*. - [d] here: authorship - [e] Emil Blank (see this volume, p. 89).

forget to let me know about Pindar, *c'est une bête ennuyeuse et assez confuse*.[a] Is he a member of the League?[b]

The copies of the *Turn-Zeitung* advised by Weydemeyer have still not arrived; there must have been some oversight on his part.

Write soon.

Your
F. E.

In the case of parcels which do not go by post, it would be best if, instead of the old No. 70, you include the old and new nos. In the address, thus:

No. 44/70, Great Ducie St., Strangeways, Manchester.

Szerelmey's thing[c] tomorrow perhaps.

First published in part in *Der Briefwechsel zwischen F. Engels und K. Marx*, Bd. 1, Stuttgart, 1913 and in full in *MEGA*, Abt. III, Bd. 1, 1929

Printed according to the original

Published in English for the first time

50

MARX TO ENGELS

IN MANCHESTER

London, 6 May 1852
28 Dean Street, Soho

Dear Frederic,

The parcel didn't go off to you because Pickford's demanded 2/6d from my wife. And the whole lot put together isn't worth that much.

The strange note enclosed herewith is a hastily made copy of a circular sent out by Messrs Kinkel and Willich to their affiliates.[132] The funniest thing about it is that one of their heads of sections invariably carries these scraps to Hebeler, the Prussian Consul-General, who pays him for them. The Prussian government, of course, no less than Kinkel-Willich, possesses the key to these

---

[a] a tedious and rather muddle-headed creature - [b] the Communist League - [c] See this volume, p. 93.

portentous mysteries. Indeed Willich, for all his principles and scruples, has after all accepted a position on the definitive committee. Where the money is, there you will find Willich.

A *coup quelconque*[a] is intended, so much is certain. General Klapka has already left for Malta, in his pocket a commission signed by Kossuth and Mazzini appointing him general commanding the Italo-Hungarian army. I believe a start is to be made in Sicily. Unless these gentlemen suffer defeat and receive a drubbing twice a year, they feel ill at ease. That world history continues to unfold without their help, without their intervention, and without, indeed, official intervention, is something they refuse to admit. If things go wrong, as they are sure to do, Mr Mazzini will have a renewed opportunity for self-assertion in outraged letters to a Graham *quelconque*.[b][133] Nor will his digestion suffer in consequence.

I am now correcting Bangya's translation of Szemere's character-sketches[c] written in Hungarian. While the original must be splendid, it has to be laboriously reconstructed from the wretched and often almost incomprehensible translation which is constantly at loggerheads with the rules of grammar and the *consecutio temporum*.[d] This much is clear: the deposition of the Austrian dynasty which, at the time of its proclamation, was unpolitical and pernicious, was engineered by Mr Lajos Kossuth so as to secure for himself the post of governor, for he feared that, if he hesitated, he would later see it devolve unopposed on the victorious Görgey. Lajos was also responsible for the mistake of storming Ofen instead of marching on Vienna, since he was itching to celebrate with his family his triumphant entry into the capital.[134]

Apropos. I have just received a letter from Bangya. The publisher in Berlin has now made a definite offer: £25 for 5-6 sheets of character-sketches, 24 free copies. I shall receive the money from Bangya as soon as I deliver the manuscript to him. But the man wants it quickly.

My plan is as follows: for the time being I shall do a *brouillon*[e] with Dronke, which will *plus ou moins*[f] obliterate my style. So it might be possible for you and me to get the thing[g] READY in a fortnight's time. At all events you must let me have some more

---

[a] some coup or other - [b] some or other - [c] B. Szemere, *Graf Ludwig Batthyány, Arthur Görgei, Ludwig Kossuth. Politische Charakterskizzen aus dem Ungarischen Freiheitskriege.* - [d] sequence of tenses - [e] rough draft - [f] more or less - [g] K. Marx and F. Engels, *The Great Men of the Exile.*

information about Willich (during the campaign[a] and in Switzerland) in your CURRENT LETTERS.

Enclosed letter from Cluss.

Yesterday Freiligrath and I were with Trübner, the bookseller. He believes he can dispose of a number of copies of the *Revolution*[b] here in London and place a further quantity in Germany through Campe. So as soon as Weydemeyer's copies arrive, forward them here. The *Turn-Zeitung* seems to have gone astray.

Your
K. Marx

First published much abridged in *Der Briefwechsel zwischen F. Engels und K. Marx*, Bd. 1, Stuttgart, 1913 and in full in *MEGA*, Abt. III, Bd. 1, 1929

Printed according to the original

Published in English for the first time

51

ENGELS TO MARX

IN LONDON

Manchester, 7 May 1852

Dear Marx,

I return Cluss' letter herewith. In this connection it has occurred to me that now that Mr Dana is in touch with B. Bauer and Simon of Trier and is, at the same time, restricting your space on account of the presidential election, it would certainly not be out of place to give Mr Dana a taste of Yankee medicine. Cluss and a number of others should write to Mr Dana from various quarters inquiring why it is that these INCOMPARABLE articles should appear so rarely and irregularly and expressing the hope that the fault does not lie with the editorial board which, rather, might be expected to correct this situation and find it possible to publish articles by K. M. more frequently, etc., etc. Weydemeyer could very easily organise this; the only reason we need to give him is that Dana wants to restrict your space and hence a demonstration of this

---

[a] Willich's service in the Baden-Palatinate insurgent army in the spring of 1849. - [b] The issue of *Die Revolution*, in which Marx's *Eighteenth Brumaire of Louis Bonaparte* appeared.

kind is called for if we are to continue to have access to this organ. *A Barnum, Barnum et demi*.[a] If you agree, I can put this to Weydemeyer per the next STEAMER.

The circular sent out by the convention to the sections is exquisite. I'll be hanged if the St Petersburg, Warsaw, Berlin, Rome, etc., sections are situated more than 4 miles from Charing Cross. This carbonari-like, self-important, bustling, order-of-the-dayish attitude again betrays how mistaken these gentlemen are as to their ostensibly organised forces. To propose a coup just now is a *bêtise*[b] and a dirty trick. But truly, 'something has got to happen, something has got to be done'. It would be desirable for the supposed leaders of the thing to be all of them captured and shot; but needless to say the great men will make sure this doesn't happen and the heroic Willich will stay quietly in London so long as there is still money in the cashbox, credit at Schärttner's and free coats and boots *ad libitum* at the 'tailor's and shoemaker's'. That is what Mr Willich means by supplies for the army!

As for the matter of the character-sketches,[c] so far so good. The thing can be ready in a month's time. But mind you find someone reliable to make a fair copy, so that it goes out in a completely unknown hand. When you come up, bring the Americana, the complete run of the *N. Rh. Z.* and the necessary manuscript documents. My old man arrives tomorrow and is unlikely to be able to stay here for longer than 8-10 days.

I've at last received my stuff on military science from Germany. So far I have been able to read only little of it. At this stage, I should say that Mr Gustav von Hoffstetter, of wide renown, is not exactly a Napoleon but rather a thoroughly reliable commander of a battalion or so in a minor engagement. But I haven't yet finished reading his thing.[d] Not unpleasing, on the other hand, is a booklet on new fortifications in general by Küntzel, a Prussian captain of engineers[e]—both better history and more materialist than anything I have so far read in *militaribus*.[f]

Now as for Mr Willisen, be it said here that the victory at Idstedt[135] was won, not by the Danes over the Schleswig-Holsteiners, but rather by the usual tactics of common sense over

[a] *A Barnum, Barnum et demi* (Against one Barnum one and a half) is modelled on such an expression as 'à Corsaire Corsaire et demi', the idea of which is roughly 'to beat someone at his own game'. - [b] piece of stupidity - [c] K. Marx and F. Engels, *The Great Men of the Exile*. - [d] Gustav von Hoffstetter, *Tagebuch aus Italien, 1849*. - [e] H. Küntzel, *Die taktischen Elemente der neuen Fortificationen*. - [f] in the military sphere

Hegelian speculation. Willisen's book^a should really be called the *philosophy* of great wars. This in itself would indicate that it contains more philosophising than military science, that the most self-evident things are construed *a priori* with the most profound and exhaustive thoroughness and that, sandwiched between these, are the most methodical discourses on simplicity and multiplicity and such-like opposites. What can one say about military science which begins with the concept of art *en général*, then goes on to demonstrate that the art of cookery is also an art, expatiates on the relationship of art to science and finally subsumes all the rules, relationships, potentialities, etc., etc., of the art of war under the one, absolute axiom: the stronger always overcomes the weaker. Every now and again there are some nice *aperçus*^b and some useful reductions to basic principles; it would indeed be bad if there were not. As to its practical application, I haven't yet got to that, but it doesn't say much for Willisen that every one of Napoleon's greatest victories was achieved in defiance of Willisen's elementary rules, a result that your orthodox Hegelian can, of course, readily explain away without the least violence being done to those rules.

I see that Görgey's memoirs have just come out^c—but since they cost 6 talers, I doubt that I can buy them just now. With these, the material on the *military aspect* of the Hungarian war may be regarded as complete for the time being. At any rate, I shall do something on the Hungarian war, and possibly on all the wars of 1848/49.¹³⁶ As soon as I am clear in my mind about earlier military history, I shall look round for a publisher onto whom I can then shift most of the expenditure on sources.

You will have received the 30/- sent you last Saturday.

Your

F. E.

First published much abridged in *Der Briefwechsel zwischen F. Engels und K. Marx*, Bd. 1, Stuttgart, 1913 and in full in *MEGA*, Abt. III, Bd. 1, 1929

Printed according to the original

Published in English for the first time

---

^a W. Willisen, *Theorie des großen Krieges angewendet auf den russisch-polnischen Feldzug von 1831.* - ^b insights - ^c A. Görgei, *Mein Leben und Wirken in Ungarn in den Jahren 1848 und 1849.*

52

MARX TO ADOLF CLUSS[137]

IN WASHINGTON

[London, 7 and about 15 May 1852]

... Herewith you will find a wrapper, in which the contemptible, craven, half-crazed *Tellering* mailed his defamatory opus. (Address:) CHARLES MARX, THE FUTURE DICTATOR OF GERMANY.[138] Now I ask you, what is to be done with the cur? To start a public row with a lunatic of this sort would be doing him too much honour and is the whole object of his manoeuvre. Could you not send the MANIAC's wrapper to the New York postal service in my name? Or might not a sound thrashing be the simplest course? I leave the whole thing to you. Naturally any packages of the kind will in future be returned. But by indulging in this sort of gutter-snipe's trick, the cur also brings me to the notice of the English police, which, under the Tories, is far from pleasant...

Ad vocem[a] Szemere: I am not by nature inclined to be unduly trusting, least of all when it comes to the official great men of 1848/49. But in Szemere's case, it's quite a different matter. I am correcting the German translation—for he originally wrote in Hungarian—of his 'character-sketches'.[b] Every line betrays a *superior intellect*, and the rage of the democrats may be attributed to the CONTEMPT AND MOCKERY-SYSTEM which he employs with supreme skill. Although, of course, in accordance with the Hungarian line, he places, as in Antiquity, 'the fatherland and the citizen' above all else, his writing is imbued with a fundamentally critical spirit. A man who thinks and writes in this way is no Austrian agent. As for the 'DEAR COLONEL WEBB', he was negotiating with him without knowing who he was, but broke off as soon as he was informed what was afoot. The story of his fortune is very simple. Szemere himself does not possess a centime. But his wife is the daughter of a (now deceased) Austrian '*Hof-agent*' (as the Austrian *Procureurs du roi*[c] are called in Hungary); her old man possessed a fortune of a million. Throughout the 1848/49 revolution Mrs Szemere lived in Vienna with her mother. He had even ordered her to refrain from writing to him and to sever all ties with him until the old

---

[a] As to - [b] B. Szemere, *Graf Ludwig Batthyány, Arthur Görgei, Ludwig Kossuth. Politische Charakterskizzen aus dem Ungarischen Freiheitskriege.* - [c] King's prosecutors

woman's death, when she could collect *her* fortune. His old mother-in-law died at the end of 1849 and Mrs Szemere, who was, of course, in no way suspect, surreptitiously sold all her worldly goods and turned them into CASH. In this she was aided by the minister, Bach, her father's lawyer, who seized on this opportunity and surreptitiously *took his cut*. Once her fortune was liquid, Mrs Szemere converted it into bills on London and English STOCKS, obtained a passport authorising her to visit the water-cure doctor, Priessnitz, in Prussia, but instead travelled to London and thence to her husband in Paris. Those Austrians, however, could lay their hands on nothing with which to gladden their Exchequer. Well, what does all this prove? That Szemere is much too astute to make his enemies a present of a million. I have written to Sz. himself, telling him that, without mentioning Kossuth, he should make a statement about his personal circumstances which I shall get into the *New-York Tribune* for him.

The Austrian spies are in Kossuth's immediate entourage, notably Madame Pulszky. This Count Pulszky is a Galician Jew by origin. Madame Pulszky, daughter of an ultra-reactionary Jewish banker in Vienna, writes to her mater each week, and from this source the Austrian government finds out anything it wants. It may even be asked whether Count and Countess Pulszky (*The Times* regularly derided both these individuals for the ASSUMPTION of their title)[a] have not promised to lure Mr Kossuth into the snare in the hope that they may thereby retrieve their confiscated land. It is known for a fact that as a student, Pulszky denounced his comrades' demagogic activities[139] to the Austrian government...

Enclosed you will find General Klapka's declaration of principles,[140] from which you will see that he, too, is starting to rebel against Kossuth. The last part of the document means nothing more than that Klapka is going to participate in Mazzini's projected coup. I have, if I am not mistaken, already written to you about the plans for a coup hatched by Messrs Mazzini, Kossuth, etc. Nothing could be more welcome to the great powers, especially Bonaparte, and nothing **more damaging** *to ourselves*.

I have just received a letter from Cologne, dated 3 May.[b] They are asking for 200 or 250 copies of the *Brumaire*. So pray ask Weydemeyer to send me forthwith 300 copies via *Engels*. At the same time, he should advise me of the selling price. I take it that he has already dispatched the 50 copies as promised...[141]

---

[a] *The Times,* No. 20955, 10 November 1851, leader. - [b] Bermbach's letter to Marx of 3 May 1852; the original has 11 May.

To return to Klapka's document. I would beg you to keep it secret for the time being. It was given me in confidence, but with permission to publish it. I shall send it to the New York *Tribune*, and I do not want it to come into circulation before then...

Jones' STAMPED PAPER has come out and the first number has sold surprisingly well. I enclose a cutting from the Notes[a] from which you will see that he has knocked Harney out completely. Mr Harney is proceeding down the primrose path. One article in his paper, signed Spartacus,[b] attacks Chartism for being only a CLASS MOVEMENT which ought to be replaced by A GENERAL AND NATIONAL MOVEMENT, genuine Mazzinian hot air, etc., etc., etc....

Extracts from the Cologne letter[c]:

'Recently Mrs Daniels was favoured yet again with a domiciliary visit in the certain expectation that it would yield a letter from you. The Prussian police seem to be as putty in the hands of the first jackass to come along. The prisoners' case seems to be approaching its conclusion. The examination has been concluded and, for over two months, the files have been back in the possession of the local public prosecutor at the Court of Appeal where, however, they seem incapable of deciding upon the wording of a petition to the Board of indicting magistrates. It is generally rumoured that the thing will be dealt with before a special Court of Assizes in June.'

Apropos. Ask Weydemeyer if he has yet been to see Dana, who is waiting for him to pass on the information I sent him about the situation of the Cologne prisoners and the conduct of the Prussian government, before writing a LEADER on the subject.[d] He mustn't for God's sake fail to do this, if it can possibly be helped.

If you manage to bring out Freiligrath's poem against Kinkel *et Comp*[e] as a broadsheet, you will have an assured sale of 500 copies in the Rhineland alone. But the thing must be done quickly. Otherwise it will be *trop tard*.[f]

Do not allow the articles, etc., in your possession to age so much that they lose their bouquet. If you can't get them printed (Eccarius, Engels, etc.),[142] give them to some paper or other, e.g. the *Turn-Zeitung*, as you think fit. In any case, it is better they should be read than left unread.

If you can't get Freiligrath's poem printed, give it to whatever

---

a [E. Jones,] 'Current Notes', *The People's Paper*, No. 1, 8 May 1852. - b Spartacus [pseudonym of W. J. Linton], 'The Sense of the Country', *The Star of Freedom*, No. 1, 8 May 1852. - c Below is an extract from Bermbach's letter to Marx of 3 May 1852. - d *New-York Daily Tribune*, No. 3446 of 4 May 1852 used this material for its leader 'Justice of Prussia'. See also this volume, p. 115. - e F. Freiligrath, 'An Joseph Weydemeyer', I and II. - f too late

newspaper you think best.[13] If, as a party, we make no effort to be quick off the mark, we shall always arrive *post festum...*[a]

Few mortals, other than yourself, can boast of having received letters from me on 4 successive mail days; but I was anxious to show Papa Lupus which of us two is the more punctilious...

First published in part in Russian in *Voprosy istorii KPSS*, No. 3, 1962 and in full in: Marx and Engels, *Works,* Second Russian Edition, Vol. 28, Moscow, 1962

Printed according to a letter from Cluss to Weydemeyer of 31 May 1852

Published in English for the first time

53

MARX TO ENGELS

IN MANCHESTER

[London,] 13 May [1852]
28 Dean Street, Soho

Dear Engels,

Only a couple of lines today. Old Szerelmey, whose first volume is now ready, chivvies me daily about the advertisement for his book of battle reports.[b] If you can't do it now, at least send me back his *brouillon*[c] by return.

Your
K. M.

First published in *MEGA*, Abt. III, Bd. 1, 1929

Printed according to the original

Published in English for the first time

---

[a] after the event - [b] See this volume, p. 93. - [c] rough draft

54

ENGELS TO MARX

IN LONDON

Manchester, 19 May 1852

Dear Marx,

Les affaires vont bien.[a] Tomorrow or the day after my old man will be leaving again, very satisfied with his affairs. The business here is to be completely reorganised and will be run on a new basis. I have succeeded in obtaining a rise and, as soon as the contracts have been signed and my old man is out of the way, the banknote I promised you will materialise. The best thing about all this is that I am signing nothing at all; my old man was wise enough not to trust me entirely on the political score, thus perhaps safeguarding himself against becoming involved through me in any further unpleasantness. Moreover, in this case, and providing certain proprieties are observed, I can arrange to be replaced by one of my brothers in such a way that my old man would lose nothing by my departure save, perhaps, a few illusions, and it would be I, not he, who would be making the sacrifice. Let me know by return how your character-sketches[b] are going. All these changes are going to saddle me with a fair amount of work for a while, so that there would seem to be no immediate prospect of our doing very much together, and yet I should like very much to see you here as soon as possible. It would therefore be good if you and Dronke could complete the things so far as you are able, after which we could polish them off here in a few evenings. And before you come up I would make the necessary extracts about the people in question (whose names you must give me) from the documents up here, thereby enabling us to get on quickly. It has just occurred to me that it would be best for you to come at Whitsun, i.e. on the previous Friday—the day after tomorrow week—when there are general HOLIDAYS here. If the weather is fine we can go to the Isle of Man or somewhere, and if bad we shall work. But mind you come on your own. I should be very glad to see Dronkius later on, but I have no use for him just now, and he would only disturb our work.

By the way, the best thing about the new arrangement is that, as

---

[a] Things are going well. - [b] K. Marx and F. Engels, *The Great Men of the Exile.*

from 1 July, not only shall I have more money, but it will be all *mine*, so that no one will have any right to ask what use I make of it. Further details when we meet.

Your

F. E.

First published abridged in *Der Briefwech-sel zwischen F. Engels und K. Marx*, Bd. 1, Stuttgart, 1913 and in full in *MEGA*, Abt. III, Bd. 1, 1929

Printed according to the original

Published in English for the first time

55

ENGELS TO MARX

IN LONDON

Manchester, 21 May 1852

Dear Marx,

My old man has left. ALL IS RIGHT. Herewith the first half of the ten-pound note. I hope to see you here at the end of next week. Presumably a letter from you is this moment awaiting me at home but I haven't the time to go there. The second half of the note will follow either today by the second post, or tomorrow.

Your

F. E.

First published in *Der Briefwechsel zwischen F. Engels und K. Marx*, Bd. 1, Stuttgart, 1913

Printed according to the original

Published in English for the first time

56

ENGELS TO MARX

IN LONDON

Manchester, 22 May 1852

Dear Marx,

I am writing to you today simply to make sure you know that yesterday I sent direct to you by the first post 1/2 a £10 note, and that the 2nd half went off at the same time under cover to Lupus for transmission to you. I trust you have received it all right.

There is now great ELECTIONEERING ACTIVITY here—two of the WHIG FREE TRADERS[a] were put up by the Tories with the intention of ousting Bright and Gibson, and nothing goes on here but canvassing and boozing. Of course the fellows don't stand a chance, but it's going to cost them a mint of money.

Three weeks ago, as I anticipated, there was a flush of speculation on the cotton market; but since opportunities are not yet sufficiently pronounced and the spinners and merchants here were operating against it, the thing momentarily subsided again. However, it will recur before very long, as soon as the whole weight of the American crop has been delivered. Wool, too,— because of the sudden ruin of the Australian sheep-farmers— lends itself splendidly to speculation and, all things considered, there is every prospect that by the autumn speculation will be in full spate. Railway stocks, etc., etc., are again beginning to rise—the better ones continue to yield more than the 1 to $1\frac{1}{2}\%$ now still to be had from the banks in respect of deposits. In America, speculation in cotton has been well under way for the past six weeks, and the proliferation of strange new joint-stock companies now being announced all over the place indicates the extent to which capital is feeling around for *debouchés*[b] in all the big money markets. *Après tout*[c] the straws in the wind may now

---

[a] Joseph Denman and George Loch - [b] outlets - [c] After all

be seen rather more clearly and in greater quantity. *Cela sera beau.*[a]

I hope to receive a letter from you by tomorrow morning at the latest.

Your

F. E.

First published abridged in *Der Briefwechsel zwischen F. Engels und K. Marx*, Bd. 1, Stuttgart, 1913 and in full in *MEGA*, Abt. III, Bd. 1, 1929

Printed according to the original

Published in English for the first time

57

MARX TO ENGELS

IN MANCHESTER

[London,] 22 May [1852]
28 Dean Street, Soho

Dear Frederic,

The first half of the 10-pound note arrived this morning.

I intend to leave here on Friday,[b] this time by ship to Liverpool and thence to Manchester.

Apropos. Citizen Schramm[c] is travelling to America via Liverpool. Well, the fellow proposes, or so he confides to us, to descend upon you on Wednesday or Thursday. You must see if you can give him the slip.

Willich has had a rather nice adventure. Mrs von Brüningk, who provided him with free board, used to enjoy flirting with this old he-goat, as with the other ex-lieutenants. One day the blood rushes to the head of our ascetic, he makes a brutally brutish assault upon madame, and is ejected from the house with éclat. No more love! No more free board! *Nous ne voulons plus de jouisseurs.*[d]

Cherval, about whose heroism before the Paris Assizes in the matter of the *Complot allemand-français*[e] [143] you will have heard, has, as you may also have seen in the English papers (*Morning*

---

[a] It will be a fine how-do-you-do. - [b] 28 May - [c] Conrad Schramm - [d] We want no more sybarites. - [e] Franco-German plot

Advertiser), escaped from the catchpolls in prodigiously daring manner—as it later transpired, with the connivance of the police to whom he betrayed everything he knew. Even the Great Windmillers[144] were forced to throw out the hero with whom they had been parading round London.

The Cologne people have at last been referred by the Board of indicting magistrates to the Court of Assizes. Unless a special Court of Assizes is appointed, they will not appear before July.[16]

Dronke sends his regards.

Your

K.M.

First published abridged *in Der Briefwech- sel zwischen F. Engels und K. Marx*, Bd. 1, Stuttgart, 1913 and in full in *MEGA*, Abt. III, Bd. 1, 1929

Printed according to the original

Published in English for the first time

58

ENGELS TO MARX

IN LONDON

Manchester, 24 May [1852]

Dear Marx,

If you intend to wait till Friday before leaving by boat for Liverpool, you won't be here till Monday evening, perhaps not till Tuesday morning. If you are absolutely intent on coming by sea, arrange to come via Hull—a boat leaves the CITY three or four times a week at 8 o'clock in the morning and the journey doesn't take so long—you would have to leave on Wednesday morning, or Thursday morning at the latest, the FARE to Hull being 6/6d, and from Hull to here 3rd class, some seven or eight shillings. You must be here by *Friday afternoon*, so that we can leave for Liverpool at about 6 o'clock the same evening. The PARLIAMENTARY TRAIN[145] direct from London leaves too late to be any good to you on Friday. You can take the sea-route from Liverpool on the return journey.

Well, *quoi que tu fasses, il faudra que tu sois ici le vendredi, à 4 heures de l'après-midi.*[a]

Awaiting further details.[146]

Your
F. E.

The story about Willich is most entertaining. So fate has caught up with that pure and noble man after all!

First published in *MEGA*, Abt. III, Bd. 1, 1929

Printed according to the original

Published in English for the first time

59

MARX AND ENGELS TO JOSEPH WEYDEMEYER

IN NEW YORK

Manchester, 28 May 1852

Dear Weiwei,

I am staying with Engels for a few days and have found your letter here. Today you must be content with a few lines.

The main purpose of this letter is to inform you about three individuals who will be arriving in America:

1. *Heise* (of the Kassel *Hornisse*), *Willich's agent* (who, unbeknown to Kinkel with whom he is on bad terms, is seeking to spread *Willich's* renown). Apropos. Mr Willich was among the *cavaliere servante*[b] of Baroness von Brüningk who, once a week, provided him, Techow, Schimmelpfennig, etc., with free board. The Brüningk woman is a flirtatious little woman and it amuses her to tease the old he-goat, who plays the ascetic. One day he made a direct carnal *attaque* upon her and was ignominiously shown the door. Keep an eye on Heise and don't trust him out of your sight.

---

[a] whatever you do, you must be here by Friday, at four o'clock in the afternoon - [b] knights in attendance

2. *Schütz* from Mainz. Kinkelian. Member of the Committee for the Administration of the European-American National Loan.[27]

3. *Conrad Schramm.* He has in his hands a credential from us, so worded that *without you* he cannot take a step. In his relations with his brother[a] and the latter's other friends, his conduct has not always been beyond reproach. The confidence you accord him should not be *unconditional* but rather *tempered with caution.* In the adverse circumstances here he has, furthermore, gone very much *downhill,* is quite unreliable and not over-scrupulous in money-matters, tends to swagger and boast like a *commis voyageur*[b] and hence may well compromise those in his surroundings. On the other hand he has a number of good qualities. I feel it my duty to put you *au fait* in advance. You should also pass on this information to Cluss.

As to Lupus' letter, you should not take it too literally. Wolff wrote in a moment of agitation and is very well aware of the many obstacles that stood in your way.[c]

Don't forget to send me in your next a detailed report on 'Willich's Corps'[147] in New York.

My warm regards to your wife. I hope that, 'for all that',[d] your affairs will yet progress.

Dana has written to say he wants to do an essay on the Cologne people[e] as soon as you provide him with the necessary information. So go and see him. The Cologne people are to appear before a special Court of Assizes in June. Daniels is said to have consumption and Becker[f] to be half blind. Mind you settle the matter quickly with Dana and send me the article. It will provide consolation for Mrs Daniels.

Your

K. Marx

Dear Weydemeyer,

As regards Heise, I first met him in the Palatinate. A democratic loafer who lends a willing ear to bad jokes about Tom, Dick or Harry, but a no less willing hand to Tom, Dick or Harry's pompous, democratic schemes for world conquest and world

---

[a] Rudolf Schramm - [b] commercial traveller - [c] Wilhelm Wolff's letter to Weydemeyer of 16 April 1852. - [d] An allusion to F. Freiligrath's verse 'Trotz alledem!' published in the *Neue Rheinische Zeitung* on 6 June 1848. - [e] Reference to the leading article 'Justice of Prussia', based on the material sent in by Marx and published in the *New-York Daily Tribune*, No. 3446, 4 May 1852. - [f] Hermann Heinrich Becker

liberation. Recently—since his arrival in London—he has consorted exclusively with the others, never coming to see us; now, of course, wholly in the others' clutches. No time for any more. Greetings to your wife.

Your

F. E.

First published in: Marx and Engels, *Works*, First Russian Edition, Vol. XXV, Moscow, 1934

Printed according to the original

Published in English for the first time

60

MARX TO JENNY MARX

IN LONDON

Manchester, 11 June 1852
70 Great Ducie Street

Dear Heart,

I was very pleased to get your letter. By the way, you must never have any qualms about telling me all. If you, my poor little wretch, have to endure bitter reality, it is only fair that I should share that torment, at least in my thoughts. In any case, I know how unendingly resilient you are and how the slightest encouragement is enough to revive your spirits. I hope that the other £5 will reach you this week or on Monday at the latest.

I did of course pack the *Schnellpost*. But I haven't got the back numbers in which Ruge deposited the better part of his ordure. The process of curing these stock-fish[a] makes us laugh till we cry.

Though Oswald's package won't yield very much, something may be made of it. Our dear A. Ruge is incapable of writing 3 lines without compromising himself. 'Moute'[b] has already been corrected by me, unless I am mistaken.

The printer in the City seems to be a lesser *lumen*[c] who, not having a superfluity of underlings, will certainly require an

---

[a] Marx refers here to his and Engels' work on *The Great Men of the Exile*. - [b] The misprint which cropped in *The Eighteenth Brumaire of Louis Bonaparte*, VII published in *Die Revolution*, should read: *Toute*. - [c] luminary

unconscionable time to do one sheet. His paper is 3 x worse than the American, and his type likewise, this being clearly quite worn out. But you have managed the business splendidly.

Harro's pamphlet[a] is truly touching in the naivety of its stupidity! Be so kind as to cut *Engels' article* on Heinzen out of the *Brüsseler-Zeitung*[b] and send it to us,—and that very soon. If the *Kosmos* doesn't arrive, no matter. We have a letter of mine up here which contains the gist of the thing.[148]

Love and kisses to my manikins.

Your

K. M.

Engels has further pointed out that whereas, throughout the pamphlet, I always deliberately write 'Louis Bonaparte', Mr Weydemeyer has entitled it 'Louis Napoleon'.[149]

P.S.

Dear Jenny, be so kind as to tell Eccarius that he should write a short postscript to his 'Mechanics' Strike',[44] since Weydemeyer is 'considering' publishing it. We should agree to this, if only on Cluss' account.

Dear Heart, send Jones the 2 enclosed pieces, 'Chevalier Hülsemann's Farewell' and 'John Barney and the French Minister[c]', together with the short cutting about 'Cayenne'—preferably by post, unless he comes to see you.[150] I beg you not to bother Mr Pieper with such errands. To him, everything provides occasion for rodomontade and I don't want Jones—who, by the way, was responsible for making him so uppish—to regard him as my *alter ego*. Since Pieper believes the letters are written for '*the* party', he must not henceforward set eyes on any more of them.

[From Engels]

Prego il Signor Colonello Musch di gradire le mie migliori e più cordiali felicitazioni.[d]

F. Engels

First published in *MEGA*, Abt. III, Bd. 1, 1929

Printed according to the original

Published in English for the first time

---

a Harro Harring, *Historisches Fragment über die Entstehung der Arbeiter-Vereine und ihren Verfall in Communistische Speculationen.* - b F. Engels, 'The Communists and Karl Heinzen' (published in *Deutsche-Brüsseler-Zeitung*). - c Etienne Gilbert Sartiges - d Will Colonel Musch please accept my best and most cordial felicitations.

61

ENGELS TO JOSEPH WEYDEMEYER

IN NEW YORK

Manchester, 11 June 1852

Dear Weydemeyer,

We have received the first issue of the *Revolution*,[a] but we had imagined you would contrive to include Freiligrath's poem about Kinkel,[b] which would not after all have increased the cost very much. While the closeness of the print and the large format were unavoidable due to lack of funds, it is a great pity that this should have made it so difficult to read, particularly when misprints distort the meaning. But what surprises us is the difficulty you seem to have about dispatching the 300 copies we ordered other than by post. Your friends over there, Helmich and Korff, must be colossal asses indeed if they can't so much as tell you that the mail steamers also carry parcels and even heavy bales of merchandise, and that all details concerning freight, etc., etc. can be obtained at the steamship offices—not, of course, at the post office. The location of these steamship offices may be found in any newspaper announcement, beneath which there is always the name of a local business house. Moreover there are any number of forwarding agents concerned with handling such things, for example Edwards, Sandford & Co. of Liverpool and London, who also have an office in New York. You simply address the parcel as follows:

(at the top) per ... Steamer

care of Messrs Edwards, Sandford & Co.,
Liverpool

(underneath)   F. E.
care of Messrs Ermen & Engels
Manchester
Printed books, not bound.

---

[a] containing K. Marx's *Eighteenth Brumaire of Louis Bonaparte* - [b] F. Freiligrath, 'An Joseph Weydemeyer', I and II.

That's all, and sent in this way it costs only a few shillings which Ermen & Engels can stand. But it's really too bad that people like Helmich and Korff, who have been in New York so long and who, moreover, also do a certain amount of business, should be ignorant of matters with which any child over here is familiar.

The copies of the *Turn-Zeitung* have *not* yet arrived, either here or in London; you should make inquiries at your post office.

The printing costs are colossal; for £5 per sheet—scarcely more than you have had to pay—we could get the thing similarly printed in London. Paper should, after all, be cheaper over there, since here it carries a duty of $1\frac{1}{2}$d (3 cents) per 1b. Perhaps you could inquire about the price from the local wholesale paper merchants and let us know what it is.

Just send here anything destined for Europe. Marx has a German bookseller in London who is reliable and upon whom, moreover, he can keep an eye; this man will see to distribution both here, and in Germany, Switzerland, etc., etc., in return for a modest percentage. If, then, when you receive this letter you have *not* yet sent off the parcel with the 50 copies for London and 250 for Cologne, take the opportunity of including in it as many as you think appropriate, or can spare, for the German bookseller to dispose of. But should it already have gone, send nothing more until we ask for it. We shall, of course, charge a higher price here, if only to defray our costs and the bookseller's commission. 15 silver groschen is well within the means of the German philistine.

Since the second issue is to be devoted exclusively to Freiligrath's poems, it is presumably already in print. These things, particularly the Kinkel poem, should not be held back a moment longer than is unavoidable. This should really have been published in one way or another[13] after Kinkel's return to New York; but the longer it lingers, the more it loses in topicality and, even for things which are largely written with an eye to immortality, there is a certain period during which they are especially rewarding and at their most topical. But since I deliberately write, not with an eye to immortality, but rather for the immediate present, my article on the English bourgeoisie[a] may well be somewhat long-drawn-out, especially since a work of this kind lends itself very well to piecemeal publication amongst other material in a newspaper or weekly; in a review, however, where because of its very length it takes up most of the space, it would not be topical or interesting enough for the American-German public. Besides, Mr Derby may

---

[a] See this volume, p. 55.

very well topple before August, and that's a ticklish sort of thing to prognosticate.

While beholden to Korff for his goodwill, Dronke has no intention of going to America since he has just started a wholesale business in cigar cases, etc., etc., as agent for a Parisian house. For that matter, neither Dronke nor any of the rest of us is on the same easy terms with Korff as during the first months of the *N. Rh. Z.*; we still remember all too clearly the circumstances of Korff's dismissal from the newspaper[151] and how subsequently, in New York, he published my Hungarian articles under his own name.[152]. He may be of some use to you in small ways, but you would be well advised not to trust him out of sight, and Marx is particularly anxious that Korff should not come butting in between himself and Dana, having, it seems, already caused some sort of ruction in this respect. In your letter you say that Marx will have been able to see for himself from Dana's letter how unresponsive the *Tribune* is to our cause; this passage we find totally incomprehensible since Dana had written Marx a most cordial letter in which he requested, not only further instalments of the German article,[a] but other contributions as well. It would certainly not suit us if Korff were in any way to thrust himself forward as the representative or CHAMPION of either of us in personal matters.

Since there is so much delay over the American exhibition,[128] it would be better if you were to take no further steps in respect of the leather business[b] until you have again heard from us about it. Marx is up here just now and hence cannot for the time being speak to the Hungarian.[c] For he and I are now engaged in a most interesting and amusing piece of work[d] which is to be published directly. As soon as we receive the first copies we shall send you one, then we shall also be able to discuss to what extent you can use the thing and, perhaps, make money out of it towards the production of new pamphlets, for this time it's going to be something that will indubitably sell.

Eccarius has been written to about his final instalment[e]; he will have little to add, the workers—as was to be expected—having been beaten.

Our dear, worthy Willich has suffered a grave misfortune. Once a week Baroness Brüningk used to invite the Prussian lieutenants in London and other such great men to her table, when it was her

---

[a] Engels' series of articles, *Revolution and Counter-Revolution in Germany.* - [b] See this volume, p. 95. - [c] Bangya - [d] *The Great Men of the Exile.* - [e] See this volume, p. 117.

custom to flirt with these gallant knights. This, it seems, caused the blood to rush violently to the head of our virtuous Willich, who, finding himself one day tête-à-tête with the young lady, was suddenly overwhelmed by a fit of uncontrollable lust and, quite without warning, made a somewhat brutish attack upon her. But this had in no way been madame's intention, and she ordered our paragon of knightly virtue to be thrown out of the house *sans façon*.[a]

> 'Blessed is he that virtue loves,
> Woe to him that's lost it...
>
> A wretched stripling, here am I
> Chucked out into the street [b]

and the morally pure stoic, who as a rule felt a far greater sympathy for fair-haired young tailor's apprentices than for pretty young women, may thank his stars that he did not in the end find himself back 'in the guardroom at Kassel'[c] as a result of this involuntary, instinctive outbreak of his physical ego so long kept enchained. The thing has been noted and circulated with great glee throughout London. There is, by the way, some prospect that you may have this gallant fellow in New York before too long. Over here the man 'who enjoyed the respect of all parties and even of his enemies', is daily losing more ground. He maintains relations with Kinkel and Schapper, his right and left hand props, only with reluctance (and in Kinkel's case on pecuniary grounds), for he hates them both and they him; he has several times received rough treatment at the hands of the inferior refugees, since when he has given them up. After this latest business he will never again be allowed into houses where there are young women, in addition to which he has now lost his aura of virtue. On the other hand he hears talk of how the men of Willich's Corps in New York stick together and he has the gallant Weitling there—hence, and more particularly when the flow of money from the loan fund[27] begins to dry up, he will probably make himself scarce. Indeed, he has already sent out an apostle in the shape of Heise from Kassel—this fellow forms part of his *personal* entourage. In addition he is now dispatching another harbinger, poor old Mirbach, who fell into his clutches through sheer, bitter necessity and, as a result of his total ignorance of the emigration's antecedents and his theoretical confusion, was naturally dazzled by

---

[a] without further ado - [b] Heine, 'Klagelied eines altdeutschen Jünglings' (*Romanzen*). - [c] ibid.

such fine airs. He is *au fond*^a a very good fellow, a political
nonentity, but otherwise honourable and, militarily speaking, I find
him 10 times preferable to all the London great men. He used to
call on Marx, but never unchaperoned by that lout Imandt and
that philistine jackass Schily, so that it was never possible to talk to
him frankly.

In America our Willich would be in his element; the old crew in
New York, which by now must have run completely wild and
disintegrated into ROWDIES AND LOAFERS, would very soon grow sick of
him and beat him black and blue—even over here his relationship
with the swine finally degenerated into the low vulgarity of a mob
of rogues bickering over plunder—while his friend, that experienced trickster Weitling, would likewise ensure him a brilliant
future.

But I must close now. Marx sends his regards—many regards
from us both to your wife.

Your
F. E.

First published in: Marx and Engels,
Works, First Russian Edition, Vol. XXV,
Moscow, 1934

Printed according to the original

Published in English for the first
time

62

MARX TO ADOLF CLUSS [153]

IN WASHINGTON

Manchester, [before 26 June 1852]

... Napoleon II^b is getting into more and more of a scrape.
Apart from his other new taxes, the jackass has got caught up in
the same snare as the provisional government,[154]—that is, by
imposing a new tax on the peasants; an increase of 25% on the
existing succession duty and the CONVEYANCE OF LANDED PROPERTY. He is

---

^a at bottom - ^b Napoleon III, whom Marx ironically calls 'the second'.

moving quickly. True socialism is being achieved by a most fatuous acceptance, if not an intensification of, the old French financial procedures...

First published in: Marx and Engels, *Works*, Second Russian Edition, Vol. 28, Moscow, 1962

Printed according to a letter from Cluss to Weydemeyer of 13 July 1852

Published in English for the first time

63

ENGELS TO MARX

IN LONDON

Manchester, 30 June 1852

Dear Marx,

Either you people down there must be working terribly hard at copying out the manuscript[a] or something unpleasant must have happened, otherwise I should undoubtedly have heard from you by now. *En attendant,*[b] herewith a letter along with cuttings from Weydemeyer.

Your little wallet with the letter from Cologne has come to light. I haven't got it with me today, otherwise I should have enclosed it. Warmest regards—in haste.

Your
F. E.

First published in *MEGA*, Abt. III, Bd. 1, Berlin, 1929

Printed according to the original

Published in English for the first time

---

[a] K. Marx and F. Engels, *The Great Men of the Exile.* - [b] Meanwhile

64

MARX TO ENGELS

IN MANCHESTER

[London,] 3 July 1852
28 Dean Street, Soho

Dear Engels,

I am late, but I have come.[a] How the delay came about, you will see from the tale recounted below:

In London, the manuscript[b] was copied out at once. By Monday noon[c] it was all ready and complete. I dictated it by turns to my wife and Dronke. At midday on Wednesday I received the money. Bangya deducted the £7 about which you know. Add to that what was owed Dronke for his collaboration. This left an amount that did not even suffice for household needs. Strohn's CIRCUMSTANCES were such that he could not pay. And then came a run of exceptional ill-luck.

Klose's wife, long ailing and wasting away in hospital, was discharged by the dirty dogs at the precise moment she was entering her final crisis, and died in his house three days ago. Not a centime available, funeral expenses, etc. Freiligrath could do nothing, having just bled all his acquaintances in order to help send Heilberg's wife and child back to Breslau, keep Heilberg himself alive and, finally, get him into hospital. Thus the thing devolved on me, and a vast amount of time and trouble it cost me before it was settled. _Maintenant_[d] all is peace and quiet again.

The 'gang' are racking their brains over our pamphlet. Notably the Meyen-bug,[e] who is in a cold sweat. He is 'quite unable to recall the least trespass against us'. Willich has had me sounded as to whether the Brüningk affair appears in it. The thought makes him exceedingly uneasy.

'The true course' of this curious happening would now appear to be as follows:

First, as you know, Willich denied it outright. His 2nd version ran: 'Mrs Brüningk has sought to corrupt him _politically_. Used Mr _von_ Willich left and right, and other such means of corruption.' It

---

[a] The German original is reminiscent of Schiller, _Die Piccolomini_, Act I, Scene 1. - [b] K. Marx and F. Engels, _The Great Men of the Exile._ - [c] 28 June - [d] Now - [e] Eduard Meyen (see present edition, Vol. 11, p. 306).

was with 'moral intent', therefore, that he created a diversion in the region of her private parts.

But now our partisan leader has put yet another construction on the case. 'The Brüningk woman (or so Imandt once told him) is a Russian spy. She tries to entrap young refugees. Old Willich stood in her way. Hence the anecdote intended to ruin him in the eyes of the émigrés. How political, deliberate and diabolical was this trumped-up "anecdote", emerges from the very fact of its having been Mrs Brüningk's own husband who circulated the rumour of the outrage for the sole purpose of discrediting Willich.'

But that is not all. The chivalrous Schimmelpfennig maintains that Willich invented the spy story to conceal the insubordination of his 'cazzo'.[a] As things now stand, the issue remains undecided between these two worthies, and Willich, taking refuge in one lie after another, is well and truly compromising himself.

The cuckold Brüningk reminds me of a nice joke I found a few days ago in one of Machiavelli's commedia:

> Nicia (cuckold): Chi è San cu cu?
> Ligurio: È il più honorato santo che sia in Francia.[b]

Willich and Kinkel mightily worried about how best to effect a revolution on £1,200. Schurz, Schimmelpfennig, Strodtmann, etc., are drawing further and further away from Kinkel.

Not even 100 horsepower could drag Willich away from the coffre-fort.[c]

Kinkel, knowing that Imandt and I see each other, calls on Imandt a week ago and says, 'What a pity it was my Economy had not yet come out, so that one might at last have a positive basis to go on.' Imandt questions him about Freiligrath's poem.[d] 'Never read such things,' retorts Godofredus.

The most ludicrous thing about it is that, having existed for years solely by abusing us the curs now declare it beneath 'our dignity' and 'station' to write such t-t-tittle-tattle. Les drôles![e]

However, a new prospect has opened up before the wretched Willich-Kinkel, the pair who are to effect the revolution. Messrs Rodbertus, Kirchmann and other ambitious ministerial candidates have dispatched a legate to London. For these gentlemen, in imitation of the French, want Vogt to set up a German Carbonari association. Connections with even the most extreme of parties. Paper money is to be issued in Germany to defray the costs. Since

---

a 'organ' - b Nicia: Who is St. Cuckoo? Ligurio: The most venerated saint in France. (Machiavelli, Mandragola, Act 4, Scene IX.) - c safe - d F. Freiligrath, 'An Joseph Weydemeyer', I and II. - e The rogues!

they are, however, anxious to emerge more or less unscathed, it is the émigrés, and of 'all' parties, who are to underwrite this paper.

Schapper has been sounding me and making contrite admissions through Imandt. Replied that he must first break *publicly* with Willich, and then we should see. That was the *conditio sine qua.*[a]

You will have read about the new arrests in Paris.[155] The boobies (this time the Ruge clique) naturally had to come up with yet another pseudo-conspiracy. Their correspondent in Paris, as I was informed some considerable time ago, is one *Engländer,* a notorious police spy (in Paris) who, of course, immediately passes all their letters to the service. Not content with that, the French police have sent Simon Deutsch over here to pump Tausenau. Louis Napoleon must have a conspiracy, cost what it may.

But he has got one on his hands about which as yet he seems to know nothing. That of the Orleans family, whose agent Mr Bangya (with the assent of the Hungarian 'radicals') has now become. The plan: Bonaparte is to be caught out one evening with his drab, to whom he goes slinking behind the Englishwoman's back. A senior police officer has been suborned. Two generals are said to have been won over. Nemours himself was in Paris a fortnight ago. Large sums paid out for the distribution of anti-Louis Napoleon pamphlets.

What do you think of it? If one of the Orleans were again to visit Paris and we happened to know when, should we, *d'une manière ou d'une autre,*[b] denounce the '*vrai prince*' to the '*faux prince*'[c]? Let me have your views on the matter.

Cherval, the cur, has also handed over to the Prussians the letter sent him by Pfänder.

Au revoir

Your

K. M.

Not a word from that blessed Weydemeyer. Bonaparte will probably be in America before my pamphlet about him[d] reaches Europe. If possible, send me an article for Dana soon.[e]

Herewith the introduction to the *Dubbii amorosi* by Pietro Aretino, the forefather (but wittier) of Cassagnac.

---

[a] indispensable condition - [b] one way or another - [c] 'true prince', 'false prince' - [d] K. Marx, *The Eighteenth Brumaire of Louis Bonaparte.* - [e] Presumably, *Revolution and Counter-Revolution in Germany,* XV.

Prefazione. Magnifico utriusque Ser Agnello,
      Voi qui scribere scitis quare, quia,
      Espelle, volte fatte co'l cervello,
      Di Bartolo e Baldo notomia,
      E le leggi passate co'l castello,
      Nella vostra bizarra fantasia,
      Questi dubbii, di grazia, mi chiarite
      Ch'oggi in Bordello han mosso un gran lite.

      Vi sono genti fottenti, e fottute;
      E di potte e di cazzi notomie.
      E nei culi molt' anime perdute, etc.[a]

First published in part in *Der Briefwechsel zwischen F. Engels und K. Marx*, Bd. 1, Stuttgart, 1913 and in full in MEGA, Abt. III, Bd. 1, 1929

Printed according to the original

Published in English for the first time

65

ENGELS TO MARX

IN LONDON

Manchester, 6 July 1852

Dear Marx,

It's a good thing that the manuscript[b] has gone off. I hope that copies will arrive in 3-4 weeks' time. You must have been really in the soup if, as antidote, you had to take Pietro Aretino's *porcherie.*[c] *Cazzo di Dio, queste sono forti.*[d]

I am up to my eyes in work here. I still have eleven business letters to write today and it is nearly 7 o'clock. However, I will do an article for Dana,[e] if possible today and if not, by tomorrow evening at the latest.

---

[a] O twice magnificent Ser Agnello,
You who of all the why and wherefore
              know,
Whose mighty mind can grasp
              the fate
Of Bartolo's and Baldo's earthly frame
And whose keen fancy apprehends
              the laws
Of heavenly bodies and their course!

Dispel for me the doubts, I pray,
Which in the brothel raised strife
              today.

Some folks seduce and others
              are seduced
But one and all by lust are ruled.
How many souls through arses
              go astray...

[b] K. Marx and F. Engels, *The Great Men of the Exile.* - [c] obscenity - [d] God's prick, this is strong meat. - [e] Probably article XV from *Revolution and Counter-Revolution in Germany.*

I am just tackling Mr Görgey. At that time, drawing on *Austrian* bulletins, we of the *N. Rh. Z.* made splendidly accurate guesses as to the course of the Hungarian war, and prognostications, if cautious, proved brilliantly correct.[a] Görgey's book[b] is truly wretched, nothing could be more pettily invidious, infamously *mesquin*[c] and mediocre. The military part is good, Görgey to the life,—sudden transformation of talented ex-lieutenant into general, still bearing unmistakable traces of the company officer and tactical tyro. Hungarians who maintain that Görgey is incapable of having written this are *jackasses*. The genuine Görgeyesque and Austrian elements are as easily distinguishable here as are the two heterogeneous elements in Chenu.[156] But otherwise the book may—with some caution—very well be used as a source. The fellow's malicious mediocrity is such that he cannot help making a fool of himself, witness the affair of the proclamation of Waitzen[157] in which he reproaches Kossuth for having been shrewder in practice than in his bombastic speeches, or again, the very inept descriptions which lead the author, always involuntarily, into compromising himself. This mediocrity never permits Görgey to draw a true portrait of any one chap, but the thing has some pleasant traits and individual comments on Kossuth and most of the others. Despite the mediocrity of his malice, Görgey—as is everywhere apparent—was after all superior to any of the others—so what must the others be like!

At all events, I shall write about the Hungarian war.[136]

Judging by the facts, the Paris plot[155] would seem more likely to have emanated from our *carrément* and *crânement*[d] sinister Barthélemy, etc.—the daring artillery preparation is something *qui sent son* Willich *de vingt lieues.*[e] It is more than likely that Ruge, etc., also had a finger in the pie, but those cannons fashioned out of gas pipes and draped with tarpaulins are of Hohenzollern origin.

Your
F. E.

---

[a] F. Engels, 'The *Kölnische Zeitung* on the Magyar Struggle', 'The War in Italy and Hungary', 'Hungary' and also reviews of military operations in Hungary published in the *Neue Rheinische Zeitung* from February to May 1849. - [b] A. Görgei, *Mein Leben und Wirken in Ungarn in den Jahren 1848 und 1849.* - [c] mean - [d] fairly and squarely - [e] which smells of Willich 20 leagues away

As for the Orleans, *pourquoi pas?*[a] To see the estimable Joinville or whomsoever treated *à la* duc d'Enghien[158] would be delightful, and *pourquoi le neveu ne ferait-il pas fusiller aussi son Bourbon?*[b]

First published abridged in *Der Briefwechsel zwischen F. Engels und K. Marx*, Bd. 1, Stuttgart, 1913 and in full in *MEGA*, Abt. III, Bd. 1, 1929

Printed according to the original

Published in English for the first time

66

MARX TO ENGELS

IN MANCHESTER

[London,] 13 July 1852

Dear Engels,

There being no letter from you, I conclude that the worthy Weydemeyer must, for all that,[c] be still persevering with his 'system'. The thing's becoming really incomprehensible and, quite aside from the pecuniary loss, which is just now very perceptible, is turning me for good measure into the laughing stock of the émigré vermin and of the booksellers whom I had approached about this unfortunate affair.

I have not written an article on the elections because I feel it would be better to await the full results.[159] From what I have seen so far, it seems to me that, apart from 5-6 more votes for the Whigs, the old Parliament will rise again unchanged. The fellows are in a *cercle vicieux*[d] from which they cannot break out. The only ones to have suffered any significant losses so far are the Peelites.[73] Meanwhile, in an apologia for Graham, *The Morning Chronicle* declares that only one alternative remains, that Whigs are as incompetent as Tories, and that the only capable people, apart from Graham and his supporters, are Cobden, Bright and Co. And these should govern together. Curiously enough, the following day—as you may perhaps have seen,—*The Times* carried an article which likewise contained an apologia for Graham.[e]

---

[a] why not? - [b] why shouldn't the nephew have his Bourbon shot too? - [c] from Freiligrath's 'Trotz alledem!' - [d] vicious circle - [e] *The Times*, No. 21164, 10 July 1852, leader.

The great Techow is emigrating to Australia next week, together with Madame Schmidt-Stirner. But—and this will wound you more deeply—even *Damm* is no less eager to turn his hand to AUSTRALIAN GOLD-DIGGING. Another few months of peace, and all our 'world underminers'[a] will be busily mining for dirt in the dirt of Australia. Only Willich, firmly chained to the *coffre-fort*,[b] remains faithful to his motto: to live but BY NO MEANS work.

Bangya is now on very close terms with the Orleanist intriguer, 'de Rémusat'. Some Hungarian *quelconque*[c] warned him against the man who is said to have 'betrayed' the Germans during the *complot allemand-français*.[143] Rémusat has agents right in the Paris Préfecture. So, *sans mot dire à M. Bangya*[d] he writes asking for a report on this gentleman. The reply, which was communicated to me, stated that Bangya was *in no way suspect,* that he had got out in time, otherwise he too would have been arrested. The traitor was *'un certain Cherval, nommé Frank, mais dont le véritable nom est Crämer.'*[e]

From the outset this Cherval is said to have been hand in glove with the police. What is more, Rémusat is receiving original letters written by Cherval to the Prussian Embassy, stating that, in accordance with promises made to him in the Mazas,[160] and now that he had professed the *'principe'* of *ordre*, it was *'leur devoir'*[f] to provide him with the necessary *'moyens'*.[g] The Prussian Embassy, however, declared that since he was being *paid* as a spy by the French, and *double emploi*[h] was out of the question, he could have no claims on the Prussians. He was therefore sent to London to observe the German refugees and, in addition, to 'keep an eye on Claremont'.[161] In the latter capacity he called on Rémusat and offered him his services as an agent. Rémusat, on instructions from Paris, pretended to agree and assigned to him a go-between in the person of a valet at Claremont; this man was now entrusted with the task of misinforming the Paris police through Cherval.

So well organised is the Orleanist agitation that the fellows possess what amounts to a regular clandestine postal service by which one can send letters, parcels, and pamphlets to France as safely as innocuous matter by ordinary mail.

My main concern in all this was to procure an original letter of Cherval's relating to his connections with the Prussian Embassy.

---

[a] The original has *Weltumwühler* by analogy with *Wühler* (agitators), the name the bourgeois constitutionalists in Germany in 1848-49 applied to republican democrats. - [b] safe - [c] or other - [d] without a word to Mr Bangya - [e] a certain Cherval, known as Frank, but whose real name is Crämer - [f] principle of order, it was their duty - [g] means - [h] double employ

Such a *pièce* could topple the whole fabric of the bill of indictment.[16]

I have arranged with Bangya that, as soon as another copy has been made, *you* will receive Szemere's pamphlet in manuscript.[a] It is a document that is indispensable to your work[b] since it contains letters from Görgey, Kossuth, etc., which have not been published anywhere.

My wife is very poorly, she has a cough and is losing weight. However, the doctor says it is nothing dangerous and has, in addition to medicine, prescribed plenty of porter.

If you can manage to send me another article[c] by Friday, I will try to discount with Johnson the £5 that will then become due from Dana.

Apropos. The Domenichi *'Orlando Innamorato' riformato* is an *adaptation*. The original is very rare and only to be had in large libraries, as here. Even the Domenichi edition is rare. More readily available is the *Orlando, rifatto*[d] by Berni.[162]

Your
K. M.

First published in part in *Der Briefwechsel zwischen F. Engels und K. Marx*, Bd. 1, Stuttgart, 1913 and in full in *MEGA*, Abt. III, Bd. 1, 1929

Printed according to the original

Published in English for the first time

67

ENGELS TO MARX

IN LONDON

Manchester, 15 July 1852

Dear Marx,

As regards Weydemeyer, you concluded rightly. There hasn't been a line from him. Since we wrote and told him exactly how to send the stuff here, he seems to feel it his bounden duty to

---

[a] B. Szemere, *Graf Ludwig Batthyány, Arthur Görgei, Ludwig Kossuth. Politische Charakterskizzen...* The reference is to the German translation, which Marx helped to edit. - [b] See previous letter. - [c] Next article from the series *Revolution and Counter-Revolution in Germany*. - [d] redone

withhold any further news from us. By the way, things cannot be going very well for him and, when all's said and done, he's got to earn his daily bread.

Did you read the article 2-3 days ago in *The Morning Herald* on the various leading men in the Opposition? It could only have been written by Disraeli himself. The 'AND NOW STAND FORTH, THOU MAN OF "UNADORNED ELOQUENCE", RICHARD COBDEN' is splendid. In it Master John Bright was rightly recognised as the only dangerous fellow, although the gentlemen are not free from illusions in regard to Graham. Precisely now this unscrupulous old *ambitieux*[a] constitutes a very real danger to the Tories.

Bon voyage to the patriotic gold diggers! Thus the term 'underminer' at last acquires a true meaning and content.[b]

The new connection with Mr Rémusat is excellent. A letter from Cherval to the Prussian Embassy would be a capital document in this trial. Don't fail to get hold of one. What a long face our old friend, *le jeune,*[c] the self-important Saedt will pull,[163] if we thus reduce to chaff the fifty sheets of his bill of indictment which he has already announced to the world through the Augsburg *Allgemeine Zeitung*![d] Has Rémusat already *got* these letters? By the way, it would appear from the news in the papers, not only that Mr Manteuffel proposes to turn the Cologne trial into a magnificent political drama—with, of course, some sort of coup in the wings—but also, on the other hand, that there is absolutely no evidence, and that the weakness of the indictment has to be veiled in a cloud of rumour on the part of the police and lies on the part of their spies. Have you heard nothing more from Bangya? I return herewith the gallant fellow's letter, hitherto forgotten.

But if you get hold of Cherval's letter, is there any way of attesting it, so that its authenticity is established? Otherwise a presiding judge of this ilk would be capable of prohibiting so much as a reading of the document.

Since, as I hear, the trial is to take place on the 28th, it is important for us just now to have several reliable links with Cologne. If only we knew to what extent one can count on Bermbach's doing anything! Letters could be safely sent to him via Bradford. If we knew that Weerth was in Hamburg, the thing would be in order. I shall write to Strohn about it this very day. At the same time we might even make use of Naut, if needs be. For, contrary to all my expectations, the latter—who has left Em-

---

[a] ambitious man - [b] See this volume, p. 130. - [c] the young - [d] 'Der Communisten-Proceß', *Allgemeine Zeitung*, No. 195, 13 July 1852.

manuel's and is now an agent for a small Jewish firm in Bradford—obtained some military stuff for me from a second-hand bookseller in Cologne with *the utmost promptitude*; the mystery will be cleared up when I tell you that he wants to become an agent for Ermen & Engels and has further asked me to secure him the agency for a local twist house. I have promised him all this and shall recommend him to my old man. We can, therefore, rely on his being punctilious for as long as these negotiations last.

The military material obtained for me by Naut—clearly the library of a retired artillery officer—is coming in very handy, the more so since it is mainly concerned with the *more elementary* aspects of military science, the actual day-to-day routine, etc. That was just what was wanting. In addition, some splendid stuff on fortifications, etc., etc. I shall soon have got to the stage when I can venture to advance, even in public, an INDEPENDENT military opinion.

The Szemere piece[a] will be *extremely welcome*; but I cannot think of working it up as yet.

Herewith the article for Dana.[b] I shall now make haste to conclude the series; but you do something on England as well. If we can extract £3 a week out of the fellow, I'll be damned if we can't manage to send your wife into the country for a spell before the summer's over—that would do her more good than any amount of porter. At all events, I'm glad to hear that her indisposition is not serious.

Just give me another year's military study, and the democratic lieutenants will get the surprise of their lives.

Regards to your wife and children and Dronke and Lupus from

Your
F. E.

First published abridged in *Der Briefwechsel zwischen F. Engels und K. Marx*, Bd. 1, Stuttgart, 1913 and in full in *MEGA*, Abt. III, Bd. 1, 1929

Printed according to the original

Published in English for the first time

---

[a] See this volume, p. 131. - [b] F. Engels, *Revolution and Counter-Revolution in Germany*, XV.

68

MARX TO ENGELS

IN MANCHESTER

London, 20 July[a] 1852
28 Dean Street, Soho

Dear Engels,

Dronke will be bringing you the manuscript on Görgey,[b] admittedly a wretched, muddled affair; likewise the *Neveu de Rameau* and *Jacques le fataliste*[c] in the original.

Yesterday received a letter from Bermbach in Cologne, the gist of which is as follows:

'Latterly they have been visiting all sorts of people in various places in an attempt to find correspondence from you which, they are convinced, was to be conveyed through the agency of these persons to democrats in the Rhineland. Your friends in Cologne are at last to be brought before the Court of Assizes. The bill of indictment, a most compendious work, has been drawn up, the date for the public hearing has been fixed for the 28th of this month, and the usual preliminaries are under way. They will be tried according to the *Code pénal*, since their offence antedates the new Prussian Statute Book.[164] As I understand the case they are, *legally speaking*, in an exceptionally good position but, as you will know, before a jury the moral standpoint is all important, and in this respect there can be no denying the danger for some of the accused. For the principal defendants, Röser, Bürgers, Nothjung and Reiff, have given away far too much: they have admitted a connection with specific tendencies over a definite period; have talked of the enrolment of new members attended by certain formalities and pledges, and other such things, which in themselves do not constitute a crime, but may, depending on circumstances, have an adverse effect on the jurymen, most of whom have been chosen from the peasantry—particularly when there is such evident lack of respect for God and landed property. Grave difficulties will also arise in connection with the defence; the advocates know nothing about such matters, most are hostile on principle and dread the thought of the ten-day sitting fixed for the case. Freiligrath will be beheaded *in contumaciam*.[d]

'I have just read the bill of indictment which contains no less than 65-70 pages. If they're convicted, these people have only their own statements to blame. I doubt [there] can be any more consummate jackasses than these German working men: Reiff made some statements that were regular denunciations, and various others behaved no less ineptly. One sees what a dangerous business it is to establish connections with working men, when those connections are supposed to be kept secret. Small wonder that the fellows were so much harassed; the longer they were held in solitary confinement, the more satisfactory statements they made. That aside, facts don't come into it and, if the accused had not for the most part themselves talked so readily, there would be nothing whatever to go on. The bill of

---

[a] August in the original. - [b] B. Szemere, *Graf Ludwig Batthyány, Arthur Görgei, Ludwig Kossuth...* (reference to a part of the MS). - [c] by Denis Diderot - [d] for refusal to obey the summons

indictment contains all kinds of incidental details from which it transpires that, with the help of spies and intercepted letters, a fairly accurate knowledge has been gained of certain persons and relationships.'

So much for Bermbach.

Vis-à-vis Schimmelpfennig, Willich has retracted his statement about the B[rüningk] woman. Schimmelpfennig has now put it about that he was seeking to destroy Mrs Brüningk's virtue by *magnetising* her. The *vertueux*[a] Willich.

A certain Cœurderoy (*d'ailleurs très bon républicain*),[b] who has already published a little pamphlet against Mazzini, Ledru, L. Blanc, Cabet, etc.,[c] is about to bring out what amounts to a book on the entire French emigration.[d]

Proudhon is publishing a new work.[e] Religion, the State, etc., having become impossible, only 'individuals' remain, a discovery he has lifted from Stirner.[f]

That jackass W[eydemeyer]'s impardonable procrastination has put me in such straits that today I can't even afford a STAMP for this letter.

Your

K. M.

First published slightly abridged in *Der Briefwechsel zwischen F. Engels und K. Marx*, Bd. 1, Stuttgart, 1913 and in full in *MEGA*, Abt. III, Bd. 1, 1929

Printed according to the original

Published in English for the first time

69

MARX TO ADOLF CLUSS [165]

IN WASHINGTON

[London, 20 July 1852]

... With a difference of at most 10 votes in favour of either Whigs or Tories, the elections here will produce the same old Parliament. The *cercle vicieux*[g] is complete. The same old

---

[a] virtuous - [b] in other respects a very good republican (an allusion to *cœur du roi*—king's heart) - [c] E. Cœurderoy, O. Vauthier, *La Barrière du Combat qui vient de se livrer entre les citoyens Mazzini, Ledru-Rollin, Louis Blanc, Étienne Cabet, Pierre Leroux, Martin Nadaud, Mallarmet, A. Bianchi (de Lille) et autres hercules du nord.* - [d] E. Cœurderoy, *De la révolution dans l'homme et dans la société.* - [e] P. J. Proudhon, *La révolution sociale démontrée par le coup d'état du 2 décembre.* - [f] An allusion to M. Stirner's *Der Einzige und sein Eigenthum.* - [g] vicious circle

constituents produce the same old Parliament. In that Parliament what have hitherto been the ruling parties are rotting from within, mutually offsetting and paralysing each other, so that they are compelled to appeal yet again to their constituents and so on, *ad infinitum*, until the circle is broken from without by the pressure of the masses, and that may soon be the case. At no previous election has the conflict between the real majority and the official majority of voters created by the electoral privileges been so glaringly in evidence. You should know that at every English election voting is done 1. by a SHOW OF HANDS when the whole population votes, and 2. by a POLL, the decisive one, in which only the enfranchised vote. Those NOMINATED by the SHOW OF HANDS do not include a *single* Member of Parliament, while those returned by the POLL (i.e. really ELECTED), do not include anyone nominated by the SHOW OF HANDS. Take Halifax, for example, where Wood, the Whig Minister (Finance) was opposing E. Jones. At the SHOW OF HANDS, Wood was hissed. Jones received 14,000 votes and was carried in triumph through the town. At the POLL, Wood was elected while Jones received only 36 votes.

There is little new to report about émigré affairs. But for a few louts, Willich stands more and more isolated, no one believing in his probity any longer. As I have told you, Reichenbach, though he resigned from the committee long ago, *refuses* to hand out a *penny* from the loan until a definitive committee has been formed. In his eyes, Willich and Kinkel are as unacceptable as the handful of blackguards who elected them. Reichenbach *est un honnête bourgeois, qui prend sa responsabilité au sérieux.*[a]

The French emigration has split into 3 camps: 1. Revolution (Ledru). 2. Delegation (the more progressive). 3. 1,500 opponents of both, the plebs or, as the aristocrats used to call them, the '*populean*'. A certain Cœurderoy (*d'ailleurs très bon républicain*)[b] has published a pamphlet against Mazzini-Ledru and Cabet-Blanc and is shortly to bring out something else. You will receive both when they appear.

Yesterday a letter from Cologne, from which the following[c]:

'Latterly they have been visiting various places in an attempt to find correspondence from you which, they are convinced, was to be conveyed through the agency of these persons to democrats in the Rhineland. Your friends are at last to be brought before the Court of Assizes. The bill of indictment, a most compendious work, has been drawn up, the date for the public hearing has been fixed for the 28th of this month, and the usual preliminaries are under way. As I

---

[a] is an honest bourgeois who takes his responsibility seriously - [b] in other respects a very good republican (an allusion to *cœur du roi*—king's heart) - [c] Marx quotes here Bermbach's letter of 9 July 1852 (see also this volume, pp. 134-35).

understand the case they are, *legally speaking*, in an exceptionally good position but, as you will know, before a jury the moral standpoint is all important, and in this respect there can be no denying the danger for some of the accused. For the principal defendants, Röser, Bürgers, Nothjung and Reiff, have given away far too much: they have admitted a connection with specific tendencies over a definite period; have talked of the enrolment of new members attended by certain formalities and pledges, and other such things, which in themselves, however, do not constitute a crime, but may, depending on circumstances, have an adverse effect on the jurymen, most of whom belong to the peasantry, particularly when there is such evident lack of respect for God and landed property. Grave difficulties will also arise in connection with the defence; the advocates know nothing about such matters, most are hostile on principle and dread the thought of the ten-day sitting fixed for the case. It should not be forgotten that, on the occasion of the Assizes, proceedings will be taken *in contumaciam*[a] against F. Freiligrath, at present in London. So Freiligrath will shortly be able to parade round London as a German poet who has been beheaded in effigy.—

'P.S. I have just read the bill of indictment which contains no less than 65-70 pages. If they're convicted, these people have only their own statements to blame. I doubt there can be any more consummate jackasses than these working men: Reiff made statements that were almost regular denunciations, and various others behaved no less ineptly. Small wonder that the fellows were so much harassed; the longer they have been held in solitary confinement, the more satisfactory statements they made. That aside, facts don't come into it.'

Voilà our Straubingers,[61] it's tough that world history should have to be made with people such as these...

First published in part in Russian in *Voprosy istorii KPSS*, No. 3, Moscow, 1962 and in full in: Marx and Engels, *Works*, Second Russian Edition, Vol. 28, Moscow, 1962

Printed according to a letter from Cluss to Weydemeyer of 6 August 1852

Published in English in full for the first time

70

ENGELS TO MARX

IN LONDON

Manchester, 22 July 1852

Dear Marx,

Enclosed the article for Dana.[b] The information sent by Bermbach is not pleasant; if only those who have *not* chattered manage to get off! The trial, by the way, is directed *autant*[c] against us as against the Cologne people; we too shall have some rough

---

[a] for refusal to obey the summons. - [b] F. Engels, *Revolution and Counter-Revolution in Germany*, XVI. - [c] as much

treatment, especially since *le jeune*[a] Saedt now believes that he will be able to avenge himself with impunity.[163]

Could you perhaps get hold of Cœurderoy's things for me? I.e. if they're worth the trouble, and contain anything more than mere rhetoric.

Our Worcell, as I learn from Smitt,[b] really was a count and a protagonist of the Volhynian insurrection; he distinguished himself by being cut off and leading a kind of robber band in the woods for some 3-4 weeks, until taken off to Poland by Różzycki; our Sznayde commanded some cavalry—from what I know so far—without distinction. A work by Mierosławski on the Polish campaign, which came out in Berlin in 1847,[c] is very highly spoken of by Smitt.[d] This Mierosławski is certainly the most eminent among Poles and is likely to make a name for himself.

Mind you don't forget the English article![e]

I am expecting Drunkel[f] this evening, together with a bag of books. I am particularly in need of the *N. Rh. Z.* just now and hope he is bringing it.

Warm regards to your wife and children.

Your
F. E.

First published slightly abridged in *Der Briefwechsel zwischen F. Engels und K. Marx*, Bd. 1, Stuttgart, 1913 and in full in *MEGA*, Abt. III, Bd. 1, 1929

Printed according to the original

Published in English for the first time

71

MARX TO GOTTFRIED KINKEL[166]

IN LONDON

[Rough copy]

[London,] 22 July 1852
5 Sutton Street, Soho
Office of *The People's Paper*

To Dr J. G. Kinkel

You are alleged, or so I am informed, to have ventured the following statement before Anneke or others at Cincinnati: 'Marx and Engels...'

---

[a] the young - [b] F. Smitt, *Geschichte des polnischen Aufstandes und Krieges in den Jahren 1830 und 1831.* - [c] L. Mierosławski, *Kritische Darstellung des Feldzuges vom Jahre 1831.* - [d] F. Smitt, op. cit., Dritter Theil, S. XI-XII. - [e] See this volume, p. 145. - [f] Ernst Dronke

I await your answer by return of post.
Silence will be regarded as an admission.

Dr K. M.

First published in *MEGA*, Abt. III, Bd. 1, 1929

Printed according to the original

Published in English for the first time

72

MARX TO ADOLF CLUSS [167]

IN WASHINGTON

[London, 30 July 1852]

... Huzel's letter [168] was greeted with Homeric laughter. It gave rise to the following intermezzos:

5 Sutton Str., Soho
Office of *The People's Paper*

'To Dr Johann Gottfried Kinkel [169]

'You are alleged, or so I am informed, to have ventured the following statement before Anneke or other Germans at Cincinnati: "Marx and Engels etc." (there follows the treasonable passage). I await your answer *by return of post*. Silence will be regarded as an admission.

Dr Karl Marx' [a]

This note was kept deliberately vague: 'alleged ... Anneke *or* other Germans', etc. in order to leave Mr Kinkel plenty of latitude for ambiguities. The following reply arrived *by return*:

1 Henstridge Villas, St. John's Wood,
24th July 1852

To Dr Karl Marx

Since the article about me was published under your auspices [170] during my imprisonment, I have wanted to have nothing more to do with you. If you believe that you can, through the testimony of Anneke or other honourable men, rather

---

[a] See also this volume, p. 149.

than through anonymous insinuations, provide proof that I untruthfully said or published anything detrimental to your own or Mr Engels' honour, I must point out to you, as I would to anyone with whom I have neither personal nor political contacts, the usual way which, under the law, is open to everyone who feels himself insulted or libelled. Except in this way, I shall have no further dealings with you.

Gottfried Kinkel

I have not succeeded in making the final stroke of the pen[a] as in the original. *N'est-ce pas*[b] very cunning? I am to have recourse to an English court on account of insults offered at Cincinnati. And how coolly everything is rejected that might smack of a duel and the like.

Since I could only assume that the worthy Gottfried Kinkel, who drops the Johann when in public, would refuse to accept further letters bearing a Soho postmark, I hit upon the following ruse. I asked Ernest Jones to write the address and Lupus to post the letter itself in Windsor, where he had business. Inside the envelope, Gottfried found a second little *billet-doux*, its margin adorned with a posy of forget-me-nots and roses printed in colour and with the following content:

24th July 1852
5 Sutton Str., Soho
Office of The People's Paper

'To Dr Johann etc. Kinkel

'In juxtaposition
with a written statement, now before me, by your *guarantor* Huzel, whom at Cincinnati you cravenly required to give his word of honour to keep silent about your mendacious gossip there, a promise which, however, was given only conditionally by Huzel;

'with a letter, likewise before me, written at some time by Dr Gottfried Kinkel *in his own hand* to his ex-guarantor Cluss,[171] in which the same Kinkel boasts of his intention to enter into *political* relations with me:

'your letter—and this is precisely why it was *provoked*—provides a new and striking proof that the said Kinkel is a cleric whose baseness is only equalled by his cowardice.

Dr Karl Marx'[172]

---

[a] An imitation of the flourishes in Kinkel's signature. - [b] Is it not

This last was self-complacently pocketed by Mr 'Johann etc.' and is now circulating among the ranks of the émigrés. But the cream of the jest will only become plain to Kinkel later on, with the appearance of the first instalment of *The Great Men of the Exile*. Namely, that, shortly *before* this fearsome attack on Gottfried, I diverted myself by doing him direct and personal injury, while at the same time justifying myself in the eyes of the émigré *louts*. To that end I needed something 'in black and white' from Johann etc.

Now for greater matters.—Mazzini, no less, has for the past few days been dashing round like mad in an attempt to bring about an agreement between all those who officially make up the bourgeois emigration here. Also betook himself to Johann etc. And with the following result: Mazzini, Kossuth, Ledru-Rollin and Kinkel constitute Europe's Executive. Each member of this authority has the right to co-opt 2 subjects of his nationality. However, the decision as to these co-options rests with the majority among the four originals, i.e. *Mazzini*. Accordingly, co-opted among the Germans are A. Ruge and A. Goegg. Who among the other nationalities, I don't yet know. Kinkel, for his part, is said to have laid down 2 conditions: 1. a demand of 20,000 dollars for his loan. This I hold to be a *fabrication*. 2. The continued and independent existence of the Kinkel-Willich, etc. finance committee. This is no more than formal deference to Willich, for in fact it has already been decided to transfer the entire loan fund to A. Goegg. Finally, Kinkel & Co. will most humbly recognise the Revolutionary League in America.[173] This is the latest turn of events. How far they have progressed towards concluding this important treaty or whether they are still lingering over the preliminaries I do not know. *In any case the thing must be noised abroad in America*, with particular emphasis on the following. At the last guarantors' meeting in London, in *May 1852*, when the Kinkel-Willich committee was definitively elected, Kinkel most solemnly declared on his **word of honour** that if A. Ruge were elected to the committee, he himself would walk out, for he would never serve on the same committee as a man who had publicly described him as an agent of the Prince of Prussia.[a]

Secondly: What will Weitling & Co. say, if the dollars raised in America by Kinkel are expended by the Finance Minister, A. Goegg? For this is what is intended, in order to subsidise 'K. Heinzen's' *Janus* and to put into circulation the immortal articles of Ruge, Heinzen, etc.

---

[a] See this volume, pp. 96 and 150-51.

As for Mazzini, this wily enthusiast is steadily descending to the level of an Italian 'Gustav Struve' or some such. For the past 4 years he has been shouting 'Action, action'. Now it so happens that the Austrian police in Italy are running in 600 Mazzinists whose correspondence is conducted on pocket handkerchiefs in invisible ink. But these people have no wish to be detained and their family connections are extensive. So Mr Mazzini has received from Italy a letter announcing their intention to take 'action' in real earnest and hit out. All at once, and *post festum,* [a] 'sober reason' stirs in the bosom of the bombastic man of action, and he adjures them for God's sake to lie low, since on their own they can do nothing, the country is swarming with foreign soldiers, and similar *loci communes* [b] none of which are either more or less true now than they were in 1849. Action, action! *Italia farà da sè!* [c]

A few days ago Lupus met an Italian member of Mazzini's committee and taxed him with most of these absurdities. What of it? retorts the Roman, more than 600 people are killed in a battle. However, since the Italians fear that in this way they will BY AND BY be caught, shot or locked up, and since this or that victim of his exhortations is sending relatives to London, our man of action is afraid that some misunderstanding may lead to his being stabbed by a deluded and frenzied fellow-countryman; so every night he changes his lodgings on the pretext of having to hide from the Austrians. Yet it is not Austrians but 'deluded' Italians from whom he abjectly slinks into hiding. Surely this antipope deserves the gallows? To harass, tease, wear down a nation in this way! The inevitable result, particularly in the case of a people like the Italians, is a state of appalling, passive dejection, of complete and utter collapse.

Our people were to have appeared before the JURY in Cologne yesterday, but suddenly came the announcement of a further adjournment because one of the witnesses for the prosecution, Schulz, a police official in Berlin, had fallen ill. So if Mr Schulz were to die, the defendants might well remain under preliminary investigation until doomsday. In the meantime Becker is going blind and Daniels is getting consumption. *C'est par trop infâme.* [d] In all this, the bourgeois press is playing a most abominable role.

I saw the notice of adjournment in the *Kölnische Zeitung.* [e] A few days earlier I had received the following report from Cologne. [f]

---

[a] after the event - [b] commonplaces - [c] Italy will manage on her own! - [d] It's too iniquitous. - [e] [Report from Cologne of 26 July,] *Kölnische Zeitung*, No. 183, 27 July 1852. - [f] Below is a passage from Bermbach's letter to Marx of mid-July 1852.

'When Becker was arrested the following letters from you were seized; those of 8.2.51, 21.2.51 and 9.4.51. From the latter the ensuing passages have been picked out by the prosecution as exceptionally incriminating: "Herewith the jolly scribble from the School of Kinkel. 15 shillings have accumulated here f.t.l.[a] 10 shillings are still outstanding, having been promised but not yet collected. I shall proceed in the manner you indicate. So debit me with £1. For owing to the reduced circumstances of the member who should pay it, five shillings cannot be collected." The prosecution makes out that the letters f.t.l. stand for "For the League", while Becker claims that they are an abbreviation indicating an arrangement made between him and yourself concerning the acquisition of cheaper *literature* for you in London. That passage constitutes one of the chief items in the indictment, since there is otherwise hardly any evidence, unless fabricated, against B. Again, the indictment, starting in the year 1831, traces the rise of the Communist League from an association of Germans in Paris which underwent various modifications under the names "League of Germans",[174] "League of the Just",[175] but continued uninterruptedly right up to the present society now appearing in the dock. This information apparently derives from data provided by the Hanoverian government. The prosecution attaches no importance whatever to the split in London in 1850[15]; in their opinion this was simply a personal squabble, the whole lot of them were, after all, pursuing the same criminal aims and shared the same views and would, moreover, act in concert at the hour of decision. Thus, besides the two addresses previously published in the press, a 3rd has been incorporated in the indictment; this address is said to be dated June or July 1850[176] and to have been intercepted in Leipzig.

'The only statements of any note are those of the witnesses Haupt, who gave a fairly detailed and comprehensive story, and Hentze, an ex-lieutenant, who to some extent attacked Becker. On Saturday Erhardt, a cashier with Stein, the banker, was arrested on the same charge. He is said to be slightly compromised by reason of the recommendation he gave to Nothjung and of a few letters discovered on the latter which seemed to indicate some understanding between the two... By the way, so nicely have the jurymen been selected that, if you consider the odds, the State could not be better placed.'

The most important news politically is the treaty concluded between Prussia, Austria and Russia during the Czar's[b] visit to Vienna.[177] It was first announced in *The Morning Chronicle* the day before yesterday. Yesterday there was a reprint of it in *The Times*,[c] so you will be able to read it for yourself. Here the election results are such that the Tories, who will drop the Corn Law question, possess a large counter-revolutionary majority on all other issues and this Cabinet will, I believe, give way before nothing short of a more or less revolutionary manifestation. The bourgeois now realise what a blunder they made in failing to draw the political conclusions from their anti-Corn Law victory in 1846. *Ils y penseront*.[d] My list of printing errors for the *Brumaire* will soon

---

[a] Here 'F.d.B.' in German means 'für die Bücher'. Below it is taken to mean 'für den Bund'. - [b] Nicholas I. - [c] 'Secret Treaty of the Three Northern Powers' (from *The Morning Chronicle*, No. 26705, 28 July 1852), *The Times*, No. 21180, 29 July 1852. - [d] They'll think of it.

moulder away; had I realised this would happen, I should have done better to send you for postage the money thus expended. But as Spinoza tells us, it is a comfort to consider all things *sub specie aeterni*.[a]

First published in part in *Voprosy istorii KPSS*, No. 3, Moscow, 1962 and in full in: Marx and Engels, *Works*, Second Russian Edition, Vol. 28, Moscow, 1962

Printed according to a letter from Cluss to Weydemeyer of 16 August 1852

Published in English for the first time

73

MARX TO ADOLF CLUSS [178]

IN WASHINGTON

[London, beginning of August 1852]

... Now the secret is out, namely the reason why the Cologne people have yet again failed to appear. The principal witness, Haupt, the traitor from Hamburg, has taken himself off to Brazil. The 2nd most important witness, a journeyman tailor, has likewise shown a clean pair of heels. This leaves the government without even the semblance of a proof. The scoundrels are taking their revenge by prolonging the period of preventive detention....

First published in: Marx and Engels, *Works*, Second Russian Edition, Vol. 28, Moscow, 1962

Printed according to a letter from Cluss to Weydemeyer of 15 October 1852

Published in English for the first time

---

[a] from the viewpoint of eternity

74

MARX TO ENGELS

IN MANCHESTER

[London,] 2 August 1852

Dear Engels,

Herewith the stuff for Dana.[179] We must assail the fellow from all sides, the more so since that old *farceur*, Ruge, has actually deposited one of his stylistic excretions in a recent number.[a]

The Cologne affair has been adjourned by the court for 3 months at the request of the public prosecutor.[b] In other words, the principal witnesses have slipped through his fingers, Haupt to Brazil and a journeyman tailor to some *lieu inconnu*.[c]

Do you think that Dana might take offence because of the *similarity in the names* of the English and American Whigs?[180]

A detailed dispatch, probably, tomorrow.

Your
K. M.

First published abridged in *Der Briefwechsel zwischen F. Engels und K. Marx*, Bd. 1, Stuttgart, 1913 and in full in *MEGA*, Abt. III, Bd. 1, 1929

Printed according to the original

Published in English for the first time

75

MARX TO ENGELS

IN MANCHESTER

[London,] 5 August 1852
28 Dean Street, Soho

Dear Engels,

Don't forget to let me have the *rest of the thing*[d] by *Tuesday*. The section on the Tories is too short by itself. This time there is a twofold reason why the portions sent to Dana should not be too niggardly. 1. In Cincinnati that blackguard Heinzen is siding with

---

[a] A. Ruge, 'The Public Law of Europe', *New-York Daily Tribune*, No. 3506, 14 July 1852. - [b] Saedt - [c] place unknown - [d] See previous letter.

the Whigs against the Democrats, because he rightly believes this ELECTIONEERING TIME is the best moment at which to sell himself. *Greeley* reported in the *Tribune* the speech Heinzen made there, and went on to praise the man.[a] So storm clouds are threatening *me* from that quarter. 2. Having for weeks, and particularly for the past fortnight, been forced to spend 6 hours a day chasing after 6d for grub, on top of which I am again being pestered by my LANDLADY, I had no other alternative but to write to Johnson yesterday inquiring whether he would discount a bill on the *Tribune* for me. Should the man agree to do what I ask, which is still *in dubio*,[b] I shall have to inform Dana, and if we send him short articles, he will think he is being fleeced and will cast me out of the temple, since he now has such a plentiful SUPPLY from Heinzen, Ruge and B. Bauer. What is even more unfortunate, I see from today's *Times* that the *Daily Tribune* is protectionist.[c] So it's all VERY OMINOUS. We must send the fellow something as quickly as possible before he countermands. I can't yet send off my dispatch[d] since I have a frightful headache—not, however, from the effects of PALE ALE.

It's regrettable that Dronke will not be here on Saturday.[e] Goegg has called a *general* meeting of refugees for that day and the little man's presence would have been very desirable. For Pieper isn't the right person. At all events, Dronke must see to it that he is here when the rabble arrives from Berlin, for I cannot cope with these blackguards all by myself.

I have all manner of stuff from Cluss, too, to send you, which you will receive as soon as you send me a few STAMPS; otherwise the trash will cost you double and *pour le moment*[f] I haven't a penny to send.

Salut.

Your
K. M.

First published abridged in *Der Briefwechsel zwischen F. Engels und K. Marx*, Bd. 1, Stuttgart, 1913 and in full in *MEGA*, Abt. III, Bd. 1, 1929

Printed according to the original

Published in English for the first time

---

[a] 'A German View of American "Democracy"', *New-York Daily Tribune*, No. 3505, 13 July 1852. - [b] in doubt - [c] 'The Approaching Election in the United States', *The Times*, No. 21186, 5 August 1852. - [d] for Engels to translate (see this volume, p. 145) - [e] 7 August - [f] for the time being

76

ENGELS TO MARX

IN LONDON

[Manchester,] Friday, 6 August 1852

Dear Marx,

You will have got back the first half of the article[a] in English and German yesterday afternoon. The second[b] you shall have on Tuesday morning. As for being thrown out of the *Tribune*, you need have no worries.[c] We are too firmly ensconced there. Furthermore, to the Yankees, this European politicising is mere dilettantism in which he who writes best and with the greatest *esprit* comes out on top. *Heinzen* can do us no harm; if he's bought by the Whigs, it means that he will obey them, not that he will give the orders. Ruge, Bauer, etc., etc., in addition to ourselves ensure that the *Tribune* has an 'all-round' character. As for protectionism, it does no harm. American Whigs are all industrial protectionists, but this by no means implies that they belong to the landed aristocracy, Derby variety. Nor are they so stupid not to know just as well as does List that FREE TRADE suits English industry better than anything else. By the way, I could at a pinch insert a word here and there to that effect with the FREETRADERS, which you could cross out if not to your liking. But there's really no need for it.

I thought you had long since settled the discounting affair with Johnson and very much hope something will come of it. As for me, I get deeper in the mire financially every day. While I much enjoy having Papa Dronke here, it is impossible to work of an evening, and so a fair amount of money is being frittered away; on top of that there are current DISBURSEMENTS besides £20 owing to the business, which make things very tight. Dronke intends to return next week (at the beginning), after which I shall do a spell of hard work, having sufficient material here, and then, by the end of September, I shall again have some money at my disposal—a few pounds in September[d] for sure. Most unfortunately, in an evil hour Mr Pindar also asked me for a loan. He is still keeping afloat on three lessons a week and seems to have

---

[a] K. Marx, 'The Elections in England.—Tories and Whigs'. - [b] K. Marx, 'The Chartists'. - [c] See previous letter. - [d] December in the original.

fallen touchingly in love—*pauvre garçon, il faut l'avoir vu sous l'empire de l'émotion plus ou moins vierge.*[a]

Moreover, towards the end of June I was unable, owing to all sorts of circumstances, to charge up to my old man a number of extras which have now been placed to my account. Meanwhile, we are busy with the balance sheet; actually it is no concern of mine, but it will at least give me some indication of how far I can go. If it turns out well—which I shall know in some 4-6 weeks' time, I might be able to chance something, in which case you will at once receive some money. Only this month, because of the £20 or £25 I owe the business, I am absolutely stuck.

I don't know how I can arrange to do an article on GERMANY for Dana behind Dronke's back—he knows nothing about the matter.[181] At the office I have my hands completely full until 7 o'clock in the evening, so I can't do it there. *Cependant je verrai.*[b]

Warmest regards to your wife and children from

Your
F. E.

Enclosed STAMPS to the value of 9/- and a few pence.

Dronke asks me to tell you that he will probably be coming at the beginning of next week.

First published in *Der Briefwechsel zwischen F. Engels und K. Marx*, Bd. 1, Stuttgart, 1913

Printed according to the original

Published in English for the first time

77

MARX TO ENGELS [182]

IN MANCHESTER

[London,] 6 August 1852
28 Dean Street, Soho

Dear Engels,

D'abord,[c] then, the incident with Johann Gottfried Kinkel.[d]

You will see from one of the enclosed letters from Cluss that Mr Kinkel stated in a BOURGEOIS CIRCLE in Cincinnati: 'Marx and Engels

---

[a] poor lad, you ought to see him in the throes of more or less virginal emotion - [b] However, I shall see. - [c] To begin with - [d] See this volume, pp. 138-39.

are no revolutionaries, they're a couple of blackguards who have been thrown out of public houses by the workers in London'.[183] Knowing my Gottfried, I began by sending him the following note in which I pretended to be not quite sure of the facts, thereby giving him fresh occasion for ambiguities:

'5 Sutton Street, Soho, Office of *The People's Paper,*
'22 July 1852

'To Dr Johann Gottfried Kinkel

'You are alleged, or so I am informed, to have ventured the following statement before Anneke or other Germans at Cincinnati (the passage follows). I await your explanation by return of post. Silence will be regarded as an admission.

Dr K. Marx'

Kinkel sent the following note by return:

'To Dr Karl Marx
    Since the article about me was published under your auspices during my imprisonment, I have wanted to have nothing more to do with you. If you believe that you can, through the testimony of Anneke or other honourable men, rather than through anonymous insinuations, provide proof that I untruthfully said or published anything detrimental to your own or Mr Engels' honour, I must point out to you, as I would to anyone with whom I have neither personal nor political contacts, the usual way which, under the law, is open to everyone who feels himself insulted or libelled. Except in this way, I shall have no further dealings with you.

Gottfried Kinkel

Since it was evident from this scrawl that Mr Gottfried would neither accept letters bearing a Soho postmark nor admit messengers, I got Lupus to post a note to him from Windsor on paper of the kind used for a *billet-doux,* bearing a posy of roses and forget-me-nots printed in colour, and having the following content:

'To Dr Johann etc. Kinkel

'In juxtaposition
with a written statement, now before me, by your *guarantor* Huzel whom you cravenly required at Cincinnati to give his word of honour to keep silent about your mendacious gossip there, a promise which, however, was given only conditionally by Huzel;
    'with a letter, likewise before me, written some time earlier by Dr Gottfried Kinkel *in his own hand* to his *ex-guarantor* Cluss, in which

the same Kinkel boasts of his intention to enter into *political* relations with me:

'your letter—and this is precisely why ¬it was provoked—provides a new and striking proof that the said Kinkel is a *cleric whose baseness is only equalled by his cowardice.*

Dr Karl Marx'

This last was swallowed in silence by Mr Johann etc. who, since then, has carefully avoided letting us hear anything more from him.

Kossuth's secret circular, which Cluss speaks of in his last letter, you will find in English in tomorrow's issue of Jones' PAPER.[184] Hence I am not enclosing it.

The meeting of Kinkel's guarantors took place on Tuesday 3 August. The chief item was the following: Reichenbach is guarding the exchequer like a Cerberus. The £200 so far spent by Kinkel and Willich was *received* from Gerstenberg, etc., against the revolutionary deposits. Statutorily, they may dispose of these only after at least 3 people have been nominated by the guarantors. And Reichenbach insists on observance of this formality. To remedy the inconvenience, Kinkel and Willich had decided to have Techow as the third nominee. True, Techow is sailing for Australia in 3 weeks' time. But, under the statutes of the loan, once the committee had its full complement of 3 members, it could on its own authority propose two more. Hence, the sole purpose of Techow's nomination was 1. to make Reichenbach hand over the exchequer, 2. to enable them later on to bring in 2 men of straw in Techow's place. However, the meeting immediately decided against Techow on the grounds that he was only being used as a cover and was leaving for Australia. Kinkel and Willich were told that their conduct of affairs was unsatisfactory, that they inspired no confidence and that they must submit a detailed account concerning the expenditure of the £200 before it could be ratified. This last and other decisions are to be SETTLED today, Friday the 6th, at a further guarantors' meeting.

At the sitting on the 3rd, Reichenbach proposed that the £1,000 be deposited in the Bank of England and left untouched until the outbreak of the revolution. Löwe (in alliance with Ruge) proposed that the money be handed over to the Revolutionary League in America.[173]

And although Kinkel himself stated, in the enclosed note to Huzel, that Ruge falsely suspected him of being an agent of the

Prince of Prussia,[185] and although he, upon the strength of that, *pledged his word* at the guarantors' meeting last May that he would never sit on the same committee as Ruge, our Gottfried now declares himself ready, for the sake of the cause, to act *in concert* with Goegg, Ruge, etc. and to administer the money in concert with them, in order to get a hand in the administration at all. Willich, however, now convinced that the £1,000 will not, like the 200 already spent, produce any further windfalls for him is said to have decided to emigrate to America, whither he has already been preceded by the trusty Gebert and Dietz.

Last week Papa Goegg again convened his Agitation Club.[26] An exact count revealed that it consisted of exactly 8 people, the place of Sigel and Fickler, who had disappeared, being taken by the newly-joined Oswald and Dralle. In addition it was found that, though Goegg had in the meantime acquired great fame as Kossuth's servant and has rendered 'sterling service' as an agitator for the Revolutionary League, he had otherwise not brought back even enough cash to cover the debts 'incurred to defray travelling expenses'. In these doubtful circumstances the agitators[a] felt compelled to attempt an alliance with Kinkel, in order that they might with decorum get at the £1,000. Kinkel likewise sees therein the last chance of avoiding an irreversible divorce from the £1,000. With the secret purpose of furthering this design, Goegg has convened a *general* meeting of refugees for tomorrow, the 7th, at Schärttner's. Ostensibly to report on his *grands œuvres*.[b] In fact, to be swept by general acclaim into an alliance with Kinkel and the £1,000. This may now not be accomplished.

But a third complication arises now, whose immediate effect is to debar both sides, Kinkel and Goegg, from the 'exchequer'. *To be precise, on the one hand, our Eduard Meyen is agitating for the money to be used to launch a big LONDON WEEKLY PAPER.* And, on the other, the 'critical' Edgar Bauer, who had barely heard of the predicament in which the £1,000 found itself, before he too crept forth and, taking up position behind Schily, Imandt, Schimmelpfennig, etc., also solicited a newspaper for himself. Imandt, etc., see this as the only means of rescuing the money from Kinkel and Goegg. Edgar Bauer adopts towards these people the appearance of a 'harmless humorist'.

I shall obtain an exact account of today's sitting since Imandt is now an L.M.[c] To revert to the one of the 3rd, I would mention the following: After questions of high policy had been dealt with,

---

[a] members of the Agitation Club - [b] great works - [c] Communist League member

the chivalrous Schimmelpfennig arose; certain persons had, he said, put it about that the Brüningk woman was a spy and he now declared them to be vile calumniators. Kinkel denied that he for his part had ever made any such assertion. (He had in fact made it to the whoreson Kamm of Bonn when the latter passed this way.) Willich, on whom all eyes were turned, sat tight and said nothing. *Techow* declared that it was even more vile when such suspicions were bandied about by persons who, for a whole year, had enjoyed the Brüningk woman's hospitality. It was their duty rather to refute such a talk whenever they got wind of it.

All eyes were turned on Willich. Willich did not stir, but throughout the whole of this sitting, which saw the fading of so many 'golden' dreams, is said to have been the very personification of 'unhappy consciousness'.

Well, enough of that crap for today.·

I have just received the enclosed letter from Freiligrath, from which it appears that cur Johnson remains adamant.[a] Hence I am utterly at a loss what to do and my position is becoming abominable.

So honest Goegg has sent Freiligrath an invitation! He's one they can still never do without, but in the end they will have to.

My regards to the mandrake.[b]

Your
K. M.

It seems unlikely that your letter will arrive today, it being already 2 in the afternoon.

Enclosed letters from *Cluss*:
1. 20 June.
2. 4 July.
3. 8 July, with Kinkel's circular.
4. Kinkel's circular of 2 August.
5. Cincinnati, 6 February,[c] letter from Kinkel to Huzel.
6. Letter from Hillgärtner to Huzel.
7. Letter from Cluss of 22 July.

First published in part in *Der Briefwechsel zwischen F. Engels und K. Marx*, Bd. 1, Stuttgart, 1913 and in full in *MEGA*, Abt. III, Bd. 1, 1929

Printed according to the original

Published in English for the first time

---

[a] See this volume, p. 147. - [b] Ernst Dronke - [c] April in the original

78

ENGELS TO MARX

IN LONDON

[Manchester,] Monday evening [9 August 1852]

Dear Marx,

I've done a stupid thing. In its MAIL TABLE the *Daily News* does not mention any American STEAMER for Wednesday—so I succumbed to the Sunday indolence so natural to a *commerçant*.[a] And today I see from a commercial circular that a STEAMER is in fact leaving the day after tomorrow. I have begun to work,[b] but nothing is ready. I have Pindar coming to see me this evening and even if I sent him away, I doubt whether I should get anything done in the few hours before the last post. *Donc*[c] you and I have been duped. But I shall never again make the mistake of believing the commercial intelligence provided by the organ of the bourgeoisie.

Your
F. E.

First published in *MEGA*, Abt. III, Bd. 1, 1929

Printed according to the original

Published in English for the first time

79

MARX TO ENGELS[182]

IN MANCHESTER

London, 10 August 1852
28 Dean Street, Soho

Dear Engels,

First, I enclose the original text of Kossuth's SECRET CIRCULAR.[184]

Next, the report 1. on the guarantors' sitting of 6 August, 2. on Goegg's meeting of 7 August.

---

[a] businessman - [b] Apparently on the English translation of Marx's article, 'The Chartists'. - [c] So

As to 1. Present: Kinkel, Willich, Reichenbach, Löwe of Calbe, Meyen, Schurz (not Techow this time), Schimmelpfennig, Imandt; I know of no others. Not forgetting Schärttner.

Kinkel had had the indispensable third member (Techow) of the alliance[a] elected in America and Switzerland. There still remained the participation in the election of the 12-15 London guarantors. Here, as I told you, the election of Techow fell through and then he declared that he could not accept as he was leaving for Australia.[b]

Kinkel proposed to proceed with a new election of the third man. Fell through again.

Löwe of Calbe: First: 'The German loan has miscarried because the political circumstances (May 1852[186]) in view of which it was undertaken are no longer present, and the presupposed amount of 20,000 dollars has not been raised.' *Second:* 'The monies to be returned to the American committees.'

The first part of this motion was carried, the second rejected.

Imandt: 'If the majority of the remaining guarantors share my view, the money to hand should be used to publish a German newspaper in London.' 'Reichenbach will remain TRUSTEE of the money.' 'A committee is to be elected consisting of Reichenbach, Löwe and Schimmelpfennig, and Kinkel and Willich will hand over to it the lists of the guarantors in America and Switzerland; the previous committee has nothing more to do with the matter; the new committee will advise the guarantors abroad of the resolutions taken and will obtain their opinion.'

Reichenbach supported Imandt's motions, all were carried. Kinkel and Willich protested on the grounds that the disposal of the money did not rest solely with the body of guarantors. Only the donors of the money, or respectively the finance committees set up in America, could exercise the right of disposal.

Sic transit gloria.[c] Willich is more determined than ever to go to America, provided he can raise the fare.

As to 2. Meeting called by Finance Minister Goegg, back from America without finances.

Present: *In the chair: 'Damm' himself* (not yet slipped off to Australia). *Goegg. Ronge. Dr Strauss. Sigel,* the other one.[d] *Franck* (from Vienna). *Oswald. Dralle.* (These all 'agitators'.[e]) *Kinkel. Schurz. Meyen. Willich. Imandt. Schily. Becker.* One of Schärttner's

---

[a] A paraphrase of the expression 'in eurem Bunde der dritte' from Schiller's poem 'Der Bürgschaft'. - [b] America in the original. See this volume, p. 150. - [c] Thus passes the glory. - [d] Albert Sigel - [e] members of the Agitation Club

waiters. The tipsy Lumpenproletarian *Herweg* from Neuss. Candidate *Hentze* from Königsberg. *Garthe.* A *stripling* (unknown) from Vienna.

Goegg opened the sitting, described his activity in America, owing to which birth was given to a revolutionary league,[173] an act as a result of which the American Republic was supposed to be 'tumbled' and hence birth to be given to a German-Baden republic—the victory of the American Democrats over the Whigs to be ensured, etc. The modest young man further asserted (an opinion *attested* by the newly arrived candidate of philosophy Hentze) that Germans in all provinces stood with their eyes fixed on London so that, at the crucial moment when those present at the meeting fell into each other's arms, they could let out a thunderous hurrah that would resound across the ocean a thousand times o'er. Hence he demanded that the meeting constitute itself a branch of the Revolutionary League and no longer leave their poor compatriots to languish in that attitude of expectancy.

Imandt: Thanked Goegg for his information on American conditions. Suggested moreover that the meeting should disperse, since only a general and publicly convened meeting of refugees could take a decision.

Damm ruled him out of order.

Kinkel: (Already during Goegg's eloquent speech, this sensitive poet-martyr had, by rolling his eyes, signified his irrevocable determination to spread out his arms in reconciliation). He, too, was aware that Germany was looking to them. He was in a position to clasp the conciliatory hand. As a sacrifice to the cause, he would forget the grave injustice he had suffered. He, too, was aware that not only the liberation of Germany, but also the revolutionising of America, lay in their hands. None so great, said he, in an allusion to Ruge's 'agent of the Prince of Prussia',[a] as he who mastered himself. However he, for his part, demanded that the Revolutionary League should also now guarantee his loan. Even though he and the 'honourable' Willich might not see eye to eye politically, nevertheless they would, he believed, have achieved great things together.

Imandt: Respected the Christian humility of Kinkel who had forgotten that Ruge had called him an agent of the Prince of Prussia, who had, for sheer love of the revolution, had repressed the indignation in his burning breast which, 2 months earlier

---

[a] See this volume, pp. 150-51.

(May), had prompted, in the presence of the guarantors, the solemn declaration: 'as a good republican, he could only regard as injurious to his honour the suggestion that he should go with Ruge, his wicked detractor, and, rather than reconcile himself with the wicked Ruge, would retire from all political activity'. It was out of Christian humility that Kinkel had drained the bitter cup which Fickler had prepared for him with his horribly insulting letters (in one of those letters Fickler had described him as 'a turkey strutting on a dung-heap'); he had become, as indeed Goegg's friends maintained he had always been, simple of heart if he could bring himself to fall into the arms of his American rivals. The 'union' between Messrs Kinkel and Goegg was a fine thing, for although it really had no other purpose than that the former with the help of the latter should strive to get the upper hand in the administration of the loan funds, and that the latter with the help of the former should seek to worm his way into that administration, yet a peace agreement between two men of such stature might nevertheless ensure that the political parties throughout the world similarly became reconciled, that the constitutionalist held out his hand to the republican and the socialist to the republican, that henceforward the proletarians would no longer be exploited by the bourgeois and, in short, that everyone would embrace every one else and shout hip-hip-hurray. For the fact of Kinkel's having said in America that he regarded the proletarians as cannon fodder (as once in Bonn and Cologne he had adulated Cavaignac) and this, despite his alliance with the 'honourable' Willich, did not affect the issue. There was at most one trifling matter outstanding: like all people who, instead of studying the difference between the various parties and championing their interests, indulged in scatter-brained folly about uniting opposing elements, Kinkel could be reproached with a total lack of principle, etc. He would further draw Kinkel's attention to the fact that he could at most conclude agreements on his behalf, but not on behalf of the body of guarantors. Finally, Imandt moved that the Revolutionary League in America be left to its own devices and that all should go home. Whereupon Imandt went.

Incidents: Damm constantly interrupted Imandt and wanted to rule him out of order. As a Rhinelander, the tipsy *Herweg* felt obliged, so long as Imandt was present, to manifest approbation and, while Imandt was speaking of 'great men', he 'lorgnetted' the company with his pipe. During the passage about 'the proletarians', the painter, *Franck,* rose in indignation and said: 'I can't stand it any more. I *grunt.*' Imandt replied that this was something he had in common with other animals, whereupon Franck decamped. Kinkel denied the 'cannon fodder'. Imandt told the whole story about Schnauffer and the *Wecker*, whereat Kinkel fell silent. At the word 'Cavaignac', he again broke in: 'Citizen Imandt, when did the *Bonner Zeitung* appear?' Imandt: It was all the same to him whether it had been before or after the June insurrection. He had read about the thing himself.

Conclusion: The sitting went on for 2 more hours. Goegg pleaded that they should join the Revolutionary League, at least temporarily. The afore-mentioned stripling from Vienna declared anyone who delayed in joining by so much as an hour to be a 'traitor to his country'. Nevertheless, after the majority had rejected *every*, I repeat, *every motion*, the company went home without having founded a branch of the American-European-Australian Revolutionary League.

Your
K. M.

First published in part in *Der Briefwechsel zwischen F. Engels und K. Marx*, Bd. 1, Stuttgart, 1913 and in full in *MEGA*, Abt. III, Bd. 1, 1929

Printed according to the original

Published in English for the first time

80

ENGELS TO MARX

IN LONDON

[Manchester,] 16 August 1852

Dear Marx,

This evening I have been promised the £2 borrowed from me a short while ago; if I get it, I shall send you it at once tomorrow by P.O. order and shall also write at great length.

Since we've heard nothing further from Weydemeyer and, according to Cluss' letters, the things seem at last to have been sent off,[a] it might be advisable for us to inquire from Edwards, Sanford and Co. in Liverpool whether they have received any

---

[a] Copies of the *Revolution* containing Marx's *Eighteenth Brumaire of Louis Bonaparte*, see this volume, p. 160.

packages. If you hear nothing more (last night the STEAMER had not yet arrived), I, at any rate, could do that.

From your report it would seem that the resolutions of 3 [August] have for the present snatched the money from Mr Kinkel's grasp.[a] Mr Imandt does pretty well for himself after his own fashion. *C'est drôle, quand un Schapper nous échappe, un Imandt est toujours sûr de revenir à nous.*[b] But he is at any rate a *deus minimorum gentium, canis domesticus communismi germanici,*[c] and as such is useful, since we have now learnt to keep lesser folk of this kind on a short rein.

The noble Willich's bosom must be much lacerated now that separation from the emigration's *coffre-fort*[d] has sprung the last band holding his noble consciousness together. He must, moreover, have notified his trusties over there long ago of his arrival since the latter, on the strength of an important letter from Willich, have already convened big extraordinary general meetings. Mr Willich will become head of the LOAFERS and ROWDIES there, and as such will have a rare opportunity of distinguishing himself. What is more, he will also find his old enemy Schramm[e] there, and that will lead to some pretty rows.

How delectable that Mr Kossuth has actually already caused companies to be drilled and Napoleon-Sigel is playing the instructor of the recruits. What an unspeakable swindler this Kossuth is; driving him out of America was one of the most splendid coups ever perpetrated by Cluss.[184]

By the way I shall very soon be doing the Hungarian campaign[f] and shall write direct to Brockhaus this very week. If he has no faith in my military qualifications, I shall arrange previously to do one or two cogent articles for the *Gegenwart* so that he can see what there is to them. Dronke's connection with Brockhaus is very good and must be exploited. For Brockhaus is after all one of the more tractable booksellers. *Nous allons voir.*[g]

I was interrupted while writing the article for Dana[h] last Thursday and shall, if possible, make up for it by doing 2 this week. I also expect something more from you on England.[187] Last week there could be little thought of work. While Dronke was here

---

[a] See this volume, pp. 149-50. - [b] It's curious, whenever we lose a Schapper, an Imandt is always sure to come back to us (pun on Schapper and *échappe*). - [c] god of the minor nation, house-dog of German communism - [d] strong-box - [e] Conrad Schramm - [f] See this volume, pp. 104 and 128. - [g] We shall see. - [h] for the series *Revolution and Counter-Revolution in Germany*

I had neglected much of what I had previously been doing. Now I am gradually getting back in TRAIN.

Regards to your wife and children.

Your
F. E.

First published considerably abridged in *Der Briefwechsel zwischen F. Engels und K. Marx*, Bd. 1, Stuttgart, 1913 and in full in *MEGA*, Abt. III, Bd. 1, Berlin, 1929

Printed according to the original

Published in English for the first time

81

MARX TO ENGELS [188]

IN MANCHESTER

London, 19 August 1852
28 Dean Street, Soho

Dear Engels,

I had 10/- handed to me by Dronke. Yesterday £2 by post. However welcome the money was, I find it most *ennuyant*[a] that you should squeeze yourself dry for me, and this at a moment when you yourself are *plus ou moins*[b] in a fix.

As regards the Hungarian war, you would probably do well to have a look also at the following:

The Fortress of Komarom (Comorn) during the War of Independence in Hungary, by Colonel Sigismund Thaly. Translated (from the German) by William Rushton. James Madden, Leadenhead Street.

As regards works on military matters, since you intend to go thoroughly into the whole LINE, I would cite the following in case you might consider one or another of them worth acquiring:

Carrion-Nisas: *Essai sur l'historie générale de l'art militaire etc.* Paris 1824.

Kausler: *Kriegsgeschichte aller Völker.* Ulm 1825. *Wörterbuch und Atlas der Schlachten.* 1825 and 1831. (The only two general military histories. Said to be meagre.)

Guerard: *Encyclopädie der Kriegskunst.* 2nd ed. Vienna 1833.

---

[a] annoying - [b] more or less

Handbibliothek für Offiziere über das Ganze der Kriegslehre für Eingeweihte und Laien von einer Gesellschaft Preußischer Offiziere. Berlin 1828.

J.A.M.-r (Millerbacher): *Das Kriegswesen der Römer, nach antiken Denkmalen geordnet von Ottenberger.* Prague 1824.

Löhr: *Das Kriegswesen der Griechen und Römer.* 2nd ed. Würzburg 1830.

Blesson: *Geschichte des Belagerungskriegs.* Berlin 1821.

Hoyer: *Geschichte der Kriegskunst.* Göttingen 1797.

Chambray: *Die Veränderungen in der Kriegskunst von 1700-1815.* German. Berlin 1830.

Stenzel: *Geschichte der Kriegsverfassung Deutschlands, besonders im Mittelalter.* Berlin 1820.

Barthold: *George v. Frundsberg.* Hamburg 1833.

Letters have arrived from Cluss which I shall send you as soon as I have shown them to Lupus and the little League.[189]

As regards Weydemeyer, Cluss writes as follows[a]:

'Not long ago, after some goading on my part, Weydemeyer wrote that he would have to put serious pressure on Korff who was supposed to have sent off the 50 *Brumaires*.[b] Weydemeyer has, I believe, small sums owing to him from Korff and will therefore have charged him with the dispatch, and/or payment of the postal costs.

'The remaining 300 *Brumaires* ... not yet dispatched ... He claims that 500 copies are still held at the printers as a security and he hasn't yet been able to redeem them, etc. ... *Financially*, for one thing I *cannot* under any circumstances intervene just now, and for another I *would* not *wish* to do so even if I could. For time and again I have been told that such and such a sum would resolve everything, and time and again such and such a sum has been provided and resolved nothing. When the *Revolution* began, we were told to have faith and send in advance-payments without delay. I at once sent subscriptions to the tune of 10 dollars, which *I*, of course, subsequently lost... Later it was said that the periodical was being put on its feet again and I was to find 20 dollars to that end; 18 dollars went off forthwith, 15 dollars from me personally and 3 dollars subscriptions. *Instead of being used to carry on the business*, this went to pay for the same old stupid bag of tricks, i.e. for the first 2 issues which had been sent out at random. The *Brumaire* arrived. Weydemeyer in despair. I told him I would instantly contribute 25-30 dollars if that would help, otherwise he was to send me the manuscript. Send me 25 dollars, he says; I do so. After a while it transpires that only 500 copies can be printed with the money available; no good, I tell him, how much more would it cost to print 1,000? 20 dollars, comes the reply, and the next day the money is already on its way.

'Now the poems[c] arrive; *they* are to be printed in New York; when I insist that the nonsense must cease and the printing begin, I get the poems back, it having unfortunately proved impossible to print them just now in New York. I· at once

---

[a] Cluss to Marx, 5 August 1852. - [b] K. Marx, *The Eighteenth Brumaire of Louis Bonaparte.* - [c] F. Freiligrath, 'An Joseph Weydemeyer', I and II.

have them printed and bound for some 15 dollars (400 copies[a]) and send the stuff off in all haste so that it can be disposed of at the choral festival just then taking place in New York. They were touted round by *one solitary* vendor[b] who is said to have actually disposed of 60 (!) copies. So the printing of the 2nd thousand (I had left the type set up), the money for which Weydemeyer had promised to provide as he had already informed me, was, of course, stopped; and in the same way, the whole business appears to have remained inert and lifeless in his hands ever since.

'I shall write and tell Weydemeyer that, in so far as *I* am financially involved in this affair, I want you to use it in Europe for further publications in the interests of the party, or in any other way *you yourself* think fit, hence that so far as my share in all this is concerned, to send no money to America. In the case of the poems, I alone am involved, and so I alone have the final say in the matter.

'I shall therefore stake everything on getting the stuff sent off.'

Isn't that an exact replica of our Brussels-Westphalian *aventure*?[190] Last week I wrote to F. Streit in Coburg about the printing of the *Brumaire;* he deals in articles of this kind.[191]

Apropos. No. 15[c] appeared in the *Tribune.*

In St Louis, Heinzen is now figuring for a change as an 'aristocrat of the intellect' (sic), ludicrous second-hand rehash of Feuerbach-Stirner; and since the Revolutionary League[173] is going to pot, the 'aristocrat of the intellect' proposes a 'humanist' union.

In addition I have the following to report:

On the 3rd, Kinkel and the *coffre-fort*[d] were duly divorced. Reichenbach deposited the money in the Bank of England in his own name.

At this gathering Kinkel feigned ignorance of the meeting convoked by Goegg and hence challenged Imandt in public to read out in public the invitation he had received. On the 6th, however, Goegg, turning to Kinkel, remarked: 'in accordance with the arrangement I made with you at your house'. Willich was not present.

Hentze, the candidate, endorsed all his own remarks by adding: 'as a D. Phil. I ought to know'.

Goegg explained how his Revolutionary League 1. provided a stay and support for Germans in America, 2. might, by influencing the elections, sway American policy and induce the United States to adopt a policy of intervention. On the material side, too, a start had been made. Contributions of one cent per week. Boxes in all public houses. Gottfried declared himself in agreement with all this. Only, he opined, contributions of a dollar would be preferable to contributions of a cent, no one in America

---

[a] Cluss says 1,000 in his letter. - [b] Helmich - [c] F. Engels, *Revolution and Counter-Revolution in Germany*, XV. - [d] strong-box

having sufficient patriotic devotion to count up the cents. He also came out against BOXES.

Quoth the great Kinkel, staring hard at Imandt the while:

'Despite all the calumnies that have been spread against me, I can stand up with *unruffled* brow and say that I have never spoken ill of any exiled fellow citizen—not a single one.'[a]

Consequence: Since Kinkel had no money, but only his esteemed person, to offer by way of dowry, the latter was spurned, despite all his boot-licking and self-humiliation. The eight dynasts organised themselves into a Revolutionary League off their own bat and without co-opting Kinkel. The *malheureux!*[b]

Schmolze, a born painter, is said to have done a rather nice set of cartoons, Kinkel as King Lear and Willich as the Fool. Also a cartoon in which Willich, as a sloth, squats in a fruit-tree while Mrs Schärttner on the ground shakes the tree to dislodge him.

Willich has been stupid enough to extend his ostracism to the honourable and elderly Mr 'Schily' and to expel him from his little League [189] for all sorts of imaginary crimes. Schily is appealing to a general meeting. Today is the day of the ordeal. For his part Schily accuses Willich of '*unmistakable insanity*', as a proof of which he will this evening produce a letter from *Heise,* Willich's alleged friend in Liverpool, wherein *Heise* describes *Willich as mentally deranged.*

Last week friend Jones came within an ace of losing his newspaper.[c] Every week a deficit. At odds with the committee [192] and with the 2 citizens who have so far been putting up the money. Sudden reprieve. MacGowan has taken over publication, will make good the weekly deficit, and Jones is now ensconced in the office of the old *Northern Star.* MacGowan has sacked Harney, and the idiot bought the old *Star* from him for £40.

According to the *Gazette Agricole,* the next harvest in France will be ¹/₃ BELOW THE AVERAGE which in France, according to J. B. Say,= FAMINE.[d] In Germany a middling harvest. In England there is already an outflow of gold from the Bank for corn purchases. At the same time, wild speculation in the City. Last week, bankruptcies on the STOCK EXCHANGE. Finally, in North America, as I see from the *New-York Herald,* the wildest of wild speculation in RAILWAYS, BANKS, housing, unprecedented expansion of the credit

---

[a] Indirectly addressing to Marx in this way, Kinkel tried to justify himself in the face of the accusations moved against him, see this volume, p. 149. - [b] Poor thing! - [c] *The People's Paper* - [d] J. B. Say, *Cours complet d'économie politique pratique,* Paris, 1840, p. 394.

system, etc. Is that not APPROACHING CRISIS? The revolution may come sooner than we would like. Nothing could be worse than the revolutionaries having to provide bread.

Your
K. M.

First published considerably abridged in *Der Briefwechsel zwischen F. Engels und K. Marx,* Bd. 1, Stuttgart, 1913 and in full in *MEGA*, Abt. III, Bd. 1, Berlin, 1929

Printed according to the original

Published in English in full for the first time

82

MARX TO HEINRICH BROCKHAUS

IN LEIPZIG

London, 19 August 1852
28 Dean Street, Soho

Dear Sir,

I am writing to you to ask whether you could use in your *Gegenwart* a paper on 'Recent Literature on the Economy in England, from 1830-1852'. So far as I am aware, no work of this kind has yet been published either in English or in German. It would cover 1. general works on political economy, 2. specialised writings which appeared during that period, in so far as they relate to really important controversies, for instance on population, the colonies, the banking question, protective tariffs and free trade, etc.

Should you feel inclined to fall in with this proposal, I should have to know the length prescribed for such a paper by the economics of your publication, since the subdivision of the whole would have to be arranged accordingly.

Another paper which might perhaps be pertinent just now is 'The Present State of the Parties', i.e. those that will confront each other in the next Parliament. Awaiting your reply, I am

Yours faithfully
Dr K. Marx

First published in: Marx and Engels, *Works,* First Russian Edition, Vol. XXV, Moscow, 1934

Printed according to the original

Published in English for the first time

83

ENGELS TO MARX

IN LONDON

[Manchester, 24 August 1852]

Dear Marx,

This evening I shall translate the final part of your article [193] and shall do the article on 'Germany'[a] tomorrow or Thursday. Charles[b] has gone away for a few days and I have a great deal to do in the office so that by evening my mind is often in a whirl.

Thanks for the suggestions on military history.[c] Could you sometime have a look in the British Museum to see if they have 1. The *Oesterreichische Militärische Zeitschrift* from 1848 onwards, 2. the Prussian *Militär-Wochenblatt*, the Berlin *Wehr-Zeitung*, 3. any other military periodicals, especially reviews, including French ones—from 1848 onwards? Also a set of the Augsburg *Allg. Ztg.*, particularly from 1850. I need these things very badly and, if it could somehow be arranged, would find time to work through them there, when I have got to that stage.

The excerpt from Cluss' letter[d] shows up *père*[e] Weydemeyer in an even more Westphalian light [194] than we had ever expected. Bielefeld *tout pur.*[f] It beats everything.

Johann Gottfried's[g] end is pleasing indeed. All that is left to the noble fellow is the cold comfort of knowing that he has done his duty and swollen the STOCK OF BULLION in the Bank of England. Furthermore, in fixing a new date for the liberation of the world, he had based himself, not on vague trade crises, but on hard, ineluctable fact, namely a spurious document in *The Morning Chronicle*!

The Willich-Schily farce[h] must have been a hilarious performance. *Pauvre*[i] Willich, how often during his harassment by the philistines must he have wished himself back in red Wolff's[j] company!

So Harney's star of freedom has faded away? [195]

There seems little doubt about the advent of the crisis, even if the recent bankruptcies were no more than precursors. Unfortunately the harvests in north-east Germany, Poland and Russia

---

[a] for the series *Revolution and Counter-Revolution in Germany* - [b] Roesgen - [c] See this volume, pp. 159-60. - [d] ibid., pp. 160-61. - [e] Father - [f] pure, unalloyed - [g] Gottfried Kinkel is ironically called after his wife 'Johanna'. - [h] See this volume, p. 162. - [i] Poor. - [j] Ferdinand Wolff

show signs of being passable, and in places even good. Here the recent good weather has likewise borne fruit. But France is still in the soup, and that's enough to be going on with.

The minor PANIC in the money market appears to be over, CONSOLS and RAILWAY SHARES are again rising merrily, MONEY IS EASIER, speculation is still pretty evenly distributed over CORN, COTTON, STEAM BOATS, MINING OPERATIONS, etc., etc. But cotton has already become a very risky proposition; despite what is so far a very promising crop, prices are rising continuously, merely as a result of high consumption and the possibility of a brief cotton shortage before fresh imports can arrive. Anyway I don't believe that the crisis will this time be preceded by a regular *rage* for speculation; if circumstances are favourable in other respects, a few mails bringing bad news from India, a PANIC in New York, etc., will very soon prove that many a virtuous citizen has been up to all kinds of sharp practice on the quiet. And these crucial ill-tidings from overstocked markets must surely come soon. Massive shipments continue to leave for China and India, and yet the advices are nothing out of the ordinary; indeed, Calcutta is DECIDEDLY OVER-STOCKED, and here and there NATIVE DEALERS are going bankrupt. I don't believe that PROSPERITY will continue beyond October or November—even Peter Ermen is becoming worried.

At all events, whether a revolution is immediately produced—immediately, i.e. in 6-8 months—very largely depends on the intensity of the crisis. The poor harvest in France makes it look as though something is going to happen there; but if the crisis becomes chronic and the harvest turns out after all a little better than expected, we might even have to wait until 1854. I admit that I should like another year in which to swot, having still a good deal of stuff to get through.

Australia also does some harm. First, directly through her gold and the stoppage of all her other exports, as also through the correspondingly heavier imports of all COMMODITIES and the fact that she is draining off the SURPLUS POPULATION here AT THE RATE OF 5,000 A WEEK. California and Australia are two cases which were not foreseen in the *Manifesto*[a]: creation of large new markets out of nothing. They will have to be included.   Your

                                                  F. E.

First published abridged in *Der Briefwech-sel zwischen F. Engels und K. Marx*, Bd. 1, Stuttgart, 1913 and in full in *MEGA*, Abt. III, Bd. 1, Berlin, 1929

Printed according to the original

Published in English for the first time

[a] K. Marx and F. Engels, *Manifesto of the Communist Party*.

84

MARX TO ENGELS

IN MANCHESTER

[London,] 27 August 1852
28 Dean Street, Soho

Dear Frederick,

You will find enclosed:

1. Letter from Massol to me. The man upon whom he exerts influence is Proudhon, and the book which he regards as the happy (!) fruit of that influence is the latter's most recent book on Louis Bonaparte.[a] I shall be writing about this in one of my next letters.

2. Cluss' letter, an excerpt from which you have already had.[b]

3. A highly interesting letter from Jakob Huzel about Godofredus.[196]

4. A scribble by Goegg in the *Schweizerische National-Zeitung.*

5. and 6. 'Draft of a treaty of union' between Kinkel, Willich and Goegg. A circular letter from the first-named gentlemen to their American committees and guarantors.[197]

The whole is a cry of distress from Kinkel-Willich. They wish 1. to remove the inflexible Reichenbach from the proximity of the Holy Grail[198] so that they may use the funds 'with the utmost dispatch'.

2. Now that Kinkel no longer has an army behind him he wants to join the so-called Revolutionary League with £1,000 behind him, expecting the said League to show its gratitude by electing him to its highest committee.

3. Willich, hard-pressed and in an untenable position, wants to go to America once he has, as he puts it, 'solved *one* more problem'. The problem is to feather a parasitical swindler's nest for himself in America by handing over the £1,000 to the Revolutionary League and by joining same.

More next time. *Salut!*

Your
K. M.

First published in *Der Briefwechsel zwischen F. Engels und K. Marx*, Bd. 1, Stuttgart, 1913

Printed according to the original

Published in English for the first time

---

[a] P. J. Proudhon, *La révolution sociale démontrée par le coup d'état du 2 décembre.* - [b] See this volume, pp. 160-61.

85

MARX TO PETER IMANDT

IN LONDON

[London,] 27 August 1852
28 Dean Street, Soho

Dear Imandt,

2 truly memorable memoranda![197] If that's not champion drivel[a] ... or however the saying goes.

However, in your place I would *reply to the lads*[199]:

At your guarantors' meeting you nominated a committee (provisional), consisting of Reichenbach, Löwe and Schurz, to settle matters. You were to await that committee's report. Kinkel and Willich were in no way empowered either to ask questions or to receive answers. Their threat that anyone in Europe failing to answer by 1 September (extremely short notice) would be held to be in agreement with them, is merely an attempt by them and Co., after their failure at the meeting, to *take over the administration of the funds* by stealth. You should protest against this procedure and say you will, if necessary, publish your protest with your full reasons for it.

At the same time I would write to *Reichenbach*:

Repeat the foregoing and declare that he must see to it that *not a centime* is paid out until *the committee nominated by yourselves* has submitted *its report*. Draw his attention to a few of the chief points of the document, but more especially to the following:

'In order that we may make use of the funds if need arise, we propose that the guarantors in America accord us with the utmost dispatch the right to co-opt a third colleague. In which case we should elect either Goegg or some other local member of the Revolutionary League, etc.'[200]

I.e. what the gentlemen have in mind is to get the money out of Reichenbach's hands 'with the utmost dispatch' because great 'need has now arisen' for Willich and Co. to 'make use of the funds'.

You could slip into both these letters a few jokes about the 'treaty of union'.[b]

---

[a] Marx uses the German saying: 'Wenn das nicht gut für die Wanzen ist, so weiß ich nicht, was besser ist.' - [b] See this volume, p. 166.

Return me the documents as soon as possible, so that I can send reports to Germany and America (for which the next post leaves on Tuesday[a]) 'with the utmost dispatch'.
Salut.

Your
K. M.

First published in: Marx and Engels, *Works*, Second Russian Edition, Vol. 28, Moscow, 1962

Printed according to the original

Published in English for the first time

86

MARX TO ENGELS [182]

IN MANCHESTER

London, 30 August 1852
28 Dean Street, Soho

Dear Engels,

You will have seen from the documents I sent you how Kinkel-Willich are manoeuvring.[b] They are ignoring their deposition by the guarantors in their immediate vicinity and are endeavouring to obtain individual votes by stealth, which is partly why *Schurz* left for America immediately after the 12th. (A further object is to set up kindergartens there, of the Friends of Light.[201]) What the gentlemen have in mind is at long last to play a real role in the *administration of the funds*, from which they threaten to resign if not given their way. The *point d'argent*[c] is this. The chaps have spent £200, which would hardly be ratified here. Hence the attempt to obtain from America, directly and 'with the utmost dispatch', authority to make use of the funds or to co-opt a third colleague so that they may act as a properly constituted body. They have, after their usual fashion, set about things very artfully. First, they sent the documents to America and Switzerland, *behind* the backs of the London guarantors. Then the letters were delivered to the latter on the 26th (although dated 11 and 12), with the remark that silence would be taken for consent.

---

[a] 31 August - [b] See this volume, p. 166. - [c] money matter

But since there is a possibility that the majority of the guarantors, even in America and Switzerland, might vote against these gentlemen, they have, on the quiet, called a meeting of guarantors (friends of Kinkel) for 14 or 15 September in Antwerp, in order to safeguard themselves against all eventualities by means of an alleged congress resolution.

The nature of their much-vaunted 'strong' organisations in Germany will be plain to you from the following.

As you know, Gebert has *allegedly* left for America. *Tout le monde le croit*.[a] But this is how things really stand.

At the beginning of this month Kinkel-Willich sent an emissary to Germany, i.e. *Gebert*, the tipsy journeyman tailor. In Magdeburg he assembled a so-called communist community; for 3 consecutive days discussions were held, 26-30 members taking part; in the chair was one *Hammel*; during the debates Marx and Engels were attacked with much acrimony;—in addition to various administrative and organisational questions there arose the question of how and in what manner a printing-house might be set up. They succeeded in finding an impoverished printer of books with a business in or near Magdeburg and concluded an agreement with him. He placed his office at their disposal for propaganda, the name of the firm being retained. In return he was paid 100 talers down and given a bill of exchange for 350 talers, maturing in a year's time reckoning from now.

The police knew about everything, beginning with Gebert's departure, and had him followed everywhere. They had their informant at the loutish gathering in Magdeburg. They don't intend to pull him in until he has completed his mission and compromised as many people as possible. The affair is most unfortunate for our prisoners in Cologne. If Gebert is pulled in, etc., I think the time would be ripe to denounce the fellows publicly and to issue a warning about them, namely that, from a secure hiding-place, they are playing into the hands of the German governments, especially the Prussian, for the purpose of pseudo-agitation and self-aggrandisement. I notified Cologne immediately. I can tell you only *by word of mouth* how I found out about the business.[202] Over here, too, secrecy of mails is somewhat problematic.

Willich is quite gone to the dogs. He can no longer borrow from anyone on the strength of the imminence of '*the great day*'. A few days ago his friend Schärttner told him *coram publico*[b] that '*free*'

---

[a] Everybody believes this. - [b] in public

grub and booze must now cease. He turned red as a turkey-cock and the implacable Schärttner, promptly suiting action to word, insisted on his paying cash for the pots he had just imbibed. However Willich still obtains some, if inadequate, sustenance by tumbling his old philistine of a landlady. That, too, has become notorious and no one any longer believes in the asceticism of this Sancho Panza. When, together with Johann,[a] etc., he writes, 'the time of the pen is past, the time of the sword has come',[203] this last should read IN PLAIN GERMAN: 'The time of *fencing* has come.'[b]

Techow, the revolutionary general, is only sailing for Australia in a few days, accompanied by Madame Stirner[c] and his fiancée. As you know, he has for some time been staying here *with* the Stirner woman. But then his fiancée arrives, a person of substance. Upon becoming aware of this, the Schmidt woman declares she will stand down. But now the fiancée, on learning that Techow has been living with the Schmidt woman, declares she no longer wants him and sends for her *potential* fiancé, an East Prussian farmer. Nevertheless he lives in the same house as herself, and the fiancé (the other one) an hour away from London. Poor Buridan-Techow!

A few days ago *Pyat* (Félix) called a reunion of his French adherents and laid before them a programme which is now to be published. Needless to say, 'God' had had a hand in it. One of those present objected to 'Cod' finding lodgment in a revolutionary programme. In conformity with *gouvernement direct,*[d] Pyat put it *to the vote.* 'God' got by with a majority of 7. *L'être suprême est sauvé encore une fois.*[e] God doth not forsake his own, as the saying used to go. Now it is: God's own do not forsake him. One good turn deserves another.

For a long time General Vetter was not seen in London; no one knew where he had gone. The *mystère* has now been cleared up. Vetter was travelling on an American passport, in which he figures as a painter, accompanied by his mistress, a singer named Ferenczi. He passed for an artist. She gave concerts at all places of importance and thus he travelled from Genoa and Milan to Rome, Naples and Palermo. Mazzini-Kossuth had provided him with PASSWORDS and recommendations. This gave him access to clandestine circles in Italy, while his ostensible TRADE introduced him into

---

[a] Kinkel - [b] Play on the word *Fechten,* which, besides 'fencing', can also mean 'door-to-door begging'. - [c] wife of Caspar Schmidt, whose pen-name was Max Stirner - [d] direct government - [e] The Supreme Being is saved once again.

the higher *cercles*.[a] He came back here some time ago and submitted a report to the 'European' Central Committee.[103] (*Notabene:* Darasz died and was buried last week.) In brief, to the great mortification of the 'pious' Mazzini, *L'Italie s'est tout à fait matérialisée. On n'y parle que commerce, affaires, soies, huiles et autres misères mondaines. Les bourgeois calculent d'une manière terriblement positive les pertes que la révolution de Mars les a fait subir et ne pensent qu'à se reprendre sur le présent. Quant à l'initiative insurrectionnelle ils sont heureux de la laisser aux Français, à ce peuple frivole et sensualiste. La seule chose, dont ils ont peur, c'est que les Français ne se hâtent trop.*

Tu penses bien, mon cher, quel coup de foudre pour l'archange Mazzini. Le général Vetter, nommé déjà comme commandant supérieur des forces Mazzini-Kossuthiennes leur a déclaré que les choses étant ainsi, il ne saurait mieux faire que de passer avec sa maîtresse en Amérique. Au bout du compte, le malheureux Mazzini est convenu avec Kossuth de vouloir bien laisser aux Français l'initiative insurrectionnelle.[b]

Not to the *vile multitude*,[c] however, but to Bonaparte.

I have had a letter from Paris[d] about this and other matters:

'Kiss, Kossuth's ambassador, has entered into relations here, not only with the Orleanists, but also with the Bonapartists. Kiss is acquainted with Jérôme's[e] sons. On the strength of this formal acquaintanceship, he was able to bamboozle Kossuth into concluding with the French government an alliance favourable to Hungary. The whimsical agitator fell into the trap and to this end dispatched Kiss to Paris, provided with *gulden*. Kiss enjoys himself in coffee and *other* houses, from time to time appears in the antechamber of Pierre Bonaparte, pulls the wool over the latter's eyes, writes splendid reports to Kossuth, and Hungary's liberation is no longer in doubt. These revolutionaries par excellence send agents to conclude a life and death alliance with a "*tyrant*"!'

---

[a] circles - [b] Italy has grown wholly materialist. The sole topics of conversation there are commerce, business, silks, oils and other wretchedly mundane things. The bourgeois reckon in the most dreadfully positive way the losses they incurred as a result of the March revolution and think only how they may recoup them from the present. As for insurrectionary initiative, they are glad to leave this to that frivolous and sensual people, the French. Their only fear is that the French might be in too much hurry.

You can imagine, my friend, what a thunderbolt this was to the Archangel Mazzini. General Vetter, already appointed commander-in-chief of the Mazzini-Kossuthian forces, told them that in the circumstances he could do no better than betake himself to America with his mistress. In the final count, the unfortunate Mazzini agreed with Kossuth that insurrectionary initiative was best left to the French. - [c] These words were used by Thiers in his speech in the Legislative Assembly on 24 May 1850, *Le Moniteur universel*, No. 145, 25 May 1850. - [d] from Zerffi - [e] Jérôme Bonaparte

Mais ce n'est pas tout.[a]

I have it from a reliable source that that old fool Lelewel and Thaddäus Gorzowski have been here on behalf of the Polish 'Centralisation'.[204] They submitted to Kossuth-Mazzini an insurrectionary plan of which Bonaparte's co-operation is the PIVOT. These old jackasses of conspirators are always putting their foot in it. They had, and continue to have, as agent here a certain Count Lanckorónski or some such. This lad (lives at 7 Harington Street, Hampstead Road) is a *Russian* agent, and *their* insurrectionary plan was done the honour of being amended beforehand in Petersburg.[205]

Your
K. M.

First published abridged in *Der Briefwechsel zwischen F. Engels und K. Marx*, Bd. 1, Stuttgart, 1913 and in full in *MEGA*, Abt. III, Bd. 1, Berlin, 1929

Printed according to the original

Published in English for the first time

87

MARX TO ADOLF CLUSS[206]

IN WASHINGTON

[London, 30 August 1852]

... This is how the gentlemen[b] have manoeuvring. They are ignoring their deposition by the guarantors in their immediate vicinity who have seen through them, and are endeavouring to obtain individual votes by stealth, which is partly why Schurz left for America. (A further object is to set up kindergartens there, after the style of the Friends of Light.[201]) They, who up till now have been vainly angling for unrestricted access to the administra-

---

a But that's not all. - b Kinkel and Willich

tion of the funds—which Reichenbach is withholding from them—are behaving as though they propose to withdraw from it *now*, unless allowed to do as they please. What they really want is *to get at it.*

The *point d'argent*[a] is as follows: The chaps have spent £200, which would hardly be ratified here. By this coup, by the special powers they have received from the other guarantors, they hope to get the money out of Reichenbach's clutches and, above all, *to make good the £200.* This was their ploy: First, they send the documents of 11 and 12 August to America and Switzerland, *behind the backs of the London guarantors.* Then the letter was delivered to the latter on the 26th with the instruction that, if they failed to answer by 1 September, their silence would be taken for consent.

What will Weitling say on learning that the money will now be indirectly finding its way to the worthy Heinzen? The gentlemen were likewise careful not to mention that, despite Kinkel's recommendation and Goegg's pleading, the Revolutionary League's attempt to establish itself over here was a lamentable failure. Not a man allowed himself to be moved by them. What they now call the Revolutionary League in London is Ruge's clearly circumscribed following, seven in number, which formerly went by the name of Agitation Club. The said league comprises the following gentlemen: Ruge, Goegg, Franck (Vienna), Ronge, Tausenau, Sigel (the other one)[b]; Oswald, the tobacconist, and the arrogant Tralle have joined in place of Gen. Sigel and Fickler.

Tralle was denounced by Dulon in person because, at a time of peril, he ratted on his little Bremen paper.[c]

Willich is completely and utterly gone to the dogs. Schärttner has refused him his free meals and publicly shown him the door. He now proposes to go to America, where he hopes to be given a kind welcome from the Revolutionary League in return for his intention to bring them the £1,000 by way of a dowry. Schärttner had been solicitously accepted into the central authority of Willich's league. Willich's position in London has become completely untenable; his parasitical existence is over once and for all. It would do no harm were these plans and grand designs of the patriots made public.

In the Kinkel-Willich document you will find the beautiful

---

[a] money matter - [b] Albert Sigel - [c] *Bremer Tages-Chronik*

axiom: 'The time of the pen is past, the time of the sword has come'[203]; this should read IN PLAIN GERMAN, and in a higher sense, the time of 'fencing' has come.[a]

In a few days' time the revolutionary general Techow is leaving for Australia with Madame Schmidt (Stirner's wife). He has been living with her in this country for some time. But along comes his fiancée, on learning which Mrs Schmidt declares she will stand down. Then his affianced acquires another 'fiancé' and says she doesn't want Techow any more because of his having lived with the Schmidt woman, and that she is going to marry the other man. Nevertheless he lives in the same house as herself, and the fiancé (the other one) a few miles outside London. Poor Buridan-Techow!

Madame Pulszky was terribly put out, one of the American papers in which you mentioned her having arrived over here.

A propos. Szemere has sent his manuscript[b] to Webb; but first he got a written agreement that it must be published as it stands. Let me solve the Szemere mystère for you. The chap is very tight-fisted, which is why he would rather get Webb to print his thing than do so himself, as he could perfectly well do...[207]

... A few days ago Félix Pyat called a reunion of his French adherents and laid before them a programme which is now to be published. 'God' had had a hand in it. One of those present objected to God finding lodgment in a revolutionary programme. In conformity with the gouvernement direct principle, Pyat put it to the vote. 'God' got by with a majority of 7. L'être suprême est sauvé encore une fois.[c] God doth not forsake his own, the saying used to go. Now it is: God's own do not forsake him. One good turn deserves another...[208]

First published in: Marx and Engels, Works, Second Russian Edition, Vol. 50, Moscow, 1980

Printed according to Cluss' letter to Weydemeyer of 21 September 1852

Published in English for the first time

---

[a] Play on the word, Fechten, which, besides 'fencing', can also mean 'door-to-door begging'. - [b] B. Szemere, Graf Ludwig Batthyány, Arthur Görgei, Ludwig Kossuth... - [c] The Supreme Being is saved once again.

88

MARX TO ENGELS

IN MANCHESTER

[London,] 2 September 1852
28 Dean Street, Soho

Dear Engels,

From the enclosed pissabed letter from the great Weydemeyer, you will see how matters stand. With it the brute sent 10 copies.[a] I have not yet had an answer from Mr F. Streit,[b] *ce qui est de très mauvais augure.*[c] There is now some, if little, prospect of its being published in English by a London bookseller. For the time being I am to give him the first chapter by way of a sample. I have therefore had it translated by Pieper. The translation is swarming with mistakes and omissions. However, its correction will not be such an imposition on you as the boring task of translation.[d] I would like you to write an English preface of not more than 10 lines, saying that this paper originally appeared in the form of newspaper articles between the end of December and the beginning of February, that it was published as a pamphlet in New York on 1 May, that a 2nd edition is now to appear in Germany,[209] and that it was the first anti-Bonaparte paper to appear; the few details no longer of relevance may be accounted for by its date of origin.

E. Jones is a thoroughly egotistical rascal. For 2 months he has been dangling before me the promise that he will do a translation (for his journal[e]). For my part, I have done him nothing but favours. In spite of my own money bothers I have spent days with him traipsing all over the place in connection with his paper's financial affairs. All the foreign intelligence *exclusive* to his *pauvre*[f] little paper came from me. Whenever he got into a scrape with his committees,[192] opponents, etc., he came running to me, and my advice invariably got him out of it. Finally, when his journal became altogether too deplorable, I gave him my EDITORIAL SUPPORT for several weeks, and indeed the wretched thing gained some 100 additional subscribers in London.

---

[a] K. Marx, *The Eighteenth Brumaire of Louis Bonaparte.* - [b] See this volume, p. 161. - [c] which is a very bad sign - [d] See this volume, p. 179. - [e] *The People's Paper* - [f] wretched

He, for his part, does not even observe the common civilities. Help him concoct his journal today and he'll forget to send you a copy tomorrow, but this *forgetfulness* recurs every seven days since his paper does not come out twice a week.

I have told him it's all very well to be an egotist but he should be so in a civilised way and not so inanely. Since, however, the paper is the only Chartist organ, I shall not break with him but LET HIM SHIFT FOR HIMSELF for a few weeks.

Your
K. M.

First published abridged in *Der Briefwech-sel zwischen F. Engels und K. Marx*, Bd. 1, Stuttgart, 1913 and in full in *MEGA*, Abt. III, Bd. 1, Berlin, 1929

Printed according to the original

Published in English for the first time

89

MARX TO ADOLF CLUSS[210]

IN WASHINGTON

[London, 3 September 1852]

It has been put about here that *Gebert*, a bottle-loving journeyman tailor and a myrmidon of Willich's, had left for America. That is not so. At the beginning of August Kinkel and Willich sent him to Germany as their emissary.

As these people harp on 'organisations' in their circular—the last one to the guarantors—and on the whole have no connections in Germany, the remnants of the Communist League there who for one reason or another have no contact with Cologne were to provide a semblance of, and pretext for, such 'organisations'.[a] And then the gentlemen also had to account for the sum of £200. Hence a certain sum of money had to be spent in one quarter or another in such a manner that it could decently be described as 'revolutionary expenditure'. They hoped the remainder of what had been spent could then be more easily passed off. Finally, Marx, Engels and co. were to be destroyed (sic) in the eyes of working men in Germany. Kinkel thought that, having begged

---

[a] See this volume, p. 169.

and lied his way into the esteem of the remnants of the Communist League, he could palm off the latter on to his bourgeois guarantors as a *bourgeois-democratic* connection. Willich, the representative imposed upon the German workers by himself and Kinkel, at last saw a chance of creating for himself a real following of workers in Germany.

To continue. In Magdeburg, Gebert assembled a so-called communist community; for 3 consecutive days discussions were held, 26-30 members taking part; in the chair was one Hammel (*nomen omen*[a]); during the debates Marx and Engels were attacked with much acrimony, the main task laid down being to destroy them, their influence and their 'doctrines'. (Brother Hammel may not find this last so easy.) In addition to various administrative and organisational questions, there arose the question of how and in what manner a printing-house might be set up. They succeeded in finding an impoverished printer of books with a business in or near Magdeburg and concluded an agreement with him. He placed his office at their disposal for propaganda, the name of the firm being retained as it was. In return he was paid 100 talers down and given a bill of exchange for 350 talers, which he is to receive after *one* year.

Thus the revolutionary funds are to serve the purpose of propaganda for that creature, Kinkel-Willich, and of promoting intrigue to split up the 'organisations' in Germany.

But the best is still to come. The Prussian police *were informed of everything* from the moment the innocuous Gebert left London, whereas everyone here imagined he had slipped off to America. The government had its informant at the loutish assembly at Magdeburg; he took down the entire debate in shorthand. Gebert, who has now gone to Berlin, had a Prussian policeman in train. He is not allowed out of sight for an instant. The government intend to allow him to fulfil his mission, by which time he will have compromised dozens of others besides himself.

I have this intelligence—Willich, too, has been bragging about his 'agents' in Germany—from a Prussian police headquarters in which I have planted a *séid*.[b] [202]

Qu'en dis-tu?[c] So these knaves are providing the Prussian government with an opportunity to introduce fresh complications into the Cologne trial, etc.

---

[a] The name is significant (Hammel means sheep). - [b] a devoted follower - [c] What do you say to that?

And to what purpose? To cover up their shady accounts, to disguise the pointlessness of all their revolutionary committee doings hitherto, to excite their feeble spirits against their foes, etc., etc. Just now the thing *must still be kept secret*. But as soon as you see that Gebert has been pulled in, or that arrests of 'communists' have begun, let fire without waiting to hear anything more....

First published in: Marx and Engels, *Works*, Second Russian Edition, Vol. 28, Moscow, 1962

Printed according to Cluss' letter to Weydemeyer of 26 March 1853

Published in English for the first time

90

MARX TO ADOLF CLUSS[211]

IN WASHINGTON

[London, after 5 September 1852]

... Enclosed copy of a manuscript from Paris by Häfner[212] (sometime editor of the *Constitution*, the only tolerable newspaper in Vienna). This man once allowed himself to be misused to bluster against me in the *Hamburger Nachrichten* in the interests of Kinkel. The manuscript was not addressed to me but to an acquaintance of mine in Paris,[a] through whose 'indiscretion' it came into my hands, probably not wholly without the author's prior knowledge. Hence, you can make use of the document if opportunity arises, but only in such a way as to omit everything that might betray its *origin*, or rather directly indicate it. Though he may have a hump both fore and aft, little Häfner writes and thinks better and has a great deal more to him than many a straight-limbed revolutionary philistine...

First published in: Marx and Engels, *Works*, Second Russian Edition, Vol. 28, Moscow, 1962

Printed according to Cluss' letter to Weydemeyer of 28 September 1852

Published in English for the first time

---

[a] Zerffi

91

ENGELS TO MARX

IN LONDON

[Manchester,] Tuesday, 7 September 1852

Dear Marx,

I am having a great deal of trouble over Pieper's translation.[a] The beginning is particularly difficult to translate and *l'aimable candidat*[b] Pieper seems to have given rein to charming lightheartedness. If possible, I'll let you have it on Thursday.

Pindar has been involved in a romance up here. I don't know whether I have already told you this, but recently I went to his house and found his mother there, A VERY RESPECTABLE OLD ENGLISH LADY, with a young lady of very un-English appearance whom I took to be a Russian. Last Friday I asked Pindar whether this *krasnàvitza* (*beauté*) was his wife or his sister— *ni l'un ni l'autre*,[c] was the reply. On Monday his mother comes to my house: her dear Edward had gone, vanished. I wasn't in but, hearing about it, at once went to see her. *Je trouve la digne mère en pleurs*[d] and am told the following: In Petersburg Pindar fell madly in love with a Swede (or Finn) with whom, it seems, he ran away after his father's death. He married her in England—'her' being the afore-said *krasnàvitza*. In London he makes the acquaintance of a Frenchwoman—an erstwhile Parisian whore and mistress of an English Grub Street dramatist by the name of Taylor, says his mother who, of course, makes her out to be a thoroughly bad lot. He gives her lessons, and the quiet candidate becomes amorously entangled with her. His wife discovers the affair (in the meantime his mother had come over from Kronstadt with some money and had made her peace with the Swedish woman) and, to wean Pindar from the Frenchwoman, the whole family moves to Liverpool. But again he sends for the lady of joy, and the Swede, evidently a woman of great patience and tenacity, finds out once more. Fresh migration to Manchester, where the mother finally establishes herself and even buys 2 houses (she is living on what remains, after her

---

a See this volume, p. 175. - b the amiable candidate - c neither the one nor the other - d I find the worthy mother in tears

fritterings, of the former Pindar fortune, made in the TIMBER AND BISCUIT TRADE). Here again, however, Pindar sends for his French-woman—she has undoubtedly visited him three times, as I know from the fact that on each occasion he regularly touched me for a loan and as regularly paid me back afterwards. But last Saturday he brought things to a head by running away with her—as his mother maintains, to Australia, but either New York or simply Paris would seem more probable to me. He took from the FUNDS £190 belonging to him and promptly lost £20 in the omnibus (the waiter in the hotel where the Frenchwoman was staying thinks that she relieved him of it). The fellow had money enough, his mother kept him in everything and he had £100 pocket money.

Yesterday the Swede followed him to Liverpool. I am curious to know what comes of it.

For the rest of his life the poor devil will be plagued by this foolish early marriage to his Swedish ideal— *voilà ce qui a toujours pesé sur lui.*[a] With a little more experience and *savoir-faire,* he could have kept his Frenchwoman very nicely here on his £100, but how is a fellow to gain experience if at 21 he falls madly in love with a Swede, runs away with her and enters into respectable wedlock! If the silly boy had only told me about the affair, it would have been easy enough to straighten things out. But to go and let himself in for a *plus ou moins*[b] enduring, at any rate serious, affair with a Frenchwoman *à l'étranger,*[c] and to run away with her— *quelle bêtise! Elle lui en fera voir, ma foi,*[d] especially if he has really gone to Australia. Besides, his mater is a terribly kind and soft-hearted person and God knows what he couldn't have got her to agree to. But just as Kinkel sees betrothal,[e] so Pindar would seem to see elopement, as the essence of every love affair.

Your news about Vetter, etc. and the London people is splendid. I am returning Massol's letter[f] and also Weydemeyer's— Cluss' I shall keep here *jusqu'à nouvel ordre.*[g] What about the articles for Dana? Pindar's absence gives me more time; I am now doing Russian more *con amore sine ira el studio,*[h] and can already manage a little. At the moment things military are AT A DISCOUNT. Office work very lively.

---

[a] that's what has always weighed him down - [b] more or less - [c] abroad - [d] how stupid! Upon my soul, she'll lead him a pretty dance - [e] Allusion to the facts from Kinkel's biography made fun of in the pamphlet *The Great Men of the Exile.* - [f] See this volume, pp. 166 and 182. - [g] until further order - [h] with love, without undue zeal (the latter part from Tacitus, *Annals,* I, i)

As soon as I possibly can, i.e. in a few days' time, I shall send you £2 which is all I can screw out for the moment.

Your
F. E.

First published abridged in *Der Briefwechsel zwischen F. Engels und K. Marx*, Bd. 1, Stuttgart, 1913 and in full in *MEGA*, Abt. III, Bd. 1, Berlin, 1929

Printed according to the original

Published in English for the first time

92

MARX TO ENGELS[213]

IN MANCHESTER

London, 8 September 1852
28 Dean Street, Soho

Dear Engels,

Your letter today found us in a state of great agitation.

My wife is ill. Little Jenny is ill. Lenchen[a] has some sort of nervous fever. I could not and cannot call the doctor because I have no money to buy medicine. For the past 8-10 days I have been feeding the FAMILY solely on bread and potatoes, but whether I shall be able to get hold of any today is doubtful. Such a diet is not, of course, beneficial in present climatic conditions. I have not written any articles for Dana because I didn't have a PENNY to go and read the papers. By the way, as soon as you send No. XIX, I shall write and give you my views on No. XX, i.e. a résumé of the present dirty business.[214]

When I was with you[146] and you told me you would be able to find me a somewhat larger sum by the end of August, I wrote and told my wife that to reassure her. Your letter of 3-4 weeks ago[b] hinted that there were no great prospects, but still left some. Accordingly I had put off all creditors—who, as you know, are

---

[a] Helene Demuth. - [b] See this volume, pp. 147-48.

always paid by dribs and drabs—until the beginning of September. Now the storm is breaking out on all sides.

I have tried everything, but in vain. First I am cheated out of £15 by that cur Weydemeyer. I write to Streit[a] in Germany (because he had written to Dronke in Switzerland). The brute does not deign to answer. I approach Brockhaus[b] and offer him an article of entirely innocuous contents for the *Gegenwart.* He sends a very polite letter of refusal. Finally I spend the whole of last week trailing round with an Englishman[c] who said he would find someone to discount the bills on Dana for me. *Pour le roi de Prusse.*[d]

The best and most desirable thing that could happen would be for the LANDLADY to throw me out. Then I would at least be quit of the sum of £22. But such complaisance is hardly to be expected of her. On top of that, debts are still outstanding to the baker, the milkman, the tea chap, the GREENGROCER, the butcher. How am I to get out of this infernal mess? Finally, and this was most hateful of all, but essential if we were not to kick the bucket, I have, over the last 8-10 days, touched some German types for a few shillings and pence.

You'll have seen from my letters that, as usual, when I myself am in the shit and not just hearing about it at second-hand, I plough through it with complete indifference. Yet, *que faire?*[e] My house is a hospital and so worrying is the crisis that it compels me to devote all my attention to it. *Que faire?*

Meanwhile Mr Goegg is again on a pleasure trip to America, STEAMER FIRST CLASS. Mr Proudhon has pocketed a few 100,000 fr. for his anti-Napoleon[f] and Papa Massol has been generous enough to leave the *miner, fouiller,*[g] etc., to me.[215] *Je le remercie bien.*[h]

Your

K. M.

First published in *Der Briefwechsel zwischen F. Engels und K. Marx,* Bd. 1, Stuttgart, 1913

Printed according to the original

---

[a] See this volume, p. 161. - [b] ibid., p. 163. - [c] Poenisch - [d] Literally: for the king of Prussia, i.e. for nothing - [e] what's to be done? - [f] P. J. Proudhon, *La révolution sociale démontrée par le coup d'état du 2 décembre.* - [g] digging and rummaging - [h] I thank him very much.

93

MARX TO ENGELS

IN MANCHESTER

[London,] 9 September 1852
28 Dean Street, Soho

Dear Engels,

Received, the £4 Sperlinge.[a]

I have again written to my mater and think that at least it may do some good.[191]

Besides, I have today made another attempt, which I trust will at long last succeed, to obtain the money on Dana, for I am very hard-pressed, *et je n'ai pas à perdre du temps.*[b]

The doctor has just been and prescribed something for the whole FAMILY *excepté moi.*[c] My wife is getting better; little Laura's condition is worst of all.

You have no idea what a silly ass Pieper is!

Every day he asks me whether you have sent the thing[d] back yet and *what* you had to say about his outstanding piece of work. Of course I couldn't tell him and now the clown imagines that out of envy I am withholding the praises you showered on him.

Today, when I went out to call the doctor, I ran into the humbug. 'Has Engels written and sent the translation?' Not yet, I told him, to which Pieper replied: 'But he will, *for I myself* have written to him.' Should you reply you might point out to him that there is no call for him to have any say in *my* transactions with *you.*

Enclosed a memorandum from Paris[212]; it fell into the hands of a friend of mine[e] there who sent me a copy of it, and I have made a further copy for the Manchester archives.[216]

Your

K. M.

First published considerably abridged in *Der Briefwechsel zwischen F. Engels und K. Marx*, Bd. 1, Stuttgart, 1913 and in full in *MEGA*, Abt. III, Bd. 1, Berlin, 1929

Printed according to the original

Published in English for the first time

---

[a] Marx wrote *Sperlinge* (sparrows) instead of 'sterling'. - [b] and I must lose no time - [c] except me - [d] Translation into English of the first chapter of Marx's work *The Eighteenth Brumaire of Louis Bonaparte* made by Pieper (see this volume, p. 175). - [e] Zerffi

94

ENGELS TO MARX

IN LONDON

[Manchester,] 14 September 1852

Dear Marx,

Pieper has written asking me to send him the corrected translation[a] by *return of post. Cela me convenait bien.*[b] I had a pain in the abdomen and was unfit for any kind of work. Tell him that if he wants answers to his letters, the least he can do is give his address; Pieper, Esq., is not as well known as all that in London, even if he has become a clerk at 25/-a week. Apart from that, there's no reason why he shouldn't go on with the translation, but he must take a little more trouble or, if he can't, at least leave blank spaces to be filled in by me, when he strikes a difficult patch, which is after all better than writing nonsense out of sheer carelessness. His pretext for writing to me, by the way, was simply that he didn't know whether I thought him capable of doing the thing at all. He shall have a detailed list of his principal mistakes, with comments.[c]

I might be able to get the thing done tonight and tomorrow evening, as I am now feeling better.

For the rest, his letter faithfully echoed everything he had heard at your house and which I, of course, already knew.

I take it that Pindar has been to see you? He wrote to me from London and is on his way to Paris. I shall write to him this evening. I have also made the acquaintance of his Swede or Finn; *c'est une oie, petite bourgeoise au plus haut degré, qui paraît s'être bientôt consolée du départ de son époux.*[d] He was right to give the creature the slip. I shall visit his mater once or twice more for appearances' sake and then drop the whole thing; *c'est embêtant*[e] to listen to the cold-blooded little witch maligning her husband.

I hope the discounting affair turned out all right and that things at home are going a little better. I am now thinking up a new way of saving a few pounds; if it succeeds, I shall probably be able to

---

[a] K. Marx, *The Eighteenth Brumaire of Louis Bonaparte* (see this volume, pp. 175 and 183). - [b] That suited me very well. - [c] See this volume, pp. 190-93. - [d] she's a goose, petty bourgeois to the marrow, who seems quickly to have consoled herself for her husband's departure - [e] it's a bore

send you something more by the beginning of next month—i.e. in about 14-16 days. It depends partly on whether my brother-in-law[a] comes here and if so, when.

Enclosed two things from Weydemeyer; you might let me have the *Lithogr*.[217] back some time for the archives. Häfner's memorandum[212] is interesting, though obviously written for our consumption—*c'est une pétition*.

Best wishes to your wife and children.

Your

F. E.

You'll be glad to see that Heinzen is on his last legs.[218]

First published abridged in *Der Briefwechsel zwischen F. Engels und K. Marx*, Bd. 1, Stuttgart, 1913 and in full in *MEGA*, Abt. III, Bd. 1, Berlin, 1929

Printed according to the original

Published in English for the first time

95

MARX TO ENGELS

IN MANCHESTER

London, 18 September 1852
28 Dean Street, Soho

Dear Engels,

If you delay sending back the translation[b] for another few days, the possibility of getting it taken will be absolutely nil. Interest in Bonaparte, having again attained a peak,[219] is now giving way to fresh topics, as always happens in London.

The discounting affair has come to naught after a week spent on a wild goose-chase with a rascal from the CITY *nommé*[c] Poenisch. I therefore wrote to Dana yesterday.[191] At the same time I told him that there were only two more articles, 19 and 20, to come ON GERMANY. As soon as you send me 19[d] I shall write to you

---

[a] Emil Blank - [b] of the first chapter of Marx's work *The Eighteenth Brumaire of Louis Bonaparte* (see this volume, pp. 175 and 183) - [c] named - [d] F. Engels, *Revolution and Counter-Revolution in Germany*, XIX.

again, giving my views on 20, the concluding one. Within the next few days the Customs Union business, too, will have been decided, and without it 20 cannot be finished.[220]

Physically, my wife is lower than ever before, i.e. sheer debility. On doctor's orders she has been taking a spoonful of brandy every hour for the past 3 days. There is however some improvement, inasmuch as she has at least got up today. She has been in bed for a week. Little Laura is convalescent, the others ALL RIGHT. I shall not be able to write at length before next week. This week has been wasted on abortive business errands and the most nauseous wrangling *cum creditoribus*.[a]

Your
K. M.

With next week's letter I shall also return the documents.[b] Let me have Massol's letter back.

First published in *Der Briefwechsel zwischen F. Engels und K. Marx*, Bd. 1, Stuttgart, 1913

Printed according to the original
Published in English for the first time

96

ENGELS TO MARX

IN LONDON

[Manchester,] 20 September 1852

Dear Marx,

I didn't know that you were in such a hurry for the translation[c] and let the thing slide for a bit because, as I said,[d] I wasn't well, and also because I wanted to tease Pieper a little for having been so pressing. However, I immediately set to work yesterday and would have finished had not the aging Mr Schily[e] walked into my room at about 2 in the afternoon. He wishes to open a factory in

---

[a] with creditors - [b] See this volume, p. 185. - [c] into English of the first chapter of K. Marx's work *The Eighteenth Brumaire of Louis Bonaparte* - [d] See this volume, p. 184. - [e] Victor

Liverpool for the production of a purported patent soda which would yield 400-500 per cent clear profit and might, depending on circumstances, produce $4\,{}^1/_2$ million talers a year. He wanted to discuss this fantastic plan with me—and was all ready to fall for the swindle with a few thousand talers which his brother says he will procure for him. Mr Heise is in it too, but is investing nothing but his talents. After the dispassionate advice he has received here, the noble Schily will probably keep his hands off the thing and will take advantage of a possible opening as Liverpool human cargo agent for a fleecer of emigrants in Le Havre. Mr Heise once had a natty little plan whereby the funds of the National Loan were to be used for this soda swindle; the work was to be carried on democratically and the millions thus raked in[a] devoted to the liberation of Europe. It is a pity that nothing came of this scheme, which would seem to have foundered largely on the impossibility of mustering thirty refugees able to *hold their tongues.*

I was, of course, under an obligation to get the noble Schily tipsy—*il n'y avait pas moyen à y échapper.*[b] It's some time since I encountered such an innocuous beast. The stupidity and ignorance and thoughtlessness of such a man of principle has to be seen to be believed. When he had become a little tipsy—I was engaged in an argument with a third German, Charles'[c] cousin—he shouted incessantly, although very good-humouredly: Don't you believe that; Engels believes in nothing, there's nothing at all Engels believes in, none of the fellows of the *N. Rh. Z.* believe in anything, no one can fathom them. There's nothing at all Engels believes in! I, of course, replied that the fellows of the *N. Rh. Z.* did not find it in the least difficult to fathom the likes of him. This morning the worthy fellow, after a sober handshake, set course for Liverpool again, and by tonight the translation will be finished. But I get dreadfully held up over the thing since I have to make a new translation of all the more difficult bits without exception— Pieper makes shift with a literal translation in every case, the result being utter nonsense. There are, by the way, some bits which are almost impossible to translate.

However, I will do my utmost to have finished by tonight so that you can have it tomorrow.

Your

F. E.

---

[a] An ironical reminiscence of Schiller's words 'Seid umschlungen, Millionen!' in his ode 'An die Freude' ('To Joy'). - [b] there was no escaping it - [c] Roesgen

If at all possible, I shall send you another pound within the next few days.

First published considerably abridged in *Der Briefwechsel zwischen F. Engels und K. Marx*, Bd. 1, Stuttgart, 1913 and in full in *MEGA*, Abt. III, Bd. 1, Berlin, 1929

Printed according to the original

Published in English for the first time

97

ENGELS TO MARX[221]

IN LONDON

[Manchester, 23 September 1852]

Dear Marx,

The day before yesterday I sent you the translation[a] and a Post Office order for a pound. A few more pounds will follow at the beginning of October—i.e. in 9-10 days. I should like to send you more at a time because, then even though the total amount is the same in the end, it has the advantage of enabling you to plan your expenditure more methodically, but my own pecuniary circumstances are in such a muddle just now that I never know exactly how much I shall need for the month, and hence pounds only become available singly, so it seems best to send them to you straight away. Next month I shall put things on a business-like footing, after which I shall soon be able to make some rough estimates.

From the enclosed memorandum you will see that Pieper has made a number of fairly bad howlers—I haven't, of course, enumerated his transgressions against grammar and Donatus,[b] *cela n'aurait jamais fini.*[c] You may give it to him if you think it would do any good; otherwise, if it might lead him to abandon the translation, you had better keep it. Should he grumble over this or that correction, you can always use it as an opportunity to point out his imperfections.

Individual bits are, by the way, almost untranslatable.

---

[a] into English of the first chapter of K. Marx's work *The Eighteenth Brumaire of Louis Bonaparte* - [b] Fourth-century Roman grammarian. - [c] there'd have been no end to it

Incidentally, it might also be advisable for the bookseller to see the *last* chapter in particular; he would then be vastly more impressed; I suggest that Pieper might translate it and you send it straight on to me; having already looked at it with this in mind, I am not wholly unprepared and progress would therefore be rapid. Even if it can't be published now, the translation must be completed; the chap[a] will soon become Emperor,[222] and that would provide another splendid opportunity for adding a postscript.

I am going straight home to finish the article for the *Tribune*[b] so that it catches the 2nd post and you can send it off by tomorrow's STEAMER. What prospect is there of a new English article for Dana?

I trust the brandy has set your wife on her feet again—warm regards to her and your children, also Dronke and Lupus.

Your
F. E.

Massol's letter with the article for Dana by the 2nd post—I haven't got it here.

Did you see the statistics from Horner, the FACTORY INSPECTOR, on the growth of the cotton industry in yesterday's *Times* and day-before-yesterday's *Daily News?*[c]

Oct. 1850-Oct. 1851—
2,300 horsepower in newly built factories
1,400 horsepower in extensions to existing factories
3,700 horsepower increase in the Manchester district

and the cotton industry alone.[223] The following particulars reveal that during that period there were factories still under construction which would require some 4,000 horsepower and which will now have been completed. Since that time, work has undoubtedly begun on factories of 3,000-4,000 horsepower, more than half of which might be completed by the end of the year; if we assume that the increase between Jan. 1848 and Oct. 1850, i.e. $2^3/_4$ years, is no more than 4,000 horsepower, the steam-power of the Lancashire cotton industry will have risen between 1848 and the end of 1852 by 3,700+4,000+1,500+4,000=13,200 horsepower.

---

a Louis Bonaparte - b F. Engels, *Revolution and Counter-Revolution in Germany*, XIX. - c 'Cotton Manufactures', *The Times*, No. 21227, 22 September 1852; 'Progress of Cotton Manufactures', *The Daily News*, No. 1975, 20 September 1852.

In 1842 the total steam-power of the cotton industry in Lancashire amounted to 30,000 and in 1845 (end) to 40,000 horsepower; in 1846/47 there was little installed, hence almost 55,000 horsepower, nearly twice that of 1842, will now be in use.

On top of that there is hydraulic power—about 10,000 horsepower (1842) which has barely increased, hydraulic energy having been fairly well exploited for some time past. From this it may be seen where prosperity's additional capital has gone. For that matter the crisis cannot be very far off, although *here* excess over-speculation is almost entirely confined to *omnibuses*.

Memorandum on the Translation of the 1st Chapter

Ad generalia[a]:

1. Pieper is evidently more used to writing English spontaneously than to translating. Hence, if he wants for a word, he should guard all the more against having recourse to that worst of all known aids, the *dictionary*, which, in 99 cases out of 100, will regularly provide him with the most inappropriate word and invariably gives rise to a disastrous jumbling of synonyms, examples of which follow.

2. Pieper should study elementary English grammar, in which he makes a number of mistakes—especially as regards the use of the article. There are also spelling mistakes.

3. Above all Pieper must guard against falling into the Cockney's petty-bourgeois floridity of style, of which there are some irritating examples.

4. Pieper uses too many words of French derivation, which are, it is true, sometimes convenient because their vaguer, more abstract meaning is often of help in a quandary. But this emasculates the choicest turns of speech and often renders them completely incomprehensible to an Englishman. In almost every case, where vivid, sensuous images occur in the original, there is a no less sensuous, vivid expression of *Saxon* derivation, which at once makes the thing plain to an Englishman.

5. Where there are difficult bits, it would be better to leave blanks to be filled in, rather than—on the plea of literal translation—put in things which Pieper himself knows full well to be sheer nonsense.

6. The main criticism of the translation, and which sums up 1-5, is gross carelessness. There are passages enough to prove that, if

---

[a] In general

he really tries, Pieper is reasonably capable, but such superficiality, in the first place, makes more work for *himself* and secondly twice as much for me. Some passages are quite admirable, or could be so, had he tried a little harder.

Ad specialia[a]:

schuldenbeladene Lieutnants[b]: here the word lieutenant can only mean 'representative'. In English and French a lieutenant is not, as in German, primarily a figure of fun;

unmittelbar gegebne, vorhandene und überlieferte Umstände[c]: CIRCUMSTANCES IMMEDIATELY GIVEN AND DELIVERED. Pieper himself was very well aware that this translation made nonsense. 'DELIVERED' can here only mean 'delivered of a child';

sich und die Dinge umzuwälzen: THE REVOLUTION *OF THEIR OWN PERSONS.* This revolution can be nothing other than a somersault;

A NEW LANGUAGE (*eine neue Sprache*) means a *newly invented* language. At most, A LANGUAGE NEW *TO THEM.*

MIDDLE CLASS SOCIETY for *bürgerliche Gesellschaft* is not strictly grammatical or logically correct; it is as if one were to translate *feudale Gesellschaft* as NOBILITY SOCIETY. An educated Englishman would not say this. One would have to say BOURGEOIS SOCIETY or, depending on circumstances, COMMERCIAL AND INDUSTRIAL SOCIETY, to which one might append the following note: *By Bourgeois Society, we understand that phase of social development in which the Bourgeoisie, the Middle Class, the class of industrial and commercial Capitalists, is, socially and politically, the ruling class; which is now the case more or less in all the civilized countries of Europe and America. By the expressions: Bourgeois society, and: industrial and commercial society, we therefore propose to designate the same stage of social development; the first expression referring, however, more to the fact of the middle class being the ruling class, in opposition either to the class whose rule it superseded (the feudal nobility), or to those classes which it succeeds in keeping under its social and political dominion (the proletariat or industrial working class, the rural population, etc., etc.)—while the designation of commercial and industrial society more particularly bears upon the mode of production and distribution characteristic of this phase of social history.*

To ARRIVE AT ITS OWN CONTENTS (*bei ihrem eignen Inhalt anzukommen*) can only mean: to arrive AT THE CONTENTS OF ITS OWN STOMACH.

---

[a] In particular - [b] debt-ridden lieutenants (this expression was omitted in the 1869 second German edition of *The Eighteenth Brumaire of Louis Bonaparte*) - [c] circumstances immediately given, existing and handed down

OLD SOCIETY (*alte Gesellschaft*) won't do in English and at most means feudal rather than bourgeois society. Owen's writings have been forgotten; and whenever he mentions OLD SOCIETY, it is always accompanied by a plan and elevation (if possible in colour) of the NEW SOCIETY, SO THAT THERE CAN BE NO MISTAKE; WHICH IS NOT TO BE EXPECTED NOW-A-DAYS.

SET IN FIERY DIAMONDS (*in Feuerbrillanten gefasst*[a]) is nonsensical in English, since in English usage it is diamonds *themselves* that are set, and FIERY DIAMONDS is in any case something of a hyperbole.

STORM AND PRESSURE PERIOD does not translate *Sturm- und Drang-periode*[b 224] but *Sturm- und Drückperiode*.

A FUTURE THAT WAS TO COME (*die Zukunft, die ihnen bevorsteht*[c]) is nonsense, as Pieper himself knows (EVERY FUTURE BEING TO COME), and altogether in the style of Moses & Son,[d] as in an earlier bit where '*die Geister der Vergangenheit*'[e] is rendered as THE SPIRITS OF THOSE THAT HAVE BEEN.

THE CIRCLE SHOULD BE INCREASED (*erweitert werden*[f] p. 4, bottom).[g] *Un cercle est élargi, il n'est pas* AGRANDI.[h]

THE GENERAL INDEX (*der allgemeine Inhalt der modernen Revolution*[i]) means the general *list* of contents of modern revolution! *Le citoyen Pieper le savait, du reste, aussi bien que moi.*[j]

AS IT COULD BUT BE, *wie es nicht anders sein konnte*—*lapsus pennae*; should read 'AS IT COULD NOT BUT BE'; otherwise it would mean: *wie es kaum sein konnte*.

UNWIELDINESS (p. 5, top in the orig.) is *Unbehülflichkeit* in the *passive* sense, 'inertia' in physics but, applied to persons, can only mean that they cannot move for fat. *Unbeholfenheit*, used of persons, in the *active* sense, means CLUMSINESS. This mistake was suggested to Pieper by his dictionary.

CONSTITUTIONAL STANDARD (*die Nationalversammlung sollte die Resultate der Revolution auf den* bürgerlichen *Maßstab reduzieren*[k]). *C'est un peu fort*[l] that, in order to evade the difficulty of translating '*bürgerlich*', Citoyen Pieper should everywhere render it as 'CONSTITUTIONAL' because '*konstitutionelle Republik*' and '*bürgerliche Republik*' are used synonymously. *Je demande un peu,*[m] what does CONSTITUTION-

---

a set in sparkling brilliants - b Storm and Stress period - c the future that is in store for it - d A hint at Moses Hess. - e the spirits of the past - f be widened - g Here and below Engels refers to the first edition of Marx's *Eighteenth Brumaire of Louis Bonaparte*, published in New York in 1852. - h A circle is *widened*, it is not *increased*. - i the general content of modern revolution - j For that matter Citizen Pieper knew it as well as I do. - k the National Assembly was to reduce the results of the revolution to the bourgeois scale - l That's too bad - m I ask you

AL mean in this context? It becomes even more delectable later on, when *bürgerliche Gesellschaft* figures *sans façon*[a] as CONSTITUTIONAL SOCIETY. *C'est assommant.*[b]

FOR EVER AND THE DURATION (*für die ganze Dauer des Zyklus*[c]). Why not rather FOR EVER AND A DAY, as the saying goes?

UTOPIAN JUGGLES (*utopische Flausen*). JUGGLES means legerdemain, not flights of fancy.

TRANSPORTED WITHOUT *JUDGMENT* means *déporté contre le sens commun*, transported in defiance of common sense and should read without TRIAL.

TO PASS AS A REAL EVENT doesn't mean '*um überhaupt als ein Ereignis passieren zu können*',[d] but to pass for something that *has really happened.*

FOUNDED doesn't mean *fondu*[e] but *fondé.* It has nothing to do with the illogical but accepted term CONFOUNDED for *confondu.*

All these are things which Pieper, if only he paid a little attention, would know as well as I do but, as already mentioned, it is easier to translate difficult things oneself than to correct a translation that is carelessly thrown together and dodges the difficulties. If he tried a little harder, he could translate quite well.

First published in full in: Marx and Engels, *Works,* Second Russian Edition, Vol. 28, Moscow, 1962

Printed according to the original

Published in English for the first time

98

MARX TO ENGELS

IN MANCHESTER

[London,] 23 September 1852
28 Dean Street, Soho

Dear Engels,

Received the £1 and the corrected translation.[f] You went to too much trouble over the latter. If the thing is passable (success will depend on this No. 1), you must take it easier: I mean, forget about figures of speech or other inessentials, if difficult to translate.

---

a without more ado - b It's infuriating. - c for the entire duration of the cycle - d to be able to pass for an event at all - e melted - f See previous letter.

Weerth has been here since Sunday. On Saturday he leaves for Manchester where he will spend 3 or 4 weeks before disappearing to the West Indies, etc.

Enclosed:

1. A letter in Schurz's handwriting, found in the pocket of a waistcoat which Kinkel gave to a refugee of our acquaintance.

2. Letter from Cluss.

3. Two excerpts from the revelations about the émigrés, first published in the *Karlsruher Zeitung* and then reprinted by the Augsburg *Allgemeine Zeitung*, etc.,[a] in case you haven't seen the things yourself.

Dr Piali (in Paris) writes *inter alia*:

'Kossuth intends to go into action in October. From here, Kiss has been giving Kossuth all manner of assurances which probably belong to the realm of fable yet could, given the fabulous nature of circumstances here, *actually be possible.* Kossuth is said to have received a note from Bonaparte *in his own hand* summoning him *to Paris.* A word-for-word copy of this note is believed to be circulating throughout the counties of Hungary. Everything in Hungary is in readiness for an all-out blow by Kossuth. Even Royal and Imperial officials are involved in the great conspiracy...'[225]

'Countess Kinski, née Zichy, has been arrested for infanticide. The child was fathered by Dr Chaises,' (our well-known shit[b]), 'a Polish Jew, etc. Madame Beckmann (wife of the police spy and newspaper correspondent) will figure as *dame de compagnie*[c] at the hearing before the Assizes.'

As for the Kossuth affair, it is quite possible that Bonaparte is setting snares for him in order to curry favour with Austria.

Piali has got Häfner to enter into correspondence with Ruge-Tausenau, so that now it is just as if we were corresponding with Mr Arnold direct. In this way we shall learn at first hand about the *mystères des grands hommes.*[d]

The *Volksverein,*[226] 8 man strong, (out of which, according to W's[e] letter to you, Ruge, with well-known virtuosity, formed 3 committees) is now (Ronge and Dralle included) trailing round the City on the pretext of simultaneously founding a 'free community'. What the devil has that German-Catholic, Ronge, to do with 'free communities'?[227] A few German-Catholic and, in particular, Jewish merchants have put their names on the list, if only in the form of

---

[a] 'Die deutsche revolutionäre Propaganda in London und die Revolutionsanleihe', *Karlsruher Zeitung,* Nos. 208-210, 212, 214, 217-220, 224; 3-22 September 1852. And also in the *Allgemeine Zeitung,* Nos. 255-257, 11-13 September 1852. - [b] As pronounced by Germans, 'Chaises' closely resembles Scheiße—shit. - [c] lady companion - [d] mysteries of the great men - [e] presumably Wolff

initial letters, and contributed a few pounds, as was actually envisaged.

Willich, for his part, now makes a public collection every Saturday at the Great Windmill Street Society,[24] ostensibly towards the cost of correspondence.

What do you say to the ovations accorded Bonaparte in the provinces?[228] The French are indeed making ignominious fools of themselves.

The Customs Union[220] seems to me to be on the brink of certain collapse. Austrian bankruptcy shows itself still capable of dealing with Prussian prosperity.

I see that Dana has accepted the article.[a] The *Staatszeitung* (New York) has already published an excerpt in German.

Old Wellington's death came at the right time. At a moment of crisis the old bull would still have commanded an authority grown legendary. With him and Peel the COMMON SENSE OF OLD ENGLAND has been DULY buried.

So our 'people' are to appear on 4 October.[16] Bürgers admits everything, at least so far as he himself is concerned. In keeping with his profession, he will defend himself '*on principle*'. During the examination he placed on record a 30-sheet memorandum on the 'essence of communism'.[229] *Honi soit qui mal y pense.*[230] Daniels is said to be fairly well. The prosecutor will begin by reverting to the St.-Simonists; attorney Schneider will attempt TO BEAT him by beginning with Babeuf. We can consider ourselves lucky if neither of them harks back as far as the Incas or Lycurgus.

Pindar, whose *mystères*[b] I found most entertaining, did not come to see me. Your ADVENTURES WITH OLD Schily were exquisite.[c]

Ad vocem[d] Jones. Though I personally have little to say in his favour, I and the whole lot of us stood by him last week—he came pestering me again because *il y avait crise.*[e] The other fellows had summoned two or three meetings for the purpose of tabling a motion, namely 'THAT THIS MEETING IS OF OPINION, THAT NO CONFIDENCE CAN BE PLACED IN THE SUCCESS OF ANY DEMOCRATIC MOVEMENT WHILE MR ERNEST JONES IS CONNECTED THEREWITH'.[f] They HAVE BEEN BEATEN, and that right thoroughly.[231] The jackasses first tried to throw financial dirt at him. In this they failed. Then they attacked him for the same reason that we support him, *because* he *stirs up* 'UNFRIENDLY FEELINGS

AMONGST THE DIFFERENT CLASSES'. For Harney-Holyoake, Hunt of the *Leader*, Newton (CO-OPERATIVE) *et tutti quanti*[a] have united to found a 'NATIONAL PARTY'. This NATIONAL PARTY wants GENERAL SUFFRAGE, BUT NOT CHARTISM.[232] The same old story. But before they launched their campaign Jones was to BE CRUSHED. They have RATHER miscalculated He has raised the price of his paper[b] by a penny without losing a single subscriber.

Your
K. M.

First published abridged in *Der Briefwechsel zwischen F. Engels und K. Marx*, Bd. 1, Stuttgart, 1913 and in full in *MEGA*, Abt. III, Bd. 1, Berlin, 1929

Printed according to the original

Published in English for the first time

99

ENGELS TO MARX[84]

IN LONDON

[Manchester,] 24 September 1852

Dear Marx,

Encl. I return the envelope of the letter received from you today; an attempt, incidentally abortive, seems to have been made to break it open.

The translation[c] and Massol's letter went off yesterday evening by the 2nd post.

Cluss' description of Kinkel and Co.'s reception by the German Yankees is really nice. The chaps in the Alleghenies are the very spit of those in the Black Forest and the Taunus.

I haven't read the revelations in the German papers[d]—in fact, yesterday was the first time in some while that I saw a German paper.

The *crapauds*[e] are in clover.[233] The workers would appear *après tout*[f] to have become utterly bourgeoisified as a result of the present PROSPERITY and the prospect of *la gloire de l'empire*.[g] They

---

[a] and all the rest - [b] *The People's Paper* - [c] into English of the first chapter of Marx's work *The Eighteenth Brumaire of Louis Bonaparte* - [d] See this volume, p. 194. - [e] philistines - [f] after all - [g] imperial glory

will have to be severely chastened by crises if they are to be good for anything again *soon*. Should the next crisis be a mild one, Bonaparte will be able to weather it. But it looks as though it is going to be damned serious. No crisis is worse than when over-speculation develops slowly in the sphere of production, so that its results take as many years to mature as they would months on the stock and commodity exchanges. And it was not just the COMMON SENSE of Old England that was buried along with old Wellington, but OLD ENGLAND herself, in the person of her sole surviving representative. All that remains are SPORTING CHARACTERS without a *suite*,[a] like Derby, and Jewish swindlers like Disraeli— who are caricatures of the old Tories in exactly the same way as is Monsieur Bonaparte of his uncle.[b] There'll be a merry dance here when the crisis comes, and one can only hope that it will last long enough to develop into a chronic condition with acute periods, as it did in 1837/42. From what is known of him, by the way, old Wellington would have been a truly formidable military leader in case of insurrection—the fellow studied diligently, read all the military treatises with the utmost zeal and was pretty well-versed in his subject. Nor would he have balked at extreme means.

From what you tell me, the Cologne trial threatens to be terribly *ennuyant*.[c] Unhappy Heinrich,[d] with his defence 'on principle'! He will demand that his 30 sheets be read in court and, if he gets his way, will be *perdu*.[e] The jury will never forgive him for having bored them so. The prosecution, by the way, seems to be out of luck. For Haupt is off to Brazil, the anonymous journeyman tailor has similarly vanished and seems unlike to reappear, and now the police official,[f] because of whose illness the whole affair was adjourned in July, must needs go and die on them. But what will such good fortune be worth if Heinrich elucidates the thing from the philosophical standpoint?

So the gallant Schurz is carping at Kossuth for preaching the gospel of action, after he and Co. have for years eked out a bare living from this same gospel! IT IS ALL VERY WELL to try and settle Kossuth's hash because he takes the lion's share, but it's really very stupid to write things of that sort when the whole world knows better.

That Kossuth will commit some folly seems most probable; what has *le malheureux*[g] got after all but battered saddles, outranged

---

a following - b Napoleon I - c tedious - d Bürgers (see this volume, p. 195) - e lost - f Schulz - g the unfortunate man muskets, companies drilled by Sigel, and Klapka and Garibaldi? (The latter commands the Italo-Hungarian fleet in the Pacific Ocean to wit one merchantman plying between Lima and Canton under the Peruvian flag.)

Your

F. E.

First published abridged in *Der Briefwechsel zwischen F. Engels und K. Marx*, Bd. 1, Stuttgart, 1913 and in full in *MEGA*, Abt. III, Bd. 1, Berlin, 1929

Printed according to the original

Published in English in full for the first time

100

MARX TO ENGELS [234]

IN MANCHESTER

London, 28 September 1852
28 Dean Street, Soho

Dear Engels,

You have not had a letter from me for some time. The main cause of this is Weerth who—not I might say, to my unalloyed delight—has *plus ou moins*[a] monopolised my evenings which are usually given over to writing. As you know, I'm very fond of Weerth, *mais*[b] it's embarrassing, when one's up to one's neck in trouble, to have to face so fine a gentleman, *auquel il faut cacher les parties trop honteuses.*[c] Such a relationship creates twice as much *gêne*[d] and I hope he will leave for Manchester tomorrow and will on his return find me in circumstances that will enable me to consort with him *franchement.*[e] However, I don't believe that, aside from my wife's ill-health, he had any inkling of my predicament.

I have given him a big parcel to take to you. It contains documents that belong in the archives[216]; some, if not most of them are already familiar to you.

Enclosed the extract from a letter from Barthélemy to Willich. Barthélemy gave this letter to a Frenchman by the name of

___

[a] more or less - [b] but - [c] from whom the most shameful aspects must be concealed - [d] embarrassment - [e] frankly

Durand to take to Willich. Durand, unable to read the signature, asked Dronke if he would see to it that Willich got the letter. Dronke of course agreed, came to my house, and Lupus, who is a great artist in this line, opened the letter most expertly. Dronke copied out all that was of note—the rest mere twaddle. *Que penses-tu de ce brave Barthélemy, 'auquel il est impossible de se résigner à laisser Bonaparte jouir paisiblement de son triomphe'.*[a] Tremble, O Byzantium![b] As to the alleged letter from Blanqui, this strikes me as a piece of melodramatic falsehood on the sinister Barthélemy's part. For what news does he give of Blanqui? That the situation of the *prisonniers de Belle-Ile est bien triste.*[c] If that is all Blanqui had to divulge to him, he would have done better to keep his *libri tristium*[d] to himself. Incidentally, Barthélemy's whole letter shows that he is completely out of touch with the French emigration and the French societies in France.

In order that you, too, may 'adopt to some extent the standpoint of world history'[e] I enclose an article from the Augsburg *Allgemeine* on the spy A. Majer who, here in London, was actually 'chucked out of the house' by his bosom friends, Willich and Schapper.

I have, I presume, already told you that Herzen is here and is sending round memoirs against Herwegh,[235] who has not only cuckolded him but has extorted 80,000 fr. from him.

I have not yet been able to do any work on an article or even on the draft of the final instalment of the German article.[214] So engrossed have I been by the incessant correspondence arising out of my domestic troubles that it is 3 weeks since I went to the library—which I also forbore from doing in order to sustain my wife during what was for her a ghastly time.

Apropos!

There is *no doubt* that the Orleanist conspiracy shows greater activity, scope and prospects every day. The gentlemen have coalesced with Cavaignac, Charras, Lamoricière, Bedeau. Of L. Bonaparte's aides-de-camp 3 have been bought, i.e. substantial sums have been deposited on their behalf in the Bank of England. The following contract has been entered into with the out-and-out

---

[a] What do you think of the honest Barthélemy 'who finds it impossible to resign himself to allow Bonaparte to enjoy his triumph in peace'. - [b] Words from Donizetti's opera *Belisario,* libretto by S. Cammarano, Act II, Scene 3. - [c] the prisoners on Belle-Ile is *very sad.* - [d] tale of woe (an allusion to Ovid's *Tristia*) - [e] From Jordan's speech in the Frankfurt National Assembly (July 1848) (see 'The Frankfurt Assembly Debates the Polish Question', present edition, Vol. 7, pp. 360-64).

republicans. *Firstly:* Formation of a provisional government consisting solely of *generals. Secondly:* By way of guarantee, Cavaignac is to receive Marseilles, Lamoricière Lyons, Charras Paris, Bedeau Strasbourg. *Thirdly:* At the preliminary elections the people will be called on by the provisional government to decide whether they want the constitution of 1830 and the Orleans dynasty, or the constitution of 1848 and a president. In the latter case, Joinville will come forward as a candidate.

The Jew, Fould, is in constant touch with the Orleans. The undertaking has been tentatively fixed for the month of March, when Bonaparte will, if necessary, be assassinated by his aides-de-camp. But they would prefer Bonaparte to have become emperor first and done further damage to himself.

I myself have talked to the Orleanist agent[a] who travels freely to and fro between Paris and London. The day before yesterday he and Bangya went to see the Duc d'Aumale.

I see from a letter of Piali's that, at a private audience in London, Lord Palmerston told a fugitive Italian noblewoman[b] all manner of comforting things about Italy, and held out what was to him the no less 'comforting' prospect of becoming British prime minister within the space of a year. How addicted to lies and *vanité* is old age! Incidentally on one point at least Mr Palmerston did not mince his words. In case of insurrection Lombardy and Venice must, he said, at once unite with Piedmont. The pipe-dreams of an 'Italian republic' must be left to 'the future'.[236]

Dronke, inmate of the MODEL LODGING HOUSE, says he is sorry he has not written. 'He has his reasons.'

Your

K. M.

There is no doubt that an attempt, obviously clumsy and unsuccessful, was made to open my last envelope, which you returned to me.

First published slightly abridged in *Der Briefwechsel zwischen F. Engels und K. Marx*, Bd. 1, Stuttgart, 1913 and in full in *MEGA*, Abt. III, Bd. 1, Berlin, 1929

Printed according to the original

Published in English in full for the first time

---

[a] Rémusat - [b] Marquise Visconti

101

ENGELS TO MARX

IN LONDON

[Manchester, after 28 September 1852]

Dear Marx,

Have still not seen or heard anything of Weerth. Why the devil should you feel ill at ease with the fellow? In any case, he knows quite well that you've been down on your luck for years and he also knows how things are now, if only from the fact that you're still stuck in those old lodgings.

I have been removed, i.e. my old landlady has removed, and has carted me with her *sans façon*.[a] It's two doors away, so in future address letters to *No. 48* (new numbering) instead of No. 70.

In haste,
Your
F. E.

First published in *MEGA*, Abt. III, Bd. 1, Berlin, 1929

Printed according to the original

Published in English for the first time

102

ENGELS TO MARX

IN LONDON

[Manchester,] 4 October 1852
48 Great Ducie Street

Dear Marx,

Encl. £2. 10. -. Give the 10/- to Dronke, who has searched out a very valuable Slav book[b] for me—the amount by which he beat the fellow down is his commission for the discovery; *puisqu'il est commerçant, il faut le traiter selon les principes du commerce.*[c] But tell

---

[a] without more ado - [b] R. A. Fröhlich, *Kurzgefaßte tabellarisch bearbeitete Anleitung zur schnellen Erlernung der vier slavischen Hauptsprachen.* - [c] Since he's a businessman he has to be treated in accordance with business principles.

him to go and post the book to me at once in a plain wrapper like a newspaper, with 6 STAMPS if it weighs less than a pound, and 12 STAMPS if it weighs more, N.B., if it's 1 volume; otherwise 6 STAMPS for each volume, in which case it would be best to send it in a parcel, unstamped, by Pickford & Co. or Carver & Co. If you can discover Carver & Co's office (I believe they are known down there as Chaplin, Horne & Carver or Chaplin, Horne & Co.), it had best go through them to Friedrich Engels, CARE OF Ermen & Engels—they are our CARRIERS. Indeed, this is always the best way to send me parcels.

As soon as I can see my way somewhat more clearly this month, you shall get more. There are a few debts to be paid, how many I don't yet know. On this will depend how much I can send you.

Weerth is in Bradford. He won't be here for a week, yet.

Le roman Pindar prend une tournure tout à fait bourgeoise.[a] The poor boy is already suffering from remorse. Because I have given him no news of his wife and mother since the *fifteenth of September,* he is bombarding me with letters and threatening to write to them direct for news! The fellow seems to imagine that I spend all my days there, as though the Finnish features and Scandinavian-Germanic heart of his cold-blooded better half were as bewitching to me as they were and still are to him. By his *evasion,*[b] Master Pindar had once more gone up a little in my estimation, but these letters bring him right down again. He is a Slav through and through, sentimental in his frivolity and even in his beastliness, servile and arrogant; and he has nothing of the Englishman save in exaggerated—being a Russian, he must exaggerate—taciturnity. Recently the fellow had grown somewhat more garrulous, yet when the long-closed sluice gates finally opened, nothing came out but *fadaise.*[c] On top of that the lovelorn Pindar has exceedingly unsavoury appetites and likes nothing better than to discuss unnatural discoveries. He's wholly uncultivated and withal pedantic, knowing absolutely nothing except a language or two; *en matière de science,*[d] even the most ordinary mathematics, physics and other school subjects, and especially in history of the most elementary kind, he is utterly ignorant. *Ce n'est que son silence acharné qui ait pu faire croire qu'il soit profond.*[e] He is *ni plus ni moins*[f] than a little Russian bourgeois with the appetites of the

---

[a] Pindar's romance is taking an altogether bourgeois turn. - [b] running away - [c] fiddle-faddle - [d] in the field of science - [e] It's only his obstinate silence which has lent him a semblance of profundity. - [f] neither more nor less

Russian nobility, lazy, dilettante, soft-hearted, would-be blasé and at the same time, alas, a born pedagogue. For as long as I could, I tried to maintain a good opinion of the fellow, but it can't be done. What can one say of an individual who, on reading Balzac's fiction for the first time (and the *Cabinet des antiques* and *Père Goriot* at that) considers it infinitely beneath him and dismisses it with the utmost contempt as something commonplace and quite unoriginal, yet a week after running away, and apparently in all seriousness, writes from London to his deserted wife in the following platitudious terms: 'My dearest Ida, appearances are against me, but believe me, my heart is still entirely yours!' There you have the fellow in a nutshell. Though the Swede may possess his heart, as is proved also by his letters to me, he intends that no one but the Frenchwoman shall be presented with his cock. So far as he is concerned, the real piquancy of the whole affair lies in this clash, this Slavonic, sentimental, vulgar contradiction. The Swede, however, has much more sense; she tells anyone who will listen that he can do what he likes with his heart provided he keeps his carnality at home. Besides, the fellow's lack of ideas and worldly wisdom contrast ludicrously with the spiritual pretensions he harbours as a Russian. He has understood neither the *Manifesto*[a] nor Balzac; of that he has given me ample and frequent proof. He doesn't know German, no doubt of that, since he fails to understand the simplest things. I also greatly doubt whether he knows French. Once the *mystère* with which he held one's interest has gone, nothing remains but *une existence manquée*.[b] Yet in his letters the fellow tries to spin out the *mystère* that has long since been unveiled; it's ridiculous. You'll see! Within three months *gospodin*[c] Pindar will be back again, *bon fils, bon époux, bon bourgeois, plus taciturne que jamais,*[d] and will continue as before to squander what remains of his mother's fortune without making the slightest attempt to set his hand to anything or study anything. And a fellow like that goes and runs away with an experienced Parisienne—she'll make him rue the day.

The latest story about the truthful Willich's falsehood is good indeed.[e]

---

[a] K. Marx and F. Engels, *Manifesto of the Communist Party.* - [b] wasted existence - [c] Mr - [d] a good son, a good husband, a good bourgeois, more taciturn than ever - [e] See this volume, p. 195.

I am also writing to Dronke so that the book will not get lost.[237]

Your

F. E.

First published in part in *Der Briefwechsel zwischen F. Engels und K. Marx*, Bd. 1, Stuttgart, 1913 and in full in *MEGA*, Abt. III, Bd. 1, Berlin, 1929

Printed according to the original

Published in English for the first time

103

MARX TO ADOLF CLUSS

IN WASHINGTON

London, 5 October 1852
28 Dean Street, Soho

Dear Cluss,

Your letter of 16 September[a] arrived very late today. I am therefore sending only a few lines in reply, since you ask for an answer by return. Next Friday a rather more substantial report will be going off to you.[b] My information about the Brüningk woman (she's not a spy but corresponds with her aunt, the Princess Lieven, in Paris, who is notoriously one) came from Bangya. The latter, however, has *very important reasons* for not being named. If he were, he would forfeit many 'sources of information' which, being important to us, must be preserved.

You can write and tell Schnauffer that he merely has to answer that no further authorities need be cited since his (Brüningk's) two *friends, Kinkel and Willich,* have themselves been spreading it about in London that Mrs von Brüningk has suspect political connections.

That *Willich* has been saying things of this kind is so well known that Schimmelpfennig has taken him to task about it. If necessary, witnesses can be cited to support this.

Kinkel voiced this suspicion outright, e.g. to his friend Kamm,

---

[a] 26 September in the original. - [b] See next letter.

the brushmaker (from Bonn), when the latter passed through here on his way to America. Kamm helped to spread it further.

(Willich, of course, did not discover that the woman was suspect until after she had dropped him.)

Your
K. M.

First published in: Marx and Engels, *Works*, First Russian Edition, Vol. XXV, Moscow, 1934

Printed according to the original

Published in English for the first time

104

MARX TO ADOLF CLUSS

IN WASHINGTON

[London,] 8 October 1852
28 Dean Street, Soho

Dear Cluss,

So necessary have your weekly letters become to me that I am far from satisfied with your change of method and, out of vexation at your silence, have likewise remained silent.

You'll have had my letter about Brüningk.[a] We must— *et nous sommes dans le vrai*[b]—repay the shameless Gottfried[c] in kind. According to Imandt's last report of the London guarantors' meeting,[d] extracts of which appeared in the *Wecker, Techow* (now departed for Australia) rose and said: '...those in particular who had enjoyed Brüningk's hospitality should be ashamed of themselves for spreading calumnies about Mrs von Brüningk.' Kinkel, of the unashamedly unruffled brow, protested his innocence, although Imandt could have proved that he was lying. Willich sat as though nailed to his seat.

As regards the second matter, that of remuneration,[e] I can do nothing further since my informant, Biskamp (*whom I would beg*

---

[a] See previous letter. - [b] and we are in the right - [c] Kinkel - [d] See this volume, pp. 161-62. - [e] ibid., p. 96.

you not to name) has settled in France and I have no correspondence with him. However, salary or no salary, this much is certain:

1. that Kinkel and Willich spent £200 and failed adequately to account for it to the London guarantors' congress;

2. Willich, on the pretext of meeting the cost of correspondence, remunerated himself for as long as he could;

3. that when Kinkel—proof of his purity in money matters—arrived in Paris after his escape[238] he immediately approached one of the leaders of the Slav-German etc. revolutionary committee there and informed him in confidence that it would be desirable if the German democrats in Paris were to give him a welcoming supper which he would then get the press to trumpet abroad. (*As in fact later happened.*) To the remark: where is the money coming from? Gottfried replied that it could be taken out of the revolutionary committee funds. To the further remark that there was no money in the exchequer but rather a considerable deficit, Gottfried opined that the member (Bangya) to whom he was speaking could advance it, he himself being so frightfully popular in Germany that money would come flowing in. Subsequently this same Kinkel got Bangya to advance him 500 fr. for his *personal use* on the account of the revolutionary committee. *His* reçu[a] *is still in existence.* He has not repaid it to this very day.

I have seen the *reçu.* But Bangya insists on not being named, likewise Häfner, who was also present. These people are right. The object of Kinkel's policy is by means of bare-faced denials (that the man is lying is proved by the business with me[b] and with *Dr Wiss,* whom he forced to make a *public statement* by asserting that he had no connection with the 'loan in his name'. See *New-Yorker Deutsche Zeitung* and Wiss' own statement therein.[239] Cite *this last* fact), his object, I say, is to compel me to show my hand and BY AND BY to discover whence I draw the information with which to catch him out. This, he thinks, would draw my sting. *Ça ne va pas.*[c]

You'll be able to follow in the *Kölnische Zeitung* the proceedings against our friends that opened on the 4th of this month in the Court of Assizes. The jury is damn bad. It consists of big landowners and big capitalists, viz: Regierungsrat von Münch-Bellinghausen, Häbling von Lanzenauer, Freiherr von Fürstenberg, von Bianca, von Tesseler, vom Rath; Joest (the biggest manufacturer—sugar—in Cologne); Herstadt (one of the leading

---

[a] receipt - [b] See this volume, pp. 149-50. - [c] That won't do.

bankers in Cologne), D. Leiden (big capitalist). Finally Leven (wine merchant) and Professor Kräusler.

Have my last two articles on the GENERAL ELECTION appeared in the *Tribune*[a]? The first two caused a great stir here in England. Jones reproduced them.[b]

Enclosed you will find:

1. Letter from Imandt.

2. Copy of an article from *The Morning Advertiser* of 6 October,[c] in which the luckless Ruge-Ronge endeavour to *assert* themselves. The League here[d] would now ask you to write by return a letter to *The Morning Advertiser* (signed Dr Smyth OR SOMETHING LIKE THAT) in which you make fun of the German LONE STAR which has neither LONE nor STAR, and reassure *The Morning Advertiser* about the threat to America presented by this soap-bubble that has long since burst there. (Copy to be sent to us.)[240]

3. A letter from Massol in Paris,[241] which please return. Massol is one of the cleverest of the *older* Frenchmen (those of the forties), former St Simonist, Proudhonist, etc. *The man and the book* he alludes to are Proudhon and his book on Bonaparte.[e]

It seems to me that you people should now go for Heinzen in such a way as to torture him by pointing out how, since '47, this oaf has systematically ignored every attack relating to matters of principle (as, of late, that of Weydemeyer and subsequently your own[242]), only to reappear a few months later as much of a charlatan as ever, *quasi re bene gesta*.[f]

Your
K. M.

N. B. The morsel of erudition (striking in view of Heinzen's well-known ignorance) which he reveals in treating of the historical development of marriage, was borrowed by the unhappy man from G. Jung, *Geschichte der Frauen,* Part 1, Frankfurt am Main 1850. Jung himself drew his material from:

C. Meiners, *Geschichte des weiblichen Geschlechts,* 4 vols. Hanover 1788-1800, and from:

---

[a] K. Marx, 'Corruption at Elections' and 'Results of the Elections'. - [b] K. Marx, 'The Elections in England.— Tories and Whigs' and 'The Chartists' published in the *New-York Daily Tribune* and reproduced in *The People's Paper,* Nos. 22 and 23, 2 and 9 October 1852. - [c] 'The German "Lone Star"', *The Morning Advertiser,* No. 19122, 6 October 1852. - [d] The London District of the Communist League - [e] P. J. Proudhon, *La révolution sociale démontrée par le coup d'état du 2 décembre* (see this volume, p. 166). - [f] just as though nothing had happened

J. A. de Ségur, *Les femmes* etc., 3 vols. Paris 1803, and sprinkled it with Hegelian-Young German sauce.

Meiners and Ségur drew on:

Alexander (W.), *History of Women* etc., 2 vols. London 1782, 3rd ed.

Thomas (de l'Ac. franç.), *Essai sur le caractère etc. des femmes* etc., Paris 1773.

For the manner in which the Hegelian school finally sums the thing up—that old buffoon Ruge, now apparently in his dotage, is too stupid to count—see:

Unger (J.), *Die Ehe in ihrer welthistorischen Entwicklung.* Vienna 1850.

This 'bibliography' will enable you not only to deprive the unhappy Heinzen of all desire to pass off as new discoveries a few platitudes filched from the socialists but also to provide the German-American public, if interested in the subject, with the sources where the material may be found.   ,

First published in: Marx and Engels, *Works,* First Russian Edition, Vol. XXV, Moscow, 1934

Printed according to the original

Published in English for the first time

105

ENGELS TO MARX

IN LONDON

[Manchester,] Sunday, 10 October 1852

Dear Marx,

I am fed up with the perpetual delays over the pamphlet.[a] Month after month we are told it will appear and it never does. One excuse after another is trotted out and then dropped. Finally it is said to be definitely coming out at Michaelmas. *La Trinité se passe, Marlbrough ne revient pas.*[b] Quite the contrary, for now we hear *the* man is dead and Bangya doesn't know what has become

---

[a] K. Marx and F. Engels, *The Great Men of the Exile.* - [b] Trinity goes by but Marlbrough does not return (from a French satirical song composed during the War of the Spanish Succession).

of the manuscript. It's too maddening. We must at long last insist on being told the plain truth. The thing's getting more suspicious every day. I don't, and you certainly don't, want our joint work to fall into the wrong hands. We wrote it for the benefit of the public, and not for the private delectation of the police in Berlin or anywhere else, and if Bangya proves intractable, I intend to act off my own bat. Our clerk Charles,[a] whom you know, is going to the Continent next week, via Hamburg and Berlin. I have asked him to inquire carefully into the matter in Berlin and, if the week he is spending there should not suffice, to enlist the help of our local agent. But I'll wager that we'll see what's at the bottom of this stink. What is all this about Eisermann or Eisenmann, the bookseller of whom there is no trace whatever in the directory of booksellers? But tracking down the 'editor of the former *Constitutionelle Zeitung*' should not prove difficult. If things aren't in order, it is absolutely essential that we make a *public statement*, and that in all the more widely read German papers, so that the same trick won't be played on us as was played on Blanqui with the *pièce*[b] Taschereau.[243] As for Bangya's mystery-mongering, it is, in this instance at least, utterly uncalled-for, and having, for my part, had enough of TERGIVERSATION, I shall now take what steps I think fit.

Papa Kinkel is coming up here to give German lectures under the auspices of third and fourth rate poetical Jews. *Cela sera beau.*[c] The secretary of the Athenaeum[244] tried to induce me to subscribe with the remark: 'WHEREVER THERE WAS SOMETHING LIKE A CHEQUERED LIFE, WERE IT ONLY AN ESCAPE FROM A SHIPWRECK OR SO, THERE WAS ALWAYS A NATURAL AND FAIR GROUND FOR SYMPATHY.' *Voilà les arguments qu'on emploie pour lui mendier un auditoire.*[d]

No other news. Write and tell me if you hear anything more about the affair of the pamphlet, but it's hardly likely to affect my decision respecting Charles. Warmest regards to your wife and children.

Your
F. E.

First published in *MEGA,* Abt. III, Bd. 1, Berlin, 1929

Printed according to the original

Published in English for the first time

---

[a] Roesgen - [b] document - [c] That will be nice. - [d] Such are the arguments used to obtain an audience for him.

106

MARX TO ENGELS

IN MANCHESTER

[London,] 12 October [1852]
28 Dean Street, Soho

Dear Frederic,

More about your letter later.

Enclosed:

1. A document, 'The German Loan Star Society', smuggled into the *Advertiser*[a] by Ruge-Ronge.

2. A cutting from Weydemeyer's *Lithographierte Correspondenz* about the effect of this dangerous 'SOCIETY' on their League congress at Wheeling.[245]

3. An article for Dana.[246] But the whole of it must go off, as I have a mass of political stuff for next time. I had a bad headache when I was scribbling the thing. So don't be afraid to deal with it FREELY in translating.

You may have read the infamous article in yesterday's *Times*, a contribution dated Berlin.[b] All the cur has done is to translate from the *Neue Preussische Zeitung* (the Cologne trial) and add one or two scurrilous comments from his own STOCK.[247]

Your

K. Marx

First published in *MEGA*, Abt. III, Bd. 1, Berlin, 1929

Printed according to the original

Published in English for the first time

---

[a] 'The German "Lone Star"', *The Morning Advertiser*, No. 19122, 6 October 1852. Here Marx puns on the title of the article and the attempt of the American Revolutionary League to raise a loan. - [b] 'From our own correspondent' in the section 'Prussia', *The Times*, No. 21243, 11 October 1852.

107

ENGELS TO MARX

IN LONDON

[Manchester, 14 October 1852]

Dear Marx,

It is physically impossible to translate the whole article for you. I received it this morning. Have been so busy at the office all day that I didn't know whether I was coming or going. This evening took tea at 7-8 and just glanced through the thing. Then got down to translating. Now—11.30—have done the part I am sending you,[a] up to the natural break in the article. At 12 o'clock it must be in the post. So, you see, you will get as much as can possibly be done.

The rest[b] will be translated directly—next week you can send it either via Southampton or on Friday.[c] In the meantime finish off your next article; part of it might be able to go on Friday, if not, the following Tuesday, when there is another YANKEE STEAMER. So it doesn't really matter. But make sure I get the manuscript *early*; I am expecting Weerth any day and will then have to try to make best use of my time, since my days are more than fully taken up with business.

Regards to your wife and children, Dronke, Lupus, Freiligrath.

Your
F. E.

Mark my word, the Cologne people won't get off. What a cur the presiding judge[d] is to bait Bürgers so.[248]

First published in *Der Briefwechsel zwischen F. Engels und K. Marx*, Bd. 1, Stuttgart, 1913

Printed according to the original

Published in English for the first time

---

a K. Marx, 'Pauperism and Free Trade.—The Approaching Commercial Crisis'. - b K. Marx, 'Political Consequences of the Commercial Excitement'. - c 22 October - d Göbel

108

ENGELS TO MARX

IN LONDON

M[anchester,] 18 October 1852

Dear Marx,

Herewith the remainder of the recent[a] article.[b] Yesterday I also received the next one.[249] You can at once dispatch VIA LIVERPOOL PER UNITED STATES MAIL STEAMER the piece I am posting you today; the *Pacific* sails on Wednesday morning. You will be getting some more on Friday.[c]

You really must stop making your articles so long. Dana cannot possibly *want* more than 1-1$^1/_2$ columns, it would be too much for one number. I shall again have to split this new article, but it's difficult to do and I don't yet know where. Five-7 pages in your wife's handwriting is *quite enough* and if you give more in one article, Dana won't even thank you for it.

Bürgers and Röser, and perhaps Otto and Nothjung likewise, seem to me pretty well done for. There doesn't appear to be anything at all against Daniels, Becker[d] or Jacobi, and I hope that these at least will get off. Becker has extricated himself with great effrontery. The more these are exonerated the greater, I think, will be the zeal with which the judges and jury will set about the compromised men; the injured bourgeoisie and the injured State want their victims.

The edges of the seals on all the letters I am getting from you show signs of having been gone over with a hot iron but, so far as I can judge, *pour le roi de Prusse.*[e] The gum on the envelope prevents them from getting inside.

Weerth is here, has brought me the parcel, and sends his regards to you all. Szemere's manuscript on Kossuth is far better than the one on Görgey—he's a match for Kossuth. I have not yet

---

[a] Barely legible in the original. - [b] K. Marx, 'Political Consequences of the Commercial Excitement'. - [c] 22 October - [d] Hermann Becker - [e] literally: for the king of Prussia; figuratively: in vain

been able to look at Pieper's translation,[a] being very busy at the office and dog-tired most evenings.

Warmest regards to your wife.

Your
F. E.

First published in *Der Briefwechsel zwischen F. Engels und K. Marx,* Bd. 1, Stuttgart, 1913

Printed according to the original

Published in English for the first time

109

MARX TO A. von BRÜNINGK

IN LONDON

[Rough copy]

[London,] 18 October 1852
28 Dean Street, Soho

To Baron A. von Brüningk

I have received by today's post the *Baltimore Wecker* dated 27 September 1852, together with your statement. Since I, as *one* of the correspondents of A. Cluss in Washington, am directly involved in this matter, I would request you to appoint a meeting-place for Thursday or Friday (of this week).[b] I for my part shall bring a witness with me and would therefore request you to do likewise, but would point out in advance that the said witness may not be either *Ruge, Ronge, Kinkel,* or *Willich,* since these gentlemen are *implicated* in the matter now pending, nor can it be Mr *Schimmelpfennig.* When in Paris, that gentleman swore in so many words to 'destroy me by *slander* of every possible description'. While I do not believe in his destructive ability, I cannot, in view of this assertion, possibly consent to meet him.

---

[a] into English of Marx's *Eighteenth Brumaire of Louis Bonaparte,* I - [b] 21 or 22 October

I shall then explain to you my connection with the *Baltimore* article[250] and, should my explanation not suffice, I shall be prepared to give you the satisfaction customary among gentlemen.

Yours truly
Dr Karl Marx

First published in: Marx and Engels, *Works,* First Russian Edition, Vol. XXV, Moscow, 1934

Printed according to the original

Published in English for the first time

110

MARX TO ENGELS

IN MANCHESTER

London, 20 October 1852
28 Dean Street, Soho

Dear Engels,

I recommend most highly to you the bearer of these lines, Colonel Pleyel. Although I am not personally acquainted with him, he is most 'highly recommended' by Colonel Bangya whom, of course, you know.

Your
K. Marx

First published in *MEGA,* Abt. III, Bd. 1, Berlin, 1929

Printed according to the original

Published in English for the first time

111

ENGELS TO MARX

IN LONDON

[Manchester, 22 October 1852]

Dear Marx,

If you want to count on receiving the articles for Dana punctually in future, you must take care not to send me Hungarian COLONELS, especially of a Thursday night. Yesterday the fellow[a] took up the whole of my evening and intends to come back today—he is pretty well-versed in a number of subjects, military included, and is the most interesting Hungarian I have met so far, but he is also a German-Austrian aristocrat.

So we are now recognised by the State, and even by the police, as 'intelligent' people, teste[b] Stieber. A fine business. The way that stupid Stieber tries to shuffle off responsibility for his own spy, Cherval, onto our chaps![251] Have you any idea why Kothes and Bermbach have been arrested?[c] Those two, of all people—it's ominous! But we shall discipline Haupt.[252] Weerth will find out where he is in South America and, on his arrival there, will unmask him. To that end we shall have to get hold of the *Kölnische Ztg.* or some other paper containing his statements. Could you not attend to this? Do everything you can; it would really be splendid to make the rascal feel the power of the *Neue Rheinische Zeitung* as far away as Brazil.

More in a day or two, and also translations.[253]

Your
F. E.

First published abridged in *Der Briefwechsel Zwischen F. Engels und K. Marx,* Bd. 1, Stuttgart, 1913 and in full in *MEGA,* Abt. III, Bd. 1, Berlin, 1929

Printed according to the original

Published in English for the first time

112

MARX TO ENGELS

IN MANCHESTER

[London,] 25 October 1852
28 Dean Street, Soho

Dear Engels,

We must make some other arrangements about our correspondence. We undoubtedly have a *fellow*-reader in Derby's Ministry. Moreover, there is again someone keeping watch, or at least attempting to do so, outside my house (of an evening). Hence I

---

a Pleyel - b witness - c See this volume, p. 216.

can write and tell you nothing I deem it inadvisable for the Prussian government to learn at this moment.

Dana is treating me very badly. I wrote to him about 6 weeks ago, telling him exactly how things stood with me and that I must be paid *by return* for the articles I had sent. He has regularly published the articles but has not yet sent the money. I, of course, must continue punctiliously, notwithstanding. Otherwise it is I who will suffer in the end.

Now, as much as 5 weeks ago, I mollified my LANDLORD with my prospects in America. Today the fellow calls and makes a fearful scene in front of me and the HOUSEKEEPER. Upon my finally resorting to the *ultima ratio*,[a] i.e. abuse, he retired, threatening that if I didn't produce any money this week, he would throw me out into the street, but first would land me with a BROKER.

4-5 days ago 130 copies of the *Brumaire* arrived from Cluss. As yet I have been unable to get them from the customs because this would mean paying 10/9d. As soon as I've got the stuff out, I'll send it to the place you know and at once draw a bill on the same. With this and the Dana business I now have over £30 outstanding, yet often have to lose an entire day for a shilling. I assure you that, when I consider my wife's sufferings and my own impotence, I feel like consigning myself to the devil.

Kothes and Bermbach were arrested because I had sent the latter through the former a work necessary to the defence, which (despite thin paper and small pearl type) was somewhat bulky.[254] The government thought it had made a splendid catch. But on the closer examination *jeune*[b] Saedt raised heaven and earth to have the thing suppressed, for the document contained curious STRICTURES on the capability, etc., of *jeune* Saedt and could, if communicated to the juries, only help to acquit the *accusés*.[c]

In the *Neue Preussische Zeitung*, 'G. Weerth' is said to be a member of the Central Authority in Cologne, and, indeed, this is cited from the bill of indictment.

Tell Weerth that I have heard nothing from Duncker.[255]

Your

K. M.

As soon as the trial is over, and whatever its outcome, we two must bring out one or two sheets, 'For the Enlightenment of the

---

[a] last resort - [b] young - [c] accused

Public'. No such favourable moment to address the *nation en large*[a] will ever recur. Furthermore, we must not tolerate any semblance of RIDICULE which not even the moral dignity and scientific profundity of the gentle Heinrich[b] are capable of dispelling.

Cherval has himself written to the German Workers' Society in London[24]: saying that he 'is a *spy*, but in the noble sense of "Cooper's spy"'.[c] I have conveyed the necessary explanation to one of the lawyers[d] by a safe route.

We should already start casting about with a view to the publication on the 'Cologne trial' mooted above. I think it would be best if you were to write to Campe asking him to give you the name of a *reliable agent*, should he himself be too afraid. Since your credit is good, the agent can be told that he will receive the money in, say, 3 months' time (against a bill), if he has not in the meantime repaid himself from the sales (as he certainly will do). For that matter, the cost of printing this sort of stuff would amount at most to 25 talers.

Vale![e] And think the matter over. We cannot remain silent and if we don't see to the printing in good time, we shall again miss the boat. We should, of course, have to make sure that the agent is not downright dishonest, for the thing will even have 'commercial' value.

First published abridged in *Der Briefwechsel zwischen F. Engels und K. Marx*, Bd. 1, Stuttgart, 1913 and in full in *MEGA*, Abt. III, Bd. 1, Berlin, 1929

Printed according to the original

Published in English for the first time

113

MARX TO ENGELS

IN MANCHESTER

[London,] 26 October [1852]

Dear Engels,

Tomorrow morning Weerth will find, along with this scrawl, a letter from me addressed to him at Steinthal's and enclosed in it another to Schneider II,[256] *which you should attend to forthwith.* The

---

[a] nation at large - [b] Bürgers - [c] Harvey Birch, character in F. Cooper's *Spy.* - [d] Schneider II. The letter has not been found. - [e] Farewell.

thing is of the utmost importance and must not be delayed for an instant. So please neither of you embark on your daily round until you have read the thing and sent it off.

Your

K. M.

First published in *Der Briefwechsel zwischen F. Engels und K. Marx*, Bd. 1, Stuttgart, 1913

Printed according to the original

Published in English for the first time

114

ENGELS TO MARX

IN LONDON

Manchester, 27 October 1852

D. M.,

When I wrote yesterday,[257] I had only cursorily read Stieber's statements and was therefore most agreeably surprised today when your document[a] gave a turn to the case which *now* no longer makes me despair of the acquittal of *all* the accused. *En effet,*[b] Stieber will be utterly discredited. I made a further copy of the thing and dispatched it to Cologne by 2 different and very good routes[258]; I also did what should already have been done in London, namely affixed the 2 notes in Hirsch's handwriting[259] to the original with sealing-wax, at the same time recording the fact by appending my signature so that, if the worst comes to the worst, they cannot be detained unless the whole thing is detained. I have now discovered several more ways of communicating with Cologne and, although there is a 99% chance that the things will reach Schneider safely and on the same day by the first two routes (which, however, cannot be used again), it might be advisable for you to send me a 3rd copy, *authenticated by you*, with *fresh* samples of Hirsch's handwriting, which I could then send by yet another route. Anyway, the Prussians *cannot* detain this thing; it would mean criminal proceedings against those involved.

---

[a] See previous letter. - [b] Indeed

Your letter received today had been tampered with, not all 4 corners of the envelope being properly secured by the seal. Whether the one to St.ª had also been tampered with is difficult to say, for the firm had opened the outer cover. But it proved so easy to open that I am inclined to assume that here too someone had already been at it. So the Steinthal address is no longer any good either. Write to our old friend, James Belfield, Golden Lion, Deansgate, Manchester, with 'F. E.', no more, on the inside envelope. In the case of very important and dangerous things, do as I am now doing: Make up a parcel of anything with your letter inside it, and send it to my house per Pickford & Co.; alternatively, per Chaplin, Horne & Carver, addressed to me at Ermen & Engels, unstamped. That is perfectly safe. But see that the addresses, particularly if sent by post, are written by turns in different hands and, when parcels are sent by carrier, don't have them always taken to the office from the same place by the same person. Then the latter way will be perfectly safe. So you must either give me a safe address in London to which I can send things in this way, or get someone with an unsuspicious landlord to assume a false name, à la Williams, or let me know whether Lupus is still at 4 Broad Street and Dronke at the Model Lodging House, and where any of our other reliable people live so that I can use different addresses.

By employing all these methods alternately we shall achieve adequate security. In addition, to make it less conspicuous, you should send letters containing matters of no consequence direct by post, and I shall do the same.

Copying out the document has made such demands on my time that I really don't know whether I shall be able to keep my word in the *fullest* sense as regards Dana and Friday's[b] STEAMER. At all events, *something* will be forthcoming. You might bear in mind that a lengthy spell of more or less uninterrupted chaste living is again causing me to burgeon like mad at a certain spot, and at times prevents me from sitting down; *il faut que cela finisse.*[c]

The statement made by old Justizrat Müller will have put Stieber into a blue funk over his original minutes.[260] It also reveals how incensed jurists over there must be by the infamies of the police which Stieber, in his old-Prussian ignorance of Rhenish law, judicial procedure and Rhenish public opinion, is so unashamedly

---

a Steinthal, see this volume, p. 217. - b 29 October. Engels had in mind the translation of Marx's two articles: 'Political Parties and Prospects' and 'Attempts to Form a New Opposition Party'. - c this must cease

proclaiming from the house-tops with childish glee at his own cleverness. *C'est de bonne augure.*[a]

It's a pretty state of affairs: the police steal, forge, break into desks, perjure themselves, give false evidence and, withal, claim this privilege vis-à-vis communists who are *hors la société*[b]! This, and the way in which the police, at their most rascally, are usurping all the functions of the prosecution, pushing Saedt into the background, and submitting unauthenticated scraps of paper, mere rumours, reports and hearsay, as things legally proven, as evidence—*c'est trop fort!*[c] It's bound to have an effect.

Your
F. E.

First published in *Der Briefwechsel zwischen F. Engels und K. Marx*, Bd. 1, Stuttgart, 1913

Printed according to the original

Published in English for the first time

115

MARX TO ENGELS

IN MANCHESTER

London, 27 October 1852
28 Dean Street, Soho

Dear Engels,

I wrote and told you that I would compose a 'Lithographed Circular' about the 'Cologne trial'.[d] That 'L. C.' has now become a pamphlet of some 3 sheets.[261] The thing cannot be lithographed now for two reasons: firstly, such an extensive lithograph would prove very expensive while yielding *nothing,* for one could not in all decency sell a lithographed circular of this kind. Secondly, nobody could read or be expected to read, a lithograph of 3 printed sheets.

So the only thing to do is to get the thing printed. IMPOSSIBLE in Germany. London is the only conceivable place. It will also be

---

[a] It's a good portent. - [b] outside society - [c] it's too much! - [d] See this volume, p. 217.

possible to obtain *credit* if only I am in a position to make a part payment in advance. I would like you to discuss the matter with Weerth and Strohn. But not a day is to be lost. If the thing doesn't come out now, it will no longer be of any interest. My pamphlet is not a vindication of principles, but rather a denunciation of the Prussian government based on the facts and the course of events. Needless to say, I myself am incapable of contributing so much as a centime to the thing. Yesterday I pawned a coat dating back to my Liverpool days in order to buy writing paper.

The Empire is progressing splendidly.[262] Bonaparte knows better than anyone how to ensure that this time the commercial crisis will hit France even more cruelly than England.

Your
K. M.

First published in *Der Briefwechsel zwischen F. Engels und K. Marx*, Bd. 1, Stuttgart, 1913

Printed according to the original

Published in English for the first time

116

MARX TO ENGELS

IN MANCHESTER

[London,] 28 October 1852
28 Dean Street, Soho

Have received the money and, today, a parcel with the letter.[a] In my last to you and Weerth[b] I deliberately refrained from mentioning anything which, had the letter been opened, might have further enlightened the Prussian government as to the steps we have taken against them. Today I shall give you a detailed account. I believe we have laid a countermine that will blow the whole governmental humbug sky high. Those Prussians shall see *qu'ils ont à faire à plus fort.*[c]

On Monday Schneider II will be receiving via Düsseldorf (addressed to a merchant, an acquaintance of Freiligrath's) a letter

---

[a] See this volume, pp. 218-20. - [b] ibid., p. 217. - [c] that they're up against somebody stronger

from me,[263] the content of which is briefly as follows: 1. In 1847,[264] when I was in *Brussels,* Cherval was admitted into the League[a] in London by Mr Schapper and at the latter's suggestion. Not, therefore, in 1848 by me in Cologne. 2. From the late spring of 1848 to the summer of 1850 Cherval lived continuously in London, as his HOUSEKEEPERS can testify. Hence, he did not spend this period in Paris as a propagandist. 3. Not until the summer of 1850 did he go to Paris. The papers found on him and the statements he made before the Paris Assizes prove that he was Schapper-Willich's agent and our enemy.

That Cherval was a *police spy* is borne out by the following: 1. His miraculous escape (along with Gipperich) from prison in Paris immediately after sentence. 2. His unmolested stay in London although a *common* criminal. 3. Mr de Rémusat (I have authorised Schneider to name him if necessary) tells me that Cherval offered him his services as an agent for the Prince of Orleans; thereupon he, Rémusat, wrote to Paris and was sent the following documents (to be kept for a few hours, so that copies might be made; these he showed me), from which it emerges that Cherval was first a Prussian police spy and is now a Bonapartist one. The Prussian police reject his demand for money on the grounds of *'double emploi'*[b] and the fact that he is being paid by the French.[265]

Finally, I provided Schneider with a few simple explanations on points of theory which will enable him to distinguish between the Schapper-Willich documents and our own and to show how they differ.

Besides the letter to Schneider II sent off by you,[c] the same document went via Frankfurt am Main (where it was posted by old Ebner who obtained a *reçu*[d]) to the lawyer, von Hontheim; this was on Tuesday.[e] The same package contained: 1. A letter from Becker to me, with both London and Cologne postmarks, from which it emerges that our correspondence was primarily concerned with the book-trade.[266] 2. Two enclosures from Daniels to me in Becker's letter, which relate solely to his manuscript.[267] 3. Two excerpts from Hirsch's minutes.[268] 4. An excerpt from *The People's Paper* in which by good fortune Cherval actually gives his address. 5. Letters from Mr Stieber (in his own hand) to me[269] at the time of the *Neue Rheinische Zeitung*; see p. 3 of this letter.

On Tuesday evening a letter from Schneider arrived with an occasional traveller; from this it transpires that his first, sent by

---

[a] the League of the Just - [b] double employ - [c] See this volume, pp. 217 and 218. - [d] receipt - [e] 26 October

post, was intercepted. However, he received a registered letter from here, written to him at my request by Dronke, in which he was told that 6-8 weeks ago *Hentze* was over here at Willich's, that Willich was entertained by him and that Willich himself boasted that he had given Hentze instructions about how to proceed against us. Schneider writes that all the lawyers are convinced that the documents are bogus, and he urgently asks for proof of this and, in particular, of the fact that Mrs Daniels never wrote to me.

For want of money *nothing* could have been done on Wednesday, but luckily your £2 arrived. I therefore went to the [Great] Marlborough Street POLICE COURT (BEFORE MR WINGHAM, MAGISTRATE OF THE METROPOLITAN DISTRICT, who asked for an account of the affair and *furieusement* declared himself *for* us and *against* the Prussian government) where I had two things authenticated:

1. The handwriting of Rings and Liebknecht; according to Schneider II's letter they signed nearly *all* Hirsch's minutes. As you know, Rings is barely able to write and as a taker of minutes was therefore a splendid choice on Hirsch's part.[259]

2. I got the landlord of the pub where we hold our meetings to testify that, since March, the 'SOCIETY OF DR MARX' (I'm the only one the fellow knows), some 16-18 strong, has been regularly foregathering once a week and no more, namely on Wednesdays, and that neither he nor his WAITER[s] have ever seen us put pen to paper. The stuff about Wednesdays was also testified by a neighbour of his, a German baker and householder.

Both documents, bearing the seal of the POLICE COURT, have been written out in *duplicate*. The first copy of the same I sent via [...] to G. Jung who, by a stroke of good fortune, wrote to me 3 days ago saying that he was living in Frankfurt am Main, and giving his address. Jung will take the things to Cologne himself or send them by express delivery. The letter he received is addressed to Schneider II and contains, besides the documents mentioned and authenticated by the police court: a) A copy of the first letter to Schneider[270] along with 2 more copies of excerpts from Hirsch's minutes. b) Excerpt from a letter from Becker to myself, the reverse side of which fortunately bears London and Cologne postmarks. To quote Becker's own words (the bit I have sent contains no more than this):

'Willich is sending me the funniest letters; I do not reply, but this does not prevent him from describing his latest plans for a revolution. He has appointed me to revolutionise the Cologne garrison!!! The other day we laughed till the tears came. His idiocy will spell disaster for x people, for a single letter would suffice to guarantee the salaries of a hundred Demagogue[139] judges for three years. As soon as I have completed the revolution in Cologne he would have no objection to assuming the leadership for all subsequent operations. Very kind of him! Fraternal greetings. Your Becker."[271]

c) Three letters from Bermbach to me which reveal the nature of our correspondence and one of which (that of March) also contains an answer to my letter[272] about Hirsch, the denunciation of Mrs Daniels and the consequent searching of her house.[a] This letter proves that she did not correspond with me. d) Copy of the letter from Stieber. e) Instructions to Schneider, in which I inform him among other things that the *authenticated documents* (or *duplicate*) will be sent on Thursday (28 October) by registered post from London direct to his address, and that he will at the same time receive the *certificate of registration* via Düsseldorf from W., the merchant. So if the government detain it this time, we can show that we have caught them *au flagrant délit*[b] while they, for their part, will have deprived the defence of nothing more than a duplicate.

In the *Advertiser* next Saturday (30 October) you will find a short statement on the infamous articles in *The Times*[c] and *The Daily News*. It will be signed: 'F. Engels, F. Freiligrath, K. Marx, W. Wolff.' Also in several weeklies.[d]

This time, I think, the Prussian government will be discredited in a manner not even they have ever experienced, and will see for themselves that the people they are dealing with are not blundering democrats. Through Stieber's intervention they have saved our fellows. Even Bermbach's arrest is a stroke of luck. For otherwise his letters could not have been sent over there. He would have strenuously objected for fear of being placed in temporary custody. Now that he's in jug everything's ALL RIGHT.

Père Barthélemy, born for the galleys, will make the acquaintance of Van Diemen's Land[273] this time for a change.[274] One of this fellow's dirty tricks is his persistent refusal to admit the facts, thereby implicating the seconds yet further. However, 2 have already stated that they were Cournet's seconds. As the gallows loom larger, no doubt the 3rd will forswear his *dévouement*[e] and likewise admit to having been a second.

A few days ago the guarantors met at Reichenbach's, all being present save for Kinkel and Willich who have been more or less expelled. Reichenbach, Löwe of Calbe, Imandt, Schimmelpfennig,

---

[a] See this volume, p. 107. - [b] red-handed - [c] 'From our own correspondent' in the section 'Prussia', *The Times,* No. 21243, 11 October 1852. - [d] K. Marx and F. Engels, 'Public Statement to the Editors of the English Press'. - [e] loyalty

Meyen, Oppenheim. Reichenbach, and the rest along with him, resolved to return the money to the donors. Reichenbach stated that their main reason was as follows:

'Willich and Kinkel are engaged in downright *escroquerie.*[a] Thousands of notes bearing his (Reichenbach's) signature are still circulating in America and they are disposing of them at a discount through their agents, pocketing the proceeds and using them for private purposes.'

Only the winding up of the whole filthy business would provide him with the pretext for exposing in public the *escroquerie* being perpetrated in his name, and forestalling any further embezzlement. You can see what those respectable citizens Willich and Kinkel have come to. *Des escrocs ... voilà le dernier mot.*[b]

Best regards to Weerth.

Your

K. M.

Safe addresses down here in my next.[c]

'No. 177 of the *Neue Rheinische Zeitung* contains a news item from your correspondent in Frankfurt am Main dated December 21 in which a base lie is reported to the effect that being a police spy I went to Frankfurt to try to discover the murderers of Prince Lichnowski and General Auerswald. I was in fact in Frankfurt on the 21st but stayed only one day and as you can see from the accompanying certificate I was engaged in purely private business on behalf of a lady from here, Frau von Schwezler. I have long since returned to Berlin and resumed my work as defence counsel. I would refer you moreover to the official correction in this matter that has already appeared in No. 338 of the *Frankfurter Oberpostamts-Zeitung* of December 22[d] and in No. 248 of the Berlin *National-Zeitung.* I believe that I may expect from your respect for the truth that you will print the enclosed correction in your paper without delay and that you will also give me the name of your slanderous informant in accordance with your legal obligations, for I cannot possibly permit such a libel to go unpunished, otherwise I shall regretfully be compelled to proceed against your editorial board.

'I believe that in recent times democracy is indebted to no one more than *myself.* It was I who rescued hundreds of democrats who had been charged from the nets of the criminal courts. It was I who even while a state of siege was proclaimed here persistently and fearlessly challenged the authorities (and do so to this very day), while all the cowardly and contemptible fellows (the so-called democrats) had long since fled the field. When democratic organs treat me in this fashion it is scarcely an encouragement to me to make further efforts.

'The real joke, however, in the present case lies in the clumsiness of the organs of democracy. The rumour that I went to Frankfurt as a police agent was spread

---

[a] swindling - [b] Swindlers ... that's all there is to be said. - [c] The text of Stieber's letter to Marx is in Mrs Marx's hand. - [d] The letter has 21. The newspaper of 22 December carried a news item datelined 'Frankfurt, 21. Dec. Berichtigung'.

first by that notorious organ of reaction, the *Neue Preussische Zeitung,* in order to undermine my activities as defence counsel that gave that paper such offence. The other Berlin papers have long since corrected this report. But the democratic papers are so inept that they parrot this stupid lie. If I had wished to go to Frankfurt as a spy it would certainly not be announced beforehand in every newspaper. And how could Prussia send a police official to Frankfurt which has enough competent officials of its own? Stupidity has always been the failing of the democrats and their opponents' cunning has always brought them to victory.

'It is likewise a contemptible lie to say that years ago I was a police spy in Silesia. At that time I was openly employed as a police officer and as such I did my duty. Contemptible lies have been circulated about me. If anyone can prove that I insinuated my way into his favour let him come forth and do so. Anyone can make assertions and tell lies.—I think of you as an honest, decent man and so I expect from you a satisfactory answer by return of post. The democratic papers are generally in disrepute here because of the many lies they publish. I hope that you are a man of a different stamp.

Respectfully yours,
Stieber, Doctor at Law, etc.,
Berlin, Ritterstrasse 65.

'Berlin, December 26, 1848'[275]

'I herewith certify that last week Dr Stieber travelled to Frankfurt and Wiesbaden on my behalf in order to settle a private lawsuit.

Widow of the late President von Schwezler von Lecton,
Dame of the Order of Louise.'[a]

Seal

Now I would ask you to write the following message to Schneider, and dispatch it *without delay* by the 3rd route to Cologne indicated in your letter.[b]

'While it is true that Stieber *bought* the 14-16 documents belonging to the Willich-Schapper clique, he did at the same time *steal* them. For he incited a certain *Reuter* to steal in return for cash. It was some time since Reuter had actually been a 'police official' but he had OCCASIONALLY been a SPY paid *à la tâche*[c] by the Prussian embassy. He had *never* belonged to a communist society, not even the public German Workers' Society in London.[24] Reuter lived in the same house as Dietz, secretary and archivist to the Willich-Schapper central authority.[276] Reuter broke into Dietz's

---

[a] Here Marx wrote 'Verte' (see over). - [b] See this volume, pp. 218-19. - [c] by the job

bureau and handed over the papers to somebody, either Stieber or Schulz. The affair came out long before proceedings began in the Cologne Court of Assizes. For while under arrest in Hanover, Stechan was confronted by the examining magistrate with several letters he had written to Dietz in the latter's capacity as secretary to the refugee committee presided over by Schapper.[277] As everyone knows, Stechan then escaped from prison. Once in London, he wrote to Hanover demanding those letters so that he could proceed against *Reuter* in the English courts:

'1. For forced entry and theft.

'2. For *false evidence*. For he maintains that in his letter—which has now also been placed before the Cologne jurymen by Stieber—the words "530 talers, 500 for the leaders" are an *interpolation* for which the police were responsible. At the time, all he had sent to London was 30 talers, nor had he said a word about *leaders*.

'Needless to say, the Hanoverian court did not accede to Stechan's demand. The said Reuter stole all the documents by breaking into Dietz's bureau. Dietz and the Schapper clique did not find out about the matter until Stechan arrived here.'

I have this moment received your parcel, my dear Engels. *So there is no need for you to copy out the above.* I shall send it myself direct, in one of the envelopes I have received.

Tell Weerth that he is now permanently assured of one of the 'ministerial' appointments put at my disposal by Stieber, if he doesn't prefer the post of ambassador to Paris that was intended for him.[278]

Your

K. M.

If you have *important* things to tell me, address the letter to: A. Johnson, Esq., (Bullion Office, Bank of England).

First published abridged in *Der Briefwechsel zwischen F. Engels und K. Marx*, Bd. 1, Stuttgart, 1913 and in full in *MEGA*, Abt. III, Bd. 1, Berlin, 1929

Printed according to the original

Published in English for the first time

117

ENGELS TO MARX

IN LONDON

Manchester, 28 October 1852

Dear Marx,

Yesterday I sent you a volume of Dureau de la Malle[a] and a letter per Carver & Co.[b] Enclosed herewith you will find various covers done up to look like commercial ones, and enclosed therein envelopes for Hontheim and Esser I, who are less likely than Schneider to arouse the suspicions of the philistines. If you think it advisable, you can always enclose a sealed envelope for Schneider. However, I don't see why you shouldn't every now and again write a line or two to the other defence counsel to make them feel that they are important. I also enclose a commercial seal; your old one bearing Weydemeyer's arms and the clumsy S are useless. When writing to Manchester also use any other old SIXPENNY seal.

Every so often send Schneider a relatively unimportant letter by registered post so as to mislead the fellows and make them believe that we have dropped our clandestine methods for want of addresses.

There can be no doubt that the citizens whose addresses you will find here will see to it that the letters reach their destination.

You should draw counsel's attention to the obvious CRIMES and *délits*[c] committed by the police and make sure they enter a plea for Stieber's arrest on grounds of perjury and false evidence; the fellow has effectively committed PERJURY in the case of your letter to Kothes.[279]

By this evening's post a letter about more humdrum matters.

Your
F. E.

First published in *Der Briefwechsel zwischen F. Engels und K. Marx*, Bd. 1, Stuttgart, 1913

Printed according to the original

Published in English for the first time

---

[a] A. J. Dureau de La Malle, *Économie politique des Romains*. - [b] See this volume, pp. 218-20. - [c] offences

118

ENGELS TO MARX

IN LONDON

Manchester, 28 October 1852
By the 2nd post

Dear Marx,

Herewith 1 article for Dana—the thing couldn't be broken off at any other point.[a] If I manage to finish the whole lot this evening, I shall take it[b] to the post later. In the meantime this will do so that you may at least have *something* on time. For that matter, Dana will have to be content with $^3/_4$ à $^4/_5$ of a column for a change, especially if he pays so slowly.

It wouldn't surprise me at all if the Cologne trial were to last another month. There does not seem to have been a sitting on Monday, maybe because one of the accused or a couple of jurymen were unwell, or because everyone needed two consecutive days of rest. Especially with all the fine witnesses, none of whom can give any evidence. Mr Hentze has really been taken down a peg; Weerth met the gallant man in Hamburg, whereupon he railed against you most frightfully— *cela t'acquitte de toute obligation envers lui*.[c] Moreover, he admitted frankly that, if he was angry, it was for philistine reasons.

So write direct—by REGISTERED LETTER—to one of the lawyers, pointing out that the prosecution has been taken completely out of the hands of Mr Saedt and put into those of Stieber, the police spy who, with the Public Prosecutor's tacit consent, is advancing wholly novel legal theories, namely:

1. that it is a crime if, from abroad, someone morally involved in the trial provides a lawyer with documents and other information for the benefit of the accused, and exposes for what they are the lies of the police told by a fellow like Stieber; that it is likewise a crime to receive such letters;

2. that the police, on the other hand, have the right not only to permit themselves all manner of crimes, but actually to boast openly before the court and the public of:

---

[a] K. Marx, 'Political Parties and Prospects'. - [b] K. Marx, 'Attempts to Form a New Opposition Party'. - [c] that relieves you of any obligation towards him

a) *Forced entry and theft*—the breaking open of Dietz's bureau and the purloining of the documents therein.

b) *Incitement thereto*, avowedly by offers of cash; likewise *bribery*.

c) *Theft of documents* belonging to the defence, inasmuch as part of your memorandum to the lawyers was excised and detained; I won't even mention their tampering with letters, because afterwards the fellows did at least try to give it a semblance of legality.

d) *False testimony* and *perjury*, inasmuch as Mr Stieber deliberately represented the Cologne people as being the accomplices and associates of Cherval, etc., as he himself knew better and subsequently admitted it; notably inasmuch as he stated on oath that a letter sent through the post had not reached Cologne until 19 October, when in fact it was already there on the 15th; inasmuch as he cooked up all those lies about the special courier, etc.

e) *Forgery*, inasmuch as the alleged minutes were fabricated by the police themselves and submitted as genuine, whereas we were deprived of all means of providing the defence with counter-evidence.

And so on.

If the lawyers conduct themselves boldly and adroitly, the case might end, not in a verdict against the Cologne people, but in the arrest of Mr Stieber for perjury and various other Prussian crimes against the godless French *Code pénal*.[164]

There was something else I wanted to write to you about but I forgot it completely when I started chatting with Weerth, who has just got home.

I have just heard from him that Mrs Daniels has also been called as a witness for the defence—*tant mieux*.[a] The minutes will come to a glorious end. And *ce pauvre*[b] Bermbach would appear to have been unceremoniously bundled into the dock with the rest. What can they want of this poor, innocent devil?

Your

F. E.

First published in *Der Briefwechsel zwischen F. Engels und K. Marx*, Bd. 1, Stuttgart, 1913

Printed according to the original

Published in English for the first time

---

[a] so much the better - [b] that poor

119

ENGELS TO MARX

IN LONDON

[Manchester, 31 October 1852]

Dear Marx,

The way the case has been opened, it can hardly go wrong. The letter from Stieber[a] is a discovery that's worth more than all the gold-mines in Australia. What luck that the *malheureux*[b] Nothjung kept these old *N. Rh. Z.* papers and sent them to London at the time! I only hope the thing arrives; for not even the Chief Public Prosecutor would consider it a crime to suppress stuff of that kind. You'd have done better not to send this letter by registered mail but in some other way. There's still a possibility that something may go wrong between Frankfurt and Cologne and, even though the copy provides a fair amount of proof, the original is still all-important. Somebody should have taken it to Cologne, or else it should have gone by express delivery. However, I hope all will be well.

The other documents are likewise admirable, and we shall now raise a really tremendous hullabaloo.

Yesterday, for safety's sake, I sent a letter to v. Hontheim,[280] for posting in Amsterdam, in which I gave him a summary of what you had written in the letter intended for Schneider,[c] and told him about the non-arrival of Schneider's letter addressed to Dronke. 4 copies, then, and one summary.

Today I shall send another copy of Stieber's letter to Cologne by a different route, likewise dispatch to the Rhine Province cuttings containing the article in Friday's *Advertiser*,[d] and the statement in Saturday's,[e] and shall in general throw at the bourgeoisie items of information about the crimes of the police.

Now for some suggestions:

1. In view of the highly equivocal—and, as it now behoves us to show, in passages unequivocal—nature of the only incriminating pieces of evidence, your evidence and that of Lupus, Pieper, etc., etc., if given *on oath* and *authenticated*, is of great importance. It

---

[a] See this volume, pp. 225-26. - [b] unhappy - [c] See this volume, p. 217. - [d] 'Germany. From our own correspondent. Cologne, Oct. 27', *The Morning Advertiser*, No. 19142, 29 October 1852. - [e] K. Marx and F. Engels, 'Public Statement to the Editors of the English Press'.

does not matter what the Public Prosecutor says, the jury regards ourselves and the accused as GENTLEMEN. Now nothing could be easier than for 2 or 3 of you to go to Wingham and there record *on oath* those matters relating to London which all of you know about. For example:

a) that to the best of your knowledge there is no such person as *H.* Liebknecht, but only a *W.* Liebknecht, and that you people have never known any H. L.;

b) that you yourself never received a letter from Mrs Daniels;

c) that, aside from the Wednesday meetings, you did not hold any other meetings—on Thursdays in any other pub,—and

d) that you declare the evidence, contained in Hirsch's minutes as to speeches, lectures, etc., etc., allegedly given by yourselves, to be UTTERLY UNTRUE;

e) that the scrap of paper found with the red catechism and regarded by the Public Prosecutor as being in your handwriting, did not emanate from you[281]—

and anything else in the latest proceedings and Stieber's first statements which seems untrue and worth refuting.

When all this has been recorded on oath before Wingham, he will draw up an ordinary affidavit—you might as well take a draft in English along with you—and you should ask him to hand it to a POLICEMAN, who will accompany you to Hebeler, the Prussian consul in the City; the latter *must* certify Wingham's signature, *otherwise he will forfeit his exequatur.* 2 copies of this, drawn up as above, can then be dispatched to Cologne and cannot fail to have an effect. I regard this as extremely important, for it means that *all* the legal formalities have been complied with and that the thing is a legal document. Should Hebeler nonetheless refuse to sign, go to any NOTARY PUBLIC, who will certify it[282] (the latter procedure was indicated to my old man in a similar case by the Prussian authorities).

2. Yesterday I received a lengthy dissertation from Dronke about Bangya.[283] I must confess that, in view of those wretched lies about our manuscript,[a] in view of Duncker's letter sent you on Tuesday by Weerth,[284] and assuming that it is true he addressed the last letter but one to Kothes, I find no reason to doubt that he is a Prussian spy. The fact that he keeps in with the Hungarians is no proof of the contrary; if he refers us to the Hungarians, he will likewise refer the Hungarians to us. This matter must be

---

[a] K. Marx and F. Engels, *The Great Men of the Exile.*

investigated without fail and as expeditiously as possible. And if, within *vingt-quatre heures*,[a] Mr Bangya fails to provide satisfactory information as to the whereabouts of the manuscript, the previous *address* of the alleged Eisermann, giving street and no., and about his highly questionable means of subsistence, I would strongly recommend that counsel in Cologne ask Stieber outright what he knows about a certain Colonel Bangya. After the revelations that have already been made, Mr Stieber will no longer dare to give false evidence, since he cannot know what will be coming next; at the same time Schneider should be informed about the business of the manuscript so that he can pass the story on to the court, after which no further statement need be made for the time being.

3. A few people from Stechan's workers' society,[25] committee members, etc., might also go to the magistrate, not with little scraps of paper, but with whole pages, or as large samples as possible, of Hirsch's handwriting, and *declare on oath* that these are in Hirsch's hand. *Cela vaut infiniment mieux*[b] than mere unauthenticated cuttings.

On Monday we shall see that some more money is sent to you, so that none of you will get into difficulties. *Your own* affidavit could be dispatched last of all—which would have certain advantages; but we must ensure that everything arrives before the cross-examination of the witnesses is over.

Don't forget to let me have a few safe addresses as soon as you can.

Stechan's statement about the forgery[c] must also be sworn before a magistrate. *Cela pourra avoir de brillants résultats.*[d]

Kinkel has today been sneaking round the Exchange here, in tow of a RABBLE of local German Jews. However, we have been putting a few ideas in our people's heads and, here as in Bradford, Weerth will make things pretty hot for him.

Could you not obtain direct evidence of Kinkel's *escroquerie*[e] from Reichenbach through Imandt or someone, and send copies of it to the *Examiner and Times*, the *Guardian*, or the *Courier* here, and also to the Bradford papers? Such direct evidence, of course, that the fellows need have no fear of a LIBEL action. You might also send it to Dr J. W. Hudson, secretary of the Manchester Athenaeum.[244]

Strohn is back in Bradford, somewhat indisposed, and will be coming here on Wednesday or Thursday. I am writing to him

---

[a] twenty-four hours - [b] That is worth infinitely more. - [c] See this volume, p. 227. - [d] That could have splendid results. - [e] Swindle

today and will provide him with adequate instructions[285] so that, when you send him things, you can count on his attending to them efficiently and in such a way as not to clash with *my* arrangements. The main thing is that none of the commercial addresses should be used more than *once*.

We must take things to such lengths that in future people will no longer talk about 'stealing' but 'stiebering'.[a]

Then, too, there is the lawyer Schürmann, one of the defence counsel, whose address can be used for enclosures. Schneider is really too risky.

There's another reason why the Bangya affair is important: Granted that the original minute-book was *not* in Hirsch's hand, but copied—what then? Stieber has sworn in any case that he doesn't know Hirsch.

Should the Cologne people be sentenced after all, which I regard as exceedingly unlikely if we go on doing everything in our power to send over all available information and documents, we must write something without fail. If they are acquitted, I believe that this would merely soften down the government's defeat. Meanwhile we can only wait and see. Above all an exact copy must be taken of every document, affidavit, etc., all of them fully authenticated, etc., etc., for these things will provide a splendid series of *pièces justificatives*.

Dronke has asked me for 10/- as he is ill and down on his luck. Let him have it, or perhaps a bit more, when the next lot of money arrives, i.e. on Tuesday.

You had best send me the addresses per Pickford or Carver.
Regards to all and write soon.

Your
F. E.

Up here we are keeping a careful register of all outgoing documents, with dates, how sent, etc.[286]

First published considerably abridged in *Der Briefwechsel zwischen F. Engels und K. Marx*, Bd. 1, Stuttgart, 1913 and in full in *MEGA*, Abt. III, Bd. 1, Berlin, 1929

Printed according to the original

Published in English for the first time

---

[a] In the original there is a pun on *Diebereien* (thefts, stealing) and *Stiebereien* from the name Stieber.

120

MARX TO ENGELS

IN MANCHESTER

London, 2 November 1852
28 Dean Street, Soho

Dear Frederic,

Received your letter together with £5. 10/- given to Dronke.

The time when we had to be coy about writing openly to each other's actual addresses is now past. On Saturday (30 October) the lawyers received the bulk of the documents, on Sunday, the second letter from Frankfurt, and yesterday my last letter with the DECLARATION before the magistrate.[a] Today I have sent by registered post direct to Schneider II the declaration[b] which appeared in today's *Morning Advertiser*, not so much because there was still any necessity to do so, as to show the Prussian government that we possess the means to insist on the integrity of its mails or, failing that, to expose it before the London public.

The lawyers received all they needed in good time, i.e. *before* the prosecution *closed* its case. At present I am of the opinion that, unless some incident should prolong the trial and thus necessitate renewed intervention on our part, *nothing* more should go off to Cologne.

Herewith a letter from Imandt to Cluss, which contains more details about Kinkel's and Willich's *escroquerie*.[c] Up till now I hadn't had time to read the letter and had done no more than have it copied out for you by Pieper. It went off to Washington last Friday.[d]

Fleury, a merchant in the CITY, says that he can bear witness that he and other businessmen have been invited by Kinkel and Willich to purchase Loan Notes.

Just now that *chevalier d'industrie*,[e] Willich, is living on the bounty of the Russian, Herzen.

From what Freiligrath told me yesterday, it would appear that, before his departure for Manchester, Kinkel had been grovelling with renewed zeal before a crowd of CITY ALDERMEN, merchants, etc., in his role of fund-raiser, rhetorician and lesson-giver.

---

a Wingham - b K. Marx, 'The Trials at Cologne. To the Editor of *The Morning Advertiser*'. - c swindle - d 29 October - e swindler

As for the scrap of paper wrongly attributed to me,[287] all I still need is the *address of Moses Hess,* who is living in Liège. For I am going to write to him and say: 'Tell me who it was you gave the *Catechism* to and who hawked it round Germany. Otherwise I shall denounce you as a FORGER in the *Indépendance.'* Moses is bound to spill the beans, if it transpires that on this occasion it was not the police but Kinkel-Willich who imitated my handwriting, I shall have them up in court here for imitating another's hand.

Don't forget to send me the last bit for Dana.[a] Parliament assembles on Thursday.[b] The article is already somewhat out-of-date. But *after* Friday it will be completely worthless.

Kind regards to Weerth and Strohn.

Your
K. M.

The merchant, Fleury, further testifies that, *almost every week,* Willich extorts *pounds* from him and his English friends on the plea that he needs this for the refugees. Now, it can be proved that Willich-Kinkel rudely turn away *all* refugees with the remark that they have not a centime to spare for such purposes. Willich tells them that he hasn't enough himself for his daily bread; Kinkel points with emotion to his children, and at most gives away a waistcoat cast off by the late Julius, the absent Schurz or his own august person.

First published considerably abridged in *Der Briefwechsel zwischen F. Engels und K. Marx,* Bd. 1, Stuttgart, 1913 and in full in *MEGA,* Abt. III, Bd. 1, Berlin, 1929

Printed according to the original

Published in English for the first time

121

MARX TO ENGELS[c]

IN MANCHESTER

London, 4 November 1852 (?)

Dear Engels,

I am having to dictate these few lines to you today since the perfidious haemorrhoids will not let me sit down.

---

[a] K. Marx, 'Attempts to Form a New Opposition Party'. - [b] 4 November - [c] The letter is written in Mrs Marx's hand. Marx himself inserted only the year with a question mark and signed the letter.

Enclosed a letter from Schneider which arrived yesterday evening and 1 letter from Collmann to Bangya[288] which kindly send back.

As you see, Szemere wants to have his manuscript[a] back.

Vehse told me yesterday that Weerth had arranged an appointment with him in London but had got the date wrong: I duly explained things to him.

Your

K. M.

[From Mrs Marx]

Warm regards from the secretary, Marx's spouse.

Kossuth is furious with Marx for having told Dana about his DODGE with Bonaparte, Vetter, etc.; Dana has made this material into a fulminating article.[b]

First published in *Der Briefwechsel zwischen F. Engels und K. Marx*, Bd. 1, Stuttgart, 1913

Printed according to the original

Published in English for the first time

122

ENGELS TO MARX

IN LONDON

[Manchester, 5-6 November,] 1852,[c] Friday

Dear Marx,

I am glad to hear that I am not the only sufferer. Strohn was here yesterday and the day before which, of course, meant some hard drinking; he left at three this morning and will have sailed today, I hope. For me this was the *coup de grâce* and means that today I shall be no good at all. For the same reason you won't get a translation today, not that it matters, since there's bound to be some steamer or other from Southampton which the thing[d] can go by and there certainly won't be even a Speech from the Throne in Parliament before the 11th.

---

[a] B. Szemere, *Graf Ludwig Batthyány, Arthur Görgei, Ludwig Kossuth...* - [b] K. Marx, 'Movements of Mazzini and Kossuth.—League with Louis Napoleon.—Palmerston'. - [c] The year was added later by Engels. - [d] K. Marx, 'Attempts to Form a New Opposition Party'.

So the documents, including the original of Stieber's letter,[a] arrived safely. Things will liven up once the gallant Public Prosecutor has done. One might strain one's faculties to the utmost, yet never succeed in producing inanities such as those uttered by Seckendorf. Because Engels has stated in print that the best communists made the most courageous soldiers,[b] it follows that Bürgers must be convicted of conspiracy. What the cross-examination evidently implies is that the accused harboured the *intent—suspect de suspicion d'incivisme*[c]—hence that it is a matter of *perfect indifference* whether or not the accused belongs to the League[d]—in other words, Mr Seckendorf, despairing of a verdict against Daniels and Co., positively invites the jury to acquit Bürgers and Röser too! To have become so utterly addle-pated, the fellow must have been swilling strong BRANDY AND WATER every evening for at least a week. Nowhere in all this mummery is there a single word TO THE PURPOSE. Incidentally, ever since the presiding judge[e] released particulars of the cross-examination, I have not for a moment doubted Bürgers' and the others' acquittal. Neither his plaintive manifesto[f] nor his circular tour could possibly be transmogrified into an 'enterprise' whereby the constitution, etc.[289] Or are the annals of history to read thus: 'In May 1851, at the time the Crystal Palace[290] was opened in London, the tailor Nothjung travelled from Berlin to Leipzig in order to overthrow the Prussian constitution and start a civil war.' In any case, the minute book has been set aside and, from Strohn's account, some of the jurymen are quite decent, namely v. Rath, v. Bianca, Leven, Leiden, Herstadt and one other.

I also believe that, in view of the way the case is turning out, we ought at all costs to publish something. But it would be advisable, if not essential, for Schneider and one of the accused to come over to London after the trial, in which case I should arrange to come up there for a Saturday and Sunday. Then, when all has been discussed, you could go back with me and the manuscript could be ready within a few days. Meanwhile, write to old Ebner, asking

---

[a] See this volume, pp. 225-26. - [b] Engels refers to the words 'the most resolute Communists made the most courageous soldiers' in his work *The Campaign for the German Imperial Constitution* (see present edition, Vol. 10, p. 226). - [c] under suspicion of suspected civic disloyalty - [d] the Communist League - [e] Göbel - [f] The Manifesto of the Cologne Central Authority of the Communist League of 1 December 1850 drawn up by Bürgers and others. The text of the Manifesto was confiscated during the arrest of the Communist League members and published in the *Dresdner Journal und Anzeiger*, No. 171, 22 June and the *Kölnische Zeitung*, No. 150, 24 June 1851.

him whether he couldn't place this little pamphlet with Löwenthal—so far as I am concerned, we could go halves with him, both as regards profits and losses.

As for Bangya, the most immediate case against him necessarily falls to the ground if it is established that he did not address the last letter but one to Kothes.[a] I was completely flabbergasted when Dronke said in his letter that it was Bangya who had addressed the last letter but one, i.e. the last letter to have *arrived safely*. How did the *fiévreuse*[b] little man come to invent such a story? But the Collmann business looks fishy too.[288] This letter of Collmann's is written *in exactly the same hand* as the earlier ones from Eisermann[c]; I shall send it back to you tomorrow, but it seems to me that *we ought to hold on to it. Il y a là un faux.*[d] Before long we shall know through Weerth what is the matter with Collmann[e]; in the meantime you should ask Bangya to explain how Mr Collmann comes to be writing under a false name, etc., and why 'the man', and what man, died, and how it is that he has now suddenly come to life again. And find out from Mr Bangya the name of 'the commission agent' in London whom he 'knows' according to one of the letters. And, so that Dronke may also have something to do, get him to make inquiries with a German bookseller about Collmann.

It is most odd that all the letters should arrive by carrier; there's never a postmark on them, and their tone is always so perfunctory and nonchalant that one can't help smelling a rat. This one again has been written from 'a friend's at an inn'. None of this seems at all BUSINESSLIKE, any more than does the absurd evasion that it is *his* business when the manuscript[f] should be published. Enough. Even if in this instance Bangya is acting as honourably as can be expected of a mendacious Slav, it nevertheless seems to me that his friend in Berlin is an archscoundrel. Now, however, everything should be cleared up since Mr C. figures here as the immediate owner of the manuscript, and also as publisher. If there is no bookseller of this name, that clinches the matter.

Anyway, the notion that a publisher can leave a manuscript lying in his drawer for years is a novel one and hardly smacks of the book-trade. To my mind, that story about the children's books is also a DODGE; in England such muck never comes out at Christmas time. Moreover, it is written in such a vague and disjointed way

---

[a] See this volume, pp. 216 and 232. - [b] feverish - [c] See this volume, pp. 237 and 256. - [d] There's a forgery there. - [e] See this volume, pp. 251-52. - [f] K. Marx and F. Engels, *The Great Men of the Exile.*

that Bangya could not possibly infer a firm order from it. Nor does one write at an inn on such rotten paper, which looks more likely to come from a Prussian government office. *Enfin, nous verrons.*[a]

However, *I* myself can't possibly write to Bangya at this point, since I have no details of what happened between you and him, what he said to you, what other letters he may have shown you, etc. But we've got him now.

Saturday, 6 November

For physical reasons I did not manage to send off the foregoing yesterday. Since then I have read another 'Stieberiad' in the *Kölnische Zeitung.*[b] So the original minute-book has been dropped and in its stead H. Liebknecht has risen from the dead in the shape of a cash receipt. Monsieur Hirsch and company—for there must be a number of them—seem to have well and truly done the stupid Prussian police out of a lot of money. *Il valait bien la peine,*[c] their sending a police lieutenant[d] to London merely to find themselves imposed upon in this manner and, on top of that, fobbed off with the information about the *most secret* meeting at your house.[291]

But what is all this about Dronke's friend, Fleury, whom we here find openly and unequivocally described as a police spy? This will deflect some of the little man's wrath from Bangya. It would also seem that someone has blabbed about Stieber's letter, not that it matters; the way Stieber himself is drawing attention to this document and speaking of 'infamous calumnies' can only serve to enhance its effect.

Weerth is in Liverpool and will not be back for several hours so that I shall have to hold on to the letters from Schneider and Bangya[e] until tomorrow.

'By his own admission, Bürgers worked for the *Neue Rheinische Zeitung'.*[f]

That, of course, is enough to send him to the gallows. I've never heard anything like it before.

---

[a] Anyway, we shall see. - [b] 'Assisen-Procedur gegen D. Herm. Becker und Genossen. Anklage wegen hochverrätherischen Complottes', *Kölnische Zeitung,* No. 283, 4 November 1852. - [c] It was hardly worth the trouble. - [d] Goldheim - [e] See this volume, p. 237. - [f] 'Assisen-Procedur gegen D. Herm. Becker und Genossen...'

This evening, no doubt, the *Kölnische Zeitung* will bring the first news that the tide has turned. The lawyers were perfectly right to keep everything back, if only they now really put their shoulders to the wheel.

Your
F. E.

Don't forget to send me *by return* copies of Freiligrath's poems about Kinkel.[a] We have already people in Bradford who want to ask him to read them aloud.

Hirsch must still be here, at least, he was *positivement*[b] here last week, for I saw him at the Athenaeum.[244] Another chap who is the spit image of him was here as well and this confused me at first. Perhaps he has a post here, or is looking for one? By the way, when you were last here[292] we met a fellow once in Broughton who cried 'Good morning, Marx', and we couldn't place him. It was Hirsch! So the fellow goes 'on tour'. As soon as the trial is over, he must be given a good drubbing.

First published considerably abridged in *Der Briefwechsel zwischen F. Engels und K. Marx*, Bd. 1, Stuttgart, 1913 and in full in *MEGA*, Abt. III, Bd. 1, Berlin, 1929

Printed according to the original

Published in English for the first time

123

MARX TO ENGELS

IN MANCHESTER

[London,] 10 November 1852
28 Dean Street, Soho

Dear Engels,

Enclosed my wife's report[c] on yesterday's Robert Blum meeting.[293] She was with Imandt in the gallery of the Freemason's Tavern where it was held.

As far as Bangya is concerned, just hold on to Collmann's letter. Whenever he inquires after it, I shall say I kept forgetting to ask you to send it back. Had there been intentional deception on Bangya's part he would have supplied the incriminating evidence himself. So much is clear. Originally Bangya was accused of having betrayed the Paris conspiracy[143] and later of double-dealing in the Cologne affair. In both instances the contrary has proved to be the case. According to Schneider's letter, Kothes' address[a] would appear to have been betrayed by one of Kothes' own acquaintances.[294] Finally, as regards our pamphlet,[b] Weerth will by now have made inquiries about Collmann's address and the thing will inevitably be cleared up. I have given Bangya a letter to Collmann in which I point out that, though his publication date for the pamphlet is contractually agreed, there is no contractual agreement forbidding us to publish the original manuscript—still in our possession—in Brussels or New York, should we so desire. Nor is there any contractual agreement forbidding publication in a fortnight of the 2nd part by another bookseller under a separate title if it is ready and of itself constitutes a complete whole, etc.[295]

Now for the Cologne affair.

Had I been in Bürgers' etc. place, I should never have allowed Mr Becker[c] to flaunt himself so brazenly and at the expense of everyone else as *l'homme supérieur,*[d] or to debase as he did the character of the whole proceedings, much to the delight of the democrats. To defend oneself is one thing but quite another to deliver an apologia for oneself at others' expense. Becker is one of the revolution's epigones, possessed of a great deal of cunning but little intelligence and well able to calculate just how he can trick his way up to become a great man. His talents remain those *d'un infiniment petit.*[e]

As you already know, the government has, out of sheer desperation, resorted to heroic means, namely Goldheim's retro-spective report,[291] only to find itself once again ensnared.

Goldheim's testimony furnished 2 data: 'Greif' and 'Fleury'.

I therefore instituted inquiries about Greif (*to which end I myself engaged a Prussian informer*). In this way I obtained his address and found out that he lived at 17 Victoria Road, Kensington. This, however, is Mr Fleury's house. Hence it was established that Greif lives with Fleury. It further transpired that Greif's official position here is not that of 'police lieutenant' but of attaché to the Prussian

---

[a] See this volume, p. 232. - [b] K. Marx and F. Engels, *The Great Men of the Exile.* - [c] Hermann Becker - [d] the superior man - [e] of an infinitely small one

Embassy. Finally, that on Saturday, 6 November, he left here for a few weeks. Probably to go to Cologne. By his own account, he left because he was afraid of the Marxians, because Fleury had swindled him, etc.

So much was now clear: Greif was Fleury's superior and Fleury Hirsch's superior. And so, indeed, it has turned out.

On the other hand, Imandt and Dronke called on Fleury on Friday, 5 November, *Kölnische Zeitung* in hand. He, of course, feigned surprise, said he knew no one by the name of Greif, expressed his readiness to make any statement in the presence of a magistrate, but first wanted to consult his lawyer, made two appointments for Saturday, 6 November, one for 2 and the other for 4 o'clock, but took good care not to turn up and so gained for the police one more day on which we were unable to operate, apart from sending a few preliminary letters to Cologne. Finally, on Sunday, 7 November, Dronke and Imandt extracted from him a statement which you will see in the *Kölnische*.[296] I shall send you a copy but cannot at this moment lay hands on it. Having his statement safely in their pockets, they told him he was a spy, that Greif was living at his place, that we had known all about it and had been hoodwinking the police, whereas they had believed they were hoodwinking us. He, of course, continued to protest his innocence.

Finally I sent round some fellows (among them the tipsy General Herweg) to track down Hirsch's lodgings. It transpired that he also lived in Kensington, not far from Fleury.

One more thing before I go on. The *whole of Goldheim's testimony* becomes perfectly explicable if you consider that, 1. Goldheim was here on *30 October* (Saturday) and, in company with Alberts, secretary at the Prussian Embassy, went to see Greif and Fleury; 2. that on the *morning of that same 30 October* our statement about the forthcoming revelations[a] appeared in 5 English papers; 3. that Fleury had arranged a rendez-vous with Imandt and Dronke for *that same 30 October* because Dronke was to take over French lesson for him instead of Imandt. 4. But that *before* Stieber made the revelations about London at his *2nd* interrogation and *immediately* after his *first* interrogation on the subject of Cherval, etc., I had sent to the *Kölnische Zeitung*, the *Frankfurter Journal* and the *National-Zeitung, a statement* in which Stieber was already threatened with the disclosure of his *letter* to me.[b] Admittedly this

---

[a] K. Marx and F. Engels, 'Public Statement to the Editors of the English Press'. - [b] See this volume, pp. 225-26.

statement did not appear in any of the papers. But both post office and police had incontestably taken note of it.[297]

This provides a highly prosaic explanation for Stieber's 'clairvoyance' and the omniscience of his police agents in London. Everything else Goldheim said was *fabulae*.[a] I have conveyed such information as is necessary about these things to Cologne by *diverse* channels, together with Fleury's statement.[b]

But the best is yet to come.

It was, of course, my intention to take out a WARRANT against Hirsch, for which purpose I made inquiries about his lodgings. But it was not till Saturday that I obtained the address. I felt sure that, if I could get the WARRANT against Hirsch, he would implicate Fleury, and Fleury Greif.

What happens? On Friday Willich, very secretively, betakes himself with Hirsch to the court in Bow Street where, in Schärttner's presence, he obtains from Hirsch what is purported to be a written confession in triplicate stating *that some six months ago he and Fleury fabricated the spurious minutes,* he then sends off the 3 documents, 1. to Göbel, the presiding judge at the Assizes, 2. to Schneider, 3. to the *Kölnische Zeitung*—and gives Hirsch the money to *escape*, indeed, even has him accompanied to the steamer, ostensibly so that he can confess in person in Cologne.

We all only heard of this through the inquiry we had set on foot about Hirsch, and partly, too, at Bow Street, where we went to take out the WARRANT. Schapper himself told Liebknecht that Willich had breathed *not a word* to him of all this. Thus, our intention of initiating proceedings of our own in London was thwarted by Mr Willich's sleight of hand. To what end? The answer is very simple if we reflect that for the past year he has been the merchant Fleury's *homme entretenu*[c] and that *in any case, therefore, some highly compromising things must have emerged had we had Fleury apprehended.*

An instance, by the by, of the high esteem in which this man Fleury (I have *never* set eyes on him) is held by the democrats—*Techow, leaving for Australia and already on board ship, wrote him a letter in which he commended him for having both heart and head in the right place.*

The money Hirsch was given for his journey by Willich had *undoubtedly* been handed to the latter for this purpose by Fleury.

Hirsch has admitted that he tried to copy Liebknecht's writing and that he was working under the direction of the merchant Fleury (this cur is, besides, a *man of substance* and has married into

----

[a] fabrication - [b] See this volume, p. 235. - [c] kept man

a very *respectable* English Quaker family), just as Fleury himself was under the direction of Greif. This confirms in every particular what I deduced straight away from the content and dates of the original minute-book published in the *Kölnische Zeitung*, and which none of the lawyers has hitherto duly exploited.[298]

To my mind there is no doubt that the Cologne accused will *all*, without exception, be acquitted.

I should be grateful if you could write and tell *Strohn* that he would greatly oblige me if he could send me a few pounds *forthwith*. Of the £4.10/- received through you, nearly £3 has been spent on errands, informers, etc. Our impoverished League friends naturally took advantage of the many errands, appointments, etc., to tot up pretty substantial *faux frais de production*ᵃ for beer, cigars, omnibuses, etc., which I, of course, had to make good.

You will be receiving Freiligrath's poems.ᵇ

Apropos, Reichenbach has issued a *'Lithographed Statement'*[299] to all American papers in which a dirty trick is played on Willich-Kinkel. It discloses that Kinkel claimed, *inter alia*, £200 for his journey alone. I shall get hold of the document and let you have it for the archives.[216]

Your
K. M.

Greetings to Weerth. Vehse left yesterday. Have already written to Frankfurt about our pamphlet.[300] Unless we write something, Becker will seize upon all this business *ad majorem gloriam Beckeri.*ᶜ

First published considerably abridged in *Der Briefwechsel zwischen F. Engels und K. Marx*, Bd. 1, Stuttgart, 1913 and in full in *MEGA*, Abt. III, Bd. 1, Berlin, 1929

Printed according to the original

Published in English for the first time

ᵃ false expenses - ᵇ F. Freiligrath, 'An Joseph Weydemeyer', I and II. - ᶜ to the greater glory of Becker

124

MARX TO ENGELS

IN MANCHESTER

London, 16 November 1852
28 Dean Street, Soho

Dear Engels,

If you can, do a *Tribune* article on the Cologne affair[a] for Friday. You are now as familiar with all the material as myself and, for the past 4-5 weeks I have so neglected my domestic pother for the sake of PUBLIC BUSINESS that, with the best will in the world, I shall not be able to get down to work this week.

You haven't told me whether you received the Reichenbach circular[299] sent off to you last week.

This evening we are to discuss a statement for the English Press on the Cologne affair.[b] There will hardly be time to send it for you to see beforehand. However, if you could do one to reach me by *Thursday morning*,[c] that would be even better.

Regards to Weerth.

Your
K. M.

At the Ruge meeting[293] on the 9th, messages were received from Kossuth-Mazzini pleading sickness. However, on the 10th they put in an appearance at the 'Friends of Italy'.[301] Ledru did not make his excuses at all.

First published slightly abridged in *Der Briefwechsel zwischen F. Engels und K. Marx*, Bd. 1, Stuttgart, 1913 and in full in *MEGA*, Abt. III, Bd. 1, Berlin, 1929

Printed according to the original

Published in English for the first time

---

[a] F. Engels, 'The Late Trial at Cologne'. - [b] K. Marx and F. Engels, 'A Final Declaration on the Late Cologne Trials'. - [c] 18 November

125

MARX TO ENGELS[302]

IN MANCHESTER

London, 19 November 1852
28 Dean Street, Soho

Dear Engels,

Last Wednesday,[a] at my suggestion, the League here[b] *disbanded*; similarly the continued existence of the League on the Continent was *declared* to be *no longer expedient*. In any case, since the arrest of Bürgers-Röser, it had to all intents and purposes already ceased to exist there. Enclosed a statement for the *English* papers,[c] to complement our first one.[d] You should, however, put it into better and CONCISER *English*. I no longer have the German original.[e] [303] In addition I am writing for a lithographed article a detailed account of the dirty tricks played by the police,[f] and also an appeal to America for money for the prisoners and their families. Treasurer Freiligrath. Signed by all our people.[304]

The article for the *Tribune*,[g] however, is dependent on the time at your disposal. You must return the enclosed statement, or rather an amended version of the same, *as soon as possible*, since not a day longer is to be lost where the London press is concerned.

Regards to Weerth.

Your
K. Marx

First published in part in *Die Neue Zeit*, Ergänzungshefte, No. 12, 12 April, Stuttgart, 1922 and in full in: Karl Marx/Friedrich Engels, *Briefwechsel*, Bd. 1, Moskau-Leningrad, 1935

Printed according to the author's copy in a notebook for 1860

Published in English for the first time

---

[a] 17 November - [b] the London District of the Communist League - [c] K. Marx and F. Engels, 'A Final Declaration on the Late Cologne Trials'. - [d] K. Marx and F. Engels, 'Public Statement to the Editors of the English Press'. - [e] K. Marx and F. Engels, 'Erklärung', London, 18 November 1852, *New-Yorker Criminal-Zeitung*, No. 39, 10 December 1852. - [f] K. Marx, *Revelations Concerning the Communist Trial in Cologne*. - [g] F. Engels, 'The Late Trial at Cologne'.

126

ENGELS TO MARIE BLANK

IN LONDON

Manchester, 22 November 1852

Dear Marie,

I really must beg your pardon most humbly for not having already long since replied to your first letter. But at the office where I was formerly in the habit of dealing with my private correspondence, I now have so much to do that there can no longer be any question of that, and at home, *mon Dieu*,[a] my writing materials are always in such poor shape (as, e.g., my calligraphic experiments at the beginning of this letter go to show) that I can hardly bring myself to grapple with them. Nevertheless, I am doing so this evening in the hope that you will marvel at my sense of duty and regard my bad handwriting as yet another token of my brotherly love.

There was, besides, another reason that prevented me from writing to you. Namely the fact that, when you were in Germany, it occurred to me that there was something I wanted to ask you about; but when you came back I couldn't for the life of me remember what it was. You will understand that such lack of character, or rather such lack of memory, was bound to arouse considerable qualms of conscience in a self-respecting man. In all sincerity I must confess that I could not bring myself to write to you so long as I had not got to the bottom of this weighty matter. But your second letter, and the increased mental activity induced by a WELSH RABBIT and a few glasses of SHERRY, have at last brought me up to the mark again and I now recall what it was I wished to ask you. The matter in question is as follows: Did I, at Christmas or at Easter, leave two cotton shirts at your house? For these have long been missing from my wardrobe and if you have found them I should be quite glad, inasmuch as this would demonstrate that I am not at all a slipshod person.

You ask me what my wishes are. *Ma chère soeur*,[b] it's some time since I indulged in wishes, for nothing comes of them. Besides which, I really have no talent for it, for if by chance I catch myself being weak enough to wish for anything, it always turns out to be

---

[a] My God - [b] My dear sister

something I can't have and it would therefore be better for me to get out of the habit of wishing altogether. As you see, even on this subject I cannot help relapsing into the moral tone of Ecclesiastes, SO THE LESS WE SAY ABOUT IT, THE BETTER IT WILL BE. If, therefore, you intend to put me under an obligation by providing yet another token of your love this Christmas, my bungling and untutored talent in the matter of wishing is unlikely to be of much assistance to you, though I console myself with the thought that you do not in fact require such assistance, *à en juger par le passé.*[a]

I am glad to hear that you are all flourishing. Apart from a couple of colds I, too, have been pretty well on the whole; in particular there was no recurrence of toothache with the change of season and I hope it's now a thing of the past. I am still living in Strangeways, though a few doors further away,[b] but am considering leaving this district next month and moving a bit closer to Little Germany[305]; it really is too lonesome here and this winter I shall, for a change, allow myself a little entertainment, in so far as such a thing is possible in this smoky place. For six months past I have not had a single opportunity to make use of my acknowledged gift for mixing a lobster salad—*quelle horreur*[c]; it makes one get quite rusty. Anyhow, I shall have to write another book next spring, probably in English, about the Hungarian war[136] or the novels of Mr Balzac, lately deceased, or about something else. This, however, is a great secret, otherwise I wouldn't breathe a word to you about it.

What is Elise[d] up to? If she's a good cook, and can darn stockings, she might well come over here after Christmas and keep house for me. Now that Gottfried[e] (or is it Franz[f]?) the lute-player has set up house on his own, I am virtually under an obligation to follow suit to outshine him, which is very easy, for Elise would undoubtedly be able to do the honours of the house quite famously, while all your old stick-in-the-mud bachelor has is an ancient, crotchety, six-foot-tall, skin-and-bone, intimidating, snarling, blear-eyed, doddery, unkempt, ex-kitchen maid of a housekeeper, but never a wife, despite his gallantries at concerts, balls and suchlike; *pauvre bonhomme que Dieu le bénisse!*[g]

Come to that, it's time I stopped, for I am beginning to say all manner of horrid things about my fellow-men, if not about a

---

a to go by the past - b Strangeways, 48 Great Ducie Street. See this volume, p. 201. - c how   frightful - d Engels'   sister - e Gottfried   Ermen - f Franz Ermen - g may God bless him, poor fellow

member of the firm, and this one ought never to do unless there's something to be gained by it, as the Quakers say.

My greetings to Emil,[a] Elise and the children and please give my kindest regards to Mr and Mrs Heilgers. The weather was too bad and there was too much work at the office for me to come up for the funeral of the OLD DUKE[b]; we only took half a day off. In any case I shall be in town four weeks from now.

With much love,

Your

Friedrich

First published in: Marx and Engels, *Works*, Second Russian Edition, Vol. 39, Moscow, 1966

Printed according to the original

Published in English for the first time

127

ENGELS TO MARX

IN LONDON

[Manchester,] Saturday, 27 November 1852

Dear Marx,

Assuming I can raise anything towards the cost of printing the pamphlet,[c] it will be at most £2-3—at the moment I am myself in a fix. But 3 printed sheets will cost between £10 and £12, and even more with stitching, etc., etc. Unless the thing is printed on the Continent for the account of, or at least in partnership with, a bookseller, it will not get round at all. On reaching Prussia, etc., etc., it will be confiscated, and we shall be cheated by the booksellers. So we shall have to regard the money as sacrificed on this business, for there certainly won't be any return in the way of £. s. d. The question now is whether we can spend this amount upon it; or at least, whether it might not be better to condense the thing into 1-1 $\frac{1}{2}$ sheets, so that the cost is rather more commensurate with our resources. December and January are for me the two most difficult months in the whole year; I can hardly

---

[a] Blank - [b] The Duke of Wellington - [c] K. Marx, *Revelations Concerning the Communist Trial in Cologne.*

consider making any further contribution to the cost before February. If we have it printed on credit, the printer will, as with Weydemeyer, end up by withholding copies until he has been paid.[306] And whatever we do, we must begin by finding out what prospects there are of its being distributed; at the moment there would seem to be virtually none.

Weerth is coming up to London tomorrow and sails from Southampton on 2 December. His OUTFIT cost him a great deal of money. Strohn, too, will shortly be travelling to London and thence to the Continent. The travelling expenses he must incur in establishing himself (on foreign capital to boot, or so I hear) are so heavy that we shall not be able to squeeze anything out of him either. So we are all of us in a fix.

It is my opinion that, unless you have reasonably good channels of distribution through booksellers, the thing won't even be heard of, and, like all literature published by émigrés, will go before anyone in Germany has a chance to see it. And that is very bad—even worse, in some ways, than if nothing were done at all. For it would provide public proof that we are dependent on hole-and-corner German emigrant printing presses and are powerless to get anything done. We were able to disassociate ourselves from the fiasco of Bürgers' circular[a] by withdrawing into our literary sanctum, but even this could be compromised were we to admit literary impotence in such a way. The Prussian government would be delighted to see us reduced in matters of publicity to the same expedients as were available to the demagogues of 1831 during their exile,[307] i.e. virtually zero. Lamentable though this is, it would, I think, be better, if *we* at least did not blazon it abroad. Furthermore, now that the new crime of treasonable correspondence [...] has been recognised by the jury, we could not send a single copy to the Rhine Province, which would be the chief market, without compromising hundreds of people.

I shall send you the money on 1 or 2 December. Consider the matter once more and, if you still think it would be better to print the pamphlet in this way rather than not at all, you should at least try so to arrange things that we do not run into difficulties over payments for, as I have said, I can commit myself to nothing before February.

Weerth may already have written and told you that Mr Chr.

---

[a] The Manifesto of the Cologne Central Authority of the Communist League of 1 December 1850 drawn up by Bürgers and others. See also this volume, p. 238.

Coilmann *is not to be found* at the address indicated, 58 or 59 Neue Königsstrasse or, for that matter, in Berlin, nor does anyone know a bookseller of that name.[a] *Après tout, il paraît pourtant qu'on a voulu nous jouer.*[b] For the time being I shall not let Mr Bangya have any of the stuff back. So Schulz, the 'commercial traveller', and the dead policeman,[c] were one and the same person after all!

Warmest regards to your wife and children. I shall be in London in somewhat over a fortnight.

Your
F. E.

First published abridged in *Der Briefwech-sel zwischen F. Engels und K. Marx*, Bd. 1, Stuttgart, 1913 and in full in *MEGA*, Abt. III, Bd. 1, Berlin, 1929

Printed according to the original

Published in English for the first time

128

ENGELS TO MARX

IN LONDON

Manchester, Monday, 29 November 1852

Dear Marx,

I've been toiling over the enclosed article[d] until one o'clock in the morning, but another post goes at 9 a.m. I'll try it as an experiment and see whether you get it in time for the STEAMER (Tuesday evening per first MAIL to Liverpool); if not, you'll have to send it by Friday's steamer.

Tomorrow I have to go out of town. If I'm back early enough I shall send you some money.

Shall I be getting an article on England for the *Tribune* soon? I am now able to work again.

Cobden seems to have been disappointed in the ministerial hopes

---

[a] See this volume, p. 239. - [b] It looks as though they have been trying to hoodwink us after all. - [c] A pun on Schultz—the name and *Polizeischulz*—a police official. - [d] F. Engels, 'The Late Trial at Cologne'.

Adolph Bermbach

Ernest Jones

he had pinned on Graham and Russell; the latter would appear to be giving him the cold shoulder. I can see no other explanation for his rage on Friday.[a] Not since 1844 has the fellow spoken with such fury. HE IS A DISAPPOINTED DEMAGOGUE AGAIN for as long as this continues. By the way, it's a good thing the Tories were in a majority, for now we shall get to hear about Disraeli's budget after all.[308] If the chap's knowledge and intelligence were greater and his cunning and thieving propensities less, nothing would be easier than to arrange a FREE TRADE BUDGET for the FREE TRADERS that would make them see stars. If only the fellows hold out until the crisis comes! We are *décidément* in EXCITEMENT. Although even this is still going very *piano piano* But no matter. The six pages of JOINT-STOCK prospectuses in today's *Daily News*—on the strength of which it thinks to outshine *The Times*—are bound to have an effect, likewise the 50-80 or so foreign railway, gold mining, steamship, etc., etc., companies. Inevitably this will create a taste 'for more'. Fortunately the only circumstance which might have brought over-production in the cotton industry to a premature end has now been eliminated; the new crop will be *far in excess of 3 million bales,* i.e. the biggest there has ever been, and cotton is again going down; so there'll be no shortage of raw material. Only let the corn harvest fail next year and we shall see a merry dance. But unless it does so, it is difficult to say whether anything decisive will happen as early as next year, given the abnormal conditions, given the mushroom growth of the markets in Australia and California where, as there are hardly any women and children, one individual consumes perhaps four times as much as elsewhere and gold is freely squandered in the towns, given the new market which the Calcutta houses are already exploiting in Burma, given the way Bombay and Karachi are expanding their trade with North-East India and the adjacent territories (particularly so in the case of the latter), etc.

Your

F. E.

First published in *Der Briefwechsel zwischen F. Engels und K. Marx,* Bd. 1, Stuttgart, 1913

Printed according to the original

Published in English for the first time

---

[a] R. Cobden, [Speech in the House of Commons on 26 November 1852,] *The Times,* No. 21284, 27 November 1852.

129

MARX TO KARL EDUARD VEHSE

IN DRESDEN

[Rough copy]

[London, end of November 1852]

Sir,

No doubt you thought it unusual that I, a stranger, should have written to you like an old friend.[191] For this you must ascribe the blame to Weerth and Reinhardt. However, I realise that I was thoroughly mistaken. As an acquaintance of Campe's, that old usurer, *parjure*[a] and maid-wife-widower, you must have been aware that this individual is one of my mortal enemies, and hence you had no right to offer him my pamphlet,[b] thereby affording him the opportunity he desired of conveying his impertinences to me indirectly and at no risk to himself. I am not personally acquainted with the individual, although possessed of some specific information about him. The fact that I am engaged in a fight *à mort*[c] with the SHAM LIBERALS is enough to expose me to his intrigues which, *il en peut être sûr,*[d] I shall answer when the time is ripe.

In the second place you had no right whatever, upon receiving an inquiry from me, to write to Mr Bangya. So far as I am aware, it was I who introduced you to Mr Bangya, but in no sense did I present him as my confident in private matters. And it is strange to have Campe's insolence conveyed to me through a 3rd party whom Mr Campe—I have this on the authority of Weerth here and shall inform Bangya accordingly—declares to be a *spy*.

Should this letter cause you offence, you need only come to London; you know where I live and may be assured that you will always find me prepared to give you the satisfaction customary in such cases.

Dr K. Marx

First published in: Marx and Engels, *Works*, First Russian Edition, Vol. XXV, Moscow, 1934

Printed according to the original

Published in English for the first time

---

[a] perjurer - [b] Apparently K. Marx and F. Engels, *The Great Men of the Exile*. - [c] to the death - [d] he may be sure of it

130

MARX TO ENGELS

IN MANCHESTER

London, 3 December 1852
28 Dean Street, Soho

Dear Frederic,

You would long ago have had an answer to your letter (enclosing the article for Dana[a]), had I not been occupied with the dictation of the final version of my pamphlet,[b] and then delayed by visits from Weerth, Strohn, Damm, etc.

In all probability the pamphlet will be printed in Switzerland by Schabelitz JUNIOR, who has left his old man and set up his own bookshop. Moreover, if Cluss thinks he can recoup the cost of production, he can have the thing printed in Washington. Printed it *must* be, if only so that it may be available as a public document after the outbreak of the revolution. I have made some further, very interesting discoveries about the Cherval conspiracy, etc., which I hope you will be reading in print.[309]

Weerth called on Sunday evening, and found me very busy and not in the best of moods. He asked me 'what did I propose, actually, to write about the Cologne affair?'—and this in somewhat superior, nasal tones. I asked 'what did he propose to do in the West Indies?' and, after a quarter of an hour or so, he made off. On Tuesday evening he reappeared and said he had not wished to come back, actually, but had yielded to Freiligrath's insistence. For on Sunday I had seemed to him very busy and out of temper. I took the liberty of pointing out to Mr Weerth that, for 9/10ths of the time I had known him, he had always been out of temper and MALCONTENT, which was something he couldn't say of me. After I had given him a piece of my mind, he pulled himself together and became the old Weerth again. He seems to me to have become damned bourgeoisified and to be taking his career too much 'au sérieux'.[c] Strohn at least is the same as ever, and *pas trop fin*.[d]

[a] F. Engels, 'The Late Trial at Cologne'. - [b] K. Marx, *Revelations Concerning the Communist Trial in Cologne*. - [c] seriously - [d] not too clever

10*

Today Mr Bangya has received the following letter from me[a]:
'I have today received from Engels a letter containing some highly curious pieces of information.[b]

'Engels has not written to the address indicated by you for, as he points out, what is actually proved by an answer to a letter that is sent not direct but only poste restante, through the medium of a second address?

'Instead, Engels asked some business friends in Berlin to make inquiries. After the most painstaking investigations they now tell him that:

'1. no such firm as Collmann exists.

'2. no such person as Collmann exists at the address indicated, 58 or 59 Neue Königsstr.

'3. no one at all by the name of Collmann is to be found in Berlin.

'Engels further draws my attention to the fact that the two letters signed Eisermann and the letter signed Collmann were written by the same hand, that all 3 possess the unusual quality of being loose bits of paper bearing no postmark, that in the first two Eisermann, and in the third Collmann, figures directly as publisher, etc., and that on pretexts that are mutually incompatible the thing has been allowed to drag on for nearly 7 months.[310]

'Now that Collmann has proved to be as much of an illusion as was previously the non-existent publisher of the *Constitutionelle Zeitung* Eisermann, I ask you yourself, how can all these contradictions, improbabilities and mysteries over something so simple as the publication of a pamphlet[c] be *rationally* explained?

'"Trust" will not conjure away facts, nor do people who respect one another demand unquestioning faith of one another.

'I confess that, the more I turn this matter over in my mind, the more I am compelled, even with the best will in the world, to find it damned *obscure;* also that, were it not for my feelings of friendship towards you, I would unhesitatingly echo Engels' concluding remark: "*Après tout il paraît pourtant qu'on a voulu nous jouer.*"[d]

Yours etc.,

Marx

---

[a] See this volume, pp. 257-58. - [b] ibid., p. 252. - [c] K. Marx and F. Engels, *The Great Men of the Exile.* - [d] 'It looks as though they have been trying to hoodwink us after all.'

'P.S. Engels finally draws my attention to the fact that, even were the manuscript in question to reappear for a few days in London,[311] absolutely nothing would be proved and nothing gained. What could it prove, save the existence and identity of the manuscript, of which nobody is in doubt.'

Tomorrow we shall see what reply comes from Mr Bangya.

Bonaparte is spending some glorious months honeymooning with his empire. The fellow has always lived on tick. Simply make loan institutions in France as universal and as accessible as possible to all classes of Frenchmen—and the whole world will believe that the millennium is here. On top of that, a bank of one's own, no less, for STOCKJOBBERY and RAILWAY HUMBUG.[312] The fellow never changes. Not for one moment does the *chevalier d'industrie*[a] deny the pretender, or vice versa. If he doesn't go to war and that right soon, he'll founder on his finances. How good that Proudhon's plans for salvation should find realisation in the only form in which they are practicable—that of the credit racket and more or less barefaced fraud.

I am looking forward very much to your arrival here.[313]

Your

K. Marx

First published considerably abridged in *Der Briefwechsel zwischen F. Engels und K. Marx*, Bd. 1, Stuttgart, 1913 and in full in *MEGA*, Abt. III, Bd. 1, Berlin, 1929

Printed according to the original

Published in English for the first time

131

MARX TO JÁNOS BANGYA

IN LONDON

[Rough copy]

London, 3 December 1852
28 Dean Street, Soho

Dear Bangya,

I have today received from Engels a letter containing some highly curious pieces of information.[b]

Engels has not written to the address indicated by you for, as he points out, what is actually proved by an answer to a letter that is

---

[a] swindler - [b] See this volume, p. 252.

sent not direct but only poste restante, through the medium of a 2nd address?

Instead, Engels asked some business friends in Berlin to make inquiries. After the most painstaking investigations they now tell him that:

1. no such firm as Collmann exists;

2. no Collmann exists at the address indicated, 58 or 59 Neue Königsstr. and

3. no one at all by the name of Collmann is to be found in Berlin.

Engels further draws my attention to the fact that the two letters signed Eisermann and the letter signed Collmann were written by the *same* hand, that all 3 possess the unusual quality of being loose bits of paper bearing no postmark, that in the first 2 Eisermann, and in the 3rd Collmann, figures directly as *publisher*, etc., and that on pretexts that are mutually incompatible the thing has been allowed to drag on for nearly 7 months. Now that Collmann has proved to be as much of an illusion as was previously the non-existent publisher of the *Constitutionelle Zeitung*, Eisermann, I ask you yourself, how can all these contradictions, improbabilities and mysteries over something so simple as the publication of a pamphlet be *rationally* explained?

'Trust' will not dispose of facts, nor do people who respect one another demand unquestioning faith of one another.

I confess that, the more I turn this matter over in my mind, the more I am compelled, even with the best will in the world, to find it damned *obscure*; also that, were it not for my feelings of friendship towards you, I would unhesitatingly echo Engels' concluding remark: '*Après tout il paraît pourtant qu'on a voulu nous jouer.*'[a]

Yours ever,

K. Marx

P.S. Engels finally draws my attention to the fact that, even were the manuscript in question to reappear for a few days in London,[311] absolutely nothing would be proved and nothing gained. What could it prove, save the existence and identity of the manuscript, of which nobody is in doubt.

First published in *MEGA*, Abt. III, Bd. 1, Berlin, 1929

Printed according to the original

Published in English for the first time

---

[a] 'It looks as though they have been trying to hoodwink us after all.'

132

MARX TO ADOLF CLUSS[314]

IN WASHINGTON

[London,] 7 December 1852

... Enclosed you will find: 1. A manuscript of mine: *Revelations Concerning the Communist Trial in Cologne.* This manuscript went off to Switzerland yesterday to be printed there and thence pitched into Germany as *étrennes*[a] for the Prussian gentlemen. You should have it printed locally[315] *if* you believe that sales in America will enable you to recoup at least the *production costs,* if more, *tant mieux.*[b] In which case, advance notices should appear in the Press to whet people's curiosity. If the pamphlet does come out in America, it should be published *anonymously,* as in Switzerland. To appreciate to the full the humour of the thing, you must know that its author, for want of anything decent to wear on his backside and feet, is as good as interned and, moreover, is and continues to be threatened with *truly ghastly misère*[c] engulfing *his family* at any moment. The trial dragged me even deeper into the mire, since for 5 weeks, instead of working for my livelihood, I had to work for the party against the government's machinations. On top of that, it has completely alienated the German booksellers with whom I had hoped to conclude a contract for my Economy.[45] Finally, Bermbach's arrest has deprived me of the prospect of making anything out of the *Brumaires* sent through you—300 had been ordered through him as long ago as May. So it's a pretty kettle of fish.[d]

Here in London I have made it generally known that the pamphlet is to be printed in North America, if only so that we can make an incursion from Switzerland behind the Prussians' backs. They suspect that something is afoot and by now will have ordered the *douaniers*[e] and police in Hamburg, Bremen and Lübeck to be on the qui-vive.

2. Herewith also an appeal for money for the Cologne prisoners

---

[a] New Year's gifts - [b] so much the better - [c] poverty - [d] The original has 'Holland in Not' (Holland in distress)—an expression used by the Dutch during the struggle for independence (1572-1609), to call out their fellow-countrymen to pierce the dykes and drive away the Spanish invaders. - [e] customs men

and their families.[a] See that it appears in various papers. It might also be a good idea for you to form committees over there. Here it is a matter of a party demonstration. You will observe that Ernest Jones actually appears as a party member. In an introductory note, signed by you both, you might specially emphasise that this is not a case of begging for the revolution Kinkel-fashion, etc., but rather of a *definite* party aim whose fulfilment is demanded by the honour of the workers' party.

A longish statement (signed by me, Lupus, Freiligrath and Engels) about the government's infamies at the Cologne trial has appeared in various London papers.[b] What especially riles the Prussian Embassy is the fact that the most *distinguished* and *respectable* London weeklies, the *Spectator* and the *Examiner*, have accepted this unvarnished denunciation of the Prussian government.

The Morning Advertiser did not print your letter[c]; can it have smelt a rat?

The item from the *Abendzeitung* received from you today, according to which I, etc., the police, etc., is a scurrility on the part of Mr M. Gross, who has been put up to it by some Willichian or other in New York. You will see from my manuscript what kind of role this 'honourable' Willich plays in the Cologne trial. I have kept a good deal back, partly so as not to impair the literary scheme of the whole, and partly for use as fresh ammunition should the fellow—which I hardly dare hope—have the courage to reply.

I am tickled by Fickler's letters. Blind, who is now living here with his wife, tells me that, during the industrial exhibition,[316] Fickler, good, honest Fickler, rented a large house and furnished it sumptuously for the purpose of reletting. The speculation misfired. Not only did Fickler make off to America to escape his creditors. He also made off without breathing a word of his plans to his marriageable daughter who lived with him, and without leaving her a single centime. She, of course, was thrown out of the house. What became of her after that, no one knows. Good, honest Fickler!

As regards Proudhon, you are both right.[317] Massol's delusions were due to the fact that Proudhon, with his usual industrial

---

[a] K. Marx and F. Engels, 'Appeal for Support of the Men Sentenced in Cologne'. - [b] K. Marx and F. Engels, 'A Final Declaration on the Late Cologne Trials'. - [c] See this volume, p. 207.

quackery, adopted as *his* 'latest discoveries' some of my ideas, e.g., that there is *no such thing as absolute knowledge,* that everything is explicable in terms of material conditions, etc., etc. In his book on Louis Bonaparte[a] he openly admits what I had to deduce for myself first from his *Philosophie de la Misère,* namely, that his ideal is the *petit bourgeois.*[b] France, he says, consists of 3 classes: 1. Bourgeoisie; 2. Middle class (*petit bourgeois*); 3. Proletariat. Now the purpose of history, and of revolution in particular, is to dissolve classes 1 and 3, the extremes, in class 2, the happy mean, this being effected by Proudhonian credit transactions, the final result of which is the abolition of interest in its various forms.

General Vetter will be looking up Weydemeyer in New York and yourself in Washington.

Ad vocem[c] *Kossuth.* When I learnt through what you sent about the initial scandal in the German-American Press over my 'PRIVATE CORRESPONDENCE' in the *Tribune,*[d] I sent a statement[e] to the *Tribune,* signed 'YOUR PRIVATE CORRESPONDENT' of which herewith a summary[f]:

But to continue. On receiving from you the cutting in which one of Kossuth's secretaries describes me as an infamous calumniator, etc., and at the same time works for Pierre,[g] etc., I informed Mr Kossuth of the contents of my first statement to the *Tribune* and asked the gentleman for a definitive explanation. Whereupon Kossuth replied 1. *on his word of honour,* that he has no secretary; that possibly Benningsen in America, his one-time clerk of chancery, had arrogated this office to himself; and 2. that the first he had heard of the alleged statement had been through me (I having sent him the *corpus delicti,* the slip of paper contained in your letter); 3. that he was grateful for my 'WARNING' and would again invite me to meet him somewhere on neutral ground.

Next Friday I shall convey points 1 and 2 to the *Tribune* again.[h] Keep me *au fait* with this affair.

Ad vocem Kinkel. Well, Kinkel has been roving around lecturing on modern poetry, etc., in Bradford and Manchester where, like the clerical, aesthetic, liberal parasite he is, he paid court to the German Jews. People who attended his lectures have informed me

---

[a] P. J. Proudhon, *La révolution sociale démontrée par le coup d'état du 2 décembre.* - [b] K. Marx, *The Poverty of Philosophy* (see present edition, Vol. 6, p. 190). - [c] re - [d] K. Marx, 'Movements of Mazzini and Kossuth.—League with Louis Napoleon.—Palmerston'. On details see this volume, pp. 268-69. - [e] K. Marx, 'Kossuth, Mazzini, and Louis Napoleon'. - [f] Note by Cluss in the original: (there follows the piece you know). - [g] Pierre Napoleon Bonaparte.- [h] K. Marx, 'A Reply to Kossuth's "Secretary"'.

on his aesthetic derring-do as follows: he announces that he will be giving a *lecture on Goethe's Faust* in Bradford, admittance 3/- per head. Hall packed. Great expectations. And what does Gottfried do? Reads them *Faust* from cover to cover, and calls this a lecture *on 'Faust'*! Needless to say, Gottfried was wily enough to save up this *piece of cheating* for the very last lecture. In Manchester Gottfried declared:

'Goethe is *no* poet, he rhymes "*erbötig*" with "*Venedig*"; but *Immermann* is the greatest of all German poets.'

And again:

'I would venture to say that, of the more recent German poets, 3 in particular have enjoyed the favour of the public—Herwegh, Freiligrath and—if I would venture to say—*Gottfried Kinkel.*'

But easy-going Gottfried also lectured on politics, e.g. on the parties in North America. Here is what he said in Manchester and Bradford:

'True, I announced that I was going to speak about the American parties, e.g. Democrats, Whigs, Free Soilers,[318] etc. But in fact there are no more parties left in America, than there are in Europe. There remains only the *one great party of the liberals,* as would also become apparent in Germany, if only the defeated party were allowed to resume its former position.'

Finally *Gottfried* spoke about the *Mormons*[319] of whom, among other things, he declared:

'He who wishes to be rid of all earthly cares should betake himself to the Mormons', etc.

His pronouncements even led people in Bradford to believe that he was a *Mormon agent*. Be that as it may, Gottfried Kinkel left the two manufacturing towns profoundly convinced that he *must never show his face there again*.

At the Assizes in Cologne Becker[a] has discredited both himself and the party. It had been mutually agreed from the outset that he would come forward as a non-League[b] member, so as not to lose the good-will of the democratic petty bourgeoisie. But being very weak in theory and pretty strong in the matter of petty ambition, he was all of a sudden overcome by vertigo. He wanted to play the great man of democracy at the communists' expense. Not only did he want to get off scot-free, but also carry off in

---

[a] Hermann Becker - [b] The Communist League

person what laurels were to be won at the trial. He is not only as shameless as ever, he is growing despicable.

In conclusion, a few words on France. Bonaparte, who has always lived on tick, believes that there is no better way of bringing about the golden age in France than by making loan institutions universal, and as accessible as possible to all classes.[312] His transactions have a twofold advantage: They pave the way for an atrocious financial crisis, and demonstrate what results from Proudhon's credit manoeuvres when they are put into practice and not confined to theoretical day-dreams, namely a stock-jobbing swindle unparalleled since the days of John Law.

The Orleanists—I know one of their agents[a] very well—are tremendously active. Thiers is here at the moment. They have many allies in the army and in Bonaparte's immediate entourage. They intend to murder him (in January) in his bed. *Nous verrons.*[b] At all events, I shall be notified a fortnight *before* the attempt, and shall in turn notify the revolutionary proletarian party in Paris through the secret society of '*frères et amis*'[c][320] to which I belong. If the Orleanists pull the chestnuts out of the fire, they must in no case be allowed to eat them.

Should Heinzen, etc., brag about Becker's performance in Cologne, thereby compromising us all, you must publish a statement signed with your name, to the effect that Becker was a member of the communist society[d] and that shortly before his arrest, he invited me to write a paper *against* the democrats, but asked me not to reply to the attacks of Heinzen and Ruge, those wretched allies of Müller-Tellering. Of course, you should only make use of this weapon *if absolutely necessary.* In which case you declare outright that Becker took the stage as arranged, but grossly over-acted, did not play his part *skilfully enough*—which is all that he can be reproached with.

K. M.

First published in part in *Die Neue Zeit,* Bd. 2, No. 31, Stuttgart, 1906-07 and in full in: Marx and Engels, *Works,* First Russian Edition, Vol. XXV, Moscow, 1934

Printed according to the letter from Cluss to Weydemeyer of 6-7 January 1853

Published in English in full for the first time

---

[a] Presumably, F. M. Rémusat. - [b] We shall see. - [c] brothers and friends - [d] the Communist Leauge

133

MARX TO ENGELS

IN MANCHESTER

London, 14 December 1852
28 Dean Street, Soho

Dear Engels,

Like you, I have been suffering all this while from piles. But this time they did not, in my case, reach the 'perfidious' stage, since they luckily occurred during the time of lean kine. If necessary you should use leeches. *C'est le grand moyen.*[a]

The money arrived a week ago yesterday.

From the following copy of a letter from Schabelitz jnr. you will see how things stand with the *Revelations Concerning the Communist Trial in Cologne.*

'Basle, 11 December 1852

'Dear Marx,

'I received the manuscript intact day before yesterday, and today am already going through the first sheet of proofs. The pamphlet is SPLENDIDLY set in a completely new type and will appear in 16mo. We shall get the proofs as best we can. The whole will amount to 70-80 printed pages and we could, I think, fix the price at 10 silver groschen per copy, since part at any rate of the edition (2,000 copies) is likely to be confiscated. The main consignment will go to the Rhine Province. I feel sure the pamphlet will create a tremendous sensation, for it is a masterpiece. There were four of us reading through the manuscript, two highly competent and discriminating men'

(do you suppose Schabelitz numbers himself among the 'competent'?)

'and we were all unanimous in our praise of it. It certainly constitutes a "memorial" to the Prussian government.

'With kind regards to the Marx party.

Yours
J. Schabelitz'

This last is an allusion to certain misgivings of mine lest Schabelitz should take offence at the rough treatment meted out to the Willich-Schapper party, to which he himself *plus ou moins*[b] belonged.

---

[a] That's the drastic means. - [b] more or less

Secrecy being all-important if the thing is not to be confiscated as soon as it reaches the German border, I have been putting it about here that a pamphlet on the Cologne affair is to appear in America.

In order not to overburden you in your present haemorrhoidal condition I got Pieper to translate *tant bien que mal*[a] a critique of Disraeli's budget[b] written for Dana and it went off to America last Friday.[c]

Excuse me for not writing more this time. I have the most infernal headache.

Your

K. Marx

First published in *Der Briefwechsel zwischen F. Engels und K. Marx*, Bd. 1, Stuttgart, 1913

Printed according to the original

Published in English for the first time

134

MARX TO ADOLF CLUSS[321]

IN WASHINGTON

[London,] 14 December 1852

... No more than a few lines today. Brüningk has written to me. I replied in writing,[322] telling him that Kinkel and Willich were the *instigators of the rumour* and that I had alluded to, but not named them, in my letter to you.

Should Kinkel issue a public denial in the American Press, I shall publish the whole correspondence and/or the record of what happened between him, myself and J. Huzel,[d] as proof of his veracity and his courageous vindication of the imputations he had made.

Should Brüningk demand that you recant or publicly attack you for 'deliberate distortion of the material with which I provided you', confine yourself to the following points: 1. You could perfectly well have concluded that Mrs von Brüningk was an agent whom *even* her friends suspected her of being one,[e] the more so

---

[a] as well as he was able - [b] K. Marx, 'Parliament.—Vote of November 26.—Disraeli's Budget'. - [c] 10 December 1852 - [d] See this volume, pp. 139-40 and 149-50. - [e] ibid., pp. 125, 152, 204 and 205.

since she was an agent for the notorious Russian agent, Princess von Lieven.

2. You had all the less reason to stand on ceremony since Schimmelpfennig—Mrs von Brüningk's crony—had established the principle that Marx and Co. were to be *calumniated*.

3. You might have issued a statement yourself had Brüningk approached the *Wecker* direct, and then yourself instead of dragging in the miserable Ruge-Ronges. *Ça suffira.*[a]

Ad vocem[b] *E. Jones.* Jones is now RISING rapidly. Harney's paper—and J.'s rival—*The Star of Freedom, set* some 3 weeks ago.

Ad vocem Kinkel-Willich. The effrontery of these two fellows' anti-Reichenbach statement surpasses all bounds.

1. Reichenbach acted too leniently in respect of these fellows in concealing the *real* reason which above all motivated his action.[323] For in America Loan Notes bearing Reichenbach's signature still continue to circulate. *Kinkel and Willich* got their agents in America to *convert them into silver,* even at a discount, and send *the proceeds direct* to them, long after they had been disowned *qua* financial committee by the London guarantors; similarly, they hawked these notes round London. *At no time have they accounted for* the sums thus received. It was *downright escroquerie*[c] and Reichenbach deemed a statement necessary in order to clear himself of all responsibility for it.

2. The *German* papers *applauded* the resolution to return the money to America, Kinkel coming in for especial *praise*. The rascal received these bourgeois plaudits in silence—nor, in Bradford and Manchester, did he show any inclination whatever to confess his *opposition* to the said resolution. He seeks to appear respectable to bourgeoisie in Germany in order to make money, and poses as a believer in revolution before the revolutionary philistines in America in order to wrest from the clutches of the Cerberus Reichenbach the money he has swindled from them.

3. Willich pins his faith to the distance between America and London. Over here the fellow is regarded by all the refugees as a proven spy and a rogue unmasked. He believes that in America he will still be able to play the treasurer of the revolution.

Hirsch has told a working men's club in Blamich Street[d] that Willich is his accomplice. He himself, the sly Hirsch (!!!) says, is a spy in the interests of democracy, but Willich in the interests of the police, no less. Willich's society heard about this. Questions

---

[a] That will be enough. - [b] re - [c] swindle - [d] In the original there is a question mark above this word.

were asked, etc. (you may have read about it already in my *Revelations*).[324] He could think of nothing better than to remove with a minute nucleus of his society to another establishment where *visitors were not admitted,* and to shift his own domicile to a remote corner of London. These two blackguards must now be unmasked in America as well. Here they are completely done for.

Ad vocem Goegg. Goegg, who for months was telling everyone that he attended the Wheeling Congress,[245] was in Strassburg at the time, getting together what remained of his fortune, £300. Now, in company with Ronge, he is setting up kindergartens and similar German-Catholic[227] educational establishments.

Your
K. M.

First published in: Marx and Engels, *Works,* First Russian Edition, Vol. XXV, Moscow, 1934

Published according to the letter from Cluss to Weydemeyer of 6-7 January 1853

Published in English for the first time

135

MARX TO GUSTAV ZERFFI

IN PARIS

London, 28 December 1852
28 Dean Street, Soho

Dear Friend,

Sincerest thanks for your letter.

There were two circumstances which enabled Bangya to hoodwink me for so long. *Firstly,* his acquaintanceship with Szemere, whom I instantly recognised as *l'esprit fort*[a] of Hungary from his manuscript on Görgey, Kossuth, etc.,[b] also,. your friendship with Bangya, since you inspired me with complete

---

[a] brains - [b] B. Szemere, *Graf Ludwig Batthyány, Arthur Görgei, Ludwig Kossuth...*

confidence, despite the fact that we have known each other for so short a time. *Secondly:* So long as I was able, I attributed the inconsistencies, lies, etc., to Bangya's urge, which manifests itself at the slightest occasion, to shroud his activities in mystery and play at hide-and-seek not only with others but actually with himself.

At this very moment I am still inclined to believe that he is not a true spy; rather, as you rightly say, his function as *'intermediary'* between the various parties and as political match-maker has led him into dubious ways.

But first a point that is of particular concern to yourself.

Szirmay is certainly an agent of Kossuth's. His mission, or so I have gathered from some unguarded remarks, is to establish contact with Bonaparte through Mr de Maupas. A short time previously Kossuth had tried to raise a loan of $1\,^1/_2$ million from the Orleanists through the agency of Bangya and Malingre, his correspondent in Paris, but had met with a rebuff.

To return to Bangya.

I have with my own eyes seen a *commission* made out by Kossuth and countersigned by Szirmay, by which Bangya is appointed prefect of police *in partibus,* as it were, by Kossuth—as chief of an anti-government counterpolice force. On the one hand, my fears over otherwise suspect contacts and acquaintanceships of Bangya's were allayed by this commission, for it gave them an air of being official connections which, if exploited with skill, could be of use to our party; thus I myself have obtained from him some details of importance concerning the Prussian government. On the other hand, I asked him outright: 'How can you reconcile your relationship with Kossuth and your relationship with Szemere?' He replied very candidly that firstly he was acting in Szemere's interest, and then the latter had *authorised* his relationship with Kossuth. I therefore never again alluded to the subject.

Bangya several times invited me on Kossuth's behalf to visit the latter. I replied that I lived at such and such a place and that, if Mr Kossuth wished to speak to me, he need only take the trouble of coming to see me. Kossuth then suggested that we should meet on neutral ground.[a] I left the matter pending. In the meantime, however, an article of mine appeared anonymously in the *Tribune* (New York), in which I attacked Kossuth, Mazzini, etc., with especial reference to the intrigues in Paris conducted through Kiss, etc.[b] Frightful hullabaloo in the American Press! Kossuth

---

[a] See this volume, p. 261. - [b] K. Marx, 'Movements of Mazzini and Kossuth.—League with Louis Napoleon.—Palmerston'.

contacting the tyrant! IMPOSSIBLE! Bangya, questioned by Szirmay, named me as the author, whereupon I personally told Mr Szirmay, that *I* was indeed the author. Also that, so far as I was aware, I was at complete liberty to write anything I chose about and against Mr Kossuth. Shortly afterwards I received from America newspapers in which Kossuth had had me denounced 'as a calumniator' by a supposed 'private secretary' of *Monsieur le Gouverneur.* I then, via Bangya, requested Mr Kossuth to state whether this démenti had originated with him, in which case I would chastise him with scorpions, whereas hitherto I had merely touched him with a rod.[a] Kossuth replied, through Szirmay, 1. that he knew nothing about the statement, 2. that he had no private secretary, and repeated his invitation, which I ignored, to meet him on neutral ground. I, for my part, published in the *Tribune* Kossuth's statement to me,[b] and there, for the time being, the matter rests, although the entire inept and insipid German-American press is still buzzing with it. Nevertheless, the storm of indignation evoked by his article against me shows that Kossuth will be *perdu*[c] the moment the fact of his alliance with Bonaparte is established.

I am now wholly of the opinion that we should both of us observe the *utmost discretion* for, as soon as Bangya knows that we have seen through him, he could do you and Szemere harm, perhaps considerable harm, particularly as regards your remaining in Paris. Moreover, were Bangya to be in any way publicly unmasked *before* the manuscript[d] appears, it could at best only make me look ridiculous. Finally, I believe it is important—until the point has been reached at which we can publicly unmask him—that a close watch be kept on Mr Bangya. This is particularly important while he remains in Paris. He is astoundingly indiscreet and, if only to retain your confidence, will keep you and Szemere informed of every move made by the various parties he serves.

My attitude towards him, therefore, will be cool and reserved—as he can only expect after his latest coup—but I shall not let him know either the full extent of my suspicion or that I am 'secretly' corresponding with you.

Bangya himself, in the note enclosed in his anonymous friend's letter, writes:

'I think you are now at liberty to have the work published elsewhere.'

---

[a] A reference to 1 Kings 12:11. - [b] K. Marx, 'A Reply to Kossuth's "Secretary"'. - [c] lost - [d] K. Marx and F. Engels, *The Great Men of the Exile.*

In giving this advice, which, by the by, is merely the echo of a threat I made him,[a] he is, I think, trying to cover his rear.

However, I fully agree with Szemere and yourself that it is high time this was done. The only difficulty lies in the execution. A pamphlet of mine, *Revelations Concerning the Communist Trial in Cologne* has just been brought out by a Swiss bookseller.[325] (I shall arrange for 2 copies to be sent to you and Szemere as soon as possible.) This same bookseller is busy with an edition of my *18th Brumaire* for Germany.[326] There is no prospect of inducing him to embark on a third undertaking. No bookseller in Germany now dares to publish anything of mine. Hence my only recourse would be to print it *at my own expense,* which, in my present circumstances, is impossible. And yet the thing is *vital.* I shall consider what can be done.

You will see from the *Revelations* that Greif is a thoroughly infamous creature. In December 1851 he visited Paris *in connection with the Franco-German plot*[143] and in order to establish a *spurious connection* between my friends in Cologne and the idiots in Paris.[327]

However, it is true that, while Greif was still here in London, Bangya received *money from Berlin* regularly on the 3rd or 4th of each month. Do you know from what sources he is drawing this money?

Our watchword in this business should be: '*à Corsaire Corsaire et demi*'.[b] Should Bangya show signs of becoming 'dangerous', all we have to do is remind him that his connections with Malingre and the Orleanists have placed him at our mercy.

Write soon, and assure Szemere that in me he has a sincere admirer.

Yours

Ch. Williams[c]

First published in: Marx and Engels, *Works,* First Russian Edition, Vol. XXV, Moscow, 1934

Printed according to the original

Published in English for the first time

---

[a] See this volume, pp. 257-58. - [b] Set a thief to catch a thief. - [c] Marx's pseudonym

1853

136

ENGELS TO MARX

IN LONDON

Manchester, 11 January 1853

Dear Marx,

I had hoped that I might have been able to call in on you again yesterday on my way to the station for, as a result of a somewhat unpleasantly outspoken letter about my prolonged absence[313] and the work accumulating up here, I was compelled all of a sudden to pack my bags and hasten back to the office. Having scandalously neglected my business in the CITY, I had to settle it yesterday at the last moment. This held me up so long that I had no option but to set course *recta via*[a] if I was to appear today, as I needs must, AT A DECENT HOUR at the office; anyhow, I would have turned up at your house at a time in the evening when all your disciples are wont to foregather there, in which case I couldn't have answered for the consequences, i.e. pots at Göhringer's, Zimmermann's, Wood's and other night haunts.

It would be best if you were to make a PARCEL of the letters from Cluss, etc., etc., American newspapers and other such stuff, and send it per Pickford & Co., or Chaplin, Horne & Co., addressed to me here at Ermen & Engels, so that the firm pays the carriage.

Waiting for me here was a letter from Madier, in passable English, about a patent of his which might have some impact on our industry. Whether or not the thing is any good, he has all sorts of grand ideas; however, I'll see what I can do. If the invention is a *good* one, it will earn him a hefty sum, the market being almost unlimited. Should you happen to run into him, tell him I should have written to him one of these days, but I am again more than fully occupied.

---

[a] direct

I wish some of our lads in London would really settle down to a *plus ou moins*[a] steady job, for they're becoming inveterate loafers and, once you get that way, it's 10 to one you'll be tipsy for 36 hours at the least, as has twice happened to me, to the great astonishment of my sister.[b]

In the spring or early summer I shall again come up to London. Hasn't that thing[c] arrived from Schabelitz yet?

Warm regards to your wife and children and to the tipsy crew likewise.

Your

F. E.

First published abridged in *Der Briefwechsel zwischen F. Engels und K. Marx*, Bd. 1, Stuttgart, 1913 and in full in *MEGA*, Abt. III, Bd. 1, Berlin 1929

Printed according to the original

Published in English for the first time

137

MARX TO ENGELS

IN MANCHESTER

[London,] 21 January 1853

Dear Engels,

If *at all possible,* kindly translate the whole of the enclosed[d] and send it off *direct from Manchester* (*signing it with my name*) via Liverpool or Southampton, depending on sailings, to 'A. Dana, One of the Editors of the "New-York Tribune", New York'.

This is how matters stand:

Now that our misfortunes here have reached a CLIMAX, I have drawn £20 on Greeley for 10 articles (*including the enclosed*) and have written, telling him that the copyist has not quite finished copying the article (which must therefore be dated Friday), *and that it will be sent off to him on Tuesday.* I have charged him £2 per article, which is what Dana promised in his letter of 16 December

---

[a] more or less - [b] Marie Blank - [c] K. Marx, *Revelations Concerning the Communist Trial in Cologne* (see this volume, p. 264). - [d] K. Marx, 'Elections.—Financial Clouds.—The Duchess of Sutherland and Slavery'.

1851, a promise he has so far failed to keep (in respect of CURRENT LETTERS).[328]

The little Jew Bamberger has not yet given me a centime but I have his *promise* and shall by degrees extract at least £15 from him against the bill (pending its arrival).

Now that we are charging £2, the above article must be sent off in its *entirety.* The piece about the Duchess of Sutherland will cause an uproar in America.

Apropos, Blind has already dunned me twice for Herzen's book.[a] So you must return it to me.

It is 2 o'clock in the morning. Hence I cannot now have this letter STAMPED, and must send it off unstamped.

Your

K. M.

First published abridged in *Der Briefwechsel zwischen F. Engels und K. Marx,* Bd. 1, Stuttgart, 1913 and in full in *MEGA,* Abt. III, Bd. 1, Berlin, 1929

Printed according to the original

Published in English for the first time

138

MARX TO ADOLF CLUSS[329]

IN WASHINGTON

[London,] 21 January 1853

... Yesterday I read a letter from Heinzen to Bamberger. He complains of money troubles and says he has been *forced* to resign from the *Janus.* As regards Dr Kellner, he was for a time correspondent of the *Neue Rheinische Zeitung.* You should see if you can't make contact with him *d'une manière ou d'une autre.*[b] Once Weydemeyer has put out feelers, your first step might be to send him a 'pithy' article... The wretched Willich, who is done for here, sailed for America last week as Kinkel's agent; so it is important that *at least* those parts of the pamphlet[c] which relate to him should appear in the press. It would be best if you could arrange

---

[a] A. Herzen, *Du développement des idées révolutionnaires en Russie.* - [b] in one way or another - [c] K. Marx, *Revelations Concerning the Communist Trial in Cologne.*

for the pamphlet to be published in magazines; it has already come out in Switzerland, so it is no longer so important. Could not *Börnstein,* who wants to catch us with 'his bait', also be of some use in this matter? From what I know of him and his *compagnon*[a] Bernays, they will be much tickled by the account of the trickery of the police. I think it *politic* to establish contact with these people. I can assure you that if Bernays finds the means—and we must provide him with it—to re-establish contact with us, I could have these two chaps eating out of my hand. Have you heard nothing more from *Schramm*[b] or, on the other side, from *Tellering?*...

First published in Marx and Engels, *Works,* Second Russian Edition, Vol. 28, Moscow, 1962

Printed according to the letter from Cluss to Weydemeyer of 17 February 1853

Published in English for the first time

139

MARX TO ENGELS

IN MANCHESTER

London, 29 January 1853
28 Dean Street, Soho

Dear Engels,

Have received the £3 and the manuscript you returned.

You must excuse me for not having written for so long, the explanation being PRESSURE FROM WITHOUT.

About a fortnight ago Willich pushed off to America as Kinkel's agent.

Mrs von Brüningk was buried a few days since.

As a result of clumsy manoeuvring by the Parliamentarians Reichenbach and Löwe, and negligence on Imandt's part, the £1,000 have again fallen into the hands of Mr Kinkel in the sense that the money has been deposited in the Bank of England in *his* name and Reichenbach is to hand over the certificate of deposit to him in May, unless the guarantors should decide otherwise. Such decisions are, of course, now quite worthless.

---

[a] companion - [b] Conrad Schramm

Mr Bangya has been in Paris for the past three weeks. Liebknecht has obtained a very good post with the Jew Oppenheim. The rest of the folk, Imandt EXCEPTED, still at a loose end. Schabelitz did not have the pamphlet[a] ready until 11 January. About 6 sheets. But he seems unwilling to send anything to London until the thing has been successfully dispatched to every part of Germany and receipt acknowledged.

The gentlemen in Cologne, notably Daniels, persist in maintaining a dignified silence. The answer to our having subordinated all business to their affair for the space of 4-5 weeks.

In the enclosed cutting from the *Arbeiterrepublik*[b] (editor Weitling) you will see the venom which this tailor king and dictator of the 'Communia' colony[330] expends upon the communist trial in Cologne and the Marx party and Co.

Yesterday I ventured for the first time to write an article *in English* for Dana.[c] Pieper made some corrections and, once I have a good grammar and write away gamely, I should do *passablement*[d] well.

Two apropos:

D'abord.[e] Blind is incessantly dunning me for Herzen's book.[f]

Second: Don't forget to enclose in your next Reichenbach's circular and his statement of accounts.[299] Dronke needs it to establish himself as a new correspondent.[g]

The state of the winter crops being what it is, I feel convinced that the crisis WILL BECOME DUE. So long as the STAPLE ARTICLE, FOOD, remains tolerably ABUNDANT and cheap, and what with Australia, etc., the thing could have been a long time in coming. Now a STOP will be put to all that. Incidentally, is it not somewhat unusual to find e.g. *The Economist vindicating* the Bank of England's most recent DISCOUNT REGULATION, on the ground that its purpose is 'TO PREVENT THE *EXPORTATION OF CAPITAL*'[h]? We know very well what is intended. But could one not trouble one's FREE TRADER's conscience by asking: Do you also wish to PREVENT 'EXPORTATION OF CAPITAL' in the form of COTTONS, YARNS, etc.? Why, then, in the form OF GOLD? Is the FREE-TRADE ECONOMY destined to revert to MERCANTILISM pure and simple and regard the EFFLUX and INFLUX OF GOLD as the *nervus rerum*[i]?

---

[a] K. Marx, *Revelations Concerning the Communist Trial in Cologne.* - [b] 'Schlußbemerkung zum Kölner Kommunistenprozeß', *Republik der Arbeiter*, No. 52, 25 December 1852. - [c] K. Marx, 'Capital Punishment.—Mr. Cobden's Pamphlet.—Regulations of the Bank of England'. - [d] passably - [e] Firstly. - [f] A. Herzen, *Du développement des idées révolutionnaires en Russie.* - [g] See this volume, p. 282. - [h] 'The Bank of England and the Rate of Discount', *The Economist*, No. 491, 22 January 1853. - [i] prime mover

Since Bonaparte's last speech[a] all the talk in the City has been of war. I have also had a letter from old Ebner in Frankfurt in which he speaks of the terror inspired in Germany's pampered puppets, especially the diplomats in Frankfurt am Main, by Bonaparte's wedding speech. The doltishness of our compatriots was brought home to me yesterday by, *inter alia,* the *Frankfurter Journal* in which a correspondent writing from Heidelberg remarks that, what with a propagandist war in the offing and Bonaparte throwing in his lot with 'democracy', the authorities must already be ruing their prosecution of the great Gervinus.[331] I fear that Crapulinski[b] will be hailed as 'friend and saviour' by German peasants and philistines. Apparently the vocation of this burlesque figure is to stand all traditional ranks and parties on their heads and turn them into a laughing-stock.

What is the effect of a bad harvest on an *incipient* war?

Let me know, too, what the position is in the MANUFACTURING DEPARTMENT, particularly in cotton.

Jones' paper[c] is again *en ascendant.*[d]

Cobden's pamphlet[e] and the MANCHESTER PEACE CONFERENCE[332] are, I feel, utterly nonsensical at the present time. So now you know, says Palmerston's journal, *The Morning Post,* these bourgeois parvenus are totally incapable of governing a country; that's a thing only the aristocracy can do.[f] *The Morning Herald* publishes a letter addressed to itself and written, or so it *asserts,* at Bonaparte's own dictation, in which the latter says he would come to England only if the QUEEN needed 200,000 of his 'heroes of order' to combat the perilous growth of democracy. Which democracy, says the *Herald,* is you, Mr Cobden, you and associates.

Concerning *The Times,* I have been given the following, fairly reliable, particulars which may be of interest to you:

Mr *Walter,* MP for Nottingham, is still the PAPER'S constitutional monarch, still its PRINCIPAL SHAREHOLDER. Mr *Mowbray Morris* is *The Times's* LORD OF EXCHEQUER, its FINANCIAL AND POLITICAL MANAGER—a very adventurous and 'RECKLESS' FELLOW. Mr *Delane* JUNIOR (a friend of Disraeli's) is SECRETARY FOR THE HOME OFFICE. His father is EDITOR OF THE *Morning Chronicle.* Mr *Dasent* is SECRETARY OF FOREIGN AFFAIRS. In

---

[a] [Speech of Napoleon III in the Senate on 22 January 1853 on the occasion of his marriage to Eugénie de Montijo,] *Le Moniteur universel,* No. 23, 23 January 1853. - [b] i.e. Napoleon III thus called after a character in Heine's satirical poem 'Zwei Ritter'. - [c] *The People's Paper* - [d] in the ascendant - [e] R. Cobden, *1793 and 1853. In Three Letters.* - [f] 'London, Friday, Jan. 28, 1853' (leader), *The Morning Post,* No. 24681, 28 January 1853; 'The Peace and Arbitration Conference', *The Morning Post,* No. 24682, 29 January 1853.

addition, *The Times* has A SORT OF PRIVY COUNCIL, the most important member being Mr *Lowe*, MP for Kidderminster, an albino with pink eyes and white hair. He is said to be very talented and particularly knowledgeable about financial matters. Next to him comes Mr *Henry Reeve*, an admirer of Orleanist statesmen, who holds a minor post in the STATISTICAL DEPARTMENT of the BOARD OF TRADE. Mr *Lampon* writes the MONEY ARTICLE, but otherwise has no influence on the direction of the whole.

According to a letter from Zerffi, it is generally believed in Paris that Bonaparte is plotting with the Sultan against Austria and Russia in the Montenegro affair.[333]

Vale faveque.[a]

K. Marx

[Note written on an enclosed illustration
from an unknown Italian book]

Which Italian town does the above female belong to?

First published slightly abridged in *Der Briefwechsel zwischen F. Engels und K. Marx*, Bd. 1, Stuttgart, 1913 and in full in *MEGA*, Abt. III, Bd. 1, Berlin, 1929

Printed according to the original

Published in English for the first time

140

MARX TO J. G. MAYER[334]

IN LONDON

[London, after 3 February 1853]

Charles Williams presents his compliments to Mr Mayer and he[b] takes the liberty to transmit him the enclosed letter for Mr Szemere.

First published in: Marx and Engels, *Works*, Second Russian Edition, Vol. 50, Moscow, 1981

Reproduced from the original

Published in English for the first time

---

[a] Good-bye and farewell. - [b] Here the words 'will be much obliged' are crossed out in the original.

141

ENGELS TO MARX

IN LONDON

[Manchester,] 11 February 1853

Dear Marx,

Well, here it is, the *grande affaire*[a] of Messrs Kossuth and Mazzini.[335] Our news up here is very incomplete but my own view is that tomorrow or on Monday we shall certainly hear that all is over. Milan is first-rate terrain for street-fighting, few straight streets, none connecting with the other, almost everywhere narrow, crooked alleys with tall, massive stone houses, each a fortress in itself, their walls often 3-5 feet or more thick and virtually impossible to breach, the *rez-de-chaussée*[b] windows provided with iron grills (almost invariably) as here and there in Cologne. But much good will all this do—they don't stand a chance. After 1849 Radetzky ordered the restoration of the old citadel's fortifications and, if the work is complete—and there has been time enough for this—Milan will belong to the Austrians so long as they occupy the citadel which is impregnable to insurgents unless abetted by a military insurrection. The fact that no further news is forthcoming from Bellinzona whence, from time immemorial, the Tessinese have inundated the world with lies in support of every Italian movement,[336] argues strongly against the spread of the insurrection in the surrounding region.

I regard the whole business as very *mal à propos*[c] since its only *point d'appui,* apart from Austrian tyranny IN GENERAL, is the commotion in Montenegro[333] where also, *après tout,*[d] Turkish 'order' is bound to prevail over Homeric Czernogorzan barbarism. Thus these great dictators, having allowed themselves to be bamboozled, altogether *à la* Seiler, by the usual diplomatic melodramas, invoke the world-historical importance of the 'oriental question'! They are obviously counting on some sort of WINDFALL

---

[a] great affair - [b] ground floor - [c] untimely - [d] after all

from Louis Napoleon but, unless everything turns out otherwise than expected, he will leave them to stew in their own juice and treat them as anarchists. It would further seem probable that, as with all insurrections organised in advance, the moment of outbreak is liable to be determined far more by the pettiest of local incidents than by crucial events.

Mazzini does at least seem to be on the spot; it could hardly be otherwise. However stupid his bombastic proclamation, it may well prove something of a hit with the grandiloquent Italians. On the other hand we have Kossuth, that man of boundless activity! *Celui-là est absolument mort, après cela.*[a] Such absurd pretensions cannot be trumpeted with impunity in the year of our Lord 1853. However preposterous Mazzini's abstract passion for insurrection may appear on this occasion, the man comes off splendidly when compared with the worthy Kossuth, who reassumes the role he played at Vidin[337] and, from the safety of the rear, decrees the liberation of the fatherland from nothing, with nothing, for nothing. The fellow really is a *lâche* and a *misérable.*[b]

Now we shall see what the Italian peasants will do; even if, by some unheard of and incredible stroke of luck, *père* Mazzini, his bourgeois and his aristocrats, should succeed, they might still be in for something very unpleasant at their hands; and should the Austrians find an opportunity to unleash these same peasants against the aristocracy they will not hesitate to do so.

The Austrians must still have 120,000 men in Italy; how, in the face of this, a rebellion can be staged unless there are mutinies among the troops, I cannot conceive. And I refuse to believe that there could be Honved[c] mutinies *in Italy,* even on Kossuth's orders,[d] this would demand events of greater magnitude, while 3 years of discipline and peace have enabled the Austrians to flog many an unyielding Honved posterior into tractability.

The whole business is of importance, I think, only as a symptom; a reaction has set in against the state of oppression obtaining since '49 and, naturally, at the most sensitive spot. The thing has made a great impact here, and the philistines are beginning to agree that this year will not elapse without trouble.

---

[a] After this the man will be completely and utterly done for. - [b] a coward and a wretch - [c] soldiers of the Hungarian national army during the 1848-49 revolution; here: Hungarian soldiers serving in the Austrian army. - [d] An allusion to the so-called Milan proclamation 'In the Name of the Hungarian Nation.—To the Soldiers Quartered in Italy (February 1853)', *The Times,* No. 21348, 10 February 1853 (see this volume, pp. 280, 283 and 290).

Now for a poor CORN AND COTTON harvest, financial difficulties and all that goes with them, and *nous verrons!*[a]

Have you had the £3 I sent you last week—on Thursday or Friday?

Your
F. E.

First published in *Der Briefwechsel zwischen F. Engels und K. Marx*, Bd. 1, Stuttgart, 1913

Printed according to the original

Published in English for the first time

142

MARX TO ENGELS [338]

IN MANCHESTER

[London,] 23 February 1853

Dear Engels,

I have been *sérieusement*[b] indisposed; for the 'perfidious Prussians' have not permitted me either to stand, sit or lie down. Hence my long silence and my failure so much as to acknowledge the money.

You will have seen that Kossuth, through an American filibuster, Captain Mayne Reid, has disavowed his alleged Milan proclamation.[c][339] Well, yesterday Szemere wrote to me from Paris, saying he knew *for certain* that the proclamation was *authentic*, as was evident in any case from its contents. *The Leader* (pro-Mazzini)

*'deems it his duty to caution his readers, that this affair lies entirely between Mr Kossuth and Mr Mazzini and that the latter is *absent* from England'.*[d]

You will yourself have seen, in *The Daily News*, Della Rocco's statement[e] aimed directly at Agostini, but also indirectly at

---

[a] we shall see - [b] seriously - [c] 'In the Name of the Hungarian Nation.—To the Soldiers Quartered in Italy (February 1853)', *The Times*, No. 21348, 10 February 1853. - [d] Cf. 'Kossuth and the Milan Revolt', *The Leader*, No. 152, 19 February 1853. - [e] Della Rocco, 'Mazzini's Proclamation. (To the Editor of *The Daily News*)', *The Daily News*, No. 2107, 21 February 1853.

Kossuth.[340] The *par nobile fratrum*[a] seems to have fallen out. Kossuth is as false as he is cowardly.

You have rated Mazzini too high if you imagine he was present in person at Milan. At critical moments like these he absents himself from England so that he may be suspected of being in the theatre of war.

Pitiable finale though the Milan business is to Mazzini's eternal plotting, and despite my conviction that he has done himself personal injury, I am sure that the revolutionary movement as a whole will benefit by what is happening. I.e., by the brutal manner in which the Austrians are exploiting [...]. Had Radetzky followed Strassoldo's example, had he praised the Milanese citizenry for their 'orderly conduct', had he described the whole thing as the wretched uprising of a few 'MISCREANTS' and, as a token of his confidence, appeared to loosen the reins a little, the revolutionary party would have been discredited in the eyes of the whole world. But as it is, by introducing a system of wholesale plunder, he is turning Italy into the 'revolutionary crater' which Mazzini, for all his declaiming, was unable to conjure into existence.

And another thing. Could any one of us have believed that, after its 4 years of victory, military preparations and rodomontade, reaction should feel itself so infinitely weak that, at the first sign of a riot, it lets out a scream of genuine terror? The fellows' belief in revolution is unshakable. Once again they have testified to the whole world how insecure they feel. Whereas *realiter*[b] the 'emigration' is totally bankrupt and impotent, they loudly proclaim its power through all government papers and encourage the belief that a net of conspiracy is closing in from all sides on the worthy citizens.

Ad vocem[c] Bangya. Is presently in Paris. I now possess actual proof that the gallant fellow is an agent of the Austrian government. He bought his way back to France by accepting a clandestine post in the ·French Police Ministry. At the same time he is in Paris as official agent for Kossuth, who wants money from Bonaparte. In Paris, by the by, the fellow has woven a net in which he himself will become ensnared. As to our manuscript,[d] he sold it to Greif, who was travelling under the name of 'Schulz'. Incidentally, both of them misled the government into believing that they had 'managed to procure'—note the professional term—this 'document' from the archives of a 'secret society'.

---

[a] noble pair of brothers (Horace, *Satires*, II, 3) - [b] in reality - [c] re - [d] K. Marx and F. Engels, *The Great Men of the Exile*.

Still no news from Schabelitz, save that the thing[a] is circulating in Germany. He still doesn't dare send anything here, for fear that the French police will open the parcel and denounce the business to the Prussian police.

I have heard from a *reliable* source, *mais c'est un secret*[b] (which Napoleon doubtless knows as well as I do), that Ledru intends to go into action in Paris in 3-4 weeks. I have been told by an eye-witness that the first news of the rising in Milan created a great sensation in Paris. Gatherings in the streets, etc., not to rebel but to confer. On the whole the FRENCHMEN here are well content that Mr Mazzini should have discredited himself by his 'ACTION'. They see themselves avenged.[c]

Thanks to Cluss our appeal on behalf of the Cologne people[d]—6 lines long—has appeared in all the American papers, in each case under the auspices of the local gymnastic club.[120] *Nous [verrons]*.[e] Our dear acquaintances in Cologne itself have as yet given no sign of life. That's caution for you! One of them, ex-lieutenant Steffen, who figured as a defence witness at the Cologne trial, is here and promptly found himself a teaching post in Friedländer's establishment. Blind is dunning me daily for the *Herzen,*[f] as is Dronke for Reichenbach's circular.[299] This is essential to Dronke since he wants to become a correspondent of the *Volkshalle* in Cologne under another name.

What do you think of the lively sympathy shown by the clerics of the Established Church towards the unfortunate Ten Hours Movement[341]? Always the same old game. On Saturday I'll send you a parcel containing all the remaining newspapers, and letters from Cluss.

Of all LITTLE FINALITY JOHN'S[g] PERFORMANCES, the last was probably the most classical.[342] Even *The Times* was forced to admit that JOHNNY EXCITES 'MIGHTILY LITTLE ENTHUSIASM'[h]

Mrs Harney[i] is dead. Likewise Mrs von Brüningk. A short while ago there was an exchange of letters between myself and

---

[a] K. Marx, *Revelations Concerning the Communist Trial in Cologne.* - [b] but it's a secret - [c] See this volume, p. 73. - [d] K. Marx and F. Engels, 'Appeal for Support of the Men Sentenced in Cologne', *New-Yorker Criminal-Zeitung*, No. 45, 21 January 1853. - [e] We shall see. - [f] A. Herzen, *Du développement des idées révolutionnaires en Russie.* - [g] Nickname given by the Radicals to John Russell who qualified the 1832 Parliamentary Reform as finality of Britain's constitutional development. - [h] *The Times,* No. 21350, 12 February 1853 [leader]. - [i] Mary

Brüningk, in which everything hinged on Kinkel and Willich.[a] As I have already told you, Willich sailed for America 4 weeks ago. *Salut.*

Your
K. M.

First published considerably abridged in *Der Briefwechsel zwischen F. Engels und K. Marx*, Bd. 1, Stuttgart, 1913 and in full in *MEGA*, Abt. III, Bd. 1, Berlin, 1929

Printed according to the original

Published in English in full for the first time

143

ENGELS TO MARX

IN LONDON

[Manchester, 10 March 1853]

Dear Marx,

Yesterday I sent off one half of a fiver to you and, at the same time, the other half under cover to Dronke. I'm really in a fix; in February I had to fork out some £50 to repay debts, etc., and there'll be another £30 or so to be paid out this month and next. Otherwise I'd have sent you more. A reform of my PERSONAL EXPENSES is urgently called for and, in a week or a fortnight's time, I shall move into cheaper LODGINGS and also resort to less potent liquor so as to prepare myself for the great moment when the balance is struck. Last year, thank God, I gobbled up half of my old man's profits from the business here. As soon as my old man's arrival becomes imminent, I shall remove to select LODGINGS, buy select cigars and wines, etc., so that we can impress him. *Voilà la vie.*[b]

By his statements,[c] Monsieur Kossuth has utterly ruined himself in the eyes of people up here, German as well as English. Mazzini likewise, by the insurrection itself [335] and by his sordid way of

---

[a] See this volume, pp. 213-14. - [b] That's life. - [c] Two statements by Kossuth published in various English newspapers in February and March 1853 which denied his participation in the Milan uprising. See, in particular, 'M. M. Kossuth and Mazzini and *The Times*' and 'A Letter from Kossuth', *The Daily News*, Nos. 2105 and 2117, 18 February and 4 March 1853.

starting a fracas with the cowardly murder of individual soldiers, this being particularly abhorrent to the English. It would be difficult to imagine anything more craven and blackguardly than these two letters of Kossuth's and withal the constant pretension: I AM A PLAIN, HONEST MAN. The gentlemen should, by the way, beware: given the evidence, *ce cher*[a] Aberdeen is just the sort of man to have them locked up and prosecuted without more ado and whether, after all this, they could be quite so sure of an acquittal, I do not know.

The MINISTRY OF ALL THE TALENTS [343] TURNS OUT A COMPLETE HUMBUG. Johnny,[b] more shrunken than ever; the great Gladstone, a self-complacent know-all *à la* Mevissen; Aberdeen, full of diplomatic-toryistic reminiscences and consummate courtier; the late messiah Peel's apostle John, Sidney Herbert, a wholly incompetent Secretary at War,—they're a fine LOT. At the same time they all feel somewhat out of place, except for shameless old Palmerston, who is at home everywhere and, witness the Mazzini debate in both Houses,[344] as MUTINOUS as ever. Indeed, ever since the debate on Greece,[345] the Militia Bill[62] and the debate on the Address,[346] he has been *de facto* LEADER OF THE HOUSE OF COMMONS, and it is bitterly ironical that, for form's sake, poor Johnny should be given this post. But when, in this capacity, Johnny goes on to ask for a salary, it is carrying effrontery beyond all bounds; however a new post is, of course, a godsend to both parties. I shall be curious to see Master Gladstone's budget; what he said about the ESTIMATES and Hume's Tariff motion [347] leads one to expect that he will leave everything more or less as it was, which is about all that is likely to result from this patriotic coalition ministry. Meanwhile, the tales of corruption during the last election are really capital and will doubtless necessitate some sort of Reform Bill during the next session. If, by then, TRADE has deteriorated and the Continent bestirs itself, we can expect some fine goings-on.

I now have at home the book by Urquhart,[c] the mad MP who denounces Palmerston as being in the pay of Russia. The explanation is a simple one: the fellow's a Celtic Scot with a Saxon-Scottish upbringing, by inclination a Romantic, by upbringing a FREE-TRADER. This chap went to Greece as a Philhellene[348] and, after 3 years of fighting the Turks, proceeded to Turkey and went into raptures about these self-same Turks. He enthuses over Islam on the principle, 'if I wasn't a Calvinist, I could only be a

---

[a] that dear - [b] Russell - [c] [D. Urquhart,] *Turkey and Its Resources: Its Municipal Organization and Free Trade...*

Mohammedan'. Turks, particularly those of the Ottoman Empire in its heyday, are the most perfect nation on earth in every possible way. The Turkish language is the most perfect and melodious in the world. All the foolish talk of barbarism, cruelty and absurd barbaric arrogance stems solely from European ignorance of Turkey and from the biased calumnies of Greek dragomans. If a European is maltreated in Turkey, he has only himself to blame; your Turk hates neither the religion of the Frank, nor his character, but only his narrow trousers. Imitation of Turkish architecture, etiquette, etc. is strongly recommended. The author himself was several times kicked in the bottom by Turks, but subsequently realised that he alone was to blame. Contact with Europeans, and attempts at civilisation, have only enervated and disorganised the Turks. The Turkish Constitution in its 'purity' is the finest there is, and is almost superior to the English. The Turk enjoys SELF-GOVERNMENT through customs going back a thousand years and through the Koran. The Sultan, far from being a 'despot', is more circumscribed than the MOST GRACIOUS QUEEN.[a] Freedom of religion exists *only* in Turkey. In this paradise there are no class differences, class struggles or political parties, nor can there be, for in matters of internal politics all are of the same mind. Nowhere is there less centralisation than in Turkey. In short, only the Turk is a gentleman and freedom exists only in Turkey.

The Czar[b] is now intriguing against this happy land through the agency of Greek clerics, and England has constantly allowed this same Czar to lead her by the nose. England must support Turkey, etc., etc., and other commonplaces as hoary as they are trivial. On the whole this book is highly entertaining. The really choice thing about it is that it forms the basis for the entire policy of the English, anti-Palmerston liberals, e.g. all the articles in *The Daily News* on the Turkish mummery are simply paraphrases of Urquhart who, *qua* FREE-TRADER, enjoys absolute confidence, although he blames the English for destroying Thessaly's industry with their imports—but in a HIGHLANDER a certain licence may be permitted.

There is one good aspect to it, namely that *The Times,* even though primarily in the Russian interest, is at long last attacking the old philistine nonsense about Turkey's integrity.[c] The asinine *Daily News* which, in its blinkered bourgeois way, can see no

---

[a] Victoria - [b] Nicholas I - [c] *The Times,* Nos. 21365 and 21369, 2 and 7 March 1853, leaders.

further than the end of its nose, is whining about betrayal but can offer nothing better to counter it than the same old diplomatic rubbish.[a][349] If the fun goes on much longer, the gentlemen will soon have to resort to other arguments and come round to the view that only a continental revolution can put an end to the mess. Surely even the most egregious philistines must in due course come to realise that, without one, absolutely nothing can be solved.

The Austro-Prussian tariff business[350] is the only step forward Germany has succeeded in making—*et encore*[b]! The thing has so many strings attached, and so many vital issues have been left to later committees, while the actual tariff reductions are so minimal, that little will come of it. Come the great industrial crisis, and the whole trade agreement will vanish into thin air in the face of the general débâcle.

Here all that happens is thieving, broken bones on the railways, and flying up in the air. The local philistines are quite dumbfounded by the extraordinary events of the past week. Fortunately cotton is going down, which is why nothing is happening on the Exchange and people can concern themselves to their heart's content with these momentous occurrences. The spinning mills and most of the weaving mills are still fully occupied, but in coarse calicoes (DOMESTICS) there is *total stagnation* and, as from Monday, all factories in this trade will be working only 3 days a week.

Regards to your wife and children.

Dronke will have received the Reichenbach thing.[c]

Your
F. E.

Will get the Herzen[d] one of these days; the snag is that just now I'm unable to write to my brother-in-law.[e]

First published considerably abridged in *Der Briefwechsel zwischen F. Engels und K. Marx*, Bd. 1, Stuttgart, 1913 and in full in *MEGA*, Abt. III, Bd. 1, Berlin, 1929

Printed according to the original

Published in English for the first time

---

[a] *The Daily News*, No. 2117, 4 March 1853 (see this volume, p. 283). - [b] Here: and that's not much. - [c] See this volume, pp. 245 and 275. - [d] A. Herzen, *Du développement des idées révolutionnaires en Russie* (see this volume, pp. 273 and 275). - [e] Emil Blank

144

MARX TO ENGELS

IN MANCHESTER

[London,] 10 March 1853

Dear Engels,

Received the £5.

This week I was within an inch of kicking the bucket. From hepatitis, or something very similar. This is hereditary in my family. My old man[a] died of it. During the 4 years I have been in England there hasn't been a sign of the thing and I thought it had gone for good. But now the worst is over and, what is more, *sans médecin*.[b] But I am still somewhat knocked up.

Yesterday I received the following *'pleasing'* letter from Basle:

'Basle, 7 March 1853. 9 o'clock in the morning.

Dear Marx,

I have just heard that the whole consignment of *Revelations*,[c] amounting to 2,000 copies, which has been lying in a village on the other side of the border for the past 6 weeks, was intercepted yesterday while being conveyed elsewhere. What will happen now, I do not know; first of all, a complaint lodged by the Baden government with the Federal Council, then, no doubt, my arrest or at least commitment for trial, etc. In either case, a terrific shindy! This briefly for your information; further communications, should I be prevented from making them myself, will reach you through a third party. When writing to me, address the envelope: "Mad. Brenner-Guéniard, magasin de modes, Basle" and, on the sealed enclosure for me, simply write "For Jacques". I shall deposit the manuscript on the *coup d'état*[d] in a safe place. Adieu. Before long, I hope, I shall be able to tell you more than I now know. Let me have a safe address; yours and Bamberger's are probably known.

Yours
Jacques[e]

Well, *qu'en pensez-vous, mon cher maître renard?*[f] Has the 'Suisse'[g] sold me to the Prussian government for cash? 6 weeks in a village on the other side of the border, the affectation of fear, not a word

---

[a] Heinrich Marx - [b] without a doctor - [c] K. Marx, *Revelations Concerning the Communist Trial in Cologne*. - [d] K. Marx, *The Eighteenth Brumaire of Louis Bonaparte*. - [e] Schabelitz - [f] What do you think of it, dear Master Renard? - [g] Swiss

about the copies still in Switzerland, not a copy sent here despite my insistence!

It's enough to put one off writing altogether. This constant toil *pour le roi de Prusse*[a]!

Que faire?[b] For the 'Suisse' must not be allowed to get away with it like this.

Quant à[c] Dana, he has *honoured* my bill. Originally the 'worthy' Bamberger gave me £5 against it, but then kept me traipsing to and fro between here and the City for a fortnight, and it was not until this week that he finally paid out, after weeks of 'moaning' (literally) on the part of my landlady. Since then I have sent 7 more articles to the *Tribune* and another one goes off tomorrow.[351] I could now begin to see my way out of the wood but for the accursed *dette consolidée*[d] hanging round my neck. And even this would have been largely paid off had that wretched Swiss not precipitated me again into *néant*.[e]

To keep in with Dana I shall now be forced to write a somewhat longer article on *haute politique*.[f] In other words, the *détestable question orientale*, regarding which a miserable YANKEE here is trying to compete with me in the *Tribune*.[352] But this QUESTION is primarily military and geographical, hence outside my *département*. So you must once more *exécuter*.[g] What is to become of the Turkish Empire is something I have no clue about. I cannot therefore present a general perspective.

However, for a newspaper article—in which, by the by, you must do your best to skirt the QUESTION as such in favour of its military, geographical and historical aspects—it seems to me that you should touch on the following basic points, which arise directly out of Montenegro[333]:

1. Despite all the chicanery and the political twaddle in the Press, the *question orientale* will never be the *occasion* for a European war. The diplomatists will keep quietly tinkering at it until here, too, a general hullabaloo puts an end to their tinkering.

2. ENCROACHMENTS OF RUSSIA in Turkey. Austria's greed. France's ambitions. England's interests. Commercial and military significance of this bone of contention.

3. Should there be a general hullabaloo, Turkey will compel England to come in on the revolutionary side, an Anglo-Russian clash being inevitable in such a case.

---

[a] for the king of Prussia, i.e. for nothing. - [b] What's to be done? - [c] As for - [d] consolidated debt - [e] void - [f] high politics - [g] put yourself out

4. Inevitable disintegration of Mussulman Empire. *D'une manière ou de l'autre*[a] will fall into the hands of European civilisation.

At the present, you should dwell more particularly on the Montenegro affair, on the deplorable role England is now officially playing in it. The Sultan only yielded because France and England did not pledge their help. In this affair, both countries used the *entente cordiale* to mask their competing for the favours of the Holy Alliance.[353] You should point out that the ruling oligarchy in England is bound to fall if only because it has become incapable of performing its traditional role abroad, namely maintaining the pre-eminence of the English *nation* vis-à-vis the Continent.[354]

Tout ça est très pauvre, mais enfin, il me faut un ou deux articles sur cette question pour tuer mon concurrent.[b]

Your
K. M.

Your translation of my Sutherland article[c] is splendid. I myself would seem to possess some talent for writing in English, if only I had a Flügel,[d] a grammar, and a better man than Mr Pieper to correct my work.

Today I shall again write to the Continent. Should I succeed, now that there's nothing doing with Schabelitz, in scraping together at least enough money to ensure my wife's peace of mind until a second bill has been drawn on Dana and returned—this time I intend to get him up to £30—I might perhaps come and spend a few days with you in April, *pour restituer mes forces.*[e] Then we could, for once, chat undisturbed about present conditions, which in my view must soon lead to an EARTHQUAKE.

According to *The Morning Post*, manufacturers in Lancashire have put all their hands on SHORT TIME, PROSPERITY is drawing to an end, etc.[f] What is the situation in this respect?

Your
K. M.

It's already 11.30 and Dronke has still not brought me No. II[g]. No doubt the fellow is still in bed. What milksops these chaps are!

---

a One way or another - b All this is very weak, but after all I must have one or two articles on this question to dispose of my rival [Pulzsky]. - c K. Marx, 'Elections.—Financial Clouds.—The Duchess of Sutherland and Slavery'. - d J. G. Flügel, J. Sporschil, *Vollständiges Englisch-Deutsches und Deutsch-Englisches Wörterbuch.* - e to restore my strength - f 'Manchester Manufactures.—A Grave Fact', *The Morning Post*, No. 24712, 5 March 1853. - g The other half of the £5 note (see this volume, p. 283).

With their idleness, lack of stamina and inability to sustain any PRESSURE FROM WITHOUT, they are absolutely hopeless. We must recruit our party entirely anew. Cluss is a good man. Reinhardt in Paris is hardworking. Lassalle, despite his many 'buts', is *dur*[a] and energetic. Pieper would not be without his uses if he possessed less childish *vanité* and more *esprit de suite*.[b] Imandt and Liebknecht are tenacious, and each is useful in his own way. But that doesn't add up to a party. Ex-lieutenant Steffen, ex-witness at the Cologne trial, at present a schoolmaster in an establishment near London, seems to me efficient. Lupus GROWS FROM DAY TO DAY OLDER AND BECOMES MORE CROTCHETY. Dronke is and ever will be a 'congenial loafer'.

First published abridged in *Der Briefwechsel zwischen F. Engels und K. Marx*, Bd. 1, Stuttgart, 1913 and in full in *MEGA*, Abt. III, Bd. 1, Berlin, 1929

Printed according to the original

Published in English for the first time

145

MARX TO BERTALAN SZEMERE

London, 10 March 1853[c]

I have received your last lines. You will have read Kossuth's various statements.[d] Even before Mazzini's statement[e] was published I knew that he [Kossuth] had written a most *embittered private letter* about Kossuth to one of his friends here, an Englishman.[f] In connection with this I wrote the following to the *Daily New-York Tribune*:* 'As Mr Mazzini himself has now broken the ice I may as well state that Kossuth disowned his own document[g] under the pressure of his Paris friends. This is not the first symptom, in Kossuth's past career, of vacillating weakness, inextricable contradictions and false duplicity. He possesses all the attractive virtues, but also all the feminine faults, of the *Artist* character. He is a great artist *"en paroles"*.[h] I recommend Mr

---

[a] hard - [b] singleness of mind - [c] The original has 1852. - [d] Two statements published in various English newspapers denied his participation in the Milan uprising. See in particular: 'M. M. Kossuth and Mazzini and *The Times*', 'A Letter from Kossuth', *The Daily News*, Nos. 2105 and 2117, 18 February and 4 March 1853. See also this volume, pp. 283-84. - [e] 'A letter from Mazzini', *The Daily News*, No. 2115, 2 March 1853. - [f] Mayne Reid - [g] L. Kossuth, 'In the Name of the Hungarian Nation.—To the Soldiers Quartered in Italy (February 1853)', *The Times*, No. 21348, 10 February 1853. - [h] in words

Szemere's lately published biographies *'Batthyány, Görgey and Kossuth* to those who, unwilling to bow to popular superstition, are anxious to form a matter-of-fact judgment.'*[a] I *sign* all my articles. Attacks will now follow, so I shall have an opportunity to go deeper *en matière*.[b] I should be obliged if you would communicate to me in good time any news you hear about the emigrants, particularly as regards the *par nobile fratrum*.[c] With a couple of pieces of such information I can always buy myself the right to deal with the *matter itself* in the *Tribune*.

Quant à[d] Zerffi, whom I have not seen for a fortnight, I told him at any rate that if I knew Kossuth personally I would have felt it was my duty to warn him against Bangya. It seems to me that Zerffi is talkative and somewhat indiscreet. But I do not by any means believe that he is to be placed on the same level as Bangya, but that he is much more honourable.

2,000 copies of my *Revelations Concerning the Cologne Trial* (sent to Switzerland on 6 December 1852)[e] were *confiscated* on the Baden border 3 months later. I am convinced that Bangya had something to do with that too. *C'est un infâme qu'il faut écraser*.[f]

Pulszky went to America about 4 weeks ago. I think Kossuth sent him there to restore the renown he has lost with the Press and to intrigue against his *opponents*. Pulszky will try to get me too a bad name with the *New-York Tribune*, but I prophesy no great success for him.

I remain yours most respectfully
Ch. Williams

First published in the journal *Magyar Tudomany*, No. 4, 1978

Printed according to the original

Published in English for the first time

---

[a] K. Marx, 'Forced Emigration.—Kossuth and Mazzini.—The Refugee Question.—Election Bribery in England.—Mr. Cobden' (see present edition, Vol. 11, p. 532.) - [b] into the matter - [c] noble pair of brothers (Horace, *Satires,* II, 3) - [d] As for - [e] See this volume, pp. 264-65. - [f] He is the infamous thing that must be crushed.—From the expression *Ecrasez l'infâme* frequently repeated by Voltaire in his letters of 1759-68. By the infamous thing he meant the Catholic Church.

146

ENGELS TO MARX

IN LONDON

[Manchester, 11 March 1853]

Dear Marx,

You shall have the articles within a few days[a]; I see that my CONSIDERATION of Urquhart[b] was opportune. Unfortunately it's too late for tomorrow's STEAMER, since I can hardly have finished at the office before 8 o'clock and some preparation is, of course, still necessary. It's grand that *père* Dana is now paying £2 and promptly honouring bills; *avec ça*,[c] we shall at last be out of the wood. Incidentally, I would never have believed that you had sent off seven English articles in such a short space of time[d]; when you come up here, which I much look forward to, you will learn more English in a week than in 6 weeks with Mr Pieper.

As for Monsieur Jacques,[e] it is more than likely that the little man wants to imitate the trick played on the Baden government by Mr Jenni (whom he greatly resembles), namely sell part of the edition[f] to the German governments, and afterwards do business so much the better with what is left. I don't believe he is so bad as to have sold the whole lot outright. Booksellers established in Basle may be justified in feeling nervous; the Basle government won't stand any nonsense and is on neighbourly terms with Baden. But mind you insist on his sending you forthwith per *messagerie*, i. e. by train, a packet of at least a few copies addressed direct to London or, if you like, to me, CARE OF Ermen & Engels, Manchester. Nobody would think of opening such a packet, and even were this to happen, the cat is in any case already out of the bag. It's fishy that he should so far have refused to let a *single copy* out of his hands. Surely he must know some manufacturer in Basle who sends ribbons, etc., etc., to London, and could include some in a consignment.

There's nothing more to the Lancashire story in *The Morning Post* than what I told you in my yesterday's letter.[g] In answer to an inquiry of ours about prices, Houldsworth and Murray, the two

---

[a] See this volume, pp. 288-89. - [b] ibid., pp. 284-85. - [c] with that - [d] See this volume, p. 288. - [e] Schabelitz (ibid., pp. 287-88). - [f] K. Marx, *Revelations Concerning .the Communist Trial in Cologne.* - [g] Engels to Marx, 10 March 1853, see this volume, p. 286.

leading fine spinners in England, told us yesterday that it was useless to quote any prices since they were booked up a long way ahead and could not accept a single new order. Between them these two have about 150,000-200,000 mule spindles in operation. In coarse WATER-TWIST, on the other hand, No. 6/16, business is very slack precisely because of conditions in DOMESTICS which are sticking not only here but also in America and Germany.

We must destroy the competing YANKEE[a] with a great SHOW of omniscience. I shall take a look at a few more books on Turkey of which there are quite a LOT in the Athenaeum.[244]

It is not very pleasant to hear about the DECLINE of our friends. Nor will it be pleasant if these *citoyens*[b] go into the next affair as wise as, but no wiser than, they emerged from the last one, though when it comes to the point, the 'best' of them will no doubt pull themselves together. After Cluss, Lassalle is by far the most useful of the lot, and will be all the more so from the moment *où les biens du comte Hatzfeldt seront irrévocablement réunis au domaine public.*[c][355] He may have his foibles, but he also has *esprit de parti et ambition,*[d] and we are already aware that he will always make official business a pretext for indulging his lesser appetites and pursuing his own little private affairs. As for recruiting, that's the way it is; once we are back in Germany we shall, I think, find plenty of talented young fellows who have, in the meantime, and not without result, tasted the forbidden fruit. If we had had the means to conduct propaganda scientifically and steadily for the space of 2 or 3 years, writing books about *n'importe quoi,*[e] as we did before 1848, we should have been appreciably better off. But that was impossible, and now the storm is already brewing. You ought to finish your Economy[45]; later on, as soon as we have a newspaper, we could bring it out in WEEKLY NUMBERS, and what the *populus*[f] could not understand, the *discipuli* would expound *tant bien que mal, mais cependant non sans effet.*[g] This would provide all our by then restored associations with a basis for debate.

That Dana is paying £2 per article without demur is the best proof of how firmly ensconced you are at the *Tribune.* Anyway, there is a certain advantage in our being the only one of all the parties of European revolution to have expounded its ideas before the *English*-American public. The YANKEES know absolutely nothing

---

[a] Pulszky (see this volume, p. 288). - [b] citizens - [c] when Count Hatzfeldt's property reverts irrevocably to public ownership - [d] party spirit and ambition - [e] no matter what - [f] people - [g] disciples would expound after a fashion but not, however, without profit

about the rest, for all Kossuth's twaddle amounted to was money for, and intervention on behalf of, the great man Kossuth. Doubtless Monsieur Bamberger will advance more against the next bill, the first having been paid so promptly.

Your
F. E.

First published in *MEGA*, Abt. III, Bd. 1, Berlin, 1929

Printed according to the original

Published in English for the first time

147

MARX TO ENGELS

IN MANCHESTER

[London,] 22[-23] March 1853

Dear Engels,

Your article on Turkey[a] splendid. Sent off.

I don't know if you have seen the following comments in a recent number of *The Economist* on the 'VALUE OF TURKEY'.

* 'While our commerce with Austria and Russia is either stationary or on the decline, with Turkey it is rapidly increasing. We are not able to state what proportion of our exports may find their way to Austria through Germany, but we believe it [is] only small. Our direct trade with Austria is absolutely insignificant. Our exports of British produces to her Adriatic ports (the only ones she has) were not given separately from those to the rest of Italy till 1846, when they reached £721,981. In 1850 they had fallen to £607,755 and in 1851 had risen to £812,942. Our exports to Russia were on the average of 1840 and 1841: £1,605,000, in 1846 and 1847, £1,785,000, and in 1850 and 1851, £1,372,000.' 'Our exports to the

---

[a] See section on Turkey in the article by Marx and Engels, 'British Politics.—Disraeli.—The Refugees.—Mazzini in London.—Turkey'.

Turkish dominions, including Egypt, Syria, Palestine, Moldavia and Wallachia, have progressed as follows:

£		£		£	
1840	1,440,592	1844	3,271,333	1848	3,626,241
1841	1,885,840	1845	3,134,759	1849	3,569,023
1842	2,068,842	1846	2,707,571	1850	3,762,480
1843	2,548,321	1847	3,530,589	1851	3,548,959

Our exports are therefore *threefold* those to Russia and nearly double those to Russia and Austria together.'*[356]

So much for *The Economist*.[a]

There must be a considerable row going on about the 'TURKISH QUESTION' within the English Ministry itself, for the tune being piped by Palmerston's journal, *The Morning Post*, is altogether different from that in *The Times*.

Disraeli has happily been deposed from his LEADERSHIP of the 'GREAT CONSERVATIVE PARTY' and his place taken by Sir John Pakington, A MOURNFUL MAN OTHERWISE. It is the first time since 1828 that the Tory party has possessed a 'LEADER' no less mediocre than its rank and file.

You will have seen that during the last division on the Clergy Reserves Bill, when the worthy Russell himself PROPOSED THE OMISSION OF THE 3RD of his 3 original CLAUSES, it was only the votes of the conservative minority that secured victory for the Ministry.[357] A bad sign, that.

Mazzini has been here for a few days, but for the time being incognito.

That the 'GOOD ABERDEEN'[b] is much inclined to pick on the refugees will be evident to you from the fact that last week the English police took a kind of census of refugees. Two or three detectives IN PLAIN CLOTHES went from SQUARE to SQUARE and from street to street, jotting down information, most of it culled from neighbours or nearby *ale-house keepers*. In exceptional cases, however—e.g. at Pulszky's, the blackguard himself being now in America—they actually pushed their way into the homes of the refugees on the pretext that a theft, etc., had been committed, and scrutinised their papers.

---

[a] 'Turkey and Its Value', *The Economist*, No. 498, 12 March 1853. - [b] Marx quotes Louis Philippe.

The estimable Barthélemy got away with 2 months' imprisonment.[274] The fellow had the effrontery to have Ledru-Rollin informed he would shoot him down like a dog. To this Ledru replied that he would never exchange shots with such a man. Barthélemy, for his part, retorted that, if he wanted to induce a man to exchange shots with him, he knew very well how to do it—tested methods being to box his ears in public, spit in his face, etc. Whereat Ledru sent word that, in such a case, Barthélemy would become acquainted with his stick and with an English MAGISTRATE. This Barthélemy seems intent on becoming the Rinaldo Rinaldini of the emigration. Some ambition!

Père Willich has landed in New York. Friend Weitling organised a banquet for him attended by 300 persons, at which Willich appeared in a vast red sash, made a long speech to the effect that bread is worth more than liberty, and was presented by Weitling with a *sword.* Then Weitling took the floor and proceeded to prove that Jesus Christ was the first communist and his successor none other than the well-known Wilhelm Weitling.

I have received a letter from Schabelitz, which I enclose and from which it emerges 1. that, though he has not betrayed us politically, he has behaved very stupidly indeed; 2. that he meant, and still means, to swindle me, at least commercially. Originally, and under the contract, he was to run off only 2,000 copies.[a] From his letter it appears that he has run off more. How many, he has still not divulged. At the same time Dronke has received an answer from Dr Feddersen to whom he had written about the matter. Feddersen confirms Schabelitz's letter, but at the same time states that, in his opinion, nothing would come of a judicial inquiry concerning Schabelitz. The question is, *what is to be done?* The Prussian government wants to hush the whole thing up, so much so that the Foreign Minister[b] is looking for a *Theory of Communism* allegedly published by me in Basle. So even the title is to be kept from the public. *Que faire?*[c]

Schabelitz sent me 2 copies, 1 direct to me and 1 to Freiligrath, which together cost me 15/-. A fine *return!* So far I have not been able to drag the copies away from the gang. But I think I might succeed in getting hold of one by Wednesday (tomorrow) and will send it with the parcel that has long been waiting to go off to you.

Zerffi is here. He fled from Paris during the razzia on foreign correspondents. He believes that friend Bangya (who, by the by

---

[a] of Marx's *Revelations Concerning the Communist Trial in Cologne* - [b] Presumably Manteuffel. - [c] What's to be done?

and *en passant*, is said to be finding life difficult and intends to return here in May) had denounced him as the author of a number of articles in the *Kölnische Zeitung* compromising to the '*Blonde Souveraine*'.[a] Zerffi is a chatterbox, but his opinions on conditions in Hungary are more independent and accurate than any I have yet heard expressed by refugees from that country. This may be due to the fact that he is no Magyar born and bred, but a 'Swabian', and not only a Swabian but the son of a Hanover Jew, whose name was probably Cerf and was magyarised as Zerffi.

What wretchedly indolent dogs our people in Germany are! Not a word has come through from the fellows. By now they'll have seen from the newspapers that a pamphlet has been published about their case. But they don't so much as inquire about it. There's no responsiveness, no *élan* about the chaps. Old women— *voilà tout.*[b]

A funny piece of news in *La Nation* will hardly have come your way in Manchester. That angel Montijo suffers, it seems, from a most indelicate complaint. She is passionately addicted to *farting* and is incapable, even in company, of suppressing it. At one time she resorted to horse-riding as a remedy. But this having now been forbidden her by Bonaparte, she 'vents' herself. *Ce n'est qu'un bruit, un petit murmure, un rien,*[c] *mais enfin, vous savez que les Français ont le nez au plus petit vent.*[d]

Is there no news of Weerth in Manchester yet?

Your
K. M.

23 March. Yesterday, in response to our appeal[e] consisting of three lines and all our names, Freiligrath, the treasurer, received from the gymnastic club in Washington the sum of £20 17s. for the Cologne people.

Schimmelpfennig has inherited £1,000 from the Brüningk woman.

First published abridged in *Der Briefwechsel zwischen F. Engels und K. Marx*, Bd. 1, Stuttgart, 1913 and in full in *MEGA*, Abt. III, Bd. 1, Berlin, 1929

Printed according to the original

Published in English for the first time

---

[a] Eugénie Montijo, Napoleon III's wife - [b] that's all - [c] A paraphrase of Don Bazile's words in Beaumarchais' *Le barbier de Séville, ou la précaution inutile*, Act II, Scene VIII. - [d] It's only a noise, a faint murmur, a nothing, but then, you know, the French are sensitive to the slightest puff of wind. - [e] K. Marx and F. Engels, 'Appeal for Support of the Men Sentenced in Cologne' (see also this volume, p. 282).

148

MARX TO ADOLF CLUSS[234]

IN WASHINGTON

London, 25 March 1853[a]
28 Dean Street, Soho

Dear Cluss,

Your complaints about our (or at least my) laziness in the matter of writing are not WHOLLY justified. I used to write—save when ill—once a week. It was you who first replaced this with a different system, and often just sent newspapers in the interval instead of letters. There are ALL IN ALL 3 letters from you that have remained unanswered. Of those 3, two came on the same day, one enclosed with the money sent to Freiligrath, one direct to myself. Hence, only 2 unanswered letters.[358] If you go back to writing once *every* week, whether at length or briefly, I too will again adopt this regular MANNER. Or rather, I shall do so without waiting. But then I shall expect the same of you.

Schabelitz has now written to me at length. He had printed the *Revelations* pamphlet 2 months ago and, for the space of 5 weeks, left it lying at Weil, a Baden village on the other side of the border. Instead of posting a reliable man there, the jackass went and left everything to the smuggler who, having gradually extracted from him a substantial sum of money, ended up by giving himself away to the Baden government. The rest you will have seen in the last issue of the *Tribune*.[b] But you will be even more convinced of the interest taken by the Prussian government in this pamphlet, and hence of its importance to the 'Fatherland', when I tell you that the heroic Stieber has not only become police superintendent in Berlin but is co-opted onto every ministerial council concerned with precautionary measures against revolutionaries and revolutionary activities. I am almost beside myself with anger at the pamphlet's temporary suppression. You for your part would not appear to have handled matters on this occasion with your usual felicity. The *Neu-England-Zeitung* may take a year to get it out by thus printing it in dribs and drabs,[359] whereas it devotes whole columns to the *'figure de fouine'*[c] of the wretched Ruge who, over here, has still not succeeded in acquiring

---

[a] In the original, 1852. - [b] K. Marx, 'Kossuth and Mazzini.—Intrigues of the Prussian Government.—Austro-Prussian Commercial Treaty.— *The Times* and the Refugees'. - [c] weasel-like features

more than a 'strictly circumscribed train' of 5 persons. Why didn't you put the thing into the *Demokrat,* a *much more widely read* organ, to which you yourself contribute? Next time you write you must tell me frankly whether or not the thing can be produced as a pamphlet in America. It would be for *European consumption* and would be tossed into Prussia via Hamburg. If I were not utterly devoid of means I would arrange for it to be printed in Altona forthwith. It is not partiality to the little lampoon, but my perfect knowledge of conditions in Prussia which prompts me to say that, at the present moment, we could deal our beloved Prussians no more telling blow.

Don't lose sight of that blackguard Willich. He is the most rabid of enemies and an idiot into the bargain.

Pulszky has not come among you simply to engage in high politics. He has also been sent across the ocean for the purpose of appeasing General Vetter who, having become DISAFFECTED, is intriguing from America against the 'GREAT Kossuth'. To my amazement I see in the *Daily Tribune,* received from you today, that it has accepted my attacks upon Kossuth-Mazzini.[a] I had thought this highly improbable, the more so since Greeley's WHITE-RED-BLACK FRIEND, the Jew Pulszky,[b] is over there.

Szemere wrote to me from Paris giving me the news I published in the *Tribune,* namely that there had been a lengthy conference between Kossuth and his Parisian PARTISANS about his now 'DISOWNED PROCLAMATION'[c] and that they forced the miserable little man to make a disavowal.

Barthélemy, Willich's friend, whom you will remember from his duel with Schramm[360] (the latter, by the by, lives in Cincinnati whence he has written once), has received a 2 months' sentence for fighting a duel on English soil in the course of which he killed Cournet. He got off so lightly, despite the sordid DISCLOSURES which were made during the trial, because according to English law, seconds are punished as severely as duellists and also because they didn't want to make the poor devil pay the full penalty for what he had done. The fellow had the effrontery when in prison to have a message sent to Ledru saying that as soon as he came out he would shoot him down like a dog. Ledru replied that he would

---

[a] K. Marx, 'The Attack on Francis Joseph.—The Milan Riot.—British Politics.—Disraeli's Speech.—Napoleon's Will'. - [b] An allusion to F. and Th. Pulszky, *White, Red, Black Sketches of Society in the United States During the Visit of Their Guest,* Vols. 1-3, London, 1853. - [c] K. Marx, 'Forced Emigration.—Kossuth and Mazzini.—The Refugee Question.—Election Bribery in England.—Mr. Cobden's (see also this volume, p. 280).

not exchange shots with such a scoundrel. *Barthélemy*: He was very well able to induce a man to exchange shots with him by boxing his ears in the open street, and other such tested methods. *Ledru* (riposte): That being so, he would regale him with his stick.

The winsome warrior, Schimmelpfennig, has inherited £1,000 sterling[a] from the Brüningk woman. Indeed, *Monsieur le Lieutenant* had appointed himself to the post of sycophant, nursery-maid, fan-bearer, political oracle, companion, admirer, boots, and any other agreeable function you may care to name.

Reichenbach wants to go to America, as does—up to a point—Kalb of Löwe,[b] the first as a farmer, the second as a doctor.

In the West, the most important, if least conspicuous event, has been the burial of Madame Raspail in Paris[c]. The unexpected turn-out of 20,000 proletarians IN FULL DRESS utterly dumbfounded the Bonapartists. So you can see that the proletarian lion isn't dead. For Ledru, too, the event was a most bitter pill. Raspail is his arch-enemy.

One more FACT. Don't blame me if it is unaesthetic. The *'blonde souveraine'*, Montijo-Lola,[d] is subject to a most repellent constitutional complaint—incessant *farting*. It is known as tympoptanomania. Formerly she used to combat the 'ACCIDENT' with energetic horse-riding which Bonaparte has now forbidden her on the grounds that it is beneath her station. Thus at several *'réunions'* her *'détonations fortes'*[e] have even brought blushes to the cheeks of braided Décembraillards.[f] And that is saying a great deal. *Ce n'est qu'un petit bruit, un murmure, un rien*[g]; *mais enfin, vous savez que les Français ont le nez au plus petit vent.*[h]

In a year *at the most* you will, I think, be with us. *Les choses marchent.*[i]

Your

K. M.

First published in: Marx and Engels, *Works*, First Russian Edition, Vol. XXV, Moscow, 1934

Printed according to the original

Published in English in full for the first time

---

[a] For 'sterling', Marx wrote in jest *'Sperling'*—sparrow. - [b] Marx jokingly transposed personal and place-names, misspelling the latter, to give 'Calf of Lion'. - [c] on 13 March - [d] An analogy between the Empress Eugénie and Lola Montez, a well-known dancer and adventurer. - [e] loud reports - [f] Omnibus word meaning 'loud-mouthed men of December' (the time of Louis Napoleon's coup). - [g] A paraphrase of Don Bazile's words in Beaumarchais' *Le barbier de Séville, ou la précaution inutile*, Act II, Scene VIII. - [h] It's only a small noise, a murmur, a nothing; but then, you know, the French are sensitive to the slightest puff of wind. - [i] Things are moving.

149

ENGELS TO MARX

IN LONDON

[Manchester,] Sunday, 10 April [1853]

Dear Marx,

I return herewith Cluss' letter.[361] And there, it seems, the matter will have to rest until we have before us the whole of Hirsch's document,[a] and also his first statement[b] which Weydemeyer has retained (do you know anything more about this?). The Bangya business isn't very nice; however, *au bout du compte*,[c] it is better to settle it·now than later. According to what you write you have full proof against Bangya to hand now, and, of course, there is also Zerffi to vouch for the Greif business.[d] Knowing as we do now what is coming, we have time to prepare a proper answer.[e] I shall look out Bangya's and the fictitious Collmann's letters.[f] So far as I am concerned, the pamphlet[g] can be printed in America.

Some of the things in Hirsch's statement are perfectly correct, e.g. concerning your letter from Manchester.[362] At the same time, of course, he does his fair share of lying and keeping things under his hat. For instance, he forgets to say that he followed you to Manchester, clearly not by accident, and that, meeting us one Sunday in the Bury New Road with another loafer, he called out quite loudly as he went by: 'Good morning, Marx!' You will recall that we wondered who it might be; *ce fut notre cher Hirsch*.[h] Likewise the affair of Mrs Daniels' letter and the domiciliary visit.[260]

It is curious how many spies *à la* Cooper[363] seem to be turning up just now. Chenu, Cherval, Hirsch. It's a good thing Hirsch now testifies that Bangya was never able to report anything about you except personal tittle-tattle.

Inquiries must be made about the persons mentioned. Lanckoroński is clearly none other than the 'Count L.' denounced by

---

a W. Hirsch, 'Die Opfer der Moucharderie. Rechtfertigungsschrift', *Belletristisches Journal und New-Yorker Criminal-Zeitung*, Nos. 3-6, 1, 8, 15 and 22 April 1853. - b W. Hirsch, 'Erklärung [of 12 January 1852]', *Belletristisches Journal und New-Yorker Criminal-Zeitung*, No. 7, 29 April 1853. - c after all - d See this volume, pp. 242-45. - e K. Marx, 'Hirsch's Confessions'. - f See this volume, pp. 239, 256 and 258. - g K. Marx and F. Engels, *The Great Men of the Exile*. - h It was our dear Hirsch.

you as a Russian agent in the Kossuth-Bonaparte article.[a] As far as Bangya is concerned, we are fully covered by Kossuth and Szemere and, if he possessed a manuscript of Szemere's,[b] why not one of ours?[c] It's an excellent thing that we have *always* kept *everything* that came our way.

Apropos. Not long ago Dronke made a terrible fuss about my not providing him AT A MOMENT'S NOTICE with the Reichenbach circular[299] and now, in the parcel of American papers, I find it reproduced at least ten times. Couldn't the lazy devil have searched it out himself?

Pour revenir.[d] I don't believe anything can be done publicly for the time being, i.e. until we've had a thorough examination of the documents; preliminary steps, no more—for instance, finding out where the document came from, the present whereabouts of Hirsch and what he is doing and, if necessary, confronting the fellow in order to extract another written statement from him. I shall also take immediate steps to find out more about the business of Fleury and the theft[364]; unfortunately my informant, a personal acquaintance of his, is ill. Mind you send me without delay the requisite personal description, etc., etc.

Today I have leafed through most of the American papers sent to me. Much is very amusing but, when there's such a pile of them, it's a very trying and stultifying job. By comparison, Cluss' letters are a delight. I see that the *Revelations* are already appearing in the *Neu-England-Zeitung*[365]; it's really too bad of Weydemeyer not to have got them into the *Criminal-Zeitung*. The least he can now do is to catch up with the main content—drop him a heavy hint to that effect by the next STEAMER, otherwise it may never occur to him.

I have not yet read the pile of (New York) *Demokrats* in which Weydemeyer publishes his articles; I'm saving them up for this evening.

Between ourselves, I am now pretty well convinced that it was, after all, Monsieur Bangya who betrayed Kothes' address.[e] It's a good thing nobody knows about it.

If the business of Hirsch and Bangya becomes any more involved, there'll be another job for us to do when you come up.

---

[a] K. Marx, 'Movements of Mazzini and Kossuth.—League with Louis Napoleon.—Palmerston'. - [b] B. Szemere, *Graf Ludwig Batthyány, Arthur Görgei, Ludwig Kossuth...* - [c] K. Marx and F. Engels, *The Great Men of the Exile*. - [d] To return. - [e] See this volume, pp. 232 and 239.

What are your prospects of a visit? I am counting on seeing you here in May at the latest.

You will have had my Friday's letter[366] and with it £3. Warm regards to your wife.

Your
F. E.

First published abridged in *Der Briefwechsel zwischen F. Engels und K. Marx*, Bd. 1, Stuttgart, 1913 and in full in *MEGA*, Abt. III, Bd. 1, Berlin, 1929

Printed according to the original

Published in English for the first time

150

ENGELS TO JOSEPH WEYDEMEYER[1]

IN NEW YORK

Manchester, 12 April 1853

Dear Weydemeyer,

Herewith Marx's statement on Hirsch's *Confessions*[a] which you should *immediately* get into *as many papers as you can.* If you send Cluss a copy at once, he will undoubtedly be able to take over a large part of the task. It would, I think, do no harm if you were to append the words, 'The undersigned express their full agreement with the above, E. Dronke, F. Engels'. As far as the business of the manuscript[b] is concerned, and relations with Bangya generally, we are just as responsible as Marx and it would not be right if we were to let him bear the responsibility alone. The copy that was handed over[c] is partly in Dronke's hand, the original almost entirely in mine. There is now a prospect of the thing being published in Switzerland.

This statement was composed solely on the strength of the excerpts made by you and sent to us by Cluss.[d] Whether the remainder contains anything that will necessitate a further statement, we cannot, of course, yet say, but doubtless you'll have

---

[a] K. Marx, 'Hirsch's Confessions'. - [b] K. Marx and F. Engels, *The Great Men of the Exile*. - [c] to Bangya - [d] excerpts from Hirsch's article 'Die Opfer der Moucharderie. Rechtfertigungsschrift', then being prepared for the press.

extracted everything relating to ourselves. In a few days' time you will, I trust, send us the whole thing in print.

As for Bangya, we have him completely in our power. The fellow's so deeply implicated that he is utterly done for. Fresh grounds for suspicion kept cropping up and, in order to cover himself he was compelled to show Marx little by little his entire hoard of documents from Kossuth, Szemere, etc. This is how I come to possess the original manuscript of Szemere's pamphlet on Kossuth and Görgey. Mr Kossuth, then, has been badly compromised through Mr. Bangya. This magyarised Slav's petty cunning was foiled by Marx's tenacity and the skill with which he implicated him. *We,* and no one else (save perhaps Szemere, up to a point), now possess complete documentary evidence as to Bangya's character, but what purpose would be served by raising the alarm just now? The fellow is said to be returning to London in May, and then we can press him hard and possibly extract a great deal more useful information. All manner of things have been going on between Willich and Hirsch which are still very far from clear and if, as you maintain, it was through Kinkel's agency that Hirsch's manuscript found its way over there, this again conjures up the most bizarre speculations. *Il faut tâcher d'y voir clair,*[a] and Bangya can be useful there. So don't say anything about it for the moment; that apart, let the Hungarian gentlemen themselves come forward for once and speak their minds, Kossuth in particular. Why should we give them a helping hand? If they make fools of themselves in a public statement, *tant mieux,*[b] then it will be our turn.

The émigrés are carrying on as disreputably as ever, though with less public offence than hitherto. When I was in London at Christmas-time,[313] we used to mingle *sans façon* with the crowd in the Kinkel-Willich-Ruge pubs, something we could scarcely have done 6 months earlier without risking a brawl. Often the small fry would come up to us quite amiably and patiently allow us to twit them, particularly the gallant Meyen-Julius Vindex.[c] Amongst our own people, everything is still much the same. Lupus is said to be keeping himself very much to himself. Dronke has been angling for a clerk's post these past six months and now there's a scheme afoot to get him one in Bradford, $2^{1}/_{2}$ hours by railway from here. Weerth, when I last heard from him, was in St Thomas in the West Indies, where he had survived the yellow fever season. Red

---

[a] We must try to clarify this - [b] so much the better - [c] An analogy between Eduard Meyen and the Roman general Julius Vindex.

Wolf[a] who, as you know, is a husband and father, takes his wife and child out on jaunts and seldom puts in an appearance. Freiligrath is still living in Hackney and engages in commerce under the auspices of Mr Oxenford.[b] As for myself, I have made substantial progress this past winter in Slavonic languages and military affairs and, by the end of the year, shall have a passable knowledge of Russian and South Slav.[c] In Cologne I accoutred myself at little expense with the library of a retired Prussian artillery officer and for a time felt myself quite the bombardier again, what with the old Plümicke,[d] the Brigade Training Manual and other well-thumbed volumes which you will remember. However, Prussian military literature is positively the worst there is, the only tolerable stuff being what was written with the campaigns of 1813/15 still fresh in mind. But after 1822 this gives way to a repulsively pretentious pedantry, to a bogus omniscience, which is the very devil. Quite recently a number of passable things have again appeared in Prussia, but not many. Unfortunately the French stuff is completely inaccessible to me owing to my unfamiliarity with specialised literature.

I have swotted up pretty well on the old campaigns (i.e. after 1792); the Napoleonic ones are so simple that it would be difficult to go wrong on them. However, *au bout du compte*[e] Jomini gives the best account of them; despite many fine things, I can't really bring myself to like that natural genius, Clausewitz.[367] For the immediate future, i.e. for *us*, the Russian campaign of 1812 is the most important, the only one where important strategic problems still remain to be solved; Germany and Italy do not admit of any lines of action other than those laid down by Napoleon, whereas in Russia everything is still very confused. The question whether, originally, Napoleon's plan of operations in 1812 was to march directly on Moscow or, during the first campaign, simply advance as far as the Dnieper and Dvina, repeats itself for us with the question as to what a revolutionary army should do in the event of a successful offensive against Russia. This question—accidents apart, of course, and assuming no more than an approximately equal balance of forces—can be solved, or so it has seemed to me up till now, only by water—in the Sound and in the Dardanelles, at Petersburg, Riga and Odessa. Apart also, of course, from *internal* movements in Russia—and an aristocratic-bourgeois

---

[a] Ferdinand Wolff - [b] i.e. Oxford - [c] Serbo-Croat - [d] J. C. Plümicke, *Handbuch für die Königlich Preußischen Artillerie-Offiziere.* - [e] in the final analysis

revolution in Petersburg with a resulting civil war in the interior is a possibility. Mr Herzen has made things much easier for himself (*Du progrès des idées révolutionnaires en Russie*[a]) by positing, Hegel-fashion, a democratic-social-communist-Proudhonist Republic of Russia under the triumvirate Bakunin-Herzen-Golovin, so that it cannot possibly fail. Meanwhile it is by no means certain that Bakunin is still alive and in any case Russia, with its huge expanses and sparse population, is a country that is very difficult to conquer. As to the former Polish provinces on this side of the Dvina and Dnieper, I want to hear nothing more of them, knowing as I do that the peasants there are all Ukrainians, only the aristocracy and some of the people in the towns being Polish, and that to the peasant there, as in Ukrainian Galicia in 1846,[368] the restoration of Poland is synonymous with the restoration of the old ruling aristocracy, its powers unimpaired. In all these countries, outside the kingdom of Poland proper, there are barely 500,000 Poles!

It is a good thing, by the way, that this time the revolution should have found a respectable antagonist in Russia and not such spineless scarecrows of opponents[b] as in the year 1848.

In the meantime all sorts of symptoms keep appearing. Prosperity in cotton has reached such heights as to become vertiginous, whereas certain branches of the cotton industry (coarse qualities, DOMESTICS) are completely stagnant. Speculators hope to escape this vertigo by promoting it *en gros*[c] solely in America and France (railways with English money), but over here piecemeal in penny packets, thus by degrees spreading the condition to *all* articles. The quite abnormal weather we've had here during the winter and spring must have damaged the corn and if, as usually happens, the summer is also abnormal, it will spell ruin to the harvest. To my mind the present prosperity cannot last beyond the autumn. In the meantime the 3rd English ministry in 12 months—and, indeed, the last one that will be possible without the direct intervention of the radical bourgeoisie—is falling into disrepute. One after another Whigs, Tories and Coalitionists come to grief as a result, not of a tax deficit, but of a SURPLUS.[369] That typifies the whole policy of the old parties and also their extreme impotence. If the present ministers tumble, it will no longer be possible to govern England without

---

[a] A. Herzen, *Du développement des idées révolutionnaires en Russie*. - [b] governments of numerous German states - [c] wholesale

considerably extending the *pays légal*[a]; hence, this is likely to come about at the beginning of the crisis.

The protracted tedium of prosperity has made it almost impossible for the unhappy Bonaparte to maintain his dignity; the world is bored and he bores the world. Unfortunately he cannot remarry every 4 weeks. This trickster, drunkard and cheat will come to grief through having to make a pretence of putting Engel's *Fürstenspiegel* into practice. The vagabond as 'father of the fatherland'! He is *aux abois*.[b] Yet he can't even start a war: everywhere serried ranks bristling with bayonets as soon as he makes the slightest move. And then this period of tranquillity affords the peasants most desirable time in which to reflect upon how the man who promised to subdue Paris for the peasants' benefit is now using the peasants' money to embellish Paris and how, despite everything, mortgages and taxes are going up rather than down. In short, this time the thing is being methodically prepared, and that's very promising.

In Prussia the government has raised a veritable hornet's nest among the bourgeoisie with its income tax. The bureaucrats have increased the rates of tax in the most barefaced manner, and you can imagine the glee with which those egregious quillpushers are now poking their noses into the trade secrets and ledgers of all the merchants. Even my old man, a dyed-in-the-wool Prussian, is fuming with rage. These fellows must now endure to the bitter end the blessings of a constitutional, fatherly, Prussian *gouverne-ment à bon marché*.[c] Prussia's national debt,—some 67 mill. talers before 1848,—must since have swollen to four times that amount, and already they are wanting to borrow again! One can only assume that the portly monarch[d] would cheerfully sweat now, as once he sweated during the March days,[e] if only he were to be guaranteed this credit for the rest of his mortal life. Yet Louis Napoleon has helped him set the Customs Union on its feet again, Austria, fearing war, has drawn in her horns,[370] 'and now, Lord, lettest thou thy servant depart in peace into the grave'![f]

The Austrians are doing everything in their power to set things in motion again in Italy, a country which, before the Milan uprising,[335] was completely given over to commerce and prosperity in so far as this was compatible with taxation; and if everything goes on like this for another few months, Europe will be in a splendid state of readiness, needing only the jog of a crisis. On top

---

a franchise - b at bay - c cheap government - d Frederick William IV - e of 1848 (beginning of the revolution in Prussia) - f Luke 2:29

of this, one must consider that prosperity, unprecedented in its scope and duration—having begun early in 1849—has restored the strength of the exhausted parties (in so far as these were not beyond repair, like the monarchist party in France) much more quickly than was the case after 1830, for example, when trading conditions long remained unsettled and, on the whole, indifferent. In 1848, too, only the Paris proletariat, and later Hungary and Italy, were exhausted by severe struggles; after June 1848, the insurrections that took place in France were hardly worth speaking of and, in the final count, *ruined* only the old monarchist parties. Add to this the curious result produced by the movement in *all* countries, a result in no way serious or significant save for the colossal historical irony and the concentration of Russian military resources; and in view of all this, it seems to me that, even taking the most sober view, the present state of affairs cannot possibly continue beyond the spring of 1854.

How splendid it is that on this occasion *our party* is taking the stage under wholly different auspices. All the socialist stupidities which one still had to advocate in 1848 vis-à-vis the pure democrats and the South German republicans, the vapourings of L. Blanc, etc., and, indeed, even the things *we* were compelled to propound if only to find *points d'appui* for our views in the confused state of affairs in Germany—all this is already being advocated by our respected opponents, by Ruge, Heinzen, Kinkel and so forth. The preliminaries to proletarian revolution, the measures by which the field of battle is being made ready and the way cleared for us—a single and indivisible republic, etc., things which originally *we* had to advocate *in the teeth* of those whose natural, normal calling it should have been to implement, or at least demand them,—all this is now *convenu*,[a] has been learnt by the gentlemen. This time we shall start off straight away with the *Manifesto*,[b] thanks largely to the Cologne trial in which German communism (most notably through Röser) has passed its matriculation.

All this, of course, relates merely to theory; in practice we shall, as always, be reduced to insisting above all on resolute measures and absolute ruthlessness. And that's the pity of it. I have a feeling that one fine day, thanks to the helplessness and spinelessness of all the others, our party will find itself forced into power, whereupon it will have to enact things that are not immediately in

---

[a] agreed - [b] K. Marx and F. Engels, *Manifesto of the Communist Party*.

our own, but rather in the general, revolutionary and specifically petty-bourgeois interest; in which event, spurred on by the proletarian *populus* and bound by our own published statements and plans—more or less wrongly interpreted and more or less impulsively pushed through in the midst of party strife—we shall find ourselves compelled to make communist experiments and leaps which no one knows better than ourselves to be untimely. One then proceeds to lose one's head—only *physiquement parlant*[a] I hope—, a reaction sets in and, until such time as the world is capable of passing *historical* judgment of this kind of thing, one will be regarded, not only as a brute beast, which wouldn't matter a rap, but also as *bête*,[b] and that's far worse. I don't very well see how it could happen otherwise. In a backward country such as Germany which possesses an advanced party and which, together with an advanced country such as France, becomes involved in an advanced revolution, at the first serious conflict, and as soon as there is *real danger,* the turn of the advanced party will inevitably come, and this in any case will be *before* its normal time. However, none of this matters a rap; the main thing is that, should this happen, our party's rehabilitation in history will already have been substantiated in advance in its *literature.*

We shall, by the way, cut a far more respectable figure on the stage than last time. In the first place we are happily rid of all the old idlers in the persons of Schapper, Willich and Co., secondly, we have grown somewhat stronger, thirdly, we can count on the rising generation in Germany (if nothing else, the Cologne trial is enough to guarantee us this), and finally we have all of us benefited substantially in exile. There are, of course, some amongst us who proceed on the principle: 'What need is there for us to swot? That's what *père* Marx is there for, it's his business to know everything.' But in general the Marx party does do a good deal of swotting, and one only has to look at the way the other émigré jackasses snap up this or that new catchword, thereby becoming more bemused than ever, to realise that our party's superiority has increased both absolutely and relatively. As indeed it must, for *la besogne sera rude.*[c]

I should like to have time before the next revolution to study and describe thoroughly at least the campaigns of 1848 and 1849 in Italy and Hungary. Generally speaking, I have a pretty clear notion of the business, despite imperfect maps, etc. But the very

---

[a] physically speaking - [b] stupid - [c] it will be a tough business

accuracy of detail required to depict it calls for a great deal of trouble and expense. On both occasions the Italians behaved like nincompoops. Willisen's account and analysis, while accurate on the whole, is often silly,[a] and the total superiority of Austrian strategy, which he stresses as early as 1848, only becomes apparent in the Novara campaign,[371] without doubt the most brilliantly fought affair in Europe since Napoleon's day (*outside* Europe, however, the feats performed by old General Napier in India in 1842 are of quite another order and, indeed, reminiscent of Alexander the Great; on the whole I regard Charles Napier as the foremost living general). Strange in Italy, just as in Baden in 1849, is the traditional superstitious belief in positions occupied during the campaigns of the 1790s. Nothing would have induced Mr Sigel to fight anywhere save in the position made classical by Moreau, and Charles Albert's belief in the Virgin Mary's virginity was no more steadfast than his belief in the miraculous powers of the plateau of Rivoli. So immutable was this conviction in Italy that the Austrians commenced every important manoeuvre with a feint attack on Rivoli and *every time* the Piedmontese fell into the trap. The joke is, of course, that the relative positions and lines of communication were quite different.

Despite everything, Monsieur Görgey remains the only fellow in Hungary who was superior to everyone else and to whom everyone else was hostile out of sheer envy; I think it probable that had not Görgey, despite his great military talents, been a very vain, petty chap, this for the most part stupid hostility would have finally turned him into a traitor. Ever since the Világos affair[372]— entirely justified in *military* (but *not* revolutionary) terms—the fellows have subjected Görgey to such a plethora of insane accusations that the chap almost compels one's interest. The actual 'betrayal' took place after the relief of Komarom,[373] before the Russians got there, and for this Kossuth is just as much to blame as Görgey. A cloud of uncertainty still envelops Bayer, Görgey's Chief of the General Staff, who is now in London. From the memoirs of Görgey[b] and other sources, it would seem that it was *he* who inspired Görgey's *strategic* plans. From what Pleyel told me, Bayer is the principal author of the official *Austrian* book on the campaign.[c] (Bayer was captured in Pest and escaped); it is said

---

[a] W. Willisen, *Der italienische Feldzug des Jahres 1848.* - [b] A. Görgei, *Mein Leben und Wirken in Ungarn in den Jahren 1848* und 1849. - [c] Presumably *Sammlung der für Ungarn erlassenen Allerhöchsten Manifeste und Proklamationen, dann der Kundmachungen der Oberbefehlshaber der kaiserlichen Armee in Ungarn.*

to be excellent, but I haven't yet been able to get hold of it. Görgey speaks of Klapka with great respect, but everyone admits that he was very weak. Perczel is regarded as a jackass, the 'democratic' Hungarian general. Old Bem always thought of himself only as a good partisan and commander of a detached corps intended for a definite purpose; so far as I can judge, this is all he was, but to a superlative degree. He did two stupid things, once with his fruitless expedition into the blue after Banat; next, during the great Russian invasion when he repeated, literally, the highly professional manoeuvre he had successfully executed before Hermannstadt and was trounced in consequence.[374] *Père* Dembiński, however, was an incorrigible visionary and braggart, a partisan who believed himself born to conduct great campaigns and embarked on the maddest enterprises. Smitt's Polish Campaign of 1831[a] contains some good stories about him.

Apropos. Could you give me a short description of Cologne's fortifications with a few drawings—rough sketches—done from memory? If I remember rightly, the main wall is bastioned and the forts are said to be of the Montalembert type; is that so, and how many of them are there? You can use any military engineering terms, since I have some quite passable manuals and drawings here. Do you know details of any other Prussian fortresses? I am fairly familiar with Coblenz (Ehrenbreitstein, at least), and have seen a plan of Mainz. What interests me particularly is the manner in which the new Montalembert structures are built in Germany; it's impossible to find out anything about this owing to Prussian secretiveness.

Write soon. Warmest regards to your wife[b] and to Cluss from

Your

F. Engels.

First published in part in *Die Neue Zeit,* Bd. 2, No. 31, Stuttgart, 1906-07 and in full in: Marx and Engels, *Works,* First Russian Edition, Vol. XXV, Moscow, 1934

Printed according to the original

Published in English in full for the first time

---

[a] F. Smitt, *Geschichte des polnischen Aufstandes und Krieges in den Jahren 1830 und 1831.* - [b] Louise

151

MARX TO ADOLF CLUSS [375]

IN WASHINGTON

[London, 17 April 1853]

... Today I have received the first 5 numbers[a] from New York, whether from Weydemeyer or from Kellner I do not know. With most of them I was already familiar through you. This is at least a *decent* paper—a rare thing in America—and a working man's paper. However, I cannot say I very much care for the chief editor's affected effusions concerning *'questions personnelles'* which are at one and the same time party questions, or for his pseudo-naive gentility and biblical portentousness. But you have to take this newspaper as it comes. What I liked best of all was Weydemeyer's introduction to his 'Ökonomische Skizzen'. Good stuff that. I have approached our people here; Dronke and Pieper have, I think, already sent something. I shall speak to Jones. On the whole it is difficult to get contributions. I myself have too much to do. The others unfortunately are still somewhat put off by their earlier experiences. Lupus is in a wretched state. Eccarius has to work away at his tailoring from 5 in the morning until 8 at night and is in a dangerously hectic condition. Engels, when not stuck in the office, is completely taken up with his studies, and probably he too has not yet got over the wrongs he thinks he has suffered at the hands of the American Press. Our party is, alas, very *pauvre*.[b] I shall also approach ex-lieutenant Steffen, ex-witness for the defence at the Cologne trial, presently a schoolmaster in the vicinity of London. He has more spare time than anyone else and is very capable.

Pieper has still not finished the articles you want, which explains why you haven't yet had them.[376]

As for the Hirsch affair,[c] a statement[d] IMMEDIATELY went off to Engels via Engels, which, etc., etc. I've known for 6 months or more that there was something fishy about Bangya. I didn't break with the fellow until, like the jackass he is, he had let me find out all about his connections, handed over all documents that put me

---

[a] of *Die Reform* - [b] poor - [c] See this volume, pp. 301-02. - [d] K. Marx, 'Hirsch's Confessions'.

in the right and him in the wrong, and generally placed himself at my mercy. I threw him out months ago at Szemere's.

My suspicions of Willich have only been confirmed by his latest step. *D'abord,*[a] I know that he and Kinkel paid and continue to pay Hirsch out of revolutionary funds! Then, at the Cologne trial, soon after it began, he boasted to Fleury (who in turn passed it on to Imandt) that he had in his possession a letter of mine to Bangya dated Manchester. I challenged Bangya about this at the time. He said he was willing to be confronted with Fleury. On being informed of this by Imandt at my behest, Fleury retracted. Thus at that time Willich was illicitly consorting with Hirsch. He knew that Hirsch was illicitly consorting with Greif and that his *friend* Fleury was a spy. It was through these fellows that he got hold of my letter. The 'gallant worthy'—for whom, *en passant,*[b] free meat and drink is *le dernier but*[c]—wanted to set a trap for me, and to that end became embroiled in intrigues with *mouchards.*[d]

True, he sent Hirsch to Cologne. True, I heard later that Hirsch was in Cologne. But why did he send Hirsch to Cologne, and when did he send him there? *Firstly,* when it was already too late. 2. When the police in Cologne had themselves denounced his friend Fleury. 3. When he himself, having become suspect, wished to rehabilitate himself as a 'magnanimous worthy' by means of this theatrical coup. This was Hirsch's own account of the affair on his return...

Reichenbach and family, 'clever' Lieutenant Schimmelpfennig complete with wife and Brüningk legacy of £1,000, and lastly, the artist Schmolze, set sail today for America. *Bon voyage!* But Reichenbach's flight has deprived poor Lupus of the last of his lessons. It's most unfortunate for him. He's no Kinkel. Nor does he know how to lick the boots of the bourgeois like the future 'President of the German Republic' and his 'consort',[e] both of them consummate sycophants, humbugs and parasites. The amiable Gottfried has so far succeeded in ingratiating himself that he has been accorded the use of one of London University's lecture rooms to repeat before a London audience his old series of lectures on Christian art in the Middle Ages. He is giving them *free* and gratis in the hope that he will be able to worm his way into the post of Professor of Aesthetics at London University. He delivers them in ABOMINABLE English, *reading* from a manuscript. Though welcomed with applause at the beginning of the series, he

---

[a] In the first place - [b] in passing - [c] the ultimate aim - [d] police spies - [e] Johanna Kinkel

subsequently proved such a complete failure that not even the organised claque of Jewish aesthetics-mongers could save him. Edgar Bauer, who was present—Kinkel gave his first lecture last Tuesday—told me all about it. It seems to have been a truly nauseating and wretched performance.

First published in: Marx and Engels, *Works,* Second Russian Edition, Vol. 28, Moscow, 1962

Printed according to the letter from Cluss to Weydemeyer of 3 May 1853

Published in English in full for the first time

152

MARX TO ENGELS

IN MANCHESTER

[London,] 23 April 1853
28 Dean Street, Soho

Dear Engels,

The Pieper business is true.[377] Bangya is here again, also Stieber and Goldheim. *Please return enclosed pencilled note immediately.*[a] *Qu'en dis-tu?*[b]

I now have a further £30 to draw on New York. Bamberger refused to budge, but I have something else in prospect. If it materialises, I shall visit you from 1 to 7 May, *supposé* [c] I shan't be in your way.

If you have the time, I should very much like to have an article on *Switzerland* [378] by Friday.[d] You have dealt with the subject any number of times, whereas I am not familiar with the personalities, etc. But it should be an article *without* a sequel. *One* article on Switzerland is enough for a country of that size.

Your
K. M.

First published abridged in *Der Briefwechsel zwischen F. Engels und K. Marx,* Bd. 1, Stuttgart, 1913 and in full in *MEGA,* Abt. III, Bd. 1, Berlin, 1929

Printed according to the original

Published in English for the first time

---

[a] See this volume, p. 316. - [b] What do you say to that? - [c] supposing - [d] 29 April

153

MARX TO ENGELS

IN MANCHESTER

[London,] 26 April 1853

DEAR Frederic,

I fear that nothing will come of my proposed trip.[a] Bamberger cannot discount the bill for me and Friedländer, who half-promised to do so, has now definitely refused. I have written to Strohn about it,[379] but look on this as a mere formality which I complied with *pour acquit de conscience*[b] and for my wife's sake, without expecting anything to come of it.

A paper of mine for the *Tribune* (which included the *first* Turkish article)[c] about Mazzini's presence here—again denied by his friends but on his orders, I think—was made the basis for a short LEADER on Mazzini's lucky escape, followed by the comment:

* 'In this connection we may properly pay a tribute to the remarkable ability of the correspondent by whom this interesting piece of intelligence is furnished. Mr Marx has very decided opinions of his own, with some of which we are far from agreeing, but those who do not read his letters neglect one of the most instructive sources of information on the great questions of current European politics.' * [d]

As you see, I am firmly in the saddle. I have in addition had a most interesting letter from Cluss with 2 issues containing Hirsch's confessions[e] (not yet concluded). I'm not sending the stuff yet since there's still a chance that something might happen to enable me to come myself and bring the things with me. Anyhow, I won't come without notifying you beforehand. When is your old man arriving? I'd rather not cannon into him.

If only Dana would advise me of a business house here, as I have asked him three times to do, I should at least be over the worst.

Ad vocem[f] Hirsch: Originally I was of the same opinion[g] as yourself, but the matter is somewhat different. Stieber and Goldheim are definitely here, their purpose being to 'link'

---

a See this volume, pp. 303 and 314. - b to salve my conscience - c K. Marx and F. Engels, 'British Politics.—Disraeli.—The Refugees.—Mazzini in London.—Turkey'. - d *New-York Daily Tribune*, No. 3736, 7 April 1853. - e W. Hirsch, 'Die Opfer der Moucharderie. Rechtfertigungsschrift', *Belletristisches Journal und New-Yorker Criminal-Zeitung*, presumably Nos. 3 and 4, 1 and 8 April 1853. - f re - g See this volume, pp. 301-02.

Kossuth's gunpowder plot with Berlin.[380]. The same fellow who wrote me the anonymous scrawl,[a] wrote on the same day to Schärttner and Göhringer word-for-word as follows:

'London, 21.4.53

Announcement

Recent arrivals: Police Commissioner Stieber and the Jew Goldheim, a police lieutenant, both of Berlin (P.T.O.)

Description

Stieber	the Jew Goldheim
Medium height (about 5)	about 6'
Hair: black, short	black, short
Moustache: ditto, ditto	ditto, ditto
Complexion: sallow and muddy	sallow, puffy features
Wears dark, narrow trousers, a blue sack, a collapsible stuff hat, and spectacles.	Wears black trousers, a light yellow sack, black hat.

N.B. Both of them regularly go about together and are accompanied by *Hirsch*, a commercial assistant from Hamburg, and Haering, a postal clerk from Willich's birth-place. Today Stieber and Goldheim had a meeting with Bangya. Stieber and Goldheim visit the Prussian Embassy regularly every day between 11 and 3.'

I believe the author to be Henry de L'Aspée, friend and compatriot of O. Dietz, that same aggrieved policeman who, you will recall, was to have [a meeting] with us after your arrival here for the purpose of making further revelations. You can see what headway 'Hirsch' is making. Nothing could be more inopportune for Willich-Kinkel.

FAREWELL.

Your

K. M.

As to the pound,[b] I shall give them each 10/-, since so far as I know there's some prospect of Pieper's getting his money without a lawsuit. The poor devil is hellish syphilitic and at the same time in rotten CIRCUMSTANCES and too featherbrained to look after himself.

First published abridged in *Der Briefwechsel Zwischen F. Engels und K. Marx,* Bd. 1, Stuttgart, 1913 and in full in: Marx and Engels, *Works,* Second Russian Edition, Vol. 28, Moscow, 1962

Printed according to the original

Published in English for the first time

---

[a] See this volume, p. 314. - [b] Reference to the help given to Dronke and Pieper.

154

MARX TO ADOLF CLUSS

IN WASHINGTON

[London, 26 April 1853]

Dear Cluss,

You must by now have received three letters from me.[381] Enclosed a Jones *Paper*, containing an anti-*Times* article by 'Englishman'.[a]

If the *Cologne Revelations* have not yet been printed as a pamphlet, or *'gratis'* as such by the *Neu-England-Zeitung*, do nothing more about it, as it is now too late.

Willich has written to Herzen (the Russian) to say that everything is going 'splendidly', that he has achieved 'great results' and will soon be returning.

Mr *Hentze,* for one, is again implicated in the Berlin business.[b] In any case, as Willich-Kinkel's agent, he would have been possessed of old proclamations and revolutionary recipes. Furthermore, he was destined by these great men to be military commander of Berlin.

The local Rollinists[c] are blushing for shame over Ruge's proclamation of which they were informed by us. In no case had Ledru given Ruge permission to publish this discreditable letter. Ruge extorted the letter from Ledru through the latter's ex-servant, the ex-Palatinate lawyer, and ex-French deputy, *Savoye*—one-time pedlar of German *adjectiva*.[382] At all events, Ledru has sunk lower than ever before.

Your
K. M.

First published in: Marx and Engels, *Works,* First Russian Edition, Vol. XXV, Moscow, 1934

Printed according to the original

Published in English for the first time

---

a 'The Base and Brutal *Times*', *The People's Paper*, No. 51, 23 April 1853. Englishman—pen-name of Alfred Richards. - b See this volume, pp. 315-16.- c followers of Ledru-Rollin

155

MARX TO JOSEPH WEYDEMEYER

IN NEW YORK

[London,] 26 April 1853
28 Dean Street, Soho

Dear Weydemeyer,

On 21 April I received the anonymous scrawl set out *below*. An identical anonymous letter was sent to the democratic tavern-keepers, Schärttner and Göringer. *I have* ASCERTAINED *the facts contained therein.* I think you should publish the thing (you may name Schärttner and Göringer) along with a few introductory remarks dated London. Messrs Stieber and Goldheim have come over here in order to '*link*' Kossuth's apocryphal gunpowder plot with the Berlin affair.[a] From the following you will note to what extent the 'contrite' Hirsch continues to be 'A Victim of Moucharderie'.[b] Let us hope the blackguard doesn't succeed in finding fresh victims in Berlin. I think this business will prove his complete undoing in America. Cluss will have received what follows below at the same time as yourself. We were all very taken with your 2 articles in the *Reform*.[c] Only see to it that Kellner doesn't exploit you without a fitting *quid pro quo* in terms of political influence. Well, here is a *word-for-word* copy of the letter received by Schärttner, etc.:

'London, 21.4.53

Announcement

Recent arrivals: Police Commissioner Stieber and the Jew Goldheim, a police lieutenant, both of Berlin.

Description

Stieber	*the Jew Goldheim*
Medium height (about 5′)	about 6′
Hair: black, short	black, short
Moustache: ditto, ditto	ditto, ditto
Complexion: sallow and muddy	sallow, puffy features
Wears dark, narrow trousers, a blue sack, a collapsible stuff hat, and spectacles.	Wears black trousers, a light yellow sack, black hat.

---

[a] See this volume, pp. 315-16. - [b] An allusion to Hirsch's 'Die Opfer der Moucharderie...' - [c] Weydemeyer, 'Nationalökonomische Skizzen'.

N.B. Both of them regularly go about together and are accompanied by *Hirsch*, a commercial assistant from Hamburg, and *Haering*, a one-time postal clerk from Willich's birth-place. Today Stieber and Goldheim had a meeting with Bangya. Stieber or Goldheim visit the Prussian Embassy regularly every day between 11 and 3.'

Today's *Times* reports the presence here of Stieber and Goldheim.[a]

Many regards to you and your wife.

Your
K. M.

As that fire-eater Heinzen has again had the audacity in his *Volk* to invoke the 'Chartists'—who simply want universal suffrage without having to bother their heads over communists or odious class distinctions, I think it high time you published in the *Reform* the letter written to you by Ernest Jones.[82]

First published in. Marx and Engels, *Works*, First Russian Edition, Vol. XXV, Moscow, 1934

Printed according to the original

Published in English for the first time

156

ENGELS TO MARX [383]

IN LONDON

[Manchester,] 26 April 1853

Dear Marx,

Herewith the article[378] and pound sterling. Even though one of the two CLAIMANTS[b] may suffer, fob him off until next week.

The sooner you come yourself, the better. The bedroom in my house is ready.

Trade appears to be falling off already in France. In particular, direct imports of cotton from America have decreased. The

---

[a] [Report from a Berlin correspondent of 22 April,] *The Times*, No. 21412, 26 April 1853. - [b] Dronke and Pieper, see this volume, p. 321.

figures for American exports are as follows: from 1 September to 6 April of each year.

	1853	1852	1851	1850
To England	1,100,000	930,000	757,000	592,000
„ France	257,000	302,000	246,000	192,000
All other countries	204,000	189,000	163,000	105,000

In other words, France is the *only* country which, despite the enormous American crop, has taken *less* than last year and barely more than in 1851, the year of political gloom, *où l'ordre et la société allaient s'engloutir dans le gouffre socialiste*.[a] Imports in 1852 show the momentarily magical effect of the coup d'état, 1853 shows the reverse. Something was still being shipped from Liverpool to Havre, but not as much as formerly. In other respects too, industry in France would not appear to be exactly flourishing. This time the thing seems to be really serious, and connected especially with the ousting of French articles from foreign markets by domestic manufactures. The colossal proscriptions of workers in 1851/52 are beginning to bear fruit; I am convinced that they have contributed quite specifically to the expansion and improvement of the English and American factories producing Paris articles, bronzes, etc. Today it is a thousand times more difficult than before to drive the proletariat across the border with impunity on the pretext of order. Even if there were complete peace, French industry would inevitably go to the dogs owing to this perpetual exploitation of conspiracy as a *moyen de gouvernement*,[b] and the constantly renewed proscription of the proletariat; the English and the Yankees certainly know how to take advantage of the more useful amongst these.

When, then, will you be coming?

Your
F. E.

First published abridged in *Der Briefwech-sel zwischen F. Engels und K. Marx*, Bd. 1, Stuttgart, 1913 and in full in *MEGA*, Abt. III, Bd. 1, Berlin, 1929

Printed according to the original

Published in English in full for the first time

---

[a] when order and society were about to be swallowed up in the socialist abyss - [b] means of government

157

MARX TO ENGELS

IN MANCHESTER

[London,] 27 April 1853
28 Dean Street, Soho

Dear Engels,

I have just been with Freiligrath to see Gerstenberg and there is some prospect of having the bill discounted by Friday or at least of obtaining an advance on it. No go with Strohn, OF COURSE. So there is still a possibility of coming to you—which I greatly wish to do.

I should be obliged if you would answer *by return* the following enquiry little Bamberger asked me to pass on to you (the fellow might come in useful now or at any time):

Madapolams for the Italian market ⎫ Good houses to
Printed calicos ....ditto ⎬ buy from in
Straw manufacturing houses ....ditto ⎭ Manchester

Received the article [378] and £1 for Pieper and Dronke.

I know now for certain that my information about Mazzini's presence in London[a] was correct.

Hirsch was at the Russian consul's the day before yesterday, and on the same day at Fleury's house with Stieber and Goldheim.

Your
K. M.

First published abridged in *Der Briefwechsel zwischen F. Engels und K. Marx*, Bd. 1, Stuttgart, 1913 and in full in *MEGA*, Abt. III, Bd. 1, Berlin, 1929

Printed according to the original

Published in English for the first time

---

[a] See this volume, p. 281.

158

ENGELS TO MARX

IN LONDON

[Manchester,] Wednesday, [27 April 1853]

Dear Marx,

If there is nothing better you can do about the bill, send it to me by return (in time for Friday's American post). I think I can get it cashed for you by a Yankee or at any rate advance you £10 against it pending receipt of the balance—i.e., you can't have the money before 1 May, but on *2 May* you will receive the £10 *without fail.* Write and tell me whether in these circumstances you will be able to come here, and do come if at all possible; then you can send the money to your wife yourself.

At any rate, keep me informed, so that I'm NOT OUT OF THE WAY when you arrive.

P. Ermen's old library will again be at our disposal.

Your
F. E

First published in *MEGA*, Abt. III, Bd. 1, Berlin, 1929

Printed according to the original

Published in English for the first time

159

MARX TO ENGELS

IN MANCHESTER

[London,] 28 April 1853
28 Dean Street, Soho

Dear Engels,

Today Freiligrath and I went to Gerstenberg's again. He gave me a 'sealed' letter of recommendation to Spielmann in Lombard Street. Refusal. As a prominent Kinkelian, Gerstenberg was not, of course, in earnest.

I am now sending you the bill which, with the stuff[a] that goes off tomorrow, amounts to £32.

Bamberger is willing to lend me £2 so that I can leave a few shillings with my wife and use the rest for my journey to you. *I shall leave on Saturday morning.*[b] Tomorrow is impossible.

Your
K. Marx

First published in *Der Briefwechsel zwischen F. Engels und K. Marx*, Bd. 1, Stuttgart, 1913

Printed according to the original

Published in English for the first time

160

ENGELS TÓ MARX

IN LONDON

[Manchester,] Friday, 20 May 1853

Dear Marx,

Herewith the latest news from America. I still have several copies of the *Criminal-Zeitung* containing the statements by Weydemeyer and yourself,[c] which I shall send at the beginning of next week so that you and the others can make use of them; I shall keep one copy here for Dronke and the archives.

Freiligrath will, perhaps, be so good as to notify Weydemeyer or Lièvre of the receipt of the £25 enclosed herewith,[384] it being too late for me to write to Weydemeyer today. But how the fellows have managed to convert $125 into £25 is a mystery to me, for according to the last New York rate of 4 May sterling was standing at 54d.=109³/₄ cents, thus, even at 110 cents, $125=£25. 11s. 4d., hence there has been a loss of ³/₂d. for every dollar on the rate of exchange.

My old man has at last written to me. As I expected: for God's

---

[a] K. Marx and F. Engels, 'The Rocket Affair.—The Swiss Insurrection', and F. Engels, 'Political Position of the Swiss Republic'. - [b] 30 April. Marx stayed with Engels in Manchester till 19 May. - [c] J. Weydemeyer, 'Der "demokratische" Mouchard', *Belletristisches Journal und New-Yorker Criminal-Zeitung*, No. 7, 29 April 1853, and K. Marx, 'Hirsch's Confessions'.

sake avoid a row, wait till he comes and then takes me to the Exchange. Business is too good to permit of an almighty rumpus. So far as I'm concerned that's perfectly in order provided my worthy papa has nothing against it; what do *I* care about the wretched affair?

Your

F. E.

First published in *Der Briefwechsel zwischen F. Engels und K. Marx*, Bd. 1, Stuttgart, 1913

Printed according to the original

Published in English for the first time

161

MARX TO ENGELS

IN MANCHESTER

[London,] 21 May 1853
28 Dean Street, Soho

Dear Engels,

Today the bill for £25 goes off to Freiligrath, who will immediately notify Lièvre of its receipt.[a]

Herewith Wolff's[b] address; he is still sulking. By the by, now that so much has been brought out into the open, I have become convinced that Dronke has been purveying the most abject lies, rumours and gossip at my expense. The only activity, indeed, of which this self-important midget and WOULD-BE Blanqui was capable. His addiction to tittle-tattle had turned him into such a dyed-in-the-wool liar that he himself no longer knew what he was saying or had said.

Don't for God's sake send me *any more* copies of Weydemeyer's statement or my own.[c] Here alone I have 14 of each which I received the day before yesterday. It would have been more to the point had Weydemeyer sent at least 2 or 3 copies of 'Hirsch's' revelations.[d] E.g., Schabelitz could make use of 1 in Switzerland

---

[a] See previous letter. - [b] Wilhelm Wolff - [c] J. Weydemeyer, 'Der "demokratische" Mouchard' and K. Marx, 'Hirsch's Confessions'. - [d] W. Hirsch, 'Die Opfer der Moucharderie...'

should further proceedings be taken against him. I like the inevitable Weydemeyerian misprint, where Bangya is made to say *'Ähnliches'*[a] instead of *'Rühmliches'*.[b]

Nothing else of interest here. I have not seen Blind recently. Have you sent him his Herzen[c]?

The People's Paper is on the up and up and, for the time being, financially secure. Jones is convening mass meetings for 19 June *et seq.* at Blackstone Edge, Skurcoat Moor, Mount Sorrell and Nottingham Forest.[385]

Apropos. I was only able to give Pieper 10/-, Strohn having shown me the wrong RAILWAY GUIDE which caused me to miss the PARLIAMENTARY TRAIN,[145] so that I had to travel 2nd class.[386]

Write to me soon.

Your

K. M.

First published abridged in *Der Briefwechsel zwischen F. Engels und K. Marx*, Bd. 1, Stuttgart, 1913 and in full in *MEGA*, Abt. III, Bd. 1, Berlin, 1929

Printed according to the original

Published in English for the first time

162

ENGELS TO MARX[387]

IN LONDON

[Manchester, before 28 May 1853]

Dear Marx,

So the bomb is at long last about to go off, as you will see from the enclosed scrappy proof[d] and Weydemeyer's letter. Willich's manner of extricating himself is strange, at any rate; you will undoubtedly be much amused by these lame circumlocutions and the awkward and embarrassed style. The fellow's been hard hit. But papa Schramm[e] would seem to have gravely insulted him in

---

[a] similar - [b] glorious - [c] A. Herzen, *Du développement des idées révolutionnaires en Russie.* - [d] Proofs of Willich's statement published in *Belletristisches Journal und New-Yorker Criminal-Zeitung*, No. 9, 13 May 1853. - [e] Conrad Schramm

Cincinnati; all grist to the mill. One thing we may be sure of is that the only effect of *this* statement will be to compromise the chivalrous one even more.

So *just because* the *New-Yorker-Criminal Zeitung*!!!!! has published attacks upon him, the gallant Willich feels compelled to break his heroic silence.

'Putting the case at its *highest*[a]!' In Willich's case bodies do not fall *downwards* but *upwards*! Good-bye to gravity! The fellow's quite mad. The same old tale of assassination too! We shall now see the aforesaid Schramm leap promptly into the lists, statement in hand.[388]

To put your mind at rest, I can inform you that the *Neu-England-Ztg.* today advised me of the dispatch of 420 copies of *Revelations*[b] to my address, so they may be here tomorrow or, if the parcel didn't go off by the last STEAMER, in a week at the most. The fellows have the effrontery to send me a letter signed semi-anonymously 'Office of the *N.-E.-Z.*' inviting me to contribute. That's the last straw!

At all events, it's a good thing that we now possess in the *Reform*[389] an organ in which, if the worst comes to the worst, we can still make ourselves heard in the polemic against Willich and Co. As a result of the rumpus, Kellner is becoming more and more embroiled.

Weydemeyer's misprint shouldn't surprise you. After all, you must know that when Weydemeyer does something, it is always 'similar' rather than 'glorious'.[c]

The little fellow[d] is coming here next Sunday. I am curious to see how he is shaping as a clerk in Bradford. At all events the good Buckup seems to be working him very hard.

Yesterday I read the book on Arabian inscriptions which I told you about.[390] The thing is not without interest, repulsive though it is to find the parson and biblical apologist forever peeping through. His greatest triumph is to show that *Gibbon* made some mistakes in the field of ancient geography, from which he also concludes that Gibbon's theology was deplorable. The thing is called *The Historical Geography of Arabia*, by the Reverend Charles Forster. The best things to emerge from it are:

1. The supposed genealogy of Noah, Abraham, etc., to be found in Genesis is a fairly accurate enumeration of the Beduin

---

[a] Case in German=*Fall*. The pun cannot be reproduced in English. - [b] K. Marx, *Revelations Concerning the Communist Trial in Cologne.* - [c] See this volume, p. 325. - [d] Ernst Dronke

tribes of the time, according to the degree of their dialectal relationships, etc. As we all know, Beduin tribes continue to this day to call themselves Beni Saled, Beni Yusuf, etc., i.e. sons of so and so. This nomenclature, which owes its origins to the early patriarchal mode of existence, ultimately leads up to this type of genealogy. The enumeration in Genesis is *plus ou moins*[a] confirmed by ancient geographers, while more recent travellers have shown that most of the old names still exist, though in dialectally altered form. But from this it emerges that the Jews themselves were no more than a small Beduin tribe like the others, which was brought into conflict with the other Beduins by local conditions, agriculture, etc.

2. As for the great Arab invasion, you will remember our discussion when we concluded that, like the Mongols, the Beduins carried out periodic invasions and that the Assyrian and Babylonian Empires were founded by Beduin tribes on the very same spot as, later, the Caliphate of Baghdad. The founders of the Babylonian Empire, the Chaldeans, still exist under the same name, Beni Chaled, and in the same locality. The rapid construction of large cities, such as Nineveh and Babylon, happened in just the same way as the creation in India only 300 years ago of similar giant cities, Agra, Delhi, Lahore, Muttan, by the Afghan and/or Tartar invasions. In this way the Mohammedan invasion loses much of its distinctive character.

3. In the South-West, where the Arabs settled, they appear to have been a civilised people like the Egyptians, Assyrians, etc., as is evident from their buildings. This also explains many things about the Mohammedan invasion. So far as the religious fraud is concerned, the ancient inscriptions in the South, in which the ancient Arab national tradition of monotheism (as with the American Indians) still predominates, a tradition of which the Hebrew is only a *small part*, would seem to indicate that Mohammed's religious revolution, like *every* religious movement, was *formally a reaction*, a would-be return to what was old and simple.

It is now quite clear to me that the Jews' so-called Holy Writ is nothing more than a record of ancient Arab religious and tribal traditions, modified by the Jews' early separation from their tribally related but nomadic neighbours. The circumstance of Palestine's being surrounded on the Arabian side by nothing but desert, i.e. the land of the Beduins, explains its separate

---

[a] more or less

development. But the ancient Arabian inscriptions and traditions and the Koran, as well as the ease with which all genealogies, etc., can now be unravelled, show that the main content was Arab, or rather, generally Semitic, as in our case the *Edda*[391] and the German heroic saga.

Your

F. E.

First published abridged in *Der Briefwechsel zwischen F. Engels und K. Marx*, Bd. 1, Stuttgart, 1913 and in full in *MEGA*, Abt. III, Bd. 1, Berlin, 1929

Printed according to the original

Published in English in full for the first time

163

ENGELS TO MARX

IN LONDON

Manchester, 31 May 1853

Dear Marx,

The bill on Dana has been paid; we shall have the money tomorrow and shall send it you without delay; Charles[a] missed the chap twice today. There will be some loss on the rate of exchange, but less, I think, than if the bill were to be negotiated in London.

The parcel of pamphlets[b] has also arrived and will go off tomorrow. I shall keep 8 or 10 up here. It is fairly heavy and cost £1 16/- which you can add on to the selling price. DUTY alone was 18/-, so, all things considered, it was a good thing it was addressed to me.

The little man[c] was here on Saturday and seems to be making out better than was to be expected. Buckup told Strohn that he was quite satisfied with him and that he had quickly familiarised himself with the work. I gave him a little sermon about punctuality; anyhow, conditions at Buckup's office are as favourable as he could wish. He is already doing book-keeping and, if he continues to do well for 3 or 4 months, will have a secure berth.

---

[a] Roesgen - [b] Marx's *Revelations Concerning the Communist Trial in Cologne* published in Boston. - [c] Ernst Dronke

Strohn has gone to the Continent again; he left on Saturday. It was a good thing that he was on the spot for the first fortnight. Nothing new from America this week.

Your

F. E.

First published in *Der Briefwechsel zwischen F. Engels und K. Marx*, Bd. 1, Stuttgart, 1913

Printed according to the original

Published in English for the first time

164

ENGELS TO MARX

IN LONDON

[Manchester, 1 June 1853]

Dear Marx,

Herewith half the £20 note,—P/E 90 138. The other half by the 2nd post as I don't know any other address.

The fellow who cashed the bill has gone away for a few days, which means we can't get the money. But so as not to keep you waiting I have got hold of this £20. Settlement of the bill, then, will be effected early next week.

The dirty dog[a] has docked us about £18 for cigars and wine bought from him partly by Charles[b] as a speculation and partly by me for my own consumption, so this has also involved paying debts.

Yesterday I read your article on *The Times* and the refugees (with the quotation from Dante)[c] in an old number of the *Tribune* published at the beginning of April. *Je t'en fais mon compliment.*[d] The English isn't merely good; it's brilliant. Every now and again there's a key word which doesn't fit in quite *coulant*[e] enough, but

---

[a] Gottfried Ermen - [b] Roesgen - [c] K. Marx, 'Kossuth and Mazzini.—Intrigues of the Prussian Government.—Austro-Prussian Commercial Treaty.—*The Times* and the Refugees'. - [d] I congratulate you. - [e] smoothly

that's about the worst that can be said of the article. Pieper is hardly in evidence at all and I can't conceive what you still need him for.

Your

F. E.

First published in *Der Briefwechsel zwischen F. Engels und K. Marx*, Bd. 1, Stuttgart, 1913

Printed according to the original

Published in English for the first time

165

MARX TO ENGELS [84]

IN MANCHESTER

[London,] 2 June 1853
28 Dean Street, Soho

Dear Frederic,

The first half of the £20 note has turned up. I am writing this before going to the Museum,[a] i.e. at a very early hour.

I would have sent you long ago the enclosed great Willich's statement to the *Neu-England-Zeitung*[b] had I not assumed that you'd had the thing from Weydemeyer. In *conception* this second statement is pure, GENUINE Willich. Others write 'essays', he writes 'facts',[392] and only if one has been on a 'personal footing' with him does the calumny lose its sting. It is the manoeuvre of your petty partisan. He does not answer for his own Hirsch.[c] Rather, he explains to the public Marx's 'motives' for *not* refuting his Hirsch. And now he has discovered a terrain where he can operate with a measure of virtuosity. And it is with 'reluctance' that the noble man reveals the facts to the 'public'. Needless to say, he has preferred to whisper them to the philistines in the privacy of the beer-parlour

---

[a] The library of the British Museum. - [b] A. Willich, 'An die Redaktion der *Neu-England-Zeitung*, Louisville, den 2. Mai 1853', *Neu-England-Zeitung*, No. 62, 13 May 1853. - [c] An allusion to Willich's help in publishing Hirsch's 'Die Opfer der Moucharderie...' (For details see K. Marx, 'The Knight of the Noble Consciousness', present edition, Vol. 12, pp. 481 and 498-99).

and, for the past three years, to peddle them 'contraband-wise' throughout two hemispheres, *juvante Kinkelio*.[a] Then his man-oeuvring to keep the public on tenterhooks. They forget the facts among which he twists and turns and eagerly await the facts which are to demolish the 'critical authors'. And the noble man is 'distinguished' withal, as befits a 'public figure'. When he does reply, it will not be to Marx's uncouth 'agents' but to the 'ingenious' quill-pushers themselves. Finally, he gives the public to understand that what makes his opponents so cocksure is their belief in his 'decision' to retire and, with a roll of drums, this important personage proceeds to announce that he has 'changed' his mind.

Tout ça n'est pas trop mal pour un vieux sous-lieutenant.[b] But as for the style of statement No. 2—bad as it is, it is nevertheless apocryphal. Other hands have been at work on it, probably those of Madame Anneke. At all events, the necessary supplement to Tellering's pamphlet will now be published by Mr Willich[c] and, the dirty business having been once placed before the public, *il faut aller jusqu'au bout*.[d] If Weydemeyer, Cluss and Co. operate with skill, they should now be able to put a spoke in Willich's wheel and ruin the impact and novelty of the surprises he is holding in store for the public. *Nous verrons.*[e]

The praise you accord to my 'budding' English,[f] I find most encouraging. What I chiefly lack is first, assurance as to grammar and secondly, skill in using various secondary idioms which alone enable one to write with any pungency. Mr *Tribune* has given special prominence to a note about my 2nd article on Gladstone's Budget,[g] drawing the attention of readers to my 'MASTERLY EXPOSITION' and going on to say that NOWHERE have they seen 'A MORE ABLE CRITICISM' and do 'NOT EXPECT TO SEE ONE'.[h] Well, that is ALL RIGHT. But in the following article it proceeds to make an ass of me by printing under my name a heading of mine[i] which is quite trifling and intentionally so, whereas it appropriates your 'Swiss' thing.[j] I shall write and tell Dana that, 'flattering' though it may be if they occasionally use my things for a LEADER, they would oblige me by

---

[a] with Kinkel's assistance - [b] Not too bad for an old second lieutenant. - [c] E. [Müller-]Tellering, *Vorgeschmack in die künftige deutsche Diktatur von Marx und Engels.* - [d] it must be taken to its conclusion - [e] We shall see. - [f] See this volume, pp. 329-30. - [g] K. Marx, 'Riot at Constantinople.—German Table Moving.—The Budget'. - [h] *New-York Daily Tribune*, No. 3761, 6 May 1853, leader. See also present edition, Vol. 12, Note 57. - [i] Section 'The Rocket Affair' in Marx's and Engels' 'The Rocket Affair.—The Swiss Insurrection'. - [j] F. Engels, 'Political Position of the Swiss Republic' published over Marx's signature.

not putting my name to trifles.[393] I have now sent the jackasses, amongst other things, 2 articles on 'China' with reference to England.[a] If you have the time and happen to feel like writing about something—Switzerland, the East, France, England or COTTON, or *Denmark,* say—you should do so on occasion, for I am now slogging away with an eye to the fellow's money-bags in order to make good the 3 WEEKS I have lost. If you send me something from time to time—*de omnibus rebus*[b]—I shall always be able to place it, for as you know, I am the fellows' 'maid of all work', and it's always easy to relate one thing to another and to every day. Παντα εν παντα.[c]

As regards the Hebrews and Arabs,[d] I found yor letter most interesting. It can, by the by, be shown that 1. in the case of all eastern tribes there has been, since the dawn of history, a *general* relationship between the SETTLEMENT of one section and the continued nomadism of the others. 2. In Mohammed's time the trade route from Europe to Asia underwent considerable modification, and the cities of Arabia, which had had a large share of the trade with India, etc., suffered a commercial decline—a fact which at all events contributed to the process. 3. So far as religion is concerned, the question may be reduced to a general and hence easily answerable one: Why does the history of the East *appear* as a history of religions?

On the subject of the growth of eastern cities one could hardly find anything more brilliant, comprehensive or striking than *Voyages contenant la description des états du Grand Mogol, etc.* by old François Bernier (for 9 years Aurangzeb's physician). He provides in addition a very nice account of military organisation and the manner in which these large armies fed themselves, etc. Concerning both these he remarks *inter alia*:

'The main body consists of cavalry, the infantry not being so numerous as is commonly supposed si ce n'est qu'avec les véritables gens de guerre, on ne confond tous ces gens de service et de bazars ou marchés qui suivent l'armée; car, en ce cas-là, je croirais bien qu'ils auraient raison de mettre les 2 et 300 000 hommes dans l'armée seule qui est avec le roi, et quelquefois encore davantage, comme quand on est assuré qu'il sera longtemps absent de la ville capitale; ce qui ne semblera pas si fort étonnant à qui saura l'étrange embarras de tentes, de cuisines, de hardes, de meubles et de femmes même assez souvent, et par conséquent d'éléphans, de chameaux, de bœufs, de chevaux, de portefaix, de fourrageurs, vivandiers, marchands de toutes sortes et de serviteurs qui traînent après soi ces

---

[a] K. Marx, 'Revolution in China and in Europe'. The *Tribune* editors may have included both articles in this one publication. - [b] anything under the sun - [c] All in all. - [d] See this volume, pp. 326-28.

armées, et à qui saura l'état et gouvernement particulier du pays, à savoir que le *roi est le seul et unique propriétaire de toutes les terres* du royaume, d'où vient par une certaine suite nécessaire que toute *une ville capitale* comme Delhi ou Agra ne vit presque que de la milice, et est par conséquent obligée de suivre le roi quand il va en campagne pour quelque temps, ces villes-là n'étant ni ne pouvant être rien moins qu'un Paris, mais *n'étant proprement qu'un camp d'armée* un peu mieux et plus commodément placé qu'en rase campagne.'[a]

In reference to the Grand Mogul's march on Kashmir, with an army 400,000 strong, he writes:

'La difficulté est de savoir d'où et comment peut subsister une si grande armée en campagne, une si grande quantité d'hommes et d'animaux. Il ne faut pour cela que supposer, ce qui est très vrai, que les Indiens sont fort sobres et fort simples dans leur manger, et que de tout ce grand nombre de cavaliers il n'y a pas la dixième, ni même la vingtième partie, qui, dans la marche, mange de la viande; pourvu qu'ils aient leur kicheris ou mélange de riz et d'autres légumes, sur lesquels ils versent du beurre roux quand ils sont cuits, ils sont contents. Il faut encore savoir que les chameaux résistent extrêmement au travail, à la faim et à la soif, vivent de peu et mangent de tout, et qu'aussitôt que l'armée est arrivée, les chameliers les mênent brouter à la campagne, où ils mangent tout ce qu'ils attrapent; de plus que les mêmes marchands qui entretiennent les bazars dans Delhi, sont obligés de les entretenir dans les campagnes, ebenso die petits marchands etc. ... enfin à l'égard du fourrage, tous ces pauvres gens s'en vont rôdant de tous les côtés dans les villages pour en acheter et y gagner quelque chose, et que leur grand et ordinaire refuge est de raper, avec une espèce de truelle, les campagnes entières, battre ou laver cette petite herbe qu'ils ont rapée, et l'apporter vendre à l'armée...'[b]

Bernier rightly sees all the manifestations of the East—he mentions Turkey, Persia and Hindustan—as having a common

---

[a] 'unless all those serving-people and bazaar or market folk who follow the army are taken for true warriors; for, if such were the case, there would, I think, be good reason to put at 2 to 300,000 men the strength of that army alone that is with the king, and sometimes even more, as, for example, when it is known that he will be long absent from the capital city; which would not, indeed, seem so very surprising to anyone familiar with all the strange impedimenta of tents, kitchen, clothing, furniture, and even women quite often, and, consequently, elephants, camels, oxen, horses, porters, foragers, sutlers, merchants of all kinds and servants who follow in the wake of these armies, nor to anyone familiar with the conditions and government peculiar to the country, namely that the *king is the sole and unique proprietor of all the lands* in the kingdom, whence it necessarily follows that every *capital city*, such as Delhi or Agra, fixes almost wholly on the militia and is therefore obliged to follow the king whenever he goes campaigning for a time, these cities neither being, nor indeed able to be, in any respect a Paris, but *being really nothing but an army encampment* rather better and more commodiously situated than if it were in the open country.' (Marx's italics.) - [b] 'How and upon what so great an army can subsist in the field, or so large a concourse of men and animals, is difficult to conceive. To that end one can only surmise, and such is indeed the case, that the Indians are very sober and very simple in what they eat and that, of this

basis, namely the *absence of private landed property*. This is the real *clef*,[a] even to the eastern heaven.

It would seem to be no go with Borchardt[394]; nevertheless I think the fellow might be prepared to try and obtain recommendations for Lupus from Steinthal, etc., to London merchants. So much, at least, you could compel him to do, and it would mean a great deal to Lupus.

What do you think about the failure of the hudibrastic Rodolpho[b] Gladstone's 'FINANCIAL SCHEME FOR REDUCING THE NATIONAL DEBT'?[c]

The day before yesterday the *Journal des Débats* revealed the true secret of Russia's impudence. The Continent, it says, must either expose its independence to danger from Russia, or it must expose itself to war, and that is *'la révolution sociale'*. What the wretched *Débats* forgets, however, is that Russia is no less afraid of revolution than Mr Bertin, and that the whole question now is who can most convincingly simulate 'non-fear'. But England and France—the official ones—are so abject that Nicholas, if he sticks to his guns, will be able to do what he likes.

Vale faveque.[d]

C. M.

Have written to Lassalle, who will probably be READY to take receipt of a few 100 copies of the pamphlet[e] and distribute them

---

great number of horsemen, not one tenth, nay, not even one twentieth, eats meat during the march; provided they have their khichri, or mess of rice and other vegetables, whereon they pour brown butter when cooked, they are content. It should also be known that camels are extremely resistant to work, hunger and thirst, live on very little and eat anything and that, as soon as the army reaches camp, the camel-drivers lead them out to graze in the countryside, where they eat everything that comes their way; further, that the same merchants that keep the bazaars in Delhi are obliged to keep them in the field also, likewise the lesser merchants, etc. ... finally, concerning forage, all these poor people go roving in every direction to the villages to buy the same and to earn something there, and that their chief and habitual recourse is to scratch up whole stretches of country with a kind of trowel, pounding and washing the little herbs thus scratched up, and taking them to the army for sale...'

[a] key - [b] An allusion to Ralpho—a character in Samuel Butler's satirical poem *Hudibras*. - [c] Marx described Gladstone's financial schemes in 'The New Financial Juggle; or Gladstone and the Pennies', 'Achievements of the Ministry', 'Affairs in Holland.—Denmark.—Conversion of the British Debt.—India, Turkey and Russia', 'The Russian Humbug.—Gladstone's Failure.—Sir Charles Wood's East India Reforms'. - [d] Good-bye and farewell. - [e] K. Marx, *Revelations Concerning the Communist Trial in Cologne* (Boston edition).

in Germany. The question now is how are we to get them across? When I was in Manchester[386] Charles[a] suggested it might be done by including them in a consignment of merchandise. You might ask him about this again.

P.S. There's been a delay over the posting of this letter and so I can include an acknowledgment of the parcel of books and the other half of the NOTE.

First published abridged in *Der Briefwech-sel zwischen F. Engels und K. Marx*, Bd. 1, Stuttgart, 1913 and in full in *MEGA*, Abt. III, Bd. 1, Berlin, 1929

Printed according to the original

Published in English in full for the first time

166

ENGELS TO MARX[338]

IN LONDON

Manchester, 6 June [1853,] evening

Dear Marx,

I had intended to write to you by the first post today, but was detained at the office until 8 o'clock. You will have received both Weydemeyer's and Cluss' anti-Willich statements in the *Criminal Zeitung*,[b] i.e. direct from America. If not, write to me at once. As usual, papa Weydemeyer is too long-winded, very seldom makes a point, then promptly blunts it with his style, and unfolds his well-known lack of verve with rare composure. Nevertheless, the man has done his best, the story about Hentze, the 'comrade-in-arms', and the influence of others on Hirsch's pen is nicely fashioned; his incredible style and his composure, regarded over there as impassibility, will appeal to the philistines, and his performance can, on the whole, be regarded as satisfactory. Cluss' statement, on the other hand, pleases me enormously. In every line we hear the chuckle of *l'homme supérieur*[c] who, through 'personal contact' with Willich, has, as it were, become physically

---

[a] Roesgen - [b] J. Weydemeyer, 'Weiters in der Willich-Hirsch'schen Angelegenheit'; A. Cluss, 'An die Redaktion der *New-Yorker Criminal-Zeitung*', *Belletristisches Journal und New-Yorker Criminal-Zeitung*, No. 10, 20 May 1853. - [c] the superior man

conscious of his superiority. For lightness of style, this surpasses everything that Cluss has ever written. Never a clumsy turn of phrase, not a trace of *gêne*[a] or embarrassment. How well it becomes him thus to ape the worthy citizen of benevolent mien who nevertheless betrays the cloven hoof at every turn. How splendid, the sentence about 'revolutionary agencies' being 'a swindle' off which, according to Willich, he lives. The chivalrous one will have been surprised to find among the uncouth 'agents'[395] a fellow who is so dashing, so adroit, so aggressive by nature and yet so unassumingly noble in his bearing, and who returns thrust for thrust *a tempo*[b] so subtly—far more subtly and deftly than himself. If only Willich had the discernment to discover this! But irritation and due reflection will, I trust, give him a little more insight.

It is obvious that we shall have to see this dirty business through to the bitter end. The more resolutely we tackle it the better. You'll find, by the way, that it won't be so bad after all. The chivalrous one has promised vastly more than he can fulfil. We shall hear of assassination attempts, etc., the Schramm affair will be glamorously tricked out,[c] and such chimeras will be evoked as will cause us to stare at one another in amazement, not having the faintest idea what the man is actually talking about; at worst he will tell the story about Marx and Engels arriving drunk one evening at Great Windmill Street[24] (*vide* Kinkel in Cincinnati, *coram* Huzelio[d]). If he goes as far as that, I shall tell the scandal-loving American public what the Besançon Company[396] used to talk about when Willich and the *formosus*[e] pastor Corydon Rau[f] were not present. *Au bout du compte*,[g] what can a brute of this kind find to tax us with? Mark my word, it will be just as *pauvre*[h] as Tellering's smear.[i]

I shall be seeing Borchardt within the next few days. If any recommendations are to be had, you can trust me to get them.[j] But I hardly imagine that Steinthal, etc., have connections of the sort in London. It's almost wholly outside their line of business. Besides, if only for fear of making a fool of himself, the fellow will attempt to put off doing anything about it up here. If it were not for Lupus, I'd consign the chap, etc. I can't abide him, with his

---

[a] constraint - [b] in good time - [c] See this volume, pp. 325-26. - [d] in Huzel's presence (ibid., pp. 148-50) - [e] comely - [f] Officer Rau is compared to shepherd Corydon, a character in pastoral poems who suffers from unrequited love. - [g] Come to that - [h] poor - [i] An allusion to [Müller-]Tellering's *Vorgeschmack in die künftige deutsche Diktatur von Marx und Engels.* - [j] See this volume, p. 334.

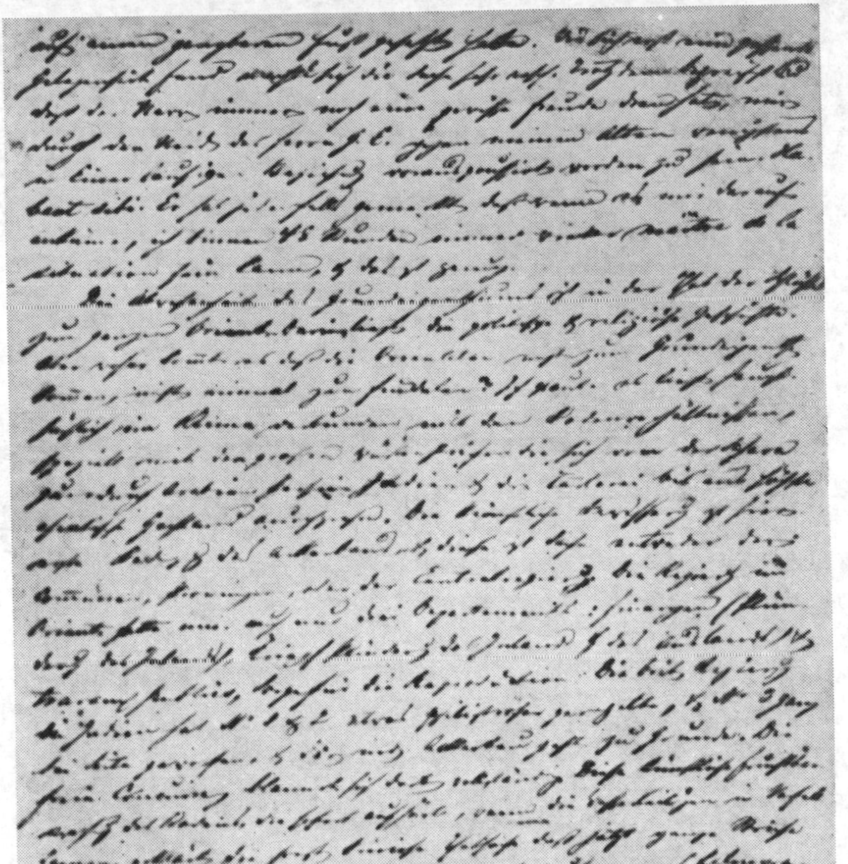

Third page of Engels' letter to Marx of 6 June 1853

smooth, self-important, vainglorious, deceitful charlatan's physiognomy.

If Lassalle has given you a good, neutral address in Düsseldorf, you can send me 100 copies.[a] We shall arrange for them to be packed in bales of twist by firms up here; but they should not be addressed to Lassalle himself, since the packages will go to Gladbach, Elberfeld and so on, where they *will have to be stamped* and sent by *post* to Düsseldorf. However, we cannot entrust a package for Lassalle or the Hatzfeldt woman to any local firm, because, 1. they all employ at least *one* Rhinelander who knows all the gossip, or 2. if that goes off all right, the recipients of the bales will get to know about it, or 3. at the very best the postal authorities will take a look at the things before delivering them. We have a good address in Cologne, but are not, alas, very well acquainted with the people who are the principal buyers *here* for the firm in Cologne, and hence cannot expect them to do any smuggling. Indeed, what we shall tell the people here is that the packages contain presents for the fair sex.

From all this you will gather that I am once again on passable terms with Charles.[b] The affair was settled with great dispatch at the first suitable opportunity. Nevertheless you will realise that the fool derives a certain pleasure from having been given preference over myself in one rotten respect at least, because of Mr Gottfried Ermen's envy of my old man. *Habeat sibi.*[c] He at any rate realises that if I so choose, I can become *maître de la situation*[d] within 48 hours, and that's sufficient.

The absence of landed property is indeed the key to the whole of the East.[397] Therein lies its political and religious history. But how to explain the fact that orientals never reached the stage of landed property, not even the feudal kind? This is, I think, largely due to the climate, combined with the nature of the land, more especially the great stretches of desert extending from the Sahara right across Arabia, Persia, India and Tartary[398] to the highest of the Asiatic uplands. Here artificial irrigation is the first prerequisite for agriculture, and this is the responsibility either of the communes, the provinces or the central government. In the East, the government has always consisted of 3 departments only: Finance (pillage at home), War (pillage at home and abroad), and *travaux publics*,[e] provision for reproduction. The British govern-

---

a K. Marx, *Revelations Concerning the Communist Trial in Cologne* (see this volume, p. 334). - b Roesgen - c Let him have it. - d master of the situation - e public works

ment in India has put a somewhat narrower interpretation on nos. 1 and 2 while completely neglecting no. 3, so that Indian agriculture is going to wrack and ruin. Free competition is proving an absolute fiasco there. The fact that the land was made fertile by artificial means and immediately ceased to be so when the conduits fell into disrepair, explains the otherwise curious circumstance that vast expanses are now arid wastes which once were magnificently cultivated (Palmyra, Petra, the ruins in the Yemen, any number of localities in Egypt, Persia, Hindustan); it explains the fact that one single war of devastation could depopulate and entirely strip a country of its civilisation for centuries to come. This, I believe, also accounts for the destruction of southern Arabian trade before Mohammed's time, a circumstance very rightly regarded by you as one of the mainsprings of the Mohammedan revolution.[a] I am not sufficiently well acquainted with the history of trade during the first six centuries A.D. to be able to judge to what extent general material conditions in the world made the trade route via Persia to the Black Sea and to Syria and Asia Minor via the Persian Gulf preferable to the Red Sea route. But one significant factor, at any rate, must have been the relative safety of the caravans in the well-ordered Persian Empire under the Sassanids, whereas between 200 and 600 A.D. the Yemen was almost continuously being subjugated, overrun and pillaged by the Abyssinians. By the seventh century the cities of southern Arabia, still flourishing in Roman times, had become a veritable wilderness of ruins; in the course of 500 years what were purely mythical, legendary traditions regarding their origin had been appropriated by the neighbouring Beduins, (cf. the Koran and the Arab historian Novaïri), and the alphabet in which the local inscriptions had been written was almost wholly unknown although *there was no other,* so that *de facto writing* had fallen into oblivion. Things of this kind presuppose, not only a SUPERSEDING, probably due to general trading conditions, but outright violent destruction such as could only be explained by the Ethiopian invasion. The expulsion of the Abyssinians did not take place until about 40 years before Mohammed, and was plainly the first act of the Arabs' awakening national consciousness, which was further aroused by Persian invasions from the North penetrating almost as far as Mecca. I shall not be tackling the history of Mohammed himself for a few days yet; so far it seems to me to have the character of a Beduin reaction against the settled, albeit decadent urban fellaheen whose religion by then was

---

[a] See this volume, p. 332.

also much debased, combining as it did a degenerate form of nature worship with a degenerate form of Judaism and Christianity.

Old Bernier's stuff[a] is really very fine. It's a real pleasure to get back to something written by a sensible, lucid old Frenchman who constantly hits the nail on the head *sans avoir l'air de s'en apercevoir*.[b]

Since I am in any case tied up with the eastern mummery for some weeks, I have made use of the opportunity to learn Persian. I am put off Arabic, partly by my inborn hatred of Semitic languages, partly by the impossibility of getting anywhere, without considerable expenditure of time, in so extensive a language—one which has 4,000 roots and goes back over 2,000-3,000 years. By comparison, Persian is absolute child's play. Were it not for that damned Arabic alphabet in which every half dozen letters looks like every other half dozen and the vowels are not written, I would undertake to learn the entire grammar within 48 hours. This for the better encouragement of Pieper should he feel the urge to imitate me in this poor joke. I have set myself a maximum of three weeks for Persian, so if he stakes two months on it he'll best me anyway. What a pity Weitling can't speak Persian; he would then have his *langue universelle toute trouvée*[c] since it is, to my knowledge, the only language where 'me' and 'to me' are never at odds, the dative and accusative always being the same.[399]

It is, by the way, rather pleasing to read dissolute old Hafiz in the original language, which sounds quite passable and, in his grammar,[d] old Sir William Jones likes to cite as examples dubious Persian jokes, subsequently translated into Greek verse in his *Commentariis poeseos asiaticae*, because even in Latin they seem to him too obscene. These commentaries, Jones' *Works*, Vol. II, *De poesi erotica*, will amuse you. Persian prose, on the other hand, is deadly dull. E.g. the *Rauzât-us-safâ* by the noble Mirkhond, who recounts the Persian epic in very flowery but vacuous language. Of Alexander the Great, he says that the name Iskander, in the Ionian language, is Akshid Rus (like Iskander, a corrupt version of Alexandros); it means much the same as *filusuf*, which derives from *fila*, love, and *sufa*, wisdom, 'Iskander' thus being synonymous with 'friend of wisdom'.

---

[a] F. Bernier, *Voyages contenant la description des états du Grand Mogol, de l'Indoustan, du Royaume de Cachemire, etc.* See also this volume, pp. 332-34. - [b] without appearing to be aware of it - [c] universal language ready-made - [d] W. Jones, *A Grammar of the Persian Language.*

Of a RETIRED king he says: 'He beat the drum of abdication with the drumsticks of retirement', as will *père* Willich, should he involve himself any more deeply in the literary fray. Willich will also suffer the same fate as King Afrasiab of Turan when deserted by his troops and of whom Mirkhond says: 'He gnawed the nails of horror with the teeth of desperation until the blood of vanquished consciousness welled forth from the finger-tips of shame.'

More tomorrow.

First published abridged in *Der Briefwechsel zwischen F. Engels und K. Marx*, Bd. 1, Stuttgart, 1913 and in full in *MEGA*, Abt. III, Bd. 1, Berlin, 1929

Printed according to the original

Published in English in full for the first time

167

ENGELS TO MARX

IN LONDON

Manchester, 9 June 1853

Dear Marx,

So that Pieper may see he hasn't been forgotten, inform him of the following. In yesterday's *Manchester Guardian* there was the offer of a post as CORRESPONDING CLERK AND BOOKKEEPER. He might contrive to get £180 a year; from what I hear, it is with a Jew here, Leo Schuster. Pieper should at once write a letter addressed to:

Box B 47,
Post Office,
Manchester

and beginning: Monsieur, etc.

The letter had best be written in French, since French and German are required. He should say he thinks he can fill the post, that he comes from Hanover, is aged such-and-such, and last worked for so-and-so in London, from whom inquiries may be made as to his character and qualifications. He can conduct correspondence in German, French and English and, if needs be, in Italian, is rather less familiar (if indeed this is the case) with bookkeeping; he must say that he lost his post because the partner's son had joined, etc., then what sort of a business it was, but that he could without doubt quickly familiarise himself with all types of merchandise business in the Manchester TRADE. *Le tout sans phrase, aussi simplement raconté que possible.*

J'ai l'honneur de me souscrire',
or else, '*Mr., votre très dévoué',*[a] etc.

Nothing more. If they consider him, he will probably be summoned to Schuster's London house, and then it will be up to him. But he *must write straight away, by the first post tomorrow.*

Herewith £1. 18. 6d., the balance of the £32. The fellow only deducted 18 pence for collecting charges but, on the other hand, all Charles[b] and I owed him.

You will have received the bill from America the day before yesterday.

Whether Pieper can give Rothschild as a reference, you people in London will be best able to judge; if so, it might do no harm, for the fact that Pieper is no BRED CLERK will emerge at the very first interview when they ask him where he worked before. But he must be sure of what Rothschild is going to say and, perhaps, see him beforehand.

Your
F. E.

Copie d'Annonce.[c]

* Wanted in a Shipping House a Bookkeeper and Corresponding Clerk. A knowledge of German and French absolutely required. Address Box B 47, P. Off. Manchester.*

[To refer to me would do *no good whatever,* indeed it might do harm. Pieper, of course, should not let Schuster see that he knows *who* inserted the advertisement to which he should refer as his reason for applying.]

First published in *MEGA*, Abt. III, Bd. 1, Berlin, 1929

Printed according to the original

Published in English for the first time

---

[a] The whole without frills and told as simply as possible. 'I have the honour to sign myself', or else, 'I am, sir, your most obedient'. - [b] Roesgen. See this volume, p. 344. - [c] The memo is in pencil; the last paragraph is barely legible.

168

MARX TO ENGELS[338]

IN MANCHESTER

London, 14 June 1853
28 Dean Street, Soho

Dear Frederic,

Having been prevented by all sorts of business and domestic affairs, I have only today got round to replying to your two letters[a] and acknowledging receipt of the American money (handed over to Freiligrath),[b] likewise the balance of the American *Tribune* money. If that's the sort of business relationship you and Charles[c] had with your 'intermediary', then you've been up to some trick for my sake. For since it was not that fellow, but you, who advanced the money against the bill, you and Charles could just as well have sent the bill to America without the fellow. At least, that's how it seems to me.

I did *not* inform Pieper of your news for the following reasons: Pieper was becoming more and more of a wreck and some 8 or 10 days ago I took him to task about the state of his health. It then transpired that his illness was going *de pis en pis*[d] at the hands of his English quack. I therefore suggested I should take him straight to *Bartholomew*'s Hospital—the London hospital at which the foremost and most renowned doctors treat the public for nothing. He came with me. An ancient Hippocrates, after examining the *corpus delicti* and questioning him about his former TREATMENT, told him: 'YOU HAVE BEEN A FOOL', explaining at the same time that he would be 'DOWN' within three months if he did not follow his instructions to the letter. The efficacy of the new treatment was immediately apparent and in 2 weeks the man will be *sain et sauf*.[e] The case was too serious for the treatment to be interrupted, and anyhow Freiligrath has a post in view for Pieper. If nothing comes of it, I shall let you know.

Rumpf, our jolly tailor, is now shut up in a *lunatic asylum.* Some 5 months ago, in order to extricate himself from a social quandary, *le malheureux*[f] married an *elderly* woman, became excessively respectable, foreswore all spirits and worked like a

---

[a] of 6 and 9 June - [b] See this volume, p. 323. - [c] Roesgen - [d] from bad to worse - [e] safe and sound - [f] the wretched man

carthorse. About a week since he took to drinking again, sent for me a couple of days ago, revealed that he had discovered 'the means of making the whole world happy, that I was to be his minister, etc., etc. He has been in the ASYLUM since yesterday. It's a pity about the fellow.

In *The Leader*—which, by the by, has become a purely bourgeois sheet—*Ruge* has announced that he will be giving *lectures* on German philosophy in London.[a] Needless to say he takes this opportunity to give himself a puff. E.g. 'Where style is concerned, there is only one man whom the German people set alongside him—*Lessing*.' In the same issue of *The Leader*, the Russian *Herzen* advertises his collected works[b] adding that, together with the Polish Committee, he is to set up a Russo-Polish propaganda press here in London.[400]

One of the enclosed letters from Cluss[401] will reveal to you the nature of the main blow with which Willich is threatening me. He refers to the £20 *borrowed* by me from the Refugee Committee at a time when I myself was distrained because my Chelsea landlady,[402] although I had paid her, had not paid her LANDLORD,—a debt which I *repaid* down to the last farthing by the necessary INSTALMENTS.[403] You must now advise me what tactics to adopt. If that's how the good Willich thinks he's going to do me in, he must be a regular '*bonhomme*'.[c]

Carey, the American political economist, has brought out a new book, *Slavery at Home and Abroad.* Here 'SLAVERY' covers all forms of servitude, WAGE-SLAVERY , etc. He has sent me his book in which he quotes me repeatedly (from the *Tribune*) now as 'A RECENT ENGLISH WRITER', now as 'CORRESPONDENCE OF THE *NEW-YORK TRIBUNE*'.[404] As I have told you before, this man, in his earlier works, propounds the 'harmony' of the bourgeoisie's economic foundations and attributes all MISCHIEF to unnecessary interference by the State. The State was his *bête noire.* He is now playing a different tune. All ills are blamed on the centralising effect of big industry. But this centralising effect is in turn blamed on England, who has made herself the WORKSHOP of the world and has forced all other countries to revert to brutish agriculture divorced from manufacturing. In its turn, responsibility for England's sins is laid on the theory of Ricardo-Malthus, and specially Ricardo's theory of rent. The necessary consequence both of Ricardo's theory and of industrial

---

centralisation would be communism. And to obviate all this, to counter centralisation with localisation and the union,—a union scattered throughout the land—of factory and farm, our ULTRA-FREE-TRADER finally recommends—*protective tariffs*. To obviate the effects of bourgeois industry, responsibility for which he lays on England, his recourse, as a genuine Yankee, is to speed up this process in America itself by artificial means. For the rest, his opposition to England drives him into *Sismondian* praise of the petty bourgeoisie in Switzerland, Germany, China, etc. And this is the chap who used to deride France for her resemblance to China. The only thing of definite interest in the book is the comparison between Negro slavery as formerly practised by the English in Jamaica and elsewhere, and Negro slavery in the United States. He demonstrates how the main STOCK of Negroes in Jamaica always consisted of freshly imported BARBARIANS, since their treatment by the English meant not only that the Negro population was not maintained, but also that $^2/_3$ of the yearly imports always went to waste, whereas the present generation of Negroes in America is a native product, more or less Yankeefied, English speaking, etc., and hence *capable of being emancipated*.

The *Tribune*, needless to say, is puffing Carey's book for all it's worth.[a] Both, indeed, have this in common, that, in the guise of Sismondian-philanthropic-socialist anti-industrialism, they represent the protectionist, i.e. industrial, bourgeoisie of America. That is also the key to the mystery why the *Tribune*, despite all its 'isms'[b] and socialist flourishes, manages to be the 'LEADING JOURNAL' in the United States.

Your article on Switzerland[c] was, of course, a direct swipe at the *Tribune*'s 'LEADERS' (anti-centralisation, etc.) and *their* man Carey. I continued this clandestine campaign in my first article on India,[d] in which England's destruction of native industries is described as *revolutionary*. This they will find very SHOCKING. Incidentally the whole administration of India by the British was detestable and still remains so today.

The stationary nature of this part of Asia, despite all the aimless activity on the political surface, can be completely explained by two mutually supporting circumstances: 1. The PUBLIC WORKS system of the central government and, 2. Alongside this, the entire

---

[a] See reviews 'Slavery and Emancipation' and 'New Publications', *New-York Daily Tribune*, No. 3771, 18 May 1853. - [b] An allusion to Horace Greeley's article 'Isms' in the *New-York Daily Tribune*, No. 3747, 20 April 1853. - [c] F. Engels, 'Political Position of the Swiss Republic'. - [d] K. Marx, 'The British Rule in India'.

Empire which, apart from a few large cities, is an agglomeration of VILLAGES, each with its own distinct organisation and each forming its own small world. A parliamentary report described these VILLAGES as follows[a]:

* 'A village, geographically considered, is a tract of country comprising some 100 or 1000 acres of arable and waste lands: politically viewed, it resembles a corporation or township. Every village is, and appears always to have been, in fact, a separate community or republic. Officials: 1. the *Potail*, Goud, Mundil etc. as he is termed in different languages, is the head inhabitant, who has generally the superintendence of the affairs of the village, settles the disputes of the inhabitants, attends to the police, and performs the duty of collecting the revenue within the village... 2. The *Curnum*, Shanboag, or Putwaree, is the register. 3. The *Taliary* or *Sthulwar* and 4. the *Totie*, are severally the watchmen of the village and of the crops. 5. the *Neerguntee* distributes the water of the streams or reservoirs in just proportion to the several fields. 6. The *Joshee*, or astrologer, announces the seed-times and harvests, and the lucky or unlucky days or hours for all the operation of farming. 7. The *smith*, and 8. the *carpenter* frame the rude instruments of husbandry, and the ruder dwellings of the farmer. 9. The *potter* fabricates the only utensils of the village. 10. The *waterman* keeps clean the few garments... 11. The *barber*, 12. *the silversmith*, who often combines the function of village *poet* and *schoolmaster*. Then the *Brahmin*, for worship. Under this simple form of municipal government the inhabitants of the country have lived from time immemorial. The boundaries of the villages have been but seldom altered; and although the villages themselves have been sometimes injured, and even desolated by war, famine and disease; the same name, the same limits, the same interests, and even the same families, have continued for ages. The inhabitants give themselves no trouble about the breaking up and division of kingdoms, while the village remains entire, they care not to what power it is transferred, or to what sovereign it devolves. Its internal economy remains unchanged.'*

The post of Potail is mostly hereditary. In some of these COMMUNITIES the LANDS of the VILLAGE CULTIVATED IN COMMON, in most of them EACH OCCUPANT TILLS HIS OWN FIELD. Within the same, slavery and the caste system. WASTE LANDS FOR COMMON PASTURE. Home-weaving and spinning by wives and daughters. These idyllic republics, of which only the VILLAGE *boundaries* are jealously guarded against neighbouring VILLAGES, continue to exist in well-nigh PERFECT form in the NORTH-WESTERN PARTS OF INDIA only recently occupied by the English. No more solid basis for Asiatic despotism and stagnation is, I think, conceivable. And however much the English may have Irelandised the country, the breaking up of the archetypal forms was the *conditio sine qua non* for Europeanisation. The TAX-GATHERER alone could not have brought this about. Another essential factor was the destruction of the ancient industries, which robbed these villages of their SELF-SUPPORTING character.

---

[a] Marx quotes presumably from the Fifth Report from the Select Committee on the Affairs of the East India Company, 1812.

In Bali, an island off the east coast of Java, this Hindu organisation still intact, alongside Hindu religion, its traces, like those of Hindu influence, discernible all over Java. So far as the *property question* is concerned, this is a great *bone of contention* among English writers on India. In the broken mountainous terrain south of the Kistna, however, there appears to have been property in land. In Java, on the other hand, as noted in the *History of Java* by a former *English* governor, Sir Stamford Raffles, the sovereign [was] absolute LANDLORD throughout the country 'WHERE RENT TO ANY CONSIDERABLE AMOUNT WAS ATTAINABLE'. At all events, the Mohammedans seem to have been the first in the whole of Asia to have established the principle of 'no property in land'.

Regarding the above-mentioned VILLAGES, I should note that they already feature in the Manu,[405] according to which the whole organisation rests on them. 10 are administered by a senior COLLECTOR, then 100, then 1,000.

Write soon.

Your
K. M.

First published considerably abridged in *Der Briefwechsel zwischen F. Engels und K. Marx*, Bd. I, Stuttgart, 1913 and in full in *MEGA*, Abt. III, Bd. 1, Berlin, 1929

Printed according to the original

Published in English in full for the first time

169

MARX TO ADOLF CLUSS [406]

IN WASHINGTON

[London, about 14 June 1853]

... On the other hand, a reply must be given,[a] and that can best be done by third parties. In which case you need feel no compunction about entering into personal matters and regaling the brutal democratic 'temperament' with a few pungent 'anecdotes'...[407]

---

[a] to Willich. See this volume, pp. 330-31.

In dealings with the *Reform* I would recommend, besides shrewdness, *une modération extrême*.[a] This clever-clever philistine[b] who, in Hesse—and Hesse was his world—represented nothing except the demiurge of this, his world: the petty bourgeois, and who now assumes the air of one who, from the very start, has represented the proletariat on a 'materialist basis'—this smiling nonentity who, with Solomon-like dicta, 'stresses' his shrewdness and remarkable composure vis-à-vis rebellious parties—this incarnation of a marginal gloss to 'Heise's articles'; this fellow, then, does not, of course, interest me—he repels me. But you people helped to make the paper. It appears in New York.

Half Germany will come to New York for the Exhibition.[128] You have no other paper in New York. Might it not, then, be impolitic to throw over Kellner and the paper? It would in the end be doing the fellows another favour. Pretend to be naive. Go on writing; you couldn't do him a worse turn. Do not emancipate him from influences which, as everything goes to show, have been damnably irksome to him. Do as the Prussian bourgeois do. The government and its Manteuffel twist and turn in vain to rid themselves of the friendship of those bourgeois. The latter, for their part, pretend to believe in the constitutionality of their government, and *le gouvernement est constituonnel malgré lui-même*[c]: that's *worldly wisdom* for you.

The *Neu-England-Zeitung* is equally unreliable and likely to remain so. Mr Schläger, a pedant replete with platitudes, a presumptious bore who always knows better (à la Kellner, '*le mieux est le plus grand ennemi du bien*[d]'), has written to Pieper suggesting I write for the *N.-E.-Z.* about the necessary transition from the bourgeois to the communist mode of production.

Citizen Marx with his 'schematising and organising' intellect would, it seems, be well suited to this task set him by Citizen Schläger, but Citizen Marx must 'forego his abstract language' and write in the same manner as all, etc. Worthy Citizen Schläger! In the same letter he enjoins Pieper on no account to attack Citizens Ruge and Heinzen (*he regularly deletes such passages*) since the 'élite of his readers' (just think what the others must be like!) are Heinzenites, and the *N.-E.-Z.* is destined (literally) to inherit the readers of the *Janus*. Mighty Citizen Schläger! Almighty Pompey! Nevertheless, I have advised Pieper to go on writing for Schläger.

---

[a] extreme moderation - [b] Gottlieb Kellner - [c] and the government is constitutional despite itself - [d] 'the better is the greatest enemy of the good'

Le motif est très simple.[a] We are not doing our enemies a favour by writing for them. *Tout au contraire.*[b] We could hardly play them a worse trick...

First published in part in *Die Neue Zeit,* Bd. 2, Nr. 31, Stuttgart, 1906-07 and in full in: Marx and Engels, *Works,* Second Russian Edition, Vol. 28, Moscow, 1962

Printed according to a letter from Cluss to Weydemeyer of 28 June 1853

Published in English in full for the first time

170

MARX TO ENGELS

IN MANCHESTER

[London,] 29 June 1853
28 Dean Street, Soho

Dear Engels,

My sister[c] and her newly wedded husband[d], who is sailing from here to the Cape of Good Hope as a GENERAL DEALER, have unexpectedly descended on me. This, combined with the work for the *Tribune* and some unpleasantness to be cleared up in America, has made considerable demands on my time. The couple set out tomorrow, I believe. I hear from Imandt that your mother is expected in London, from which I conclude that you, too, will turn up soon.

Enclosed Lassalle's instructions for the dispatch of the copies[e] to Germany. My wife will undertake their dispatch to Manchester. I hope that you people will then take care of the matter up there. Haven't you seen anything of Jones? He's roaming about in your part of the world and is said to have brought off a MONSTER MEETING in Halifax.[408]

Last Wednesday, much to my astonishment, I received a very peevish letter from Cluss, in which he said someone had written telling him that Pieper had described him to Schläger—him and Arnold—as 'subordinate agents', and himself, on the contrary, as the one who supplied news 'at first-hand', etc., etc. Fortunately

---

[a] The reason is very simple. - [b] Quite the contrary. - [c] Louise - [d] Jaan Carel Juta - [e] K. Marx, *Revelations Concerning the Communist Trial in Cologne.*

there isn't *a word of truth* in the whole thing, which is merely an attempt by Willich, Anneke, Weitling and Co.'s party to sow dissension amongst our own ranks, and, more particularly, to neutralise 'that most unpleasant man, Cluss'. The necessary explanations were, of course, dispatched across the water at once.[409] I am unable to find Cluss' first letter, but enclose the 2nd.

Before leaving for Manchester[410] I borrowed £2 from the little Jew Bamberger. The fellow keeps sending me strongly-worded reminders, if not threats. *Mais nous verrons.*[a] By Friday I shall have £20 to draw on New York. But again the question is how?

Enclosed the *nec plus ultra*[b] of Heinzen's now sanguinary cowardice and aversion to 'ordinary methods of warfare'.[c]

I was mistaken about the 'Swiss article',[d] Dana having divided the thing into two parts,[e] but published both under my name.

Until next time, then. My worthy sister and brother-in-law have just come in. My sister is very stout and will sweat damnably while crossing the Equator.

Your
K. M.

First published in *Der Briefwechsel zwischen F. Engels und K. Marx,* Bd. 1, Stuttgart, 1913

Printed according to the original

Published in English for the first time

171

MARX TO ENGELS

IN MANCHESTER

[London,] 8 July 1853
28 Dean Street, Soho

Dear Engels,

Dr Jacobi, the bearer of this note, was one of the accused at the 'communist trial in Cologne'.[16]

I'm at a loss to understand whether your continued silence is due to illness, pique, overwork or what.

---

[a] But we shall see. - [b] uttermost - [c] K. Heinzen's pamphlet *Mord und Freiheit.* - [d] See this volume, p. 331. - [e] K. Marx and F. Engels. 'The Rocket Affair.—The Swiss Insurrection'; F. Engels, 'Political Position of the Swiss Republic'.

Yesterday I drew £24 on Dana at Spielmann's in Lombard Street; Spielmann will pay me in 5 weeks as soon as the bill is returned. In the meantime I shall have another very bad spell to go through, the more so since a number of valuable things now in pawn will have to be repledged or else they will be forfeited, and that is, of course, impossible *dans un moment*[a] when the wherewithal even for *les choses les plus nécessaires*[b] is lacking. However, I'm now well-accustomed to being in the soup and all that that entails.

In any case write and tell me why you're not writing. I hope, AT ALL EVENTS, that you are not ill.

Your
K. M.

[On the back of the letter]

Friedrich Engels. 48 Great Ducie Street, *Manchester*

First published (except the text on the back of the letter) in *Der Briefwechsel zwischen F. Engels und K. Marx*, Bd. 1, Stuttgart, 1913 and in full in: Marx and Engels, *Works*, Second Russian Edition, Vol. 28, Moscow, 1962

Printed according to the original

Published in English for the first time

172

ENGELS TO MARX

IN LONDON

Manchester, Saturday, 9 July [1853]

Dear Marx,

At four o'clock this morning my old landlady roused me from my slumbers saying there was a gentleman wanting to speak to me. Dragging myself out of bed, I went to the door where I found a little man with a CAB, a colossal trunk and a travelling bag, who told me his name was Jacobi and that you and Pieper had sent him to me. Marx *and* Pieper! I thought. Who the devil can this

---

[a] at a moment - [b] the most necessary things

Jacobi be? Is he the illegitimate son of one in Königsberg[a] or what? Until finally the little man pulled your letter[b] out of his pocket, somewhat taken aback at not being instantly welcomed with open arms, stranger though he was—whereupon it occurred to me that he was, as your letter confirmed, the communist trial Jacobi to whom I hadn't given a thought, believing him long since well and truly lodged in a Prussian prison cell. *Que faire?*[c] I took him in, together with his belongings and, drunk with sleep, chatted with him for half an hour before offering him my sofa to sleep on, for the house was CRAMMED FULL of people. Luckily my old man is out of town until tomorrow and so, this very morning, I took the good party martyr by the collar, engaged lodgings for him and forbade him to show his face here until my old man's departure raises the interdict.

This warlike[d] Westphalian way of behaving, the doltishness of spending a whole week in London and then choosing a train that arrives in the middle of the night and, on the pretext of not knowing what's what, turning a man's house upside down and imposing himself, all this was no more calculated to predispose me in his favour than was the discreet question put to me at the very outset as to how I stood with my old man. Further exchanges have raised the fellow in my estimation a little, but not very much. He proposes to call on Borchardt with letters from you *and* Kinkel (almost beats Marx *and* Pieper), to burst in on little Heckscher without ceremony and without an introduction in the hope that the latter will immediately provide him with all possible information about his TRADE and, for sheer joy at the prospect of fresh 'scientific' intercourse, make half his practice over to his new competitor—and other such philistine conceits. His foolishness in going to Kinkel will do him more harm than good. Kinkel gives him letters not to Mr but to *Mrs* Schunck, a piece of effrontery which is also a gross and direct breach of English etiquette, and again, if Mr Kinkel, who was fed and paid cash for his buffooneries on German literature, if Monsieur Gottfried, I say, believes he can send letters of recommendation (other than fund-raising licences) *d'égal à égal*[e] to these merchants, he's damned well mistaken. Apart from that, Monsieur Jacobi, *à ce qu'il me paraît,*[f] is not the man to make his fortune here.

As soon as my old man has left, I'll send you some money. I

[a] Dr Johann Jacoby - [b] See previous letter. - [c] What's to be done? - [d] Marx uses the word 'kriegisch', which may mean 'warlike' or may be a pun on the name 'Kriege'. - [e] as between equals - [f] or so it seems to me

can't very well take anything before that, since I run the risk every day that he will check my accounts, which alone would be enough to provoke a lively argument of the kind I prefer to settle in writing.

The idea that I am not writing because of 'pique' made me laugh. *De quoi donc?*[a]

Regards to your wife and children and do your best to stick it out, at least until my hands are free again—within the week, I hope.

Your
F. E.

First published abridged in *Der Briefwechsel zwischen F. Engels und K. Marx*, Bd. 1, Stuttgart, 1913 and in full in *MEGA*, Abt. III, Bd. 1, Berlin, 1929

Printed according to the original

Published in English for the first time

173

MARX TO ENGELS

IN MANCHESTER

[London,] 18 July 1853
28 Dean Street, Soho

Dear Engels,

The day before yesterday I got a letter from Lassalle, who is now in a state of suspense, imagining letters have been intercepted, etc. It would have been good had you advised me whether or not the parcel had gone off to him.[b] Lassalle is still the only one who dares correspond with London, and we must therefore be careful not to put him off. So I would ask you to let me know what the position is about the parcel. The time of its dispatch is of importance to me in another way, i.e. because upon it depends the time of the RETURN.

The last mail brought my wife a most friendly and obliging letter from A. Dana[411] in which he states that he *cannot possibly* advise us of a business house in London and that AT ALL INSTANCES bills drawn by me will be promptly honoured. He says that my

---

[a] What about? - [b] See this volume, p. 350.

articles are 'HIGHLY VALUED BY THE PROPRIETORS OF THE *TRIBUNE* AND THE PUBLIC', and sets *no* limit on the quantity we send him.

In the debate on ADVERTISEMENT DUTY [412]—about a fortnight ago, I think—Mr Bright was loud in his praises of the *New-York Tribune* and gave an analysis of one of its numbers[a]—the very one containing my article on the budget.[b] This is what he said about it:

> * 'From Great Britain there is an elaborate disquisition on the Right Honourable Gentleman's[c] budget, doing him justice in some parts, but not in others, and doing certainly, as far as the Manchester School[63] was concerned, no justice whatever.'*[d]

As regards Jacobi, you must not allow yourself to be deterred by the gaucherie and inexperience of a 23-year-old stripling from the District of Minden who has spent 2 years in jug. He has a good background. I have read his doctoral dissertation[413] and was 'MUCH PLEASED WITH IT'.

Your
K. M.

Jones has held some very important meetings which have even attracted the attention of the bourgeois press.[414]

First published in *Der Briefwechsel zwischen F. Engels und K. Marx*, Bd. 1, Stuttgart, 1913

Printed according to the original

Published in English for the first time

174

MARX TO ENGELS

IN MANCHESTER

[London,] 18 August 1853
28 Dean Street, Soho

Dear Engels,

Lupus will *probably* obtain a good post in Liverpool. In which case he will go there via Manchester. The snag is that he won't be paid until the end of the quarter. However, he hopes that you and

---

[a] *New-York Daily Tribune*, No. 3761, 6 May 1853. - [b] K. Marx, 'Riot at Constantinople.—German Table Moving.—The Budget'. - [c] Gladstone - [d] J. Bright, Speech in the House of Commons on 1 July 1853, *The Times*, No. 21470, 2 July 1853.

Strohn between you may be able to help him. Has Strohn returned?

Needless to say, that mischief-monger Dronke is writing the most pompous letters to all and sundry, e.g. to Imandt, saying that 'he has made arrangements for Lupus' emigration to America'. *Entre nous*[a] I should say the little shop-assistant, anxious to inflate his own importance at small cost to himself, has given Lupus to understand that it was *he* rather than you who took the matter in hand. At least I thought I could detect a certain chilliness towards Manchester ON THE PART OF Wolff. Dronke is *cancan*[b] incarnate, NO DOUBT ABOUT THAT. *Experto crede,* etc.[c]

You absolutely must at once send *Pieper* at least sufficient to buy himself a coat and trousers. Shabby as he now is, he cannot possibly take advantage of opportunities that come his way, however favourable. He has become unpresentable. Moreover, you promised him this when [you] left.[415] He's putting a brave face on his misfortunes. But there's a limit to everything.

[I have] been particularly unlucky over money transactions. I now have current bills on America—two of them—amounting to £42 and yet cannot command above 42 farthings, though having to provide means of subsistence not [only] for myself but also for Pieper. The first bill of £24 I gave to Mr Spielmann; he told me to come back in five weeks' time. That was seven weeks ago. Besides, this wretched traipsing to and from the City invariably takes up my Mondays and Thursdays, the very days when I have to be preparing Tuesday's and Friday's articles. Each time Spielmann turns me away with the remark, uttered in Jewishly nasal tones: 'Nah nahtice yet.' In the case of such 'small' amounts, he says, his correspondents write only at their convenience, and, if I had needed the money straight away, I should have said beforehand that I would pay the *postage* for a special letter, etc., etc. This means daily unpleasantnesses, not only for me but for my wife who, counting on the prompt arrival of the money, had given definite promises to sundry creditors, and now the curs are laying siege to the house. Meanwhile, I am writing away like the devil. It would be fine if you could send me an article or two in between whiles, thus giving me the time to write something better. ³/₄ of my time is taken up chasing after PENNIES.

Heise is here just now; as a person the fellow's not at all bad. Mr Kossuth is presently making a fool of himself as correspondent

---

[a] Between ourselves - [b] gossip - [c] Experto crede Roberto.—Trust Roberto who has had experience (from a comic poem by Antoine Arena).

of the *Daily New-York Times.* In the *Advertiser* 4 letters by D. Urquhart on the eastern question[a] contained much that was interesting, despite quirks and quiddities. WE HAVE BEEN STRIKING against Jones for the past two weeks.

Your
K. M.

First published in *Der Briefwechsel zwischen F. Engels und K. Marx,* Bd. 1, Stuttgart, 1913

Printed according to the original

Published in English for the first time

175

ENGELS TO MARX

IN LONDON

[Manchester,] Wednesday, 24 August 1853

Dear Marx,

I'll send some money tomorrow if I *possibly can.* Your letter arrived on Saturday too late for anything to be done, this week there have been all sorts of complications, but tomorrow things will, I think, have improved, and our old bookkeeper has been forewarned.

The little man[b] was here on Saturday. That he had been gossiping was evident to me from the moment he wrote to Borchardt. He had sent him Lupus' most *discreditable* letter in which the latter makes an outright and most earnest appeal to the 'generosity' of the Jews in Bradford. *C'était une lettre à brûler de suite*[c]; Borchardt at once magnanimously sent Lupus alms, to wit the sum of *one pound,*—not that he wasn't very decent about it, WHICH HE COULD WELL AFFORD to be, seeing that it released him from all his obligations. I must confess that this letter of Lupus' left a *very bad* taste in my mouth, but not so bad as the little man's tactlessness in letting it fall into Borchardt's clutches. Anyway I duly hauled him over the coals for it.

---

[a] D. Urquhart, 'What Means "Protection" of the Greek Church?', 'Time in Diplomacy.—The "European Recognition"', 'The Relative Power of Russia and Great Britain', 'War between England and France', published as letters to the editor in *The Morning Advertiser* of 11, 12, 15 and 16 August 1853. - [b] Ernst Dronke - [c] It was a letter that ought to have been burnt forthwith.

Enfin c'est fait.[a] If Lupus is going to Liverpool, see to it that he comes here first, if possible on a Friday, in which case I shall arrange a rendez-vous with the little man. If, as Dronke proposes, Lupus first goes to Bradford, the *cancan*[b] will only proliferate.

You know that Jacobi intends to go to America. The chap's altogether *trop mou*[c] and even philistines get the impression that he's a helpless sort of creature. I don't believe he'll ever obtain a practice, however much he may pine for one. Besides one can't help laughing when one remembers that the chap's still a virgin.

Your
F. E.

First published in *MEGA*, Abt. III, Bd. 1, Berlin, 1929

Printed according to the original

Published in English for the first time

176

MARX TO JAMES GRANT, EDITOR OF *THE MORNING ADVERTISER*[416]

IN LONDON

London, August 31st, 1853

To the Editor of *The Morning Advertiser.*

Sir,

You will much oblige me by inserting the following in Your highly esteemed paper.

Your obedient servant
Dr. Karl Marx
(28 Dean Street, Soho)

First published in: Marx and Engels, *Works*, First Russian Edition, Vol. XXI, Moscow, 1929

Reproduced from a copy in Mrs Marx's hand

Published in English for the first time

---

[a] Well, it's done. - [b] gossip - [c] too soft

177

MARX TO ENGELS

IN MANCHESTER

[London,] 3 September[a] 1853
28 Dean Street, Soho

Dear Engels,

I have not written to you for a long-time, even to acknowledge receipt of the £5 (of which £2.10 was paid to Pieper and £1.10 to Lupus), the reason being that a lot of indescribable muck has taken up MY TIME AND MY ENERGIES. On 7 July I gave my bill to Spielmann.[b] On 31 August[c] the lad told me—after I had been to see him 7 times—that the bill had got lost, that I must make out another one for him, etc. So I had managed for weeks by pawning everything, down to *the last item*, and had made a further appointment for 31 August[c] with all my creditors whom I had been putting off since July. As I have no resources other than the income from the *Tribune,* you will understand my situation and that I have neither the time nor the inclination for correspondence.

Tell Jacobi, if he's still there, that I have written to Weydemeyer, etc., on his behalf.[417]

My reason for writing to you today is the following:

So far as I know you do not read *The Morning Advertiser.* This paper, which belongs to the 'UNITED VICTUALLERS', carried an apology of Bakunin by a 'FOREIGN CORRESPONDENT' (Mr *Golovin,* I think).[d] In the same *Morning Advertiser* an anonymous *F. M.* expressed suspicion that Bakunin was a Russian spy and doing very nicely, etc., etc.[e] To this *Golovin* and *Herzen* replied, pointing out that this same calumny had already appeared in 1848 in a 'GERMAN PAPER', which PAPER 'HAD EVEN VENTURED TO APPEAL TO THE TESTIMONY OF GEORGE SAND'.[f]

Three days ago 'Dr Arnold Ruge' chipped in, remarking that this German paper was the *New Rhenish Gazette*[g] whose EDITOR, 'Dr

---

[a] The original has '2 September'. - [b] See this volume, pp. 352 and 356. - [c] The original has 'September'. - [d] [I. Golovin,] 'Europe.—A Single Man', *The Morning Advertiser,* No. 19394, 19 August 1853. - [e] F. M. [Francis Marx], 'The Russian Agent, Bakunin. To the Editor of *The Morning Advertiser*', *The Morning Advertiser,* No. 19397, 23 August 1853. - [f] I. Golovin, A Herzen, S. Worcell, 'The Russian Agent, Bakunin. To the Editor of *The Morning Advertiser*', *The Morning Advertiser,* No. 19398, 24 August 1853. - [g] *Neue Rheinische Zeitung*

Marx', had known just as well as any other democrat that these calumnies were false.[a]

In yesterday's *Morning Advertiser* I published a statement[b] to the effect that:

MESSRS Golovin AND Herzen had CHOSEN TO CONNECT THE *NEW RH. G.* EDITED BY ME IN 1848 AND '49 with their polemic with F. M. about Bakunin, etc. Now, I CARE NOTHING ABOUT THE INSINUATIONS OF MESSRS Herzen AND Golovin. But etc., etc. 'PERMIT ME TO STATE THE FACTS OF THE CASE'. There follows an enumeration of the facts:

'that on 5 July 1848 we received letters from Paris, one from the Havas Bureau, the other from a POLISH REFUGEE (which is what I call Ewerbeck), both STATING that George Sand possesses letters compromising Bakunin AS BEING LATELY ENTERED INTO RELATIONS WITH THE RUSSIAN GOVERNMENT';

'that on 6 July we published this letter,[c] not the one from the Havas Bureau, but from our Paris correspondent';

'that Bakunin, replying in the *Neue Oder-Zeitung*,[d] *prior* to our correspondence, states that similar rumours had been circulating in Breslau, that they emanated from the Russian embassies and that he could refute them in no better way than by appealing to George Sand'[418];

'that on 3 August Kościelski brought to the *Rheinische Zeitung* a letter addressed by George Sand to its editor, which was published the same day[e] with the following introductory remarks[f]:' (here follows an extract from the *Neue Rheinische Zeitung*[g]);

'that at the end of August I passed through Berlin, saw Bakunin and renewed my old friendship with him';

'that on 15 October (or thereabouts) the *Rheinische Zeitung* stood up for Bakunin against the Prussian ministry which had ordered his expulsion'[h];

'that in February ('49) the *Rheinische Zeitung* published a LEADING ARTICLE on Bakunin the opening words of which were, "Bakunin is our friend!",[i] etc.';

---

[a] A. Ruge, 'Michael Bakunin. To the Editor of *The Morning Advertiser*', *The Morning Advertiser*, No. 19404, 31 August 1853. - [b] K. Marx, 'Michael Bakunin. To the Editor of *The Morning Advertiser*', *The Morning Advertiser*, No. 19406, 2 September 1853. - [c] [H. Ewerbeck,] 'Bakunin', *Neue Rheinische Zeitung*, No. 36, 6 July 1848. - [d] M. Bakunin, [Open Letter,] *Allgemeine Oder-Zeitung*, No. 151, 12 July 1848. This was the title under which the *Neue Oder-Zeitung* appeared in 1846-49. - [e] *Neue Rheinische Zeitung*, No. 64, 3 August 1848. - [f] ibid. - [g] See present edition, Vol. 12, p. 285. - [h] [Report on Bakunin's Expulsion, 10 October,] *Neue Rheinische Zeitung*, No. 115, 13 October 1848. - [i] F. Engels, 'Democratic Pan-Slavism', *Neue Rheinische Zeitung*, No. 222, 15 February 1849 (see present edition, Vol. 8, p. 363).

'that in the *New-York Tribune* I PAID BAKUNIN THE TRIBUTE DUE TO HIM
FOR HIS PARTICIPATION IN OUR MOVEMENTS,'[a] etc., etc.

My statement concludes with the words:

*'As to F. M. proceeding as he does from the fixed idea that
continental revolutions are fostering the secret plans of Russia, he
must, if he pretends to anything like consistency, condemn not
only Bakunin but every continental Revolutionist, as a Russian
agent. In his eyes Revolution itself is a Russian agent. Why not
Bakunin?'*

Well, in *today's* issue the blackguard Golovin does not dare give
his name but, under the rubric 'FROM A FOREIGN CORRESPONDENT',
publishes the following piece in *The Morning Advertiser:*

* *How to Write History*[b]
(From a Foreign Correspondent)

Bakunin is a Russian agent—Bakunin is not a Russian agent. Bakunin died in
the prison of Schlüsselburg, after having endured much ill-treatment—Bakunin is
not dead: he still lives. He is made a soldier, and sent to the Caucasus—no, he is
not made a soldier: he remains detained in the citadel of St. Peter and St. Paul.
Such are the contradictory news which the press has given in turn, concerning
Michael Bakunin. In these days of extensive publicity we only arrive at the true by
affirming the false; but, has it at least been proved that Bakunin has not been in
the military pay of Russia?

There are people who do not know that humanity makes men mutually
responsible—that in extricating Germany from the influence which Russia
exercises over it, we *re-act* upon the latter country, and plunge it *anew* into its
despotism, until it becomes vulnerable to revolution. Such people it would be idle
to attempt to persuade that Bakunin is one of the purest and most generous
representatives of progressive cosmopolitism.

'Calumniate, calumniate,' says a *French* proverb, and 'something will always
remain.' The calumny against Bakunin, countenanced in 1848 by one of his
friends, has been reproduced in 1853 by an unknown person. 'One is never
betrayed but by one's own connexion', says another proverb: 'and it is better to deal
with a wise enemy than with a stupid friend.' The conservative journals have not
become the organ of the calumny insinuated against Bakunin. A friendly journal
undertook that care.

Revolutionary feeling must be but slightly developed when it can be forgotten,
as M. Marx has forgotten, that Bakunin is not of the stuff of which police-spies are
made. Why, at least, did he not, as is the custom of the English papers, why did he
not simply publish the letter of the Polish refugee which denounced Bakunin? He
would have retained the regret of seeing his name associated with a false
accusation.*

---

[a] F. Engels, *Revolution and Counter-Revolution in Germany*, XVIII, *New-York Daily
Tribune*, No. 3576, 2 October 1852 (see present edition, Vol. 11, p. 90). Engels'
articles were published over Marx's signature. - [b] Golovin's item in *The Morning
Advertiser*, No. 19407 of 3 September 1853 is copied in Pieper's hand.

I intend to answer the chap as follows (see below) and would like you to return this to me *promptly* (by Monday if possible), with the style put to rights.[419]

At the same time the point arises whether you and Dronke, as EDITORS of the *New Rhenish Gazette*, might not wish to make a statement. Clique versus clique. On the other side are only Ruge, Herzen and Golovin. Bakunin himself has dubbed the latter '*un polisson*'.[a] One of Nicholas' most zealous admirers in 1843 and '44, he became a democrat because he *believed* he had become suspect, nor has he dared return to Russia. This last is the sum total of his heroism.

I for my part suggest a statement, the *substance* of which would be as follows:

* It is better to deal with a wise enemy, than with a stupid friend,' Bakunin would have exclaimed, if he was ever to read the letter of the 'foreign' Sancho Pansa who, in your Saturday's paper,[b] indulges in his proverbial commonplaces.

Is he not a 'stupid friend' who reproaches me with *not* having done by what doing I would according to himself have '*retained* the regret of seeing my name associated with a false accusation'?

Is he not a 'stupid friend' who is astonished of what every schoolboy knows that truth is established by controversy and that historical facts are to be extricated from contradictory statements?

When the *N. Rh. G.* brought the Paris letter Bakunin was at liberty. If he was right to be satisfied with the public explanations of the *N. Rh. G.* in 1848,[c] is it not a 'stupid friend' who pretends to find fault with them in 1853? If he was wrong in renewing his intimate relations with the Editor of the *N. Rh. G.*, is it not 'stupid' on the part of a pretended friend to reveal his weakness to the public?

Is he not a 'stupid friend' who thinks necessary to 'plunge Russia anew in its despotism' as if she had ever emerged from it?

Is he not a 'stupid friend' who calls the Latin proverb 'calumniare audacter'[d] a French proverb?

Is he not a 'stupid friend' who cannot understand why the 'conservative journals did not like to *publish* the calumnies' which were *secretly* spread against Bakunin throughout Germany while the most revolutionary paper of Germany was obliged to publish them?

---

[a] a lout - [b] [I. Golovin,] *How to Write History* (From a Foreign Correspondent.) - [c] A reference to George Sand's letter of 20 July 1848 and the editorial introductory remarks published in the *Neue Rheinische Zeitung*, No. 64, 3 August 1848. See also this volume, p. 360. - [d] calumniate boldly

Is he not a 'stupid friend' who ignores that 'revolutionary feeling' at its highest pitch made the 'lois des suspects'[420] and beheaded the Dantons and the Desmoulins and the Anacharsis Cloots?

Is he not a 'stupid friend' who dared not accuse *The Morning Advertiser* for having inserted the letter of F. M. while Bakunin is incarcerated at St. Petersburg at the same time accusing the *N. Rh. G.* for having inserted a similar letter in 1848 when Bakunin was free and not yet reduced to the misery of being defended by a 'stupid friend'?

Is he not a 'stupid friend' who makes the name of Bakunin a pretext for calumniating the friends of Bakunin while he is cautiously withholding his own name?*

A prompt answer, then. The matter is urgent.

Your

K. M.

First published in *Der Briefwechsel zwischen F. Engels und K. Marx*, Bd. 1, Stuttgart, 1913

Printed according to the original

Published in English for the first time

178

MARX TO ENGELS

IN MANCHESTER

[London,] 7 September 1853
28 Dean Street, Soho

Dear Frederic,

Your letter did, indeed, arrive too late.[421] I condensed the stuff[a] by cutting out unnecessary pathos, tidied it up a bit, and sent it to the amiable organ of the united 'LICENSED VICTUALLERS'[b] on Monday. Not inserted. At the same time, however, this highly consistent paper published a short *letter* 'FROM A NATIVE CORRESPONDENT' (presumably D. Urquhart) in its Monday issue, in which its own 'FOREIGN CORRESPONDENT' was quite plainly unmasked as a 'RUSSIAN AGENT', while

---

[a] See previous letter. - [b] *The Morning Advertiser*

Bakunin himself was not exactly made out to be a saint.[a] Probably *The Morning Advertiser* rejected my riposte[419] because less confused than that of the 'NATIVE'. Now the thing is to come out in *The People's Paper.*[b]

It was through a mere *lapsus linguae*[c]—out of long habit—that I mentioned Mr Dronke in my letter to you. I don't believe that 'little' Blanqui's[d] words are of any consequence, or that we shall gain anything by an appendix.

The worthy little man has stirred up such a mighty pother that 1. Lupus has never said a word to me about his departure,[422] although I had long since learnt of it through you; 2. that this same Lupus is always very guarded in his references to you; 3. that last *night* I was treated to a scene which was hardly creditable.

I was busy at work. Wife and children in the room. In comes Lupus with portentous tread—to take his leave at last, I supposed, for not once in my house had he let fall a word about his impending departure.

A year earlier I had borrowed a little Spanish grammar from him, by *Franceson,* maybe 120 pages.[e] So far as I could recall, I had returned the trashy object 5 months before. Or else, Dronke had pinched it.

The old gentleman had already asked my wife and Lenchen about the thing on two previous occasions and had been told that they would look for it.

Last night, then—the fellow was snappish from the moment he came in—I told him in as soothing tones as possible that I couldn't find the damned thing, that I had looked for it everywhere and believed I had returned it to him, etc., etc. 'You've *sold* it!' came the boorish, uncouth, insolent reply. (I'd wager a sovereign that nowhere in London could anyone get 2 FARTHINGS for the rubbish.) I, of course, jump to my feet, an altercation ensues, stubborn as a mule he persists in his nonsense, insults me '*au sein de ma famille*'.[f] As you know, I'm willing to put up with a great deal from an old man in his dotage who has become venerable as a party tradition. However, there are limits. I believe the old fool was taken aback when at last I bared my teeth at him.

All this is the result of Dronke's intrigues, too constant an

---

[a] D. Urquhart, 'Indeed?' [From a native correspondent,] *The Morning Advertiser,* No. 19408, 5 September 1853. - [b] K. Marx, 'To the Editor of *The People's Paper'*. - [c] slip of the tongue - [d] i.e. Dronke's - [e] C. F. Franceson, *Grammatik der spanischen Sprache.* - [f] in the bosom of my family.

indulgence in gin, and the evaporation of the cerebral juices. Perhaps the sea air will have a beneficial effect on his thinking organ. One may, perhaps, lay claim to the privilege of being an 'old blusterer', but one should not abuse it. My own lot is no bed of roses, nor can I in consequence regard his worldly worries as an EXCUSE.

The hobby-horse presently being ridden by those wretched Russians, in both the *Tribune* and the London *Advertiser* (though differing in person and form), is that the Russian *people* is democratic through and through, whilst official Russia (Csar and bureaucracy) is exclusively German, likewise the aristocracy.[423]

So Germany must be fought in Russia, not Russia in Germany.

You know more about Russia than I do,—and if you can find time to challenge this nonsense (it's just the same as when the Teutonic jackasses blamed the French for the despotism of Frederick II, etc., as if backward thralls haven't always needed civilised thralls to train them) you would greatly oblige me. In the *Tribune*, of course.

Your

K. M.

Write to me at greater length about the *state of commerce*—in *English* at once.

I have made a diplomatic reply to the enclosed letter from Klein, which I send to you for safe keeping.[424] It is impossible to correspond from London. The factory workers should keep themselves *entirely* to themselves and not make contact with philistines or other handicraftsmen in Cologne, Düsseldorf, etc. If they wish to send someone over here once a year to get good advice, we should have no objection.

First published abridged in *Der Briefwechsel zwischen F. Engels und K. Marx*, Bd. 1, Stuttgart, 1913 and in full in *MEGA*, Abt. III, Bd. 1, Berlin, 1929

Printed according to the original

Published in English for the first time

179

MARX TO ADOLF CLUSS [425]

IN WASHINGTON

[London,] 15 September 1853

... I have today received the latest number of the *Reform* containing your piece from Quebec,[a] and Kellner's apology of the self-same Poesche,[b] whose insipid WOULD-BE jokes about the 'cranky' proponents of the 'class struggle'[c] appeared in the *Neu-England-Zeitung* of 3 September, which reached me at the same time. You started sending me extra copies of the *Reform* at the very time I began to get them again regularly; on the other hand, I haven't been receiving the *Tribune* regularly and it is important that I should. For example, I haven't got the article in which I refer to the exchange of diplomatic notes on Denmark,[d] or the article in which I characterise the relationships of landed property[e]....

I think it is time you made a fresh start in the polemic and picked a few holes in the jejune arguments of Goepp-Poesche, discoverers of the *material view* though *their* materialism is that of the man-in-the-street. Our opponents are becoming uppish, something which could not have happened at least in the days of the *Neue Rheinische Zeitung*. That pedant Schläger, who more or [less] took to his heels at the time of the '48 revolution and hawked his genius in America, still regularly sends me his *N.-E.-Z.*, no doubt in order to demonstrate *ad oculos*[f] what fine fellows they are. Has there ever before been a rag in which stupidity and vanity were so nicely coupled with presumption?

Kellner is too much of a slow-coach, he seems unable to understand that polemics are essential to any journal as long as it

---

a [A. Cluss,] 'White Mountains (Summit-House), 21 August 1853', *Die Reform*, No. 44, 31 August 1853. - b In the article 'Die neue Welt' published in the same issue of *Die Reform* G. T. Kellner gave a review of *The New Rome. The United States of the World* by Th. Poesche and Ch. Goepp. - c Th. Poesche, 'Die "Klassenkämpfer".'- d K. Marx, 'In the House of Commons.—The Press on the Eastern Question.—The Czar's Manifesto.—Denmark'. - e K. Marx, 'The War Question.—Doings of Parliament.—India'. - f unmistakably

has to STRUGGLE. On top of that he has an unfortunate proclivity always to praise his enemies 2 days before they regale him with kicks. Thus Heinzen and Poesche; the latter, by the by, used his sorry article on the circulation of money to convey the sort of information one gets from encyclopedias...[426]

At any rate I find that things have begun to move sooner than I should have liked (I think the COMMERCIAL DOWNFALL will begin in the spring as in 1847). I had always hoped that, before that happened, I might somehow contrive to withdraw into solitude for a few months and work at my Economy.[45] It seems that this isn't to be. I find perpetual hackwork for the newspapers tiresome. It is time-consuming, distracting and, in the end, amounts to very little. However independent one may think oneself, one is tied to the newspaper and its readers, especially when, like myself, one is paid in cash. Purely learned work is something totally different, and the honour of figuring beside an A.P.C.,[a] a LADY CORRESPONDENT and an archbishop is CERTAINLY not to be envied.

Carl Wilh. Klein (of Solingen, a working man) has asked me to put you in touch with him. His address is———He's a capable chap. He set up a Working Men's Association and, from what he tells me in his letter, the *Gradaus* has come under its influence.[424] Pieper writes to him from here and, if you can possibly find the time, you must give him support from Washington.

Papa Blind is continuing his[b]... articles with much fervour in the *N.-E.-Z.* and congratulates himself and his EDITOR and *vice versa* on the unexampled achievements which cannot fail to inspire respect in Brüggemann of the *Kölnische Zeitung.*

Only a few lines today. EVENTS there have been none, if you except the onset of *cholera morbus* in London:

Your
K. M.

First published in part in *Die Neue Zeit,* Bd. 2, Nr. 31, Stuttgart, 1906-07 and in full in: Marx and Engels, *Works,* Second Russian Edition, Vol. 28, Moscow, 1962

Printed according to a letter from Cluss to Weydemeyer of 3 October 1853

Published in English for the first time

---

[a] Pulszky - [b] Insertion by Cluss: illegible.

180

MARX TO ENGELS

IN MANCHESTER

[London,] 17 September 1853
28 Dean Street, Soho

DEAR Frederic,

You're becoming damned taciturn.

Since I was expecting YOUR ARTICLE yesterday, all I had done was to make up a heading from the most recent news and, since the letter didn't come, one lot of correspondence went by the board.

I really must ask for your co-operation for the fortnight beginning today. For today *Pieper* is going, not into a monastery exactly, but into the German Hospital, a sort of medical prison, where he is to spend a fortnight or 3 weeks being thoroughly cured of the painful consequences of his carnal lust. Since I have in any case forfeited 3 or 4 articles through having to traipse off to that rotten Spielmann,[a] I must now write something every Tuesday and Friday so that the next bill I draw is not too paltry. There is a possibility of Freiligrath's finding a business friend who will regularly discount them for me.

If you can manage to do something in between times, I shall send you the other stuff to look through, in which case you will only have to preface or conclude it with the latest news you may have seen about TURKEY in the *Débats,* say, or some particularly important telegraphic dispatch, before sending the stuff to Liverpool.

I expect an article[427] from you for Tuesday.[b]

I think it important that something be said about the position of the armies, etc. There's a great deal of nonsense in the English papers, e.g. Omer Pasha is said to be crossing the Danube, etc.

I have already sent off two articles about the commercial crisis, 1 last Friday week about the Bank of England, its DISCOUNT and the effect of Peel's Act, or rather intended effect.[c] 1 last Tuesday on the price of corn, signs OF OVERPRODUCTION, etc.[d]

---

[a] See this volume, p. 356. - [b] 20 September - [c] 9 September. K. Marx, 'The Vienna Note.—The United States and Europe.—Letters from Shumla.—Peel's Bank Act'. - [d] 13 September. K. Marx, 'Political Movements.—Scarcity of Bread in Europe'.

I think it important to have more details about the MANUFACTURING DISTRICTS.

Enclosed something further by the *Tribune* man[a] and '*on*' him by the EDITORS of the *Tribune*. It would seem, by the by, that he is not a Russian AFTER ALL, but A GERMAN.

The abolition of the advertisement duty means that Jones' advertisements now bring him in £3 a week—the PAPER[b] IS ARRIVING TO THE PAYING POINT. This could also provide Pieper with a source of income.

When you write, you must also tell me about Lupus' travels. I heard later that he didn't push off from here until last Saturday.[c]

FAREWELL.

Your
K. M.

Enclosed another cutting from the worthy *Neu-England-Zeitung.*[d]

First published in *Der Briefwechsel zwischen F. Engels und K. Marx*, Bd. 1, Stuttgart, 1913	Printed according to the original Published in English for the first time

181

ENGELS TO MARX

IN LONDON

Manchester, 19 September 1853

Dear Marx,

What has hitherto been stopping me from working and writing has been the presence of the 'old gent'[e] who is temporarily encamped with me. There was no berth to be had on the SCREW-STEAMER and Borchardt was also very much in favour of his trying to get lessons here first; moreover, there were prospects for him in Liverpool as well. Anyway, he intends to try his luck here

---

[a] Pulszky (see this volume, p. 288). - [b] *The People's Paper* - [c] 10 September - [d] Presumably Th. Poesche's 'Klassenkämpfer', *Neu-England-Zeitung*, 3 September 1853. - [e] Wilhelm Wolff

and, in view of his curmudgeonly behaviour towards you in London,[a] I would sooner not let him see how the *Tribune* articles sometimes come into being. There are a few openings here and, after confabulating with Borchardt and me yesterday, he has set out today to look around, which means that I shall have the evening to myself and hence will be able to concoct for you an article on the state of business hereabout, which will go off by the second post.[427] The Russian one will follow as soon as possible—I believe the author[b] to be a German Balt or half Pole; clearly the chap has a great deal of material, so we must be cautious, but all the same we may very well be able to catch him out. Or might it even be Löwe, who wrote to Nesselrode in the *Deutsche Londoner Zeitung?*[c] To judge by the occasional prolixity and the tittle-tattle, here and there, this could well be so.

The *Reform* is arriving very irregularly. Have you heard anything from Cluss?

N. B. Since Lupus, as I see from your letter[d] today, made off without any kind of leave-taking, he will naturally not be allowed to set eyes on anything you send me—*il reste parfaitement en dehors de tout*[e] and, were it not for Borchardt, who got together £10 for his journey and is showing him kindness in other ways, my behaviour towards Monsieur Lupus would be somewhat cooler. Especially since the fellow, though as stubborn as ever, has lost his stoicism and become very dependent on those from whom he derives some advantage. *Il est même devenu un peu flatteur*[f]—and how!

However, we shall see whether a better position, if such is to be found here, doesn't soon bring the old gent to his senses again, in which case he'll have to ask your forgiveness as well.

Now I am off home to work.

> Your
> F. E.

First published abridged in *Der Briefwechsel zwischen F. Engels und K. Marx*, Bd. 1, Stuttgart, 1913 and in full in *MEGA*, Abt. III, Bd. 1, Berlin, 1929

Printed according to the original

Published in English for the first time

---

[a] See this volume, pp. 364-65. - [b] Adam Gurowski (see this volume, p. 365). - [c] 'Junius II' [Löwe], 'An den Graf Nesselrode', *Deutsche Londoner Zeitung*, Nos. 264 and 266, 19 April and 3 May 1850. - [d] See this volume, p. 369. - [e] he's left out of absolutely everything - [f] He's even become a bit of a flatterer

182

MARX TO KARL BLIND

IN LONDON

[London,] 26 September 1853
28 Dean Street, Soho

Dear Blind,

My wife and I were surprised to hear about that piece of infamy in Baden,[a] although one could hardly expect anything good to come from such a quarter. You may be assured of our deepest concern regarding all matters affecting you and FAMILY.

Quant à[b] Jones, I fear he has gone away. I haven't seen him for weeks. However, I shall try and find out this very day whether or not and whether he received your letter. More about this tomorrow, I hope. Kind regards from my family to yours.

Your
K. Marx

I should have come out to see you long ago had not a mass of *petites misères*[c] invariably intervened.

First published in *International Review for Social History*, Vol. IV, Leiden, 1939

Printed according to the original

Published in English for the first time

183

MARX TO ENGELS

IN MANCHESTER

[London,] 28 September[d] 1853
28 Dean Street, Soho

Dear Engels,

Herewith a letter from Weydemeyer, several from Cluss, a statement of Mr Willich's,[e] a letter from Mazzini to Mrs Mott (abolitionist) in America.

---

[a] See this volume, pp. 372-73 and 377-78. - [b] As for - [c] little tribulations - [d] The original has 'August'. - [e] A. Willich, [To the Editors of the *Belletristisches Journal und New-Yorker Criminal-Zeitung*, 28 August 1853], *Belletristisches Journal und New-Yorker Criminal-Zeitung*, No. 25, 2 September 1853.

I have split your essay into 2 and rewritten it as 2 essays[a] which I have sent to New York, my wife acting as secretary.

Pieper has had his throat *cauterised* in the German Hospital. A little board hangs at the foot of his bed bearing the ominous message: Wilhelm Pieper *syphilis secundaris.* He is subjected to rigorous discipline, which is salutary for him.

W. Wolff has written to his confidant, Rings. He is going to try his luck in Manchester until the end of October. If he hasn't found anything by then, he will move on. For the time being, he says, he is living at number such and such, Great Ducie Street,[b] at '*another's* expense'. He does *not* name *you at all,* which will give you an idea how obstinate and petty the OLD CHAP can be. After the way he grumbled about you he is, of course, ashamed to admit that he has any obligation towards you. *Quant à nous autres,*[c] I don't know what he may have told Rings in his letter, since the latter says nothing about it.

I should like to clear up the matter with Mr Dronke,[d] having now learnt that he sold Pieper's *Ricardo,* likewise a German history of political economy belonging to the working man, Lochner, etc., etc. Needless to say this has reinforced my STRONG SUSPICIONS about him.

Before he left, Mr Wolff gave Imandt also an account—and a very garbled one coloured by philistine indignation—of his insolent onslaught upon me.[e] What annoys me is the excessive consideration I have always shown the old blusterer instead of baring my teeth at him.

Les choses marchent merveilleusement.[f] All h[ell] will be let loose in France when the financial bubble bursts.

In the *Reform* there is a melancholic, stylised article by Jacobi about the end of the world.[g]

Don't let these lines fall into the wrong hands.

Your
K. M.

Apropos. Yesterday I received a few lines from Blind. He will now have to reconcile himself to abandoning his democratic hauteur in the knife and fork question.[428] He has lost his case and

[a] K. Marx, 'The Western Powers and Turkey.—Symptoms of Economic Crisis', 'Panic on the London Stock Exchange.—Strikes' written in co-authorship with Engels. - [b] at Engels - [c] As for the rest of us - [d] See this volume, p. 364. - [e] ibid., pp. 364-65. - [f] Things are going splendidly. - [g] A. Jacobi, 'Ueber den Untergang der Erde', *Die Reform,* Nos. 44-48, 31 August, 3, 7, 10 and 14 September 1853.

the whole of his wife's[a] fortune has been temporarily sequestered. So there will be no more subsidies. I feel sorry for him, despite the absurd manner he thought fit to adopt.

Have you been following the story about Bakunin in *The Morning Advertiser*?[b] Urquhart wrote an article in this connection[c] in which he suggests that Bakunin is suspect 1. because he's A RUSSIAN and 2. because he's 'A REVOLUTIONIST'; he goes on to assert that there are no honest revolutionaries among the Russians and that their would-be democratic writings (a swipe at Herzen and that *polisson*[d] Golovin) prove absolutely nothing; and finally, he tells the continental revolutionaries that, if they take Russians into their confidence, they are no less traitors than their governments. The Russians, it would seem, then sent into the fray an *Englishman* (Richards), who nourishes a grudge against Urquhart, the latter having, on grounds of seniority, elbowed him out of the topic '*The Times* and *Turkey*' in *The Morning Advertiser*. Richards maintains[e] that to declare Bakunin a SPY is just as PREPOSTEROUS as TO IMPEACH PALMERSTON FOR BEING BRIBED BY RUSSIA; he invokes the testimony of both Ruge and myself,[f] praises Herzen's '*idées révolutionnaires*',[g] etc. Yesterday it was the turn of A. B., another minion of Urquhart's, who declared[h] that he was acquainted with all the writings of '*la jeune Russie*',[i] and that they proved the rightness of Urquhart's views, pan-slavism, etc.

At all events, *les intrigants russes*[j] will realise that here it isn't as easy as in the *pauvre*[k] French democracy, to give themselves airs, gain INFLUENCE and behave as though they were a kind of aristocracy within the revolutionary emigration. Here it supposes hard knocks. What service have the jackasses done Bakunin save to have him seriously accused in public while themselves receiving a slap in the face?

First published abridged in *Der Briefwechsel zwischen F. Engels und K. Marx*, Bd. 1, Stuttgart, 1913 and in full in *MEGA*, Abt. III, Bd. 1, Berlin, 1929

Printed according to the original

Published in English for the first time

---

[a] Friederike Blind - [b] See this volume, pp. 359-63. - [c] D. Urquhart, 'Indeed?', *The Morning Advertiser*, No. 19408, 5 September 1853. - [d] lout - [e] A. B. Richards, 'Michel Bakounine and His Accuser. To the Editor of *The Morning Advertiser*', *The Morning Advertiser*, No. 19426, 26 September 1853. - [f] K. Marx, 'Michael Bakunin'. - [g] A. Herzen, *Du développement des idées révolutionnaires en Russie*. - [h] A. B., 'Revolutionary Russians. To the Editor of *The Morning Advertiser*', *The Morning Advertiser*, No. 19427, 27 September 1853. - [i] young Russia - [j] the Russian intriguers - [k] poor

184

ENGELS TO MARX

IN LONDON

[Manchester,] 29 September 1853

Dear Marx,

Herewith the article on the Turkish armies.[a] If you tell me what you are sending tomorrow on the STRIKES in Lancashire and the STATE OF TRADE,[429] I shall be able to link on to that and let you have a further REPORT on these matters by Tuesday.[b][430] The local MANUFACTURERS and MERCHANTS are at great pains to convince one another that things are not too bad, and the *Guardian* does what it can, but it's ALL SHAM AND HUMBUG. Since last week ordinary yarns are down by between $^1/_4$d and $^3/_8$d per pound, i.e. at 9d a fall in value of 3-4$^1/_2$%, at 8d of 3-6%, at 7d of 4-7%; in the same period COTTON fell by about $^1/_8$. STOCKS are accumulating and the HOME TRADE DEMAND is also falling off. There has been such frightful overspeculation in the Australian trade that 80,000 barrels of American flour were reconsigned *to this country* from Australia at a freight charge of 8/- per barrel. In 4 weeks' time the Australian CRASH should be well under way. All that the 'good news' from India amounts to is that the rise in prices over there and the fall in prices here added together still leave a loss on exports to that market. Nothing is flourishing save TRADE with America and speculation in corn. In Upbridge, *80/- per quarter* is already being paid for first quality wheat. CORN LOOKING UP, YARN LOOKING DOWN, and the Turkish rot IN THE FAIREST POSSIBLE WAY OF BORING OUR MERCHANTS ALL WINTER OVER.

MANUFACTURED GOODS are also coming down smartly, and here STOCKS are far more catastrophic than in the case of yarn. The manufacturers' decision to stop work thus kills two birds with one stone: 1. it disarms the workers, 2. it cuts down production. The fellows in Preston are sure to receive a general vote of thanks, if not compensation.[431] In Ashton, Stalybridge and Glossop, the manufacturers are also considering a stoppage, and some here as well. However there is a snag to it, namely that it only benefits those who don't stop, and only harms those who do.

If Borchardt is to be believed, Lupus has some prospect of

---

[a] F. Engels, 'The Russians in Turkey'. - [b] 4 October

obtaining a post as corresponding clerk. The old gent is studying Russian and the like and is as enthusiastic as ever over the Turkish question, of which I wish him joy.

My regards to your wife and children.

Your
F. E.

What do you think of Jacobi's melancholic and virtuous views about the end of the world?[a]

First published in *Der Briefwechsel zwischen F. Engels und K. Marx*, Bd. 1, Stuttgart, 1913

Printed according to the original

Published in English for the first time

185

MARX TO ENGELS

IN MANCHESTER

[London,] 30 September 1853
28 Dean Street, Soho

Dear Frederic,

Your piece on the war[b] is capital. I myself had serious MISGIVINGS about the westward advance of the RUSSIAN FORCES but did not, of course, dare TRUST TO MY JUDGEMENT in such matters. I have already written a whole series of STRIKE articles,[c] produced at intervals throughout the 6 months during which the thing has been going on. Now, however, the affair has taken a new TURN. In the article where I used your STRIKE-GENERALITIES,[d] I have mentioned a host of

---

[a] A. Jacobi, 'Ueber den Untergang der Erde'. - [b] F. Engels, 'The Russians in Turkey'. - [c] K. Marx, 'English Prosperity.—Strikes.—The Turkish Question.—India', 'Russian Policy Against Turkey.—Chartism', 'Financial Failure of Government.—Cabs.—Ireland.—The Russian Question', 'Rise in the Price of Corn.—Cholera.—Strikes.—Sailors' Movement', 'Panic on the London Stock Exchange.—Strikes'. - [d] K. Marx, 'Panic on the London Stock Exchange.—Strikes' (written in co-authorship with Engels) (see this volume, p. 372).

STRIKE-LOCALITIES by *name*, also the Preston [431] and Wigan [432] affairs. I couldn't get hold of any particulars about Manchester. I have depicted the manoeuvring in Preston (very briefly, mind you) 1. as an attempt by the manufacturers to use the operatives, whose demands are forcing the closure of the MILLS, to *cover* their *retreat* from over-production; 2. as an attempt to STARVE THE OPERATIVES INTO SUBMISSION.

As you can see, my HISTORY OF STRIKES goes no further than last Tuesday[a] and doesn't touch on Manchester.

You might, perhaps, expand somewhat the notes on yarn and COTTON prices and, if possible, the price of GOODS, so that they amount to at least one paragraph of an article.[430]

In each article, besides the subject proper, I naturally have to follow step by step the Russian Notes and England's FOREIGN POLICY (and right brave it is!), since the *jackasses* in New York consider this to be of prime importance and, AFTER ALL, nothing is easier to write about than this business of HIGH politics.

Next Tuesday *week* I shall have finished an article on the 'ORIENTAL CHURCH', and *next Friday week* the first of three articles on Denmark where next month the various assemblies of estates will be again taking the stage.[433]

Should there be any military MOVEMENT, I shall count on receiving immediate information from the Ministry of War[b] in Manchester, and the same applies to COTTONS and YARNS which are wretchedly covered by the papers down here.

Above all I want to slay the fellows with my pen, the moment being propitious, and if at the same time you keep me supplied with material, I can spin out the various themes over longer periods. What is more, without my secretary[c] I feel a little nervous about my English.

No regards to Lupus.

Your

K. M.

First published in *Der Briefwechsel zwischen F. Engels und K. Marx*, Bd. 1, Stuttgart, 1913

Printed according to the original

Published in English for the first time

---

[a] 27 September - [b] i.e. Engels - [c] Pieper

186

MARX TO JOSEPH WEYDEMEYER[434]

IN NEW YORK

[London, beginning of October 1853]

... Blind has suddenly become aware that the knife and fork question[428] is just as important as a South German view of the Turkish question. As you know, this gentleman had grown very grand, very much the *homme d'état*,[a] very much the superior émigré. You will also know that an article of Pieper's poking fun at Russia[b]—a frivolous scrawl well-suited to the *Neu-England-Zeitung* and such as could only have been concocted on the spur of the moment by a homeless waif—caused Blind to loose off in the *Neu-England-Zeitung* no fewer than 3 articles within 2 months, more or less fraternising (true love never fades) with Heinzen, etc. Hence his relations with us were strained. When I say 'us' I except Mr Lupus, who was naturally drawn to Blind by his *Morning Advertiser* sympathies and who, for some time past, has generally evinced a curious tendency to snarl at his so-called party friends and sympathise with political philistines. A few days ago then, Mr Blind reappears, bringing my wife a letter to Cluss, i.e. for Wolff who had written him a fond letter of farewell in which he invited him to correspond and left him Cluss' address.[435] Needless to say, my wife informed him that England for the present was still harbouring the great Turkophile.[c] But that was not, of course, the reason why our ex-friend of Falstaffian proportions had called. The court in Baden has sequestered the entire fortune of the children by his first marriage (the 2nd was contracted in the 13th *arrondissement*) until such time as they are handed over to the Jews in Germany to be given a Jewish upbringing. Thus Mr Blind has been reduced to $^1/_4$ of his or his wife's[d] income and he now regards the 'knife and fork question' as worthy of consideration, *even before* the Turkish War has been decided and Petersburg taken by

---

a statesman - b Probably Pieper's report from London of 31 May in *Die Reform*, No. 22, 15 June 1853. - c See this volume, pp. 369-70 and 372. - d Friederike

storm. In these much changed circumstances, and needing the assistance of the advocate *Jones* (Ernest), he once again remembered that I exist, which, of course, is damned flattering to me[a]...

First published in: Marx and Engels, *Works*, Second Russian Edition, Vol. 28, Moscow, 1962

Printed according to the original

Published in English for the first time

187

MARX TO ADOLF CLUSS

IN WASHINGTON

[London,] 5 October 1853
28 Dean Street, Soho

Dear Cluss,

That I have writer's itch, and this in the 'loftier sense of the term', you must needs conclude from the fact that I am writing to you today although—as so often nowadays—I have been working without a break for thirty hours on end.

D'abord,[b] I want you, if it is at all possible, to get the German press to publish my *Palmerston article.*[436]

On the 17th Jones will be setting forth on another tour of the manufacturing districts and tomorrow evening will call in here to get material for a campaign against that great HUMBUG.[437] It is comic that we are forced to teach the English their own history.

Willich's journeymen's association (the London one),[c] already demoralised since our resignation, has now become too much of a good thing even for that HIPPOPOTAMUS Schapper, who has also withdrawn.

Quant à[d] Carey and Ricardo's theory of rent[438]:

1) If we assume—as Carey would have it—that rent is simply another form of profit on capital or, still more precisely, of *interest*, this does not disprove but merely *simplifies* Ricardo's theory. The economic antithesis, in the most general sense, would simply coincide with the *antithesis* of capital and wage labour, PROFIT (and INTEREST) ON ONE SIDE and WAGES ON THE OTHER. The antithesis to capital *within* property would be eliminated (in so far as we disregard,

---

[a] See this volume, pp. 371 and 372-73. - [b] First - [c] German Workers' Educational Society - [d] As for

Die Reform of 2 November 1853 with Marx's article 'Palmerston' translated by Cluss

d'abord, the antithesis between individual *kinds* of capital determined by the *division of labour,* and then, the antithesis between
individual capitalists), but the antithesis *to* property would be all
the more comprehensive.

2) I am of course aware that, in an attempt to complete his
theory, the worthy Carey also reduces *profit* (interest included) to
wages in a *different* form. *D'abord,* is not Protestantism, for
example, merely a *different* form of religion from Catholicism?
Does the antithesis, the contradiction, the struggle between them
cease—and that is what you are dealing with—because they are
both *religions?* Thus, even assuming that profit and wages are
simply 2 *different* forms of the return on labour, the result is not
to reconcile them but merely to reduce their *difference* to a
simplified expression.

But how does he define their *otherness?* Profit is the wages for
past labour. Wages are the profit on *immediate present labour. Eh
bien!*[a] How does this avail him? For it is precisely from its
thraldom, from its slavery to *past, materialised* labour that present,
i.e. *actual* labour seeks to emerge, and from its thraldom to the
product of labour that *labour* seeks to be emancipated. The old
feudal laws were also *at one time* the present expression of popular
activity. Is that any reason why we should be subjugated by them
now?

At *best,* therefore, he is merely changing the phrase 'oppression
of labour by capital', into the phrase 'oppression of present labour
by past labour'.

There still remains the question, '*How* do I gain possession of
past labour?' By labour? No. By inheritance on the one hand and,
on the other, by the *fraudulent* exchange of past for present
labour. If past labour were exchanged for an equal quantity of
present labour, the owner of past labour could continue to
consume only so long as he had aliquot portions to exchange and,
at a given moment, would himself have to start working again.

3) Carey has himself wholly failed to understand Ricardo's
theory of rent when he maintains that it is based on the successive
deterioration of land. Ricardo—as I have proved in my book against
Proudhon[b]—falls into the common error of all other bourgeois
economists, when he passes off the form of landed property as an
'eternal natural law' of history in general, whereas it is the product
of purely industrial circumstances. His theory is true only of

---

[a] Well! - [b] K. Marx, *The Poverty of Philosophy. Answer to the 'Philosophy of Poverty' by
M. Proudhon.* On critique of Ricardo's theory of rent see Chapter II, § 4: 'Property
or Rent'.

bourgeois society in a condition of full development. Rent, in its *commercial* form—the only one he mentions—does not otherwise exist at all. It therefore leaves him unaffected to maintain that at *various* historical epochs it was not the worse, but rather the better, lands that were SUCCESSIVELY cultivated. The *historically better* land of one period does not count as land at all for the other[s]. Moreover, Ricardo does not speak only of the *natural* properties of the soil, but also of its *situation,* a social product, a social attribute.

The *fertility of the soil,* as I have likewise already said in the *Anti-Proudhon,* is something purely relative. Changes in the soil's fertility and its *degree* in relation to society, and that is the only aspect of fertility with which we are concerned, depend on changes in the science of chemistry and its application to agronomy.

4) *Assuming* a given condition of society, not any society, but one of full bourgeois development, with a populous countryside [...] etc., even this part of Ricardo's theory—*unessential* to his system—is correct.

Firstly. Types of land, with an equal infusion of *capital* and equally well situated for markets; how can their rents be differentiated? Merely by their *natural* fertility. This constitutes the *level* of rent.

On this assumption, when will a corn field of inferior quality be cultivated or a less productive coal-mine be exploited? When the price of corn or coal has risen so high as to enable the less productive ones to be cultivated or exploited. *Hence the cost of production of the* **poorer** *land determines the rent of the richer.* (This is Ricardo's Law.)

Secondly. Does this exclude a *constant increase* in fertility? Hence, does it include Malthus? By no means.

If 1 is the best land, followed by 2, 3, 4, etc., and fertility is increased tenfold, the relation between 1, 2, 3, 4, etc., remains as before. Were fertility to become so great as a result of chemical discoveries that 1, 2 and 3 sufficed, land 4 would no longer be cultivated. The cost of production of land 3 (let it $=3$) would then determine the rent. When land 4 (let its production costs $=4$) still had to be brought under cultivation, the rent of land 1 (let its production costs $=1$)$=4-1=3$. The rent of land $3=3-1=2$. The rent of land $2=2-1=1$. Now, however, the rent of 1 would $=2$, that of 2 would $=1$ and that of 3 would $=0$. Should the fertility of the land so increase that only 1, the best land, had to be cultivated, rent would *disappear completely.*

5) Ricardo's theory is based not on the doctrine of rent, but on the law that the *price of a commodity* is determined by *its cost of production*. That law, however, should not be understood as meaning that the price of *individual* commodities is determined by their cost of production. Rather, the commodity produced under the most unfavourable circumstances, and made *necessary* because of the demand for it, determines the price of all *other commodities of the same kind*. E.g. if demand is so great that flour, the production price of which is 20/-a QUARTER, can be placed on the market, then a qr. of flour costing 19, 18, 17, 15, etc., to produce is also sold at 20/-. The amount by which the market price, regulated by the cost of production of the *dearest* QUARTER to be placed on the market, exceeds the production costs of the less expensively produced flour, regulates the rent. What, then, gives rise to rent? Not the land, as supposed by Ricardo, but the *market price* and the laws by which it is regulated. If the quarter, which costs only 15/-(profit included) were sold, not at 20/-, but at 15, it could not carry a rent of 5. Why, then, does it do so? Because the market price is regulated by the flour the cost of production of which =20. In order that this may be placed on the market, *20* must be the *general* market price. Hence, if rent is to be overthrown, it must not be interpreted philanthropically; rather the laws of *market price* and thus of prices generally and thus the whole FRAMEWORK of the bourgeois economy must be overthrown.

So much for today on this subject.

Your

K. M. [439]

On types of land having the same properties and an equally favourable situation, the rent will, however, be determined *merely* by the proportion of capital wedded to the land. Nor does Ricardo deny this. Rent is then merely interest on *capital fixe*.[a] To say that, in cases in which rent does not exist in an actual, *specific* sense, its *specific* antithesis to capital and labour does not exist either, is no less true than to say that, where there is neither labour nor investment of capital, no antithesis between capital and wage labour exists. Instead there is, in the case under consideration, an antithesis between profit and interest, between rentiers (in the ordinary sense) and industrial capitalists. The less the tenant pays

---

a fixed capital

14*

the man whose capital is wedded to the land, the greater will be his profit and vice versa. The tenant and his LANDLORD (even though the latter simply draws interest on the capital employed on the land) would thus be as much at loggerheads as before.

The case most favourable to Carey is as follows:

Let the *product* of labour, the profit and interest =2, rent =1, wages =2. Now if, as a result of a rise in the productivity of labour, the *product* doubles and =10, the rent might =2, profit and interest =4, wages =4. To that extent it could be said that every kind of revenue may increase at no *expense to labour* and without landowner, capitalist and worker being mutually at loggerheads. But:

1) Assuming this most favourable instance to be real, all it means is that the antitheses—rent, profit, wages—all three, become more marked without losing any of their qualitative position relative to one another;

2) *Relatively* they can only rise or fall *at each other's* expense. In the foregoing example, the proportion =1:2:2. Does not the ratio remain the same if it =2:4:4? A change in this *relative* income would occur if, for example, wages were to =5, profit =3, and rent =2. The profit would then have *fallen* relatively, although in absolute terms it would have risen.

3) It is *par trop*[a] naive to suggest that, if the *total product of labour* rises, the three classes among whom it is to be shared will share *equally* in that growth. If profit were to rise by 20%, the workers would have to strike to obtain a 2% rise in WAGES.

4) *The conditions that govern an increase in the total product preclude such relatively equal increase from the outset.* If the increase is due to a better division of labour, or to a greater employment of machinery, the worker is, from the outset, placed at a disadvantage vis-à-vis the capitalist. If it be due to increased fertility of the soil, the landowner is worse off vis-à-vis the capitalist.

First published in: Marx and Engels, *Works*, Second Russian Edition, Vol. 50, Moscow, 1981

Printed according to the original[b]

Published in English for the first time

---

[a] altogether too - [b] The original is kept in the Marx Memorial House in Trier.

188

MARX TO ENGELS

IN MANCHESTER

London, 8 October 1853
28 Dean Street, Soho

Dear Engels,

D'abord[a] I must ask you—if you can—to send by return at least a minimum of money. Two weeks ago Spielmann finally paid up after deducting nearly £2. In the meantime, of course, debts had mounted up so much, so many of our absolute essentials had found their way to the pawnbroker's and the family had grown so shabby, that for the past 10 days there hasn't been a sou in the house. I now possess proof that I have been cheated by Spielmann, but *à quoi bon*[b]? At my request the firm in New York returned me the bill together with a letter from which it emerges that payment was made *as early as 22 July*, whereas I didn't receive the money until the end of September. I now have a further £24 to draw. (Since Pieper's incarceration I have sent in 6 articles, among them a fulminating *acte d'accusation*[c] of Palmerston, in which I trace his career from 1808 to 1832.[d] I shall hardly be able to deliver the sequel by Tuesday, since there are a great many Blue Books and *Hansards* to be consulted and Friday and today were utterly wasted in traipsing around after money. I wrote Friday's article[e] during the night, dictated it to my wife from 7 to 11 in the morning, then took Shanks's pony to the City.) Freiligrath has promised—and will do everything he can to that end, i.e. endorse it himself, etc.—to discount the bill for me with Bischoffshcim, but is unable to arrange the matter for another 8 to 10 days. Such is the *casus belli*. I shall have to see how I can get through the next few days. Credit is not available for food (excepting hot drinks and appurtenances). On top of that there'll

---

a First - b what's the use? - c indictment - d K. Marx, 'Lord Palmerston'. First Article written on 4 October 1853 was published in the *New-York Daily Tribune*, No. 3902, 19 October 1853 as a leading article 'I. Palmerston'. - e 7 October. K. Marx, 'The War Question.—Financial Matters.—Strikes'.

be Pieper who will probably come out of hospital tomorrow—*peut-être.*[a] As soon as I got my money I sent him £3, but the jackass entrusted it to Liebknecht for safekeeping and will now find there's not a farthing left.

Of the many pleasures I have experienced during my years here, the greatest have consistently been provided by so-called party friends—red Wolff,[b] Lupus, Dronke, etc. Today Freiligrath told me that Franz Joseph Daniels is in London and had been to see him with red Wolff. He, Daniels, declared he wouldn't come to see me because my association with Bangya had brought about his brother's[c] arrest which would not otherwise have occurred. Bangya first called on me in February 1852, and Daniels was locked up in May 1851! A very retrospective effect, then. All this infamous gossip (the reward for my trouble and loss of time, and such-like agreeable consequences of the trial[d]) is, of course, eagerly seized upon as an excuse for their own lamentable behaviour towards me and their cowardly retreat. However this vile business is attributable solely to the bandying about of ill-natured remarks by Messrs Dronke and W. Wolff who have kept for themselves the easier part, i.e. *cancan,*[e] being otherwise perfectly content to leave the work to me.

If my life was an easy, or at least a carefree one, I wouldn't, of course, give a fig for these scurrilities. But when, year after year, the bourgeois mire is laced with this and similar kinds of mire, *c'est un peu fort.*[f] I propose at the next opportunity to declare *publicly* that I have nothing whatever to do with *any party.* I no longer feel inclined to allow myself to be insulted by any old party jackass on so-called party grounds.

You can see how necessary it is to get my pamphlet[g] into Germany. Since you can't do it yourself, let me have Strohn's address and I will take the matter up with him.

I would also much like to hear at last what Mr Dronke has to say about the book.[h] As for Mr Lupus, he apparently wishes to make up for his servility towards his bourgeois patrons by being abominably insolent towards myself. I can assure him that he has by no means settled this matter by boasting to Imandt that, on the pretext of coming to say good-bye, he had vented his philistine spleen on me.

---

[a] perhaps - [b] Ferdinand - [c] Roland Daniels - [d] Cologne communist trial - [e] malicious gossip - [f] it's a bit too much - [g] K. Marx, *Revelations Concerning the Communist Trial in Cologne.* - [h] See this volume, p. 364.

Enclosed a letter from Cluss. In his essay against the *Neu-England-Zeitung*[a] he has—aptly as I think—pieced together sundry passages from my letters about Carey, etc.[438]

Your

K. M.

First published abridged in *Der Briefwechsel zwischen F. Engels und K. Marx*, Bd. 1, Stuttgart, 1913 and in full in *MEGA*, Abt. III, Bd. 1, Berlin, 1929

Printed according to the original

Published in English for the first time

189

MARX TO ENGELS

IN MANCHESTER

[London,] 12 October 1853

Dear Engels,

£2 received. It was all the more welcome as Oxford, Freiligrath's principal, is not yet back from his travels, and thus the matter has been delayed.[b]

As regards the *Tribune*, I shall have Article II on Palmerston[c] READY for Friday.[d] Article III, the final one, which covers the period 1848-53, calls for so many Blue Books and PARLIAMENTARY DEBATES that I can't possibly have it ready by Tuesday,[e] particularly with Sunday FALLING OUT AS FAR AS THE BRITISH MUSEUM IS CONCERNED. So it would be of enormous use to me and would also save me time if you could supply me with something for Tuesday. But what? I really don't know. Perhaps current affairs, to which I would simply append the most recent news. Perhaps, if you have kept up with the subject—not very much is WANTED FOR MESSRS GREELEY AND MC ELRATH —the influence of the impending crisis on DOING AWAY WITH THE BONAPARTE REGIME. I think it high time that attention was drawn to France where, after all, the catastrophe will break out. Failure of

---

a A. Cluss, 'Das "beste Blatt der Union" und seine "besten Männer" und Nationalökonomen', *Die Reform,* Nos. 48-51, 14, 17, 21 and 24 September 1853. - b See this volume, p. 385. - c K. Marx, 'Lord Palmerston', Art. II sent on 14 October was published in the *New-York Daily Tribune,* No. 3916, 4 November 1853 as a leading article under the title 'II. Palmerston and Russia'. - d 14 October - e 18 October

the corn and grape harvests. Paris, with its lower bread prices, attracting workers from all over France and thus recruiting the revolutionary army, while these new arrivals depress the already falling WAGES of the Parisians. Bread RIOTS in Alsace-Lorraine, Champagne. Grumbling by the peasants over the preference given to Paris, by the workers over the expensive wooing of the army, by the bourgeois over forcible interference with economic laws for the benefit of the workers. Falling demand, particularly for luxury articles. CLOSING of WORKSHOPS beginning. In contrast to the general *misère,* LAVISH EXPENDITURE and stock-jobbing by the Bonaparte family. HOLLOWNESS of the entire credit system, turned into nothing more or less than a colossal institutionalised racket under the direction of the Lumpenproletariat emperor and the Jew Fould. *Bourse,* bank, railways, mortgage banks and any other institutionalised racket you may care to name. The last days of the Louis Philippe regime all over again, but with all the beastliness and none of the REDEEMING FEATURES of the Empire and the Restoration.

PRESSURE of the government on the Bank. Tax collector mulcting the land more rigorously than ever. Vast difference between the advance estimates and the actual budget. All municipal administrations atrociously in debt—because PROSPERITY has to be propped up. Then the influence of the ORIENTAL QUESTION on FUNDS, with the court itself dangerously exploiting fluctuations in the stocks. DEMORALISATION of the army. Special stress should be laid on the fact that none of the manifestos, proclamations, etc., by Ledru, L. Blanc and other kindred spirits of all complexions have succeeded in removing the evil, whereas the social and economic crisis is setting the whole caboodle in motion, etc. etc. I don't know, of course, whether the subject will appeal to you. At any rate let me know whether or not I can expect an *articulum*[a] by Tuesday, so that I can act accordingly.[440]

Your
K. M.

In last week's *Economist*—(Saturday's, so really this week's) there's all sorts of stuff in its Paris Correspondence.[b]

First published in *Der Briefwechsel zwischen F. Engels und K. Marx,* Bd. 1, Stuttgart, 1913

Printed according to the original

Published in English for the first time

---

[a] article - [b] 'Foreign Correspondence', *The Economist,* No. 528, 8 October 1853.

190

MARX TO KARL BLIND

IN LONDON

London, 13 October 1853
28 [Dean Street], Soho

Dear Blind,

Immediately after you called on me, I went to see Freiligrath in order to secure his good offices in getting my bill discounted. Freiligrath did indeed undertake to do this, but has so far not managed to arrange the thing since his principal[a]—whom he needs for the transaction and who has been expected back these past 8-10 days—has not yet returned. Thus I am *sans sous*[b]— although I have almost £30 to draw. Yet the thing must be settled within a few days.

As I was unable to obtain this money against my bill, I looked round elsewhere so that I could send you the £1 forthwith, but was everywhere met with a snub.

So, like myself, you will have to be patient for a few days and will, I am sure, realise that nothing could be more vexing to me than my present inability to settle the matter immediately.

Quant à[c] Jones, I can't understand anything. Since you were here he has been to see me twice and *positively* assured me he had written to you. It's not his way to lie about *such* things. Can his letter have been intercepted? He'll be here again tomorrow, when I shall get him to write to you in my presence. Then I shall myself take the letter to the post. He is leaving on Monday.[d]

Warm regards to you and your wife.

Your

K. Marx

First published in *International Review for Social History*, Vol. IV, Leiden, 1939

Printed according to the original

Published in English for the first time

---

[a] Oxford - [b] penniless - [c] As for - [d] 17 October. See this volume, p. 378.

191

MARX TO ADOLF CLUSS [441]

IN WASHINGTON

London, 18 October 1853
28 Dean Street, Soho

Dear Cluss,

You really did [...] too much in going to the trouble of copying out the Chinese thing.[a] AT THOSE EXPENSES I would certainly not have had the impertinence to ask you for the article.[442] Dana copied my stuff almost word for word, watering down this and that and, with rare tact, *deleting* anything of an audacious nature. NEVER MIND. IT IS A BUSINESS OF HIS, NOT OF MINE. In one of my Indian articles[b] he also amended the bit where I speak of cholera as 'THE INDIAN'S *REVENGE* UPON THE WESTERN WORLD' to 'INDIA'S *RAVAGES*' which is nonsense. *En passant*[c] Freiligrath solicited that 'revenge' for a poem about cholera upon which he is still at work.

Again, in another of my articles on India,[d] dealing with the princes there, he transmogrified 'THE SKELETON OF ETIQUETTE' into 'THE SECLUSION (PITIFUL!) OF ETIQUETTE'. NEVER MIND! Provided he pays.

My wife has also compromised me by putting Rinaldo for Ruggiero and Alcide for Alcine[e] in the first article on Palmerston. These are '*les petites misères*'[f] of an *écrivain*[g] whose own handwriting is illegible.[443] But it's a bitter pill for a man who knows his Ariosto from A to Z in the original. *Divino*[h] Ariosto!

It's a big jump from Ariosto to Klein, or rather a long fall, and a *casus obliquus*[i] at that. Papa Klein wrote to me—not a word, of course, about his upsets and rows—asking for recommendations to you and Weydemeyer. In my reply (Pieper has not written him a *single line quant à vous*[j]) I did not, of course, in any way suggest

---

[a] K. Marx, 'Revolution in China and in Europe'. - [b] K. Marx, 'The War Question.—Doings of Parliament.—India' (see present edition, Vol. 12, p. 216). - [c] By the way - [d] K. Marx, 'The Russo-Turkish Difficulty.—Ducking and Dodging of the British Cabinet.—Nesselrode's Last Note.—The East India Question' (see present edition, Vol. 12, p. 200). - [e] Rinaldo Rinaldino—title character in the novel by August Vulpius; Ruggiero and Alcina—characters in *L'Orlando furioso* by Ariosto. - [f] little miseries - [g] writer - [h] sublime - [i] oblique fall. A pun, the German word *Fall* meaning either 'fall' or 'case'. - [j] concerning you

that Weydemeyer *was unfriendly* to me.[a] How could anyone suppose me capable of such stupidity and baseness? Mr Klein would have had to conclude from my harmless remark about Cluss' being 'our party's *most* talented and energetic representative in America',[b] that I was denying all talent and energy to Weydemeyer. However, such sophisticated word-juggling is beyond the reach of Klein's intellect. Hence all his remark amounts to is a piece of nonsense invented in order to give vent to his annoyance. NOTWITHSTANDING ALL THIS, YOU ARE RIGHT, SIR, IN HAVING WRITTEN TO MR SNUG.[c]

Klein really does wield some influence over the Solingen workers, and they are the best in the Rhine province. I, *pour ma part*,[d] have never, either drunk or sober, expressed the view that the *workers* are fit only for cannonfodder, although the *louts*, among whom little Klein[e] is evidently coming to rank himself, are, to my mind, barely fit even for that. It would be as well to treat little Klein with your accustomed DISCRETION as a tool that may perhaps (?), IN TIME OF ACTION, be of use to us.

Have forwarded the letter to Pieper. There's nothing doing with the *Gradaus* for it doesn't pay, and Pieper is too badly off to write *gratis*.

As regards the *Reform*, I shall see what I can get the others to do. The only one from whom any real support can be expected is *Engels*. Red Wolff[f] is married and a retailer of HOUSEHOLD WORDS for Prutz, Gutzkow and Cotta, not worth a FARTHING to us just now. Lupus no longer writes; he's so obstinate that he cannot be made to forget the unfortunate business of Weydemeyer's *Revolution*.[2] Dronke, presently a clerk in Bradford, idle as a grisette. Weerth, travelling about South and North America on business for nearly a year now. Engels really has too much work, but being a veritable walking encyclopaedia, he's capable, drunk or sober, of working at any hour of the day or night, is a fast writer and devilish QUICK in the uptake, so he at least can be expected to do something in this respect.

I was greatly tickled by Heinzen's heroic deed. Should you people give the fellow another dressing down, concentrate on his crass ignorance, and the pains the wretched man is at to

---

a See this volume, p. 365. - b Cf. Marx to Joseph Weydemeyer, 19 December 1851, present edition, Vol. 38, p. 519. - c Klein, ironically called Snug after a character in Shakespeare's *Midsummer Night's Dream*. - d for my part - e A play on the words *klein* (little) and *Klein* (personal name). - f Ferdinand Wolff

appropriate his opponents' catch-words when they're already stale and fit for nothing. Delectable, the chap's aspirations to *dignity*, and then his scraps! Serves him right!

Rent. In the *Misère*[a] I cite an example of how in England, land which, at a certain stage of science, was regarded as barren, is, at a more advanced stage, considered fertile. I can adduce as a general fact that, throughout the middle ages, esp. in Germany, *heavy clay soil* was cultivated by preference as being *naturally* more fertile. In the past 4-5 decades, however, owing to the introduction of potatoes, sheep-farming and the resulting manuring, etc., *light sandy soil* has taken pride of place, esp. since it involves no EXPENSES OF DRAINAGE, etc., and on the other hand its deficiencies can easily be made good by means of chemical fertilisers. From this, then, it may be seen how *relative* 'fertility' is, even '*natural*' fertility, and at the same time how ill-informed Mr Carey is, even from the point of view of history, when he expresses the opinion that the *most barren* land is always the first to be brought under cultivation.[b] What leads him to that conclusion? The fact that tropical swamps are damned fertile but reclaimable only by civilisation. A tropical swamp, however, is productive not so much of herbs as of weeds. Civilisation clearly originates in those regions where *wheat* grows wild, as was the case in part of Asia Minor, etc. Such land is rightly described as *naturally* fertile by historians—and not land yielding poisonous vegetation and requiring more strenuous cultivation if it is to become fertile *for* human beings. Fertility is not, after all, absolute but merely a relation of the land to human requirements.

Ricardo's law only holds good within *bourgeois* society. Hence it is where the relationship of the bourgeois to the land is purely that *of a bourgeois*, and every peasant,—or feudal—or patriarchal, relationship is cast aside that the law applies in its purest form, hence above all in the *mining* of precious metals, and in *colonies* where *commercial crops*, e.g. sugar, coffee, etc., are grown. More about this another time. In both instances the exploitation of the land is regarded and pursued by the bourgeois *de prime abord*[c] as a purely commercial concern.

Though I'm not afraid of those curs of Russians in so far as

---

[a] K. Marx, *The Poverty of Philosophy. Answer to the 'Philosophy of Poverty' by M. Proudhon.* - [b] H. Ch. Carey, *The Past, the Present, and the Future*, Philadelphia, 1848, pp. 48-49. - [c] first and foremost

Europe is concerned—they are going to put us Germans in queer street. Between the Kalmuks and the *crapauds*[a] we are in a cleft stick.

Herewith copy of *The People's Paper.*

Vale faveque,[b]

Your

K. M.

First published in part in: Marx and Engels, *Works,* First Russian Edition, Vol. XXV, Moscow, 1934 and *Voprosy istorii KPSS,* No. 3, Moscow, 1962 and in full in: Marx and Engels, *Works,* Second Russian Edition, Vol. 50, Moscow, 1981

Printed according to the original[c]

Published in English for the first time

192

MARX TO ENGELS

IN MANCHESTER

[London,] 28 October 1853
28 Dean Street, Soho

Dear Frederic,

Mes remerciements pour les deux articles.[d] I fear you have been too biassed by Mr Smitt[e] in favour of Russia's military achievements. *D'abord,*[f] as regards the 1828-29 campaign, it was a wretched affair in the opinion of most *contemporains*[g]; I base myself *inter alia,* on the REPORT submitted to the Duke of Wellington by his ADC and published in *The Portfolio.*[h] The fortresses were bought rather than stormed. In general, BRIBERY played a major role in the campaign.

---

[a] Marx used this word for French philistines. - [b] Good-bye and farewell. - [c] The original is kept in the Marx Memorial House in Trier. - [d] My thanks for the two articles (F. Engels, 'Movements of the Armies in Turkey' and 'The Holy War'). - [e] F. Smitt, *Geschichte des polnischen Aufstandes und Krieges in den Jahren 1830 und 1831.* - [f] To begin with - [g] contemporaries - [h] F. R. Chesney, 'Précis of a Report on the Russian Campaign of 1828 and 1829, drawn up for the information of the Duke of Wellington', *The Portfolio,* No. 26, 20 July 1836.

After passing through the Balkans, Diebitsch was not sure whether he had come to conquer or to be miserably cut off and captured. What saved him was BRIBERY, this time of one of the Pashas in command, and the UTTER DISSOLUTION of THE TURKISH ARMY. Russia began the war when the fleet had been destroyed off Navarino [444] and the Turkish army's traditional organisation had been destroyed by Mahmud and no new one had yet been established. In any case, circumstances are different now.

Over the past 2 weeks the *Débats* has been publishing articles on the campaigns of '28-'29, which, however, I have not read. I shall look out further material at the library.

Pieper has been out of hospital for a week—and is doubly occupied, 1. as correspondent of the *Washington Union*, arranged by Cluss and 2. as CLERK (from 9-5) at 25/- A WEEK with a *crapaud*[a] in the City. Hence of no further use to me. *Tant mieux*[b] for him. I'm glad he's out of the mire.

I am sending you the continuation of the Palmerston.[c] Jones has asked me for the next instalment. I have sent an article for this once [d] but with the proviso that he would get no more if he didn't put an end to the abominable printing errors (this time glaring to the point of distortion). The manuscript was written very neatly.

Rings, stricken by *madness*, has spent several days in the WORKHOUSE and is still in a critical condition. Drink was to blame, *quorum magna pars*[e] the merry-making Lupus who debauched him with gin AFTER HE HAD SHUT UP HIS SHOP. Withal the man's too full-blooded to remain idle and has not yet succeeded in finding any fresh occupation. It's damnable the way the fellows all go mad on us.

Herewith Heinzen's *tour de force*.

Your

K. M.

First published abridged in *Der Briefwechsel zwischen F. Engels und K. Marx*, Bd. 1, Stuttgart, 1913 and in full in *MEGA*, Abt. III, Bd. 1, Berlin, 1929

Printed according to the original

Published in English for the first time

---

[a] philistine - [b] So much the better - [c] K. Marx, Article III of the 'Palmerston' series: 'A Chapter of Modern History', *New-York Daily Tribune*. - [d] K. Marx, 'Lord Palmerston', Art. III, *The People's Paper*. - [e] a large part being played by Virgil, *Aeneid*, II) ·

193

MARX TO ENGELS

IN MANCHESTER

[London,] 2 November 1853
28 Dean Street, Soho

Dear Engels,

You must let me have something by the day after tomorrow, even if only 1 or 2 pages (if you are short of time) on the CROSSING of the DANUBE by the Turks when they took Kalafat. Yesterday I reported the news[a] as VERY DOUBTFUL. But it seems likely to be confirmed and tomorrow's papers will at any rate tell you how things stand. Now that scientific opinions are beginning to be expressed on the subject, I can neither remain silent nor discuss it from the standpoint of 'sound common sense'.[b] According to the news in the French press, *Shamyl* has roundly trounced the Russians and is actually threatening Tiflis, while General Vorontsov has written to his government informing it that, once he is threatened from 2 sides, he will not be able to hold Georgia without substantial reinforcements.

Of late the *Tribune* has been considerably exercising its annexationist policy. To begin with your first military article was annexed as a LEADER, then my Palmerston,[c] further instalments of which are thus foredoomed to annexation. Strange though it may seem to you, by following exactly in the footsteps of the NOBLE VISCOUNT during the past 20 years, I have come to the same conclusion as that monomaniac Urquhart—namely that for several decades Palmerston has been in the pay of Russia. As soon as you have read the further instalments of my article (especially the bits about the Turko-Syrian conflict[d]) I would like to have your views on the subject. I am glad that chance should have led me to take a closer look at the foreign policy—diplomatic—of the past 20 years. We had very much neglected this aspect, and one ought to know with whom one is dealing.

---

[a] K. Marx, 'War.—Strikes.—Dearth'. - [b] An allusion to Heinzen's *'der gesunde Menschenverstand'* (sound common sense). See K. Marx, 'Moralising Criticism and Critical Morality', present edition, Vol. 6, pp. 317, 330 and 337. - [c] F. Engels, 'The Russians in Turkey'; K. Marx, 'I. Palmerston', *New-York Daily Tribune*, No. 3902, 19 October 1853. An allusion to the fact that the newspaper editors had not named the author. [d] K. Marx, Article III of the 'Palmerston' series: 'A Chapter of Modern History', *New-York Daily Tribune*.

Diplomacy as a whole is nothing but Stieber, Bangya and Co. reproduced on a large scale.

The *New-York Enquirer,* edited by General Webb (I haven't read the article myself), has attacked the *Tribune* LEADER got from you.[a] The thing, it says, is scientifically correct, but a Turkish war is waged according to different principles. Turks would go into the attack whatever the circumstances, etc.

How is the Factory Pro-le-ta-ri-at doing?

Your

K. M.

First published in *Der Briefwechsel zwischen F. Engels und K. Marx,* Bd. 1, Stuttgart, 1913

Printed according to the original

Published in English for the first time

194

MARX TO ENGELS

IN MANCHESTER

[London,] 6 November [1853]
28 Dean Street, Soho

Dear Engels,

Herewith the great Karl Heinzen's invective against myself and communism in his *Herold des Westens.*

Also a letter from Cluss. From it you will see that Willich's fiery rocket[b] is arriving by the next post. The worst of it is that the fellows will be peddling their lampoon throughout the whole of Germany while my pamphlet[c] reposes quietly in Manchester and London—and that in Heinzen they once more possess a vociferous sounding-board, whereas a few months ago the only organ at Willich's disposal was the *Criminal-Zeitung.* When the trash arrives I shall let you have it immediately, so that you can write and tell me what you think we ought to do.

You will see from Cluss' letter how things stand with the *Reform.*[445] Get the 'old man'[d] and Dronke to write for it. They have

---

[a] F. Engels, 'The Russians in Turkey'. - [b] A. Willich, 'Doctor Karl Marx und seine "Enthüllungen"', *Belletristisches Journal und New-Yorker Criminal-Zeitung,* Nos. 33 and 34, 28 October and 4 November 1853. - [c] K. Marx, *Revelations Concerning the Communist Trial in Cologne.* - [d] Wilhelm Wolff

plenty of WASTE TIME. Whether it would be advisable for us two to contribute direct is a moot point.

Weerth's letter *horriblement* insipid, despite all his striving after wit.

Your

K. M.

First published in *Der Briefwechsel zwischen F. Engels und K. Marx*, Bd. 1, Stuttgart, 1913

Printed according to the original

Published in English for the first time

195

MARX TO ADOLF CLUSS [446]

IN WASHINGTON

[London, mid-November 1853]

... As regards the *Reform*, I shall see what can be done in Germany and Paris. Pieper is now in *business* and spends from 9 in the morning until 8 at night in the City. So what with his work as correspondent for the *Union*, has little time. He'll do something. If any *money* is forthcoming, I would suggest that Eccarius get some first so that he doesn't have to spend all day tailoring. In accordance with an agreement made with me, he will now be sending articles regularly. Do try and see that he gets *something*, if at all possible. With regard to his French articles, Jones is no longer printing them,[447] nor has he returned me the manuscript, which isn't therefore available *dans ce moment*,[a] Jones being away on an agitation tour. I have written to him about it, however.[448] I have also asked *Heise*. Diversity is desirable and, by consorting with us Heise will, I believe, change for the better. I have asked Lupus and Dronke through Engels.[b] Probably little will come of it. In Lupus' case, age and bachelorhood combine to lead him into mischief during this sorry interregnum.

Not yet seen Willich's damp squib.[c] The war news takes up almost my whole attention and there's no time left to think about the great Willich. Despite the electric telegraph, the NEWS arrives late, is very confused and fragmentary and has, moreover, all

---

[a] at the moment - [b] See this volume, p. 396. - [c] A. Willich, 'Doctor Karl Marx und seine "Enthüllungen"'.

passed through the hands of the Vienna police—i.e. been censored. The news from Constantinople is of course much delayed. The heroes of democracy are preparing to march. An evil omen for the Turks.

*Quant à*ᵃ Willich, I should much prefer it if I could be spared personal statements and my contribution be confined to producing, for the feuilleton of the *Reform*, a psychological—or rather, phenomenological—genre picture of this shabby philistine's 'form of consciousness'.

Last Tuesday,ᵇ at the same time as your letter, I received one from *Klein* which was, I must say, most delightfully written, witty and considered. He tells me that he, too, will make a statement against Willich, since he can prove that the man was a fraud all the time he was in London. Klein is obsessed with the idea that you people are treating him very much *de haut en bas*. I shall try and smooth out this difference.

As regards the *Tribune*, the most ingenious way of handling the thing might have been to make people believe they 'recognised my style'.⁴⁴⁹ I have become very thick with Urquhart as a result of the Palmerston article.ᶜ To help me, he has sent me several books—with which, however, I was already familiar...⁴⁵⁰

First published in *Voprosy istorii KPSS*, No. 3, Moscow, 1962

Printed according to a letter from Cluss to Weydemeyer of 7 December 1853

Published in English for the first time

196

MARX TO ENGELS

IN MANCHESTER

London, 21 November 1853
28 Dean Street, Soho

Dear Engels,

Herewith a £2 postal order for Lupus, which I have received for him from Cluss, N.B. in response to my request.

Also Willich's exceedingly sorry scrawl.ᵈ

ᵃ As regards - ᵇ Probably 8 November. - ᶜ K. Marx, 'Lord Palmerston'. - ᵈ A. Willich, 'Doctor Karl Marx und seine "Enthüllungen"'.

You and Dronke must let me have, by *Friday*[a] at the latest, *statements* on the bits which refer to myself. I shall include them in my GENERAL ANSWER[b]—in the form of statements. We must be as quick off the mark with our answer as the noble Willich was sluggish. Mind you make your statement a very humorous one.

Thanks for the Turkish article.[c] When it arrived, news of the Turkish retreat had already reached me, and I altered the thing accordingly. Do write; it's a month since you answered any of my letters with more than half a dozen lines.[451]

Your
K. M.

Won't you come up to town for Christmas and put up *here*? I now have a small room for you. You might be able to shake off the old man[d] for once.

First published in *Der Briefwechsel zwischen F. Engels und K. Marx*, Bd. 1, Stuttgart, 1913

Printed according to the original

Published in English for the first time

197

MARX TO ENGELS

IN MANCHESTER

[London,] 23 November 1853
28 Dean Street, Soho

Dear Engels,

The People's Paper had been overlooked. Enclosed herewith. The five articles that have so far appeared in Jones' paper have been compressed in the *Tribune* into three.[e]

Whatever calls there may be on your time, I must ask you to let me have for *Friday*[f] at least 2 of (your usual) pages—more is

---

[a] 25 November - [b] K. Marx, 'The Knight of the Noble Consciousness'. - [c] F. Engels, 'The Progress of the Turkish War'. - [d] Wilhelm Wolff - [e] K. Marx, 'Lord Palmerston', I-V in *The People's Paper,* corresponding to 'I. Palmerston', 'II. Palmerston and Russia' and 'III. A Chapter of Modern History' in the *New-York Daily Tribune.* - [f] Engels' article 'The War on the Danube' was sent to New York on Friday, 2 December 1853.

unnecessary—written in English so that I waste no time over translation. It seems to me that the campaign is now over for the winter; and in any case the first phase has been concluded, and hence can be disposed of with a few general remarks. So I count on at least 2 pages.

The Willich mess calls for speed—in direct contrast to his six months of shilly-shallying.[a]

Your
K. M.

Did the 'old man'[b] get the postal order for £2?

First published abridged in *Der Briefwechsel zwischen F. Engels und K. Marx*, Bd. 1, Stuttgart, 1913 and in full in *MEGA*, Abt. III, Bd. 1, Berlin, 1929

Printed according to the original

Published in English for the first time

198

MARX TO ENGELS

IN MANCHESTER

London, 2 December 1853
28 Dean Street, Soho

Dear Frederic,

Mes remerciements pour le[c] BEAUTIFUL ARTICLE.[d] In America Mr Dana will be making himself a name as a field marshal.

That you should be coming here[452] mainly to frequent the philistines again, pleases me not at all.

Mr Dronke is behaving like a wretched little mischief-monger. He tells Strohn he has sent you his statement and the newspaper,[e] and gives you to understand that both have gone to me—*have had neither.* See to it that the LITTLE MAN returns you the newspapers, at

---

[a] See this volume, pp. 396, 397 and 398. - [b] Wilhelm Wolff - [c] Thanks for the - [d] F. Engels, 'The War on the Danube'. - [e] *Belletristisches Journal und New-Yorker Criminal-Zeitung* containing Willich's article 'Doctor Karl Marx und seine "Enthüllungen"'.

all events. I have a copy of my own here, but none is required in Bradford. Not having received the trash from Dronke, I was rummaging by chance amongst some old letters when I lit upon the *corpus delicti* with the incriminating *passage* which I quote verbatim. The letter was addressed to *you*. [453] Now, should Mr Dronke use adjectival caustic to obliterate factual accuracy, he'll have only himself to blame if *I* send his letter to New York as proof that I, *du moins*,[a] am accurate. It contains some strange passages which would now undoubtedly embarrass him, e.g. concerning that 'fanatical lout Imandt', *maintenant*[b] an intimate friend to whom he writes twice weekly. Everyone knows how addicted the little man is to mischief-mongering while our backs are turned.

On Tuesday[c] I sent off my rejoinder, *The Knight of the Noble Consciousness*. He's[d] in for a surprise. Your letter[454] and others from Steffen, Miskowsky (together with Kossuth's testimony),[455] etc., all of them, of course, with your signatures, were included as integral parts of the whole.

Write soon.

Jones is under attack from *The Economist*[e] and is acquiring fame.

Apropos. Last Tuesday a Polish meeting.[456] Mazzini and Kossuth didn't come. Inane blather from Worcell. Ruge and Ledru showed themselves worthy of the company. My wife was there.[f] Also at Monday's meeting held by Poles of the democratic variety. It was announced that Harney was to be in the chair. Fearsome revolt by the 50 or 60 English working men present. Hisses, 'TRAITOR', 'DRYBONES' (as he called the Chartists), RENEGADE. A fearsome set-to. Harney did not dare take the CHAIR, was terribly mauled, buffeted, abused and, despite half a dozen attempts, never managed to speak. Needless to say, the stupid Waschlapskis[g] couldn't understand what was going on and interpreted the whole thing as 'reaction'. This spells Nemesis for Father George Julian Harney.

Your

K. M.

---

a at least - b now - c 29 November - d Willich - e 'The Labour Parliament', *The Economist*, No. 535, 26 November 1853. - f See this volume, p. 587. - g Marx calls the petty-bourgeois émigrés who attended the Polish meeting of 29 November 1853 'Waschlapskis' (Dishcloths) after a personage in Heine's satirical poem 'Zwei Ritter'.

From the enclosed letter[a] you will see that Cluss has unfortunately already answered.[b] But since my thing was ready,[c] it had to go off. One should not work for Willich *for nothing*.

First published abridged in *Der Briefwechsel zwischen F. Engels und K. Marx*, Bd. 1, Stuttgart, 1913 and in full in *MEGA*, Abt. III, Bd. 1, Berlin, 1929

Printed according to the original

Published in English for the first time

199

MARX TO ENGELS

IN MANCHESTER

[London, about 12 December 1853]

Dear Engels,

From the telegram I received from you this morning I naturally cannot tell:

1. Whether Cluss', etc., answers[d] and the issues of the *Reform* relating to Willich[e] have reached you from New York. The contrary would seem possible, since Mr Lupus, in a fatuous letter to Cluss, seeks to conceal his laziness by inveighing against *Weydemeyer*.

2. Has Dronke returned the relevant numbers of the *Criminal-Zeitung*[f]? I asked Steffen to get you to send them to him in Chester, since I can't do without the one copy I have down here. When—induced *by you*—I came in my last letter[g] to speak of the odd affair of 'the well-known gentleman, Dr Dronke's' statement, it occurred to me that the immediate upshot would be that I would get no private letters from you until the affair could be assumed to have blown over—say a week or two. At least, that is the method which, since Mr Lupus' arrival in Manchester, you have adhered to with unusual consistency in all matters concerning

---

[a] Cluss to Marx, 13 November 1853. - [b] J. Weydemeyer, A. Cluss, A. Jacobi, 'An die Redaktion der *New-Yorker Criminal-Zeitung*', *Belletristisches Journal und New-Yorker Criminal-Zeitung*, No. 37, 25 November 1853. - [c] K. Marx, 'The Knight of the Noble Consciousness'. - [d] See previous letter. - [e] 'Werbungen in New-York', 'Das Wirken der "Militär Kommission"', *Die Reform*, Nos. 87 and 88, 19 and 21 November 1853. - [f] containing Willich's 'Doctor Karl Marx und seine "Enthüllungen"' - [g] See this volume, pp. 400-01.

myself and the two gentlemen. Hence, if our correspondence is not to be reduced to mere telegraphic exchanges, it would be better if both of us were to omit in future all allusions to your friends and protégés up there.

Salut.

Your

K. M.

First published in *Der Briefwechsel zwischen F. Engels und K. Marx,* Bd. 1, Stuttgart, 1913

Printed according to the original

Published in English for the first time

200

MARX TO ENGELS

IN MANCHESTER

[London,] 14 December 1853

Dear Frederic,

As you know, everyone gets an occasional bee in his bonnet, and *nihil humani*[a] etc. Needless to say, there was never any question of 'conspiring' and suchlike nonsense.[457] You are accustomed to SOME JEALOUSY and, *au fond,*[b] the only thing that vexes me is our not being able to be together now, to work and have fun together, whereas your 'protégés' have you conveniently to hand.

Enclosed one copy of the *Knight.* The other arrived in Washington either today or yesterday. I sent the thing to Cluss so that the 2 statements[c] should not conflict, and so that he can delete anything that has already been said. A few small stylistic changes were made in the copy I sent. The last page is missing from the one I sent you; it got mislaid and contains only a few concluding remarks in a humorous vein.

Although we have heard nothing of him, Willich must be back in London again. Did you see in the *Reform* the splendid minutes of the meeting presided over by Anneke, in which not a single person

---

[a] *Homo sum, humani nihil a me alienum puto* (I am a man and I think nothing human is alien to me), Terence, *Heautontimorumenos.* - [b] at bottom - [c] J. Weydemeyer, A. Cluss, A. Jacobi, 'An die Redaktion der *New-Yorker Criminal-Zeitung'* and K. Marx, 'The Knight of the Noble Consciousness'.

declares himself willing to return to Germany as 'a revolutionary fighter under Willich's military leadership'?[a]

Quant à[b] Palmerston,[c] I could agree to a 'German' version only if I could be sure that the work would subsequently be accepted by a publisher. For I haven't a German MS, since I myself had to write the thing in English, i.e. Anglo-Saxonise the original from the word go. As regards the *Tribune* I intend to conclude with the TREATIES OF 1840 AND '41,[458] and for this I have at my disposal some very bulky BLUE BOOKS, BESIDES *Hansard* and the *Moniteur.* Have left out Palmerston's machinations in GREECE, Afghanistan, Persia and Serbia, as being of lesser importance. That would still leave the revolutionary period[459] for which the BLUE BOOKS again provide important (if considerably curtailed) material, as well as for our 'patriotic' war, etc., in Schleswig-Holstein

Concerning your Bonaparte as a captain of artillery, or writer thereon, I think you would do best to send a paper of this sort under your own name either to 1. *The Daily News,* 2. *The Examiner,* or 3. *The Westminster Review.* The first would probably be best. An article of this kind would at one fell swoop—*par coup d'état*[d]—put you in such a position vis-à-vis the London Press that you could 'press' it and at the same time, perhaps, get a chance to have your book on the Hungarian compaign[e] published in English in London, which would in any case be more profitable and effective than in POOR old Leipzig.

Needless to say, the *Tribune* is making a great splash with your articles, POOR Dana, no doubt, being regarded as their author. At the same time they have appropriated 'Palmerston', which means that, for 8 weeks past, Marx-Engels have virtually constituted the EDITORIAL STAFF of the *Tribune.*

In addition to your lengthier expositions which are appropriated by them for LEADERS and are feasible only in the case of certain important EVENTS or periods, e.g. the initial phase, then the battle of Oltenitza, etc., I should be grateful if (time permitting) you could—during the less important interludes—let me have a brief summary of the facts—1-2 pages, say—in English. I have greater difficulties—even from the *language* standpoint—with the lesser stuff than with profound (!) expositions, especially with material I have long been familiar with by reading in an *English* context, i.e. English works. I only require this, of course, when there is a

---

[a] [Report from Newark,] *Die Reform,* No. 91, 24 November 1853. - [b] As for - [c] K. Marx, 'Lord Palmerston'. - [d] by a coup d'état - [e] See this volume, pp. 104 and 309-10.

dearth of 'great' *événements*.[a] The main difficulty is the uneasiness of my critical conscience in regard to matters with which I feel I am not *à la hauteur*.[b] My competitor[c] quite simply copies out the facts (or rather what are given out as such by the London Press).

What do you think of my brother-in-law Juta's proposal, enclosed *herewith,* that we should write a monthly article for the *Zuid-Afrikaan* (Cape Town)?[460] Rotten though Juta's French may be, he's a good, sensible chap. If only you and I had set up an *English* correspondence business at the right moment in London, you wouldn't be stuck in Manchester tormented by the office, nor I tormented by debts. Incidentally, I believe that if you were to send military articles to the London papers now, you would, within a few weeks, be able to secure a permanent post which would pay as well as the Manchester business and leave you more spare time. At present the DEMAND FOR MILITARY WRITERS exceeds the supply.

It might even be asked whether *The Times* itself might not be very glad to hook a MILITARY COLLABORATOR since it is wretchedly served in this respect. It would be worth trying. For we have, of course, now reached the stage at which we regard any English newspaper merely as an emporium and it matters not a rap in which of these emporia we display our 'articles', *supposé*[d] they are not tampered with.

Your
K. M.

First published abridged in *Der Briefwechsel zwischen F. Engels und K. Marx*, Bd. 1, Stuttgart, 1913 and in full in *MEGA*, Abt. III, Bd. 1, Berlin, 1929

Printed according to the original

Published in English for the first time

---

[a] events - [b] here: fully familiar - [c] Pulszky (see this volume, p. 288) - [d] providing

1854

201

MARX TO ENGELS

IN MANCHESTER

[London,] 5 January 1854
28 Dean Street, Soho

Dear Engels,

Since the day you left,[461] the whole FAMILY has been prostrated by influenza, etc. Musch and I are still very much down. Thus through physical causes I have already been cheated of 3 articles for the *Tribune* which, considering the weather, is *dur*.[a] Let me know if you can provide me with *one* article for next week, on any subject you like. But I must know for certain *if* and *when*.[b]

Being still confined to my room, I have not, of course, been able to keep up with the newspapers. Pieper tells me that in today's *Morning Herald* there is a long article on the Russian plan of campaign.[c] The main theatre to be Asia, not Europe. They proposed to take Constantinople from the direction of Asia Minor (!) etc., etc.

Three volumes of Joseph Bonaparte's *Memoirs*[d] have so far come out. The third contains the old Napoleon's correspondence on the Peninsular campaign.[462]

Just now I was interrupted by Musch, who is raving and thrashing about, etc., in a high fever. I hope the little man will soon recover.

---

[a] hard - [b] In compliance with Marx's request Engels wrote 'The European War' on 8 January. - [c] J. B. Slick, 'To the Editor of *The Morning Herald*', *The Morning Herald*, No. 22361, 5 January 1854. - [d] J. Bonaparte, *Mémoires et correspondance politique et militaire du roi Joseph*.

Received a letter from Dana on Monday. Unable to print the article under my name[463] as it would damage the 'prestige' of the paper. Your military articles have created a great stir. A rumour is circulating in New York that they were written by General Scott.[464]

Adieu,

Your

K. M.

First published in *Der Briefwechsel zwischen F. Engels und K. Marx*, Bd. 2, Stuttgart, 1913

Printed according to the original

Published in English for the first time

202

MARX TO ENGELS

IN MANCHESTER

[London,] 10 January 1854

Dear Engels,

Last evening Urquhart sent me from Newry (Ulster) a speech which I got my wife to copy out, then added a word or two at the beginning and the end, and thus produced an article.[a] So I shall cancel yours this Friday.[b] Should there be any further INCIDENTS that belong here,[c] perhaps you would be so good as to advise me of them by *Friday morning* so that I can give the stuff the finishing touches.

The whole family, from α to ω, is still ill.

The enclosed is from Cluss. I shall send you the other part of it next time, when I shall be writing at greater length.

That swine Tucker has just sent me a message. The first edition (50,000 COPIES) of 'Palmerston' is sold out. Now the gentleman

---

[a] K. Marx, 'The Western Powers and Turkey'. - [b] 13 January - [c] The reference is to the subjects dealt with in Engels' 'The European War'.

sends word—he used not to be so condescending—that I should revise the thing for the second edition.[465] Write at once and tell me what you advise me to do.

Your

K. M.

First published in: Marx and Engels, *Works*, First Russian Edition, Vol. XXII, Moscow, 1929

Printed according to the original

Published in English for the first time

203

MARX TO ENGELS

IN MANCHESTER

[London,] 18 January 1854
28 Dean Street, Soho

Dear Frederic,

You must let me have by Friday[a] something of a general nature (it is hardly possible to be specific) about the Battle of Citale or Zitale.[b] It seems to me that:

1. The battle of Oltenitza was a *misunderstanding* which frustrated the armistice imposed by the Ambassadors on the Porte. Similarly the Battle of Citatea[466] was a *misunderstanding* which frustrated the peace proposals dictated to the Porte under the guns of the English warships.

2. The obverse of Oltenitza. In the one case the Turks entrenched, in the other the Russians, etc.

3. Same result. After a murderous set-to lasting five days, the fellows drew in their respective horns. All I see is the result. I don't know what *should* have happened. All I do know is that this is not the way *Napoleon* fought a war.

So enmeshed in their own webs have the diplomatic intriguers become that a *guerre générale*[c] is imminent. As you know, the EVENT AT Sinope—not to mention Mr Redcliffe's threats—was intended to induce the Turks to accept the Protocol of Vienna and bring Halil and Riza Pasha into the government.[467] Once all this had

---

[a] 20 January. - [b] Marx took the wrong spelling from the English newspapers; should be Citatea as below. - [c] general war

been engineered, Palmerston resigned.[468] On 19 December, *while* he was still out of office, the coalition smelt a rat and ordered a demonstration in the Black Sea. Palmerston, doubly discredited, returned to office and effected the decision of the 26th, that the *entire* fleet was to sail into the Black Sea, but to do no more than assume a *neutral* role vis-à-vis the two BELLIGERENTS; ostensibly going further than the decision of the 19th, but in fact attempting to thwart it and cut the Turks off from their Asiatic theatre of war. In the meantime, however, Mr Bonaparte, basing himself on the decision of the 19th, has already issued contrary orders and purports to *interpret* the decision of the 26th merely as an extension of the first. Palmerston, OF COURSE, had to make the best of a bad thing and preserve his reputation as an energetic patriot. In this way the fellows have got themselves into a pretty pickle and their *dissimulation* will land them in an even worse one, especially since Parliament will have to be shown on the 31st that 'energetic' steps are being taken.[469] The Note which the fellows submitted to the Turks for signature shows that the former were prepared for a total SURRENDER TO RUSSIA and that only 'misunderstandings' frustrated this good intention.[470]

My brother-in-law— *le ministre*[a]—wrote and told my mother-in-law[b] that she was unfortunately about to relive her experience of 40 years ago, namely a general war.[471]

I forwarded your letter to Steffen[472] the same day to Brussels where Steffen is still staying with his sister. I fear that, at this particular juncture, your 'Napoleon as Lieutenant of Artillery'[473] will be *rejected,* as *The Times* has had orders to refrain from any semblance of anti-Bonaparte polemics. Since he is 'our' ally, every paper will be moved by the same patriotic considerations just now. Anyway, as soon as the thing is ready, and if the papers won't have it, we shall bring it out as a pamphlet. Where my own work is concerned, I feel embarrassed about offering it to a publisher. The same *gêne*[c] would not apply to yours.

That jackass Weydemeyer has again shelved 'the noble consciousness'.[d] The main thing was speed in answering. 6 weeks too late, and the thing's SILLY. I cannot understand Cluss, and why he should always pick on me of all people to be Mr Weydemeyer's victim.

Your

K. M.

---

[a] Ferdinand von Westphalen - [b] Caroline von Westphalen - [c] embarrassment - [d] K. Marx, 'The Knight of the Noble Consciousness'.

God bless you, Brother Straubinger.[61] A MAN OF HIGHBIRTH HONOUR PEACE PROSPERITY.

SMALL WIT[a]

First published in *Der Briefwechsel zwischen F. Engels und K. Marx*, Bd. 2, Stuttgart, 1913

Printed according to the original

Published in English for the first time

204

MARX TO ENGELS

IN MANCHESTER

[London,] 25 January 1854
28 Dean Street, Soho

Dear Frederic,

Enclosed note for Lupus, who has written to me.[474] Absolution.[b]

As to the war, there will now be some snags, unless 'MISUNDERSTANDINGS' OCCUR that have nothing to do with, or run counter to, diplomacy. Reshid Pasha's Note[475] spells total SURRENDER TO RUSSIA. It even contains more concessions than the ORIGINAL VIENNA NOTE as a result of which Turkey declared war.[476] Palmerston has not returned to office in vain.[c] On the other hand, the demonstration in the BLACK SEA would seem to be a DODGE, specially contrived for the MEETING of Parliament: if Russia accepts her *own* conditions incorporated in Reshid's Note and obtains everything she has demanded, she will appear to have bowed to *force supérieure*. That, in any case, is the plan. Otherwise, would it not be absurd to inform Nicholas of the entry of the UNITED FLEETS *before* he had, or could have, pronounced upon the last VIENNA NOTE? Now only an accident of war could bring about a warlike solution. By prior agreement the Czar, far from objecting to the ENTRANCE OF THE UNITED SQUADRON, showed considerable 'TEMPER'.[477] However, there's no vouching for 'MISUNDERSTANDINGS'. They ARE EVER PROBABLE.

Today's *Times* contains a further report from the *Wanderer* on The Battle of Citatea.[d] I EXPECT YOUR OBSERVATIONS. The advance the

---

[a] Postscript in a childish hand. - [b] See this volume, p. 386. - [c] ibid., p. 409. - [d] 'Krajova, Lesser Wallachia. Jan. 11', *The Times*, No. 21647, 25 January 1854.

Russians are said to have made simultaneously at Matchin, Giurgevo and Kalafat and, indeed, the capture of Silistria, would seem MERE HUMBUG. Apropos, one more thing: your opinion, written in *English*. According to the French newspapers, the Turks intend to fortify Constantinople on the landward side.[a] Would this not be a major blow for Russia? The more so as Constantinople will always be able to communicate by sea with the Asiatic and European coasts of its EMPIRE and thus cannot be cut off from its supplies of men and materials? Large-scale fortifications would now seem to be the ANTIDOTE to large-scale warfare à la Napoleon. May this not bring about a reversion to small-scale warfare?

It is scandalous that Berlin is not being fortified.

My brother-in-law, *le ministre,* has written to my mother-in-law warning her that now, in her ripe old age, she is about to go through the same experience as in the days of Napoleon I.[b] He believes, then, that there'll be war.

Cobden, the 'UMBLE' and 'HOMELY MAN' made a considerable ass of himself in his last speech. He demonstrates that neither he nor the 'UMBLE MEN' who applaud him, are competent to govern England. The Quaker Bright will hear of nothing but the war *within.* Cobden's discovery that the social structure of England and Russia are analogous because there are Demidovs there and Derbys here, is worthy of a Palatinate revolutionary philistine from Neustadt.[478]

On Saturday Mr Pieper went to visit Meyer in Brighton. Unwelcome though he is to the latter, he is overstaying the time allotted him by Troupeau, because the 'sea air' suits him, and has, it seems, written the bourgeois a fatuous letter. The silly lad mistakes his lack of principles for genial high spirits. From Cluss' letter[479] you will see that this same 'genial' youth wanted to obtain an American passport to Constantinople, probably in the hope of becoming a kennelboy there. It's *triste*[c] that the lad should be so thoroughly pleased with himself as to do one silly thing after another and make a laughing-stock of himself.

On Tuesday[d] Bischoffsheim will be paying me another bill through Freiligrath. In the meantime I can't raise a penny, having exhausted the possibilities of the pawnbrokers, as is regularly the case. So if you could lay your hands on £1, it would be HIGHLY DESIRABLE. Moreover, 100 copies of the 'noble consciousness'[e] will be

---

[a] [Report from Constantinople of 2 January 1854,] *La Patrie,* No. 19, 19 January 1854. - [b] See this volume, p. 109. - [c] sad   [d] 31 January - [e] K. Marx, 'The Knight of the Noble Consciousness'.

arriving on Friday and I haven't the MEANS to pay the postage, since I shan't be getting any money until Tuesday.

Apropos. I am negotiating with Tucker. The next pamphlet is to be about Unkiar-Skelessi. So correct the stuff you've got (Nos. IV and V).[480] I shall then make sundry additions and send back the ALTERATIONS for you to look through.

I have received through Dana an offer from a magazine in New York, £12 per sheet, for articles on the history of German philosophy from Kant TILL NOW.[481] But they must: 1. be sarcastic and amusing; 2. contain nothing AGAINST THE RELIGIOUS FEELINGS OF THE COUNTRY. How to set about it? Now, if we 2 were together—books would be needed besides—we could quickly earn £50-£60. I wouldn't dare attempt the work on my own.

Your
K. M.

First published abridged in *Der Briefwechsel zwischen F. Engels und K. Marx,* Bd. 2, Stuttgart, 1913 and in full in: Marx and Engels, *Works,* First Russian Edition, Vol. XXII, Moscow, 1929

Printed according to the original

Published in English for the first time

205

MARX TO ENGELS

IN MANCHESTER

[London,] 9 February 1854
28 Dean Street, Soho

DEAR Frederic,

I shall be sending you today, at the same time as this, a few copies of the 'Knight'[a] and three copies of the 2nd edition of the Polish rubbish,[482] which I have corrected. Give one copy of each to Lupus and Dronke. It was stupid of me not to have corrected the printing errors (Weydemeyer also contributes his fair share) in the Syrian Palmerston thing[b] before sending it to you.[483]

I had a meeting with Urquhart.[484] He surprised me with the compliment that the articles[c] read as though written by a 'Turk',

---

[a] K. Marx, 'The Knight of the Noble Consciousness'. - [b] K. Marx, 'Lord Palmerston', Fourth Article in *The People's Paper.* - [c] K. Marx, 'Lord Palmerston'.

an opinion in which he was in no way confirmed when I told him that I was a 'REVOLUTIONIST'. He is an utter maniac. Is firmly convinced THAT HE WILL ONE DAY BE PREMIER of England. When everyone else is downtrodden, England will come to him and say: SAVE US, Urquhart! AND THEN HE WILL SAVE HER. While speaking, particularly if contradicted, he goes into FITS which I find all the more comical as I know by heart his every platitude and quotation. This made me regard his 'FITS' as EVEN somewhat SUSPECT and RATHER as a theatrical EXHIBITION. The fellow's most comical idea is this: Russia rules the world through having a specific superfluity of BRAIN. TO COPE WITH HER, a man must have the BRAIN of an Urquhart and, if one has the misfortune not to be Urquhart himself, one should at least be an Urquhartite, i.e. believe what Urquhart believes, his 'metaphysics', his 'POLITICAL ECONOMY' etc., etc. One should have been in the 'EAST', or at least have absorbed the Turkish 'spirit', etc.

If you can do something by Tuesday,[a] it would be very welcome, since I have to write to the Cape of Good Hope on *the same* day.[b]

Your
K. M.

First published abridged in *Der Briefwechsel zwischen F. Engels und K. Marx*, Bd. 2, Stuttgart, 1913 and in full in: Marx and Engels, *Works*, First Russian Edition, Vol. XXII, Moscow, 1929

Printed according to the original

Published in English for the first time

206

MARX TO ENGELS

IN MANCHESTER

[London,] 15 February 1854
28 Dean St., Soho

DEAR Frederic,

The lithographic sample enclosed herewith is all my own work.[c]

---

[a] 14 February. In compliance with Marx's request Engels sent him on 13 February the material which provided the basis for their joint article 'The War Question in Europe'. - [b] i.e. for the paper *De Zuid-Afrikaan* in Cape Town (see this volume, p. 405). - [c] See illustration facing p. 414.

Bonaparte's publication of his LETTER to 'BROTHER' Nicholas shows that he already had a negative answer in his pocket.[485]
Salut.

Your
K. M.

First published in: Marx and Engels, *Works*, First Russian Edition, Vol. XXII, Moscow, 1929

Printed according to the original

Published in English for the first time

207

MARX TO ENGELS

IN MANCHESTER

[London,] 9 March 1854
28 Dean Street, Soho

Dear Engels,

I have not written for a long time because I have had a great deal of TROUBLE at home which has even prevented me from reading the papers properly, so that I don't know whether anything of yours has yet appeared in *The Daily News* or how the whole thing is going.[a]

As yet I have got nothing, i.e. not a single farthing, out of my 'Palmerston', nor does there seem to be any prospect of my doing so. Mr Trübner has himself told me that, *quant á lui*,[b] it is a PRINCIPLE of his never to pay for the stuff he publishes. Moreover, the thing's out of date *au moment*.[c]

On Tuesday[d] I shall send the last of the sample articles to the Cape.[486] (So you must let me have *something* for the *Tribune*, PERHAPS THE GREEK REVOLUTION?)[487] Tuesday will be the last day of regular sailings to the Cape, since the company has fallen out with the government over charges.

I am faced with the repulsive prospect of enduring throughout the spring and summer the same chronic pressure as in previous years, since it is not possible for me to work off past debts with the

---

[a] See this volume, p. 404. - [b] as for him - [c] by now - [d] 14 March

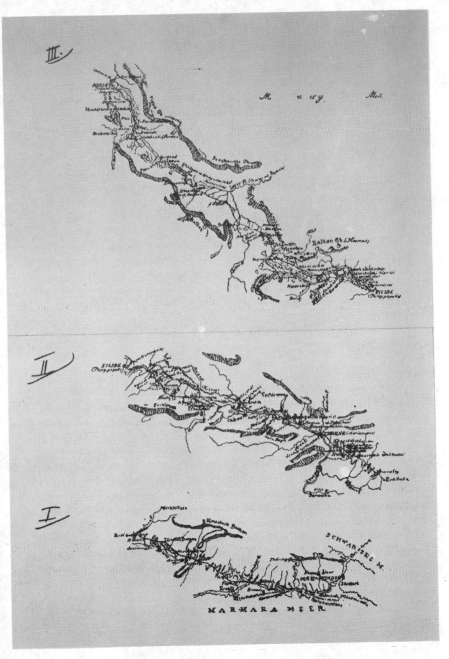

Military road from Constantinople to Nissa (lithographic sketch).
Roman figures were written in by Marx

earnings from the *Tribune* alone. From time to time I'm driven wild by the thought that I shall never get out of this mire.

You have not returned Lassalle's letter as you indicated you had in your last.[488] I *don't need it* but only want to be sure that it hasn't gone astray in the post or fallen into the wrong hands.

I have received an invitation from the LABOUR PARLIAMENT[489] to sit as HONORARY DELEGATE in Manchester (Nadaud and Louis Blanc likewise). I wrote today, thanking them for it, and made a few remarks which, according to how they are construed, could be either very extreme or very moderate.[a] I sent Jones your office address today.

The great Ruge intends to found a university (a free one) in America and, as Heinzen announces, 150 dollars has already been collected for this noble purpose.

The great Franz Sigel has become Dulon's son-in-law. What else has been happening among that crew you will discover from a parcel which will descend on you in a few days' time.

In yesterday's *Advertiser* there was a *military* (?) article by Urquhart[b] in which he maintains that the Turks should have sent their main army to the Dobrudja and assaulted the Russians from there. Cites General Valentini. I shall make sure to send you the issue.

I have written to Lassalle[490] and await further communications from him.

Tzschirner came to see me, didn't find me in, is going to America on a financial matter with his 80-year-old mother and will then settle over here. Claims he already knows you, or so Imandt says.

Your
K. M.

First published much abridged in *Der Briefwechsel zwischen F. Engels und K. Marx*, Bd. 2, Stuttgart, 1913 and in full in: Marx and Engels, *Works*, First Russian Edition, Vol. XXII, Moscow, 1929

Printed according to the original

Published in English for the first time

---

[a] K. Marx, 'Letter to the Labour Parliament'. - [b] D. Urquhart, 'What the Governments of England and Turkey Ought Severally to Do. To the Editor of *The Morning Advertiser*', *The Morning Advertiser*, No. 19566, 8 March 1854.

208

MARX TO ENGELS

IN MANCHESTER

[London, about 11 March 1854]

Dear Frederic,

Enclosed a letter from Lassalle.[491]

You would greatly oblige me by letting me have some military stuff for Tuesday.[a] The 2nd edition of *The Times*, which you'll get on Monday, contains sundry things on Shamyl, etc. If I don't produce anything on military affairs, even though it be only tittle-tattle, A.P.C.[b] will steal a march on me; he cribs unblushingly from the London newspapers.

Your

K. M.

First published in *Der Briefwechsel zwischen F. Engels und K. Marx*, Bd. 2, Stuttgart, 1913

Printed according to the original

Published in English for the first time

209

MARX TO ENGELS

IN MANCHESTER

[London,] 17th March, 1854

Dear Frederic,

I trust that you promptly consigned to the flames the letter I wrote you yesterday.[492] It was, of course, idiotic to make you in any way, I won't say answerable for Blanc, but even so much as to question you about him. In any case the whole thing's gone to pot *et il ne vaut pas*[c] your ever reverting to it.

---

a 14 March - b Aurelius Ferenc Pulszky - c and it's not worthwhile

Is the Mr John Petzler of the Labour Parliament that mad brute, the old London Petzler? Ask Heise some time.

The parcel for you has not yet gone off because I have not yet received Urquhart's article on military affairs.

Your
K. M.

First published in: Marx and Engels, *Works,* First Russian Edition, Vol. XXII, Moscow, 1929

Printed according to the original

Published in English for the first time

210

ENGELS TO MARX

IN LONDON

Manchester, 23 March 1854

Dear Marx,

I return Lassalle's letter herewith. At the time I forgot to enclose the first one, which is still here.[493] You'll have received the two half notes yesterday and the day before. T/B 58 166, Newcastle on Tyne, 17 August 1852, £5.

Lassalle's strategical operations are very diplomatic. His answer to the Enos and Rodosto affair is the foolish platitude, itself merely intended as dust in the eyes, that Constantinople must be protected[494]; if the 2 fleets and the Army of the Danube cannot protect it, then neither can 100,000 French and English. From his own standpoint, what he ought to have said was: if they are to be launched against Sevastopol or Odessa, they are, at any rate, closer to hand at Rodosto than in Malta or Toulon.

The notion that a move into Serbia would place the Austrians 'in the rear of the Turkish Army of the Danube' is basically wrong. The Austrians must make their crossing at Belgrade or not very far below it, or else enter Wallachia via Mehadia along the *left* bank of the Danube. In the first case they would find themselves in the *extension* of the Turkish left wing, in the second, to the front of it. That this would mean the immediate sacrifice of Kalafat and Vidin, with the exception of the garrison, is evident—but not that this Turkish left wing would be lost and its remnants compelled to fall back on the Shumla line. *Au contraire,*[a] 1. the *correct* tactics for the Austrians would be to march immediately on *Sofia* via Nissa, hence the correct tactics for the Turks would be to withdraw from Vidin, *likewise* to *Sofia.* Not having so far to go, they would be there *before* the Austrians and could either make a stand in the Balkans or withdraw towards Adrianople.[495]

2. Should the Austrians be stupid enough to march on Vidin, the Turks would *still* make for Sofia. This division of Omer Pasha's principal corps would not involve the fragmentation of his forces, since the new enemy would necessitate a new Adrianople-Sofia-Belgrade-Vidin operational line; thus the Turkish left wing would become an *independent* army.

3. But should Lassalle's peculiar strategy COME TO PASS, no amount of falling back on the Shumla line would avail, for the latter, having *already been outflanked* as a result of the sacrifice of *the highway* from Belgrade to Constantinople, would, on the contrary, have to be abandoned all the more precipitately in order to *assemble all available reserves at Adrianople* and advance against the first enemy to pass through the Balkans.

One can see, incidentally, that these lucubrations all emanate from that 'diplomatic source' which seems to enjoy showing off on the subject of strategic developments.

Tomorrow I shall be sending *The Daily News* a description of Kronstadt[496]; faulty though much of its fortifications may be, I'm afraid half a dozen screw ships of the line will nevertheless go to blazes before it knuckles under.

The HIGHWAYMEN have been kind enough to return Lupus his POCKET-BOOK minus 7 Prussian taler notes.[b] His philistines mean to do something towards making good the loss of his money and his watch, and he might even get some smart-money into the bargain. Borchardt is attending to his bruises, and so the thing is resolving itself.

> 'But as for the fright, the fright he got,
> There's no compensation for that.'[c]

Which is why he is somewhat *caduc*[d] and snappish, apparently in the belief that Heise and I were responsible for his foolishness, the drubbing he got and all.

---

[a] On the contrary - [b] See this volume, pp. 421 and 428. - [c] Probably a misquotation of Schiller's 'Das Lied von der Glocke'. - [d] decrepit

Who is this chap who is getting Heinzen to pass him off as an editor of the *Neue Rheinische Zeitung*?[a] See last batch of *Reforms,* No. 50 or thereabouts.

Your

F. E.

First published abridged in *Der Briefwechsel zwischen F. Engels und K. Marx*, Bd. 2, Stuttgart, 1913 and in full in: Marx and Engels, *Works,* First Russian Edition, Vol. XXII, Moscow, 1929

Printed according to the original

Published in English for the first time

211

MARX TO ENGELS

IN MANCHESTER

[London,] 29 MARCH 1854
28 Dean Street, Soho

Dear Engels,

I have not yet acknowledged receipt of the £5, or used the money for the intended purpose, or written—all for the same reason. I have been saddled with Pieper. Ten days ago he was thrown out of his lodgings and I OF COURSE had to take him in here. He has drawn a bill on the *Union* and, if it's not protested, one of the next mails from America should bring him the money. This week Freiligrath has, BESIDES, found him a German lesson which will bring in 15/- A WEEK. And he was to have secured a similar lesson at ABOUT 10/- through Meyer—who has gone back to Germany today and asks me to send you his regards. But he didn't turn up at the appointed place. Instead, he told Meyer that he was fed up with giving lessons. Feels his vocation is to be a *writer. Le malheureux!*[b]

There's still much I don't understand about Lupus' adventure.[c] Did it happen in the street? Doubtless after he'd been out on a drinking spree with you and Heise! What a DEEP IMPRESSION it made on my FAMILY you will gather from the enclosed letter of little Laura's, in which she relates the great *événement*[d] for Jenny and Edgar who were at school.

---

[a] See this volume, p. 423. - [b] Unfortunate man! - [c] See this volume, pp. 420 and 428. - [d] event

The diplomatic part of Lassalle—aside from the information, which is well done—is as bad as his military one. What he says about Palmerston is simply the gossip current on the Continent.[497]

Have you read the SECRET CORRESPONDENCE[498]? If the ministers who conducted it are allowed to conduct the war—as everything seems to indicate—the affair can only end in England's utter disgrace, although AT ALL INSTANCES the Continent will be thrown into a welcome confusion.

Enclosed an article on the war by Urquhart, of yesterday's date,[a] and cuttings from an earlier pamphlet on *his* military plans. I should like your detailed opinion of both.

One of the Prussian instructors with the Turks, whom I met by chance yesterday, says that the Turkish artillery is excellent but the army as a whole no more than an ornament, inasmuch as any vigorous action has been frustrated by Constantinople.

In your essay on the Russian RETREAT from Kalafat you say that the purpose of this manoeuvre was to set up camp in Odessa, having regard to the Anglo-French army. According to the latest news, however, it would seem that the Russians have crossed the Danube on the opposite side, or intend to do so. There might be some more detailed information to hand tomorrow, in which case you could let me have something about it the day after.[b] In my letter of the day before yesterday[499] I forbade the *Tribune,* which was really overdoing things, to annex as LEADERS anything except military pieces—*or else* omit my name altogether, since I don't want it to appear only beneath indifferent STUFF. For it is essential—and now is the moment—to show them by *military pieces* that they can*not* dispense with me.

If the *Times* commercial correspondent in Manchester has reported aright,[c] business must be in very poor shape. Serious FAILURES are expected down here any day. Likewise in Paris. It goes without saying that concerns which have long been laboriously staving off bankruptcy will choose the time when war is declared to go under with decorum.

I haven't yet seen your article in *The Daily News* and have certainly not overlooked it![496]

The *Naval and Military Gazette* maintains that the Russians bought a destructive device, invented in France and rejected by Louis Philippe's government, which continues to burn under

---

[a] D. Urquhart, 'How is the War to Be Carried on? To the Editor of *The Morning Advertiser*', *The Morning Advertiser*, No. 19583, 28 March 1854. - [b] See this volume, pp. 426-27. - [c] [Report on the cotton market in Manchester,] *The Times*, No. 21700, 28 March 1854.

water, and that they used it at Sinope, this being the explanation for the rapid and thorough destruction of the Turkish ships.

According to the *Hamburger Correspondent*, which must be regarded as a semi-Russian organ, Nicholas is to publish further documents, among them letters of Prince Albert.

No further news here. The 'Mader', mentioned by Mr Heinzen as being an editor of the *Neue Rheinische Zeitung*, is an individual quite unknown to me.[a]

Totus tuus,[b]

K. M.

I now have in my possession Hammer's *Geschichte des Osmanischen Reichs.*[500] Patience is needed to get through it. I've still got about ¼ left to read. It's at your disposal IF WANTED.

First published abridged in *Der Briefwechsel zwischen F. Engels und K. Marx*, Bd. 2, Stuttgart, 1913 and in full in: Marx and Engels, *Works*, First Russian Edition, Vol. XXII, Moscow, 1929

Printed according to the original

Published in English for the first time

212

ENGELS TO H. J. LINCOLN,
EDITOR OF *THE DAILY NEWS*[501]

IN LONDON

[Rough copy]

7 South Gate, Manchester,
30 March 1854. St. Mary's

Sir,

Perhaps I am not mistaken in supposing that at the present moment an offer to contribute to the *military department* of your paper may meet with some favour, even if the party offering his services be not, for the moment, an active member of the military profession, and though he be a foreigner to boot.

I suppose the actual qualifications of the party will be the main thing. As to these, nothing can show them better than half-a-dozen articles upon various military subjects, which you might submit to

---

[a] See this volume, p. 421. - [b] All yours

any military authority, if you should choose to do so. The higher the authority the better. I would ten times sooner be judged by Sir William Napier than by a subaltern martinet.

But I cannot expect you to give me even a trial, unless you know something more about me. I beg to state, therefore, that my military school has been the Prussian Artillery, a service which, if it is not what it might be, yet has produced the men who made 'the Turkish Artillery one of the best in Europe' as our friend Nicholas has laid it down. Later on, I had an occasion of seeing some active service during the insurrectionary war in South Germany, 1849. For many years the study of military science in all its branches has been one of my chief occupations, and the success, which my articles on the Hungarian Campaign, published at the time in the German Press, were fortunate enough to obtain, encourages me in the belief that I have not studied in vain. An acquaintance, more or less familiar, with most European languages, including Russian, Serbian, and a little Wallachian, opens to me the best sources of information and may, perhaps, prove useful to you in other respects. How far I am able to write correct and fluent English, my articles, of course, themselves must show. Any other information respecting myself I shall be happy to give, or else you may obtain it from your educational contributor Dr Watts whom I have been acquainted with for more than ten years.[502]

I have for some time past thought of making you an offer of this kind, but, considered the matter hardly worth your while as long as war was not actually declared and the whole *critique* of Danubian strategy was confined to profound disquisitions as to what share of the blame attaching to the inconceivable proceedings in Bulgaria was due to Lord Aberdeen, and what to Omer Pasha. Now the matter is different. A local war may be a mere *simulaerum* of a war; an European war must be a reality. Besides this, I avow, another reason restrained me. I was not then prepared, as I am now, with the necessary maps, plans, and special information respecting the theatre of war and the belligerent parties, and I should have been sorry to send you a single line based upon other than the very best information obtainable.

My absence, not only from the seat of war, but also (for the moment, at least) from your own headquarters circumscribes pretty nearly the sort of contributions I could offer you. They would confine themselves to descriptions of those portions of the theatre of war, where actual hostilities are going on; statements of, and observations on, the military organisation, strength, chances, and possible operations of the belligerent armies; critical remarks on actual engagements, and, from time to time, *resumés* (to use the French word) of the operations, say of a month or six weeks, according to events. As the fullest information of what has actually happened is necessary to form a correct judgment, I should very seldom have to write on the strength of mere telegraphic dispatches, but have to wait, generally, for the arrival of more detailed news; thus the loss of a day or two would be less important for my contributions, if that would make them better; and therefore my presence in London might, for a time at least, be dispensed with. In case you should wish me to extend my contributions to a wider circle, I should have no objection and await your proposals.

Should you, however, receive my offer favourably, it may be that in a couple of months I should be enabled to come to London altogether; in the meantime, I might slip over, if desired, to confer with you.

As to politics, I should mix them up as little as possible with military criticism. There is but one good line of policy in war: to go at it with the greatest rapidity and energy, to beat your opponent, and force him to submit to your terms. If the allied governments do this, I should acknowledge it; if they should cripple or tie the hands of their commanders, I should speak out against it. I do wish the Russians may get a good beating, but if they fight well, I am that much of a soldier, that I should give the devil his due. For the remainder, I should stick to the principle, that military science, like mathematics or geography, has no particular political opinion

Now for positive proposals. I do not expect that the description of Kronstadt sent herewith will enable you to form any idea of what you may expect from me. But if it should appear to you that I may be of some service to your paper, a provisional arrangement might be come to, by which you would retain your entire liberty to refuse my further collaboration, if found unsuitable, while a fair remuneration was guaranteed to me for my labour and expenses. For you cannot but know that to write on military operations, requires the possession of numerous and expensive maps and books, for which due allowance should be made as entering into the cost of production.

Supposing, then, I sent you a series of papers giving a full account of the military and naval force of Russia, its organisation, actual strength and efficiency (as far as can be ascertained), together with a military account of the theatre of war, the lines of operation and defence on the Baltic, the Black Sea, Danubian and Polish frontiers, including the system of fortresses. The enclosed Kronstadt article would form one of the series and might be postponed till its place arrived. My information upon these subjects is, I believe, first-rate, derived exclusively from printed (and not from any mysterious) sources. I could furnish an article per week, say one or two columns, and more, if required.

Should you deem this proceeding too systematical, the account of Kronstadt might be followed up by a similar one of the permanent fortifications of Sevastopol and the other Russian fortified harbours (wherever obtainable), to be concluded by some observations on the chances of naval attacks against land batteries, drawn from history and from the best theoretical sources such as Sir Howard Douglas.[a]

If you require reviews of military works, I could also undertake them. For instance Col. Chesney's *Russo-Turkish Campaigns*; for this book I am, I may say, admirably provided with materials.

I conclude this lengthy epistle in offering you, also, a few remarks on the importance or rather non-importance of the Russian passage across the Danube: these are at your service at a moment's notice.

If you take my offer into consideration, I shall be glad to receive a few lines as soon as possible so as to be enabled to set to work at once. In the meantime, etc.

First published in: Marx and Engels, *Works*, First Russian Edition, Vol. XXII, Moscow, 1929

Reproduced from the original

Published in English for the first time

213

ENGELS TO MARX

IN LONDON

Manchester, 3 April 1854

Dear Marx,

The crossing of the Danube is of a purely defensive nature. It is proof that the Russians are withdrawing from the greater part of Wallachia. They have had 7 infantry divisions in Wallachia, one in

[a] H. Douglas, *A Treatise on Naval Gunnery*, London, 1820.

reserve at Ismail and, behind it, Cheodayev's corps, making 3 more divisions. Cheodayev can, at the very best, be at Jassy. The remaining 8 divisions, including cavalry, etc., etc., amount to less than 110,000 men. Hence, with the possibility of an Anglo-French landing in their rear, it behoves them to secure the most favourable position in which they will not be cut off, and with the minimum possible sacrifice of ground. Here they had only 2 alternatives: Either a direct withdrawal to the Sereth, this and the Lower Danube being chosen as the line of defence (Fokshani, Galatz, Ismail) or, 2. a DASH to the Dobrudja, shifting the front to Kustendje, Hirsova, Oltenitza and Bucharest, with Trajan's Wall, Danube and Argish as the first line of defence, Buseo as the second, and Sereth as the third. This, at any rate, is the best plan, especially since new ground would be gained on one wing to make up for that abandoned on the other, and thus the retreat would look like an advance, and military decorum would be preserved. Possession of the Dobrudja would shorten the Russian front and, if the worst came to the worst, would leave open the line of withdrawal to Chotin on the Dniester, even if there were landings at Akkerman or Odessa.[503]

Things seem to be working out with *The Daily News.* I didn't write until last week,[a] after I had observed the English proprieties by obtaining a REFERENCE from father Watts, who also writes for it (father Watts, BY THE BY, has given up his SHOP and is now MANAGING DIRECTOR of a PEOPLE'S PROVIDENT ASSURANCE CO. in which capacity he will shortly be setting himself up in your vicinity, 47 Charing Cross [Road]. He and all his officials are letting their beards grow and look like Wasserpolacken[504]). Today I've had a letter from the CHIEF EDITOR, Lincoln, who seems altogether agreeable (I had offered to start off with articles on the Russian army, navy and fortifications), and he is eager for me to send him the articles.[505] So I don't feel at all nervous. That the fellows are in a quandary as regards things military is evident from their acceptance of Schimmelpfennigian nonsense of a kind totally incomprehensible to anyone unacquainted with Bülow's books, and my racily written and unlaboured letter will have opened up for them prospects of quite a different order. Once they have got interested in my stuff (N.B. I asked for money straight away), I intend really to impress the jackasses. Tomorrow I shall send them something no one else can provide: plans of Hirsova, Matchin, Isaktsha and Tultsha. This business has really taken a load off my mind, for a source of cash

---

[a] See this volume, pp. 423-26.

was *absolutely necessary.* If all goes well, in the summer, when my old man comes over, I shall chuck up commerce and move to London; but then I shall at any rate be coming over some time before Whitsun to make definite arrangements with the chaps.

Needless to say, Lupus had been out drinking with us. As usual, staggers off tight as a drum so that there's no holding him, loses his way, finds himself in a low pub at the opposite end of the town from where he lives. Treats 6 *maquereaux*[a] and 2 whores who were at the bar, shows his shekels, exits followed by the *maquereaux*, and so on. That's *his* ACCOUNT. However, there's more to the matter than meets the eye; for instance, on coming to his senses he didn't go home but went off with an Englishman, a total stranger, who put him up (not 200 paces from his lodgings) *moyennant*[b] one shilling. In short, *il y a là des choses que M. Lupus veut cacher, sans doute quelque vieille fille.*[c]

The story of the Russians' *boulets asphyxiants*[d] is nonsense. The French have something of the kind, but it doesn't destroy ships, merely kills people. You might send me Hammer some time, particularly about the more recent times. About Urquhart one of these days. It's bad luck about Pieper. As regards the money you can, of course, dispose of it as you please. *I* don't give a damn whether my brother-in-law[e] gets it or not.

Your
· F. E.

First published abridged in *Der Briefwechsel zwischen F. Engels und K. Marx*, Bd. 2, Stuttgart, 1913 and in full in: Marx and Engels, *Works*, First Russian Edition, Vol. XXII, Moscow, 1929

Printed according to the original

Published in English for the first time

214

MARX TO ENGELS

IN MANCHESTER

[London,] 4 April 1854
[28 Dean Street, Soho]

Dear Engels,

From Cluss' letter, enclosed herewith,[506] you will see what a worthy trick has been played on him by Dr Kellner and friend Weydemeyer. The latter, instead of enlightening him as to the

---

[a] pimps - [b] at a charge of - [c] there are things here that Mr Lupus wants to hide, doubtless some old maid - [d] asphyxiating shot (see this volume, pp. 422-23) - [e] Emil Blank

status quo, has got him into a pretty fix, a service which friend Weydemeyer regularly performs for his friends.

I am delighted about *The Daily News.* I shall have a look today and see if they've published anything yet. I HOPE, SIR, YOU WILL LEAVE MANCHESTER, SIR, FOR EVER, SIR. One gets horribly used to this SIR (or rather SAR!) when one is compelled to read the parliamentary debates each week, especially THE SPEECHES OF Lord John Russell. The fellow can be boiled down to just the 2 words: 'NOW, SAR!'

As you will see from the enclosed, Pieper has received his first bill from Washington, and yesterday evening again acquired lodgings of his own. He now struts around like a turkeycock. Not only earns money, but as an author, and not only as an author, but as a politician! For the time being he has, or at least pretends to have, forsworn London's public PETTICOATS and is on the look-out for some healthy paramour. Social standing no object. Nor yet, perhaps, age. But health. THAT IS THE THING. Experience has taught the good youth to regard the sex from a medical point of view. Depicted in a state of undress, the good youth might serve as a cautionary example. Now that he's under his own steam again, I have told him about your offer to help him should he get a negative answer or a protested bill from Weydemeyer. There could no longer be any harm in giving him your message, but the good youth who, all things considered, is *bon garçon,*[a] was deeply impressed.

At this particular juncture, just when you have opened fire in *The Daily News,* it is vital you shouldn't leave me in the lurch over the *Tribune.* Otherwise the fellows, nettled as they are by my recent statement,[b] and likewise readers of *The Daily News,* might well believe that now—when all the newspapers are anxious to make a splash with their military stuff—I am selling THE BETTER PART OF MYSELF in London and the OFFAL in New York. The fellows would be capable of chucking me out, seeing that they already have one correspondent here and one in Liverpool. Their paper would be somewhat the worse for it, but £200 to the good which, after all, is worth the trouble. Hence what is necessary above all is to tempt them once more into printing a military article as a LEADER. Then I can again be sure of them. In one of its recent issues the *N. Y. Herald* ridicules the 'MILITARY EDITOR OF THE TRIBUNE' for prescribing a plan of campaign for Omer Pasha and crying treason now that it is not carried out.

Palmerston in Three Epochs by Washington Wilks. This book

---

[a] a good lad - [b] See this volume, p. 422.

consists of two epochs. In the first, Washington Wilks has most blatantly and stupidly cribbed from my articles in the *Tribune*.ᵃ The second is a longer version of the chapter on Hungary from Urquhart's *Progress of Russia*, padded out with the help of 'Blue Books'. Wretched though the concoction is and betraying at every turn the fellow's total lack of knowledge—true plagiarist's ignorance—it has nevertheless enabled him to shoulder his way into the London MEETINGS, to gain the protection of Urquhart and his clique and to set himself up in London as a 'PUBLIC CHARACTER'.

The idea of 'betrayal' by the Ministry is beginning to spread among the philistines here and, if the fellows venture to play the same game as in 1840 and '46,[507] there may be trouble.

Your
K. Marx

First published abridged in *Der Briefwechsel zwischen F. Engels und K. Marx*, Bd. 2, Stuttgart, 1913 and in full in: Marx and Engels, *Works*, First Russian Edition, Vol. XXII, Moscow, 1929

Printed according to the original

Published in English for the first time

215

MARX TO FERDINAND LASSALLE

IN DÜSSELDORF

London, 6 April 1854
(You know the address)

Dear Lassalle,

Your letter of 7 March safely received. I should like to make a few comments, firstly on your military, and secondly on your diplomatic, VIEWS.

ad 1. To my comment[508] regarding Enos and Rodosto, you reply—agreeing in this with the English ministerial papers—that

---

ᵃ K. Marx, 'Lord Palmerston'.

Constantinople must be protected.[a] If the two fleets in the Black Sea and the Army of the Danube cannot protect it, then neither can 100,000 French and English. I do not, of course, deny that, if they are to be launched against Sevastopol or Odessa, they are closer to hand at Rodosto than in Malta or Toulon.

The notion that a move into Serbia would place the Austrians 'in the rear of the Turkish Army of the Danube' does not seem to me quite correct. The Austrians must make their crossing at Belgrade or not very far below it, or else enter Wallachia via *Mehadia* along the *left* bank of the Danube. In the first case they would find themselves in the *extension* of the Turkish left wing, in the second to the *front* of it. That this would mean the immediate sacrifice of Kalafat and Vidin, with the exception of the garrison which would remain there, is evident—but not that this Turkish left wing would be lost and its remnants compelled to fall back on the Shumla line. *Au contraire,*[b] the correct tactics for the Austrians would be to march immediately on Sofia via Nissa, hence the correct tactics for the Turks would be to withdraw from Vidin, *likewise* to Sofia. Not having so far to go, they would be there *before* the Austrians and could either make a stand in the Balkans or withdraw towards Adrianople.

Should the Austrians allow themselves to be enticed into marching on Vidin, the Turks would still make for Sofia. This division of Omer Pasha's principal corps would not involve the fragmentation of his forces, since the new enemy would necessitate a new Adrianople-Sofia-Belgrade-Vidin operational line. Thus the Turkish left wing would become an *independent* army.

Should the strategy you postulate be adopted in spite of all this, no amount of falling back on the Shumla line would avail, for the latter, having *already been outflanked* as a result of the sacrifice of *the highway* from Belgrade to Constantinople, would have to be abandoned all the more precipitately in order to assemble *all available reserves at Adrianople* and advance against the first enemy to pass through the Balkans.

ad 2. Ad vocem[c] *Palmerston.* Your view of Palmerston is the one prevailing on the Continent and among the liberal majority of the English public.[497] As for myself, I am of the unalterable opinion that Palmerston—*en passant* Princess Lieven paid his debts for him in 1827, Prince Lieven got him into the FOREIGN OFFICE in 1830 and Canning, on his deathbed, told people to beware of him—is a

---

[a] See also this volume, p. 419 - [b] On the contrary - [c] as for

Russian agent. I came to this conclusion after the most conscientious and painstaking scrutiny of the whole of his career and, indeed, of the 'Blue Books', the 'Parliamentary Debates' and the pronouncements of his own diplomatic agents.[509] Though far from amusing and very time-consuming to boot, the work has proved rewarding in so far as it provides the key to the secret diplomatic history of the past 30 years.—(*En passant.* Some of my *Tribune* articles on Palmerston have again been reprinted in London as separate pamphlets in 50,000 copies.[465])

Palmerston is no genius, a genius would not lend himself to such a role. But he is a most talented man and a consummate tactician. His artistry does not lie in serving Russia, but rather in contriving to maintain the role of a 'TRULY ENGLISH MINISTER' while so engaged. The only difference between him and Aberdeen is that Aberdeen serves Russia because he doesn't understand her, while Palmerston serves her although he does. Hence the first is Russia's avowed partisan, the second her secret agent, the first gratis, the second in return for fees received. Even if he himself now wished to do so, he could not turn *against* Russia because he is at her mercy and must live in constant fear of being immolated in Petersburg. This is the man who in 1829 condemned Aberdeen's policy as not pro-Russian enough,[a] who was told by Robert Peel in the House of Commons[b] that he didn't know whose representative he was, who sacrificed the Poles in 1831, who imposed the Treaty of Unkiar-Skelessi on the Porte in 1833,[510] who abandoned the Caucasus and the Danube estuary to Russia in 1836, who engineered the treaties of 1840 and 1841[458] and a new Holy Alliance against France, who conducted the Afghan War in the Russian interest,[511] who, in 1831, 1836 and 1840, paved the way for the incorporation of Cracow, only to protest against it in 1846, etc.[507] No matter what he engaged in, he worked against his country's commercial interests on the pretext of protecting them. E.g., in the matter of Neapolitan sulphur.[512] He frustrated advantageous trade agreements which were about to be ratified with France. This is the man who delivered up Italy and Hungary.[513] Had he merely worked against revolutionary peoples, it would have been understandable. But in questions involving exclusively British interests, he invariably contrived in *the most*

---

[a] Palmerston, [Speech in the House of Commons on 1 June 1829,] G. H. Francis, *Opinions and Policy of the Right Viscount Palmerston*, London, 1852, pp. 123-26. - [b] Probably Robert Peel's Speech in the House of Commons on 16 February 1830, ibid., p. 138.

subtle manner to betray these to Russia. Incidentally, people here are beginning to understand him. Looking forward to hearing from you soon,

Your

K. M.

First published in: *F. Lassalle. Nachgelassene Briefe und Schriften,* Bd. III, Stuttgart-Berlin, 1922

Printed according to the original

Published in English for the first time

216

MARX TO ENGELS

IN MANCHESTER

London, 19 April 1854
28 Dean Street, Soho

Dear Frederic,

In Cluss' letter, enclosed herewith, you will note on the one hand Schimmelpfennig's admiration of your military stuff—for which I am given the credit; on the other, his crafty critical reservations.[514]

Should today's report (in *The Times*) from Gorchakov and the report in the *Northern Bee*[a] on the manoeuvres on the Circassian coast[515] give you occasion to send me a LETTER for the *Tribune,* you might drop a few anonymous remarks about Schimmelpfennig's opinion which, by the by, is commanding much attention.

What is the significance of *The Times* suddenly ceasing its attacks on the ministry (*quant à la guerre*[b])?

You will see from the American newspaper cuttings that for six months the 'Central Committee'[103]—of this I received private confirmation yesterday—had had a considerable amount of money at its disposal. The letter from Karger—Ledru's famulus— in the *Pionier* shows how Ledru, and with him the entire orthodox emigration, are deceiving themselves as to the significance and future prospects of this same Ledru. He and the Germans have agreed that as soon as he is Great Khan of France, he will order a

---

[a] *Северная пчела* - [b] as regards the war

French army—but under the German command of Ruge-Blind-Goegg—to invade Germany.

Enclosed also a map of Constantinople which may be of interest to you.

Schily is off to Paris with official permission. He will represent the 'house' over there and Cornelius here.

Bangya is in Erzerum—colonel, of course—is called Moham-med Bey, has had himself circumcised, and embraced the Koran. Possibly sent to General Guyon as a spy.

Damned lovely weather. A pity one can't make better use of it.

According to a letter received yesterday from Trier, Edgar[a] is leaving Texas on a six months' trip to London and Germany.

Your
K. M.

I can see that this letter will be too bulky, so shall send the cuttings in my next.

First published abridged in *Der Briefwechsel zwischen F. Engels und K. Marx,* Bd. 2, Stuttgart, 1913 and in full in: Marx and Engels, *Works,* First Russian Edition, Vol. XXII, Moscow, 1929

Printed according to the original

Published in English for the first time

217

ENGELS TO MARX

IN LONDON

Manchester, 20 April 1854

Dear Marx,

It's all off with *The Daily News*[501] and, in fact, I have grounds for assuming that, by his indiscretion. Monsieur Pieper has played me a dirty trick which I shall not forget in a hurry. Everything was ALL RIGHT, only the fee to be settled, my article[b] *already set up in print*—I have the proof copy in my pocket. As long ago as a week last Wednesday I wrote to the fellows saying I would accept their

---

[a] Edgar von Westphalen - [b] F. Engels, 'The Russian Army'.

usual terms, and today the answer finally arrives saying that the articles are TOO PROFESSIONAL, that, much as they would like to, they cannot use them and concluding very politely with an offer of two guineas for my TROUBLE and the good advice that I should approach a MILITARY PAPER. Needless to say, I shall accept neither.[516]

I can think of only one explanation for this strange behaviour: Pieper who, to judge by a foolish letter he wrote me a week ago,[517] knew about the thing, must have been talking big about it and thus, by the well-known telegraphic medium of émigré gossip, the story came to the ears of Kinkel or some other wretched German blighter acquainted with *The Daily News* and then, of course, nothing was easier than to represent Engels, the MILITARY MAN, as no more than a former one-year volunteer, a communist and a clerk by trade, thus putting a stop to everything. The politeness of the *refus*[a] was not for my benefit, of course, but Watts's. The way the letter is written does not preclude my applying again, but only to be relegated to the PENNY-A-LINERS.

I should be greatly obliged if you could find out who let the cat out of the bag; needless to say, Mr Schimmelpfennig's eulogies[b] are a poor SET-OFF for this *échec*.[c]

On top of that, the shilly-shallying of the *Daily News* chaps has meant that in the meantime some of my sources here have become known through the German press—the Moltke,[d] which I have found enormously helpful, is now scarcely any good to me at all and in a fortnight all the rest will have gone the same way, and I wouldn't dream of risking another £5 on the thing ON SPECULATION.

I feel very much inclined to finish the articles on Russian military power and send them to *The Times*. If they published them, what an ass *The Daily News* would look! But a second *échec* would have its drawbacks, for then I should look a complete ass. That's why it's so damnable my not being in London, when everything would be perfectly simple. What do you think? Write at once and let me know.[e]

About the other things in a day or two. I can't let you have the article on the Russian bulletin[f] before the next sailing; it needs to be closely studied and compared with the map, otherwise one risks making an ass of oneself here as well.

If only you could screw more money out of the *Tribune*, I'd turn my back on the whole, rotten English press, where blackguardly German interlopers persuade stupid editors to reject the best

---

[a] refusal - [b] See this volume, p. 433. - [c] failure - [d] H. von Moltke, *Der russisch-türkische Feldzug in der europäischen Türkei 1828 und 1829.* - [e] See this volume, pp. 438-39. - [f] ibid., p. 433.

articles, and I'd send you one or two *Tribune* articles every week. But to wear our fingers to the bone writing for £200, *c'est trop fort.*[a]

Write at once and tell me what you think of this rotten business; the whole affair has put me terribly out of temper. Of all the band there's nobody we can rely on except each other.

Steffen and Dronke were here at Easter; I didn't at all care for Dronke who has acquired a revolting habit of bragging like a *commis-voyageur.*[b] The fellow's becoming a regular loafer.

Your

F. E.

First published abridged in *Der. Briefwech-sel zwischen F. Engels und K. Marx*, Bd. 2, Stuttgart, 1913 and in full in: Marx and Engels, *Works*, First Russian Edition, Vol. XXII, Moscow, 1929

Printed according to the original

Published in English for the first time

218

ENGELS TO MARX

IN LONDON

[Manchester, 21 April 1854]

Dear Marx,

I have just bought Monsieur Schimmelpfennig's pamphlets here.[c] If you would like me to review them for the *Tribune*, let me know soon. You shall have the article on the Danube crossing on Monday, unless something of greater importance crops up.[d]

Do you think Blind capable of playing a trick on me with *The Daily News*?[e] The fellow has his contacts with the paper, if I'm not mistaken. Monsieur Herzen's nonsense in today's issue of the same

---

[a] it's too much - [b] commercial traveller - [c] A. Schimmelpfennig, *The War between Turkey and Russia. A Military Sketch*. - [d] On Monday, 24 April, Engels wrote 'The Turkish War'. - [e] See this volume, p. 438.

paper[518] proves that he, too, has connections. Is there any other German officer in London who might be in collusion with the paper?

Before approaching another newspaper I shall get some more material together, which will mean a delay of perhaps 3 weeks. *N'importe*,[a] the better the stuff I have, the better my chances and, after all, the material will still be there for the *Tribune*.

If I weren't so damnably stuck for cash, I'd invite you up here. But just now it's not possible and I must first move into PRIVATE LODGINGS again. Had there been a prospect of clinching matters with *The Daily News*, I had intended to come to London for Whitsuntide but now the journey would have little point. *N'importe*, perhaps I shall come all the same.

What with the war, innumerable military works to be studied, sundry drinking bouts, etc., etc., I have of late fallen very much behind with my work at the office and, precisely because my mind was full of other things, have perpetrated a mass of blunders, all of which end up in goods being refused and other disasters. I shall now have to make up for this, for the very good reason that my old man is coming over in 3 months time; moreover I have been very remiss about corresponding with him; he's still waiting for things he should have had six months ago. I am now having to make up for all this, which means a great deal of effort. However I believe that a fortnight's hard labour in the office will see me through.

Let me have the newspaper cuttings; without them, Cluss' letter is incomprehensible.[b]

Bangya will be sending the Russians some fine reports from Erzerum. I wish the Prussians would finally go ahead and declare war on England, in which case the farce would be in full swing and my old man would not come over. I have neglected him horribly and in any case the financial aspect has all the makings of a row.

Enclosed the proof of the *Daily News* article.[c] Let me have it back soon. I'm very glad I've got the thing; the fellows won't be able to make a splash with it now.

Apropos. Is 'Bericht über die Kriegs-Operationen der Russischen Truppen gegen die Ungarischen Rebellen im Jahre 1849'[d] — (published 1851) *available* in London? And if so, who has it? I

---

[a] No matter - [b] See this volume, p. 433. - [c] F. Engels, 'The Russian Army'. - [d] written by Y. Tolstoi, published anonymously

have ordered the book but won't get it in under three weeks. If I had it I could *at once* enter into relations with *The Times*. It costs $1^1/_2$ talers, so nothing would really be lost by buying two.

Your
F. E.

First published abridged in *Der Briefwech-sel zwischen F. Engels und K. Marx*, Bd. 2, Stuttgart, 1913 and in full in: Marx and Engels, *Works*, First Russian Edition, Vol. XXII, Moscow, 1929

Printed according to the original

Published in English for the first time

219

MARX TO ENGELS [234]

IN MANCHESTER

[London,] 22 April 1854
28 Dean Street, Soho

Dear Frederic,

Pieper, at any rate, is not to blame for the business with *The Daily News*,[a] because he has had absolutely nothing to do with the émigrés for the past six months. Blind IS CONNECTED WITH THE *Advertiser*, not *The Daily News*. Herzen's crew—Krapülinski Worcell,[b] and the blackguardly Golovin—have been *positivement*[c] connected with the *D. N.* ever since Urquhart's influence got them thrown out of the *Advertiser*. Mr O. von Wenckstern has transferred from *The Times* to the *D.N.*, but is no longer in London, that JUDICIOUS PAPER having sent him as MILITARY COMMISSIONER to Omer Pasha. The belletristic blighter! It's more than likely that the fellow has introduced other German blackguards out there. However it is the Russians I chiefly suspect. So WISELY MANAGED is *The Daily News* that, as is shown by the last RETURN of newspaper stamps, its sales have plummeted since 1851 and it now ranks after the *Herald* in the newspaper hierarchy.

I consider that you should *immediately* send the article[d] to *The Times* as it stands and without waiting for one scrap of additional

---

[a] See this volume, pp. 423-26 and 427. - [b] Worcell is thus called after a character in Heine's satirical poem 'Zwei Ritter'. - [c] definitely - [d] F. Engels, 'The Fortress of Kronstadt'.

material (I shall see if the 'Bericht über die Kriegs-operationen'[a] is available here). *The Times* will still be short of material next week since the parliamentary recess, though supposed to end on 27 April, will not be over until 1 May. Hence it will be glad of anything it can get and, since the people there possess far more literary and political tact than the bunglers on the *D.N.* and would be prepared to accept an article from the devil himself if it were interesting enough, I *fermement*[b] believe that they would publish it *at once*. At the same time it would be your REVENGE on the other rag. But should your approach to *The Times* misfire— which I doubt—you may be sure that 1. nobody will hear of it, since I shan't tell a soul; 2. the reviews will be sure to take it. Finally, I would again advise you not to wait, but to send this first article *quite unchanged* to *The Times*.

As for Schimmelpfennig,[c] I think it would be doing the chap too great an honour to deal with him in the *Tribune*. I suggest that, in one of your private letters to me, you let me have sufficient to pass on to Cluss for an article in the *Reform*.

Of late the *Tribune* has again been appropriating all my articles as LEADERS and putting *my* name to nothing but rubbish. It has appropriated, for example, a detailed account of Austrian finances,[d] an article on the Greek insurrection,[e] etc. On top of that their now 'congenital' habit of making a splash with your military stuff. I *positivement* intend—as soon as Dana has replied to my last admonition[519]—to ask for a higher fee, citing in particular the EXPENSES incurred in respect of the military articles. Don't you agree? The fellows ought to pay at least £3 per article. They lay out £500 on sending Taylor to India, and the chap's reports from there are worse and shorter—what could he get to know about a country like that on a quick TRIP?—than my own sent them from here on the same subject.[520] £3 per article would enable me to get out of the mire at last.

There's been an odd business with Urquhart—whom, by the by, I have never once met in London since our first *entrevue*.[f] The ministerial *Globe* published on SATURDAY[g] [a] FURIOUS ONSLAUGHT ON HIM, saying amongst other things that, while he might pick up converts here and there, this wouldn't go on for long.

---

a See this volume, p. 437. - b firmly - c See this volume, p. 436. - d K. Marx, 'Austrian Bankruptcy'. - e K. Marx, 'The Greek Insurrection'. - f interview (see this volume, pp. 412-13). - g 15 April

* 'Where is Mr Anstey? Where Mr Monteith etc. and where that Goliath of the new revolution, Mr Marx?' 'All these gentlemen have seen the folly of their ways, and returned to the habits of good society.'*

Then, in Thursday's issue of *The Morning Advertiser, 'An Urquhartite'* declares that:

* 'If continuing to pose implicit confidence in Mr Urquhart's views be proof of folly these individuals have certainly not recovered their reason, and also must still be without the pale of good society.'*

And then proceeds to specify:

* 'Mr Marx, however, I am happy to say, is as energetic and valuable [a] supporter as ever of Mr Urquhart's.'*a

So far I've done nothing about this, but am biding my time. An opportunity will present itself for disowning Mr Urquhart. I find it all the more outrageous as he knows, since I have told him so, that I agree with him in *nothing* save the matter of Palmerston, and on that point it wasn't *he* who showed me the way. *Mais il faut attendre.*b But there is one difficulty. There is a very stupid Urquhartite by the name of Marx,c not the one meant by the *Globe*. If I publicly disown Urquhart, he'll say he didn't mean me, but the other Marx. Incidentally, it is evident from the *Globe* that Mr Palmerston has been paying me the greatest attention.

Pieper grows more vapidly complacent every day. Such is his mopping and mowing that his face is more criss-crossed with lines than a map of both the Indies. Old Malvolio! Little Jenny always refers to him now as Prince Charming, the son of Wunderhorn.d In my next I shall tell you some comical tales about 'Prince Charming' who, as his sister's letters reveal, regards himself as Byron and Leibniz rolled into one.

Salut.

Your
K. M.

First published abridged in *Der Briefwechsel zwischen F. Engels und K. Marx,* Bd. 2, Stuttgart, 1913 and in full in: Marx and Engels, *Works,* First Russian Edition, Vol. XXII, Moscow, 1929

Printed according to the original

Published in English in full for the first time

---

a 'Mr Urquhart and *The Globe*. To the Editor of *The Morning Advertiser*', *The Morning Advertiser,* No. 19603, 20 April 1854. - b But we must wait. - c Francis Marx - d Character in the introductory lines to 'Des Knaben Wunderhorn', a nineteenth-century collection of folk songs compiled by Arnim and Brentano.

220

ENGELS TO MARX

IN LONDON

[Manchester, about 24 April 1854]

Dear Marx,

It's absolutely impossible to do the things for *The Times* until I have more material, i. e. in a week or fortnight. I shall then finish them off straight away.

As regards Schimmelpfennig,[a] I shall write something with Heise. The thing must be done in such a way that the fellow can't reply, hence very accurately or not at all.

Something must be done about Heise; matters cannot continue very much longer as they are. So I am writing to Cluss today,[521] asking him to tell me whether he can put Heise in touch with an Anglo-American paper—the fellow writes passable English—and 2. whether the *Reform* could pay him. Both of these on condition that Eccarius will not suffer as a result, for he, after all, has first claim. I have informed Cluss that if there is any objection of this kind you will advise him by next Tuesday's STEAMER. At the same time I notified Cluss of the Schimmelpfennig article, so that they don't do anything stupid in New York.

I can't write another word today.

Your
F. E.

Kossuth—magnificent![522]

First published in: Marx and Engels, *Works,* First Russian Edition, Vol. XXII, Moscow, 1929

Printed according to the original

Published in English for the first time

---

[a] See this volume, pp. 436 and 439.

221

MARX TO ENGELS

IN MANCHESTER

[London,] 29 April 1854
28 Dean Street, Soho

Dear Engels,

A few days before Heise left I had a scene with him in the presence of others over 'The Knight of the Noble Consciousness'. He came out against us as the Knight's[a] steadfast (secret) supporter or AT LEAST as a venomous INDEPENDENT. The affair brewed up into a scandal. I thought it unnecessary to write to you about it 1. because you knew Heise well enough, 2. because he wrote to me, humbly asking to be recommended to you and I didn't want to give him a letter of Uriah.[b]

The man may, of course, have come over to us altogether, though I cannot regard his attaching himself to us when in need as proof of this. *At all events,* I feel that you, for your part, shouldn't get too deeply involved with Heise. Temper your trust in him and above all do not write anything *jointly* with the lad. Before he can be co-opted and thus 'set up' in the eyes of the public, MORE PROOFS OF HIS SINCERITY ARE WANTED. We have had too many beastly experiences not to have become cautious and *tant soit peu*[c] mistrustful.

Letter enclosed with cuttings from Cluss.[523]

Imandt informs me that Blanc told him you had written to Blanc saying you would be coming up here on a visit. Is there anything in it?

Your
K. M.

First published in: Marx and Engels, *Works,* First Russian Edition, Vol. XXII, Moscow, 1929

Printed according to the original

Published in English for the first time

---

[a] Willich - [b] 2 Samuel 11:14, 15. - [c] just a little

222

ENGELS TO MARX

IN LONDON

Manchester, 1 May 1854

Dear Marx,

The business of Heise is really rather disastrous.[a] If the chap had behaved dubiously in regard to *party matters*, you might at least have let me know. *As it was*, I could only suppose that, for a new convert, he was PERFECTLY SAFE. I hadn't met him before, except for a couple of days in the Palatinate; seeing him in London as part of the intimate circle and, like Meyer, apparently a special favourite of yours, I naturally concluded that the fellow had already done penance down there, had undergone his *épreuves*[b] and earned your good graces. Hitherto I have treated him accordingly and, since he had nothing to do and is in other ways a cheerful sort of chap, I've been going round with him more than with anyone else. Moreover, now that the philistines have got to know that I'm living with Mary[c] and this has got to stop, I have taken lodgings NEXT DOOR TO HIM, though I haven't yet moved in. Well, all this is exceedingly difficult to set right now, and I can see only one way of doing it: from your letter I can only conclude that you gave him a letter for me. *This I have not received.*[d] Write to me at once so that I can question him about it.

There were two reasons why I did the Schimmelpfennig article with him[524]: 1. because I wanted the fellow to be given a dressing-down without *myself* appearing to be working for the *Reform,* 2. because it was absolutely essential that Heise be given something to do to get him out of his indolent ways. The article is very good and, though marred here and there by Heise's style, gives Mr Schimmelpfennig some rough treatment. The thing can be of no further benefit to Heise, for he'll never be able to write another article of the kind; on the other hand, the business greatly impressed him by showing him how surely and on what a firm 'basis' we operate. However, even this wouldn't have happened had I been informed, and at least the fellow wouldn't have cost me so much; as it is, I have him round my neck and, *au bout du*

---

[a] See this volume, p. 442. - [b] tests - [c] Mary Burns - [d] See this volume, pp. 442 and 445.

compte,[a] am more or less responsible for his household debts, etc., etc.

As regards my visit to London, it seems very questionable. I have far too much to do at the office to be able to get away easily. However, if all had gone well with *The Daily News*,[b] I had indeed intended to come down and clinch the thing by word of mouth. That reason no longer obtains and, since the thing would cost me some £7-£8, which I can ill afford and I could only stay down there 3-4 days at the most, I shan't come if I can help it.

After Cluss' letter, returned herewith, I shall now send him the article on Schimmelpfennig to be used as circumstances dictate; if he has already become too involved with Schimmelpfennig,[525] it will at least serve to enlighten Cluss privately concerning Schimmelpfennig and at the same time help him not to become too deeply involved. As a soldier, give me Willich any day, rather than that clever-clever Schimmelpfennig who really has nothing to him except sheer vanity and arrogance, and whose entire stock of learning derives from a few common or garden manuals and textbooks.

I shall let you have another article on Turkey, military or otherwise,[c] for next Friday's[d] STEAMER. It is time we harked back to our first articles on the subject,[e] including the political aspect. Here, too, we have been splendidly vindicated by circumstances; the pertinacity of the Greek insurrection[487] and the evident uneasiness of the Turks in Bulgaria prove, *après tout*,[f] that the Christian population is starting to bestir itself and that the Turkish Empire is rapidly approaching its end. On the other hand it is symptomatic of the Turks' great weakness that the larger part of their army, as was always its wont, ran away home during the winter and that as yet no amount of reform[526] has succeeded in instilling in these fellows a soldierly spirit on the European pattern. As regards the Odessa business[527] we shall have to have some more detailed news; up till now everything has been too contradictory. Lupus is fuming at the allies for not having cut the Russians to pieces *ad majorem gloriam Aberdeeni et Bonaparti*.[g] He and Heise now vie with each other in dismaying the philistines with flat contradictions and downright rudeness. One or both of them will get a beating before long; yesterday they came close to

---

[a] in the final count - [b] See this volume, pp. 423-26 and 427. - [c] F. Engels, 'News from the European Contest'. - [d] 5 May. See this volume, p. 448. - [e] K. Marx and F. Engels, 'British Politics.—Disraeli.—The Refugees.—Mazzini in London.—Turkey'; F. Engels. 'The Real Issue in Turkey', 'The Turkish Question', 'What Is to Become of Turkey in Europe?' - [f] after all - [g] for the greater glory of Aberdeen and Bonaparte

it, whereupon I suddenly began talking in a Lancashire accent, which made the philistines laugh and provided the opportunity for a dignified retreat.

Heise, by the way, won't ever be dangerous, his writing ability is far inferior to little Dronke's, idleness is his speciality. No knowledge whatever, only a strong inclination to acquire the ABC of everything. With great difficulty he succeeded in learning the ABC of Russian, but has already forgotten it again.

Sûr ce que Dieu l'ait en sa sainte garde, habeat sibi![a]

Your
F. E.

First published much abridged in *Der Briefwechsel zwischen F. Engels und K. Marx*, Bd. 2, Stuttgart, 1913 and in full in: Marx and Engels, *Works*, First Russian Edition, Vol. XXII, Moscow, 1929

Printed according to the original

Published in English for the first time

223

MARX TO ENGELS [234]

IN MANCHESTER

[London,] 3 May 1854
28 Dean Street, Soho

Dear Frederic,

My use of the term 'letter of Uriah'[b] has caused a misunderstanding. I gave Heise *no* letter—he didn't even take his leave of me and was, incidentally, in far too tipsy a condition to do so. He wrote to me from the hole where he was lodging near Manchester, asking for my help up there. It was in this sense that I would have regarded sending you a report on him as a 'letter of Uriah', if in a somewhat 'bolder' meaning of the term. Maybe Manchester has deprived him of the main INCITEMENT of making himself out to be a 'GREAT MAN', an 'INDEPENDENT' and a 'MALCONTENT' in the eyes of

---

[a] Certain that God has him in his safe keeping—let him have him. - [b] See this volume, p. 442.

Imandt and Schily. However, all you can do now is to act diplomatically and urge the man gradually to find himself an occupation. The whole time he has been in England he has been living at other people's expense and, whenever he got a chance of earning his keep, soon gave it up. Since he now has a superfluity of time on his hands he might at least write regularly for the *Reform* which, by the by, has as yet failed to pay even Eccarius so much as a FARTHING. However, if given enough support, it should soon be in a position to pay.

Your military things—'retreat of the Russians from Kalafat' and the situation in the Dobrudja[a] have, I think, been proved splendidly right. The bombardment of Odessa [527] was, it seems, provoked by the Russians. Unless the English land troops there, little would appear to have been achieved—save to placate the bourgeois here who, inasmuch as the war is manifesting itself in the form of taxes and loans, are becoming wild about the inactivity of the ALLIED FLEETS,—PERHAPS, too, Nicholas needed a demonstration of the kind to give spice to his appeal 'to his people'.[b] There can no longer be any doubt about collusion between the Ministry here and Petersburg, now that the suppression of *a document* in the 'SECRET CORRESPONDENCE'—in which Aberdeen (1844) *accepted* the Russian proposals—has become common knowledge. I already had an inkling that something of the sort was going on behind the scenes because of the falsification of the dates and endorsements in the 'memorandum'[c] alluded to in the HOUSE OF LORDS by the Tories' EX-FOREIGN MINISTER.[d] Although the *Journal de Saint-Pétersbourg* itself censures these fellows for their *fausse position,*[e] it is clear from the 'DECLARATIONS IN COUNCIL'[f] concerning neutral, and especially Russian, shipping, that they are still agreeing their moves with Russia. Similar 'DECLARATIONS' appeared *at the same time* in St Petersburg,[528] ALMOST COUCHED IN THE *SAME* TERMS. Such a thing can't be a coincidence. The element they overlooked in their calculations is Bonaparte. No matter what sort of a chap

---

[a] F. Engels, 'The European War', 'Retreat of the Russians from Kalafat', 'Position of the Armies in Turkey'. - [b] Marx took the report about the appeal of 23 (11) April 1854 from the telegraphic dispatch 'Turkey and Russia' in *The Times,* No. 21731, 3 May 1854. - [c] K. Marx. 'The Secret Diplomatic Correspondence' (see present edition, Vol. 13, p. 99). - [d] Malmesbury, [Speech in the House of Lords on 31 March 1854,] *The Times,* No. 21704, 1 April 1854. On this see K. Marx. 'The War Debate in Parliament', present edition, Vol. 13, pp. 134-35. - [e] false position. Marx probably refers to the leading article in the *Journal de Saint-Pétersbourg,* 7 (19) March 1854, reprinted in *The Times,* No. 21702, 30 March 1854: 'France'. - [f] Victoria R. 'A Proclamation, 29 March 1854', *The Times,* No. 21702, 30 March 1854.

he may be, the question is one of life and death for him and, being a rogue by profession, he won't allow himself to be duped as was POOR Louis Philippe in 1839 and 1840.[529] When one reads the secret documents of 1830-48, one is left in no doubt that England deposed Louis Philippe and that the worthy *National*, despite and because of its blind Anglophobia, was unwittingly the principal tool of precisely English policy.

As you know, the *Tribune* prides itself on being Christian. I was all the more tickled when the fellows used for a LEADER an article of mine in which one of the chief things I held against the Turks was the fact of their having preserved Christianity,[a] although I did not of course say so quite so bluntly. INDEED, one reason why the Turks are bound to come to grief is that they have allowed Byzantine theocracy to develop in a way that not even the Greek emperors would have dreamed of. There are, in effect, only 2 religious peoples left, the Turks and the Greco-Slav population of Turkey. Both are doomed, or at least the latter, along with the clerically ordered society which has been consolidated under Turkish rule.

I have, besides, sent the *Tribune* a scandalous story about the 'Holy Sepulchre' and the 'Protectorate' in Turkey,[b] in which the historical matter will blind the fellows to the prank I play on Christianity.

I should be very glad if you could supply me with something for the *Tribune*,[c] since I am very busy studying the history of the New Greek Empire including King Otto,[530] but it will be a couple of weeks, perhaps, before I can present the result in a series of articles. *Metaxas*, who was Greek ambassador in Constantinople where he engaged in plotting — the Paris *Presse* published a pretty account of this Russo-Greek Bangyanade—was the principal tool of the INFAMOUS Capodistria.[531]

At odd moments I am going in for Spanish. Have begun with Calderón from whose *Magico prodigioso*—the Catholic Faustus— Goethe drew not just a passage here or there but whole settings for some of scenes in his *Faust*. Then—*horribile dictu*[d]—I am reading in Spanish what I'd found impossible in French, Chateaubriand's *Atala* and *René*, and some stuff by Bernardin de St-Pierre. Am now in the middle of *Don Quixote*. I find that a dictionary is more necessary in Spanish than in Italian at the start.

---

[a] K. Marx, 'The Greek Insurrection'. - [b] K. Marx, 'Declaration of War.—On the History of the Eastern Question'. - [c] See this volume, p. 448. - [d] horrible to relate

16*

By chance I have got hold of the *Archivio triennale delle cose d'Italia dall'avvenimento di Pio IX all'abbandono di Venezia* etc. It's the best thing about the Italian revolutionary party that I have read. Consists of a collection of secret and public documents, intercepted letters, etc. Nicely put together. Palmistone (as Thiers pronounces Palmerston) plays a leading role here as well. The fellow's machinations have been ubiquitous, and at all events his existence has been a very amusing one.

You still owe me a letter about Mr Urquhart's military stuff.[a] The man can be caught out only in the 'positive' SCIENCES. I.e. here and in his economics, the superficiality of which can likewise be tangibly demonstrated.

Vale faveque.[b]

K. M.

First published abridged in *Der Briefwechsel zwischen F. Engels und K. Marx*, Bd. 2, Stuttgart, 1913 and in full in: Marx and Engels, *Works*, First Russian Edition, Vol. XXII, Moscow, 1929

Printed according to the original

Published in English in full for the first time

224

MARX TO ENGELS

IN MANCHESTER

[London,] 6 May 1854
28 Dean Street, Soho

Dear Engels,

Unfortunately your 'DISPATCH'[c] did not arrive yesterday until the post office had closed, and the LETTER could not be sent to New York even against payment of the customary shilling.

The Pole Miskowsky—*vide* the 'Knight of the Noble'—has come to a very bad end. The poor devil had long been in the most wretched circumstances, had never succeeded in raising the wherewithal for the trip to Constantinople—AS HE WAS NOT ONE OF THE 'MINIONS' OF THE 'GOVERNOR'[d]—and had thus sunk to being a lumpen-proletarian in Whitechapel to whom we in the WEST END FROM TIME TO TIME sent some small aid. A few days ago the *pauvre diable*,[e]

---

[a] See this volume, p. 422 - [b] Good-bye and farewell. - [c] F. Engels, 'News from the European Contest'. - [d] Lajos Kossuth - [e] poor devil

together with six other refugees, was *burned alive* in the wooden shack he occupied with them in Whitechapel.[532] First you're reduced to beggary, then you starve, and finally you're burnt to death; what more can you expect in this 'best of worlds'.[a]

Since Wiss, Doctor of Universal Wisdom, had launched in the *Republik der Arbeiter* A FURIOUS ONSLAUGHT on our 'corrupt ideas' and mindless 'frivolity',[b] I thought it fitting to obtain from Edgar Bauer, whom I see from time to time—a *rendez-vous* invariably followed by a hangover—some information on this *lumen mundi*,[c] now a shareholder in Weitling's stables of bliss. Briefly, this is what I learned there:

Mr Wiss apparently arrived in Berlin shortly after your time.[533] He was a vain youth with a marked aversion for 'POSITIVE' knowledge, which is why he never succeeded in passing his medical examinations and threw himself passionately into the universal wisdom which was concentrated in Stehely's.[534] Initially a Brunoist[d] and then a Stirnerian, he became a member of Edgar Bauer's society of 'The Free',[535] was much interested in the emancipation of women, and resolved to become 'frivolous'. In pursuance of this aim he tumbled the landlady with whom he lodged—a midwife. The midwife then set to work on the 'frivolous' one's conscience, bemoaning the loss of her 'LESSER WALLACHIA' which damage Wiss, *le bonhomme*,[e] helped make good by cohabiting with her in 'free' marriage. Much though she esteemed Mr Wiss' money-bag, the midwife thought no less highly of the 'natural' bag of a certain working man, a lusty mechanic who lodged in the same house. Here again the great Wiss helped make good the damage by permitting the working man to work the machinery while reserving for himself the pleasure of ennobling the resulting product with the name of 'Proudhon-Fourier Wiss' and, whenever the name Proudhon was mentioned in the society of The Free, it was not the one in Paris they meant but the mechanic's OFFSPRING christened by Wiss.

Since Mr Wiss spent a great deal of money, learned nothing, and extolled free marriage, his worthy papa ceased to honour his bills, after which he lived on minor literature *à la* Meyen and loans made to him on his '*espérances*'[f] by philanthropists in Berlin. Came the revolution. Wiss became a popular orator, and one of the vice-chairmen of the democratic club, helped in by

---

[a] Voltaire, *Candide*. - [b] E. Wiß, 'Die elementaren Richtungen der Zeit', *Republik der Arbeiter*, No. 15, 8 April 1854. The article was published in instalments from March to June 1854. - [c] light of the world - [d] supporter of Bruno Bauer - [e] the worthy fellow - [f] expectations

Edgar Bauer. Next he became a contributor to the *Reform* but so dim was his light that even Ruge hid it under a bushel. *Au bout du compte*[a] Wiss hastily assumed an 'ironical attitude' to the revolution, married his midwife in bourgeois-ecclesial fashion, made things up with his old man and, together with midwife and Proudhon-Fourier Wiss, departed with his tail between his legs for America where he is prospering as a doctor, philosopher and member of the communia.[330]

Your

K. M.

First published in: Marx and Engels, *Works*, First Russian Edition, Vol. XXII, Moscow, 1929

Printed according to the original

Published in English for the first time

225

ENGELS TO MARX

IN LONDON

Manchester, 9 May 1854

Dear Marx,

I cannot understand the late arrival of the *Tribune* article.[b] The letter was specially entrusted to the messenger-boy, who took it to the post at a quarter past 7, *at the same time as the business letters,* all of which arrived punctually. Even if it had not left until the 2nd post, it should have been in your hands by 2 o'clock at the latest. I can only regard it as evidence of Mr Palmerston's solicitude for you. Since the bit about the battle has not materialised in the meantime, I can only hope you haven't sent off the article.

With regard to Urquhart's military stuff,[c] something in my next. I can, of course, deal with this subject only in notes, which I shall write straight off in English for you. You will then have to work them into your article.

The story of Dr Wiss is most edifying and Cluss will certainly ensure that it reaches the right people.[536]

As for that poor devil Miskowsky, the Noble One[d] can now say

---

[a] in the end - [b] See this volume, p. 448. - [c] ibid., pp. 422 and 448. - [d] August Willich

after all that he ultimately 'vanished without trace'.[537] When I read the story in the London papers, it immediately struck me that those who had been burnt to death were most certainly refugees.[532]

If at all possible, I shall set Heise to work—which, indeed, he cannot possibly avoid the moment I begin to hold off. The fellow's presently in Bradford, whither he was summoned by the little man[a] during the absence of the latter's principal[b] and whence, in any case, he returns in an exceedingly tipsy condition, so that he has to spend a few days in quarantine before he's good for anything. I was much tickled by the little man's little article[c] because of the care with which he retrieves and repeats all the *Neue Rheinische Zeitung*'s old chestnuts about Schleswig-Holstein, Belgium,[d] etc., etc.

Feldzug der Schleswig-Holsteinischen Armee und Marine 1850, by A. Lütgen, sometime Major, is the first sensible and comprehensive book about the Willisen episode. It confirms everything I had already deduced from preliminary studies of the affair.[e] Monsieur Willisen's original plan was a very good one,—if somewhat over-extended—so good that even the botched and belated attempt to revert to it instilled thoughts of withdrawal in the minds of the Danes, who were 36,000 strong against 26,000, almost all of their troops being already committed, whereas the Schleswig-Holsteiners had certainly $1/5$ of their troops still uncommitted. But when Monsieur Willisen actually found himself face to face with the enemy, he lost his head amidst the contradictory reports and the even more confused suggestions that were being made to him. Even the night before the battle, he detached his own reserves to a point on the left, right off the battle-field, to face an imaginary enemy and at the same time deferred the order for the attack, upon which all the dispositions had been based. Thus, concentration of reserves on the left where no enemy existed, exposure of the centre, which received the main attack, confusion on the right wing, which was to launch the main counter-attack. This alone is enough to explain the outcome, and even then he might have emerged victorious had he not too

---

[a] Ernst Dronke - [b] John Buckup - [c] E. Dronke, 'Naturgeschichte der Demokratie', *Die Reform*, 12 April 1854. - [d] Articles by Marx and Engels: 'The War Comedy,' 'The *Faedreland* on the Armistice with Denmark', 'The Armistice with Denmark', 'The Armistice "Negotiations"', 'Armistice Negotiations with Denmark Broken Off', 'The Danish-Prussian Armistice', 'Ratification of the Armistice', 'The "Model State" of Belgium', 'The "Model Constitutional State"', 'The Antwerp Death Sentences', etc. (see present edition, Vol. 7). - [e] See this volume, pp. 103-04.

hastily—as early as 8 o'clock in the morning—given everything up for lost. Even at 11 he could still have won but his horror on hearing that 2 Danish battalions were in position to the rear of his left flank (2 squadrons and 4 cannon would have sufficed to dispose of them) caused that 'strategic outflanker in maximum force' to recall the dictum 'he who outflanks is himself outflanked' and he now resolved to use all his forces to extricate himself. Our theoretician's antagonist was an old man grown grey in command, if mostly peace-time command, a mediocre pipe-clay general,[a] who was answerable not to a petty, philistine, moderate government devoid of power, but to a genuine king[b] and ministry and, if only for that reason, stood his ground more doggedly. In this way he won the battle. The success with which the weak Schleswig-Holstein detachments fought the Danes, who outnumbered them two and three to one (even according to the official Danish report), provides ample proof that the 26,000 Schleswig-Holsteiners were fully the equal of the 36,000 Danes. The chaps fought *quite splendidly*, despite the numerous raw recruits in their ranks, despite the havoc wrought throughout the entire army by Willisen's new regulations introduced only a fortnight before the campaign and, above all, despite the shortage of cadres. This army would happily have trounced twice their number of Prussians.

The bombardment of Odessa[527] was a *must* for the allies because of the insult to the flag of truce. Not much damage appears to have been done and, since they didn't land or occupy the city, it was more of a defeat than a victory. Nicest of all is the humbug that they 'sailed in the direction of Sevastopol'.[c] Incidentally, with every *Russian* action and the RETALIATION, at least apparent or attempted, this necessitates, the war is increasingly slipping from the grasp of Aberdeen and Palmerston and will gradually assume a more warlike course. As it is, Bonaparte must soon acquire *gloire* of a rather more tangible sort, even though his faithful Fridolin, Saint-Arnaud,[d] is just the man to push him further into the soup. Had this noble fellow not had a fortune to *refaire*,[e] the fortune he has already squandered away several times since 1851, he would never have gone East. But he and his ilk are just the men to ruin the best of troops by fraudulent supply contracts and then,

---

[a] Gerhard Krogh - [b] Frederick VII - [c] See 'The Black Sea. The Bombardment of Odessa', *The Morning Advertiser*, No. 19615, 4 May 1854; 'Latest Intelligence', *The Times*, No. 21734, 6 May 1854. - [d] Saint-Arnaud is compared to a character in Schiller's ballad 'Der Gang nach dem Eisenhammer'. - [e] remake

through military blunders, land them in a regular mess. I expect to see some pretty results from the campaign conducted by this *Bayard du bas-empire.*[110]

Your
F. E.

First published abridged in *Der Briefwechsel zwischen F. Engels und K. Marx,* Bd. 2, Stuttgart, 1913 and in full in: Marx and Engels, *Works,* First Russian Edition, Vol. XXII, Moscow, 1929

Printed according to the original

Published in English for the first time

226

MARX TO ENGELS[234]

IN MANCHESTER

London, 22 May 1854
28 Dean Street, Soho

Dear Engels,

It was a good thing you didn't come on Saturday.[a] My trouble—now a fortnight old—had come to a head. I could hardly speak and even laughing hurt because of a great festering boil between my nose and mouth, which this morning has at least dwindled to quite reasonable dimensions. My lips, too, which were tremendously swollen, are approximately back to normal again, etc., in short, everything indicates that I shall soon be well again. It's truly devilish, having such a wretched head for a whole fortnight. Beyond a joke. For the past week I've had to give up reading and smoking altogether and today am waiting to see if Freund will allow me to try a cigar.

To compound the misery, all three children[b] have been down with measles since last Friday (Thursday night), which means that the house has become a veritable hospital.

Herewith Cluss. Collapse of the *Reform* deplorable.[538]

---

[a] 20 May - [b] Jenny, Laura and Edgar

I rely on you to continue doing the American stint for me during *the whole of this week* since I am totally incapable of writing and have already lost £6 as a result of this wretched business, which is indeed hard to bear. I hope to have a few lines from you in the meantime.

The enclosed letter to be communicated to no one but Lupus. It would seem to be Heise's mission to compromise you in Manchester. Beware of the fellow.

Your
K. M.

First published abridged in *Der Briefwechsel zwischen F. Engels und K. Marx*, Bd. 2, Stuttgart, 1913 and in full in: Marx and Engels, *Works*, First Russian Edition, Vol. XXII, Moscow, 1929

Printed according to the original

Published in English in full for the first time

227

MARX TO FERDINAND LASSALLE[539]

IN DÜSSELDORF

London, 1 June 1854
28 Dean Street, Soho

Dear Lassalle,

I have been seriously ill these past 2 or 3 weeks and, on top of that, the 3 children[a] went down with the measles, from which they have only just recovered, so that the whole house has been turned into a hospital. I did not start going out again until 2 days ago and, since my head was the worst affected and all conversation exhausted me, I have seen no visitors during this time. The result is that I have heard little or nothing of the émigrés' activities and intentions. As you will be aware, Mazzini is in Switzerland incognito. From letters from Washington I gather that the émigrés are, as always, dreaming ambitious dreams. The confidential reports sent to America by the gentlemen here percolate back to me through a channel in Washington.[b]

In my next I may be *à même*[c] to send you the detailed information you ask for on the doings of the émigrés.[540]

---

[a] Jenny, Laura and Edgar - [b] Cluss - [c] in a position

Weerth is at present in California. It is rumoured that he is on the point of marrying a certain Miss Worbs or Worms, of Hamburg, the daughter of one of his former principals.

Even *The Times* has been poking some mild fun at the 'Cologne TRICKERS' in London who bellow from a hundred throats—bellow at the English:

> 'Softly sounding through my mind
> Many a delightful chime'[a]

or else,

> 'Lonely I am not alone'[b]

and more in similar vein.

As regards the 'Palmerston',—he is presently straining every nerve to gain complete control of the War Office, though he has a rival in the Duke of Newcastle, a Peelite—, only the first few of the articles I wrote for the *Tribune* have been printed here as pamphlets.[c] I myself prevented further publication, as pamphlets by Urquhart were appearing alternately in the same series of 'Political Fly-Sheets'[541] and I do not wish to be numbered among the followers of that gentleman with whom I have only one thing in common, viz. my views on Palmerston, but to whom in all other matters I am diametrically opposed, as became apparent at our very first meeting.[d] He is a romantic reactionary—a Turk, and would gladly guide the West back to Turkish standards and structures. I have not sent you these few short pamphlets as the cost of posting small parcels is disproportionately high. As for the substance of the matter, you are perfectly right to abide by your opinion until wholly unequivocal facts cause you to change it. What has gone to make up my own view is not this or that isolated fact—each isolated fact admitting of a variety of interpretations— but the concatenation of all the steps taken by this man, the whole context of his activities since 1829. In it I have discovered a consistent plan that assumes various and often seemingly con- tradictory forms but is always directed towards the same goal, a plan uniformly executed with the same supreme disdain.

As regards the specific points you raise, my comments are:

1. *Pacifico Expedition*.[345] In a work by one of Palmerston's former secretaries at the embassy in Athens—1836—namely the *Diplomatic History of Greece* by Mr Parish, you will find to begin

---

a Heine, 'Neuer Frühling', 6. Gedicht. - b P. A. Wolff, *Preciosa*, Act II, Scene 2. The drama provided the libretto for Weber's opera of the same title. - c K. Marx. 'Palmerston', II, III. - d See this volume, pp. 412-13.

with proof that, from 1830 onwards, Palmerston did all he could to turn Greece into a Russian province. In the end the Pacifico Expedition dropped her into Russia's lap. At the same time it also gained Palmerston popularity in England, thereby enabling him to further Russia's interests in the same year by concluding with Brunnow a treaty on the Danish succession, a treaty that was not made effective until 1852.[542] If, having done all the MISCHIEF he wanted, Palmerston gave way to France over this affair—the Greek one—, his compliance was simply 'diplomacy' vis-à-vis the English people. Papers hostile to him were already beginning to point out that in 1840 he had turned England into the ally of Russia and into the antagonist of France.

2. Recognition of the coup d'état.[a] Necessary to get Bonaparte into his toils.[74] Similarly, in connection with the Spanish troubles, he brought the Quadruple Alliance into being earlier in order to get Louis Philippe into the mire.[543]

3. The instruction of 19 June 1839—wholly justifies my view. It was not London but Paris which suggested that in no circumstances should Russia be allowed to carry out the Treaty of Unkiar-Skelessi[510] (which, by the by, was of Mr Palmerston's making). The proof—a dispatch from Soult to the Baron de Bourqueney, 30 May 1839. Similarly 17 June 1839, etc. Palmerston, who made as if to believe that the Sultan *wished* to see the Treaty of Unkiar-Skelessi put into effect and the Russians in Constantinople, sent a dispatch to Earl Granville in Paris on 19 June, enclosing his 'PROPOSED INSTRUCTIONS' of even date 'TO THE ADMIRAL, SIR ROBERT STOPFORD', in which, among many other ambiguous and inane proposals, he also instructed the Admiral if necessary 'TO FORCE THE PASSAGE OF DARDANELLES'. Soult, with great *bon sens*[b] (see dispatch from Earl Granville to Viscount Palmerston, Paris, 28 June 1839), drew Palmerston's attention to the fact that it was not the Sultan but Russia who was their enemy, that this forcing of the Dardanelles was inane and that it would suffice if the English and French ambassadors in Constantinople were to ask the Sultan— *who desired nothing better*—to permit the entry of the United Fleets into the Dardanelles. To this Palmerston could raise no objection, but put forward a proposal even more inane, whereupon Soult wrote:

'The NOBLE LORD would seem to resign himself *WITH GREAT FACILITY TO THE CONTINGENCY OF A RUSSIAN OCCUPATION OF CONSTANTINOPLE*'.

And so it goes on, Palmerston always thwarting French action

---

[a] Bonaparte's coup d'état of 2 December 1851 in France. - [b] good sense

against Russia while seeming to rage against Mohammed Ali, until Brunnow arrives in London, and the two of them conclude the treaty of 1840, subsequently ratified in the Dardanelles treaty of 1841, which was no more than a European sanction of the Treaty of Unkiar-Skelessi.[544]

I should be greatly obliged to you if you would write to me often and at length about conditions in Germany, particularly Prussia.

Your

K. M.

First published in: *F. Lassalle. Nachgelassene Briefe und Schriften.* Bd. III, Stuttgart-Berlin, 1922

Printed according to the original

Published in English for the first time

228

MARX TO ENGELS

IN MANCHESTER

London, 3 June 1854
28 Dean Street, Soho

Dear Frederic,

I am back on my feet and the children out of bed again, if not yet out of the house, but now my wife has become very unwell, probably as a result of the night vigils and nursing, and the worst of it is that instead of consulting the doctor which she refuses to do, she is dosing herself—on the pretext that two years ago when she was similarly indisposed, Freund's medicines only made her worse. If matters don't improve I shall finally have to resort to force. Thus I shan't be able to do the correspondence on Tuesday, for on *that* day Pieper's lessons prevent him from acting as secretary and, with my wife in her present state, I can't bother her with any writing. As you can see, I've become a regular Peter Schlemihl.[a] But over the years we have all enjoyed very good health on the whole and will, I hope, do so again when this crisis

---

[a] Chamisso, *Peter Schlemihl's wundersame Geschichte.*

is past. *Au fond,*[a] we can be thankful that we've all gone down one after the other.

I wrote an article[b] yesterday deriding the plan of campaign published in Thursday's *Times.*[c] However, if the French papers are to be trusted, it would not appear to be an official one. The *Moniteur* reports that Omer Pasha is hurrying to relieve Silistria.[d] Perhaps this is simply a device to keep the Parisians in good humour and to counteract the great Boichot's presence in Paris.[e] I can make little of the Russian reports or of Napier's in today's paper.[f] *Au bout*[g] the English would again appear to have achieved nothing.

Yesterday a great raw-boned chap, a democratic loafer, introduced himself to me as Dr Otto. Danish by birth. Ostensibly now expelled from Schleswig-Holstein. Took part in the 1848/49 Schleswig-Holstein and 'Thuringian' movement. Does Lupus, by any chance, possess any particular information about the man?

Have finished reading the *Archivio delle cose d'Italia.* The man's *Considerazioni*[h] at the back of the book endeavour to demonstrate the opposite of what emerges from his collection of documents, namely that the *Giovane Italia,*[545] and CONSEQUENTLY Giuseppe Mazzini, were the soul of the 1848 movement. What is particularly amusing is the final section in which he proves that the movements [must] shed their narrow, national character: FRATERNISA-TION among the various nations that came to grief in 1848/49 as a result of their isolation; Russia or the UNITED STATES OF EUROPE. At this point comes the following revelation:

'La servitù d'Italia è patto europeo: l'Italia non può esser libera che in seno a una libera Europa. Allora apparve manifesto doversi sancire, contro l'alleanza dei pochi oppressori, *l'onnipotente alleanza degli oppressi.*'[i] [*Archivio,* Vol. I, 560]

And this '*l'onnipotente alleanza degli oppressi*' was effectuated by Mazzini as follows:

---

[a] At bottom - [b] K. Marx, 'The Formation of a Special Ministry of War in Britain.—The War on the Danube.—The Economic Situation'. - [c] *The Times,* No. 21756, 1 June 1854, leader. - [d] [Report from Belgrade of 29 May 1854,] *Le Moniteur universel,* No. 151, 31 May 1854. - [e] Marx derides the pseudo-revolutionary activity of the French petty-bourgeois democrats. See this volume, pp. 461-62. - [f] Reports in *Journal de Saint-Pétersbourg* of 26 May 1854 and Napier's military reports in the section 'The Baltic Fleet' of *The Times,* No. 21758, 3 June 1854. - [g] In the end - [h] *Comments* - [i] 'Italy's servitude is a European compact: Italy can be free only in the bosom of a free Europe. Then it became manifest that *an omnipotent alliance of the oppressed* must be formed to oppose the alliance of the few oppressors.'

'Allora Mazzini compié l'ardua sua missione, dettando con Ledru-Rollin e Darasz e *Ruge*, un nuovo patto che stringa Italia, non solo alla Polonia e alla Francia, ma alla stessa Germania, serva volente finora, e quasi sacerdotessa della servitù. E così, dalle opposte parti e dalle più nemiche genti giungono i peregrini al santuario commune della libertà.'[a] [I. 560]

Have received newspapers from America, but still no letter. 'Ruge', who has concluded the '*nuovo patto*' with Mazzini, declares in Dulon's little sheet[b] that, as a result of the war against Russia, there is now a prospect of 'liberal' development in Germany and that, even though no more may be achieved than 'freedom as in England', one ought to participate in it. To adopt a pessimistic view is 'base, idle and Russian'. As you can see, the prospect of his private fortune being exhausted within the year has made the noble man ready to attach himself to any form of 'progress' and, *au cas de besoin*,[c] become 'constitutional'.

Your
K. M.

First published abridged in *Der Briefwechsel zwischen F. Engels und K. Marx*, Bd. 2, Stuttgart, 1913 and in full in: Marx and Engels, *Works*, First Russian Edition, Vol. XXII, Moscow, 1929

Printed according to the original

Published in English for the first time

229

ENGELS TO MARX

IN LONDON

Manchester, 10 June 1854

Dear Marx,

I was very sorry I was unable to send you an article for Tuesday's post,[d] but it was a *sheer impossibility* because of the many jobs to be done at the office which now absolutely preclude my

---

[a] 'Then Mazzini accomplished his arduous mission, concluded a new pact with Ledru-Rollin and Darasz and *Ruge*, binding Italy not only to Poland and France but to that same Germany, up till now the willing handmaiden, if not the priestess, of servitude. And thus pilgrims belonging to opposing sides and the most hostile peoples will unite before the common shrine of liberty.' - [b] Probably the journal *Für die freien Gemeinden*. - [c] in case of need - [d] 6 June

writing articles for you precisely on Mondays or Thursdays. On top of that, my present lodgings are almost $^3/_4$ of an hour's walk away from the post, so that nothing more can be done late at night for the second post. Hence I have to work on Saturdays and on Wednesday evenings. Tomorrow I shall send you a *comprehensive* article on the siege of Silistria[a] which ought to cause a stir; maybe, too, some notes on Napier's absurd naval frolics[546] and on the condition of the army in Bulgaria.

I am now swotting the Hungarian campaign in real earnest and shall, I think, have worked my way through all the sources by October; *come what may, I shall write the book this winter*.[b] The more I go into it, the prettier the thing gets on both sides. At present I am comparing Görgey and Windischgrätz,[547] and find that in his self-apology the latter is as mendacious as in his bulletins[548] he hasn't the courage to disown. Delightful, how each of the two adversaries tries to make his own army out to be worse than the opposing one. *Père* Windischgrätz, incidentally, proves himself the ass we know him to be—HE HAS ACTUALLY WRITTEN HIMSELF DOWN AN ASS—and was most ably abetted in his tomfoolery by men even more stupid, if such a thing is possible, than himself, namely his subordinate generals Wrbna, Csorich and, above all, the chivalrous Banus Jellačić. Görgey's cynicism enables him to record the facts much more frankly and correctly than that mendacious apologist Windischgrätz. However, it is a campaign altogether worthy of the year '48/49.

Cold feet on both sides, the old armies and the revolutionary forces both discredited. Next week I hope to receive the official Austrian book[c] and one of these days I shall go through the Brockhaus catalogues to find what sources are still required. Another thing I need is Klapka[d]; then I shall have all the principal stuff.

The thing for *The Times*[e] will be written next week; I now have all the sources and need only do a little more work on them. Could you find out in London what military periodicals are published there? Just in case of need.

Now I must go to the bookseller's if I am not to find it shut; let's hear from you soon.

---

[a] F. Engels, 'The Siege of Silistria'. - [b] See this volume, pp. 309-10. - [c] Probably *Sammlung der für Ungarn erlassenen Allerhöchsten Manifeste und Proklamationen, dann der Kundmachungen der Oberbefehlshaber der kaiserlichen Armee in Ungarn.* - [d] G. Klapka, *Memoiren. April bis Oktober 1849.* - [e] See this volume, pp. 435 and 437-38.

Dronke, drunk as usual, was run over by a CAB, and is now in bed; will be confined to his room for some 8 or 10 days, otherwise nothing serious.

I shall make inquiries about Otto.[a]

Your
F. E.

I hope your wife is well again.

First published in *Der Briefwechsel zwischen F. Engels und K. Marx*, Bd. 2, Stuttgart, 1913

Printed according to the original

Published in English for the first time

230

MARX TO ENGELS

IN MANCHESTER

London, 13 June 1854
28 Dean Street, Soho

Dear Frederic,

Enclosed letters from Cluss which you needn't return since they have already been made known to the competent people and have been answered.

The article on Silistria[b] is splendid. The request made through Austria to Russia[549] that she *promise* to evacuate the Danubian principalities (the intention being to conclude an armistice and convene a congress in Vienna on the strength of that promise) was of purely Russian inspiration. At the same time it was assumed that Silistria would quickly fall into Russian hands. The English public had been prepared for this event by the entire ministerial press. HENCE Paskievich's haste. The resistance of the Turks at Silistria upset these calculations—just as happened to a similar plan that had matured the previous autumn.

COLONEL Grach is an acquaintance of mine from Trier; not one of your Prussian instructors, but a talented ADVENTURER who went to Turkey as much as 19 or so years ago to seek his fortune.[550] A *crapaud*[c] in the know tells me that Boichot, who was caught in

---

[a] See this volume, p. 458. - [b] F. Engels, 'The Siege of Silistria'. - [c] philistine

Paris,[a] had in fact been sent to France as a political emissary by Pyat's clique and not, as Pyat declares in execrable English in the *Advertiser*,[b] to pay a visit to his old mother, whom he hadn't seen for 5 years. It's really repulsive the way the *crapauds* continually act out of character and remain addicted to these 'melodramatic' lies calculated to appeal to the hearts of the petty bourgeois. *C'est dégoûtant.*[c]

You will shortly have another consignment of *Pioniers*. Heinzen, of course, is ranting and roaring dreadfully about the defunct *Reform*, and has actually managed to trot out a quotation from Catullus, no doubt picked up from a school-book complete with crib. Also contains comical diatribes against Dulon. The great Ruge writes to them both, friend 'Dulon' and friend 'Heinzen'. He informs the latter of his grand design for the foundation of a free university in Cincinnati where Ruge intends to drone away agreeably the remainder of his days as *rector magnificus in partibus*.[d] He can hardly wait to become a professor at last, something which, for all his servility, he was unable to 'wrest' from the Saxon Minister Lindenau or, before that, from the Prussian Minister Altenstein. 'Doctorates' will also be awarded in this glorified *contrefaçon*[e] of a German university. All that is needed is dollars to the tune of 1,000,000 and 6 citizens of Cincinnati to administer the finances. In addition, a prospectus covering all disciplines. A wild omnium gatherum, *mixtum compositum*[f] of headings from Hegel's *Encyclopädie* and the table of contents from Ersch and Gruber.[g] E.g. *General Linguistics.* (Cf. Ersch and Gruber, Pott's article on the distribution of languages.) The following are to be excluded from professorial chairs: 1. Strauss and Bruno Bauer; 2. the 'Sophists' who make stuff and nonsense of philosophy; 3. not the doctrine of communism, but the 'vile personages who have betrayed the Republic and Liberty'.[551]

In one of his rotten letters Ruge extols 2 anonymous pamphlets on Palmerston—never, of course, suspecting that one of them originated with me.[h]

My wife is now confined to bed. Yesterday I at last managed to persuade her to call Dr Freund. As soon as she is at all fit to do so, he wants her to take a trip to Germany, which accords with the

---

[a] See this volume, p. 458. - [b] F. Pyat, 'The Arrest of Sergeant Boichot, at Paris, by the French Government', *The Morning Advertiser*, No. 19646, 9 June 1854. - [c] It's disgusting. - [d] vice-chancellor in exile - [e] here: version - [f] a crazy mixture - [g] *Allgemeine Encyclopädie der Wissenschaften und Künste* published by J. S. Ersch and J. G. Gruber. - [h] K. Marx, 'Palmerston and Russia'.

wishes of my mother-in-law[a] and has been impossible hitherto only on financial grounds, but will have to be engineered somehow. The children are back at school today.

Dronke's bad luck[b] is tragi-comical. The fellows seem to be playing havoc in Bradford.

Your
K. M.

First published (except the last paragraph) in *Der Briefwechsel zwischen F. Engels und K. Marx*, Bd. 2, Stuttgart, 1913 and in full in: Marx and Engels, *Works*, First Russian Edition, Vol. XXII, Moscow, 1929

Printed according to the original

Published in English for the first time

231

ENGELS TO MARX

IN LONDON

[Manchester,] 15 June 1854

Dear Marx,

Cluss' letter most amusing. I had wanted to write to you at greater length today, but now find it's too late, so will confine myself to telling you that I have not been able to finish by *today*, as I had intended, the article on relative strengths and Silistria's chances of relief. That would involve looking up a lot of old stuff and since anyhow, in view of your wife's illness, your greatest difficulty will be to have an article ready for Tuesday's steamer, I shall see what sort of a piece I can concoct for you by then.

Heise, too, is ill now; I don't yet know what ails him, but he's said to be in bed and to have all sorts of pains in his chest. Pfänder got something in his eye which will prevent him from working for a couple of days. Bad luck everywhere, *je n'y vois plus clair.*[c] Regards to your wife and children.

Your
F. E.

First published in *Der Briefwechsel zwischen F. Engels und K. Marx*, Bd. 2, Stuttgart, 1913

Printed according to the original

Published in English for the first time

---

[a] Caroline von Westphalen - [b] See this volume, p. 461. - [c] I'm quite bemused

232

MARX TO ENGELS

IN MANCHESTER

London, 21 June 1854
28 Dean Street, Soho

Dear Engels,

Your letter arrived early enough, between 2 and 3. But since I had only waited until 2, and since I had to go out of town on domestic business and my wife saw from the accompanying letter[552] that the article couldn't be sent off as it stood, it is still here. I shall use it for my Friday's article,[553] but would ask you to write to me before then—quite *briefly* if you are short of time—about the following points:

1. Is there anything new in the Turkish bulletins which appeared in yesterday's *Daily News*? Have you any more details about the events of 28 [May]-13 [June] (which is as far, I believe, as the latest, albeit fragmentary, reports go)?

2. Is there anything of military significance about the operations on the Circassian coast? No doubt the news about Shamyl needs further confirmation.[554]

3. The entry of the Austrians into Wallachia; what can be said about it from the military *point de vue*?

From the enclosed letter you will see that I'm over head and ears in bad luck. When my wife's illness was at its worst, the good Dr Freund *kept away* and sent me a bill for £26 with the request that a 'clear understanding' be reached regarding his 'professional relations' to myself. Since my wife was in a critical—and is still in a serious—condition, I was of course compelled to capitulate to the dear 'friend'[a] and promise him in writing that I would pay £8 down at the end of this month and the rest by six weekly instalments. Had the fellow not attacked me so much *à l'imprévu*,[b] he wouldn't have caught me napping like that. But what was I to do? I should have had to pay any other respectable doctor by the visit and anyhow, even were this possible, one can't change doctors like shirts in the middle of an illness, without first inquiring into their competence, etc.

So I find myself in a FIX. I know that things are tight with you as well. Do you think Dronke might be able to advance me a few

---

[a] A pun on the name Freund, which also means 'friend'. - [b] unexpectedly

pounds for the instalment due at the end of this month? When he was here last, he gave me to understand that he could be approached at a time of real crisis. However, I'd like to have your opinion first. I must in any case pay the fellow the first instalment on the agreed date, and my bill in respect of the past months has already been drawn—all of it spent needless to say, since I had £12 to pay out for the household, and the total received was considerably reduced because of unwritten articles, besides which the chemist's bills alone swallowed up a large part of the budget.

At the end of this week, if my wife feels strong enough, she, the children and Lenchen are going to spend a fortnight at Mr Seiler's villa at Edmonton. She might then be so far restored by the country air as to manage the journey to Trier.

I can assure you that these last *petites misères*[a] have turned me into A VERY DULL DOG.

Beatus ille[b] that hath no family.

Vale faveque.[c]

Your
K. M.

First published in *Der Briefwechsel zwischen F. Engels und K. Marx*, Bd. 2, Stuttgart, 1913

Printed according to the original

Published in English for the first time

233

MARX TO ENGELS

IN MANCHESTER

[London,] 27 June 1854

Dear Engels,

I should be grateful if you would write to *Dronke* forthwith. Even if I manage to get the later instalments deferred, it will be difficult, if not impossible, to do so in the case of the first one, which falls due at the end of the month. A further 8-10 days at the very outside, if I write to Freund saying my bill [of exchange] has not yet arrived.

---

[a] petty miseries - [b] Blessed is he (Horace, *Epodon*, II, 1). - [c] Good-bye and farewell.

I am sending only these few lines, as I am in the midst of concocting my article.[a] I was unable to write earlier because of the TROUBLES and the to-ing and fro-ing, etc., occasioned by the FAMILY exodus to Seiler's.

Your
K. M.

Your letter received today.[555]

First published in: Marx and Engels, *Works*, First Russian Edition, Vol. XXII, Moscow, 1929

Printed according to the original

Published in English for the first time

234

ENGELS TO MARX

IN LONDON

[Manchester,] Thursday, 6 July 1854

Dear Marx,

I hope the £5 arrived. Enclosed an article for tomorrow, which covers the first phase of the war.[b]

If the fellows are really going to send French troops to the Baltic, they *must* at least take [the] Åland [Islands]. That would be the best thing.

Enclosed a hymn. Query:

1. *What century?*
2. *Who wrote it?*

Reply by return, please.

Your
F. E.

First published abridged in *Der Briefwechsel zwischen F. Engels und K. Marx*, Bd. 2, Stuttgart, 1913 and in full in: Marx and Engels, *Works*, First Russian Edition, Vol. XXII, Moscow, 1929

Printed according to the original

Published in English for the first time

---

[a] K. Marx, 'The War.—Debate in Parliament'. - [b] F. Engels, 'The War on the Danube'.

235

MARX TO ENGELS

IN MANCHESTER

[London,] 7 July 1854
28 Dean Street, Soho

Dear Engels,

You must excuse me for not having acknowledged receipt of the £5 before. This was due to much TROUBLE at home, since my wife is leaving for Trier tomorrow, an undertaking which has called for indescribable efforts.

Your article[a] arrived *just when* I myself was concocting a scrawl on Spain.[b] I shall therefore put your article by until Tuesday,[c] the more so since Pieper is available to act as my secretary on Fridays, while on Tuesdays I now have no one to do the writing.

I had not yet had time to look at the poem. I shan't be free till after 6, when I shall send you an answer either by telegram or city post.

Your
K. M.

First published in: Marx and Engels, *Works*, First Russian Edition, Vol. XXII, Moscow, 1929

Printed according to the original

Published in English for the first time

---

[a] F. Engels, 'The War on the Danube'. - [b] K. Marx, 'The Details of the Insurrection at Madrid.—The Austro-Prussian Summons.—The New Austrian Loan.—Wallachia'. - [c] 11 July

236

ENGELS TO MARX

IN LONDON

Manchester, 20 July 1854

Dear Marx,

To judge by your total silence you must either be hard at work or making tremendous EFFORTS to raise money. *En attendant*[a] I would inform you that, after the brother of Dronke's principal[b] has been to Bradford, Dronke will be in a position to shell out some money—just how much, it is impossible to say, but about £3 or £4. The brother arrives this week, so you should be able to rely on it in, say, 3 weeks' time.

Naut has been in London, here and in Bradford and, until he ran into Dronke in the street, had kept out of everyone's way. Dronke says he is hellish slack; apparently he—Naut—only saw Daniels once or twice in the street and doesn't even know whether he's living in Cologne or out in the country. Bürgers and a tailor—who, he was unable to say—are in Glatz and said to be quite well, and Becker is in Weichselmünde.[556] Otherwise all Naut could find to say was that it would be fine if in Prussia they could have a constitution like the one in England.

Dronke, by the way, has got himself into a serious scrape, so that the money may not be forthcoming after all. For when he was here 4 or 6 weeks ago he got drunk and, at one o'clock in the morning or thereabouts, made a grab at a female in the street; she, a married, middle-class woman, boxed his ears, whereupon he KNOCKED her DOWN. True, Dronke's own version of the story is slightly different, but that is what seems to have happened. The husband arrived on the scene and went to fetch the police, who didn't want to get mixed up in it. The business was protracted by Dronke's spurious excuses and now he has finally received an ATTORNEY's letter demanding an APOLOGY AND COMPENSATION, failing which the FOREIGNER is to be made an example of. Since Buckup's brother is just due to come, you can imagine the situation. We shall try and reach an accommodation, but it will probably cost money. *Keep the matter under your hat, by the way,* otherwise I'll have instant trouble with the little man, since Imandt will promptly

_____
[a] Meanwhile - [b] Buckup

write to him about it; in general, by no means everything I write to you is intended for the crew at large.

In other ways it suits me very well that the swank and swagger of the Heise-Dronke-Imandt trio should come to an inglorious end, for otherwise one would get no respite from these people with their rumbustious drunken contentiousness. Heise, at any rate, has his SETTLER in the shape of a crooked finger which he will probably retain for the rest of his days, and Dronke, too, has doubtless had enough.

So no more from your affectionate

F. E.

First published in part in *Der Briefwechsel zwischen F. Engels und K. Marx*, Bd. 2, Stuttgart, 1913 and in full in: Marx and Engels, *Works*, First Russian Edition, Vol. XXII, Moscow, 1929

Printed according to the original

Published in English for the first time

237

MARX TO ENGELS

IN MANCHESTER

[London,] 22 July 1854

Dear Engels,

The alternative reason you suggest for my long silence[a] is the correct one. It would certainly have been preferable had swotting been the obstacle. I added another £3 to the 5 so as to pay the 'friend'[b] the first instalment and I also needed about £8 for my wife's trip, which could no longer be postponed and which called for all manner of new equipment, since she could naturally not arrive in Trier looking shabby. These extraordinary expenses again brought me into conflict with my permanent and 'decent' creditors AND SO FORTH. 'It's the old, old story.'[c]

Not a sign of life from Cluss for four weeks now.

Que dites-vous de l'Espagne?[d][557]

I must now quite definitely do something further on the military situation in Turkey. *Firstly*: The mess in Asia. *Secondly*: What I have been able to glean from the French Press concerning the latest developments on the Danube, though for lack of a map I

---

[a] See this volume, p. 468 - [b] Dr Freund. (*Freund* in German—friend.) - [c] Heine, 'Lyrisches Intermezzo', 39. - [d] What do you think of Spain?

have no idea whether or not the names are right: Between the 7th and the morning of the 8th there was a battle with the 30,000 strong Russian corps under Soimonov and Khrulov (or should it be e instead of o?). On the evening of the 7th, Khrulov had taken up position to the north of Giurgevo. During the night several Turkish corps passed above and below the town and advanced on the Russians from the rear, with the result that at daybreak Khrulov was compelled to break through, incurring severe casualties in the process. The Russians withdrew, though not in line. One element made for Frateshti, another for Calugemeni (?),[a] another eastwards for the Argish. There they took up positions and on the 9th and 10th Selim Pasha and Iskander Bey are said to have carried out a successful attack on the Russians in Frateshti. On the 9th Gorchakov moved to Dzurdzuma (?) with 20,000 men and has been bringing in fresh troops daily. His positions: On the left bank of the Argish, the crossings over which have been fortified at Fulojci (?), Falastock (?), Korotzani (?) and Prczietsheni (?). Positions of the Russian army as a whole: Left wing from Kimpolung and Kimpina (?) along the Argish to Braila and Galatz. Turks: From Kalafat through Turna, Giurgevo to Oltenitza and (?) Kalarash. From Turna to Islaz. Here Selim Pasha in contact with Iskander Bey. Main corps at Giurgevo, corps above Giurgevo constitutes an advanced post on the left of the Argish, Oltenitza and Silistria. *Thirdly*: The total strength of the Russian army, from an article in *The Morning Chronicle*[b]; but contrary to the article I estimate a battalion at no more than 550 men.

Infantry.

3 divisions of	3rd corps		(Osten-Sacken)
3 "	"	4th "	(Dannenberg I)
2 "	"	5th "	Lüders

8 divisions=16 brigades=128 battalions
Total approx. 71,000 men

Cavalry. 3 divisions of light cavalry
       1 " " " dragoons

128 squadrons each of 120 men, over 15,000
Artillery. 46 batteries (each of 10 guns = 460)
    " " ([each of] 8 guns = 368)
    Servicing crews and drivers =12,000 (?)

---

[a] Should be Calugereni. - [b] 'Prussia. From our own correspondent', *The Morning Chronicle*, No. 27321, 21 July 1854.

In addition: 10 regiments of Cossack regulars with 40 guns, 3 battalions of sappers, train with pontoons or reserve parks. ALL IN ALL:

128 battalions of infantry	=71,000
3 battalions of sappers	2,000
128 squadrons	15,000
40 pieces of artillery	13,000
train	3,000
Cossacks	8,000
Wall[achian] militia	6,000
Total	118,000

Fourthly: Items which cannot be treated humorously without a map: the hitherto snail-like progress of the French and English, who, it would seem, will *not* cross the Danube. For what purpose has St-Arnaud ordered his troops to march from Adrianople to Burgas in the present heat? The noble fellow would seem to be perpetually shuttling to and fro between Constantinople and this place or that, simply for the sake of the travelling expenses. What is the truth *realiter*[a] about the English commissariat in Varna, Devna, etc.?

If you no longer have time to write me an article for Tuesday,[b] at least send me a few notes which I can use.

Apropos. About the poem.[c] It probably derives from Gottfried, hight Kinkel, or else from a *Silesian* poet of the school of Opitz, or was it composed by Heise himself?

I enclose a manuscript snatched from a young writer; show it to no one but Lupus. Who is this young writer?

Salut.

Your
K. M.

First published considerably abridged in *Der Briefwechsel zwischen F. Engels und K. Marx*, Bd. 2, Stuttgart, 1913 and in full in: Marx and Engels, *Works*, First Russian Edition, Vol. XXII, Moscow, 1929

Printed according to the original

Published in English for the first time

---

[a] in actual fact - [b] 25 July - [c] See this volume, p. 466.

238

MARX TO ENGELS[84]

IN MANCHESTER

[London,] 27 July 1854
28 Dean Street, Soho

Dear Engels,

Je vous attends[a] for Tuesday.[558] How very boastful Mr Herbert was. This same Herbert was Vorontsov's brother-in-law and at the same time English SECRETARY AT WAR. The way the English brag as though Nasmyth and Butler had held Silistria 'single-handed' is grotesque. Have you read about Monday evening's session, when Disraeli so neatly punctured LITTLE JOHN's[b] and the *Times'* 'Sevastopol' BUBBLE with one prick of the needle?[559]

I am, *hélas*,[c] once again saddled with Pieper who looks like a HALF-STARVED sucking pig seethed in milk, after having lived for a fortnight with a whore he describes as *un bijou*.[d] He has frittered away some £20 in a fortnight and now both his purses are equally depleted. In this heat it is a bore to have the fellow hanging around one *du matin jusqu'au soir et du soir jusqu'au matin*.[e] And it disrupts one's work.

On Saturday[f] I got the following note from Papa *Tucker*:

* 'Dear Sir, There is a pretty brisk demand for the "Fly-Sheets"[541] just now. Could you send me some articles from the *Tribune* that could suit the taste of the public? The third on Palmerston would move the other two.[g] Faithfully Yours E. Tucker.' *

Incidentally I have also heard from Freiligrath that that rogue Trübner is advertising these 'Fly-Sheets' under *his* imprint. You will note that he asks for 'ARTICLES FROM THE *TRIBUNE*' in order once AGAIN to evade the question of money. Now, 1. So far as *he* is concerned, not one copy of the *Tribune* is to be had anywhere in London, since it is sent only to subscribers and back numbers cannot even be ordered from New York; 2. Without substantial additions, none of the articles would now suit. Now I must clear up the matter with the fellow and this 'easy-going' relationship

---

[a] I expect [something from] you - [b] Lord John Russell - [c] alas - [d] a jewel - [e] from morning to night and night to morning - [f] 22 July - [g] A reference to the third, fourth and fifth articles from Marx's *Lord Palmerston* which were published as two separate pamphlets.

must end. If he is agreeable, and you for your part approve, I would suggest the following:

1. Of the *Tribune* articles, I shall give him (for publication) the critique of the 'SECRET CORRESPONDENCE'.[a] For this Dronke would only have to send me the 2nd article on this, which was detained by the Post Office here. The latter gratis, 2 and 3 to be paid for in cash and on delivery of the MSS, namely.

2. A GENERAL pamphlet on Palmerston, beginning with my introduction in the *Tribune*[b] to which I should, however, add a new middle and ending.

3. A pamphlet that I would have to write in collaboration with you, i.e. on England's DIPLOMACY *and* MILITARY ACTION since war was declared. The articles which have appeared in the *Tribune* will provide us with material for both these aspects. If you agree to 3, the question arises:

How much do we ask?

After all, my articles do seem to sell better than Urquhart's who is 'happy' if his stuff in the *Advertiser* is accepted by Tucker for the 'Fly-Sheets'.

If you agree with all this—(Nos. 2 and 3 would, of course, have to be pungent enough TO PRODUCE A REAL SENSATION in London; moreover, such is the footing we are on with Tucker that we can write anything we choose without worrying about English prejudices)—then compose a letter for me putting these proposals to Mr Tucker. Not being sufficiently adept in business matters, I have deliberately avoided answering him either orally or in writing. But no time is to be lost.

A book that has interested me greatly is Thierry's *Histoire de la formation et du progrès du Tiers État,* 1853.[560] It is strange how this gentleman, *le père*[c] of the 'class struggle' in French historiography, inveighs in his Preface against the 'moderns' who, while also perceiving the antagonism between bourgeoisie and proletariat, purport to discover traces of such opposition as far back as the history of the *tiers-état*[d] prior to 1789. He is at great pains to show that the *tiers-état* comprises all social ranks and estates save the *noblesse* and *clergé* and that the bourgeoisie plays the role of representative of all these other elements. Quotes, for example, from Venetian embassy reports:

---

[a] K. Marx, 'The Documents on the Partition of Turkey' and 'The Secret Diplomatic Correspondence'. - [b] K. Marx, *Lord Palmerston,* first and second articles (entitled 'Palmerston' in the *New-York Daily Tribune*).- [c] the father - [d] Third Estate

'Questi che si chiamano li stati del regno sono di tre ordini di persone, cioè del clero, della nobiltà, e del restante di quelle persone che, per voce commune, si può chiamare *popolo*' [Thierry, *Histoire...*, Vol. I, p. III].[a]

Had Mr Thierry read our stuff, he would know that the decisive opposition between bourgeoisie and *peuple* does not, of course, crystallise until the former ceases, as *tiers-état,* to oppose the *clergé* and the *noblesse.* But as for the '*racines dans l'histoire ... d'un antagonisme né d'hier*',[b] his book provides the best proof that the origin of the '*racines*' coincided with the origin of the *tiers-état.* By the same token, this otherwise intelligent critic would have to conclude from the '*Senatus populusque Romanus*'[c] that in Rome there was never any opposition save that between the *senatus* and the *populus.* I was interested to discover from the documents he quotes that the term '*catalla, capitalia*', capital, came into being with the rise of the communes. He has, by the by, unwittingly demonstrated that the victory of the French bourgeoisie was delayed by nothing so much as the fact that it did not decide until 1789 to make COMMON CAUSE with the peasants. Although he does not generalise, he depicts very nicely, 1. how from the beginning, or at least since the rise of the towns, the French bourgeoisie has gained undue influence by constituting itself a parliament, bureaucracy, etc., and not, as in England, by commerce and *industrie* alone. This undoubtedly holds true even of present-day France. 2. From his account it may be readily shown how the class rises as the various forms in which its centre of gravity has lain at different times are ruined and with them the different sections whose influence derives from these forms. In my view, this sequence of metamorphoses leading up to the domination of the class has never before been thus presented—at least so far as the material is concerned. In regard to the *maîtrises, jurandes,*[d] etc., in short, the forms, in which the industrial bourgeoisie develops, he has, alas, restricted himself almost wholly to general, and generally known, phrases, despite the fact that here too he alone is familiar with the material. What he successfully elaborates and underlines is the conspiratorial and revolutionary nature of the municipal move-ment in the twelfth century. The German Emperors, e.g. Frederick I and Frederick II, issued edicts against these '*com-*

---

[a] 'These that call themselves the Estates of the realm are of three orders of persons, that of the clergy, of the nobility, and of the rest of those persons who, in common parlance, may be called the *people*.' - [b] 'roots in history ... of an antagonism *born yesterday*' - [c] the Senate and Roman people - [d] guilds, corpora-tions

*muniones', 'conspirationes' 'conjurationes'*ᵃ in very much the same spirit as the German Federal Diet.⁵⁶¹ E.g. in 1226 Frederick II takes it upon himself to declare null and void all *'consulats'*ᵇ and other free municipal bodies in the towns of Provence:

'Pervenit nuper ad notitiam nostram quod quarumdam civitatum, villarum et aliorum locorum universitates exᶜ proprio motu constituerunt juridictiones, potestates' (Potestad), 'consulatus, regimina et alia quaedam statuta ... et cum jam apud quasdam ... in abusum et pravam consuetudinem inoleverunt ... nos ex imperiali auctoritate tam juridictiones etc. atque concessiones super his, per comites Provinciae et Forcalquerii ab eis obtentas, ex certa scientia revocamus, et inania esse censemus' [II, 87].ᵈ

Further:

Conventiculas quoque omnes et conjurationes in civitatibus et extra ... inter civitatem et civitatem et inter personam et personam seu inter civitatem et personam, omnibus modis fieri prohibemus.' (Constitutio pacis Frederici I.)ᵉ

'Quod nulla civitas, nullum oppidum, communiones, constitutiones, colligationes, confederationes vel conjurationes aliquas, quocumque nomine censeantur, facere possent; et quod nos, sine domini sui assensu, civitatibus seu oppidis in regno nostro constitutis, auctoritatem faciendi communiones, constitutiones ... conjurationes aliquas, quaecumque nomina imponantur eisdem, non poteramus nec debebamus impertiri.' (Henrici regis sententia contra communiones civitatum.) [II, 86]ᶠ

Is that not the *raide*ᵍ German professorial style to the life—the very same which later graced the fulminations of the 'Central Commission of the Confederation'⁵⁶²? In Germany, the *'commune jurée'*ʰ penetrated no further than Trier where, in 1161, the Emperor Frederick I put a stop to it:

ᵃ communes, secret associations, sworn confederacies - ᵇ municipal councils - ᶜ The original has 'in comitatibus ipsis degentes' instead of 'ex'. - ᵈ 'It has recently been brought to our notice that the guilds of certain cities, market towns and other places have, of their own accord, constituted tribunals, authorities (the Podesta), consulates, administrations and certain other institutions of this kind ... and because, among certain of them ... such things have already developed into abuses and malpractices ... we hereby, in virtue of our imperial power, and by our sure knowledge, revoke these tribunals, etc., and also the concessions in regard to them obtained through the Counts of Provence and Forcalquier and declare them null and void.' - ᵉ 'We likewise prohibit conventions and sworn confederacies of whatever kind within the cities and without ... between city and city or between person and person or between city and person.' (Peace Charter of Frederick I.) - ᶠ 'That no city and no market town may organise communes, constitutions, unions, leagues or sworn confederacies of any kind, by whatever name they may be referred to, and that, without the assent of their lord, we neither can nor should allow the cities and market towns in our Empire the right to establish communes, constitutions ... sworn confederacies of any kind, whatever names may be conferred on them.' (Decree of King Henry against city communes.) - ᵍ stiff - ʰ sworn commune

'Communio quoque civium Trevirensium, quae et conjuratio dicitur, quam nos in civitate destruximus ... quae et postea, sicut audivimus, reiterata est, cassetur et in irritum revocetur.' [II, 88][a]

The policy pursued by the German emperors was exploited by the French *rois*[b] who secretly supported *'conjurationes'* and *'communiones'* in Lorraine, Alsace, the Dauphiné, Franche-Comté, the Lyonnais, etc., thus alienating them from the German Empire:

'Sicut ad culminis nostri pervenit notitiam, rex Franciae ... sinceritatem fidei vestrae molitur corrumpere.' (Rodolphus I, epistula ad cives de Besançon.) [II, 94][c]

The very same policy was used by the fellows to make Italian cities Guelphic.[563]

It's funny how the word *'communio'* is often reviled in just the same way as communism nowadays. Thus, for example, the priest Guibert of Nogent writes:

'Communio, novum ac pessimum nomen.'[d]

There's often something rather pathetic about the way in which the twelfth-century philistines invite the peasants to take refuge in the towns, the *communio jurata*. As, for instance, in the Charter of St Quentin:

'Eux' (the burghers of St Quentin) 'jurèrent ensement chescun quemune ayde à son juré et quemun conseil et quemune détenanche et quemune deffense. Ensement nous avons establi que quiconque en notre quemune entrera et ayde du sien nous donra, soit pour cause de fuite ou de paour des anemis ou de autre forfait ... en le quemune entrer porra, *car la porte est ouverte à tous*; et se son seigneur à tort ses choses aura détenu et ne le voudra détenir à droit, nous en exécuterons justice.' [II, 135][e]

Your

K. M.

First published slightly abridged in *Der Briefwechsel zwischen F. Engels und K. Marx*, Bd. 2, Stuttgart, 1913 and in full in: Marx and Engels, *Works*, First Russian Edition, Vol. XXII, Moscow, 1929

Printed according to the original

Published in English in full for the first time

---

[a] 'The commune of the citizens of Trier, which is also called sworn confederacy and which we have abolished in the city ... and which as we have heard was later set up anew, shall also be dissolved and declared null and void'. - [b] kings - [c] 'According to the information which has reached our Highness, the King of France ... is seeking to corrupt the sincerity of your loyalty.' (Rudolph I, Letter to the citizens of Besançon.) - [d] 'Commune, a new and thoroughly bad appellation'. - [e] 'They' (the burghers of St Quentin) 'have jointly sworn each to give common aid

239

MARX TO ENGELS

IN MANCHESTER

[London,] 8 August 1854

Dear Frederic,

I have duly received your war 'OBSERVATIONS'[a] and incorporated them IN TODAY'S LETTER.[b]

If you can possibly see your way to getting hold of some money for me I would urgently request you to do so. The £11 extra expenditure incurred over the past 6 weeks has plunged me into the utmost DESTITUTION. Moreover, Pieper, who is *sans sou,*[c] has been living and eating here all that time and will certainly be staying for another 2-3 weeks. *C'est dur.*[d]

Did you see in the papers that the 2 Turkish officers sent to that 'great' democrat Shamyl Bey by the Asiatic army were accompanied by COLONEL *Bangya?*

Your
K. M.

First published in: Marx and Engels, *Works,* First Russian Edition, Vol. XXII, Moscow, 1929

Printed according to the original

Published in English for the first time

---

to his confederate and to share with him common counsel and common responsibility and common defence. We have jointly determined that whoever shall enter our commune and give us his aid, either by reason of flight or for fear of his enemies or for some other offence ... shall be allowed into the commune, *for the gate is open to all;* and if his lord had unjustly withheld his chattels and does not wish to detain him lawfully, we shall see that justice is done.'
[a] F. Engels, 'The Attack on the Russian Forts'. - [b] K. Marx, 'Evacuation of the Danubian Principalities.—The Events in Spain.—A New Danish Constitution.—The Chartists'. - [c] penniless - [d] It is hard.

240

MARX TO ENGELS

IN MANCHESTER

[London,] 26 August 1854
28 Dean Street, Soho

Dear Engels,

My wife got back on Wednesday,[a] quite well. In the Fatherland, she tells me, everyone is down in the dumps on account of the 'uncertain conditions'.

I cannot imagine what has become of Cluss. The fellow hasn't written for months. Perhaps it's too hot over there.

It is a very good thing that you are rid of Heise. I don't see that a 'loafer' of this sort can be of any interest. I have not, of course, seen Imandt's correspondence with Dronke and Heise, but I do know that, if he takes part in their childish nonsense, he does so at most in a 'theoretical' sense. Down here, Imandt lives the life of a sober, hard-working citizen.

I have heard from Lassalle who announces triumphantly that the Hatzfeldt woman's 7, or rather 8, years' war is now over.[355] *Enfin!*[b] 'Victory' for the old woman, who would appear to have emerged from the campaign with her virtue and, what is more, her money bags, *'vierge'.*[c] Lassalle now intends to move his domicile to Berlin, but has already heard talk about difficulties with the police.

Meyer writes to tell me that the trial of the Berlin demagogues[564] (in which Gottfried's Gottfried played a part) has been quashed by the court in Berlin (which, he doesn't say), 'because *Hentze,* the principal witness for the prosecution, was "questionable"'. *Qu'en dis-tu?*[d]

I have also had a letter from Miquel in Paris. He intended to come here but first he had cholera and then a haemorrhage, whereupon his doctors suggested that he had better drop the idea of sea travel and make for home overland with all dispatch. Bad luck.

Cherval, who under the name of 'Crämer'—this time the real name was the pseudonym—had diverse experiences in Switzerland, *inter alia* engraving plates for Mr Vogt, who had taken him under his wing, is now living in Paris. I have his address.

___

[a] 23 August - [b] At last! - [c] intact - [d] What do you think of that?

Daniels has been seriously ill for months and it seems doubtful whether he'll pull through.

Reports, particularly in the *Débats,* suggest that there is a state of splendid anarchy in Spain. So far as I can gather from the papers, the Polish and Hungarian émigrés in the Turkish Asiatic army do nothing but engage in mischief, place-seeking and petty intrigues. *Toujours les mêmes.*[a]

Vale faveque.[b]

Totus tuus[c]

K. M.

First published in: Marx and Engels, *Works,* First Russian Edition, Vol. XXII, Moscow, 1929

Printed according to the original

Published in English for the first time

241

MARX TO ENGELS

IN MANCHESTER

[London,] 2 September 1854
28 Dean Street, Soho

Dear Frederic,

So now you're a member of the Exchange, and ALTOGETHER RESPECTABLE. MY GRATULATIONS. Some time I should like to hear you howling amidst that pack of wolves.

Heise has written to Imandt, telling him that factory people— where I don't know (nor does he say whether they're workers or manufacturers)—have banded together to appoint him their COMMON INSTRUCTOR, and that he can count on getting £2 a week. *Tant mieux pour lui.*[d]

My wife—as I had good reason to fear before she left—IS RATHER IN TOO INTERESTING CIRCUMSTANCES, otherwise well.

Cluss has written again at last. I enclose his letter.

Has your old man arrived yet?

It is probably time we said something in the *Tribune* about

---

[a] Always the same. - [b] Good bye and farewell. - [c] All yours - [d] So much the better for him.

military events in Asia. I have made a bit of a howler. In one of my recent LETTERS I declared the NEWS of the total defeat of the Turks at Kars to be a Vienna INVENTION.[565] True, the telegraphic dispatch was wrong, but it was nevertheless based on fact.[a]

My PRINCIPAL STUDY is now SPAIN. So far I have swotted up, mainly from Spanish sources, the 1808-14 and the 1820-23 periods. Am now coming to the years 1834-43. The thing is not without complexity. It is rather more difficult to discover exactly the springs behind developments. At any rate I made a timely start with *Don Quixote*.[b] The whole thing will amount to about 6 articles for the *Tribune,* if much condensed.[566] At least it may be counted a step forward that AT THIS MOMENT ONE'S STUDIES are paid for.

Unfortunately the Library[c] is closed from 1-7 September. Apart from other advantages, it's the only cool place in London.

Entre nous,[d] Dronke, for want of other 'intellectual' stimulus, is busily engaged in investigating 'Steffen' and, in his letters to Imandt, tears him to pieces in an attempt to render him politically 'suspect'. I had no difficulty in convincing Imandt of the total absurdity of Dronke's mischievous cavilling. *C'est absurde.*[e] I consider that in Steffen our [party] has made a very good acquisition. He has character and education. His views on comparative geography, in which he has specialised, are quite original. Unfortunately a manuscript in which he elaborated his ideas on the subject was left behind in Cologne.

What is Lupus doing? Miquel didn't come over from Paris as intended because, having had 2 attacks of cholera followed by a haemorrhage, he was finally ordered by the doctors to make his way back to Germany overland with all dispatch.

Vale faveque.[f]

K. M.

First published slightly abridged in *Der Briefwechsel zwischen F. Engels und K. Marx,* Bd. 2, Stuttgart, 1913 and in full in: Marx and Engels, *Works,* First Russian Edition, Vol. XXII, Moscow, 1929

Printed according to the original

Published in English for the first time

---

[a] Marx presumably refers to the item 'Foreign Intelligence. Wednesday evening', *The Times,* No. 21829, 25 August 1854. - [b] See this volume, p. 447. - [c] of the British Museum - [d] between ourselves - [e] It's absurd. - [f] Good-bye and farewell.

242

MARX TO ENGELS

IN MANCHESTER

London, 13 September 1854
28 Dean Street, Soho

Dear Engels,

Once again I must come knocking at your door, much though I detest doing so, but compelled by PRESSURE FROM WITHOUT. I cannot draw my bills for a few weeks yet, since IN CONSEQUENCE OF some unpleasantness he has had with Bischoffsheim in this connection, Freiligrath is no longer drawing bills of less than £25. On the whole, too, this is preferable, for while the constant drawing of· small sums may cover the *dette flottante*,[a] the fixed debt increases. On top of that, I shall have to deduct £8 for Freund from the next bill since, under the present CIRCUMSTANCES, my wife will need rather more care. The EXTRAORDINARY MEANS to which the family is wont to resort at times of crisis are AGAIN exhausted and, just as in the case of the Spanish Budget everything is in pawn.

By the by, as regards the 'budget' *en général,* I have reduced total indebtedness to under £50, i.e. about £30 less than it was at the beginning of the year. From this you can see that there have been some great financial sleights of hand. If a NEGOTIATION I have initiated with Lassalle succeeds, and he lends me £30, and you lend me the remainder, I would at last be independent again and reorganise all my domestic arrangements, whereas at present I have to pay out 25 per cent to the pawnshop alone, and in general am never able to get things in order because of arrears. As has once again been demonstrated in Trier, nothing will be achieved with my mater[567] until I can go and importune her in person.

Dans ce moment[b] the total absence of money is the more horrible—quite apart from the fact that FAMILY WANTS do not cease for an instant—as Soho is a choice district for cholera, the MOB is croaking right and left (e.g. an average of 3 per house in Broad Street), and 'victuals'[568] are the best defence against the beastly thing.

---

[a] floating debt - [b] At this moment.

So much for that. I am sending this letter to your private address because some strange combination of circumstances could cause precisely this by no means edifying epistle to fall into the wrong hands at your office.

———

As regards the *Asiatic* business, a considerable stir has been made here by the dispatches from that theatre of operations in *The Morning Chronicle*, which have also been reproduced in *The Observer* and other weeklies.[a]

I don't know whether the news about the Zouaves' cry *'A bas les singes! Il nous faut Lamoricière!'*[b] has penetrated as far as Manchester. Espinasse, the first victim of this agitation, has been recalled to France.[569]

The party has been having a run of bad luck. Steffen has lost his post in Brighton through the bankruptcy of the schoolmaster in whose establishment he was employed. It is questionable whether he will manage to get the salary already due to him. *Pieper* has lost his post as correspondent to the *Union*, since Mr Pierce has likewise gone bankrupt, and his papers get no more money for foreign correspondents. *MacGowan*, Jones' printer and source of credit, has died of cholera. A blow for Jones. ALL THIS IS NOT VERY PLEASANT.

I don't remember muck about Imandt. To inquire into it further would only make matters worse. But henceforward I shall break off the moment the gentleman makes any 'reference' to Dronke. Dronke *ne vaut pas la peine d'en parler.*[c]

Your

K. M.

First published in *Der Briefwechsel zwischen F. Engels und K. Marx*, Bd. 2, Stuttgart, 1913

Printed according to the original

Published in English for the first time

———

[a] 'The Battles of Bayazid and Kuruk-Dere', *The Morning Chronicle*, No. 27365, 7 September 1854, also reproduced in *The Observer* on 10 September. - [b] 'Down with the monkeys! We want Lamoricière!' 'Singes' also means 'bosses'. - [c] isn't worth discussing

243

MARX TO ENGELS

IN MANCHESTER

London, 22 September 1854

Dear Frederic,

Just a few lines in much haste to acknowledge due receipt. Also of your letter ON THE ASIATIC WAR on Tuesday.[570]

I have had some very important dispatches from America which I shall send you with my next letter. *Je vous attends*[a] ON TUESDAY.[571]

That fat swine Püttmann has been shipped off from here to Australia as a 'colonist', together with FAMILY.

Ebner has gone mad in Frankfurt. *Pauvre diable.*[b]

Ernest Jones has found a new printer on cheaper terms. Disraeli has written to tell him that he will bring up *all* Chartist petitions in Parliament.

The cholera epidemic, now much abated, is said to have been particularly severe in our district because * the sewers made in June, July and August, were driven through the pits where those who died of the plague 1668 (? I think) were buried *.

Your
K. M.

First published abridged in *Der Briefwechsel zwischen F. Engels und K. Marx*, Bd. 2, Stuttgart, 1913 and in full in: Marx and Engels, *Works*, First Russian Edition, Vol. XXII, Moscow, 1929

Printed according to the original

Published in English for the first time

244

MARX TO ENGELS

IN MANCHESTER

London, 29 September 1854
28 Dean Street, Soho

Dear Engels,

The enclosed letter from Dana will tell you about the *American crisis* AS FAR AS I AM AFFECTED BY IT. Upon my demanding that all or

---

[a] I expect [something from] you - [b] Poor devil.

nothing should appear under my name, they replied by confining me solely to EDITORIAL ARTICLES at half the previous rate. For the time being I have written to Dana telling him that I have not yet reached any decision[572] but shall IN THE MEANWHILE go on *as before* sending 2 articles a week, because of the Sevastopol business,[573] on the one hand, and of my SKETCHES of the Spanish Revolution in the nineteenth century on the other, which must be completed before the Cortes meets. In the meantime we can consider what definite answer to give the gentlemen.

I cannot write more than this today since I am busy just now dictating my article,[574] but should have written to you at greater length had you not announced last Tuesday week that I would be getting a 'long' letter,[575] which I have been waiting for in order to reply to it.

Salut.

Your

K. M.

First published in *Der Briefwechsel zwischen F. Engels und K. Marx*, Bd. 2, Stuttgart, 1913

Printed according to the original

Published in English for the first time

245

MARX TO ENGELS

IN MANCHESTER

London, 10 October[a] 1854
28 Dean Street, Soho

Dear Engels,

D'abord mes compliments[b] on your exceedingly GLORIOUS and SOUND CRITICISM.[c] It's a pity that this '*fait d'armes*'[d] couldn't have been accomplished in the London Press. A coup of this nature would have assured your position in that field.

Quant à notre bon[e] St-Arnaud who took good care to die at the right moment, I gave the *Tribune* a detailed biography of him[576] MONTHS AGO. Of this fellow it may assuredly be said: '*Non bis in idem.*'[f]

---

[a] November in the original. - [b] First, my congratulations - [c] F. Engels, 'The Battle of the Alma'. - [d] feat of arms - [e] As for our good - [f] Never twice on the same subject.

How to explain: 1. that the English failed to station a group of warships off the Yenikale Straits in sufficient strength to prevent the Russians crossing from Anapa, etc.? Was it not perfectly possible, indeed imperative under PRESENT CIRCUMSTANCES, to gain control of the SEA OF AZOV with small vessels in order to cut off all reinforcements by water?

2. Should not a diversion in the direction of Bessarabia have been made (by Omer Pasha) to prevent the Russians from bringing reinforcements into the Crimea from that quarter? Can negligence on this score be explained otherwise than by Anglo-Austrian diplomatic trickery?

I believe, OF COURSE, that diplomacy on the part of military commanders ceases as soon as they find themselves in a mousetrap as in the Crimea. But in all that concerns the plan as a whole, I do not believe that Palmerston has as yet ceased for one moment to evince at least his 'good will'.

In one of its recent issues, the *Tribune* is congratulated by my rival, A.P.C.,[a] for its 'SPLENDID CHARACTERISATION' of Espartero.[b] The man, of course, has no idea that he is 'complimenting' me, but at the same time a sure instinct has led him to take HOLD of a VERY SILLY concluding sentence that belongs exclusively to the *Tribune*.[577] Incidentally, they had deleted every one of my jokes about *constitutional* heroes *en général*, suspecting that, lurking behind the 'Monk-Lafayette-Espartero' trio, were certain sarcasms aimed at the noble 'Washington'. The paper's uncritical attitude is horrifying. First, they extolled Espartero as the ONLY STATESMAN OF SPAIN. Then they took my articles,[c] which treat him if anything as a comic character, and added: From this one can see that nothing is to be expected of Spain. Then, when they got the first article on Spain—mere prolegomena leading up to 1808—they believed it to constitute the whole and accordingly added on a completely heterogeneous but well-meaning conclusion urging the Spaniards to show themselves worthy of the *Tribune*'s confidence.[578] How they will handle subsequent instalments, I do not know.

Liebknecht, as you know, has been vacillating most despondently between an Englishwoman who wanted to marry him and a German woman[d] in Germany whom he wanted to marry. At last

---

[a] [F. Pulszky,] An article dated 7 September 1854 and published in the section 'The State of Europe' of the *New-York Daily Tribune*, No. 4190, 22 September 1854. - [b] K. Marx, 'Espartero'. - [c] See K. Marx, 'The Spanish Revolution.—Greece and Turkey', 'Evacuation of the Danubian Principalities.—The Events in Spain.—A New Danish Constitution.—The Chartists', 'Evacuation of Moldavia and Wallachia.—Poland.—Demands of the Spanish People'. - [d] Ernestine Landolt

the German descended on him and he married her,—in a religious as well as a civil ceremony. Both of them seem very down-in-the-mouth. His job goes west, since the people are moving away. He spent a wretched honeymoon at No. 14 Church Street in a house where he got himself heavily in debt. But who forced the ass to get married—at this of all times since he was perfectly aware of all these circumstances. The woman had in the meantime already become engaged to someone else in Germany, so at any rate the case was by no means a pressing one.

If you want to read something really funny you must try and get hold of Saturday's *Morning Advertiser*, in which the LICENSED VICTUALLERS take the present editorial board of that POTHOUSE PAPER to court.[a] Prosecution and defence both equally amusing. The first was conducted by Mr Foster who once figured as a BARRISTER in Baron Nicholson's court.[579] All the thanks Urquhart got for having extolled the LICENSED as England's party above parties were hard words and his dismissal. Never, by the way, has the curtain been raised quite so much to reveal the innermost squalor of the SHOP-KEEPER's soul.

I suppose you haven't seen Bruno Bauer's *L'Arrogance des pouvoirs occidentaux?*[b] I haven't yet managed to lay hands on it either.

Should anything important happen in the military department before Friday,[c] send me something to be *going on with*, for in that case the Spanish article, if it is to be ACCEPTABLE, will have to be preceded by a Russian one.[580]

I look forward to a letter from you soon.

Your
K. M.

First published abridged in *Der Briefwechsel zwischen F. Engels und K. Marx*, Bd. 2, Stuttgart, 1913 and in full in: Marx and Engels, *Works*, First Russian Edition, Vol. XXII, Moscow, 1929

Printed according to the original

Published in English for the first time

---

[a] 'The Incorporated Society of Licensed Victuallers', *The Morning Advertiser*, No. 19749, 7 October 1854. - [b] Presumably B. Bauer's *De la dictature occidentale*. - [c] 13 October

246

MARX TO ENGELS

IN MANCHESTER

London, 17 October 1854
28 Dean Street, Soho

Dear Engels,

Your enumeration of the Russian armed forces made today is FORMIDABLE.[a] BUT THERE REMAINS THIS ONE QUESTION TO BE ANSWERED, whether, even by exerting themselves to the utmost, they were capable of sending more than 200,000 men *outside* their own country. I am aware of no such instance.

From the standpoint of the *old* policy,—and what else do England and France advocate, even though the English Ministry is not in earnest and Napoleon III a caricature—, a distinction must be drawn between the interests of England and those of France. With the destruction of the Russian fleet in the Black Sea and the Baltic and the Russians driven out of the Crimea, the Caucasus and the provinces they had filched from Persia and Turkey, England would have ensured her supremacy at sea and her hegemony over the most cultivated part of Asia for another 50 years. It would then be just like her old self to let the continentals exhaust themselves in a seven years' and other wars—whose main theatre would be Germany and, to some extent, Italy—and, at the end of the struggle, see neither Russia nor Austria nor France supreme on the Continent. For France, on the other hand, the real struggle would only begin with the destruction of Russia's sea-power and her influence in South Asia. She would be under all the greater compulsion to break Russia's power on land in order to extend her own power on the Continent, and thus be able to cast a corresponding weight onto the scales against England. Is there any guarantee that, once England has destroyed the Russians in the BALTIC and the BLACK SEA and rendered them innocuous to herself, revolutions won't break out on the Continent and be used by England as a pretext for another official alliance with Russia against the Continent?

However, the real joke is that none of the Englishmen now in power—neither Chathams nor Pitts Jun., AND NOT EVEN Welling-

---

[a] F. Engels, 'The Military Power of Russia'.

tons—seriously pursue even the destruction of Russian sea-power and Russian influence in Turkey-Persia-Caucasus. If their HALF and HALF MEASURES compel them to do so, they may consider going *so far*; but their half-measures and villainy will probably land them in trouble, which will provoke MOVEMENTS here at home.

The following passages, quoted from the *Archives des Affaires Étrangères* in Paris—relating to the Seven Years' War [581]—show how English Ministers colluded with the enemy actually during the campaign and in matters relating to it. On 24 June 1762 the French Pompadour marshal Soubise,[a] when encamped at Wilhelmstal, had allowed himself to be surprised by the English, Prussian, Hanoverian, etc., allies and driven back across the Fulda. For *parliamentary* and *dynastic* reasons, Lord Bute, George III's Prime Minister, desired peace, but, in view of the nation's bellicose mood and its bias in favour of Frederick II, could not propose peace so long as the French persisted in letting themselves be beaten and in retreating instead of advancing. Choiseul, as you know, was then Minister of Foreign Affairs IN FRANCE. In *authentic* publications from the French archives, which I quote verbatim, we find:

'Après l'affaire du 24 Juin les *ministres anglais* écrivirent à M. de Choiseul: *Vous vous laissez battre et nous ne pouvons plus faire la paix, nous n'oserions pas la proposer au parlement*. M. de Choiseul, désolé de voir rompue la négociation, engage *le roi* à écrire à M. de Soubise: "Mon cousin, je vous écris la présente, qu'aussitôt que vous l'aurez reçue vous passiez la rivière du Fulde et que vous attaquiez les ennemis, sans compter sur les dispositions qui vous conviendront et quelque soit le succès, vous n'en serez pas responsable. Sur ce je prie Dieu etc." M. de Choiseul écrivit: "La lettre du roi, M. le Maréchal, est trop formelle pour que j'aie rien à y ajouter. Mais je puis vous dire que *quand l'armée du roi serait détruite jusqu'au dernier homme* et qu'il fût obligé d'enlever une nouvelle, *Sa Majesté n'en serait effrayée*.' " [b]

---

[a] An allusion to Marshal Soubise's liaison with Jeanne Antoinette Pompadour. - [b] 'After the affair of 24 June, the *English Ministers* wrote to M. de Choiseul: *You are permitting yourselves to be beaten and we can no longer make peace; we would not dare propose it to Parliament*. M. de Choiseul, distressed at seeing negotiations broken off, urged *the King* to write to M. de Soubise: "Dear Cousin, I am writing to you so that, immediately on receipt of this letter, you should cross the River Fulda and attack the enemy without heed for such dispositions as you might think fit and, whatever the result, you will not be held responsible. As to which, I pray God, etc." M. de Choiseul wrote: "The King's letter, M. le Maréchal, is too explicit for me to have to add anything. But I can tell you that, *should the King's Army be destroyed down to the last man* and His Majesty be obliged to raise a new one, *he would not be dismayed at it*".'

Here, then, we have the English Ministry demanding outright that an allied army, subsidised by them and consisting partly of Englishmen, should be *buffeted* by the French. They had earlier meddled in French military operations in the opposite direction because George wanted his Hanover to be spared. For in the same *extraits*[a] we read:

'En 1762 Mrs. d'Estrées et de Soubise ont commandé l'armée du haut Rhin de 150 000 hommes, établie en Hesse, à Goettinguen, Mulhouse et Eisenach; Mr. de Condé a commandé celle du bas Rhin de 30 000 hommes. La cour ne leur demandait que de conserver Cassel de Goettinguen jusqu'à la fin du novembre, d'évacuer ces deux places à cette époque pour se retirer sur l'Ohm en mettant Ziegenhayn en avant de leur première ligne. Ce plan de guerre avec puissance égale, avec 180 000 contre 80 000 serait *extraordinaire*, s'il n'avait pas été fondé sur la promesse, *que le ministère anglais nous faisait de conclure la paix avant le mois de juillet, si nous ne ferions point d'incursions dans le Hanovre.*'[b]

This latter piece of meddling by London might, at most, be regarded as normal, had the warring powers been on the point of entering into peace negotiations; the first case, on the other hand, would have cost Lord Bute his head and George, such was the mood at the time (THINK ONLY OF WILKES' AND JUNIUS'[c] LETTERS[582]), his throne but, *comme toujours*,[d] it was almost A CENTURY before the matter came to light. We encounter another such example just before the outbreak of the ANTI-JACOBIN WAR[583] when the 'liberal' Fox sent a secret emissary[e] to Catherine II telling her not to be misled by Pitt's threats, but to gobble up Poland at her leisure for, should Pitt try to go to war against Russia, he would be brought down.[584] True, Fox was then in the 'opposition' and not the Ministry, and I adduce this example simply as evidence that the 'OUTS' are no less honourable than the 'INS'.

Hence I believe that, in assessing the allies' conduct of the war—as indeed you infer from time to time in your articles—the

---

[a] extracts - [b] In 1762 Messieurs d'Estrées and de Soubise were in command of the Army of the Upper Rhine numbering 150,000 men, stationed in Hesse, at Göttingen, Mülhausen and Eisenach; M. de Condé commanded that of the Lower Rhine, numbering 30,000 men. All that the Court asked of them was to hold Cassel and Göttingen until the end of November, to evacuate those two places at that time and withdraw to the Ohm, having Ziegenhayn before their front line. Even assuming equal strengths, let alone 180,000 against 80,000, this plan of campaign would have been *extraordinary* had it not been based on a promise made to us by the *English Ministry to conclude peace before the month of July, provided that we made no incursions into Hanover.*' - [c] Philip Francis - [d] as always - [e] Robert Adair

exchanges between Downing Street (especially as long as Palmerston is there) and Petersburg MUST always BE CONSIDERED. I AM SURE that, as soon as the armies find themselves in a critical position, the generals will sh... on the Cabinet and do their best, since Messrs the generals are seldom or never let into secrets and even risk their necks—witness the example of Admiral Byng,[585] whose instructions from the Admiralty of the day were no less deplorable than those of e.g. Dundas now.

I shall try to get hold of Bauer's latest production[a] and send it to you.

I don't know whether Napier[b] and other historians of the Franco-Spanish war have presented in its true light a fact for which there is ample proof in *Spanish* works, namely that, right up to the end of the war, apart from a brief spell when Napoleon himself was in command in Spain,[586] a fully organised *republican* conspiracy existed in the French army, aimed at overthrowing Napoleon and restoring the republic. Apropos. Authentic sources suggest that the great 'Mina y Espoz'[c] was an egregious rogue, inferior to Joh. Becker, NO MILITARY TALENT AT ALL, but cunning, worldly-wise and *avant tout voleur*.[d] A careful study of Spanish revolutionary history reveals that it has taken the fellows some 40 years to subvert the material basis of the priesthood and the aristocracy, but that during this time they have also succeeded in completely revolutionising the old social order. Incidentally, the provisional governments, etc., there show about as much sense as in France, etc. Considering the hot-bloodedness of the whole race and their indifference to bloodshed, it is typical that, up to the time of the civil war of 1834-40,[587] it was precisely the revolutionary party which claimed to have a monopoly of philanthropic gentleness, and for this it was punished AGAIN and AGAIN.

Tomorrow Pieper will probably become a RESIDENT MASTER 30 miles from London. Having lost his post as correspondent to the *Union*, he is forced to accept this appointment. In view of my wife's 'condition' she will be able to do little as a secretary.

This is deplorable.

I have had another dunning letter from the 'friendly' Freund, but no reply as yet from Lassalle.

When your old man leaves again, or if he decides not to come, I

---

[a] Presumably *De la dictature occidentale* (see previous letter). - [b] W. F. P. Napier, *History of the War in the Peninsula and in the South of France, from the Year 1807 to the Year 1814.* - [c] Espoz y Mina - [d] above all a thief

should, circumstances permitting, like to come to Manchester for a time.

Still no answer from Lassalle—nine weeks now. Nothing from Cluss.

Schnauffer has died.

Your
K. M.

First published in *Der Briefwechsel zwischen F. Engels und K. Marx*, Bd. 2, Stuttgart, 1913

Printed according to the original

Published in English for the first time

247

MARX TO ENGELS

IN MANCHESTER

[London,] 25 October 1854
28 Dean Street, Soho

Dear Frederic,

Enclosed a letter from Cluss.

Schnauffer is dead.

Pieper is a RESIDENT MASTER just outside London, at Eltham, Kent. SERVANT FOR ALL WORK.

If you can let me have some military stuff for Friday,[a] so much the better. It is time to take a rational attitude to the Allies' conduct of the war.

The Mademoiselle Bürgers business is very funny.

As you already know, before she left Cologne she got herself a child, giving out that Lassalle was its father.

The post is leaving, hençe

Vale.[b]

Your
K. M.

First published in: Marx and Engels, *Works*, First Russian Edition, Vol. XXII, Moscow, 1929

Printed according to the original

Published in English for the first time

---

[a] 27 October. Engels wrote 'The Siege of Sevastopol' later, on 30 October.
[b] Farewell.

248

MARX TO ENGELS[588]

IN MANCHESTER

[London,] 26 October 1854
28 Dean Street, Soho

Dear Frederic,

While studying the Spanish muck I have got to the bottom of the worthy Chateaubriand—a style-specialist who combines in the most repellent manner the refined scepticism and Voltairianism of the eighteenth century with the refined sentimentalism and romanticism of the nineteenth. *Stylistically*, of course, such a combination was bound to be epoch-making in France, though even the style has an element of spuriousness which, for all his clever tricks, frequently leaps to the eye. As for the *political* man, he has exposed himself utterly in his *Congrès de Vérone*,[589] and the only question is whether he received 'cash' from Alexander Pavlovich[a] or whether he was bought simply by FLATTERY to which the conceited fop was more susceptible than anyone else. AT ALL INSTANCES he received the Order of St Andrew[590] from Petersburg. Everything about M. le 'Vicomte's' (?) *vanitas*, notwithstanding his now Mephistophelian, now Christian coquetting with *vanitatum vanitas*.[b] You will remember that, at the time of the Congress, Villèle was Louis XVIII's Prime Minister and Chateaubriand French envoy in Verona. His *Congrès de Vérone*, which you may at some time have read, contains documents, transactions, etc. Begins with a short history of the Span. revolution of 1820-23. As for this 'history', all I need tell you is that he transfers Madrid to the banks of the Tagus (merely so as to quote the Span. saying that this river *cria oro*[c]) and tells us that Riego led *10,000 men* (*realiter*[d] only 5,000) into the field against the 13,000 under General Freire; that Riego, having been beaten, withdrew with *15,000* men. In order to compare him with the hero of La Mancha,[e] he sends him to the Sierra Morena instead of the Sierra de Ronda. This I mention *en passant* as characteristic of his manner. Hardly a date that is right.

The best part of the joke, though, is Mr Chateaubriand's doings

---

[a] Alexander I - [b] *Vanitas vanitatum et omnia vanitas*—vanity of vanities, Ecclesiastes 1:2. - [c] breeds gold - [d] in reality - [e] Don Quixote

at the Congress of Verona, after the conclusion of which he became Foreign Minister and directed the invasion of Spain. He says *d'abord*[a]:

'Je ne me défends point d'être le principal auteur de la guerre d'Espagne'. [Chateaubriand. *Congrès de Vérone*, Vol. I, p. 11], '*Mr. de Villèle* ne voulait point les hostilités.'[b] [I, 73]

On the contrary. The text of the instructions sent by Villèle to him and Montmorency, who at the outset was also in Verona as French Foreign Minister, reads literally:

'Nous ne nous sommes pas décidés à déclarer la guerre à l'Espagne... [I, 103], Les plénipotentiaires de S. M. doivent surtout éviter de se présenter au congrès comme rapporteurs des affaires d'Espagne. Les autres puissances peuvent les connaître aussi bien que nous... Ce rôle pouvait convenir à l'Autriche au congrès de Laybach,[591] parce qu'elle avait la volonté d'envahir Naples.'[c] [I, 102-03]

The fellows do precisely the opposite of what was contained in their instructions. They 'présentent'[d] themselves as '*rapporteurs des affaires d'Espagne*'.[e] Villèle writes:

'Ils tendront à faire considérer la question d'Espagne dans ses rapports *généraux* avec l'Europe'[f] [I, 104];

they presented it from the outset as a *specifically* French matter. Villèle writes:

'L'opinion de nos plénipotentiaires sur la question de savoir ce qu'il convient au congrès de faire relativement à l'Espagne, sera que la France étant la seule puissance qui doive agir par ses troupes, elle sera seule juge de cette nécessité.'[g] [I, 103]

Whereas they took the line that:

'C'est sur la forme de ce concours moral' (of the other powers) 'et sur les mesures propres à lui assurer le *secours matériel* qui peut être réclamé par la suite, que la France croit, en définitive, nécessaire de fixer l'attention de ses augustes alliés.'[h] [I, 109]

---

[a] at first - [b] 'I do not deny having been the principal author of the war in Spain.' '*Mr. de Villèle* did not want hostilities.' - [c] 'We have not made up our minds to declare war on Spain... H. M.'s plenipotentiaries must above all avoid presenting themselves to the Congress as experts on Spanish affairs. The other powers may know as much about them as we do... Such a role may have befitted Austria at the Congress of Laibach because she was willing to invade Naples.' - [d] present - [e] experts on Spanish affairs - [f] 'Their aim must be to ensure that the Spanish question is considered in its *general* relationship to Europe' - [g] 'The opinion of our plenipotentiaries on the question of what it behoves the Congress to do in regard to Spain shall be that France, being the sole power having to engage its troops, shall also be sole judge of that necessity.' - [h] 'It is to the nature of this moral co-operation' (of the other powers) 'and to the measures calculated to assure her the *material aid* which may subsequently be demanded, that France deems it necessary finally to draw the attention of her august allies.'

From the very beginning, then, Mr Chateaubriand acted *directly counter* to the instructions he received from Paris. Secondly, he sought to *deceive* Villèle about the state of affairs in Verona. Thus, for example, he wrote to Villèle:

'Le vœu très prononcé des puissances est *pour* la guerre d'Espagne'[a] [I, 145];

He also seeks to deceive him about the prospects of the war:

'Les dernières dépêches de M. de Lagarde prouvent combien le succès serait facile.'[b] [I, 145]

On the other hand the honest fellow tells us:

'Non seulement le Congrès n'a pas poussé la France à la guerre, mais la Prusse et surtout *l'Autriche'* [I, 112] (he comments: 'le prince de Metternich, feignant d'être russe en détestant la Russie' [I, 116]) 'y étaient très opposées; *la Russie seule l'approuvait* et promettait son appui moral et *son appui matériel.'* [I, 112]

'Nous disons au président du conseil que le vœu très prononcé des puissances est pour la guerre; qu'il ne s'agit pas de l'occupation de la Péninsule; qu'il n'est question que d'un mouvement rapide; nous montrons un succès facile; et *pourtant nous savions* que le congrès de Vérone *ne voulait point* la guerre; nous *craignions* que notre mouvement ne *se prolongeât* bien au delà de l'Ebre; nous pensions qu'il nous faudrait occuper *longtemps* l'Espagne, pour faire une bonne besogne, mais nous ne révélions pas tout, *afin d'arriver à notre but,* et nous nous disions secrètement: "Une fois la Bidassoa[592] passée, il faudra bien que le président du conseil etc, aille de l'avant".'[c] [I, 173-74]

Thus he deceived Villèle in the name of the Congress, as previously he had deceived the Congress in the name of Villèle. And, not content with that, he proceeded to write to Canning, lying in the name of both and against both.

As a Minister he acted in the same manner. The following letter was written by Alexander to Pozzo di Borgo, envoy in Paris, for submission to Louis XVIII:

'L'empereur se flatte encore que la modération prévaudrait dans les conseils du *gouvernement anglais.'* If not etc., 'il regarderait l'attaque dirigée contre la France

---

[a] 'The powers are very strongly *in favour* of war in Spain.' - [b] 'The last dispatches from M. de Lagarde prove how easy success would be.' - [c] 'Not only did the Congress not urge France to go to war, but Prussia and, above all, *Austria*' (he comments: 'Prince Metternich, pretending to be Russian while detesting Russia') 'were much opposed to it; *Russia alone was in favour* and promised her moral support and *her material support.'*

'We tell the Prime Minister that the powers were strongly in favour of war; that it is not a question of occupying the Peninsula; that it is only a question of a quick move; we point to an easy success; and *yet we knew* that the Congress of Verona *did not want* war; we *feared* that our move would *carry us* far beyond the Ebro; we thought that we should have to occupy Spain *for a long time* to make a good job of it, but in order to *achieve our aim,* we did not reveal all and secretly told each other: "Once the Bidassoa has been crossed, the Prime Minister etc. will be forced to go ahead." '

comme une attaque générale contre tous les alliés et accepterait, sans hésiter, les conséquences de ce principe... **L'Empereur exhorte le roi** à consommer ses *propres'* (!) 'déterminations et à marcher avec confiance contre les hommes des troubles et des malheurs. Agissant dans cet esprit *l'Empereur rapelle la question agitée au congrès* relative à la *réunion d'une armée russe sur les frontières occidentales* de l'Empire comme moyen de sûreté européenne.'ᵃ [I, 477-78]

(At the Congress, Austria would not hear of it. For which reason the matter was temporarily dropped.)

His purpose, Chateaubriand alleges, was to procure *glory* (*gloire*) for the Restoration, and thus to pave the way for the violation of the Treaties of Vienna.⁵⁹³ Russia's support was needed against England. But how little 1. he expected of Russian help and how much 2. he feared the war, is evident from the following utterances:

'En supposant un revers en Espagne, *nous avions une révolution en France, et tous les cosaques de la terre ne nous auraient pas sauvés.*'ᵇ [I, 113]

In a letter to *La Ferronnays,* his envoy in Petersburg, he writes:

'*Nous avons mis la monarchie française sur une carte pour faire la guerre.*'ᶜ [II, 8]

(This is dated 21 April 1823.)

He further admits that they would have fallen flat on their faces if Canning had shipped a regiment or two out to Lisbon. To pave the way for this result they further saw to it that, following a row between War Minister the Duke of Bellune and General Guilleminot, the French Army suddenly found itself *sin viveres e sin medios de transporte*ᵈ after marching into Spain. Next, the pretty piece of humbug that a French victory *in the name of the Holy Alliance* and with its *appui moral*ᵉ would help liberate France from the Vienna Treaties. The 'Vicomte' is not '*si bête*'ᶠ as he here makes himself out to be. He knows very well what he is about: '*la Russie n'a point d'ambassadeur à Constantinople*'.ᵍ At the time there

---

ᵃ 'The Emperor continues to hope that moderation will prevail in the councils of the *English government.*' If not etc., 'he would regard an attack directed against France as a general attack upon all the allies and would accept without hesitation the consequences of that principle... **The Emperor exhorts the King** to implement his *own*' (!) 'decisions and to march confidently against the trouble-makers and mischief-makers. Acting in this spirit, *the Emperor recalls the question raised at the Congress* relating to the *mustering of a Russian army on the western borders* of the Empire as a means of ensuring the security of Europe. - ᵇ Assuming a reverse in Spain, we *would have had revolution in France, and not all the Cossacks in the world would have saved us.*' - ᶜ '*We have staked the fate of the French monarchy in order to wage war.*' - ᵈ without victuals and without means of transport - ᵉ moral support - ᶠ so stupid - ᵍ 'Russia has no ambassador in Constantinople'

were underhand dealings with the Greeks;[594] and war between France and England, not to speak of France's commitments in Spain and her defeat there, would have given him a free hand.

'Nous devions surtout prévoir que l'Angleterre pouvait intervenir et se poser en face de nous auprès de l'Espagne.'[a] [I, 112]

To Paris, he writes:

'Si c'est la guerre, *c'est la guerre avec l'Angleterre.*' [I, 161] 'Guerre qui pouvait devenir *européenne,* si elle venait à se compliquer d'une *guerre en Orient* et de l'attaque des colonies espagnoles par les Anglais.'[b] [I, 151]

Nor is he under any illusions about Alexander's intentions:

'Il est certain que notre triomphe **inespéré**' (!) 'lui donna quelque jalousie, car il s'était secrètement flatté que nous serions *forcés* de recourir à lui.'[c] [I, 383]

The 'triumph', then, was not what had been agreed. Besides, like the majority of Frenchmen, Chateaubriand believed the French Army to be very 'unreliable' so far as the Bourbons were concerned.

Moreover, the 'friendship' between Alexander and Louis XVIII was, as Chateaubriand himself relates, all the closer for

'Louis XVIII' having 'refusé, sous prétexte de religion et par quelque *motif offensant,* le mariage du duc de Berry avec la sœur d'Alexandre'[d] [I, 195]

and for Louis XVIII's having, for his part, known that at the Congress of Vienna (after Bonaparte's return from Elba) Mr Alexander had

'tout à coup demanda aux alliés, s'il ne serait pas bon de donner le duc d'Orléans pour roi à la France, quand on aurait une dernière fois vaincu Napoléon!'[e] [I, 196]

Having a *'grand âme de poète,'*[f] the 'Vicomte' makes the following admissions:

'Nous osons dire qu'Alexandre est devenu *notre ami.*' [I, 223]

---

[a] 'Above all we had to foresee that England might intervene and range herself against us and alongside Spain.' - [b] 'If it is war, it is *war with England.*' 'A war which might become a *European* one if complicated by *war in the East* and an attack upon the Spanish colonies by the English.' - [c] 'There can be no doubt that our **unexpected**' (!) 'triumph gave him some cause for jealousy, for he had secretly flattered himself that we would be *compelled* to have recourse to him.' - [d] 'Louis XVIII's' having 'refused, on religious grounds and for some *offensive reason,* to sanction the marriage between the Duke of Berry and Alexander's sister' - [e] 'suddenly asked the allies whether it would not be advisable to make the Duke of Orleans King of France, once Napoleon had been defeated for the last time!' - [f] great poetic soul

'Alexandre est le *seul* prince pour qui nous ayons *jamais* éprouvé un *sincère* attachement.' [I, 224]
'Louis XVIII *nous détestait.*'[a] [I, 243]

Withal it is highly entertaining to see how this '*Dieu de St. Louis*' speechifier, who had to preserve the Spanish throne for a '*petit fils de Henri IV*',[b][595] writes most *cavalièrement* to General Guilleminot telling him not to 'be deterred' from bombarding Cadiz by the fear that Ferdinand VII might be struck by shot, etc.

At all events, it is hence to this *ami intime*[c] of the great Carrel, Lamennais, Béranger, etc., that the honour belongs of having, over a period of 10 years—in the company of friend Alexander—, created the biggest mess Spain has ever known, and this at the risk of blowing his Bourbons sky-high.

Another trait of this pilgrim to the Holy Sepulchre[596]: In the *Congrès de Vérone* he himself relates how he forced Louis XVIII and Villèle to send Polignac, whom both abhorred, to London as envoy. Later, under Charles X, when he himself was envoy in Rome, he suddenly and with great *brio* announced his resignation upon the appointment of Polignac as minister because, he alleged, 'freedom' was doomed.

If you re-read the book, your contempt for the '*crapauds*'[d] and their '*grands hommes*'[e] is unlikely to diminish.

Adieu.

Your
K. M.

First published in *Der Briefwechsel zwischen F. Engels* und K. Marx, Bd. II, Stuttgart, 1913

Printed according to the original

Published in English in full for the first time

249

MARX TO ENGELS

IN MANCHESTER

London, 10 November 1854
28 Dean Street, Soho

Dear Engels,

Article splendid.[f] As regards Tuesday or Friday,[g] arrange it as you wish, although I don't yet know whether I shall have a

---

[a] We venture to say that Alexander has become our friend.' 'Alexander is the *only* prince for whom we have *ever* felt a *sincere* attachment.' 'Louis XVIII *detested us.*' - [b] Henry IV's grandson - [c] intimate friend - [d] philistines - [e] great men - [f] F. Engels, 'The Campaign in the Crimea'. - [g] 14 or 17 November

SECRETARY READY, since my wife has been confined to bed for the past three days, partly because of indisposition, partly in a fit of anger, for the worthy Dr Freund has again been bombarding us with dunning letters, which are the more odious for coming just before the impending catastrophe. GENERALLY, THE SITUATION IS NOT PLEASANT.

Père Göhringer is in the debtors' prison. His pub is closed. Bankruptcy. Hence the renewed revolutionary ardour which the noble fellow is said to have developed of late.

Pieper has to work in his institution[a] from 6 in the morning until 9 at night and to pray some 20× during that time, which 'does him good'. No smoking or drinking. Takes the boys to church, etc. He was in town for an hour a few days ago. Looked very well.

Lupus has invited Dronke to Manchester for Christmas, and Dronke has invited Imandt.

No other news.

Your
K. M.

First published in: Marx and Engels, *Works*, First Russian Edition, Vol. XXII, Moscow, 1929

Printed according to the original

Published in English for the first time

250

MARX TO ENGELS

IN MANCHESTER

London, 22 November 1854
28 Dean Street, Soho

Dear Engels,

Received the £2 YESTERDAY.

Herewith letter from Dana which will show you what use the HUMBUGS are making of the military material. The book he mentions by Ripley on the MEXICAN WAR hasn't reached me yet.[597] I shall have it fetched tomorrow, leaf through it and then send it on to you.

If you possibly can, send an article on Friday,[b] since I wrote about Spain on Tuesday[598] and, under PRESENT CIRCUMSTANCES, this

---

[a] See this volume, p. 490. - [b] 24 November

can't be done twice in one week. On the other hand, to miss an article in my very difficult financial situation would be bad from every point of view.

No sooner had the false rumours of the fall of Sevastopol arrived than His Honour, Public Prosecutor Blind, hit on the plan of holding a German meeting—which was also to be made the occasion of a declaration of principles—against Russia and the German 'prinches' and, more particularly, *ad majorem gloriam*[a] of the Public Prosecutor himself and the German emigration *in corpore*.[b] It was an occasion on which the 'chiefs' of all factions were to foregather PEACEFULLY. I and Freiligrath, of course, beat off this attack, so that at first Blind's plan was frustrated. *Mais comme les grands esprits se rencontrent*,[c] the same thing had occurred to the indefatigable Arnold Ruge—who is presently dumping all manner of rubbish in *The Morning Advertiser*—and, at his written invitation, a preparatory meeting took place, COMPOSED OF: *Vittinghof* {chiropodist; 60 years old, a Courlander speaking no known tongue; formerly servant to Count Vittinghof of Courland, now posing as his own master. This Vittinghof, according to Arnold's plan, was to take the chair; a gang of German merchants (Gerstenzweig, etc.) were to provide the money and call the meeting and, under their auspices, German refugees were to be let loose on the platform). Römer (Becker's stepfather and a notorious *mouchard*[d]). Meyen. Buchheim. Ronge. Ruge, Blind. Geck.[e]—The upshot of the meeting was that Geck and Ronge more or less 'called each other out'. Public Prosecutor Blind indignantly withdrew from the meeting because Dishcloth Ruge refused to include in the programme the phrase 'republic which unites *us all*'. Afterwards Blind called to see me—I was out—and complained 'bitterly' to my wife about the 'contempt' in which the 'German emigration' was held, and about our preventing any 'concerted' action. As if any of us were preventing the 7 or 8 jackasses from 'uniting' or 'demonstrating'. (However, if the fellows should cause a stir with their meeting and unduly compromise 'Germany' by licking English boots, it was our secret intention—as yet unknown, by the by, to Staatsrat Blind—to enlist the aid of the London Chartists and *perhaps* hold a rival meeting.)

As you can see, the 'Great Men of the Exile' are once again of the opinion that something 'has got to be done'.

---

[a] to the greater glory - [b] as a body - [c] But as great minds think alike - [d] police informer - [e] Fop, possibly ironical for Amand Goegg.

In this connection Blind also then told my wife that 'Baden alone had had the courage to proclaim a republic' etc., etc. No other news.

Your
K. M.

First published abridged in *Der Briefwechsel zwischen F. Engels und K. Marx*, Bd. 2, Stuttgart, 1913 and in full in: Marx and Engels, *Works*, First Russian Edition. Vol. XXII, Moscow, 1929

Printed according to the original

Published in English for the first time

251

MARX TO ENGELS[234]

IN MANCHESTER

[London,] 30 November 1854
28 Dean Street, Soho

Dear Engels,

You forgot to return Dana's letter[a]—very important in view of my relations with the fellows. By some oversight the first two pages were omitted from your splendid article of Tuesday's date.[b] However the substance was contained in the 5 following ones, so all that suffered was the style.

I have received from the worthy Dr Freund a third dunning letter which I enclose. How do you think I should reply to the fellow? It seems to me that *ce bon ami*[c] has a mind to take extreme measures. With the positive decline in income from the *Tribune*, as a result of which I have sunk below the level of the great Dronke, prospects for the noble Freund look gloomier than ever. The worst of it is that I shall be needing him again soon. I have been invited through Tucker to work on a Retrospective Review which is appearing here in London. However have not yet had a detailed reply about the *punctum puncti*,[d] the fee.

The day before yesterday I finally received the 2 volumes of Ripley's *Mexican War*, about 1,200 pages, large format. As a military historian, Ripley seems to me—i.e. a *strictly lay opinion*—to

---

[a] See this volume, p. 498. - [b] F. Engels, 'The Battle of Inkermann'. - [c] this good friend - [d] the crucial point

have modelled himself *plus ou moins*[a] on *Napier*. The book is sensible and, to my mind, not uncritical. Dana has certainly not read it. Otherwise he would have seen that their hero, General Scott, appears BY NO MEANS in a favourable light, NEITHER as a commander-in-chief nor as a GENTLEMAN. The thing is of particular interest to me because not long ago I was reading about Fernando Cortes' campaign in Antonio de Solis' *Conquista de Mexico*. Some very interesting comparisons might be drawn between the two *conquistas*. By the by, although the two commanders-in-chief— Taylor as well as Scott—seem very mediocre to me, the whole war was certainly a worthy prelude to the military history of the great land of the Yankees. The vast spaces in which the action took place and the small number of men with which it was conducted— more VOLUNTEERS than REGULAR ARMY at that—impart to it an 'American' originality. As for Taylor and Scott, their only merit seems to have consisted in the conviction that Yankees would always be able to extricate themselves, however great the predicament they might be landed in. I shall send you the 2 volumes early next week. Write and tell me—for they are bulky—whether by post (I am not clear about the new regulations) or PARCEL Co.

Addio

Your

K. M.

First published abridged in *Der Briefwechsel zwischen F. Engels und K. Marx*. Bd. 2, Stuttgart, 1913 and in full in: Marx and Engels, *Works*, First Russian Edition, Vol. XXII, Moscow, 1929

Printed according to the original

Published in English in full for the first time

252

MARX TO ENGELS[599]

IN MANCHESTER

[London,] 2 December 1854
28 Dean Street, Soho

Dear Engels,

I THINK NOT, SIR, that your letter[600] or so much as your name, should be linked with the worthy 'friend'.[b] (The Jew is so pressing because an exceedingly *refined* educational establishment, which he

---

[a] more or less - [b] Dr Freund

has let his wife set up in St John's Wood, has brought him to THE VERY BRINK OF BANKRUPTCY. I have just learnt the details via Cornelius.) Taking my cue from your letter, I have written to him[601] that: 1. I enclose a letter from A. Dana from which he can see how the commercial crisis in America has affected *me* and, through me, *himself*; 2. However, to cover the loss, I have established new literary contacts on the strength of which I will undertake in writing to pay him £4 on the 10th of every month, starting in January 1855. The amount still outstanding is about £17. Should Mr Freund not agree to this, then he can *prosecute*. As he cannot fail to realise, Dana's letter would protect me in any COURT. If I involve you directly, I shall forfeit 1. my whole position vis-à-vis Freund; 2. He will tell (and promptly show my letter to) the teacher in his establishment, Mr Gottfried Kinkel, who will pass it on to Mr Gerstenberg, who will pass it on to every German Jew in the City until it reaches Blanc, which would be BY NO MEANS desirable.

I had asked Lassalle whether he could not obtain some sort of literary BUSINESS for me in Germany for I must be serious IN REGARD to my decreased income and increased expenditure. Now Lassalle puts forward the following proposal,[602] as to which I should like to have your *well-considered* opinion. At the beginning of this month his cousin, Dr *M. Friedländer* will become proprietor of the *Neue Oder-Zeitung*, but—in co. with *Stein and Elsner*. I am to become the paper's London correspondent.[603] Friedländer doesn't think he would be able to pay more than 20 talers a month to begin with. But Lassalle believes he might be able to push him up to 30. *Voilà la proposition.*[a] It's a miserable pittance. However, too high a value should not be set on a little bit of work for a German hole-and-corner rag. Even so, one might pick up £40 or £50. But Elsner and Stein—there's the rub! This calls for all the more mature consideration as these gentlemen aren't Conservatives but actually *Liberals*, and more directly opposed to us than the *Neue Preussische Zeitung*. THAT IS THE QUESTION.[b] Think it over carefully.

I am sending you a copy of *The People's Paper* so that you can read about Jones' DODGE[c] with Barbès (whom, between ourselves, he took for Blanqui) and his agitation against Bonaparte for the latter's proposed visit to England.[604] The 'authorities' here are seriously concerned about the matter and the police, wherever feasible, have had the posters torn down. Even *Reynolds* and *The*

---

a That's the proposal. - b Shakespeare, *Hamlet*, Act III, Scene 1. - c 'Welcome and Protest Committee for the Reception of Barbès in London. Fraternisation of the French Democracy in London', *The People's Paper*, No. 135, 2 December 1854.

Leader[a] have denounced him for his unpatriotic sentiments. He originally had honorary members, amongst whom myself, elected to his *comité* for the anti-Bonapartist movement. I chaffed him for it, in particular pointing out that if the MOVE was to be effective here and on the Continent, it must maintain its purely English character. He recognised this, as you will see from his remarks at the preliminary meeting with the FRENCH REFUGEES.[605]

On Monday I shall send you the Ripley and Solis' *Conquista de Mexico* by the PARCEL COMP. you mentioned. Return the *latter* as soon as you no longer need it, since it doesn't belong to me. I have now read the whole of Ripley (cursorily, of course, this being sufficient for my purpose). I am no longer in any doubt—and Ripley, in his 'restrained' sarcastic style, often makes it plain—that the great Scott is nothing more than a common, petty, untalented, carping, envious cur and HUMBUG who, aware that he owed everything to the bravery of his soldiers and the SKILL of his divisional commanders, played dirty tricks in order to reap the renown himself. He appears to be as great a general as the MANY-SIDED Greeley is a great PHILOSOPHER. Throughout the campaign, the fellow made a hash of things and played the kind of tricks for which any self-respecting court martial would justifiably have had him shot. But he is America's *foremost* (in terms of *rank*) general. Which is doubtless why Dana believes in him. Without question Taylor is still worth more than Scott, as the Americ. public seems to have sensed when it made the former President of the United States and rejected the latter AGAIN AND AGAIN despite all his efforts. General Worth strikes me as the most significant of them, on which point you must let me have your opinion as soon as you have read the thing. Also, and more important, on another point. Is it not CURIOUS that Scott always remains between 2 and 10 miles from the scene of ACTIVE OPERATIONS, that he *never* appears on the battlefield *himself*, but is always simply 'OBSERVING THE PROGRESS OF EVENTS' from a safe place in the rear. He himself never appears, as Taylor certainly does, when it is necessary in the interests of the army's 'morale' for the commander-in-chief to appear. After the fierce BATTLE OF Contreras, he and all his STAFF moved up only when the whole thing was over. During the fluctuations of the BATTLE OF Molino del Rey he passed a message to the 'brave' fellows to the effect that they should stand their ground, he himself would perhaps appear in person. His 'diplomatic' talents are matched only by his military ones. If he evinces mistrust, it is always of his

---

[a] 'The British Democrats.—Louis Napoleon', *The Leader*, No. 243, 18 November 1854.

more talented divisional commanders, never of Santa Anna who leads him by the nose as though he were an aged child.

It seems to me to be typical of the war that, despite wrong or inadequate orders from their CHIEF, every division and every single small body of men at all times STUBBORNLY make for their objectives, SPONTANEOUSLY exploiting every incident, so that in the end a measure of wholeness emerges. A Yankee sense of independence and individual proficiency greater, perhaps, than that of the Anglo-Saxons.

The Spanish are already degenerate. But a degenerate Spaniard, a Mexican, is an ideal. All the Spanish vices, braggadocio, swagger and Don Quixotry, raised to the third power, but little or nothing of the steadiness which the Spaniards possess. The Mexican guerrilla war a caricature of the Spanish,[606] and even the *sauve qui peut* of the REGULAR ARMIES infinitely surpassed. But then the Spaniards have produced no talent comparable to that of Santa Anna.

Vale.[a]

Your
K. M.

Have you seen the fulminations against Heine by Jacobus Venedey—Kobes I[b] of Cologne—in the feuilleton of Saturday's *Kölnische Zeitŭng*? It's a pleasure you should not deny yourself. And Kossuth's promotion to general!!!

First published abridged in *Der Briefwechsel zwischen F. Engels und K. Marx*, Bd. 2, Stuttgart, 1913 and in full in: Marx and Engels, *Works*, First Russian Edition, Vol. XXII, Moscow, 1929

Printed according to the original

Published in English in full for the first time

253

MARX TO ENGELS

IN MANCHESTER

[London,] 8 December 1854

Dear Frederic,

I shall be putting an article[607] into the post today, although I know the post won't go. A week today I intend to do a report on Parliament. But *still* I *urgently* request you to send me *an article on*

---

[a] Farewell. - [b] Title character of a satirical poem by Heine on Venedey published in *Vermischte Schriften*.

Tuesday so that I can count on getting £2 more on Friday (when I draw the bill).[608] Even without that, there are various losses to be met. If there's nothing happening, you can do something on Austrian military power.[a]

You must write the pamphlet on the 'Teutonians and Slavism'.[609] You should also read Bauer's *England and Russia* (written in French). Gustav Diezel, too, has written a 'fat' book on the subject.[b] Do you know Freiherr von Bode's 'Statistics on Russia'? (Appeared about six months ago.)[c]

Salut.

Your

K. M.

First published in part in *Der Briefwechsel zwischen F. Engels und K. Marx,* Bd. 2, Stuttgart, 1913 and in full in: Marx and Engels, *Works,* First Russian Edition, Moscow, 1929

Printed according to the original

Published in English for the first time

254

MARX TO ENGELS

IN MANCHESTER

[London,] 15 December 1854
28 Dean Street, Soho

Dear Engels,

I have just received your note and very much look forward to seeing you here in a week's time.[610]

Article received.[d]

Barthélemy's end is a GLORIOUS one.[611] At yesterday's hearing (or rather CORONER'S INQUEST) it was said that important papers, though not relating to the assassination, had been found on him.[e] It would be annoying if these included papers from the old days, so that we seemed to be connected with a fellow who—or so the louts boasted—was 'saving up' a bullet for us in the event of our returning to Paris.

---

[a] F. Engels, 'The Military Power of Austria'. - [b] Presumably, G. Diezel, *Russland, Deutschland und die östliche Frage.* - [c] A. Bode ('Rhode' in the original), 'Notizen, gesammelt auf einer Forstreise durch einen Theil des Europäischen Russlands', *Beiträge zur Kenntniss des Russischen Reiches und der angränzenden Länder Asiens.* - [d] Engels' part of the article 'Progress of the War' written jointly with Marx. - [e] 'The Inquest', *The Times,* No. 21925, 15 December 1854.

I haven't read the Bauer, so bring it with you.

Next week I start writing for the *Neue Oder-Zeitung*. 30 talers a month for the time being. I suppose, however, that the fellows will be satisfied with three articles a week. Not having the money to buy books, I cannot possibly bid adieu to my studies at the Museum[a] in return for 30 talers a month. Much though I dislike the thing, I've accepted it for the sake of my wife's peace of mind. Her PROSPECTS, of course, are GLOOMY.

What I particularly approved of in Ripley[b] was his not giving way to enthusiastic hyperbole. The strategic mistakes made in the Mexican War would seem to be self-explanatory in view of the total absence of plan. As for the nicer tactical blunders, I, OF COURSE, understand nothing of such matters. I should think that he took Napier[c] for his model, to judge by the way he depicts the Mexicans just as Napier does the Spaniards, and in the second place strives after FAIRNESS towards the opponents.

Tomorrow I shall be saddled with Blind and wife. This 'shinishter' Russophobe and 'repelbican' still insists that Baden is the real land of the future.

Salut. And give my regards to Lupus.

Your

K. M.

First published in *Der Briefwechsel zwischen F. Engels und K. Marx*, Bd. 2, Stuttgart, 1913

Printed according to the original

Published in English for the first time

255

MARX TO MORITZ ELSNER

IN BRESLAU

London, Wednesday, 20 December 1854
28 Dean Street, Soho

Dear Elsner,

Your letter arrived here on Monday. I myself only got back today after spending a few days visiting Engels and Lupus in Manchester.

---

[a] the Library of the British Museum - [b] R. S. Ripley, *The War with Mexico*, in two volumes. - [c] W. F. P. Napier, *History of the War in the Peninsula and in the South of France, from the Year 1807 to the Year 1814*, vols. I-VI.

I shall begin work as correspondent on *Saturday*. To start off right in the middle of the *final part* of the 'preliminary' parliamentary session WOULD NOT DO. A *résumé* of this short session would make a better *entrée*. For the past two years I have been writing—i.e. for publication—only in English. German may give me some trouble at the start.

As you are aware, I edited a Prussian newspaper[a] *under censorship*—for a whole year. So I am quite familiar with the torments which the *Neue Oder-Zeitung* may have to endure under a new form of censorship, and it is these difficulties, the UNDERHAND struggle AGAINST THE ESTABLISHED POWERS which incline me to work in the interest of this paper.

So far as I am aware, and I know pretty well all the important reading-rooms in London, the *N.O.-Z.* is not available in any of them. Hence, for the time being, you'll have to send it direct to me. I might perhaps be able to introduce it into a reading-room or COFFEE-ROOM.

You would particularly oblige me if, by way of an exception, you could send me *one* issue of the *Breslauer Zeitung*. Although Edgar Bauer comes to see me every week, he has never spoken about his articles and I would like to get to know his views from one 'sample'.

Since Parliament will be going into recess, and—save for a *résumé* of its sessions and PERHAPS Of FINANCIAL MATTERS—there will be little of importance to report, I shall, if these premises hold good, write a number of consecutive articles providing a review of the conduct of the war in the Crimea so far,[612] concerning which I have seen nothing sensible, i.e. critical, either here or from Germany. Moreover, I suppose that this subject is of the greatest general interest and at the same time least liable to lead to a conflict with the indirect Royal Prussian Censorship.

Requesting you to convey my kindest regards to your wife whom I have not had the pleasure of meeting.

Yours

K. Marx

First published in: Marx and Engels, *Works*, First Russian Edition, Vol. XXV, Moscow, 1934

Printed according to the original

Published in English for the first time

---

[a] *Rheinische Zeitung*

1855

256

MARX TO ENGELS

IN MANCHESTER

[London,] 12 January 1855

Dear Frederic,

Yesterday I sent the report on TRADE and COMMERCE to the *Tribune*[a] and must now deliver two more articles if I am to pay off my overdraft with the fellows. There are two sailings next week, on Tuesday and Friday,[b] and it would be most desirable if you could let me have an article on *un sujet quelconque*[c] by Tuesday.

My wife is approaching the catastrophe with a firm tread.

Nothing new here. Götz has written to Sidney Herbert asking for an 'officer's brevet' in the apochryphal 'Foreign Legion'.[613] *Salut.*

Your
K. M.

First published in: Marx and Engels, *Works*, First Russian Edition, Vol. XXII, Moscow, 1929

Printed according to the original

Published in English for the first time

257

MARX TO ENGELS[614]

IN MANCHESTER

London, 17 January 1855

Dear Frederic,

I could not, OF COURSE, write to the *Tribune* yesterday nor can I do so for some time *à venir*[d] because yesterday morning, between

---

[a] K. Marx, 'The Commerical Crisis in Britain', I and II. - [b] 16 and 19 January - [c] some subject or other - [d] to come

6 and 7 o'clock, my wife was delivered of a *bona fide* TRAVELLER[a]—unfortunately OF THE. 'SEX' *par excellence.* If it had been a male child, well and good. Did you know that red Wolff[b] is one of the *Augsburger's* London correspondents? I found out by chance, namely by reading an article in the said paper[c] containing all manner of fatuous elucubrations on 'house' and 'home' and 'abroad'—all this to throw light on the 'ordure' with which the British troops are contending at Balaklava. I saw Freiligrath and told him that in the Augsburg *Allgemeine Zeitung* I'd read some nonsense of which only Lupus Rufus could be capable. Freiligrath thereupon confirmed that Wolff was the 'REAL, IDENTICAL Kobes'.[d]

I now have Heine's 3 volumes at home. Amongst other things he retails at some length a lie to the effect that I, etc., went to console him[e] after he had been 'attacked' in the Augsburg *A.Z.* for having accepted money from Louis Philippe.[f] The good Heine deliberately forgets that my intervention on his behalf took place at the end of 1843 [614] and thus could have no connection with FACTS which came to light *after* the February revolution of 1848.[615] BUT LET IT PASS. Worried by his evil conscience,—the old dog has a monstrous memory for such things,—he is trying to ingratiate himself.

I expect something from you on FRIDAY,[g] then. I can't write any more today, having to send out a mass of cards giving notification of the baby's birth.

Your

K. M.

First published abridged in *Der Briefwechsel zwischen F. Engels und K. Marx,* Bd. 2, Stuttgart, 1913 and in full in: Marx and Engels, *Works,* First Russian Edition, Vol. XXII, Moscow, 1929

Printed according to the original

Published in English in full for the first time

---

[a] Eleanor - [b] Ferdinand Wolff, also referred to below as Lupus Rufus meaning in Latin 'red wolf' - [c] 'Ein Beitrag zur Charakteristik der Engländer', *Allgemeine Zeitung,* No. 9, 9 January 1855. - [d] A comparison with the German journalist Venedey lampooned by Heine in his poem 'Kobes I' in 1854. - [e] Heine, 'Retrospektive Aufklärung', August 1854 (*Vermischte Schriften,* Bd. 3. Th. 2, S. 144). - [f] [Report from Paris of 22 April,] *Allgemeine Zeitung,* No. 119, 28 April 1848, supplement. - [g] 19 January

258

MARX TO ENGELS

IN MANCHESTER

[London,] 19 January 1855
28 Dean Street, Soho

Dear Engels,

Agree absolutely—and, indeed, most gratefully—to your scheme.

The parliamentary thing seems likely to misfire for reasons of time. BUT NEVER MIND.

Your yesterday's letter[616] didn't reach me until *4 o'clock this afternoon* because the ass of a postman (this is the 2nd or 3rd time it has happened, and I shall complain to the POST OFFICE) delivered it to 28 Soho Square instead of 28 Dean Street. In future address your letters to 28 Dean Street, *Soho* (*instead of Soho Square*). Because it arrived so late, I can write you no more than these few lines today.

What's this about Barthélemy? I missed it in the Augsburg paper.[a] Probably a fabrication on the part of the miserable 'Oly' or 'Ody', one of the Augsburg *Allgemeine Zeitung*'s correspondents, a blackguard from Switzerland.

Salut.

Your
K. M.

There's a tremendous panic in the City, and Freiligrath wrote yesterday telling me that even the most 'sanguine' expect things to be very bad until early spring.

First published abridged in *Der Briefwechsel zwischen F. Engels und K. Marx*, Bd. 2, Stuttgart, 1913 and in full in: Marx and Engels, *Works*, First Russian Edition, Vol. XXII, Moscow, 1929

Printed according to the original

Published in English for the first time

---

[a] i.e. 'Die Assisenverhandlung gegen Barthélemy', *Allgemeine Zeitung*, No. 9, 9 January 1855, supplement.

259

MARX TO FERDINAND LASSALLE

IN DÜSSELDORF

[London,] 23 January 1855
28 Dean Street, Soho

Dear Lassalle,

This letter would have been written a week ago had not my wife been delivered of a world citizen (female) [a] and the consequent TROUBLE left me little spare time, as you can readily imagine. However, both mother and daughter are doing well.

It is not very pleasant, *mon cher*,[b] to write in such a small [...] *au fond*,[c] all one can do is produce miniature dunghills. *Mais [n'importe]*[d] that the [...] should consider [...] and make no literary pretensions, while also hoping that none will be made.

As regards the various economic questions you put to me,[617] so far as I know there are as yet no compilations, whether official or scientific. Official figures for corn imports are, of course, to be found in the BOARD OF TRADE TABLES. But nothing else. Undoubtedly there will now be a plethora of works on these matters. A period of crisis in England is also one of theoretical research. I shall at the *earliest opportunity* compile something for you from my note-books, in which I have collected all sorts of statistical information from various sources.[618] For the present, merely the following, of a quite general nature:

Imports of Wheat and Flour

	Wheat as wheat (quarters)	Flour (reduced to quarters)
1847	2,650,000	1,808,000
1848	1,865,000	351,000
1849	4,569,000	1,129,000
1850	3,778,000	1,102,000

Thus 8,285,000 [qrs] of wheat imported during the first 2 years of FREE TRADE, and 2,226,000 in the form of flour, in all 10,511,000, or an average of more than 5 million quarters over the 2 years. This amounts to far more than 1/6 of total consumption, reckoned at 1 quarter per person per year.

---

[a] Eleanor - [b] my dear fellow - [c] at bottom - [d] But no matter

Now, can it be said that annual consumption increased to that extent? This clearly depends on the answer to another question: whether the same amount of wheat was produced in England as heretofore? This again can only be answered when we are in possession of the agricultural statistics, upon which work has only just begun. As regards Ireland and Scotland, we know that considerable amounts [of the la]nd have been turned over to pasture, etc., since the abolition of the corn tariffs.[72] [As regards Englan]d, no conclusion can be reached at present save by induction. If in England, a considerable area of land had not been withdrawn from cultivation, how came it that e.g. this year, despite a very good harvest, corn prices are higher than in the protectionist year, 1839, for instance, although the loss of imports from abroad in no way compensates for the difference between a good and a bad harvest, between, say, that of 1854 and that of 1853? How the tendency to withdraw land from cultivation has spread under FREE TRADE—mainly, no doubt, by turning it over to pasture—is evident from the following table, an *official* one (for *Ireland*):

1854 (up till November)

	Acres
[*Decrease in Ce*]*reals*	91,233
[*Green Crops*] ([Pot]atoes, roots etc.)	710
Flax	23,607
Clover	13,025
Total decrease in cultivated land	128,575

Last year (1853), on the other hand, the total decrease was only 43,867 acres. Making, for both years taken together, 172,442. This is all the more striking as the demand for *all* agricultural produce has risen in the past 2 years.

Now as regards the 'HANDS' employed in agriculture, we know that, of the 300,000 people who have emigrated every year from Great Britain since 1852, the great majority consisted of agricultural workers. We know that in 1853 the population *decreased* for the first time instead of increasing. Finally, the best proof that the number of agricultural HANDS has greatly decreased is that in 1853 wages *in rural areas* rose for the first time since 1815 and that mechanical reapers were more or less generally introduced in order to depress them again.

(Incidentally, I would point out that the free import of foreign corn has given *England's agronomy* a tre[men]dous impetus.)

What [influence] FREE TRADE has had on the price of industrial [products] is absolutely impossible to assess from the material so far available. In the woollen and linen industry, for example, the fluctuations dependent on raw material can hardly have been affected in any way by the REPEAL of the CORN-LAWS. On the whole I believe that the history of prices from 1849 to 1854 will show that the price-relations between all manufactured products and grain, as well as between individual branches of industry and the corresponding raw materials remained the same before and after the repeal of the Corn Laws (likewise the variations within each group).

As for *wages* in the factories (figures another time), it can be proved beyond doubt that the repeal of the Corn Laws, 1. has had no influence whatever on *absolute* wages, 2. has contributed to *depress* relat[ive] wages. In the year of crisis[a] wages [had] been depressed. They were *not* raised in the relatively good years 1849-52 (the latter included, at least up to the last 1/3 of the year). Why weren't they raised? Because the price of foodstuffs had *fallen.* In the course of 1852 the great emigration began, while on the other hand demand rose appreciably in the United States, Australia, India, etc. The workers then demanded a 10 per cent rise in wages and for a short time, while prosperity was at its height (until about August 1853), were able to achieve it in almost the majority of branches of industry. However, as you know, they were soon deprived of this 10 per cent rise—remember, e.g., the Preston STRIKE[431]—although corn prices were *on average* higher in 1853 and 1854 than in the protectionist years 1843-45 and 1830-37. Hence the *rise* in wages—a very *temporary* rise, for already short time is being worked again and, generally speaking, the crisis has begun—is in no way attributable to FREE TRADE, but corresponds wholly to the rise that takes place in all years of prosperity. In fact FREE TRADE simply meant that from 1849 to 1852 wages did *not* rise. Since it was possible to buy *more* food with the same wages, these were not increased. What did show a relative *increase*, therefore, was *profits.* Hence relative wages, i.e. wages in relation to profits, have in fact *fallen*—a result which I showed to be inevitable in a pamphlet[b] (FRENCH) written as long ago as 1847.

Of course, one cannot deny that the repeal of the Corn Laws may have in some degree contributed (together with the adjust-

---

[a] 1847 - [b] K. Marx, 'Speech on the Question of Free Trade'.

ment of the sugar tax, the raising of restrictions on shipping and the repeal of the protective tariffs on British North American timber) to creating new, or enlarging existing, markets for British manufactures abroad. For instance, in the United States the tendency to legislate in favour of free trade was certainly due partly to the REPEAL in England. However, too much importance should not be attached to this, since there was a decrease in English exports e.g. to Russia, whose exports to England increased enormously as a result of the REPEAL. In general, it would appear that, relatively speaking, Europe's importance as a market for English goods is steadily diminishing; since in 1854, 60 per cent of total exports (I mean total exports of *British products*, disregarding re-exports) were absorbed by the United States, Australia and India alone, a figure which does not include Britain's colonies outside Europe (excepting India).

I have jotted down the above information to provide a very general answer to your questions. I shall see what I can find in the way of definite statistical material in my note-books. As already mentioned, books will no doubt *only* begin coming out *now*...[a]

First published in: *F. Lassalle. Nachgelassene Briefe und Schriften*, Bd. III, Stuttgart-Berlin, 1922

Printed according to the original

Published in English for the first time

260

MARX TO ENGELS

IN MANCHESTER

[London,] 24 January [1855]

Dear Engels,

As you will see from today's *Times*, there is *nothing* to report about Parliament. No important debate until *Thursday evening*[b]. So there's nothing for it but to write about *'any old sujet'*.[619]
    Salut.

Your
K. M.

First published in: Marx and Engels, *Works*, First Russian Edition, Vol. XXII, Moscow, 1929

Printed according to the original

Published in English for the first time

---

[a] The end of the letter has not been preserved. - [b] 25 January

261

MARX TO ENGELS

IN MANCHESTER

[London,] 30 January 1855

Dear Frederic,

I shall send you such cuttings from the *Tribune* as you will need for a *characterisation of the Coalition*, and fill in the gaps, if any, with a few written comments.[620] I shall hardly get round to it today, since I have to send the Breslau jackasses a résumé of yesterday's frightfully long sitting.[a] Also, the BABY[b] is in a very critical condition—my wife, however, very well—so that I have been held up by DOMESTIC AFFAIRS until 1 o'clock (now). Which means that in all probability my stuff won't reach you until Thursday morning.

If Palmerston becomes premier, there'll be some high jinks.

Did you read Barthélemy's *confession* in yesterday's *Advertiser*?

Tout à vous[c]

Ch. M.

First published abridged in *Der Briefwechsel zwischen F. Engels und K. Marx*, Bd. 2, Stuttgart, 1913 and in full in: Marx and Engels, *Works*, First Russian Edition, Vol. XXII, Moscow, 1929

Printed according to the original

Published in English for the first time

262

MARX TO ENGELS

IN MANCHESTER

London, 31 January 1855

Dear Engels,

Enclosed 2 articles on Gladstone's financial policy.[621] In the first one, the chaps have clearly misprinted some figures. However, all you are really concerned with is refreshing your memory as to the SPIRIT of the whole plan.

---

[a] i.e. 'From Parliament.—From the Theatre of War' for the *Neue Oder-Zeitung*. -
[b] Eleanor - [c] All yours

Herewith a survey of the Coalition's activities:

1853

December 16.[a] Fall of Disraeli overthrown (by a majority of 19), ostensibly because of the extension of the HOUSE-TAX and the 'EXTENSION OF THE GENERAL AREA OF *DIRECT* TAXATION'. The determining factor, the Irish Brigade[622]
Coalition formed:

* 'We have now arrived at the commencement of the *political millennium*'*... (*Times*).[b]

CHRISTMAS RECESS.

February 10. Parliament reassembles. Russell's old programme of 1850. No question of a Reform Bill[623] until they reassembled the following winter.

* 'Next session is not quite so uncertain as tomorrow'* (*Times*).[c]

On the other hand, a mass of practical and administrative reforms promised: law reform, railway regulations, education, etc. Gladstone postpones his budget until *after* the EASTER RECESS.
February 18.

* 'It is no longer a Ministry of Reform: It is a Ministry of Progress, every member of which resolves to do nothing. All difficult questions are open questions'* (*Disraeli*).[d]

21 February. Clarendon FOREIGN MINISTER. Russell Minister without portfolio or salary.
February 24. Russell's Jewish bill.[624] * 'The Policy of Abstention' proclaimed on the Eastern question, is also the ministerial policy at home.*

4 April. RUSSELL'S EDUCATIONAL REFORM BILL.
7 April. Before presentation of the budget: CLADSTONE'S FINANCIAL SCHEME.
15 April. Debate in the House on the GUNPOWDER PLOT.[380] It transpires that Palmerston is acting as GENERAL INFORMER for the CONTINENTAL POLICE.
EASTER RECESS (don't know the date).
31 May. Russell insults Catholics in Parliament.[625] Irish members[e] resign from Ministry. Aberdeen's letter to them of 3 June.[f] Russell retracts.

---

[a] 1852 - [b] *The Times*, No. 21316, 4 January 1853, leader. - [c] *The Times*, No. 21349, 11 February 1853, leader. - [d] B. Disraeli, [Speech in the House of Commons on 18 February 1853,] *The Times*, No. 21356, 19 February 1853. - [e] Keogh, Sadleir, Monsell - [f] G. Aberdeen, [Letter to Mr Monsell of 3 June 1853,] *The Times*, No. 21447, 6 June 1853.

Main items in the spring and summer session:

1. *India Bill*: Ministry wishes to extend EAST INDIA COMPANY CHARTER (EXPIRING ON APRIL, 1854) by 20 years. Is *compelled* to drop this, its bill remaining in force *only provisionally* and for so long as it pleases Parliament. Apart from laying down that APPOINTMENTS IN THE CIVIL SERVICE AND SCIENTIFIC MILITARY SERVICES are to be subject to open competition, this Act confines itself to the following: Sir Charles Wood (President of the BOARD OF CONTROL) is to receive £5,000 instead of £1,200 as previously, 18 DIRECTORS instead of 24. Instead of all being nominated by the COURT OF PROPRIETORS, now 12 to be nominated by the latter and 6 by the Ministry. Salary of DIRECTORS to be once more *increased* from £300 to £500, those of the CHAIRMAN and DEPUTY CHAIRMAN to £1,000. GOVERNOR-GENERALSHIP of India to be separated from the GOVERNORSHIP of Bengal. New PRESIDENCY ON THE INDUS. Thus, instead of the inexpensive and, as practice has shown, efficient SIMPLE COMMISSIONERS, new GOVERNORS and PRESIDENTS with LUXURIOUS COUNCILS. NEW SINECURES. A few quite insignificant little reforms in the Indian judiciary.

2. *Budget.* Many of its FEATURES lifted from Disraeli, but whereas it removes EXCISE DUTIES for the benefit of the town, Disraeli did so ostensibly for the benefit of the FARMERS; thus the tea DUTY business, extension of direct taxation, etc., of Jewish[a] origin. Some of the most important decisions forced upon Gladstone after he and his opposition to them had been repeatedly *voted down* in Parliament. For instance, the abolition of the ADVERTISEMENT DUTY; the SUCCESSION DUTY. LICENSING SYSTEM, NEW REGULATION dropped after undergoing several transformations in the course of the session. Of the budget, which made its début with all the pretensions of a systematic encyclopaedia, nothing remains save a *mixtum compositum*[b] of LITTLE ITEMS. *Typical feature*: the noble Gladstone includes in his BUDGET a special BILL—abolition of STAMPS ON NEWSPAPER SUPPLEMENTS—intended to buy *The Times*, in effect making it a present of £30-40,000 a year. Since it alone issues SUPPLEMENTS, consolidates its monopoly.[c] *The Times* gratefully abandons its campaign against his INCOME TAX and today is again demanding his inclusion in the new Cabinet.

3. *Three Irish LANDLORDS and TENANTS BILLS.*[626] Introduced by the *Tory Napier*[d] under the Derby MINISTRY. Passed on 1 August after

---

[a] An allusion to Disraeli. The original has 'Israelite'. - [b] miscellany - [c] See K. Marx, 'Soap for the People, a Sop for *The Times.*—The Coalition Budget', 'Turkey and Russia.—Connivance of the Aberdeen Ministry with Russia.—The Budget.—Tax on Newspaper Supplements.—Parliamentary Corruption'. - [d] J. Napier, [Speech in the House of Commons on 22 November 1852,] *The Times*, No. 21280, 23 November 1852.

10 months' deliberation in the Commons. Aberdeen (9 August) expresses his satisfaction in the Lords at their having been burked there.[a]

4. * Parliamentary reform, national education reform, law reform (a few trifles apart) etc. *postponed*. Transportation Bill,[627] Navigation Bill * etc. inherited from the Derby Ministry. Jewish bill rejected. Nothing can truly be described as the Ministry's own [save α] *the great Cab Act* which had no sooner crossed the threshold than it required revision by Parliament because 'all the talents' of the chaps had not even sufficed to create hackney carriage regulations. β) Gladstone's conversion of the public debt,[b] the failure of which he had to admit before Parliament as early as 28 July.[628]

August 20. (Day of Parliament's prorogation—27 October.) Palmerston dismisses the Commons with the assurance that they need not worry about the Eastern affair, * 'as far as the evacuation of the principalities was concerned...* their pledge was, *"his confidence in the honour and character of the Russian Emperor", which would move him to withdraw his troops voluntarily from the principalities' *.[c]

3 December. Sinope.[629]

12 December. Note of the 4 Powers to the Porte, in which *au fond*[d] more was demanded of it than in the Vienna Note.[630]

14 December. First, Palmerston agrees in the *Conseil*[e] of Ministers to telegraph Vienna, saying the Sinope affair should not be allowed to upset the negotiations; then, in order to deceive the philistines, on

15 December, hands in his resignation, allegedly because opposed to Russell's Reform Bill. Returns to office, of course, as soon as his end attained.

1854

Mid-January. Resignation of *Sadleir,* the broker to the Irish Brigade, following scandalous disclosures before an Irish court of law. Had been Junior Lord of the Treasury. (*Later,* the virtuous Gladstone wishes to dispatch to Australia as Governor his relative, Lawley, speculator in stocks while secretary to the Chancellor of the Exchequer and betting man. Discredited in Parliament. This same

---

[a] G. Aberdeen, [Speech in the House of Lords on 9 August 1853,] *The Times,* No. 21503, 10 August 1853. - [b] Gladstone, [Speech in the House of Commons on 8 April 1853,] *The Times,* No. 21398, 9 April 1853. - [c] Palmerston, [Speech in the House of Commons on 20 August 1853,] *The Times,* No. 21513, 22 August 1853. - [d] basically - [e] Council

'virtuous' chap engages O'Flaherty, who makes off with the cash-box, and brings one *Hayward* into the Poor Law Administration on the strength of a lengthy lampoon against Disraeli. All the dirt piles up on the virtuous Gladstone.)

Beginning of February. Parliament reopens.

6 February. Palmerston announces his intention to introduce a bill for the organisation of the militia in Ireland and Scotland.[a] 28 March. War declared. Bill not introduced until *end of June.*

13 February. Russell introduces his Reform Bill, which he had made both a condition and an excuse for joining the Coalition. Withdraws it 10 weeks later with 'tears in his eyes'.[b] As a token of gratitude, again made President of the Privy Council and gets a salary.

6 March. Gladstone demands

* 'only the sum which would be required to *bring back* the 25,000 men about to leave the British shores'.*[c]

Doubles the income tax for 6 months. may 8 has again to introduce a new budget.

Mid-March. The Czar[d] forces the chaps to declare war by publishing the 'Secret and Confidential Correspondence',[631] which opens with a dispatch of 11 January 1853[e] and brands as deliberate lies all the statements made by the chaps during 1853.

7 April. Lord Grey (even then minded to become War Minister; notorious for having, as Colonial Minister, brought every English colony to the verge of rebellion) makes his speech in the Lords[f] complaining about *England's* lack of *military organisation.* This merely provides the Ministers with an opportunity— 8 June—of creating one more *post* and one more *salary* by separating the Ministry for war[g] from the Colonial Ministry without concentration of departments. *Cholera* is likewise used as a pretext to create an independent President of the 'Board of Health' and thus a new ministerial post and salary.

---

[a] Palmerston, [Speech in the House of Commons on 6 February 1854,] *The Times*, No. 21658, 7 February 1854. - [b] Russell, [Speeches in the House of Commons on 13 February and 11 April 1854,] *The Times*, Nos. 21664 and 21713, 14 February and 12 April 1854. - [c] Gladstone, [Speech in the House of Commons on 6 March 1854,] *The Times*, No. 21682, 7 March 1854. - [d] Nicholas I - [e] Sir G. H. Seymour to Lord J. Russell. St. Petersburg, 11 January 1853, *The Times*, No. 21693, 20 March 1854. - [f] Grey, [Speech in the House of Lords on 7 April 1854,] *The Times*, No. 22720, 8 April 1854. - [g] The Office of the Secretary of State for War and Colonies was divided into the War Office and the Colonial Office in 1854. The Office of the Secretary of State at War was abolished. The term 'ministry', though used by Marx, was unusual in English in this context.

May 29.

* 'Their'* (the Ministers') * 'measures were kicked overboard in a very unceremonious manner'* (*Bright*).[a]

Résumé of their domestic activities during this 2nd session: 7 major bills introduced. *3* of them * *defeated:* bill for the entire change of the law of settlement [632]; bill for public education in Scotland; bill on the entire reconstruction of Parliamentary oaths.[633] *3 withdrawn:* Bribery Prevention Bill; bill for the complete change of the civil service; measure for Parliamentary Reform. 1 bill—Oxford Parliamentary Reform Bill * passed, in very mutilated and modified form.

August 12. Prorogation of Parliament.

Extraordinary December session: Bills relating to the FOREIGN LEGION [613] and the Militia.[62]

A perusal of this list will recall enough facts to enable you to ridicule the fellows and, incidentally, cast a few aspersions on the worthy Palmerston in advance (in case he should become Premier).

First published in *Der Briefwechsel zwischen F. Engels und K. Marx*, Bd. 2, Stuttgart, 1913

Printed according to the original

Published in English for the first time

263

MARX TO ENGELS

IN MANCHESTER

[London,] 2 February 1855

Dear Frederic,

Many thanks for the article.[634] Russell has been horribly discredited by Newcastle, though that ass waxed altogether too touching at the end of his speech.[b]

---

[a] J. Bright, [Speech in the House of Commons on 29 May 1854,] *The Times*, No. 21754, 30 May 1854. - [b] H. Newcastle [Speech in the House of Lords on 1 February 1855,] *The Times*, No. 21967, 2 February 1855.

My wife is getting on satisfactorily. But all is by no means well with the child,[a] I fear.

Enclosed 1. Letter from Lassalle; 2. from Daniels; 3. the cuttings to which Lassalle refers[635]; Goldheim has been prowling about among the workers in Solingen etc. under the name of 'Lassalle'. 4. Letter from Steffen who, however, has omitted to give his Brighton address and will begin to grumble again if, *in the circumstances,* I don't reply.

As a result of the Barbès business *Jones,* of course, got mixed up with the *crapauds,*[b] and with the *crapule*[c] among them at that. So another big banquet of all nations was arranged for the February celebrations.[636] He came to see me, too, and I laughed in his face. Meanwhile his Frenchmen (a quite unknown MOB) had dug up the ex-Schapper Association[637] which did not, OF COURSE, reject such good graces. Moreover the malcontents among the Polish and Italian émigrés—who are not accounted 'superior refugees'—are said to have *organised* themselves for the purpose of sending delegates to the Committee.[638] For the fun of it, Götz and I let Jones take us to their meeting yesterday, we being designated 'observers'. He introduced us as 'OLD FRIENDS OF THE CHARTIST PARTY' who, doubtless, were entitled to satisfy their curiosity. Who was there? Various *crapauds* of the basest sort. A *Spanish* tailor or tobacco manufacturer who had 'convened himself'. *Stechan* (half crazed) and behind him three notorious German louts. Schapper himself being no longer available, Stechan, tried to ape the former's physiognomy, his morose gravity, his gesticulations, as once the butcher Legendre those of Danton. But that was not all. *Herzen* the Russian went uninvited to the previous meeting, and (himself) moved that he be nominated a member of the Committee.[639] At the meeting we attended, an obsequious letter from him was read out and, because the politically wise Frenchmen thought him *'un garçon charmant',*[d] he was admitted without further ado. The meeting, the chattering of the Frenchmen, the glazed expressions of the Germans, the gesticulations of the Spanish tailor were so awful that Jones (CHAIRMAN) 1. proposed that everyone should speak only once and for not more than ten minutes; 2. upon its being remarked that the Spaniard was not an émigré because democracy had triumphed there, he came out with an ambiguous compliment that 'he wished every émigré community in London a similar lot' so that thus 'no international committees need be maintained' here.

---

[a] Eleanor - [b] philistines (see this volume, p. 502) - [c] dregs - [d] a charming fellow

Götz and I were treated to a free comedy and we smoked furiously in our role of mute onlookers. Here one could see with one's own eyes the pass to which *'la vraie démocratie'*[a] has come.

Your

K. Marx

First published abridged in *Der Briefwech-sel zwischen F. Engels und K. Marx*, Bd. 2, Stuttgart, 1913 and in full in: Marx and Engels, *Works*, First Russian Edition, Vol. XXII, Moscow, 1929

Printed according to the original

Published in English for the first time

264

MARX TO ENGELS

IN MANCHESTER

[London,] 13 February 1855
28 Dean Street, Soho

Dear Engels,

Firstly an acknowledgement of receipt of the 'BULLION', and secondly of today's *splendid* article.[b] For the past 4-5 days I have been prevented from writing, hence also to you, by a severe inflammation of the eyes which is not yet fully cleared up: also, as a result of the cold weather my USUAL SECRETARY[c] has not risen from her bed again as quickly as is her wont. However I think that she will shortly be able to return to her post. My eye trouble was brought on by reading through my own note-books on economics,[618] the intention being, not so much to elaborate the thing, as at any rate to master the material and get it READY to work on.

I have told you how Herzen elbowed his way on to the 'International Committee'.[d] Enclosed is a letter from him in which he proffers thanks for the 'invitation' which 'was never made'. The letter was intended for publication in *The People's Paper* in order to assert his importance *coram publico*.[e] This miscarried, for I immediately wheedled the scrawl out of Jones. However Herzen has had himself nominated a steward.

---

[a] true democracy - [b] F. Engels, 'The Struggle in the Crimea'. - [c] Jenny Marx - [d] See previous letter, - [e] publicly

Also enclosed a 2nd letter, in which this committee invites me to the banquet and 'to take part in the MEETING'. I do not want to offend the *crapauds*,[a] still less the Chartists. So the question is: in *what form* I should couch my refusal. Tell me your view *by return.* The thing must be declined, 1. because such MEETINGS are, on the whole, HUMBUG; 2. because at this moment it would be to expose oneself uselessly to GOVERNMENTAL PERSECUTION, and Palmerston has his eye on me; 3. because at no time and in no place do I wish to appear alongside *Herzen*, not being of the view that OLD EUROPE should be rejuvenated with Russian blood.[640] Should one's reply, perhaps, include some reference to Herzen's presence?

Jones has done something infinitely 'stupid', indeed gone completely off the rails, in leaving the management of the affair to the *crapauds* and the German louts. He sacrificed everything to the desire to show, at a big PUBLIC MEETING, that the FOREIGN EMIGRATIONS were in the tow of the Chartists. The MEETING will be a large one and create an uproar, but as a result: 1. Urquhart and Co. (likewise *The Times* if the thing creates a sensation) will denounce the Chartists as being led by *Russian* agents. This is unavoidable. 2. It will provide the Ministry with a pretext for reviving the Aliens Bill.[75] 3. Discord within the Chartist Party. Has already broken out. A section of the London Chartists maintains that Jones has ARBITRARILY departed from the Charter and compromised their whole cause by adopting the slogan 'SOCIAL AND DEMOCRATIC REPUBLIC' when forming the branch committee which is to be the CONNECTING LINK between the Chartists and the FOREIGN EMIGRATION.[b] There is no denying the extent of Jones' energy, persistence and activity, yet he goes and spoils everything by the way he cries his wares, by his tactless striving after pretexts for agitation and his anxiety to be ahead of the time. If he can't agitate in reality, he seeks an appearance of agitation, improvises MOVEMENTS after MOVEMENTS (so that, of course, everything remains at a standstill) and periodically works himself up into a state of fictitious exaltation. I have warned him, but in vain.

Mr Golovin—Herzen's *fidus* Achates[c]—has inserted in today's *Morning Advertiser*, under the heading 'February Revolution', a small notice to the effect that

'he has heard that Herzen is to represent Russia, OR RATHER LIBERAL RUSSIA, at the banquet. His name alone betrays that he is a German, or rather a German Jew.

---

a philistines - b A reference to 'The Alliance of the Peoples. The International Committee', *The People's Paper*, No. 145, 10 February 1855. - c faithful Achates (Virgil, *Aeneid*)

In Russia the Czar is criticised for making especial use of these people. The emigration should take care not TO FALL INTO THE SAME ERROR'.[a]

If, as the Paris correspondent writes in the 2ND EDITION of today's *Morning Chronicle*,[b] Bonaparte minor[c] assumes personally the supreme command of the Army of the Rhine against Prussia, the 'campagne' might end badly for the French.

Your
K. M.

<table>
<tr><td>First published slightly abridged in Der Briefwechsel zwischen F. Engels und K. Marx, Bd. 2, Stuttgart, 1913 and in full in: Marx and Engels, Works, First Russian Edition, Vol. XXII, Moscow, 1929</td><td>Printed according to the original

Published in English for the first time</td></tr>
</table>

265

MARX TO ENGELS

IN MANCHESTER

[London,] 3 March 1855
28 Dean Street, Soho

Dear Frederic,

On Tuesday[d] you will be hearing from me at some length. Today no more than these few lines to explain the reasons for my silence:

1. Musch[e] has had a dangerous gastric fever which he has still not shaken off (this is the worst of all).

2. The BABY[f] GREW EVERY DAY WORSE and was disturbing the whole household so that a few days ago a change of wet nurse became necessary.

---

[a] I. Golovin, 'To the Editor of *The Morning Advertiser*', in the section 'February Revolution', *The Morning Advertiser*, 13 February 1855. - [b] 'Express from Paris', *The Morning Chronicle*, No. 27499, 13 February 1855. - [c] nickname of Napoleon III given to him by Victor Hugo - [d] 6 March - [e] Edgar - [f] Eleanor

3. My wife, although splendidly recovered from her confinement, has had a so-called whitlow on the index finger of her right hand. Though a minor affliction, it is extremely painful and irritating. The thing was operated upon yesterday.

4. First I had my eye trouble, now more or less over; then such a frightful cough that I had to swallow several bottles of medicine and even keep to my bed for a few days.

So you see the whole house was and, to some extent still is, a hospital.

I shall get you Herzen's stuff [641]; likewise yesterday's *People's Paper*, in which you can read about Jones' and Herzen's COMMON PROCEEDINGS.[a] Should I throw Jones out if he comes again, or should I proceed 'diplomatically'?

The doctor says I need a change of air, not having left the PRECINCTS OF SOHO SQUARE for 2 years. So I should like to visit Manchester before my wife goes to Trier again. Should you, in view of your old man's impending arrival or for any other reason, find it awkward to put me up, I could take a room in Manchester. I must at any rate—but not, of course, until everything's all right here—get away from this place for a while, since the physical staleness also stultifies my brain.

Que dites-vous de la mort de Nicholas?[b] I like the way *The Times* insinuates that his death was partly due to fright because ‘HIS WORST ENEMY’—Palmerston—has become Premier of England.[c]

Vale faveque.[d]

Totus tuus,[e]

K. M.

Have heard nothing from Cluss for months.

First published in *Der Briefwechsel zwischen F. Engels und K. Marx*, Bd. 2, Stuttgart, 1913

Printed according to the original

Published in English for the first time

---

a 'Immense Demonstration in St. Martin's Hall', *The People's Paper*, No. 148, 3 March 1855. - b What do you say to the death of Nicholas? c *The Times*, No. 21992, 3 March 1855, leader. - d Good-bye and farewell. - e All yours

266

MARX TO ENGELS [234]

IN MANCHESTER

[London,] 8 March 1855
28 Dean Street, Soho

Dear Engels,

Received the £5.

I cannot get away until COLONEL Musch is visibly recovered. However, this week he has made rapid strides towards convalescence, today the doctor was EXCEEDINGLY PLEASED, and next week everything may be ALL RIGHT. As soon as I can depart with a good conscience, I shall write to you. Next week, I imagine.

Yesterday we were informed of A VERY HAPPY EVENT, the death of my wife's uncle, aged 90.[a] As a result, my mother-in-law[b] will save an annual impost of 200 talers and my wife will get almost £100; more if the old dog hasn't made over to his housekeeper such of his money as is not entailed. Another question which will be settled is that of the Duke of Brunswick's manuscript on the Seven Years' War, for which old Scharnhorst has already offered large sums. My wife immediately registered a protest against any attempts by her brother[c] to make a present of it to 'His Most Gracious Highness'.[d] Let the Prussian state acquire it for cash BUT NOT OTHERWISE.

There is a prospect of another *possible* source of money. My wife had deposited 1,300 talers with one Grach, a banker in Trier. The fellow went bankrupt and, in her case, had acted *fraudulently*, since he was already insolvent (although unbeknown to the public) when he accepted her deposit. On the urgent plea of the wife of this Grach, my wife 'relented' and refrained from pursuing the matter in the courts. The Chief Public Prosecutor had stated that Grach would otherwise be brought before the Assizes. This Grach's wife has now inherited a large fortune and, if she keeps her promise, we can count on the recovery of at least part of the loss. In any case this will mean that the 'past' has been discharged once and for all and a weight lifted from our shoulders.

Napoleon Bonaparte's[e] pamphlet—(Girardin denies in *La Presse* that he is the *faiseur*[f])—amused me very much.[642] Despite the

---

[a] Heinrich Georg von Westphalen - [b] Caroline von Westphalen - [c] Ferdinand von Westphalen - [d] Frederick William IV - [e] Joseph Charles Paul Napoleon Bonaparte - [f] maker

attempt to present '*le prince*' in an imposing attitude, despite the French braggadocio, superficiality, and BLUNDERS in things military, the pamphlet is worth its weight in gold as a memorial to our Leroy, alias St-Arnaud, and generally as typical of the 'IMPERIAL BARNUM'[a] and his round table.

There is one point you might clear up for me about the Crimean business, namely: General Evans declared before the committee[b] that the main reason for the MELTING OF THE ARMY before Sevastopol was the absence of a road from the harbour of Balaklava; 1,000 men would have sufficed to build one in 10 days, but— *et c'est la question*[c]— ALL MEN WHO COULD HAVE BEEN SPARED WERE EMPLOYED IN THE TRENCHES, and *from the start* the extent of the lines to be captured by the English was grossly disproportionate TO THEIR NUMERICAL STRENGTH. The question is: Could the French be regarded as the CONTRIVERS of this MISCHIEF?

A short while ago I took another look at Roman history (ancient) up to the time of Augustus.[643] Internal history resolves itself PLAINLY into the struggle between small and large landed property, specifically modified, of course, by slavery relations. Debtor-creditor relations, which play so large a part from the *origines* of Roman history, figure merely as an inherent consequence of small landed property.

Today 1 saw an advertisement for 3 works by Forster, a parson, all having in common the title *Original Language*.

As you will have seen, Mr Herzen is now having himself puffed in the Augsburg *Allgemeine Zeitung* also.[d] At the same time his SPEECH (at Jones' meeting) is appearing in *The People's Paper* as a fly-sheet and in *père* Ribeyrolles' estimable *L'Homme*.[e]

Your
K. M.

First published abridged in *Der Briefwechsel zwischen F. Engels und K. Marx*, Bd. 2, Stuttgart, 1913 and in full in: Marx and Engels, *Works*, First Russian Edition, Vol. XXII, Moscow, 1929

Printed according to the original

Published in English in full for the first time

---

[a] meaning Napoleon III - [b] G. Evans de Lacy, [Evidence given before the Committee of Inquiry into the Condition of the British Army in the Crimea,] *The Times*, Nos. 21994 and 21995, 6 and 7 March 1855. - [c] and that is the question - [d] i.e. 'Der Russe Herzen', *Allgemeine Zeitung*, No. 63, 4 March 1855. - [e] Discours d'Alexandre Herzen, exilé russe, prononcé au meeting tenu le 27 février 1855 dans St. Martin's Hall, à Londres, en commémoration des grands mouvements révolutionnaires de 1848 [s. l., s. a.], published on the Island of Jersey; *L'Homme*, No. 14, 7 March 1855.

267

MARX TO ENGELS

IN MANCHESTER

[London,] 16 March 1855
28 Dean Street, Soho

Dear Engels,

I do not believe that the good Musch is going to get over his illness. You will understand how this prospect affects all of us here. My wife once again altogether DOWN. However, the issue will soon be known.

Your

K. M.

First published in *Der Briefwechsel zwischen F. Engels und K. Marx*, Bd. 2, Stuttgart, 1913

Printed according to the original

Published in English for the first time

268

MARX TO ENGELS

IN MANCHESTER

[London,] 27 March 1855
28 Dean Street, Soho

Dear Engels,

Musch has been improving visibly for the past few days and the doctor sees every reason for hope. If all goes well, Musch must go into the country straight away. He is, of course, terribly weak and wasted. The fever IS GOT RID OF and the constipation considerably abated. The real question now is whether his constitution is strong enough to undergo the whole treatment. However, I think it is. As soon as the doctor says he is out of danger, I shall come and visit you.

Dronke has arrived here and is applying for Freiligrath's post, Freiligrath having definitely broken with his principal.[a]

---

[a] Oxford

You must forgive me for not writing more than these few lines. I am dog-tired from the long night vigils, since I am Musch's nurse.

Warmest regards from the whole family, Musch included.

Tell Lupus that Furrer, the Swiss with whom he used to be in touch, has gone bankrupt and actually done his resident tutor out of £14.

Vale faveque.[a]

Totus tuus,[b]

K. M.

First published abridged in *Der Briefwechsel zwischen F. Engels und K. Marx*, Bd. 2, Stuttgart, 1913 and in full in: Marx and Engels, *Works*, First Russian Edition, Vol. XXII, Moscow, 1929

Printed according to the original

Published in English for the first time

269

MARX TO ENGELS

IN MANCHESTER

[London,] 30 March 1855
28 Dean Street, Soho

Dear Engels,

From day to day I have put off sending you a bulletin[c] because the ups and downs of the illness were such that I changed my opinion almost hourly. Latterly, however, the illness has assumed the character, hereditary in my family, of an abdominal consumption, and even the doctor seems to have given up hope. For the past week emotional stress has made my wife iller than ever before. As for myself, though my heart is bleeding and my head afire, I must, of course, maintain my composure. Never for one moment throughout his illness has the child been untrue to his own good-natured, and at the same time independent, self.

As for you, I cannot thank you enough for the kindness with

---

[a] Good-bye and farewell. - [b] All yours - [c] on Edgar Marx's condition

which you have worked in my stead, and for the sympathy you have shown towards the child.

Should there be any change for the better, I shall write to you at once.

Totus tuus,[a]

K. M.

Notabene. There's *no* sailing for America next *Tuesday*[b] and it doesn't do to send the chaps two articles at once *every time.* So give this Tuesday a miss.

First published in *Der Briefwechsel zwischen F. Engels und K. Marx*, Bd. 2, Stuttgart, 1913

Printed according to the original

Published in English for the first time

270

MARX TO ENGELS[213]

IN MANCHESTER

[London,] 6 April 1855
28 Dean Street, Soho

Dear Engels,

Poor Musch is no more. Between 5 and 6 o'clock today he fell asleep (in the literal sense) in my arms. I shall never forget how much your friendship has helped to make this ghastly time easier for us. You will understand how I grieve over the child. My wife sends her warmest regards. I might, if I come to Manchester, bring her with me for a week, in which case we should, of course, stay at an inn (or perhaps take PRIVATE LODGINGS). At any rate I must find some means of helping her over the first days.

Your

K. M.

First published in *Der Briefwechsel zwischen F. Engels und K. Marx*, Bd. 2, Stuttgart, 1913

Printed according to the original

---

[a] All yours - [b] 3 April

Edgar Marx (Musch)

271

MARX TO ENGELS[213]

IN MANCHESTER

[London,] 12 April 1855
28 Dean Street, Soho

Dear Engels,

I am thinking of coming up to Manchester with my wife on Wednesday[a]; she must have a change of scene for a few days. Unless I let you know to the contrary, Wednesday will be the day. I shall at any rate be writing again on Monday.

Needless to say, the house has been very desolate and bereft since the death of the dear child[b] who was its life and soul. I cannot tell you how we miss the child at every turn. I've already had my share of bad luck but only now do I know what real unhappiness is. I feel BROKEN DOWN. Since the funeral I have been fortunate enough to have such splitting headaches that I can neither think nor hear nor see.

Amid all the fearful torments I have recently had to endure, the thought of you and your friendship has always sustained me, as has the hope that there is still something sensible for us to do together in the world.

Your
K. M.

My wife has just brought me a line or two for you, which I enclose.

First published in *Der Briefwechsel zwischen F. Engels und K. Marx*, Bd. 2, Stuttgart, 1913

Printed according to the original

---

[a] 18 April - [b] See previous letter.

272

MARX TO ENGELS

IN MANCHESTER

[London,] 16 April [1855]

Dear Engels,

I shall be leaving with my wife for Manchester on Wednesday morning by the parliamentary train.[145]

Dronke and I have just seen Badinguet crossing Westminster Bridge.[644] A monkey in uniform.

Your

K. M.

First published in Der Briefwechsel zwischen F. Engels und K. Marx, Bd. 2, Stuttgart, 1913

Printed according to the original

Published in English for the first time

273

MARX TO MORITZ ELSNER

IN BRESLAU

[London,] 17 April 1855
28 Dean Street, Soho

Dear Elsner,

I shall be away from London for a few days in company with my wife. Dronke has kindly agreed to carry on with the articles during that time. He will today be sending you a report on Bonaparte's arrival.[a] In case I don't see him again, I am writing to you separately.

The 2 enclosed articles[b] constitute the *beginning* of a polemic against *pan-Slavism*.[609] In my view it is high time that Germany be made seriously aware of the dangers threatening her. You may

---

[a] [E. Dronke,] 'Der Besuch', *Neue Oder-Zeitung*, No. 183, 20 April 1855. -
[b] F. Engels, 'Germany and Pan-Slavism'.

print these things *when* you think fit, for they have nothing directly to do with our regular articles. However I'm convinced that there is *no time* to lose. The alarm must be sounded in Germany.

In the same context the Berlin 'Critical Criticism'[a] will be lambasted for its arrogant stupidity.

Your
K. M.

First published in: Marx and Engels, *Works*, First Russian Edition, Vol. XXV, Moscow, 1934

Printed according to the original

Published in English for the first time

274

MARX TO ENGELS

IN MANCHESTER

[London,] 16 May 1855
28 Dean Street, Soho

Dear Engels,

My wife is most unwell; the household in general still very upset. From the day we left Manchester[645] the weather here has been unremittingly awful.

Dronke, the little fool, refuses to send you the Bruno Bauer[646] until you have sent him his 'rubbers'. The 'Petermann'[b] got packed by mistake. Would already have been returned to you if I hadn't wanted to send it at the same time as the Bruno Bauer. Tell me how you wish it done. If you send the little fool his shoes, you might at the same time send me the Decker, which I forgot.[c]

I have written to Breslau.[647] No answer yet. In the meantime write and tell me in greater detail how many sheets—whether in separate volumes or ALL TOGETHER—, charges, etc.[609]

---

[a] Bruno Bauer (see also Note 535) - [b] *Mittheilungen aus Justus Perthes' geographischer Anstalt über wichtige neue Erforschungen auf dem Gesammtgebiete der Geographie*, edited by A. Petermann. - [c] C. Decker, *Der kleine Krieg, im Geiste der neueren Kriegführung, Oder: Abhandlung über die Verwendung und den Gebrauch aller drei Waffen im kleinen Kriege*.

At long last a few more *Tribunes* from Cluss, together with a couple of lines in which he indicates that he will be writing.

Herewith 1. *The Sunday Times* on the 'Soho scorpions'. 2. A cutting from *The People's Paper*ᵃ in which you may read about Mr Jones' curious negotiations with the City reformers,⁶⁴⁸ and 'how he was brought down' (clearly the chaps wanted to have the working plebs standing *in* the street *outside* their doors as mere supernumeraries, just for SHOW and to demonstrate their movement's popularity). The business is VERY CURIOUS INDEED.

Regards to Lupus.

Your
K. M.

The *Political Fly-Sheets*ᵇ have now come out as a book. In the foreword Mr Tucker thanks me *by name*ᶜ which, with an Aliens Bill⁷⁵ in the offing, is NOT QUITE RECOMMENDATORY.

First published abridged in *Der Briefwechsel zwischen F. Engels und K. Marx*, Bd. 2, Stuttgart, 1913 and in full in: Marx and Engels, *Works*, First Russian Edition, Vol. XXII, Moscow, 1929

Printed according to the original

Published in English for the first time

275

MARX TO ENGELS

IN MANCHESTER

[London,] 18 Mayᵈ 1855
28 Dean Street, Soho

Dear Engels,

My wife has been *confined to bed* since yesterday evening. As I cannot draw a bill before a week on Tuesday (next),ᵉ I should be much obliged if you could send me some money (however little).

The devil take the *Tribune*! Certainly it is now absolutely essential that it should adopt an *anti-pan-Slav* line.⁶⁴⁹ If it doesn't,

---

ᵃ i.e. E. Jones, 'Political Felony. Infamous Chicanery and Fraud of the Administrative Reform Association', *The People's Paper*, No. 158, 12 May 1855. - ᵇ See this volume, pp. 407-08, 432, 455 and 473. - ᶜ *Tucker's Political Fly-Sheets*, London, 1855, p. 1. - ᵈ March in the original. - ᵉ 22 May

one might be compelled to break with the rag, which would be disastrous.

As you will have seen in an earlier no. of the Augsburg *Allgemeine*,[a] as from next August, the great *Herzen* will be bringing out a Russian periodical here, the *Polar Star*.[b]

My warm regards to Lupus.

Your

K. M.

First published in *Der Briefwechsel zwischen F. Engels und K. Marx*, Bd. 2, Stuttgart, 1913

Printed according to the original

Published in English for the first time

276

MARX TO ENGELS

IN MANCHESTER

London, 15 June [1855]
28 Dean Street, Soho

Dear Engels,

Your article[c] just arrived (4 o'clock in the afternoon). Our inebriated postman had already passed the door when Lenchen grabbed him and took away the letter. From Dana's letter,[650] enclosed herewith, you will see that he is asking for 1. a column on the Prussian army for the *Tribune*, 2. a sheet on all the European armies for *Putnam's Review*.[d] *If you have no time* to do the latter, you must send me the material and I shall have to do it.[651] It is true that, in the latter case, my unfamiliarity with the subject would make for a sorry result, but I cannot let slip the £10 to be earned in this way, for, on the one hand, no money is yet coming in from the legacy and, on the other, expenses have been very heavy; added to which there has been a loss of earnings, since the worthy Dronke did *not* keep the *Neue Oder-Zeitung* supplied during my abscnce (despite his promise) and, as to the *Tribune* itself, there was still an overdraft outstanding (only cleared off by *today's* post[e]).

---

[a] 'Großbritannien. London, 6 Mai', *Allgemeine Zeitung*, No. 130, 10 May 1855. - [b] Полярная звезда - [c] F. Engels, 'Napoleon's War Plans'. - [d] *Putnam's Monthly* - [e] by Engels' article 'Napoleon's War Plans'

With regard to the *Petermann*,[a] I sent it to Manchester by Pfänder, together with a note, while you were away in the LAKES. Pfänder is now in Manchester again, so will be able to give you particulars.

For Lupus: Lost his bet. The pubs here open at 1 o'clock on Sundays, not half past twelve.

These lines in great haste. More in my next.

Your

K. M.

Apropos: Bruno Bauer has brought out a pamphlet on the Russian Church.[b]

First published in *Der Briefwechsel zwischen F. Engels und K. Marx*, Bd. 2, Stuttgart, 1913

Printed according to the original

Published in English for the first time

277

MARX TO ENGELS

IN MANCHESTER

[London,] 26 June 1855
28 Dean Street, Soho

Dear Engels,

I did *not* send off any article last Friday[c] because [articles dispatched] *simultaneously* from London and Manchester would have aroused the fellows' suspicions. On Tuesday (last)[d] I sent off an article of an entirely general nature on Bonaparte's diplomacy, the treaties of 1815 and the Prussian Field Marshal Knesebeck.[e] For at the Congress of Vienna the latter cracked some good jokes about the Poles.[f]

Next Friday[g] it will be virtually impossible to avoid writing a military piece about the affair at Malakhov and Redan on the anniversary of Waterloo.[652] Tomorrow and the day after I shall go

---

[a] *Mittheilungen aus Justus Perthes' geographischer Anstalt...* - [b] B. Bauer, *Die russische Kirche*, Charlottenburg, 1855. - [c] 22 June - [d] 19 June - [e] K. Marx, 'Eccentricities of Politics'. - [f] A reference to F. Knesebeck's *Denkschrift, betreffend die Gleichgewichts-Lage Europa's, beim zusammentritte des Wiener Congresses verfaßt...*, pp. 13-14. - [g] 29 June

to the library and look up something on the Spanish army. You shall have what I can find by the end of this week in any case.

Regarding your pamphlet[609] Elsner writes to me:

'You have far too lofty an idea of our booksellers if you believe that any one of them would consent to bring out something written by Engels. All those I asked refused, no doubt because they are afraid of acquiring the reputation of being revolutionary.... Should you intend making inquiries in Berlin, perhaps *Alexander Duncker* would be most likely to take the work.'

Weerth could negotiate with Duncker.[653]

The demonstration in Hyde Park on Sunday afternoon had quite a revolutionary air.[654]

This short note is written to the accompaniment of an appalling toothache which has been plaguing me for a week now.

Salut!

Your
K. M.

First published in *Der Briefwechsel zwischen F. Engels und K. Marx*, Bd. 2, Stuttgart, 1913

Printed according to the original

Published in English for the first time

278

MARX TO ENGELS

IN MANCHESTER

London, 29 June [1855]

Dear Engels,

When you have read the accompanying scraps, you will say: *multa* INSTEAD OF *multum.*[a] And rightly so. I was unable to find the most important item, viz. the number and calibre of guns for Spain, although I leafed rapidly through the whole book of *Ordenanzas.* You'll find something in this respect about the mountain artillery in one of the notes. To judge by a passage in

---

[a] *Non multa, sed multum* (not many, but much)

the Portuguese *Revista militar,* Spanish artillery is largely on a French footing as regards matériel.

I have got together all manner of stuff, some of which may be of use.

Salut.

Your

K. M.

Where *Minutoli* (Baron) quoted, reference is to his book: *Spanien und seine fortschreitende Entwicklung* etc., Berlin, 1852.

I believe it's that swine of a policeman. Was and still may be Prussian Consul General in SPAIN and Portugal.

First published in *Der Briefwechsel zwischen F. Engels und K. Marx,* Bd. 2, Stuttgart, 1913

Printed according to the original

Published in English for the first time

279

MARX TO ENGELS

IN MANCHESTER

[London,] 3 July 1855
28 Dean Street, Soho

Dear Frederic,

The £5 received on Monday.

For 3 days I have been rummaging through a mass of stuff at the Museum[651] without finding anything about the Neapolitan army save for the following, which may also be found in MacCulloch's *Dictionary Geographical, Statistical* etc.

In 1848 the army NEARLY 49,000 strong (this seems to be its war footing, as I find it given {in a *Dizionario Politico,* Turin} as 26-27,000 strong in 1840). Of these, 32,000 INFANTRY OF THE LINE, 5,000 CAVALRY, 4,000 ARTILLERY AND ENGINEERS, and 8,000 *gendarmes.* They claim to be able to increase their army to 64,237 and this is given as the official war footing.

Amalie and Roland Daniels

I discovered from *Ricciardi* that the son of Ferdinand I[a] and father of King Bomba[b] first engaged the Swiss—in 1824 or 1825—for 30 years (the Neapolitan army having aped the Spanish and mutinied) at 3 times the pay of the NATIVE ARMY. Since the government of the Two Sicilies relies on Swiss and lazzaroni at home and on the Austrian army abroad, and itself estimates at zero its badly paid, undisciplined, demoralised, cowardly army, I believe that in any survey of the European armies, this estimate made by its own government could be accepted, the army put at zero, and its strength mentioned only *en passant.*

There might be something more detailed in Mariotti. But I couldn't get hold of it as it was always 'IN HAND' whenever I asked for it.

Our family life here is still melancholy. My wife still very unwell. The memory of our poor, dear child[c] torments us, and even interposes itself in his sisters'[d] play. Such blows can only be mitigated slowly, with the passage of time. To me the loss is as poignant as on the first day and hence I can tell how much my wife is suffering. Should the Scotch money[e] arrive in time I shall spend a few weeks in Kent, where plenty of cheap and pleasantly situated places are said to be available.

The scenes in Hyde Park last Sunday were DISGUSTING, firstly because of the CONSTABLES' brutality, and secondly because of the purely passive resistance put up by the huge crowds.[655] However, things are clearly seething and fermenting and we can only hope that great disasters in the Crimea will bring them to a head.

Your

K. M.

First published abridged in *Der Briefwechsel zwischen F. Engels und K. Marx,* Bd. 2, Stuttgart, 1913 and in full in: Marx and Engels, *Works,* First Russian Edition, Vol. XXII, Moscow, 1929

Printed according to the original

Published in English for the first time

---

[a] Francis I - [b] Ferdinand II - [c] Edgar (see this volume, p. 530) - [d] Jenny and Laura - [e] an allusion to the Scottish origin of the Westphalens; see also p. 526.

280

MARX TO ENGELS

IN MANCHESTER

[London,] 17 July 1855
28 Dean Street, Soho

Dear Engels,

Strohn is here and, unfortunately, prevents me from sending an ARTICLE to the *Tribune* today. I therefore intend to send off on Friday,[a] under *Tuesday*'s date, an article on the latest ministerial crisis, and I should be very grateful if, *at the same time,* you would send me one on, say, the Prussian army (assuming that nothing occurs in the theatre of war),[b] so that 2 articles go off *at once.* For I shall be compelled to draw a bill on the *Tribune* next week, or rather *overdraw* and appreciably so at that, as I had already overdrawn last time, and this time several days have been missed.

A German returning from Yankeeland, Gustav Pöckel, brought me a line or two from Edgar[c] and more detailed news about him and other acquaintances. Of late, Edgar had been working as a farm labourer near New York and intended to sell his farm in Texas. Schramm[d] is said to be dying of consumption and is also in New York State. Ewerbeck passed through about eighteen months ago on his way to visit Cabet in Nauvoo. Fickler took over the Shakespeare Hotel after Lièvre went bankrupt, making the most of the occasion to do the dirty on him. Jacobi's[e] affairs are prospering; the Yankees like his 'serious' and 'reserved' manner. Field Marshal Blenker and a few other notorious swindlers from the days of the revolution comedy have bought up real estate with the stolen funds and, as regards swagger and brutality towards their workpeople, are said to put the Yankees completely in the shade. Heinzen has re-established himself in New York with his *Pionier.* All in all, things are going very badly for the Germans over there, at one and the same time harassed by the Maine Law, KNOW-NOTHINGS[656] and the crisis in agriculture and industry. Hence a substantial re-emigration to Germany, Canada and South America.

Through the mediation of German merchants in Paris (one of them a supporter of the *Neue Rheinische Zeitung*) *Dronke* has

---

[a] 20 July - [b] On Marx's request Engels wrote 'War Prospects'. - [c] Edgar von Westphalen - [d] Conrad Schramm - [e] Abraham Jacobi

received an affirmative reply to his application for permission to return to Paris. He proposes to set off this week, as soon as he has recouped the 'costs of production'.

Imandt is in Scotland for 4 weeks on a visit to Heise. He has placed his COTTAGE in Camberwell at my disposal in the meantime. The whole FAMILY will move there and avail themselves of the change of air until we can afford something bigger.

As to the enclosed letters:

No. I. From *Lassalle* in Paris.

No. II. I send you for your amusement Szeredy's *Asiatic Chiefs*, together with the fellow's appeal to me.[657]

No. III. Letter from Florencourt (the only one you need return). Contains an account of how things stand with the legacy.[a] You will observe on the one hand that the legacy has increased by £515, while on the other all manner of delays are militating against its rapid realisation. This Florencourt is not the notorious one,[b] but his brother.

Your

K. M.

Do you know of any book on the *êtres*[c] of LITTLE Johnny Russell?[658]

First published in *Der Briefwechsel zwischen F. Engels und K. Marx*, Bd. 2, Stuttgart, 1913

Printed according to the original

Published in English for the first time

281

MARX TO FERDINAND LASSALLE

IN PARIS

London, 28 July 1855
28 Dean Street, Soho[d]

Dear Lassalle,

I have been staying in the country for the past few weeks in a cottage lent me by a friend[e] who is away in Scotland. That is why I did not get your letter until yesterday. I have, incidentally, taken

---

[a] See this volume, pp. 526 and 541. - [b] Franz von Florencourt - [c] life and doings - [d] The letter is written in Camberwell near London but datelined London. - [e] Peter Imandt (see previous letter)

steps to have my letters forwarded to me immediately from town.

I am, of course, surprised to hear that, despite your proximity to London, you are not thinking of coming over here, if only for a few days. I hope that you will think it over again and discover how short and cheap the journey from Paris to London is. If France's doors were not hermetically closed against me, I would pay you a surprise visit in Paris.

I have several friends in Paris, but I shall not be able to send you their addresses (I am not in town at the moment of writing) until I go to Soho, where I keep them.

Bacon says that really important people have so many relations to nature and the world, so many objects of interest, that they easily get over any loss. I am not one of those important people. The death of my child [a] has shattered me to the very core and I feel the loss as keenly as on the first day. My poor wife is also completely BROKEN DOWN.

If you see Heine again, give him my regards.

Your
K. M.

First published in the *Frankfurter Zeitung*, 10 August 1913

Printed according to the original

Published in English for the first time

282

MARX TO ENGELS

IN MANCHESTER

[London,] 7 August 1855
28 Dean Street, Soho

Dear Engels,

The FAMILY (hence, for the most part, myself also) still in Camberwell. Pieper came and stayed with us for a week. I was thus prevented from writing, save for the necessary pieces for New York AND GERMANY. The article on the 'ARMIES' is splendid.[b]

From the enclosed letter from Steffen you will see what a bad state our friend Daniels and Bürgers are in. I am particularly sorry about the first. I don't know whether, in my résumé of the

---

[a] Edgar - [b] F. Engels, 'The Armies of Europe'.

report by the visitor from Yankeeland,[a] I mentioned that Conrad Schramm is consumptive and is taking a cure of ass's milk *chez* former Field Marshal Blenker.

In the past weeks I have sent the *Tribune* a series of articles—i.e. 3—about Lord John Russell in which the little man is passed in review from the very beginning.[659] However, it will soon be necessary to say SOME WORDS about the war and also, perhaps, about how the *affaire* is going in Asia.

Dronke has suffered a bitter disappointment. For it eventually transpired that the issue of a passport to Paris had been due to a misunderstanding on the part of the French Embassy; rather, express instructions had been given that he was not to be admitted into France. In a few days it will be decided whether or not he has obtained a post in Jersey.

Bonaparte has, within the bounds of pure reason, solved the problem I set him, namely 'to steal the whole of France in order to make a present of it to France again'.[b] His manoeuvrings over the loan are significant experiments in that direction.

What do you think of the Austrian concentration of troops in Italy? Have you seen the 2nd *Mémoire d'un Officier Général?*[660]

Your

K. M.

First published in: Marx and Engels, *Works*, Second Russian Edition, Vol. 28, Moscow, 1962

Printed according to the original

Published in English for the first time

283

MARX TO ENGELS

IN MANCHESTER

1 September 1855
3 York Place, Denmark,[c]
Camberwell

Dear Frederic,

Imandt has gone off to Montrose and chucked up his whole CONCERN here for the highly dubious prospect of a post in

---

[a] Pöckel (see this volume, p. 542) - [b] Marx quotes from his *Eighteenth Brumaire of Louis Bonaparte* (see present edition, Vol. 11, p. 195). - [c] Should be: Denmark street (see this volume, pp. 547 and 550).

Arbroath. I have taken over his goods and chattels and shall remain here until the arrival of the Scotch money.[a] Then I shall rent some decent lodgings. Until then I shall have to keep the house in Dean Street. The country air has suited the whole FAMILY uncommonly well, my wife especially.

Received your article[b] yesterday. The Russian report is now in all the Hamburg papers as well.

As regards *Putnam's*, we must now get a move on. In a letter I got from Dana he already evinced anxiety lest No. 2[c] should arrive too late. But it was there on time, as I see from a subsequent letter.[d] Putnam has asked for another article on 'THE IMPROVEMENTS IN MODERN WARFARE'. *The New-York Times* contains criticism which is generally favourable, but clearly grudging: off duty, Englishmen don't wear 'narrow trousers', their squadrons number more than 400 SABRES, and a ? after 'SABRES' too, and, lastly, the writer seems to be unaware that in England flogging is now restricted to 50 strokes and is inflicted only in exceptional cases. The business at Aldershot where, ABOUT 14 DAYS ago, a SOLDIER died from 30 strokes of the lash, is comment enough on the *criticus* concerning whose nonsense I have sent Dana the requisite observations.[661]

Have you been following Napier's row with Graham? The 1st article was in *The Times*, the 2nd in the *Advertiser* and the *Herald*.[662] Today the *Advertiser*'s first LEADER contains the exchange of letters between Charley and James. A reply from Graham to Napier's first articles is also, it seems, to appear in one of today's papers.

I wonder whether you have noticed that the Austrians made use of the time they were deploying their armies in Galicia to construct, under Hess' general supervision, railways of solely strategic importance; likewise fortifications directed against Russia.

I hope that you will now write and tell me something about yourself and your doings.

Your

K. M.

Unless I am mistaken, our Kościelski also appears in Pélissier's battle report.[e]

---

[a] See this volume, p. 526. - [b] F. Engels, 'The Battle of the Chernaya'. - [c] F. Engels, 'The Armies of Europe', Second Article. - [d] Dana to Marx, 7 August 1855. Dana's second letter has not been found. - [e] A. Pélissier, [Report on the Battle of the Chernaya. 18 August 1855,] *The Times*, No. 22146, 30 August 1855.

If Admiral Bruat's account in today's *Times*[a] is to be believed, the Russians are at STARVATION-POINT. At any rate, there would not as yet appear to be any shortage of spirits.

First published abridged in *Der Briefwechsel zwischen F. Engels und K. Marx*, Bd. 2, Stuttgart, 1913 and in full in: Marx and Engels, *Works*, First Russian Edition, Vol. XXII, Moscow, 1929

Printed according to the original

Published in English for the first time

284

MARX TO ENGELS

IN MANCHESTER

6 September 1855
3 York Place, Denmark *Street*
(not Hill, which is merely the
GENERAL NAME for the whole place)
Camberwell

Dear Engels,

You may already have read about the death of our friend Daniels in the *Kölnische Zeitung*.[b] He is no more nor less than a victim of the infamies of the Prussian Police. I shall be writing a few lines to his wife,[c] and you must do the same. Address: Frau Doktorin Amalie Daniels, Schildergasse, Köln. It would be desirable if Lupus did likewise. I know by experience how welcome letters from friends are at such a time. I shall write a short obituary of our poor friend for the *Tribune*. So far as the German-American Press is concerned, I think the best plan would be to insert in the New York *Neue Zeit* (nominally edited by Bernhardt, in fact by Löwe of Calbe) a brief obituary notice signed by you, Freiligrath, Lupus and myself. Also to denounce the proceedings against Bürgers.

You will have heard that O'Connor died a few days ago.

Jones' wife is mortally ill. The poor devil IS AT THIS MOMENT IN DESPERATE CIRCUMSTANCES.

A STEAMER is leaving on *Tuesday*. It is essential in the case of *Putnam's* that the thing should be in New York by 10th October at

---

[a] *The Times*, No. 22148, 1 September 1855. - [b] *Kölnische Zeitung*, 30 August 1855. - [c] See this volume, pp. 548-49.

the latest. Have you received the copy that was sent you?[a] Those inane bits of hair-splitting did not appear in the *Tribune* but in *The New-York Times*, the RIVAL PAPER.[b] As for Aldershot, the business was simply as follows: About a fortnight ago 2 privates were sentenced, one to 50 lashes, the other to 30, for 'disrespectful' behaviour towards their superiors. As is often the case, the CAT-O'-NINE-TAILS was steeped in urine. The first man had to be sent to hospital after receiving 40 lashes, and the second died shortly after receiving 30. There would appear to be no further question of an inquiry.

In *The Morning Advertiser*, Blind continues 'TO SHAKE THE DESPOTIC POWERS OF EUROPE TO THEIR VERY FOUNDATIONS'.

A German rag has reappeared in London, the actual *rédacteur en chef*[c] being the ill-famed Sigmund Engländer, of Paris police memory. Chief contributors: Ronge, the Russian Herzen and a drunkard by the name of Korn, allegedly an ex-captain.[663]

Vale.[d]

Your
K. M.

First published abridged in *Der Briefwechsel zwischen F. Engels und K. Marx*, Bd. 2, Stuttgart, 1913 and in full in: Marx and Engels, *Works*, First Russian Edition, Vol. XXII, Moscow, 1929

Printed according to the original

Published in English for the first time

285

MARX TO AMALIE DANIELS

IN COLOGNE

London, 6 September 1855
28 Dean Street, Soho

My Dear Mrs Daniels,
It is impossible to describe the grief I felt on hearing that dear, unforgettable Roland had passed away. Although the latest news reaching me through Steffen had been far from reassuring,[e] I did

---

[a] *Putnam's Monthly* for August 1855, containing the first article in Engels' series 'The Armies of Europe', which is referred to here. - [b] See this volume, p. 546. - [c] chief editor - [d] Farewell. - [e] See this volume, pp. 544-45.

not for all that ever abandon hope of your excellent husband's recovery. His was a sensitive, finely-tuned and altogether noble nature—character, talents and physical appearance in rare harmony. Seen amongst the others in Cologne, Daniels always seemed to me like the statue of a Greek god deposited by some freak of fate in the midst of a crowd of Hottentots. His premature decease is an irreparable loss not only to his family and friends but also to science, in which he gave promise of the finest achievements, and to the great, suffering mass of humanity, who possessed in him a loyal champion.

I am sufficiently acquainted with your heroic nature to be convinced that imperishable grief will not prevent you from remaining the loyal guardian of the beloved pledges left you by Roland. In his sons you will compensate the world twice over for the loss of the father.

The news of this new loss has revived in my wife such vivid memories of the death of our only little son[a] that her state of mind does not permit of her writing to you just now. She is weeping and lamenting like a child.

Consolation I will not venture to offer you since I myself am and shall remain inconsolable for [the] loss of a friend who was more dear to me personally than any other. Grief such as this cannot be alleviated, but only shared. As soon as I get over my first stormy emotions, I shall send an obituary to the *New-York Tribune* for the many friends of the departed in America. It is to be hoped that circumstances will some day permit us to wreak upon those guilty of cutting short his career vengeance of a kind sterner than that of an obituary.

You will need no assurance on my part that you can always count on me as a loyal and devoted friend.

With my heartfelt sympathy,

Yours

K. Marx

First published in: Marx and Engels, *Works*, First Russian Edition, Vol. XXV, Moscow, 1934

Printed according to the original

Published in English for the first time

---

[a] Edgar

286

MARX TO ENGELS

IN MANCHESTER

11 September 1855
3 York Place, Denmark Street,
Camberwell

Dear Engels,

Like the Russians, I have been compelled by *force supérieure* TO EVACUATE THE SOUTHERN SIDE without, however, blowing everything up behind me.[664] Indeed, my garrison will remain quietly here, whither I also propose to return IN A WEEK OR SO. In other words, I am obliged to withdraw to Manchester for a few days and shall arrive there *tomorrow evening.* I shall have to stay there *incognito,* so don't let anyone know about my presence—Lupus, OF COURSE, EXCEPTED, should you by chance see him.

I have amended your letter[a] just received, to accord with the latest telegraphic dispatches.
Salut.

Your
K. M.

First published in *Der Briefwechsel zwischen F. Engels und K. Marx*, Bd. 2, Stuttgart, 1913

Printed according to the original

Published in English for the first time

287

MARX TO MORITZ ELSNER[665]

IN BRESLAU

London, 11 September 1855
28 Dean Street, Soho[b]

Dear Elsner,

It was *impossible* for me to write last week because of legal proceedings taken against me by the worthy Dr Freund. He has actually compelled me to leave London for a week or so. During

---

[a] F. Engels, 'The Fall of Sevastopol'. - [b] The letter is written in Camberwell but datelined London.

Moritz Elsner

the parliamentary recess this does not, of course, impair my efficiency as a correspondent. This month, therefore, you should not put me on your books until 11 September.

It goes without saying that, should your paper cease to pay yet still remain *viable*, my contributions will be at your disposal then as now.

Considering the difficult circumstances and the limited space at your disposal, your paper is, in my opinion, edited with great skill and tact, and in such a way that the intelligent reader may read between the lines. Nothing can be more fatuous than to censure you for receiving 'constitutional' money. Some very 'constitutional' citizens paid in shares for the *Neue Rheinische Zeitung.* If these gentlemen subsequently came to regret it, they were at least never forbidden by the editorial board to go on paying.

If I were not so afraid of compromising this or that acquaintance by the mere fact of corresponding with him, I should long since have written to the Rhine Province in the interests of your paper. At all events, Lassalle did wrong in failing to draw attention to the *Neue Oder-Zeitung* in Cologne, etc. Circumstances would have allowed him to do so.

Should the *N. O.-Z.* go under, we shall have to console ourselves with the thought that all our present doings, activities and beginnings are purely provisional and no more than a *pis aller.*
With kindest regards.

                                              Yours
                                              K. M.

A German weekly rag has been started in London, its founder being the French ex(?)-policeman and Viennese refugee, Sigmund Engländer. Contributors: the *Russian* Herzen, Johannes Ronge and a drunkard by the name of Korn, allegedly a *capitaine.*[663]

First published in: Marx and Engels, *Works,* First Russian Edition, Vol. XXV, Moscow, 1934

Printed according to the original

Published in English for the first time

288

MARX TO MORITZ ELSNER

IN BRESLAU

Manchester, 8 November 1855
34 Butler Street, Green Keys

Dear Elsner,

I have received both your letters,[666] the first somewhat belatedly because my wife accidentally delayed sending it on to Manchester. After receiving your first letter I thought you had resigned from the *Neue Oder-Zeitung* and for that reason at once ceased to send any articles. When your second letter arrived I was suffering from such a FIT of toothache—which persisted until a few days ago—that I could no more write than I could hear or see.

I passed on your letter of 7 October not only to friends but also to adversaries, and the latter seemed thoroughly taken aback. That I and my friends are in no way affected by the dogmas of Messrs Temme and Simon of Breslau you will readily believe without any further assurance from me.

I do not see Hoyoll, but Lupus does—from time to time. Patriotism has led this Hoyoll to introduce the *Breslauer Zeitung* into the Athenaeum[244] here, a circumstance which threatens to drive our little Wolff[a] out of what is virtually the only home of the Muses in Manchester.

I have conveyed your greetings to Borchardt, whom I know well. Borchardt maintains a regular and intimate correspondence with Citizen Simon of Breslau. Upon his first asking me whether I knew that the *N. O.-Z.* lived in sin with the constitutionals, I replied: '*Qu'est ce que ça me fait?*[b] Don't you know that, in my view, constitutionals and democrats, at least of the Prussian variety, are all much of a muchness? And is a distinction now to be drawn between democrats who have accepted one royal imposition while rejecting another and those who, having submitted to the one, also submit to the other?[667] The *N. O.-Z.* expresses the most extreme views possible in the present condition of the Press. What more do you ask?'

I have had letters from particularly well-informed people in Paris. According to them, the Empire's stock is sinking lower and

---

a Wilhelm Wolff - b What's that to me?

lower. In the *faubourgs* the slogan, '*Celui-ci s'en ira*'[a] is said to be on everyone's lips. Indeed, the gravity of the situation may be deduced from two PUBLIC FACTS: the speech made by Rouland, the *procurateur-général*,[b] and Granier de Cassagnac's article in the *Constitutionnel*, '*Sur les terreurs de la* Révolution future'.[c] The probability of the latter is beyond doubt even to Mr Granier.

As for the scandal here over the 'refugee question' (Jersey, etc.), there's more smoke to it than fire.[668] PUBLIC OPINION has definitely turned against the GOVERNMENT and, in fact, I believe that this was *allowed for* in the latter's calculations. So crassly, with such tragi-comical mouthings, did they accede to Bonaparte's first demands, as virtually to demonstrate that further concessions were not within the power of an English government. Had they been in earnest, they would have shown themselves more adroit and not have carried out the grotesque coup so long before the opening of Parliament. Palmerston, OF COURSE, has no love for the refugees, but regards them as wind-bags to be kept to hand so that he may occasionally threaten the Continent with a '*Quos ego!*'[d] His ministerial position, by the by, is exceedingly precarious. But it will still be difficult to unseat the old fox.

When you next write, kindly send your letter to my old address, 28 Dean Street, Soho, London, since I don't know how long I shall be remaining here, and letters sent to the above address will in any case come into the hands of my wife. Ronge is running kindergartens in London along with his wife; Kinkel, no less than Johanna,[e] hopes that the revolution will not be unduly precipitate; in Brighton, Ruge gives an occasional lecture, leading the English to believe that the German language is the most debased of all; Tausenau, Meyen *et tutti quanti*[f] abuse the French émigré 'riff-raff' (not excluding Victor Hugo) for imperilling the 'right of asylum' of these 'officially authorised conspirators'.

Engels and Lupus send you their warmest regards. I haven't seen Borchardt for a fortnight.

Yours
K. M.

First published in: Marx and Engels, *Works*, First Russian Edition, Vol. XXV, Moscow, 1934

Printed according to the original

Published in English for the first time

---

[a] 'This fellow will go' (paraphrase of the eighteenth-century French revolutionary song *Ça ira!*). - [b] [G. Rouland,] Discours de M. le Procureur Général, *Journal des débats politiques et littéraires*, 5 November 1855. - [c] 'On the terrors of the *future revolution*'. - [d] 'Those whom...' (cf. Virgil, *Aeneid*, I, 135). - [e] Kinkel's wife - [f] and all the rest

289

MARX TO FERDINAND LASSALLE

IN DÜSSELDORF

Manchester, 8th November 1855
34 Butler Street, Green Keys

Dear Lassalle,

Herewith a very belated answer. In the first place, I did not get your letters[669] until later because I was in Manchester whereas the letters were in London and my wife did not know for certain whether I hadn't already left Manchester. For another thing, I was plagued by the most atrocious toothache, so much so that I experienced what Hegel demands of sensual consciousness at the stage at which it is said to override consciousness of self—viz. the inability to hear, see, and therefore also to write.

As regards your query about the book entitled: *Les mystères de la Bourse* by Coffinières, I believe that this miserable concoction is still among the books I left behind in the fatherland. During my first stay in Paris[670] the title misled me first into buying the thing and then into reading it. Mr Coffinières is a lawyer who, *au fond*,[a] knows nothing about the Bourse and merely warns against the 'legal' swindles perpetrated by the '*agents de change*'.[b] So there's nothing to be got out of the book—neither FACTS, nor theory, nor yet even entertaining anecdotes. Moreover, it is now completely out-of-date. 'Sweet Donna, let him go'—i.e. Coffinières. 'He is not worthy of thy wrath'.[c]

Weerth is now back in Manchester after a lengthy journey via the Continent (he returned from the West Indies at the end of July). In a week's time he will be off to the tropics again. It's very amusing to hear him talk. He has seen, experienced and observed much. Ranged over the better part of South, West and Central America. Crossed the Pampas on horseback. Climbed Chimborazo. Likewise stayed in California. If he no longer writes feuilletons,[671] he makes up for it by recounting them, and his audience has the benefit of vivacious gesture, mime and waggish laughter. He is, by the by, full of enthusiasm for life in the West Indies and hasn't a good

---

[a] at bottom - [b] stockbrokers - [c] Words of Leporello in Mozart's *Don Giovanni*, Act I (libretto by Lorenzo da Ponte).

word to say for the human riff-raff and the weather of this northern clime. And, INDEED, things are bad here, very bad.

You will have read in the papers about the Jersey affair[668] and the general to-do over the refugee question in England. I don't believe that this affair will take a serious turn. Nor, for that matter, do I believe that the government here had a serious end in view. Otherwise the row would have been saved up until just before the opening of Parliament. As it is, PUBLIC OPINION has been given time to swing back and, in many respects, has already done so.

Send your next letter to my *old address in London* as I'm not sure how long I shall stay up here with friend Engels. He and Lupus send you their warm regards.

Your

K. M.

First published in: *F. Lassalle, Nachgelassene Briefe und Schriften*, Bd. III, Stuttgart-Berlin, 1922

Printed according to the original

Published in English for the first time

290

MARX TO ENGELS

IN MANCHESTER

London, 7 December 1855
28 Dean Street, Soho

Dear Frederic,

Jones does not appear to be in London. At least, I haven't had an answer, either oral or written, to an urgent written enquiry.[672] Thus, since my arrival here, I have been incarcerated within 4 walls which, after all, I can't spend the whole day haranguing. But just now it would be too risky to venture out of doors.

The document[a] did not go off to the Union Bank until the day before yesterday. The delay was caused by all sorts of little things.

No reply yet from America, i.e. New York. The gentlemen would appear to be 'deliberating'.[b] No letter from Washington, but

---

[a] Presumably concerning Mrs Marx's inheritance (see this volume, p. 526). - [b] See next letter.

a *Wecker* and with it a note, patently by Cluss, attacking
Schimmelpfennig. Alas, I used up the *Wecker* during an
unconsidered moment in a place where 'hard words, soft paper,
etc.' It contained the assertion that the Germans in America were
UTILITARIANS and pursued 'bread-and-butter' because 'Mr Marx is
an economist and an abstruse one'. But in Mr Marx's case this
could be attributed to the 'Old Testament'. 'By a well-known trick'
he had 'turned "our relations" into a philosophical system'. That
thoughtful young Germans in America should follow his lead was
attributable to the fact that Germans are accustomed 'to echo
clever writers belonging to the nation of the Old Testament etc.'

Since ABOUT the time of my return here, the *Advertiser* has been
the arena for a cockfight between Herzen and an anonymous
antagonist. His antagonist reproaches him with being a humbug
and having passed himself off as a kind of Russian Silvio Pellico.[a]
Even the title of his book [673] is said to be a lie, inasmuch as he has
never been in Siberia, etc. Feeble reply from Herzen[b]: the title was
humbug on the PUBLISHER's part, he [Herzen] had not been
responsible for it and had *immediately* protested in the *Globe*,[c] etc.
against the attributes wrongly ascribed to him, etc. Whereupon his
antagonist came forth again (yesterday) and gave evidence of fresh
lies, also in respect of the *Globe*.[d] Besides this attack, however,
there was also a DEFENCE put up by an Englishman[e]. Even if Herzen
had not been in Siberia and was no Russian Silvio Pellico, his book
was nevertheless amusing, an innocuous book: *'an honest man,
look you, and soon dasht! He is a marvellous good neighbour in
sooth; and a very good bowler; but, for Alisander, alas, you see,
how 'tis.'*[f] Finally, the TUB-TUB PAPER, as is its wont, declared that the
contest was becoming too personal, etc., was now over and closed
its columns to it.[g] At all events this skirmish—even though the
assailants were hardly brilliant—will do Herzen a great deal of
harm in the eyes of the COCKNEYS.

Lina[h] has informed me of some fresh details concerning the
Cologne trial. The list of jurymen given in my pamphlet[i] quite

---

[a] 'To the Editor of *The Morning Advertiser*' signed 'One who had been deceived',
The Morning Advertiser, 29 November 1855. - [b] A. Herzen, 'My Exile in Siberia. To
the Editor of *The Morning Advertiser*', *The Morning Advertiser*, 1 December
1855. - [c] A. Herzen, 'To the Editor of the *Globe*', *The Globe and Traveller*, 25
October 1855. - [d] 'Mr Herzen's Case' (letter signed 'deceived'), *The Morning
Advertiser*, 6 December 1855. - [e] [E. Reeve,] 'To the Editor of *The Morning
Advertiser*' signed 'Content and not deceived', ibid. - [f] Shakespeare, *Love's Labour's
Lost*, V, 2. - [g] An Editors' Statement was published in *The Morning Advertiser* on 6
December 1855. - [h] Caroline Schöler - [i] K. Marx, *Revelations Concerning the Com-
munist Trial in Cologne*.

wrong, of course. Throughout the trial one of the jurymen—Joest—drew caricatures of the accused, and passed the drawings round in court. During the first week the worthy *jeune*[a] Saedt always had *a dagger* lying in front of him. At length the ironical laughter of the accused compelled him to 'wear the dagger under his gown'.[b] Can one imagine a more affected COXCOMB? Saedt with a dagger! *C'est à crever de rire.*[c]

Bürgers whiles away his time sending Mrs Daniels 'endless amounts of paper'. Also writes poetry. Exchanges not a word with his fellow-sufferer.

A London daily PENNY PAPER, *The Telegraph,* is said to have already dropped a number of HINTS about the underhand dealings of Dr Freund and his fellow-swindler, a military man.

The 2 articles received.[674]

Salut.

Your
K. M.

I almost forgot the most important point. A few weeks ago, 3 I THINK, Zitschke came to see my wife. The conversation turned to Mirbach.[d] QUOTH Zitschke: 'That old loafer had a splendid chance of a passage. I had thought him long since at sea. Then I found him sitting again at a table in Bibra's pothouse and looking very down-at-heel.' Liebknecht, too, claims to have seen him recently.

First published considerably abridged in *Der Briefwechsel zwischen F. Engels und K. Marx,* Bd. 2, Stuttgart, 1913 and in full in: Marx and Engels, *Works,* First Russian Edition, Vol. XXII, Moscow, 1929

Printed according to the original

Published in English for the first time

291

MARX TO ENGELS

IN MANCHESTER

[London,] 11 December 1855
28 Dean Street, Soho

DEAR Frederic,

From Dana's letter, enclosed herewith, you will see that our manoeuvre has succeeded.[675]

---

[a] young - [b] from F. Schiller, *Die Bürgschaft* - [c] It's enough to make you split your sides with laughter. - [d] See this volume, p. 560.

Otherwise, everything as before. I still incarcerated. Jones not yet turned up.

Bürgers will be allowed to move to another fortress if he pays the travelling expenses himself. Weerth had half promised Bürgers' mother in Cologne to send her money for him. Hasn't kept his word.

Little Dronke corresponds regularly with Freiligrath. Had a great set-to with one of the partners, was on the point of giving up his post. To make himself look important, offered it to Freiligrath.

Your

K. M.

First published in: Marx and Engels, *Works,* First Russian Edition, Vol. XXII, Moscow, 1929

Printed according to the original

Published in English for the first time

292

ENGELS TO MARX

IN LONDON

Manchester, 12 December 1855

Dear Marx,

Something can be arranged with the good *Tribune* people after all, you see, and the £200 are assured. So that a start can be made straight away, I shall do a military article this evening, then you must do a political one. Both of them can then go on Friday,[a] *hoc facit*[b] £4.

I return Dana's letter herewith.[675] *Au fond,*[c] it is all to the good that the noble Mirbach has settled down to a life of idleness in London, for after all nothing has been definitely settled with the New Yorkers about the Crimean articles.[676] At all events, I am now relieved of any indirect obligation to the chap, and *il ne me regarde plus.*[d] I have said nothing at all here about the matter, otherwise it would give Lupus qualms of conscience in the end, and next time he would turn rebellious.

---

[a] 14 December - [b] that makes - [c] At bottom - [d] he's no longer any concern of mine

Jmeyer[a] wrote to me recently, not so much to inform me that he was still awaiting a letter from you, as to let me know what to say at my brother-in-law's[b] at Christmas. He has heard nothing at all from the little man.[c]

We shall bear in mind Mr Karl Joest and his caricatures.[d] I believe I shall do an even better caricature of him when he is dangling from a lamp post.

Whether I shall be able to do an article on Tuesday[e] depends, of course, on events, which are now very few and far between. Kars and Omer Pasha will have to be my victims today; if anything happens tomorrow I shall add it on.[677]

The STRIKE is going ahead here. The MASTERS said that they were willing to pay,[f] provided the Ashton rates were taken as a basis. The HANDS replied that if the MASTERS chose Ashton, they would choose Oldham and be prepared to accept as a basis the average for the two places. Thereupon the MASTERS gave an evasive answer and proposed yet a third place in the district as a norm. This was refused and there the matter rests. The HANDS seem to me to be completely in the right; but they obviously still have in mind a few old trade union traditions whereby only this or that machine may be operated and only in the specific, time-honoured manner. But they'll soon drop this rubbish. The neighbourhood is beginning to support them.

The editor[g] of the *Guardian*, whom I've come to know, is a wise man IN HIS OWN MIND and a kind of oracle in the eyes of a number of philistines; apart from that a teller of dirty stories and a moderate carouser. He has obviously heard about me for, whenever I mention some shabby trick, he listens with attention and asks questions which show a desire to know. I shall gradually encourage the man's advances and then draw him out about the people on the *Examiner and Times*, after which I shall approach the latter rag. *Après, on avisera.*[h]

Warmest regards to your wife and children.

Your
F. E.

First published abridged in *Der Briefwechsel zwischen F. Engels und K. Marx*, Bd. 2, Stuttgart, 1913 and in full in: Marx and Engels, *Works*, First Russian Edition, Vol. XXII, Moscow, 1929

Printed according to the original

Published in English for the first time

---

[a] Joseph Meyer - [b] Emil Blank - [c] Ernst Dronke - [d] See this volume, p. 559. - [e] 18 December - [f] In the original Engels wrote *arbeiten* (to work) above *zahlen* (to pay). - [g] Jeremiah Garnett - [h] Afterwards we shall see.

293

MARX TO ENGELS[84]

IN MANCHESTER

[London,] 14 December 1855
28 Dean Street, Soho

Dear Frederic,

This confinement to my room is beginning to weigh on me. Not one breath of fresh air yet. Meanwhile, another 1,000 Germans sent off yesterday. Jones supposed to be coming today, at last.

The day before yesterday evening I had a visit, you'll never guess from whom. Edgar Bauer—whom I hadn't seen for about a year—came to see me, and with him—Bruno. He's already been here a fortnight and intends to remain ABOUT 6 MONTHS 'in order to prove his assumptions' which he can hardly fail to do, considering the way he's begun. The man has aged visibly, his forehead has broadened and the impression he now gives is more or less that of a pedantic old professor. For the present he is lodging with Edgar in a hovel SOMEWHERE ABOUT the far end of Highgate and there he squats, amidst the most profound petty-bourgeois *misère*, seeing and hearing nothing. This he takes to be London and believes that, apart from the privileged 30,000, all the English live like Edgar Bauer. Hence his hatred and 'contempt' for the country is enormous. In his view, it's like living in 'Treuenbrietzen'.[a] To anyone coming from 'Berlin', London is a veritable 'prison'. On the same occasion it also transpired that his present ideal is the 'East Frisian', 'Altenburgian' and PARTLY 'Westphalian peasant,[b] those true noblemen. He is, moreover, convinced that these clodhoppers cannot be wished away and will be the ROCKS upon which the modern, egalitarian fiddle-faddle, bemoaned by this man of the 'dissolution', will come to grief. It was most CURIOUS to hear the 'Criticism'[678] make the CONFESSION that, in the final analysis,

---

[a] Small town in Brandenburg symbolising provincialism. - [b] Pun on Bauer—a peasant and Bauer the name of Edgar.

Berthold Auerbach is its true cornerstone. He holds that, save for a few 'purely commercial towns', the towns of Germany are in decline, but that 'the country' is prospering fabulously. He knew not a thing about the rise of industry, but quietly bemoaned the fact that nothing is now being done in Germany save 'IMPROVEMENTS'.

The 'English language' is 'wretched', completely romanicised. For his consolation I proceeded to tell him that the Dutch and the Danes say the same of the German language and claim that the only fellows to have remained truly untainted by Romance are the 'Icelanders'.

The old boy has devoted much time to languages. He *speaks* Polish and declares in consequence the *Polish language* to be 'the most beautiful of all'. His linguistic studies seem to have been highly uncritical. He considers Dobrovský, for instance, to be a far 'more important man' than Grimm,[a] and calls him the father of comparative linguistics. Moreover, he has let the Poles in Berlin persuade him that OLD Lelewel has refuted Grimm's *Geschichte der deutschen Sprache* in a recent paper.

Apropos. He also told me that a fat volume (of German provenance) had appeared in Germany attacking Grimm's dictionary.[b] The whole volume consists of howlers G[rimm] is shown to have perpetrated.

Despite all his efforts to adopt a humorous attitude, his gloom and despondency over the 'present' kept obtruding. In Germany—HORRIBLE INDEED!—nothing is now read or bought save miserable compilations in the field of the natural sciences. When you come,[679] we shall have great fun with the old boy.

Köppen has been working for years on a book on Buddhism.[680] Rutenberg is the publisher of the *Staats-Anzeiger*. Mr Bergenroth, who used to drift about America (North and South) as commissioner (trade), has returned *sans argent*[c] but with an illness.

I am still waiting for the 2nd edition of *The Times* or *Morning Post*. The news may make it necessary to couch the thing on Kars in somewhat more hypothetical terms. However, this would only require quite minor alterations (a few words in the conditional).[681] I, for my part, believe that Kars has fallen.

Today there is a not uninteresting article in the *Herald*—or so my wife tells me—about Bonaparte's MISGIVINGS AS TO THE TRUE INTENTIONS OF VISCOUNT Palmerston. That Pam is in very bad odour at

---

[a] Jacob Grimm - [b] Publication of the *Deutsches Wörterbuch* was started by Jacob and Wilhelm Grimm in 1852, and completed in 1961 in the GDR. - [c] without money

court you may see from the *Times* article against Prince Albert.[a] At the same time, again the old manoeuvre of presenting Prince Albert as an encumbrance to the 'Ministry'.

Salut.

Your
K. M.

First published abridged in *Der Briefwechsel zwischen F. Engels und K. Marx,* Bd. 2, Stuttgart, 1913 and in full in: Marx and Engels, *Works,* First Russian Edition, Vol. XXII, Moscow, 1929

Printed according to the original

Published in English in full for the first time

---

[a] *The Times,* No. 22237, 14 December 1855, leader.

APPENDICES

1

JENNY MARX TO FREDERICK ENGELS

IN MANCHESTER

[London, 7 January 1852] [a]

Dear Mr Engels,

How can you imagine that I would have been angry with *you* over that little drinking spree? I was very sorry not to have seen you again before you left, for that would have enabled you to see for yourself that I was only somewhat sulky in respect of my liege lord. Besides, such interludes often have quite salutory effects, but this time *père* Marx must have caught a bad chill during his nocturnal philosophic excursion with 'the archbishop's nephew', [b] for he fell seriously ill and has up till now stayed quietly in bed. He may perhaps be able to get up a little today and apply himself to the articles for America. [c] However, I don't think he is as much restored as he imagines. For three nights he rambled in his speech and was very poorly. He asks you to convey his regards to Weerth and to tell him that he was very annoyed with him for having written no more than 2 words when forwarding Reinhardt's letter from Paris, and that he must above all fulfil his duty as a former editor of the *Neue Rheinische* and send out to America some articles from stock. [682] As for that insufferable man, [d] here, word for word, is what *père* Marx says now:

'Ever drunk as a lord; boasting about his insinuating ways with women, meaning his being kicked out of bars; from the outset raucously inciting the English public in streets and alleyways, PARLOURS, omnibuses and HA'PENNY STEAMBOATS, to take part in the great debates between Kinkel and Ruge; dragging every German by the ear to the Cranbourne Hotel; one of the most pompous ranters of

---

a This date is established on the basis of Engels' letter to Marx of 6 January 1852 (see this volume, pp. 4-5). When Engels was putting his archives in order he dated it 'Beginning of January 1852'. - b A humorous reference to Engels. - c K. Marx, *The Eighteenth Brumaire of Louis Bonaparte*. - d Lüders

the Emigrés' Club,[26] and hence also crudely venting his spleen on the out-of-the-way little church of the *N. Rh. Z.* Should he ask Weerth's protection, the latter must tell him to look for a post in one of the seven ministries to be set up by Kinkel, which should not present any difficulty in view of his great services to the great and only revolutionary party and of his influence on Kinkel's pair of court scribes, Meyen and Oppenheim. Generally speaking, should Weerth be approached by any of the blackguards, he must give them to understand that he, too, belongs to the "small, incorrigible, separatist church" of the *N. Rh. Z.*, as Meyen put it when writing to America.'

So much for my exalted patient, 'old Crosspatch'.

Yesterday a very nice letter arrived from Cluss in Washington, from which Kinkel's boundless turpitude again emerges. Unfortunately I cannot enclose it as Freiligrath took it away with him yesterday. We shall send it tomorrow. Pass on bits of it to Weerth.

Freiligrath has a new story about Kinkel's toadyism towards the democratic grocers here, which I shall now treat you to. Freiligrath applies to a *blind* German democratic merchant here for a position. He acquaints him with his commercial testimonials, whereupon the cross-eyed cheesemonger tells him: 'I have had the privilege of making Professor Kinkel's acquaintance. I attended one of his lectures, after which the Professor called on me and at once offered to come to my house of an evening and read aloud free of charge the best German poetic works. I, of course, declined this exceptional offer, not being in a position adequately to reward a man like Professor Kinkel for such services. In addition, the gentleman would have had the expense of the omnibus fares, since he lives some distance away. Nevertheless, the Professor came and read aloud to me from German poets.— Amongst which a few little things by yourself, Mr Freiligrath— whereupon he told me that you were really a man of commerce and had already held a position, etc., etc. The Professor's wife[a] also called on me and offered to sing and play to me.'—Doubtless the Professor's wife would also have obliged with dances and *poses plastiques*[b] had she not been dealing with a blind connoisseur.

The future president of the German Republic, who goes chasing after the grocers here in order to read them his divine poetry and sometimes snatch a bite of supper, all but outshines the French Krapülinski.[c]

---

[a] Johanna Kinkel - [b] living sculpture - [c] Louis Bonaparte (called after a character in Heine's 'Zwei Ritter')

It will also interest you to hear that your former chief, General Willich, has received a sound thrashing at the hands of the inferior refugees, since the latter are unable to grasp the difference between themselves and the superior refugees, and disapprove of the way the large revolutionary funds are being administered in the interests of the great men. It would further appear from Cluss' letter that Kinkel has used Willich's MYSTIFICA-TIONS and Schramm's letter[10] to provide proof in America of their connections with Cologne. It will soon be time to come out with the true story. Kinkel has apparently been putting about in America too that Marx's party presents prizes for vice in order not to become moral heroes. Musch sends Frederick his love. The girls have already gone to school. You will, perhaps, remember that Pieper made the boy a present of his fine travelling bag. Yesterday he threatened to take it back and buy him something else instead. This morning the boy hid the bag, and just now he said: 'Moor,[a] I've hiddened it well and if Pieper asks for it, I'll tell him I've given it to a poor man.' The slyboots!

Adieu.

Warmest greetings

Jenny Marx

First published in *Der Briefwechsel zwischen F. Engels und K. Marx*, Bd. I, Stuttgart, 1913

Printed according to the original

Published in English for the first time

2

JENNY MARX TO JOSEPH WEYDEMEYER[12]

IN NEW YORK

[London, 9 January 1852]

Dear Mr Weydemeyer,

For the past week my husband has been very poorly and is for the most part confined to bed. Nevertheless he has managed to finish the enclosed sequel to his article,[b] so that there may be no

---

[a] Marx's nickname - [b] K. Marx, *The Eighteenth Brumaire of Louis Bonaparte*, II.

interruption in the printing thereof, supposing a start has really been made on it.

A few days ago we had a letter from Cluss in Washington—with whom I hope you have already made contact for you will find him in all respects an excellent support—from which Kinkel's boundless turpitude again emerges. For while this hypocrite fawns on Karl's friends in the most barefaced manner and writes to them, saying 'he has emphasised the need to get in touch with Marx and the most capable members of his party' (a downright lie), *he seeks in the most perfidious way to blacken my husband's personal character* and relates the most edifying tales about him and his friends drawn from Willich's mendacious innuendoes.

Karl, who doesn't feel strong enough today to write to you himself, asks me to tell you that you should provide some information in your paper[a] about our poor friends in Cologne,[b] the more so since Kinkel's party, along with its court scribes and its rowdies and its compliant *Lithographische Korrespondenz,* deliberately passes over their existence and all their sufferings in complete silence, which is all the more infamous as it is precisely to Becker,[c] Bürgers and their erstwhile organ[d] that Kinkel owes most of his popularity. But our people languish in prisons, are hideously treated, and now will have to spend another three months in jug while the great men of the future are pocketing thousands in the name of the revolution and are already handing out future ministerial posts.

How was your dear wife[e] after the terrible voyage? What are your children doing? Have they all become more or less acclimatised?[683]

But time is getting exceedingly short. I must hurry out and post this letter. Let us hope that the conclusion of his article will be easier for my dear Karl.

Farewell for the present,

Yours

Jenny Marx

Lupus is now somewhat recovered. He, too, will send something soon, as will Engels. Insistent reminders have also gone off to

---

[a] *Die Revolution* - [b] Communist League members arrested and detained under investigation in Cologne - [c] Hermann Becker - [d] *Westdeutsche Zeitung.* See also this volume, pp. 21-22 and 34. - [e] Louise

Weerth. Red Wolff[a] has got married and, being on his honey-moon, cannot let you have anything as yet.

First published in: Marx and Engels, *Works*, First Russian Edition, Vol. XXV, Moscow, 1934

Printed according to the original

Published in English in full for the first time

3

JENNY MARX TO FREDERICK ENGELS

IN MANCHESTER

[London, 16 January 1852]

Dear Mr Engels,

As you see, I am still *en fonction*[b] as secretary. My husband has still not altogether left his bed. He was indeed very poorly. Tomorrow he will attempt to take a short walk. His illness prevented him from getting anything done for America, although he did manage to strike some sparks out of Freiligrath and Pieper. I enclose herewith a most felicitous poem of Freiligrath's.[c] Let our friend Weerth have a look at it as well. Perhaps he too will feel inspired to climb onto Pegasus. Send us the *Tribune* if you have finished with it. Next week you will receive a very nice letter from Cluss. Lupus hasn't got it just now. We hope to hear from you soon and may you enjoy your PALE ALE in the meantime.

Warm regards from the patient.

Jenny Marx

First published in: Marx and Engels, *Works*, Second Russian Edition, Vol. 28, Moscow, 1962

Printed according to the original

Published in English for the first time

---

[a] Ferdinand Wolff - [b] acting - [c] F. Freiligrath, 'An Joseph Weydemeyer', II.

4

JENNY MARX TO JOSEPH WEYDEMEYER [684]

IN NEW YORK

[London, 27 February 1852]

Dear Mr Weydemeyer,

After a week of strenuous nocturnal labours, his days being taken up with domestic affairs, my husband's eyes are so wretchedly sore that he cannot possibly write to you today and I must assume all secretarial functions. He asks me to tell you that he has been unable to read through the whole of Eccarius' article,[a] and that you yourself must correct the orphographic mistakes; for this admirable man, who writes excellently, has only just learnt his letters here and knows nothing of full-stops and commas. He is also sending you an article by a Hungarian[b] who is familiar with the innermost secrets of the Hungarian émigrés. You yourself must decide whether you can use and publish it at this moment. At all events, it is essential to keep in with the man, since he has promised to provide us later on with original contributions by Perczel, Szemere, etc., whose intimate he is. My husband thinks you should, of course, correct the worst grammatical howlers that crop up in the article, but that a few peculiarities of style which might give it the stamp of a genuine Hungarian product could do no harm at all. He further requests you to return as' soon as possible the five instalments of his paper on Napoleon[c] if you should not succeed in publishing it. We might, perhaps, be able to bring it out in a French translation, although it would really be a pity about the German version. He would greatly prefer it if you could succeed in America, since the piece is bound to sell and could also be distributed in Germany, providing as it does an historical appreciation of the most important event of the present day. I hope that there will soon be some good news from you, dear Mr Weydemeyer, to wit that your dear wife has come smoothly through the great catastrophe, and that two births have taken place under your roof—a son and a journal. My very warmest greetings to your dear wife.

Yours

Jenny Marx

---

[a] See this volume, p. 26. - [b] Bangya. See also p. 32. - [c] K. Marx, *The Eighteenth Brumaire of Louis Bonaparte*, I-V.

Jenny Marx with her daughter Jenny

Laura Marx

So that it will not take so long, you might have each of the individual articles printed separately, because the thing is of immediate interest. Later, they could be combined into one. No. 5 goes off today. Next Friday he will be sending No. 6, the final instalment.[85] As already mentioned, then, *try to publish the work as a pamphlet.* Otherwise, send the thing back, because come what may, we must get it published.

Many regards to Cluss also, and write soon telling us just how things are with you.

Lupus has just brought a brief scrawl on the latest events of the day in London.

First published in: Marx and Engels, *Works*, First Russian Edition, Vol. XXV, Moscow, 1934

Printed according to the original

5

JENNY MARX TO ADOLF CLUSS

IN WASHINGTON

London, 15 October 1852

Dear Mr Cluss,

Today my husband has appointed me his deputy and I therefore hasten to assume the duties of a *secrétaire intime.* For my husband is under such PRESSURE FROM WITHOUT AND WITHIN that he has had to traipse round all day on HOME BUSINESS and now, just gone 5, has not yet returned to dispose, more especially, of the affair Brüningk v. Cluss.[a] Do *nothing, absolutely nothing about this matter* until the next STEAMER. Imandt had meant to send a statement today proving that Willich and Kinkel had made insulting remarks about Mrs Brüningk. At the same time he will lay the blame for all the tittle-tattle at the door of that old buffoon, Ruge, presently knight-crrant and champion of princely innocence, and will do so all the more easily as the rumour indeed arose and began to spread at the very moment when the old jackass declared Kinkel to be—witness his close friend Gross—an agent of the Prince of Prussia,[b] at the same time revealing that Kinkel's release had been

---

a See this volume, p. 213. - b ibid., p. 92.

the prince's doing, but that Mrs Brüningk had also played a leading role in the affair and had put up the money for it. In Germany, these rumours were both current at once and (if Dronke's memory is to be trusted, though he cannot say for certain) it is said that in the self-same article Ruge spoke of the suspect circles frequented here by Gottfried. Well, this stupid affair is nothing but a conspiracy to avenge themselves on Marx-Cluss by imputing to them vile, anonymous gossip and slander—an art in which these curs have long since been practising with the greatest virtuosity. No sooner had the old Pomeranian[a] broken a lance for the princess than he paid a personal call on the great lady. No doubt Heinzen, too, still hopes to supplement his Whiggish source[b] by striking and exploiting a princely seam over here for his *Janus*. But how ridiculous, the way in which the rabble suddenly raises a hue and cry in two continents when, for so long, it has heaped scurrility upon scurrility, tittle-tattle upon tittle-tattle, calumny upon calumny. And withal there is really nothing to the article[250] which, at least, reveals in moderate, discreet, indeed veiled terms, what has been said bluntly and openly by her own guests. The revolting thing about it is that one would sooner keep this scum at a healthy distance than be forced to grapple with them, and over so paltry a matter to boot. My husband himself had intended to send you today an article written in his own name about how your article came to be published in the *Wecker*. But Imandt thought it absolutely essential that my husband, against whom the whole thing has been cooked up, should be left out of it, which is why he wanted to write the statement himself. Unfortunately it has not yet arrived! But you should do nothing about the matter until you receive further instructions. Meyen was saying today that Dronke, Willich and Kinkel had stated on their word of honour that they had never said anything defamatory about the woman. So the fellows had already been subjected to a cross-examination. As you see, here too, the thing is being conducted as a matter of the utmost importance. By the by, from his own viewpoint Schnauffer's reply[c] is excellent, witty and apt and, in truth, the two philosophers ought not to make so much fuss merely because a high-born lady is ill-used. Did anyone ask any questions when Ruge spread the most scurrilous, defamatory and socially ruinous rumours and things about my husband, and this at a time when

---

[a] Arnold Ruge - [b] See this volume, pp. 145-46. - [c] Editorial Statement about A. Brüningk's letter in the *Baltimore Wecker*, 27 September 1852. See also this volume, p. 204.

my husband's lips were sealed by party considerations and out of regard for his friends in Germany.

Did anyone bother whether all this grieved me almost to death, when my child[a] died, having imbibed at my breast torment, grief and care?—oh! and all the other sufferings—yet I was not called princess when I was born—but wherefore all this foolish commotion? We shall extricate ourselves somehow and prove the others responsible. But you must wait, at any rate, just one more posting-day.

The *Brumaires* have not yet arrived. My husband will send you by the next post the 2 *People's Papers* containing your articles.[b]

My brother Edgar has at last written to his mother.[c] Thanks to your kind efforts my letter reached him safely.[d] Once again, may I say how grateful I am.

One more thing. Keep Jacobus Huzel on a fairly short rein so that he doesn't kick over the traces.[e] There should be no chit-chat with the vermin since their line now is to implicate us and thus erase the memory of their past infamies. Some diplomacy is required in dealing with this bunch of purely objective, principled, honourable, worthy washerwomen.

You have, I suppose, been following the Cologne trial in the *Kölnische.* Today we received an account of Becker's[f] interrogation. Since there was nothing against him, it had been agreed to leave Becker out of the thing altogether,[g] and this will explain to you the manner of his defence, which will be eagerly seized upon by the democrats in order to claim Becker as one of their own and declare him the true hero—free, independent man of the people that he is and no blind follower of a secret society's cut-and-dried doctrine—, precisely because he is the weakest of all and has the greatest amount of democratic blood in his veins. Should that loud-mouthed Heinzen make use of this case to build up Becker, you can at once point out that the defence had been agreed upon beforehand and that, shortly before his arrest, Becker had insistently begged my husband to attack with him in his review[685] all the official democrats—Ruge, Heinzen, Kinkel, Willich, etc., etc.—and hold them up to ridicule. That he also wanted to have

---

a Heinrich Guido - b [A. Cluss, Articles on Presidential Elections in the USA published in the section.] 'Our American Correspondence', *The People's Paper,* Nos. 23 and 24, 9 and 16 October 1852. - c Caroline von Westphalen - d See this volume, p. 71. - e A reference to J. Huzel's article 'Über die Flüchtlinge in London', *Anzeiger des Westens,* September 1852. - f Hermann Becker - g See this volume, pp. 212 and 242.

Willich's imbecile letters published.ᵃ Further that, on his release, the democratic gentlemen could expect to fare no better, etc., etc. I am writing in something of a rush.

I must catch the post.

Farewell and warm regards,

Jenny Marx

Write again soon. Your letters invariably give us the greatest pleasure. My husband is always saying that if we had a few more chaps like Cluss, we might yet get something done. In the meantime, don't do too much. Best let dog eat dog, otherwise they might band together to combat the 'common enemy', the wicked, infamous blight—Marx and his clique.

First published abridged in: Marx and Engels, *Works*, First Russian Edition, Vol. XXV, Moscow, 1934 and in full in: Marx and Engels, *Works*, Second Russian Edition, Vol. 28, Moscow, 1962

Printed according to the original

Published in English for the first time

6

JENNY MARX TO ADOLF CLUSS [12]

IN WASHINGTON

[London, 30 October 1852]

Dear Mr Cluss,

You will have been following the monster trial of the communists in the *Kölnische Zeitung*. During the sitting of 23 October the whole thing took such a splendid and interesting turn, and one so favourable to the accused, that we are beginning to regain some of our confidence.[686] As you can imagine, the 'Marx party' is busy day and night and is having to throw itself into the work body and soul. This overloading with work also accounts for my again appearing before you as deputy reporter. Mr Willich's close friend, Mr Dietz, now also in America, has *contrived to have* all the documents, letters, minutes, etc., etc. of Willich's clique *stolen* from him. They were produced by the prosecution as evidence of the party's dangerous activities. In order to establish a

---

ᵃ See this volume, pp. 223-24.

link between these and the accused, they now proceeded to think up a spurious connection between my husband and the notorious spy Cherval. Thus my husband became the bridge, the spurious link, between the theoreticians of Cologne and the men of action, incendiaries and robbers, in London. Stieber and the prosecution expected wonders of this coup. It burst like a bubble. New effects had to be conjured up, hence the tissue of lies at the sitting of 23 October. Everything adduced by the police is untrue. They steal, forge, break into desks, perjure themselves, bear false witness and, withal, claim this licence *vis-à-vis* communists, who are *hors [de] la société*[a]! This and the way in which the police, at their most rascally, are usurping all the functions of the prosecution, pushing Saedt into the background, and submitting unattested scraps of paper, mere rumours, reports and hearsay, as real legally proven facts, as evidence, is truly hair-raising. We here had to supply all proofs of the forgery. Hence my husband had to work all day and late into the night. Affidavits had to be obtained from the publicans, and the handwriting of the alleged minute-takers, Liebknecht and Rings, officially authenticated to provide proof of forgery on the part of the police. Then every one of these things had to be copied out 6-8 times and dispatched by the most divers routes to Cologne, via Frankfurt, Paris, etc., since all letters to my husband as well as all letters from here to Cologne[b] are opened and detained. The whole thing has now become a struggle between the police on one side and my husband on the other—they blame him for everything, the entire revolution and even the conduct of the trial. Finally Stieber has now declared my husband to be an Austrian spy. In return, my husband looked out a glorious letter, written to him by Stieber in the *Neue Rheinische Zeitung* days, which is really damning.[c] We likewise discovered a letter from Becker in which he makes fun of Willich's imbecilities and his 'military conspiracies'.[d] Out of hatred for Becker, Willich gave directions here in London to the witness Lieutenant Hentze, from whom up till now he has been receiving alms. In short, things are about to happen which would seem unbelievable if one wasn't experiencing them oneself. All this business with the police is distracting the public, and hence the jury, from the actual prosecution of the communists, while bourgeois hatred of the dreadful incendiaries is paralysed by the HORROR inspired by the villainy of the police,—so much so that we can now even believe in

---

[a] outside society - [b] London in the original [c] See this volume, pp. 225-26. - [d] ibid., pp. 223-24.

our friends' acquittal. The struggle against official power, armed as this is with money and every kind of weapon, is not, of course, without interest and will be all the more glorious should we emerge the victors. For on their side there is money, power and everything else, whereas we were often at a loss where to get the paper on which to write our letters, etc., etc.

The enclosed statement was issued today by Freiligrath, Marx, Engels and Wolff.[a] We are sending it to the *Tribune* today. You could publish it as well.[b]

Excuse me for such a confused letter but I, too, have had some part in the intrigue and have done so much copying that my fingers are afire. Hence the muddle. Your essay in the *Turn-Zeitung*[c] has been much applauded here. My husband thought it first-rate and the style, in particular, exceptionally brilliant. There are others who prefer you in a less theoretical vein and would like you always to remain the same old humorous, light-hearted Cluss.

We have just received from Weerth and Engels whole parcels full of commercial addresses and pseudo-commercial letters so that we can send off the documents, letters, etc.[d][687]

Another load of tremendous scandal has just arrived with the *Kölnische.* Two further packages are being dispatched at once to commercial addresses. A complete office has now been set up in our house. Two or three people are writing, others running errands, others scraping PENNIES together so that the writers may continue to exist and prove the old world of officialdom guilty of the most outrageous scandal. And in between whiles my 3 merry children[e] sing and whistle, often to be harshly told off by their papa. What a bustle! Farewell, dear Mr Cluss, and write again soon to your friends.

     By permission of the higher authorities,

Jenny Marx

First published considerably abridged in *Die Neue Zeit,* Bd. 2, No. 31, Stuttgart, 1906-07 and in full in: Marx and Engels, *Works,* Second Russian Edition, Vol. 28, Moscow, 1962

Printed according to the original

Published in English in full for the first time

---

[a] K. Marx and F. Engels, 'Public Statement to the Editors of the English Press'. - [b] The *New-York Daily Tribune* did not publish this statement. Its German translation was printed in the *New-Yorker Criminal-Zeitung,* No. 37, 26 November 1852 and the *Republik der Arbeiter,* No. 49, 4 December 1852. - [c] A. Cluss, 'Die materielle Kritik und der moralisierende Standpunkt', *Turn-Zeitung,* No. 13, 1 October 1852. - [d] In the original there follows a copy made by Wilhelm Wolff of the statement mentioned above. - [e] Jenny, Laura and Edgar

7

JENNY MARX TO ADOLF CLUSS [688]

IN WASHINGTON

London, 10 March [1853]

For weeks my dear Karl has been indisposed and, during the past few days, has again been suffering from his old liver complaint which almost developed into hepatitis, a disease I find all the more frightening for its being hereditary in his family and the cause of his father's death.[a] Today he is better again, is getting his *Tribune* article into shape,[b] and has asked me to write to you. I must at once plunge into a circumstantial tale of woe which almost equals the bad luck of Weydemeyer and Cluss.[689] Please don't be angry with me if I dilate. On 6 December, at the same time as your manuscript copy of the *Revelations*,[c] my husband sent another one to Schabelitz's son in Basle. Schabelitz was delighted to receive it, wrote saying it was a masterpiece, that it ought to be across the border within a fortnight and that he would run off 2,000 copies, sell them at 15 silver groschen a piece and, after deducting the printing costs (low in Switzerland), share the profits with my husband. We would be justified in counting on at least £30 sterling—with no risk of disappointment. Moreover he intended to send 40 copies to London immediately. For 4 weeks we hear nothing. My husband writes. Answer: the printing was held up by the compositors' Christmas junketing; he intends to be across the border in a fortnight at the latest and to send us 40 copies. All we hear, and this through a third party, is that the smuggling operation has run into unexpected difficulties and that he has had to smuggle across the 1,800 copies in small parcels over a period of 14 days, but that everything will be across by about the beginning of February, when he will charge one of his own clerks with forwarding the pamphlet and distributing it to the booksellers and will send him there, but that he, however, will send us a specimen copy at once. Good. We wait expectantly for 4 weeks. Then my husband writes to inquire, believing that the pamphlets have long since reached the furthest corners of Germany and that all he need now do is draw a bill on him. Then, yesterday, the following letter arrived.[d]

---

a Heinrich Marx - b Probably Marx's and Engels' 'British Politics.—Disraeli.—The Refugees.—Mazzini in London.—Turkey'. - c K. Marx, *Revelations Concerning the Communist Trial in Cologne.* - d See also this volume, p. 287.

'Dear Marx, I have just heard that the whole consignment of *Revelations,* amounting to 2,000 copies, which *had been lying in a village on the other side of the border for the past 6 weeks,* was intercepted yesterday while being conveyed elsewhere. What will happen now, I do not know; first of all, a complaint lodged by the Baden government with the Federal Council, then, no doubt, my arrest or at least commitment for trial,etc. In either case, a terrific shindy! This briefly for your information; further communications, should I be prevented from making them *myself,* will reach you through a 3rd party. When writing to me, use the address: A modiste in Basle, *etc.*'

That's all; what do you think of it? He leaves 2,000 copies, i.e. the entire edition, lying in a village for 6 weeks, and then writes to tell us that they have been confiscated. Not a word about the copies for London, nothing about those for Switzerland, etc. Have the things been printed, did the Prussian police buy them for a hefty sum, or God knows what? Suffice it to say that this is the 2nd pamphlet to have been entirely suppressed.[690] Mr Stieber, who has become Chief of Police in Berlin and announced a *magnum opus* on conspiracies,[a] etc., and Mr Willich, owner and administrator of the American funds,[691] come out of the affair *sain et sauf*[b]; the Cologne trial has been utterly obliterated, the party is still not quite cleansed of all taint, and the government is triumphant! At this moment the pamphlet would have had the most tremendous effect. The hearts of the German police would have quaked and trembled at this THUNDERBOLT falling among them. If we had the means, we would have it printed again *au moment*[c] in Altona in order to enrage the government, but that is impossible. All that can be done now is for you to bring it out as a feuilleton in some paper or other. Could not the type then be used to produce a pamphlet which you could at once send over here? Since printing in Europe has become almost impossible but is now entirely a matter of honour for the party, you should at least have it printed *à tout prix*[d] as a feuilleton. The publication of the pamphlet is now a necessity as against *all* our enemies, and will, more than anything else, further the interests of the Cologne people and sway public opinion in their favour. Interest in them must be reawakened. Becker's[e] attempted escape failed only because of lack of interest and outside help. Above all, proof of the pamphlet's existence must be given and this can only be done by its being printed, even if only as a feuilleton on the other side of the ocean.

---

[a] Wermuth/Stieber, *Die Communisten-Verschwörungen des neunzehnten Jahrhunderts.* -
[b] safe and sound - [c] at once - [d] at all costs - [e] Hermann Becker

You can imagine what effect this news had on my husband's state of health, etc.

Jenny Marx

First published in *Voprosy istorii KPSS*, No. 3, Moscow, 1962

Printed according to a letter from Cluss to Weydemeyer of 28 March 1853

Published in English for the first time

8

JENNY MARX TO FREDERICK ENGELS

IN MANCHESTER

[London, 27 April 1853]

Dear Mr Engels,

It is for me a hateful task to have to write to you about money matters. You have already helped us all too often. But this time I have no other recourse, no other way out. I have written to Hagen in Bonn, to Georg Jung, to Cluss, to my mother-in-law,[a] to my sister[b] in Berlin. Ghastly letters! And so far not a word from a single one of them. So there's no other course left open to us. I cannot describe what things are like here. My husband has gone to the City to see Gerstenberg. You can imagine what kind of an errand that must be for him. Meanwhile I am writing these lines. Can you send us something? The baker warned us that there'd be no more bread after Friday. Yesterday when he asked: 'Is Mr Marx at home?' Musch managed to fend him off by answering: 'No, he a'nt upstairs' and then, with three loaves tucked under his arm, shot off like an arrow to tell his Moor about it.

Farewell.

Jenny Marx

First published in *Der Briefwechsel zwischen F. Engels und K. Marx*, Bd. I, Stuttgart, 1913

Printed according to the original

Published in English for the first time

---

[a] Henriette Marx - [b] probably Anna Elisabeth Franziska von Westphalen

9

ADOLF CLUSS TO JOSEPH WEYDEMEYER [692]

IN NEW YORK

Washington, May 15th 1853

... Marx has written me a very jolly letter in which he says that everyone was greatly amused by my description of the doings of Willich, that 'brother of the guild of misery'.[693] He says that, amid peals of Homeric laughter, they resolved *en grand comité*[a] to wish his 'life' as unhampered a course as possible. He remarks: 'If the lunacy of this *drôle*[b] were not intermixed and interlarded with cunning calculations as to how best to fill his belly without doing any work, he would long since have found his way to the lunatic asylum.' In return for my report, Marx is going to send me in his next a copy of the passage relating to Willich in *The Great Men of the Exile*.

Revolution and Counter-Revolution. Marx says he has no time for translation; if you or I or someone else will undertake to translate it, and if we let him know where he left off, he will take upon himself to write the whole of the conclusion.[694] Marx is of the opinion that as a pamphlet, the thing will *not* sell, and certainly not pay for itself; he would be perfectly satisfied with a feuilleton. (So whatever remains to be done would be left to us.)

Raveaux's former followers—philistines—long in need of another saint, have put red Becker[c] in Raveaux's place. *À tout seigneur tout honneur*[d]...

First published in: Marx and Engels, *Works*, Second Russian Edition, Vol. 28, Moscow, 1962

Printed according to the original

Published in English for the first time

---

[a] in full committee - [b] rascal - [c] probably Max Joseph Becker - [d] Honour to whom honour is due.

10

ADOLF CLUSS TO JOSEPH WEYDEMEYER[695]

IN NEW YORK

Washington, June 2nd 1853

... Today received a letter from Marx's wife which unfortunately I would seem to have placed *outside* my pocket when on the omnibus. Marx had just returned from Manchester (20th May).[696] He is delighted with your *Reform* article[a]; likewise your introduction[b] to Hirsch's statement.[c] Marx's only regret is that not all our things are able to appear under your auspices, but that the names of the two ciphers[d] from the *Hornisse* must be given precedence. Otherwise he is satisfied with the *Reform*. Dronke has at last obtained a post as clerk in Bradford at £10 a month.

Pieper would appear to have been shown the door by Rothschild[e] some time ago; the part he played in the communist trial makes it difficult for him to find a berth elsewhere.

Rothschild, was at university with him, has paid him nothing to date, but would do so if he possibly could; Pieper must see to this *au moment,*[f] having no other recourse.

Eccarius is still not restored.

Lupus, due to PRESSURE FROM WITHOUT, is very ill disposed...

The *Tribune* leaders on the EASTERN QUESTION are all by Marx; he wrote them without adding any of the usual NEWS trivialities so that Dana went and changed some of the longer historical expositions, etc., into Tribunese and published them as LEADERS.[g] The *Tribune* is a well-spring from which Marx cannot afford to cut himself off, hence he intends to turn a blind eye and would rather we didn't make any *direct* reference to the fact, even though he resents it—, that his *more objective* LOOKING pieces appear without his name, while the articles that do appear under his own name are no more than dregs...

First published in: Marx and Engels, *Works,* Second Russian Edition, Vol. 28, Moscow, 1962

Printed according to the original

Published in English for the first time

---

[a] J. Weydemeyer, 'Nationalökonomische Skizzen'. - [b] J. Weydemeyer, 'Der "demokratische" Mouchard'. - [c] W. Hirsch, 'Erklärung' [of 12 January 1852], *Belletristisches Journal und New-Yorker Criminal-Zeitung,* No. 7, 29 April 1853. - [d] Gottlieb Kellner and Heinrich Heise - [e] probably Wilhelm Karl Rothschild - [f] presently - [g] On the *Tribune* editors' tampering with Marx's and Engels' articles see also this volume, pp. 331-32.

11

ADOLF CLUSS TO JOSEPH WEYDEMEYER [697]

IN NEW YORK

Washington, June 14th 1853

Dear Weyd.,

Just received your letter. As regards Pieper's article, Marx wrote some time ago—4 months, perhaps—in reply to my apology for making use of one of his letters, saying that I shouldn't get such silly ideas into my head.[698] Though in no way given to flattery he had found that I only made use of his letters on rare occasions and certainly never for my own personal ends; in any case, they were deliberately written for me to make use of. I shouldn't think him so niggardly of his ideas; Pieper and red Wolff[a] are there, writing down everything he says...

First published in: Marx and Engels, *Works,* Second Russian Edition, Vol. 28, Moscow, 1962

Printed according to the original

Published in English for the first time

12

JENNY MARX TO FREDERICK ENGELS

IN MANCHESTER

[London, 9 September 1853]

Dear Mr Engels,

Imandt was here just now and told us that Dronke was studying Spanish and he *believed* he had seen him with the little grammar, 'the one that was sold'.[b] If, dear Mr Engels, you could question

---

[a] Ferdinand Wolff - [b] C. Franceson, *Grammatik der spanischen Sprache.* See this volume, p. 364.

Dronke about the wretched little book as soon as you receive this letter, Karl would be much obliged to you; for we might thus be able to clear the matter up to the confusion of Isegrim[a] before he leaves. To you it may seem funny that we should make a thing of this stupid business, but one must have experienced the whole thing to understand it—such crude, boorish tones, such churlish behaviour, such brutal shouting, such outbursts and anger in front of myself and the children. It would be splendid if the sold booklet were in the hands of a bosom friend! But do not mention Imandt's name. It is already very late and I am addressing these lines to your house to make sure they reach you tomorrow. More pleasant news. Bamberger is threatening to take proceedings over the Swiss affair.[b] Schabelitz has asked him to sue my husband because of a passage in a letter in which Karl promised to pay half the expenses if the thing sold. Please send the letter which you still have in the file.[699] Karl likewise begs you yet again to let him have the notes about the Russian and Turkish troop deployment.[c] He is continually having to write about the business since it hasn't yet been settled, and the Americans are besotted with the EASTERN QUESTION.

Today Karl has been forcing himself to write another long article on economics[d] and, being very tired, has asked me this evening to take up the pen on his behalf.

Farewell, and warmest regards from us all.

Jenny Marx

Lupus, or so we hear, is leaving tomorrow morning. He has not said good-bye to me and the children.

First published in *MEGA*, Abt. III, Bd. 1, Berlin, 1929

Printed according to the original

Published in English for the first time

---

[a] Wilhelm Wolff (a pun: Isegrim—a wolf, character in Goethe's 'Reineke Fuchs'). - [b] See this volume, pp. 579-80. - [c] ibid., p. 365. - [d] K. Marx, 'The Vienna Note.—The United States and Europe. Letters from Shumla—Peel's Bank Act'.

13

JENNY MARX TO FREDERICK ENGELS

IN MANCHESTER

[London, 24 November 1853]

Dear Mr Engels,

I have made out the POSTAL ORDER to William Wolff, with Charles Marx as the sender.[a]

The statements attacking Willich's scrawl[b] will hardly catch tomorrow's steamer since Miskowsky, 'the missing Russian officer', has not as yet been traced. He lives somewhere in Whitechapel and his address has been mislaid. Nor was it known to Kossuth, whom we approached indirectly. A messenger has just left for Whitechapel. Unluckily for the gallant Willich, the man has been back here for some months, possesses a certificate signed by Kossuth to the effect that he fought in the Hungarian campaign, and will now be able to provide a first-hand account of the duel.[700]

Père is BUSY with the next instalment of the Palmerston article,[c] and hopes to receive some small aid tomorrow.

With warmest regards.

Jenny Marx

First published in *MEGA*, Abt. III, Bd. 1, Berlin, 1929

Printed according to the original

Published in English for the first time

14

ADOLF CLUSS TO JOSEPH WEYDEMEYER

IN NEW YORK

Washington, December 12th 1853

Dear W.,

Herewith 1 article 'from Wisconsin'[d]; I think you'd be well advised to bring it out in two parts, with 'to be continued' in between.

---

[a] See this volume, p. 398 - [b] A. Willich, 'Doctor Karl Marx und seine "Enthül-lungen"'. - [c] 'Lord Palmerston', IV published in the *New-York Daily Tribune* under the title 'England and Russia'. - [d] 'Der Staat Wiskonsin' by Cluss was published in *Die Reform,* No. 109, 15 December 1853.

Just received 1 letter from Marx, *dated 28TH Nov.* Dronke, it seems, has sent you a statement which you should hold back if it is not already too late.[a] Dronke was supposed to send this statement to Marx in London, instead of which he sent it to you in New York.

Marx has answered Willich at length,[b] in very learned, 'Hegelian' fashion. Splendid, so far as I can see, and plentifully buttressed with documents; I shall probably send you the thing tomorrow, but haven't yet had time to read it through, and so do not know what to do with it. *It is voluminous.* 20 pages of LARGE NOTE-PAPER. Marx had already written it when my letter arrived informing him that we were taking care of the answer.[c] He now considers that, since it isn't every day one meets with such a lying codger as Willich, it would be RATHER DISAGREEABLE if the thing had to be shelved. He authorises me to make deletions if his article repeats what we have already said, or conflicts with ours in matters of detail.

More about this when I send you the thing.

The accompanying letter, dashed off in great haste, partly by Monsieur and partly by Madame Marx,[701] concludes as follows:

'Yesterday evening (27TH Nov.) the Waschlapskis and Schelmufs-kis[d] held a meeting.[702] Harney was IN THE CHAIR. The PEOPLE almost tore him to pieces. DOWN, DOWN, RASCAL, TRAITOR, RENEGADE, and he wasn't permitted to TAKE THE CHAIR. PEOPLE jumped onto the platform, everyone was belabouring everyone else, the Schelmufs-kis acted as Harney's GUARDS.'

Again: 'As regards the *Reform,* Karl has done everything in his power. Pieper, driven by necessity, has gone to work in a French SHOP, where he sells sunshine, i.e. the newly-invented *lampe réverbère.*[e] He *cannot* write just now. Accordingly Karl has roped in Heise and given him a subscription to the reading room since he hadn't got the required penny. He has also written to Germany asking for help.'

---

[a] See this volume, pp. 399 and 400-01. - [b] K. Marx, 'The Knight of the Noble Consciousness'. - [c] J. Weydemeyer, A. Cluss, A. Jacobi, 'An die Redaktion der *New-Yorker Criminal-Zeitung*', see also this volume, p. 402. - [d] An allusion to petty-bourgeois refugees, using names of characters in Heine's satirical poem 'Zwei Ritter'. See also this volume, p. 401. - [e] lamps with reflectors

Treat the bit about Heise as confidential.

Your

Ad. Cluss

First published in: Marx and Engels, *Works*, Second Russian Edition, Vol. 28, Moscow, 1962

Printed according to the original

Published in English for the first time

15

JENNY MARX TO FREDERICK ENGELS

IN MANCHESTER

[London, end of March 1854]

Dear Mr Engels,

Karl asks you to send Lassalle's address *by return*. You did not return Lassalle's first letter,[a] which gives it.

Warmest regards from the whole family.

Yours

Jenny Marx

First published in: Marx and Engels, *Works*, First Russian Edition, Vol. XXII, Moscow, 1929

Printed according to the original

Published in English for the first time

16

JENNY MARX TO FREDERICK ENGELS

IN MANCHESTER

London, 13 May [1854]

Dear Mr Engels,

I am sending you herewith a packet of old abusive *paperasse*[b]; and with it the very latest ordure by Wiss,[c] Dulon, etc. Some of it

---

[a] See this volume, pp. 414-17. - [b] waste paper - [c] Probably E. Wiß, 'Die elementaren Richtungen der Zeit', see also this volume, p. 449.

will amuse you. For the past five days Karl has been plagued by rheumatic pains in his teeth, ears and face, so severe that he hasn't been able to sleep a single night and today feels seriously indisposed. Nothing we tried did any good. We went through the whole pharmacopoeia, from Pfänder to Raspail. But still the same terrible pain. Not until tonight was some sweating induced by Spanish fly, opium, etc., and a slight improvement noticeable. He's not in a condition to put pen to paper, but urgently begs you, dear Mr Engels, to be sure and send him an article on Tuesday[a] so that we don't miss another whole week, as we did last. Otherwise it would make too big a hole in the money-box. Cordial regards from the whole family and from

Jenny Marx

Heise and the little man[b] have written Imandt a quite crazy letter. It reeked of brandy.

First published in: Marx and Engels, *Works*, Second Russian Edition, Vol. 28, Moscow, 1962

Printed according to the original

Published in English for the first time

17

JENNY MARX TO FREDERICK ENGELS

IN MANCHESTER

[London, 23 May 1854]
3 o'clock in the afternoon

Dear Mr Engels,

Your article[c] has just arrived. It's already been addressed and I shall put it in the post at the same time as this note. Karl was tremendously pleased when he heard the postman's portentous double KNOCK. *Voilà* Frederik,[d] £2, we're saved! he cried. Unfortunately he is still very, very unwell and asks me to tell you that he is

---

[a] 16 May. Engels wrote 'A Famous Victory' on 15 May. - [b] Ernst Dronke - [c] F. Engels, 'The War'. - [d] That's Frederic.

Lazarus and Peterkin Pint-pot rolled into one. There can be no question of writing. He labours over Gladstone's long speeches and is very annoyed at not being able to write just now when he's got enough material on Mr Gladstone and his SCHEMES. If you *possibly can, do concoct something again for Friday.*[a] Anything will do, Karl says. I truly detest bothering you in this way, but send something if possible.

I enclose herewith the latest dispatch from Cluss and would ask you to return his letter[b] and not tell Heise anything about it. The fellow chatters so and, should little Meyen or other eminent men hear anything prematurely, communications to Cluss would at once stop. It's all very amusing and the gentlemen should be allowed to carry on undisturbed.

In his last letter to Imandt, consisting of a whole lot of little snippings glued together, Heise said he had now again given up the military DODGE since the Russians waged war differently from the way the *Tribune* said; he intended to apply himself henceforward to *doux commerce.*[c]

Karl and I send our heartiest thanks for the articles, and the three little ones[d] send their love.

Yours
Jenny Marx

Our Edgar[e] is said to be loafing about in New York again and to be coming here and then going on to Germany! What a band of loafers!

First published in: Marx and Engels, *Works,* First Russian Edition, Vol. XXII, Moscow, 1929

Printed according to the original

Published in English for the first time

---

[a] 26 May. Engels wrote 'The Present Condition of the English Army—Tactics, Uniform, Commissariat, etc.' on 25 May. - [b] Probably Cluss' letter to Marx of 30 April 1854. - [c] gentle commerce - [d] Jenny, Laura and Edgar - [e] Edgar von Westphalen

NOTES
AND
INDEXES

NOTES

¹ This letter was first published in English considerably abridged in Karl Marx and Frederick Engels, *Letters to Americans. 1848-1895. A selection.* International Publishers, New York, 1953.—3, 27, 303

² This refers to Chapter I of Marx's *Eighteenth Brumaire of Louis Bonaparte*, which Marx wrote from December 1851 to March 1852, immediately following the coup d'état in France on 2 December 1851 (see present edition, Vol. 11, Note 64). It is closely linked with other works by Marx and Engels analysing the 1848-49 revolution in France (Engels' *Letters from France*, Marx's *Class Struggles in France, 1848 to 1850*, see present edition, Vol. 10) and was originally intended as a series of articles in the weekly *Die Revolution*, which Joseph Weydemeyer began preparing in December 1851 for publication in New York.

Marx and Engels considered this journal highly important for the dissemination of scientific communism and took great pains to provide Weydemeyer with material. They sent him their own articles and those of their associates—Ernest Jones, Wilhelm Pieper, Johann Georg Eccarius, Ferdinand Freiligrath, Wilhelm Wolff and others. In connection with the forthcoming publication of the journal the *Turn-Zeitung*, No. 3, carried the following announcement on 1 January 1852: 'Die Revolution, a weekly journal edited by J. Weydemeyer, associate editor of the *Neue Deutsche Zeitung* suppressed by the police in Frankfurt am Main, is published *every* Saturday in co-operation with the editorial board of the former *Neue Rheinische Zeitung* (K. Marx, Fr. Engels, Freiligrath, etc.)'.

Weydemeyer managed to put out only two issues (on 6 and 13 January 1852), following which publication ceased for lack of funds. The first issue reproduced part of 'Review, May to October 1850' published by Marx and Engels in 1850 in the *Neue Rheinische Zeitung. Politisch-ökonomische Revue* (see present edition, Vol. 10), and also announced the forthcoming publication of Marx's *Eighteenth Brumaire of Louis Bonaparte* and 'Neuste Offenbarungen des Sozialismus oder "Idée générale de la Révolution au XIXᵉ siècle, par P. J. Proudhon". Kritik von K. M.' (the latter was not written by Marx). The second issue carried the rest of the 'Review' and part of Chapter II of the *Manifesto of the Communist Party* (see present edition, Vol. 6).

Weydemeyer received Chapter I of *The Eighteenth Brumaire,* mentioned here, as well as the rest of the work, when publication had ceased, but with the help of Adolf Cluss he succeeded in bringing out two more issues of the 'non-periodic journal' *Die Revolution* in May and June 1852 which carried this work and satirical poems by Ferdinand Freiligrath (see Note 13).

Weydemeyer failed to buy up from the printer even half of the 1,000 copies of the work printed. Only about 150 copies were sent to Europe, and approximately the same number sold in the USA in 1852 and 1853. Cluss and other associates of Marx in the past revolutionary struggle in Germany (Johann Schickel, Conrad Schramm, Franz Arnold and others) greatly contributed to disseminate his work among former subscribers to *Die Revolution* in Philadelphia, Baltimore, Richmond, Cincinnati, Washington and other large cities.—3, 391

[3] Wilhelm and Ferdinand Wolff intended to write articles for *Die Revolution.* In a letter of 19 December 1851 Marx promised Weydemeyer (see present edition, Vol. 38, p. 519) to send him by the next steamer the following material: 1. *The Eighteenth Brumaire of Louis Bonaparte* by K. Marx; 2. *Der Staatsstreich in Frankreich* by Ferdinand Wolff; 3. *Nemesis* by Wilhelm Wolff. Weydemeyer announced this in the first issue of *Die Revolution* on 6 January 1852, being unaware as yet of Marx's decision not to publish Ferdinand Wolff's article.—3

[4] The reference is to the progressive newspaper, the *New-York Daily Tribune,* to which Marx contributed from August 1851 to March 1862. A large number of articles for this paper were written at his request by Engels, Marx beginning to send his own articles to New York only in August 1852. He wrote the first ones in German, and his friends, generally Engels, translated them into English. By the end of January 1853 he started writing his contributions in English.

Marx's and Engels' articles in the *New-York Daily Tribune* dealt with major questions of foreign and home policy, the working-class movement, the economic development of European countries, colonial expansion, and the national liberation movement in oppressed and dependent countries. The articles at once attracted attention by their factual information, acute political judgment and brilliant style. This was acknowledged by the editors of the *Tribune,* who wrote, in a leading article on 7 April 1853, of the need 'to pay a tribute to the remarkable ability of the correspondent'. They went on: 'Mr Marx has very decided opinions of his own, with some of which we are far from agreeing; but those who do not read his letters neglect one of the most instructive sources of information on the great questions of current European politics.' In a letter to Mrs Marx of 1 July 1853, Charles Dana, one of the editors, wrote that her husband's articles were highly thought of by the *Tribune* owners and the reading public.

Articles by Marx and Engels were widely disseminated in America, many of them being reprinted in the *Tribune's* special editions—the *New-York Weekly Tribune* and the *New-York Semi-Weekly Tribune.* Some of the *Tribune's* articles were translated into German and published in German-language American newspapers. Marx's and Engels' articles in the *Tribune* were also read in Europe. From 1853 to 1855 Marx wrote regularly for the newspaper sending, as a rule, one or two contributions every week.

Sometimes the editors of the *New-York Daily Tribune* tampered with Marx's and Engels' articles, publishing them as editorial leaders and occasionally making insertions in the text. In 1855 all Marx's and Engels' articles were published without the authors' names. Marx repeatedly protested against such practices but his financial circumstances compelled him to accept the editors' terms (see, for instance, this volume, pp. 367, 395, 404). Marx ceased contributing during the Civil War in the USA.—3

5 Marx has in mind Article VII of Engels' series *Revolution and Counter-Revolution in Germany*. These articles were printed in the *New-York Daily Tribune* over Marx's signature from 25 October 1851 to 23 October 1852. While writing them Engels constantly exchanged views with Marx who read his articles before sending them off to the newspaper.

Only in 1913, when the correspondence between Marx and Engels was published, it became known that the articles had been written by Engels. Some articles of the series were published in German refugee newspapers in America. The German translation of the first two articles appeared in the *New-Yorker Abendzeitung* at the end of October 1851 without any reference to the source; a free translation of the beginning of the first article was published in Weitling's *Republik der Arbeiter* on 1 November 1851.—3

6 In November 1851 Cluss wrote to Marx about the need to disseminate the *Neue Rheinische Zeitung. Politisch-ökonomische Revue* in America, noting that Magnus Gross, the New York distributor, was not giving it sufficient publicity. When Weydemeyer went to America, he accepted Marx's proposal that he should take upon himself the sale and distribution of the *Revue* (see present edition, Vol. 38, p. 489). On 6 February 1852 he informed Marx that he hoped to sell about 200 copies of it at $1 instead of the $4.50 fixed by the Hamburg publisher Schuberth. Marx, however, was unable to have the necessary number of copies sent over from Europe.—3

7 Engels alludes to his stay at the Marxes' in London from about 20 December 1851 to 3 January 1852 (see also this volume, p. 567).—4

8 The reference is to the special imperial patent of 31 December 1851, which abolished the constitution introduced by the Austrian Government on 4 March 1849.

When speaking about the Prussian Constitution, Engels has in mind the one promulgated on 31 January 1850, which abolished all the democratic gains of the 1848-49 revolution and was based on high property qualification and unequal representation.—5

9 Probably an allusion to Conrad Schramm who had a duel with Willich in September 1850.—6

10 At the beginning of 1851 Conrad Schramm, wishing to play a joke on Willich, sent him a letter purportedly written by Hermann Becker, a Cologne Communist League member, reflecting the views of the Willich-Schapper group. In reply Willich sent a number of letters to Becker expounding an adventurist plan of 'revolutionising' the Rhine Province. Becker informed Marx of Willich's plans in a letter of 27 January 1851. During the Cologne trial Marx made use of these letters to expose the sectarian adventurist tactics of the Willich-Schapper group (see K. Marx, *Revelations Concerning the Communist Trial in Cologne*, present edition, Vol. 11, p. 452).—6, 569

11 Engels describes here the reaction of the European Press to Louis Bonaparte's policy of unrestrained social demagogy on the one hand and increased personal power on the other after the coup d'état of 2 December 1851. On 1 January 1852, a solemn service in honour of the President for which 190,000 francs were assigned was held in Notre Dame de Paris; the eagles on state banners (symbol

of Napoleon's Empire) were restored. The Prince President moved to the royal palace of the Tuileries, where on 14 January a new Constitution was proclaimed under which all power was concentrated in the hands of the head of the State elected for a term of 10 years, the composition and legislative functions of all the higher state institutions were also placed under his control. A detailed analysis of the methods and essence of the demagogic policy pursued by Bonaparte in the social sphere and of repressions against the democratic and working-class movements is given in Marx's *Eighteenth Brumaire of Louis Bonaparte* (present edition, Vol. 11).—7

[12] This letter was published in English for the first time, slightly abridged, in Karl Marx and Frederick Engels, *Letters to Americans. 1848-1895,* International Publishers, New York, 1953.—7, 15, 40, 52, 79, 94, 569, 576

[13] The reference is to the first of the two satirical poems by Freiligrath written on Marx's request specially for *Die Revolution* on 16 and 23 January 1852. The poet ridiculed the so-called German-American loan which Kinkel tried to raise in the USA (see Note 27). Kinkel's activity in America was described by Cluss in his letters to Wilhelm Wolff of 4-6 November and to Marx in mid-December 1851.

Freiligrath's poems were published in German in the *Morgenblatt für gebildete Leser,* Nos. 10 and 27, 7 March and 4 July 1852, printed in Stuttgart and Tübingen. The first poem was also published in English in *Notes to the People,* No. 50, 10 April 1852. Both the *Morgenblatt* and *Notes to the People* carried an introduction, the contents of which were not identical in the two publications. The editors of the present edition have insufficient proof that it was Marx who wrote this introduction, though Freiligrath is known to have asked him to do so (*Freiligraths Briefwechsel mit Marx und Engels,* Berlin, 1968, Bd. I, S. 42-43).

In America the first poem was published by Cluss in English in the newspaper *The National Era,* No. 282, 27 May 1852 (reproduced from the *Notes to the People*) with additions to the introduction made by Cluss, relating it to conditions in America. *Die Revolution* did not publish the poems until June 1852.—8, 108, 119

[14] On 12 January 1852 Hirsch made a statement, but as early as February 1852 he was found to be a Prussian police spy and was expelled from the Communist League. For this reason Marx, in a letter of 20 February 1852 (see this volume, p. 41), asked Weydemeyer not to publish Hirsch's statement. When in the spring of 1853 Hirsch published his anti-Marx and Engels article 'Die Opfer der Moucharderie' in America, in an attempt to justify the splitting activity of Willich and Schapper, Cluss and Weydemeyer, in order to expose Hirsch, published his first statement in the *Belletristisches Journal und Criminal-Zeitung,* No. 7, 29 April 1853.—8, 41, 66

[15] The *Communist League* was the first German and international communist organisation of the proletariat formed under the leadership of Marx and Engels in London early in June 1847 as a result of the reorganisation of the League of the Just. The programme and organisational principles of the Communist League were drawn up with the personal participation of Marx and Engels. The League's members took an active part in the bourgeois-democratic revolutions in Europe in 1848-49.

In 1849-50, after the defeat of the revolution, the Communist League was reorganised. In the summer of 1850, disagreements of principle arose in the League's Central Authority between its majority headed by Marx and Engels and the Willich-Schapper separatist group which tried to impose on the League its adventurist tactics of immediately unleashing a revolution without taking into account the actual political situation and the practical possibilities in Germany and other European countries. After 15 September 1850 the Willich-Schapper group broke away from the League and formed an independent organisation with its own Central Authority.

Owing to police persecutions and arrests of League members in May 1851, the activities of the Communist League ceased in Germany. On 17 November 1852, soon after the Cologne Communist Trial (see Note 16), the London District, on a motion by Marx, declared the League dissolved. However, many of its members, particularly in Germany and America, continued to be active for a long time.—8, 143

16 Members of the Communist League (see Note 15) were arrested by the Prussian police in May 1851 and accused of 'treasonable conspiracy'. The accused remained in detention for about eighteen months. Eleven Communist League members (Heinrich Bürgers, Peter Nothjung, Peter Röser, Hermann Heinrich Becker, Karl Otto, Wilhelm Reiff, Friedrich Lessner, Roland Daniels, Johann Jacob Klein, Johann Erhardt and Abraham Jacobi) were brought to trial which began in Cologne on 4 October and lasted till 12 November 1852. It was rigged by the Prussian police on the basis of fabricated documents and forged evidence which included the so-called Original Minute-book of the Communist League Central Authority meetings and documents stolen by the police from the Willich-Schapper group. The trial was accompanied by an anti-communist hue and cry in the official press of Germany and other countries. On the basis of forged documents and perjury seven of the accused were sentenced to imprisonment for terms of three to six years. Marx, Engels and their friends and associates in England, Germany and America supported the Cologne prisoners in the press and supplied counsel for the defence with documents and material exposing police fabrications. The provocative actions of the prosecution and the contemptible methods of the Prussian police state were exposed by Marx in his pamphlet *Revelations Concerning the Communist Trial in Cologne* and by Engels in the article 'The Late Trial at Cologne' (see present edition, Vol. 11).—9, 113, 131, 195, 351

17 The reference is to Engels' series of articles on England written for *Die Revolution*. Two articles got lost on their way to the USA (see this volume, p. 16). Manuscripts of the last two articles have survived (see present edition, Vol. 11). The first of these was written by Engels on 23 January and published on 15 November 1852 in the *Turn-Zeitung* (New York) to which Weydemeyer contributed. The second, written on 30 January 1852, was not published during Engels' lifetime, but was used by Weydemeyer in a number of his own writings for the press.—10, 39, 80

18 Engels is expressing the wish that Wilhelm Wolff should write for *Die Revolution* on current events as he did earlier in the *Neue Rheinische Zeitung* in the column 'Aus dem Reich' ('From the German Empire').—10

19 Between February and early April 1852, in compliance with Jones' request, Engels wrote for his journal *Notes to the People* a series of articles, the first of which was entitled 'Real Causes Why the French Proletarians Remained Comparatively Inactive in December Last' (see present edition, Vol. 11). Jones received it on 5 February 1852.—11, 38

20 On 16 January 1852 Jones informed Engels about Harney's sudden refusal to write on foreign policy for *The Notes to the People*. Harney explained his position by

his friendly connections with the supporters of the parliamentary reform (see Note 28). The conflict between Jones and Harney arose at the end of 1850. Jones headed the revolutionary wing of the Chartists and worked to create a mass proletarian party in England, trying to unite all the revolutionary proletarian elements and revive Chartism on a socialist basis. Harney advocated a 'united national party' to be formed on the basis of diverse national associations, including bourgeois ones, to campaign for universal suffrage. Harney's attempts to create a 'mass party of reform' and an independent press organ completely failed by the autumn of 1852.— 11

[21] The decrees on the resignation of de Morny, Minister of the Interior, and the appointment of Persigny to this post, on the resignation of Fould, Minister of Finance, and on the confiscation of the property of the Orleans were signed by Louis Bonaparte on 22 January 1852 and published in *Le Moniteur universel* on 23 January and *Le Constitutionnel* on 24 January.— 12

[22] Pieper's article 'Die Arbeiter Assoziation in England' was written on 15 January 1852, but as *Die Revolution* had ceased to appear the article was published in *Die Reform,* Nos. 41, 42 and 44 on 20, 21 and 31 August 1853.— 13

[23] The announcement published in the *Turn-Zeitung* in connection with the starting of *Die Revolution* (see Note 2), was repeated in two issues of *Die Revolution* in January 1852. It read: '*Die Revolution* is published every Saturday, from January on, under the editorship of the undersigned and in co-operation with the editorial board of the former *Neue Rheinische Zeitung* (Marx, Engels, Freiligrath, etc.). Its task will be to present as clear a picture as possible of the class struggle which is increasingly concentrating in the Old World, to culminate in the abolition of all class distinctions. It will keep its readers abreast of all the changes occurring in the industrial and commercial relations between the different nations and classes of the people and in their political attitude towards one another, changes which prepare revolutionary explosions.
'New York, January 1852

'J. Weydemeyer'.— 13

[24] When the Communist League (see Note 15) split, and Marx, Engels and their followers withdrew from the German Workers' Educational Society in London, the spokesmen of the Willich-Schapper faction (located in Great Windmill Street) brought a suit on behalf of the Society against Heinrich Bauer and Karl Pfänder, supporters of the majority of the League's Central Authority, who, as trustees, held part of the Society's money to be used under the Central Authority's control for the needs of the League and to help political refugees. They were accused of stealing this money. A libel campaign against Bauer and Pfänder was started in the press (*Schweizerische National-Zeitung,* 7 January 1851; *Republik der Arbeiter,* New York, Nos. 19, 20 and 21 for 23 and 30 August and 6 September 1851). In the statement made on 21 January 1852 and mentioned here, Pfänder refuted the libel and said that on 20 November 1850 the court had acknowledged the charge to be invalid (see present edition, Vol. 38, Note 328).

The *German Workers' Educational Society in London* was founded in February 1840 by Karl Schapper, Joseph Moll and other members of the League of the Just. After the reorganisation of the League of the Just in the summer of 1847 and the founding of the Communist League, the latter's local communities played the leading role in the Society. In 1847 and 1849-50 Marx and Engels took an active part in the Society's work.— 14, 195, 217, 226, 336

25 This refers to the workers' society founded in London in January 1852 with Marx's support. It consisted of those who had withdrawn from the German Workers' Educational Society (see Note 24) and had the carpenter G. L. Stechan, a refugee from Hanover, as its chairman. An active part in organising this society was also played by Georg Lochner, a worker, Communist League member and close friend of Marx and Engels. The society did not survive long, many of its members, Stechan included, coming under the influence of the Willich-Schapper faction and rejoining their organisation.— 14, 72, 233

26 *Agitation* and *Emigration* were the names Marx gave to two rival German petty-bourgeois refugee organisations in London which appeared in the summer of 1851—the Agitation Union headed by Ruge and Goegg and the German Emigration Club headed by Kinkel and Willich. The aim of both these small organisations was to raise money for an 'immediate revolution' in Germany.— 14, 42, 44, 97, 151

27 The reference is to the so-called *German-American revolutionary loan* which Kinkel and other petty-bourgeois refugee leaders tried to raise among the German emigrants in Europe and America in 1851-52 to finance an 'immediate revolution' in Germany. Kinkel's trip to the USA for this purpose in September 1851-March 1852 was a failure. In a number of their works (e. g. *The Great Men of the Exile, The Knight of the Noble Consciousness,* present edition, Vols. 11 and 12), Marx and Engels ridiculed this idea of Kinkel's and denounced the attempts to produce a revolution artificially when the revolutionary movement was on the wane.— 15, 73, 115, 121

28 In January 1852 *The Northern Star* was sold by O'Connor to A. G. Flemming and D. MacGowan. In 1849 a radical political trend among the Free Traders founded the National Parliamentary and Financial Reform Association to campaign for an electoral reform (the so-called Little Charter) and a taxation reform. By opposing their programme to that of the Chartists and at the same time borrowing some of their demands though in an extremely curtailed form, the bourgeois radicals expected to split the Chartist movement and to influence the workers. The bourgeois radicals, supported in their campaign by Cobden, Bright and the reformist elements among the Chartists under O'Connor, failed and the Association ceased to exist in 1855.

In writing about a Chartist faction connected with the supporters of the financial and parliamentary reform, Marx has Harney's group in mind (see Note 20).— 15, 68, 89

29 The letter to Weydemeyer and two articles of the series on England (see Note 17) which Engels mentions have not been found.— 16

30 Engels draws an ironical parallel between the policy of Bonapartism in the social sphere and the views of German 'true socialists' (Karl Grün, Moses Hess, Hermann Kriege and others), who in the mid-1840s indulged in the sentimental preaching of love and brotherhood and of pseudo-socialist ideas, and denied the need for political struggle and a revolution. Marx and Engels criticised this ideological trend of the reactionary German petty bourgeoisie particularly in *The German Ideology* (see present edition, Vol. 5), and in the *Circular Against Kriege, German Socialism in Verse and Prose* and the *Manifesto of the Communist Party* (Vol. 6).— 17

[31] The Bonapartist coup d'état of 2 December 1851 caused a republican uprising of artisans, workers in small towns, local peasants, tradesmen and intellectuals in about 20 departments in South-East, South-West and Central France. The Bonapartists thoroughly concealed the genuine scale of the republican movement. The true character of the movement and its brutal suppression by police and troops became known only in the last years of the Second Empire (see present edition, Vol. 43, Marx to Engels, 19 December 1868).— 17

[32] Engels has in mind his article 'England' which he intended to send to Weydemeyer with the letter (see Note 17).— 18

[33] The *Roman wall* (so-called *Hadrian's Wall*) was erected in North England in the second century to defend the Roman province of Britannia against the raids of the Picts (tribes then inhabiting the territory of what is now Scotland) and extended between the Solway and the Tyne (from Carlisle to Newcastle) over a distance of about 120 kilometres. After the fall of Roman rule in the fifth century Hadrian's Wall was destroyed.— 18

[34] These are Marx's covering notes to Stechan's contributions to *Die Revolution*, which Marx promised to Weydemeyer in his letter of 23 January 1852. The material contained some concrete facts concerning the persecution of the participants in the socialist and communist movements in Germany and the position of the Communist League members, Bürgers, Becker, Daniels, Otto and others, then under investigation in Cologne, but it was not a finished article. The material reached Weydemeyer in New York before 17 February but was not used because *Die Revolution* had ceased to appear.— 19

[35] On the confiscation of the property of the Orleans, the appointment of Persigny Minister of the Interior, and the resignation of Minister of Finance Fould, see Note 21.— 21

[36] The 'glorious revolution' of 1688 in England established a constitutional monarchy based on a compromise between the landed aristocracy and the financial bourgeoisie.— 21

[37] Kossuth was given an enthusiastic reception on his arrival in England in October 1851. Some bourgeois liberals and government representatives, in particular the Foreign Secretary Palmerston, used this welcome as an excuse to eulogise British constitutional freedoms. This served as a hypocritical cover for the unseemly role played by Britain in supporting the suppression of European revolutions, including that in Hungary.

The *Great Exhibition* in London, held from 1 May to 15 October 1851, was the first world trade and industrial exhibition, and was portrayed by some as the beginning of an era of 'universal peace'.— 21

[38] The reference is to the verse added by Freiligrath to the second poem which he had written for Weydemeyer's newspaper on 23 January 1852 (see Note 13) and sent to Marx on 25 January 1852 to have his opinion:

> Das heißt: dafern Du Babel nicht beglücktest
> Endlos mit Briefen, Karten, Inseraten,
> (Plakaten gar!)—dafern Du Dich nicht bücktest,
> Und um ein Wörtlein nur von Deinen Thaten
> Feig vor der Presse krochst und *so* Dich drücktest,
> (Gleich Virtuosen oder Akrobaten,)
> Daß Dich zuletzt, nach manchem sauern Schritt,
> Wirklich in Holz die Illustrierte schnitt!

Here Freiligrath alludes to the fact that Kinkel, by flattery and fawning, succeeded in having an article about himself, together with a portrait, printed in the *Illustrated News* on 30 November 1850.

When the poem was published, the additional verse about Kinkel was not included, which means that Freiligrath complied with Marx's recommendation.—21

39 Freiligrath's second poem contained verses addressed to Hans Andersen which Marx mentions here. They were prompted by Freiligrath's grudge against Andersen who, while in London, did not recognise him when they chanced to meet. He felt all the more bitter because the Danish storyteller had enjoyed his hospitality in Germany.

When the poem was published in *Die Revolution* the editors supplied the following note to Andersen's name: 'Herr *Andersen* himself appears here not merely as an individual but as the epitome of a peculiar type of literary lion and parasite to which the revolution seemed to have dealt the death-blow but which is again coming up and boastfully asserting itself everywhere.' In *Freiligraths gesammelte Dichtungen* published in Stuttgart in 1870 (Bd. 4, S. 5-6) the poem was printed without the 11 verses devoted to Hans Christian Andersen.—22

40 In a letter to Marx of 25 January 1852 Freiligrath quoted a letter from Ebner who expressed surprise at not having received any letters from Marx and Pieper and promised to discuss with the publisher Löwenthal the possibility of printing Marx's works. It later transpired that Ebner was an Austrian police informer, of which Marx and his friends were not aware at the time.—22

41 Marx refers here to the ruling of the Board of indicting magistrates concerning the members of the Communist League arrested and detained under investigation in Cologne (see Note 16). He quotes it probably from the letter of the lawyer Bermbach received in January 1852 (it has not been found). This same letter was also used by Marx when he described the proceedings to Weydemeyer in a letter of 13 February 1852 (see this volume, p. 34).—22

42 The letters of Marx and Engels to *The Times* and *The Daily News* on the Cologne Communist Trial were not published in view of the editors' hostility to the leading figures of the revolutionary movement. The original of Engels' letter to *The Daily News* has not survived. It may be that Engels did not do the final editing (see this volume, p. 29). For Marx's and Engels' letter to *The Times* see Vol. 11 of the present edition.—24, 25

43 The *New-York Daily Tribune* published in all 19 articles of Engels' *Revolution and Counter-Revolution in Germany*. Marx intended to write the last, twentieth, article, but did not do so.—25

44 Eccarius wrote an article about the English machine-building workers' strike (see Note 79) for *Die Revolution*, but since the latter had ceased publication Weydemeyer proposed to publish the article in the *New-Yorker Demokrat*.—26, 117

45 Marx refers here to his work on political economy which he started as early as 1843. He conceived it as a critique of bourgeois political economy and an analysis of the economic structure of bourgeois society in his time and its ideological basis. His initial research resulted in the writing of *Economic and Philosophic Manuscripts of 1844* (see present edition, Vol. 3) which were to serve as a basis for the whole work. On 1 February 1845, Marx signed a contract with

Carl Leske, a Darmstadt publisher, for the publication of his two-volume 'Kritik der Politik und National-Ökonomie'. This plan did not materialise as a whole, however, because Marx was busy writing other works (*The Holy Family, The German Ideology,* etc.). The contract with Leske was cancelled in February 1847.

Marx returned to his economic studies when he was in London, in the period of emigration, after the defeat of the 1848-49 bourgeois-democratic revolutions. From the spring of 1850 onwards he regularly visited the library of the British Museum, where he made a deep and thorough study of the economy of different countries, England in particular, critically analysed works by classic bourgeois economists, and made extracts from books by English, French, American and other economists and from official documents and periodicals. The notes and extracts made by Marx in the 1850s fill several dozen special notebooks. At that period Marx was especially interested in the history of landed property and rent, the history and theory of money circulation and prices, and economic crises.

In 1851 and 1852 Marx renewed his attempts to find a publisher for his work on economics, but he could not find one either in Germany or in America.

The vast stock of facts and theoretical material on political economy accumulated between 1850 and 1853 was systematised and arranged in the manuscripts of 1857-58 (also known as the *Grundrisse*), part of which, after a further revision, was published in 1859 as the first part of *A Contribution to the Critique of Political Economy.* Work on the economic manuscripts of the 1850s was an important stage in Marx's writing his main economic treatise, *Capital,* published in 1867.—26, 46, 69, 99, 259, 293, 367

[46] Here Engels has in mind the Willich-Schapper faction (see Note 15) which existed till early 1853.—29

[47] The publication of Harney's weekly, *The Friend of the People,* the first issue of which appeared on 14 December 1850, was discontinued at the end of July 1851.

Harney seems to have sent to Marx the proofs of the first issue of the resumed publication, which came out on 7 February 1852.—30

[48] The *Amalgamated Society* of Engineers was founded in 1851. Gerald Massey's article, mentioned by Marx, was published in *The Friend of the People,* No. 1, on 7 February 1852 and entitled 'The Engineers, Operative and Co-operative'.—30

[49] The reference is to Harney's speech at the Chartist meeting in London on 3 February 1852, the opening day of the English Parliament.—31

[50] Marx may have had in mind O'Connor's speech in the Court of Chancery (2-5 February 1852) where he and the directors of the Chartist National Land Company founded in 1845 gave evidence on the Company's financial activity, and its compliance with the parliamentary Act of August 1851 which envisaged the disbanding of this Chartist organisation. O'Connor's evidence was published in *The Northern Star,* No. 744, 7 February 1852.—31

[51] The Egyptian Pasha Mohammed Ali, who had actually secured his position as independent ruler of the country and strove to secede from the Ottoman Empire, carried out a number of important socio-economic reforms in the 1820s-30s in the sphere of agrarian relations, organisation of the state apparatus, industry and the navy. In his reforms Mohammed Ali received a

certain assistance from French ruling circles who supported him in the struggle against the Sultan in order to strengthen their own position in the Middle East. On Mohammed Ali's invitation a large number of French officers, military instructors and engineers went to Egypt.—31

52 This letter (without Jenny Marx's postscript) was published in English for the first time in Karl Marx and Frederick Engels, *Letters to Americans. 1848-1895*, International Publishers, New York, 1953 and the journal *Masses and Mainstream*, New York, 1953, No. 3.

An extract from Jenny Marx's postscript was first published in *Die Neue Zeit*, Bd. 2, Nr. 29, Stuttgart, 1906-07.—33

53 Marx wanted someone to start a campaign in the American Press in defence of the accused in the Cologne Communist Trial (see Note 16). This letter was used by Cluss as a basis for a large article published in Cincinnati in the democratic newspaper, *Der Hochwächter*, No. 80, 14 April 1852. On Marx's request, Weydemeyer also delivered the material about those accused in Cologne to the *New-York Daily Tribune*, which published it considerably abridged and with some editorial remarks as a leading article 'Justice in Prussia' in No. 3446, 4 May 1852.—34

54 An allusion to the fact that Kinkel, a participant in the 1849 Baden-Palatinate uprising, was taken prisoner and sentenced to life imprisonment. In November 1850, with the help of Carl Schurz, he escaped from the prison in Spandau to England.—34

55 In a letter of 6 February 1852 (with a postscript from Cluss) Weydemeyer informed Marx of the suspension of *Die Revolution* (see Note 2) and Cluss' and his intention to continue publication of Marx's works written in London, as announced in the first issue of the journal. Weydemeyer also wrote that on 4 February 1852 Dana published in the *New-York Daily Tribune* an article by Ludwig Simon (a deputy to the Frankfurt National Assembly), 'Movements of the German Political Exiles', attacking Marx and Engels.—37, 44

56 The reference is to the former deputies of the Frankfurt National Assembly. The *Frankfurt Left*—the petty-bourgeois Left wing of the National Assembly which was convened after the March revolution in Germany and opened its session in Frankfurt on 18 May 1848. The main aim of the Assembly was to put an end to the political disunity of Germany and draw up an all-German Constitution. However it failed to take a decisive stand on the basic problems of the 1848-49 German revolution and ceased to exist on 18 June 1849.—37

57 *March associations* (thus named after the March 1848 revolution) were branches in various German towns of the Central March Association, founded in Frankfurt am Main at the end of November 1848 by Left-wing deputies to the Frankfurt National Assembly. Fröbel, Simon, Ruge, Vogt and other petty-bourgeois democratic leaders of the associations confined themselves to revolutionary phrase-mongering and displayed indecision and inconsistency in the struggle against counter-revolution, for which Marx and Engels criticised them sharply in the *Neue Rheinische Zeitung* (see K. Marx, 'The Frankfurt March Association and the *Neue Rheinische Zeitung*', present edition, Vol. 9).—37, 42, 44

58 In writing about the King of Prussia being imposed on the German people Marx had in mind the all-German central government headed by a hereditary emperor and the Imperial Parliament—the Reichstag, which were envisaged by

the Imperial Constitution drawn up by the Frankfurt Assembly. On 28 March 1849 the Assembly offered the imperial crown to Frederick William IV of Prussia but he refused to accept it from the 'people's representation'.—42, 44

[59] Karl Vogt was a member of the *Imperial Regency* of five formed in Stuttgart on 7 June 1849 by the rump of the National Assembly which moved there from Frankfurt. The attempts of the Regency to implement by parliamentary means the Imperial Constitution, drawn up by the Frankfurt Assembly and rejected by the German princes, failed.—42, 44

[60] Cluss made a statement about the congress of American guarantors of the 'German-American loan' (see Note 27) to be held in Cincinnati on 3-8 February 1852. Cluss protested against being named as one of the guarantors. On Marx's instructions he exposed the adventurism of the whole idea. Cluss dispatched the text of the statement to Marx in London at the end of February 1852 and had it published in the *Turn-Zeitung*, No. 6, 1 March 1852.—42, 70, 92

[61] *Straubinger*—German travelling journeyman. Marx and Engels ironically applied the name to some participants in the German working-class movement of the time who were connected with guild production and displayed petty-bourgeois sectarian tendencies.—43, 137, 410

[62] On 16 February 1852, amidst alarming rumours of Louis Bonaparte's intention to invade the British Isles, Russell moved in Parliament a *Local Militia Bill* for England and Wales. The government was granted the right, in the event of an enemy attack, to increase the strength of militia detachments previously used only within their respective counties and to subordinate them to the regular army command. When the Bill was discussed in the House of Commons, Palmerston moved an amendment that it should apply also to Scotland and Ireland, and that the word 'Local' be deleted. Palmerston had recently resigned from the Cabinet (see Note 74) and the adoption of the amendment moved by him was considered by Russell as an expression of non-confidence in the government and served as a pretext for Russell's resignation on 20 February 1852. The Tory Cabinet headed by Derby was formed on 23 February 1852. The Bill became law in July 1852.—44, 49, 284, 520

[63] This name was given in England to Free Traders who advocated government non-interference in economic life. In the 1840s and 1850s the Manchester men formed a separate political group which joined the Liberal Party as its Left wing in the 1860s. The centre of Free Traders' agitation headed by two textile manufacturers, Richard Cobden and John Bright, was Manchester.—44, 69, 355

[64] 'Voting by *ballot* to prevent bribery and intimidation by the bourgeoisie' was the fourth point of the People's Charter published in 1838 as the programme of the General Working Men's Association in London (see F. Engels, *The Condition of the Working-Class in England*, present edition, Vol. 4, p. 518).—45

[65] Marx's letters to Lassalle mentioned here have not been found.—46

[66] Engels replies to a letter of 9 February 1852 in which Weydemeyer acknowledged receipt of Engels' first letter dated 23 January (see this volume, pp. 15-19); Engels' earlier letters had not reached Weydemeyer.—52

[67] Engels has in mind his article 'England. I' written for *Die Revolution*. About the whole series see Note 17.—52

68 Engels recalls the time when he fought in the ranks of the revolutionary detachments of the Palatinate provisional government (its seat was in Kaiserslautern) against the Prussian troops during the campaign for the Imperial Constitution (see Note 77). Engels was an aide-de-camp of August Willich who commanded a workers' corps. This corps was covering the retreat of the Baden-Palatinate insurgent troops to Switzerland and was the last to cross the border on 12 July 1849.—52

69 The reference is to the counter-revolutionary coalition of European powers— the resurrected Holy Alliance as Engels calls it—formed during the suppression of the 1848-49 revolutions. See Marx's and Engels' article 'The New "Holy Alliance"' (present edition, Vol. 8) and Engels' 'Conditions and Prospects of a War of the Holy Alliance against France in 1852' (Vol. 10).—53

70 British troops under Wellington fought Napoleonic France during the Peninsular War, 1808-14.—53

71 Engels characterised this Bill in his article 'England. II' (see present edition, Vol. 11).—53

72 The *Anti-Corn Law League* was founded in 1838 by the manufacturers Cobden and Bright. In the interests of the industrial bourgeoisie, the League strove to repeal the Corn Laws which were introduced in England in the fifteenth century and limited or banned corn imports for the benefit of the landed aristocracy. The League's aim was to reduce corn prices on the home market and together with them workers' wages. It made wide use of the free trade slogan, demagogically preaching that the interests of workers and industrialists coincided. In 1846 the Corn Laws were repealed, which signified victory for the industrial bourgeoisie, advocates of free trade (see Note 63). That same year the League declared itself dissolved, but in fact its branches continued to exist. In February 1852, in view of the protectionist tendencies of the Derby Ministry, attempts were made to revive the League.—53, 56, 61, 69, 512

73 The *Peelites*—a group of moderate Tories who rallied around Sir Robert Peel in the 1840s and supported his policy of concessions to the commercial and industrial bourgeoisie in the economic sphere while preserving the political domination of the big landlords and financiers. In 1846, in the interests of the industrial bourgeoisie, Peel repealed the Corn Laws. This caused great dissatisfaction among the Tory protectionists and led to a split in the Tory party and the secession of the Peelites. After Peel's death (1850), the Peelites formed a political group without any definite programme; they participated in the Aberdeen Coalition Ministry (1852-55) and merged with the Liberal Party in the late 1850s and early 1860s.—54, 129

74 Palmerston, Foreign Secretary in the Whig Ministry of Russell, was dismissed because in a conversation with the French ambassador in London he had expressed his approval of the Bonapartist coup d'état of 2 December 1851, without consulting other members of the Ministry. The dismissal occurred on 19 December 1851, though in principle the British Government did not disagree with Palmerston's point of view and was the first in Europe to recognise the Bonapartist regime in France.—54, 456

75 *Aliens Bills* were occasionally passed by the British Parliament on the pretext of guarding British subjects against the allegedly hostile actions of foreigners residing in England. These Bills were in fact directed against members of the

international revolutionary-democratic and working-class movement who lived in England as political refugees.—54, 523

76 Engels did not write a special article on this subject for Weydemeyer, but expressed some of his ideas on matters of the cotton industry and the development of world trade in letters to Marx (in particular, on 2 March and 20 April 1852, see this volume, pp. 57-58 and 82-83), who in his turn shared them with his American friends. These ideas were reflected in articles by Cluss and Weydemeyer published in 1852 in American democratic periodicals, e.g. Weydemeyer's 'Die Lage Europa's' in the *Turn-Zeitung*, No. 10, 1 July 1852.—55

77 The *campaign for the Imperial Constitution,* which was adopted by the Frankfurt National Assembly (see Note 56) on 28 March 1849, was the last stage of the 1848-49 bourgeois-democratic revolution in Germany. Despite its limited character, the Constitution was a step forward in solving the problem of Germany's unification. But it was rejected by the majority of German governments. In May 1849 popular uprisings in support of the Constitution broke out in Saxony, Rhenish Prussia, Baden and the Palatinate. The insurgents received no support from the Frankfurt National Assembly and the movement was suppressed in July 1849. Engels devoted his work *The Campaign for the German Imperial Constitution* to this subject (see present edition, Vol. 10), but did not fulfil his wish to elucidate this problem in one of the articles of *Revolution and Counter-Revolution in Germany.*—56

78 In 1844, to satisfy the Austrian Government, Sir James Graham, the British Home Secretary, ordered that the letters of Italian revolutionary refugees should be handed over to the police to be opened. This was the case with the letters of the Bandiera brothers (members of the conspiratorial organisation) to Mazzini containing the plan of their expedition to Calabria. The aim of the expedition was to start an uprising in Italy against the Neapolitan Bourbons and Austrian rule. The participants in the expedition were arrested and the Bandieras executed.—56

79 The machine-building workers' strike which started in late December 1851 in several towns of South-East and Central England was organised by the Amalgamated Society of Engineers (see Note 48) with the aim of abolishing overtime and improving working conditions. The employers responded with a lock-out on a national scale. After three months' struggle the workers were defeated and compelled to resume work on the former terms.—57

80 The anonymous letter of 29 February 1852 informed Marx that he and his friends were under Prussian police surveillance and hinted that there might be a traitor in their organisation.—58

81 Marx's letter to Amalie Daniels has not been found; judging by Marx's letter to Freiligrath (see this volume, p. 23), it could have been written after 26 January 1852.—59

82 Jones' letter to Weydemeyer of 3 March 1852 was intended for *Die Revolution.* It described the condition of various classes of English society and analysed the development of class struggle in England. Judging by Weydemeyer's letter to Marx of 24 May 1853, the letter was published in the American democratic papers at the end of 1852 or beginning of 1853.—59, 60, 70, 319

83 The *National Reform League* was founded in London in 1849 by the Chartist leaders Bronterre O'Brien, G. W. M. Reynolds, the Owenite socialist Lloyd

Jones and others. The League campaigned for universal suffrage and social reforms.

The meeting was reported in *The Times*, No. 21053, 3 March 1852.—59

84 An abridged translation of this letter was first published in Karl Marx and Friedrich Engels, *Correspondence. 1846-1895*. A Selection with Commentary and Notes, Martin Lawrence Ltd., London, 1934.—60, 196, 330, 472, 562

85 Apparently, while writing the concluding part of *The Eighteenth Brumaire of Louis Bonaparte*, Marx somewhat changed his plan: the work includes not six, but seven chapters, the last of which he sent to New York on 25 March 1852 (see this volume, p. 70).—60, 573

86 The role of protectionism at the different stages of capitalist development and the influence of the Corn Laws on the economic structure and class relations in capitalist society were the subject of a special economic research by Marx. See in particular 'The Protectionists, the Free Traders and the Working Class', 'Speech on the Question of Free Trade', Marx's speech included into Engels' 'The Free Trade Congress at Brussels' (present edition, Vol. 6) and also *Capital*, Vol. III, Book III, Part VI, Chapters XXXVII and XLIII.—61

87 Marx analysed H. Ch. Carey's *Essay on the Rate of Wages* and criticised his views in *Capital*, Vol. I, Part V, Ch. XVIII and Part VI, Ch. XXII and Vol. III, Book III, Part VI, Ch. XXXVII.—62

88 In 1853 these notes were used by Cluss almost unchanged in the article 'Das "beste Blatt der Union" und seine "besten Männer" und Nationalökonomen' written against Heinzen and other petty-bourgeois democrats (see present edition, Vol. 12).—65

89 In their polemic articles against Heinzen published in the *Deutsche-Brüsseler-Zeitung* in 1847 (Engels' 'The Communists and Karl Heinzen' and Marx's 'Moralising Criticism and Critical Morality', see present edition, Vol. 6) Marx and Engels revealed the narrow-minded democratism of the German petty-bourgeois radicals, in particular their failure to understand the need for the centralisation and unification of Germany.—65

90 Hochstuhl's visit to the USA being delayed, Cluss received seven copies of the pamphlet *Zwei politische Prozesse* only in July 1852 when Conrad Schramm arrived there.—66

91 A reference to the Rules of the Communist League drawn up by the Central Authority in Cologne in December 1850 after the split in the League in September 1850 (see Note 15).—66

92 An abridged translation of this letter was first published in K. Marx and F. Engels, *Selected Correspondence*, Foreign Languages Publishing House, Moscow, 1955.—66

93 An allusion to a duel between Dronke and Sazonov, a Russian emigrant in Geneva, in early August 1851.—67

94 Engels began to study Slavonic languages (Russian, Serbo-Croatian, Slovenian and Czech) at the end of 1850 and wanted to write a comparative grammar of these languages. He studied Russian most thoroughly. Extracts made by Engels from Pushkin's *Eugene Onegin* and *The Bronze Horseman* and Griboyedov's *Wit Works Woe* have survived. In the early 1850s he made extracts from Bowring's *Specimens of the Russian Poets* on eighteenth- and early nineteenth-century poets

and writers: Lomonosov, Derzhavin, Karamzin, Zhukovsky, Krylov and others. He knew many works by Czech and Serbian authors on the history of literature and folk art and also studied the history and culture of the Slav peoples on the basis of books by West European authorities.—67

[95] Engels alludes to the portraits of George Washington, John Milton, Robert Blum and others printed in Harney's *The Friend of the People.* The portrait of Kościuszko (1746-1817), a leader in the Polish liberation movement, was printed in No. 6, 13 March 1852.—68

[96] On 14 March 1852 Louis Bonaparte decreed the conversion of the state five per cents. The holders of five per cent papers were offered reimbursement of their nominal value or their exchange for papers of the same nominal price but bringing in $4\,^1/_2$ per cent revenue. The measure was carried out with the help of the banking houses. The decree was published in *Le Moniteur universel*, No. 74, 14 March 1852.—68

[97] Marx has in mind the plan suggested by Weydemeyer (in his letter to Marx of 10 March 1852), after the weekly *Die Revolution* ceased to appear, to publish the manuscripts held by Weydemeyer as separate pamphlets. The first issue was to contain Freiligrath's poems; the second, Marx's *Eighteenth Brumaire of Louis Bonaparte;* the third, Eccarius' article on the English machine-building workers' strike; the fourth, Cluss' article on the campaign for abstention from strong drinks; the fifth, his own article against Kinkel's memorandum; the sixth, Engels' article on England, and so on. However, Weydemeyer managed to issue two pamphlets only (see Note 2).—70

[98] Weydemeyer fulfilled Marx's instructions (see present edition, Vol. 11, p. 163). Marx relates, not quite accurately, the story told by the Greek writer Athenaeus (2nd-3rd cent. A.D.) in his book *Deipnosophistai* (Dinner-Table Philosophers). The Egyptian Pharaoh Tachos, alluding to the small stature of the Spartan King Agesilaus, who had come with his troops to the Pharaoh's help, said: 'The mountain was in labour. Zeus was afraid. But the mountain has brought forth a mouse.' Agesilaus replied: 'I seem to you now only a mouse, but the time will come when I will appear to you like a lion.'—70

[99] On 23 March 1852, on Marx's instructions, Wilhelm Wolff wrote in a letter to Cluss (to be passed on to Weydemeyer) that, instead of an article against Kossuth, Szemere was going to publish a pamphlet of 10 sheets about Görgey, Batthyány and Kossuth. Attempts to find a publisher in the USA in 1852 failed however, and only in 1853 did the newspaper *Die Reform* (Nos. 18-28, 1 June-6 July) publish the second section of the article, devoted to Görgey. The book appeared in Hamburg in 1853.—70, 77

[100] Marx refers here to the German Workers' Educational Society (see Note 24) dominated at the time by supporters of Willich and Schapper. On Pfänder's statement, see Note 24.—72

[101] The reference is to preparations to start *The People's Paper.*—72

[102] In February 1852 the *Morning Courier and New-York Enquirer* published Szemere's letter against Kossuth. Cluss informed Marx and Wolff of this in a letter at the end of February 1852.—73

[103] Marx means the *Central Committee of European Democracy* founded in London in June 1850 on Mazzini's initiative. It included Ledru-Rollin, Darasz and Ruge and united bourgeois and petty-bourgeois refugees from different countries. In March 1852 the Central Committee of European Democracy actually dissolved

due to disagreements between Italian and French democratic refugees.—73, 171, 433

104 *2 December 1851*—the day of the counter-revolutionary coup d'état in France.

The *capture of Rome* was effected by French troops on 1 July 1849 as a result of the intervention of France, Austria, Spain and Naples against the Roman Republic proclaimed on 9 February 1849. After this event the republic ceased to exist.—73

105 Marx refers here to Cluss' letter of 18 March 1852. Cluss reported on the activities of German petty-bourgeois emigrants in the USA and his opposition to the Congress of Kinkel's guarantors in Pittsburgh. This statement, dated 18 February, was published in the *Baltimore Wecker* and reprinted in the *Demokratisches Tageblatt* (Cincinnati), No. 145, 20 March 1852, under the title 'Eine verdeckte Batterie'.—76

106 The reference here is to Weydemeyer's letter to Marx and Engels of 6 April 1852. The part addressed to Engels bore no date, thus giving rise to Engels' doubts.

Engels has in mind here a meeting of the German petty-bourgeois refugees convened in New York on 3 April 1852 by the representatives of the American Revolutionary League (see Note 173) and presided by Fickler. Goegg and Fickler, who vied with Kinkel in raising funds in the USA for the so-called German-American revolutionary loan (see Note 27), tried to make Kinkel's supporters agree to the association of the rival emigrant organisations. This was also reported in Cluss' letter to Wolff of 4-6 April 1852.—79

107 Judging by Weydemeyer's letter to Marx of 11 May 1852 Müller-Tellering's letter containing slanderous attacks on Marx was not accepted by the American newspapers.—80

108 The reference is to the non-periodic journal *Die Revolution* (see Note 2).—80

109 Engels was in London for a few days in mid-April 1852 (at Easter).—81

110 *Bas-empire* (Lower Empire)—the name sometimes given in historical literature to the Byzantine Empire and also to the late Roman Empire; it came to denote a state at the stage of decline and dissolution. Here it refers to the proclamation of the Second Empire in France then being prepared by Bonapartist circles and effected on 2 December 1852.—82, 453

111 Only an extract from this letter has survived, quoted by Cluss in his letter to Weydemeyer of 6 June 1852. Marx made use of the economic data contained in Engels' letter to him of 20 April 1852 (see this volume, pp. 81-83) supplementing his political conclusion: 'On the other hand, it explains the flaccid condition of politics in this country. Given such prosperity, the Tories cannot, for their part, compete with the "blessings of Free Trade", even though they are at the helm, while the Free Traders, for their part, refrain from provoking political agitation because, so long as business is flourishing, the manufacturers do not want political upheavals and disturbances.'—83

112 A short extract from this letter has survived, quoted by Cluss in his letter to Weydemeyer of 8 May 1852.—84

113 The *Society of 10 December*—a secret Bonapartist organisation founded in 1849 and consisting mainly of declassed elements, political adventurists and reactionary military. Its members were active participants in and organisers of the coup d'état on 2 December 1851. Marx gave a detailed analysis of this

society in *The Eighteenth Brumaire of Louis Bonaparte* (see present edition, Vol. 11).—88

[114] The reference here is presumably to the five chapters from Marx's *The Eighteenth Brumaire of Louis Bonaparte* dispatched by Marx to Weydemeyer in New York between January and March 1852 and, after the manuscript had been copied, returned enclosed in Weydemeyer's letter of 6 April 1852.—88

[115] A reference to the division at the second reading of the Militia Bill (see Note 62) in the House of Commons.—89

[116] In the spring of 1852 negotiations were carried on to set up a new editorial board of *The Northern Star*, a Chartist newspaper published by O'Connor from 1837 onwards. Harney turned down Jones' proposal to publish the Chartist newspaper jointly, would not let Jones buy *The Northern Star*, acquired it himself and continued the publication first under the title *The Star* and from 24 April 1852 *The Star of Freedom*. This revealed the disagreement in principle existing between Jones and Harney, the latter seeking to turn the newspaper into the mouthpiece of the Right-wing Chartists and bourgeois radicals. In May 1852, Jones started a new Chartist weekly, *The People's Paper*.—89, 93

[117] Engels wrote this letter on Weydemeyer's letter to him of 12 April 1852.—90

[118] In April 1852 Engels wrote only Article XIV; the next articles (XV-XIX), devoted to the campaign for the Imperial Constitution and the popular uprisings of 1849 in its support, were written in July-September 1852.—90

[119] Engels visited Marx in London in the first half of April 1852 and returned to Manchester about 13 April.—92

[120] *Gymnastic clubs*—organisations of German democratic emigrants, including workers, set up in the USA by former participants in the 1848-49 revolution. At a congress in Philadelphia on 5 October 1850 the gymnastic clubs united into a *Socialist Gymnastic Association* (Sozialistischer Turnverein) which maintained contacts with German workers' organisations in America and published the *Turn-Zeitung*, a newspaper to which Weydemeyer and Cluss contributed regularly in 1852 and 1853.—92, 282

[121] Marx quotes Cluss' letter to him of 15 April 1852. Cluss' previous letter of 4-6 April, mentioned here, was addressed to Wilhelm Wolff and informed him of a meeting of the German petty-bourgeois refugees held in New York on 3 April 1852 (see Note 106).—93

[122] The reference is presumably to the copies of Marx's letters of 15-22 August and 2 December 1851 to the journalist Ebner, in which he exposed the activities of Ruge, Kinkel, Willich and others (see present edition, Vol. 38). Later these literary sketches became part of the pamphlet *The Great Men of the Exile* (see Note 131). Marx's letters to Ebner became known to the Austrian police.—93

[123] An allusion to Willich's participation in the Baden-Palatinate uprising of 1849.—93

[124] In a letter of 9 April 1852 Weydemeyer informed Marx that, due to the assistance of a German emigrant worker who had donated 40 dollars, the printing of *The Eighteenth Brumaire of Louis Bonaparte* had become possible.—94

[125] The reference is to a letter Wilhelm Wolff wrote to Weydemeyer on 16 April

1852, immediately after the death of Marx's youngest daughter Franziska, in reply to Weydemeyer's letter describing the difficulties encountered in publishing *The Eighteenth Brumaire of Louis Bonaparte.*—94

126 Weydemeyer wanted to publish Pfänder's statements (see Note 24, and this volume, p. 14) in one of the issues of the planned non-periodic journal *Die Revolution;* this intention was not carried out.—94

127 This letter has not been found.—95

128 The International Industrial Exhibition in New York was held in July 1853.—95, 120, 349

129 Weydemeyer complied with Marx's request and reported this in the article 'Die Lage Europas'' published in the *Turn-Zeitung,* No. 10, 1 July 1852.—96

130 Marx presumably wrote to Cluss about the conflict between Jones and Harney (see Note 116) on 30 April 1852. This letter has not been found. Cluss mentioned it in his letter to Marx of 22-24 May 1852.—96

131 It was in early 1851 that Marx and Engels conceived the idea of publishing a satirical *exposé* of the leaders of the petty-bourgeois democratic emigration. Engels wanted to publish a series of articles about 'continental democracy' in the weekly *Friend of the People* (see present edition, Vol. 38, p. 278) and in the autumn of 1851 he began writing a satirical article about Karl Schapper. As is seen from Marx's letters to Ebner (see Note 122), he had the literary portraits of Ruge, Kinkel, Willich and others ready as early as 1851. In late April and early May 1852 he continued collecting facts and material on this subject and received great help in this from Cluss and Weydemeyer, who sent him newspaper cuttings describing activities of various emigrant organisations in America.

On the basis of the facts collected Marx and Engels drew up a political pamphlet during May and June 1852. It was tentatively entitled *The Great Men* and was to consist of two parts. Only the manuscript of the first part has survived. The pamphlet was not published during the authors' lifetime, but separate chapters became known to the émigré leaders, its 'heroes' (see this volume, p. 124). Some excerpts were sent to Cluss in America in May 1852.

A proposal to publish the manuscript was made by a Hungarian émigré, Bangya, who, as it turned out later, had been a police spy since 1851 and kept Greif, a Prussian police agent in London, fully informed about Marx. Marx learned about Bangya's actions only at the end of 1852 and publicly exposed them in the article 'Hirsch's Confessions' (see present edition, Vol. 12).

The manuscript copy that has survived was written mainly by Engels with additions by Marx. The first pages are in Dronke's hand. The pamphlet is published in Vol. 11 of the present edition.—98

132 After Kinkel's return from the USA, the committee which was to organise the 'German-American revolutionary loan' decided at its sitting in London on 16 April 1852 to reactivate the local sections. With this aim in view it distributed an instruction circular drawn up by Kinkel and Willich. Marx writes here about a copy of it made and sent to him by Bangya. On Bangya's spying activities, see Note 131.—100

133 An allusion to the fact that in 1844-45 Mazzini protested in the press against Italian revolutionary emigrants' letters being opened by the police. His pamphlet, 'Italy, Austria and the Pope. A letter to Sir James Graham', was published in May 1845 in periodicals and separately. At that time James

Graham was Home Secretary and it was on his orders that Italian revolutionary emigrants' letters were delivered to the police.— 101

134 On 14 April 1849, the Hungarian National Assembly, on Kossuth's initiative, proclaimed the independence of Hungary and the overthrow of the Habsburg dynasty. On 2 May the Defence Council was replaced by a Council of Ministers headed by Szemere. Kossuth was elected ruler of Hungary. The siege of Ofen (Buda) by the Hungarian army under Görgey lasted from 4 to 21 May 1849 and ended in the taking of the fortress. The storm was effected after the defeat of the Austrian troops near Komarom on 22 April 1849, which provided favourable conditions for the Hungarian revolutionary army to march on Vienna. See Engels' appraisal of the military operations during the siege of Buda in his article 'Buda', present edition, Vol. 17.— 101

135 The *battle of Idstedt* (a village in northern Schleswig) was fought on 24-25 July 1850 by the Schleswig-Holsteinian and Danish troops and was the concluding episode of the national liberation uprising in Schleswig-Holstein against Danish rule in 1848-50. Under public pressure the Prussian Government, together with other states of the German Confederation, started a war against Denmark in 1848, but repeatedly betrayed the insurgents and on 2 July 1850 concluded peace with Denmark, leaving the insurgents to fight alone. As a result, the duchies remained within the Kingdom of Denmark. See Engels' detailed analysis of this battle on pp. 451-52 of this volume.— 103

136 As from 1852 Engels made a thorough study of the history of warfare, planning to write a military history of the 1848-49 revolutions, the Hungarian and Italian campaigns in particular. For this purpose he studied the works by Clausewitz, Jomini, Willisen, Hoffstetter, Küntzel, Görgey and many others. However, he failed to implement his plan.— 104, 128, 249

137 These are extracts from two letters which Marx sent to Cluss in the USA on 7 May and on about 15 May 1852. The extracts were quoted by Cluss in his letter to Weydemeyer of 31 May 1852. It cannot be established with certainty when each extract was written. However, the analysis of the letters from Cluss to Marx of 22-24 May 1852 and to Weydemeyer of 25 May 1852 leads to the conclusion that the first paragraphs belong to the second letter and the rest must be from that of 7 May, though passages from the second letter are interpolated; this applies in particular to the passage containing quotations from Bermbach's letter of 3 May 1852, which could not have been received in London earlier than 13 May.— 105

138 After his expulsion from the German Workers' Educational Society in London in the spring of 1850, Müller-Tellering (on the exposure of his intrigues in that Society, see present edition, Vol. 38, pp. 229-30) wrote a lampoon— *Vorgeschmack in die künftige deutsche Diktatur von Marx und Engels*. The inscription on the envelope quoted here by Marx is a direct allusion to that publication. In compliance with Marx's wish Cluss returned to Müller-Tellering everything he had received.— 105

139 *Demagogues* is Germany were the participants in the students' opposition movement after the liberation of the country from Napoleonic rule. The name became current after the Karlsbad Conference of Ministers of the German States in August 1819, which adopted a special decision on the persecution of the demagogues.— 106, 223

140 The reference is to György Klapka's 'Political Programme' dated April 1852. Marx wrote the introductory and concluding remarks to it (see present edition, Vol. 11) planning to publish them in the *New-York Daily Tribune*. But the plan was not realised in this form. In September-November 1852 Marx had the articles 'Movements of Mazzini and Kossuth.—League with Louis Napoleon.—Palmerston' and 'Kossuth, Mazzini, and Louis Napoleon' (see present edition, Vol. 11) published in that newspaper. He warned revolutionary democrats against premature action and maintained that any reliance on support from Louis Bonaparte in the struggle to liberate Hungary and Italy from Austrian rule would only contribute to strengthening the Second Empire.—106

141 In a letter to Marx of 6 February 1852 Weydemeyer promised to dispatch the first 50 copies of *The Eighteenth Brumaire* published as a special issue of the journal *Die Revolution*. Since the printing was delayed they were dispatched through Korff much later, but Marx did not receive them. For lack of money Weydemeyer failed to buy up all the copies printed and sent only 10 copies on 13 August 1852, which reached London in early September. At the end of October 1852 Marx received 130 copies more from Cluss.—106

142 See notes 17 and 44.—107

143 In September 1851 arrests were made in France among members of local communities who belonged to the Willich-Schapper group (see Note 15). The conspiratorial tactics of this group enabled the French and Prussian police, with the help of the agent-provocateur Cherval, who headed one of the Paris communities and at the same time was in the pay of the Prussian and French police, to fabricate the case of the so-called Franco-German plot. In February 1852 the accused were sentenced on a charge of plotting a coup d'état. Cherval was allowed to escape from prison. Attempts of the Prussian police to incriminate the Communist League led by Marx and Engels failed. Marx publicly exposed these provocations in his *Revelations Concerning the Communist Trial in Cologne* and *Herr Vogt* (see present edition, vols. 11 and 17).—112, 130, 242, 270

144 The reference is to the members of the German Workers' Educational Society in London (see Note 24).—113

145 *Parliamentary trains*—a name given in England in the nineteenth century to special trains which, by a parliament act of 1844, ran daily with a speed of no less than 12 miles per hour, fares not exceeding one penny a mile.—113, 325, 534

146 Marx arrived in Manchester probably on 27 May 1852 and stayed with Engels till the second half of June. They devoted this time to writing their joint pamphlet *The Great Men of the Exile.*—114, 181

147 An allusion to the attempts of Willich's supporters (former members of the volunteers' corps during the 1849 Baden-Palatinate uprising) to form a special military unit in the USA in view of an allegedly imminent revolution in Europe. In a letter to Engels of 17 June 1852 Weydemeyer appraised these actions as an attempt to form one more makeshift organisation of petty-bourgeois emigrants.—115

148 In their pamphlet *The Great Men of the Exile* Marx and Engels made use of the assessment of the newspaper *Der Kosmos* and Ruge's and Kinkel's contributions to it which Marx gave in his letters to Engels of 21 and 28 May 1851 (see present edition, Vol. 38).—117

¹⁴⁹ The first edition of Marx's *Eighteenth Brumaire of Louis Bonaparte* put out by Weydemeyer had *The Eighteenth Brumaire of Louis Napoleon* on its title-page.— 117

¹⁵⁰ The reference is to the cuttings from American newspapers enclosed in Cluss' letter to Marx of 27 May 1852.— 117

¹⁵¹ Korff, the responsible publisher of the *Neue Rheinische Zeitung,* was dismissed as from 1 April 1849 for business incompetence, inclination to intrigues and meddling in the management of the newspaper.— 120

¹⁵² The reference is to the reviews of military operations in Hungary written by Engels and published in the *Neue Rheinische Zeitung* from February to May 1849 (see present edition, vols. 8 and 9). On 1 December 1851 Weydemeyer informed Engels that Korff had published one of these articles in the *New-Yorker Staatszeitung* in his own name.— 120

¹⁵³ All that has survived from this letter is a short extract quoted by Cluss in his letter to Weydemeyer of 13 July 1852. The following passage from Cluss' letter may give an idea of what Marx wrote in the non-extant part of his letter:

'A few days ago Marx wrote in haste some more lines from Manchester promising details next week. He has only 3 copies of *Brumaire* left.

'"The history of the war between mice and frogs" [i.e. the pamphlet *The Great Men of the Exile*] (the first notebook up to Kinkel's departure to America) will appear *anonymously*. Marx regrets that he has to interrupt his studies in order to "clear the cesspool". Nevertheless, *I* think this is very good because it will protect the next revolution to some degree against this joint swindler company. In Marx's opinion, the whole thing is done in a very lively way and will come to us as soon as it is printed. He authorises us, *if we think it economically and politically viable,* to have it published in America. Think this over for a while.'— 122

¹⁵⁴ Marx refers here to the French Provisional Government's decree of 16 March 1848 which added an extra 45 centimes to every franc of direct taxes levied on landowners (land tax, taxes on movable property, windows and doors, patents). The tax became a new burden mainly for small peasants and caused them to join the opposition to the Second French Republic.— 122

¹⁵⁵ In early July 1852 a number of French and German newspapers reported the arrests in Paris of members of a secret organisation who were making preparations for the assassination of Louis Bonaparte and aimed at restoring the republic. According to the newspapers, the arrested were mainly workers, several of whom had taken part in the June 1848 uprising. The newspapers maintained that the plot was directed by refugees in London and Brussels.— 126, 128

¹⁵⁶ Engels has in mind the fact that Adolphe Chenu, the author of *Les Conspirateurs. Les sociétés secrètes; la préfecture de police sous Caussidière; les corps-francs* (Paris, 1850), was simultaneously an organiser of secret societies during the July monarchy and a police informer, and that this was reflected in the book. Marx and Engels published a review of this book in the *Neue Rheinische Zeitung. Politisch-ökonomische Revue,* No. 4 (see present edition, Vol. 10).— 128

¹⁵⁷ This refers to two documents issued in Waitzen (Vác) by Görgey, commander of the Upper Danubian Hungarian Corps, after the surrender of Buda to the counter-revolutionary troops of the Austrian Field Marshal Windischgrätz:

'Statement of the Upper Danubian Royal Hungarian Corps' of 4 January 1849 and the address 'To the Upper Danubian Royal Hungarian Corps' of 6 January 1849. In them Görgey unjustly accused Kossuth and the Defence Council headed by the latter of deserting the capital, and in fact counterposed the Corps to the Defence Council and put forward an independent plan of conducting the war. The documents were published in A. Görgei, *Mein Leben und Wirken in Ungarn,* 1. Bd., Leipzig, 1852, S. 149-54.— 128

158 The duc d'Enghien was condemned to death on a charge of conspiring against Napoleon and was executed by firing squad on 21 March 1804.— 129

159 Marx may have made up his mind to write on this subject when he was staying with Engels in Manchester from the end of May to second half of June 1852, but he did not carry out his plan until August, when he devoted a few articles for the *New-York Daily Tribune* to analysing political parties in England and exposing the anti-popular essence of the English electoral system. These articles were 'The Elections in England.—Tories and Whigs', 'The Chartists', 'Corruption at Elections' and 'Result of the Elections' (see present edition, Vol. 11).— 129

160 The *Mazas*—a Paris prison.— 130

161 *Claremont*—a house near London, residence of Louis Philippe after his flight from France in 1848; a centre of Orleanist intrigues to restore the Orleans dynasty in France.— 130

162 *Orlando innamorato*—a chivalrous poem by Boiardo, an Italian Renaissance poet, published in Italy in 1495. In the sixteenth century, adaptations of this poem were made by Lodovico Domenichi and Francesco Berni; most popular was that of Berni which appeared in 1541 and was repeatedly republished. Boiardo's poem was republished in London in the 1830s.— 131

163 Here Engels alludes to the article 'Saedt' which he and Marx published in the *Neue Rheinische Zeitung,* No. 225, 18 February 1849. The article ridiculed the mental limitation of Saedt, a Cologne public prosecutor since 1848, in connection with his poor speech for the prosecution at the trial of Kinkel in February 1849, on a charge of insulting the Prussian garrison at Mainz.— 132, 138

164 The reference is to the Prussian criminal code introduced in April 1851. Until then the *Code pénal* introduced in 1811 in western and south-western Germany occupied by the French had been in force in Rhenish Prussia. The *Code pénal* determined the penalty for perjury, libel and similar crimes.— 134, 230

165 Only a passage of the letter has survived as it was quoted by Cluss in his letter to Weydemeyer of 6 August 1852. The date of Marx's letter, 20 July, was given by Cluss.
An abridged translation of this letter was first published in K. Marx and F. Engels, *Selected Correspondence,* Moscow, 1965.— 135

166 This rough copy of Marx's letter to Kinkel is published according to Marx's letter to Engels of 6 August 1852 (see this volume, pp. 149-50). Marx also quotes it in his letter to Cluss of 30 July 1852 (see ibid., pp. 139, 140).— 138

167 Only a passage of this letter has survived in the form of a long quotation in Cluss' letter to Weydemeyer of 16 August 1852. The date is given by Cluss.— 139

[168] In a letter to Cluss written at the end of June 1852, Huzel gave an account of Kinkel's slanderous attacks on Marx and Engels. Cluss quoted an extract from it in his letter to Marx of 4-5 July 1852 and Marx copied it in his letter to Engels of 6 August 1852 (see this volume, pp. 149-50).— 139

[169] Marx ironically calls Gottfried Kinkel Johann after his wife Johanna, who exerted a great influence on him (see Marx and Engels, *The Great Men of the Exile*, IV and V, present edition, Vol. 11).— 139

[170] This refers to the article 'Gottfried Kinkel' written by Marx and Engels in April 1850 and published unsigned in the *Neue Rheinische Zeitung. Politisch-ökonomische Revue*, No. 4, 1850 (see Note 185).— 139

[171] In a letter of 14 November 1851 Kinkel proposed that Cluss become a guarantor of the so-called German-American revolutionary loan.— 140

[172] This letter of Marx to Kinkel has survived only as quoted by Cluss in his letter to Weydemeyer of 16 August 1852 and is reproduced in Marx's letter to Engels of 6 August 1852 (see this volume, pp. 149-50). The texts are identical, with the exception of italics.— 140

[173] The *American Revolutionary League*—an organisation of German refugees in the USA set up in January 1852 by the petty-bourgeois democrats Goegg and Fickler who had arrived in the USA to raise the so-called German-American revolutionary loan (see Note 27).— 141, 150, 155, 161

[174] The reference is to the secret conspiratorial organisation of German refugees in Paris—the German People's Union (Deutscher Volksverein) set up in 1832. When it was banned in 1834, a new secret revolutionary-democratic organisation of German artisans—the Outlaws' League (Bund der Geächteten) was formed.— 143

[175] The *League of the Just* was established between 1836 and 1837 in Paris as a result of the split in the Outlaws' League and was the first political organisation of German workers and artisans. It had branches in Germany, France, Switzerland and England. Its members were greatly influenced by the ideas of utopian socialism, that of Weitling in particular. In 1847 it served as a basis for the creation of the Communist League, the first international organisation of the proletariat (see Note 15).— 143

[176] The reference is to the Addresses of the Central Authority to the League written by Marx and Engels at the end of March and in June 1850 and to the Address of the Central Authority in Cologne dated 1 December 1850 and drawn up by the associates of Marx and Engels, mainly Bürgers. The Address of the Central Authority of March 1850 and that of the Central Authority in Cologne were published in a number of German bourgeois newspapers (see *Kölnische Zeitung*, No. 156, 1 June 1851, *Dresdner Journal und Anzeiger*, No. 177, 28 June 1851, and others).— 143

[177] The reference is to the convention signed in Vienna on 20 May 1852 by the Austrian and Russian emperors and the King of Prussia in connection with the Bonapartist coup d'état in France on 2 December 1851. The signatories agreed to recognise the Bonapartist regime in France on certain conditions, which included the consent of the head of that regime to restrict the claim for power to his own lifetime and not to try to restore the Bonaparte dynasty.— 143

[178] Only a short extract of this letter has survived as quoted by Cluss in his letter to Weydemeyer of 15 October 1852.— 144

179 Marx has in mind the article on political parties in England which he wanted Engels to translate into English. This was in fact Marx's first own contribution to the *New-York Daily Tribune*. Marx wrote his first articles for the *Tribune* in German and sent them to Engels to be translated into English. Sometimes Engels divided a long article into two, which Marx then sent to the newspaper as separate articles. In this case too Engels divided the material received into two parts, which Marx sent to New York on 6 and 10 August entitled respectively: 'The Elections in England.—Tories and Whigs' and 'The Chartists' (see present edition, Vol. 11). From the end of January 1853 Marx himself wrote his articles for the paper in English.— 145

180 Marx expresses his apprehension that Dana would refuse to print the article, because in the presidential election campaign in 1852 the *New-York Daily Tribune* supported the candidature of Scott, a representative of the American Whigs.

The *Whigs*—members of a political party in the USA mainly representing the interests of the industrial and financial bourgeoisie and supported by some of the plantation owners. The party existed under this title from 1834 to 1854. The intensification of the struggle over slavery caused splits and led to regroupings in the ranks of the Whigs. The majority of them, with a section of the Democratic Party and the farmers' party (Free Soilers), formed the Republican Party, which opposed slavery. The rest of the Whigs sided with the Democratic Party, which defended the interests of the slave-owning planters.— 145

181 The series of articles *Revolution and Counter-Revolution in Germany* was published in the *New-York Daily Tribune* over Marx's signature (see Note 5).— 148

182 In the margins of this letter there were vertical lines drawn by Marx at some time which has not been ascertained.— 148, 153, 168

183 Marx learned of these facts from Cluss' letter of 4-5 July 1852.— 149

184 The reference here is to Kossuth's circular of 28 June 1852 which Marx received from Cluss together with a letter of 22 July 1852. In the circular Kossuth urged the German refugees in America, in view of the imminent presidential elections, to demand that the USA should effect an armed interference in order to carry out a revolution in Europe. To expose the adventurist nature of this appeal, Cluss had the circular published in *The New-York Herald*. This was the immediate reason for Kossuth's departure from America on 14 July 1852 as he had officially declared himself a supporter of non-interference in the home affairs of host countries. The circular was also published in *The People's Paper*, No. 14, 7 August in the section 'Foreign News' under the title 'Secret Circular by Kossuth'.— 150, 153, 158

185 The reference is to Kinkel's letter to Huzel of 6 February 1852 (see p. 152).— 151

186 Presidential elections were to be held in France in May 1852 according to the Constitution. The petty-bourgeois democratic emigrant circles hoped that democracy would win in France and Louis Bonaparte would be removed from power because the Constitution stipulated that the outgoing President could not stand for re-election. After the coup d'état of 2 December 1851, however, the question of the President being re-elected practically no longer arose.— 154

[187] About 16 August 1852 Marx sent Engels a long article, which, while being translated, was divided into two ('Corruption at Elections' and 'Result of the Elections'). On their dispatch to New York they were dated 20 and 27 August respectively (see present edition, Vol. 11).— 158

[188] This letter was first published in English abridged in K. Marx, *On America and the Civil War*, McGraw-Hill, New York, 1972. In the margins of the original there were vertical lines drawn by Marx at a time which has not been ascertained.— 159

[189] The reference here is to the separatist organisation formed by the Willich-Schapper adventurist sectarian group after the split in the Communist League (see Note 15).— 160, 162

[190] An allusion to the unsuccessful attempt made in 1846-47 to publish Marx's and Engels' work *The German Ideology* (see present edition, Vol. 5).— 161

[191] This letter of Marx's has not been found.— 161, 183, 185, 254

[192] The reference is to the London committee of *The People's Paper*, set up for financing and distribution of the paper. Its 13 members were Chartists and members of the bourgeois-radical opposition who wanted to use the newspaper in the interests of the latter.— 162, 175

[193] Engels has in mind the second part of the article on the English electoral system written by Marx about 16 August 1852 (see Note 187).— 164

[194] On the instructions of Marx and Engels, Weydemeyer took the manuscript of *The German Ideology* to Westphalia where he failed in his negotiations for its publication with Julius Meyer and Rudolph Rempel, publishers in Bielefeld (see Note 190).— 164

[195] An ironical allusion to the difficulties encountered in publishing the Chartist newspaper, *The Star of Freedom*, edited by Harney. It succeeded *The Northern Star* and ceased publication in November 1852.— 164

[196] A reference to Huzel's letter to Cluss of 20 July 1852 which Cluss sent to Marx and which contained information about Kinkel's preparations for a congress of guarantors in America in the autumn of 1852, and gave a list of European guarantors of the loan.

Huzel had a high opinion of Marx's work, *The Eighteenth Brumaire of Louis Bonaparte*, which he had read thanks to Cluss: 'I am also firmly convinced now that with his philosophy of destruction he will show us many more treasures with which we, despite all the devilish difficulties, can and must conquer the world.— In the *Eighteenth Brumaire* I find the loftiest ideas expressed in the most revolutionary way.'— 166

[197] The reference is to the two documents: 'Entwurf des Unionsvertrags' and 'An das Comité zur Förderung der deutschen Nationalanleihe und an die Garanten dieser Anleihe in Amerika. London. 12. August 1852'. The first contained the terms for a preliminary agreement to amalgamate the American Revolutionary League and the German Emigration Club (see notes 173 and 26).

The second document was an address to the committees and guarantors of the 'German-American revolutionary loan' (see Note 27). Its aim was to secure guarantors' preliminary consent to and approval of the amalgamation of these two organisations, which was to be finally formalised at the congress of the Revolutionary League at Wheeling (West Virginia) on 18 September

1852. On these documents see also this volume, pp. 168-69 and 173.—166, 167

198 The *Holy Grail*—according to a medieval legend, the cup used by Christ at the Last Supper, the object of quests by mythical figures.—166

199 This is Marx's reply to Imandt's letter of 27 August 1852. With it Imandt sent Marx the 'Entwurf des Unionsvertrags' and the circular to the guarantors of the loan (see Note 197) passed on to him by Kinkel and Willich. Enclosed also was a letter from Kinkel and Willich to Imandt of 26 August in which they asked the latter to give his opinion on the above-mentioned documents not later than 2 September 1852.

Imandt took part in the guarantors' congress; on his actions towards the exposure of Kinkel's and Willich's adventurist schemes see this volume, pp. 151-52 and 153-57.—167

200 Marx quotes from 'An das Comité zur Förderung der deutschen Nationalanleihe und an die Garanten dieser Anleihe in Amerika. London. 12. August 1852'.—167

201 The *Friends of Light (Lichtfreunde)*—a religious trend that arose in 1841 and was directed against the pietism predominant in the Lutheran Church and distinguished by extreme mysticism and bigotry.—168, 172

202 Marx learned all these facts from Bangya's letter of 30 August 1852. Bangya, being in the service of the Prussian police, tried by these means to worm his way into Marx's confidence. Marx soon became aware of Bangya's provocative activity and broke off all relations with him (see this volume, pp. 267-70).—169, 177

203 Marx alludes to a passage in the address to the guarantors of the loan issued on 12 August 1852 (see Note 197). In reply to the guarantors' proposal to found a newspaper, the document stated that revolution 'no longer needs the pen but the sword. A newspaper in London is of no use for the revolution'.—170, 174

204 The *Centralisation* was set up in 1836 as the leading executive organ of the Polish Democratic Society which arose in France in 1832 after the suppression of the national liberation insurrection of 1830-31 and united Left-wing Polish emigrants, the small nobility (*szlachta*) and the bourgeoisie. Its programme envisaged restoration of Poland's independence, abolition of the feudal obligations and the inequality of social estates, free transfer of land allotments to peasants, and a number of other progressive measures. In the summer of 1849 the seat of the Centralisation was moved to London.—172

205 The material on Vetter, Mazzini and Kossuth was used by Marx in the article 'Movements of Mazzini and Kossuth.—League with Louis Napoleon.—Palmerston' written for the *New-York Daily Tribune* (see present edition, Vol. 11).—172

206 The only part of this letter that has survived is an extract in Cluss' letter to Weydemeyer of 21 September 1852. Cluss writes: 'Herewith English notes for the *Herald*. Lexow will no doubt attend to them if you din it into him that the rotten elements and buffoons have got to be rendered harmless for the

620 Notes

revolution. The agent mentioned therein is General Vetter, a generalissimo of
the Kossuth-Mazzini army. He vanished from London for a considerable
stretch of time, no one knew where to. He was travelling on a passport in
which he figured as an American painter, and with a singer by the name of
Ferenze (his mistress). She gave concerts in all the important places. The rest
you may read in the English. Vetter has now told the "big-wigs" [i.e. Kossuth]
that, circumstances being what they are, he thinks he can do no better than go
to America with Ferenze. Mazzini *et* Kossuth are said to be resigned to their
fate and to have decided to leave the initiative to the French.—On 14 and 15
September—yet another intrigue conducted by Kinkel behind the backs of the
guarantors in London—the pro-Kinkel guarantors are to hold a meeting in
Antwerp with a view to adopting a congressional resolution that will, it is
hoped, serve as a weapon against the resolution passed by the American and
Swiss guarantors.' After this Cluss quotes fragments from Marx's letter which
are reproduced here in full.

'Notes for the *Herald*' mentioned by Cluss are a version of Marx's article
'Movements of Mazzini and Kossuth.—League with Louis Napoleon.—
Palmerston' sent by Marx to Dana presumably after 5 September 1852. When
publishing it in the *New-York Daily Tribune* the editors dated it 28 September
1852. The editors of the present edition have no information whether this
material was published in *The New-York Herald*.—172

207 Here the fragment from Marx's letter ends and is followed by a sentence which
reveals to some extent the contents of the lost part of Marx's letter: 'Marx has
now received 10 *Brumaires* and a letter from you. He does not complain about
the material damage but solely about that caused him by this troublesome affair
from the political and literary points of view; he says he must now fight his way
through with fibs.' A few lines further Cluss again quotes Marx: 'I also took
notes ... at the section meeting there.'—174

208 Cluss does not say that this paragraph is by Marx, but textually it almost
coincides with Marx's letter to Engels of 30 August 1852 (see this volume, p.
170).—174

209 The plans to have Marx's *Eighteenth Brumaire of Louis Bonaparte* republished in
Germany and published in English did not materialise at that time. The second
edition appeared only in 1869 in Hamburg.—175

210 The only part of this letter that has survived is an extract quoted by Cluss in
his letter to Weydemeyer of 26 March 1853.—176

211 The only part of this letter that has survived is an extract quoted by Cluss in
his letter to Weydemeyer of 28 September 1852.—178

212 In a memorandum entitled 'Drei Jahre in Paris', L. Häfner, a German
petty-bourgeois refugee, gave his opinion of the German émigrés in Paris in
1849-51.—178, 183, 185

213 This letter was published in English in full for the first time in *The Letters of
Karl Marx*, selected and translated with explanatory notes and an introduction
by Saul K. Padover, Prentice-Hall, Inc., Englewood Cliff, New Jersey,
1979.—181, 530, 533

214 Marx did not carry out his intention to write a concluding article to Engels'

Revolution and Counter-Revolution in Germany. The last, twentieth, article of the series did not appear in the *New-York Daily Tribune.* The 1896 English edition and a number of subsequent editions had as the concluding article Engels' 'The Late Trial at Cologne' (see present edition, Vol. 11) which did not belong to this series of articles.—181, 199

215 Marx alludes to a passage in Massol's letter of 25 July 1852. Massol informed Marx that Proudhon had published a book on the coup d'état in France on 2 December 1851 and stressed that Proudhon was only a populariser, while Marx was engaged in a serious analysis of the events: 'Dig, search, keep at it; that is your lot, let French mouths do the vulgarising'.—182

216 The *Manchester archives*—documents of the Communist League, letters and other materials relating to the revolutionary activity of Marx and Engels kept at Engels' house.—183, 198, 245

217 The reference is to the information bulletin *Lithographierte Correspondenz* published by Weydemeyer in New York from August to October 1852.—185

218 Engels has in mind the state of Heinzen's New York newspaper *Janus* which published attacks on the Communist League and carried insinuations against Marx and Engels personally.—185

219 The reference is to the great fuss in the newspapers over Louis Bonaparte's tour of France on 14-16 September 1852, whose purpose was to secure support in the provinces, among the French clergy in particular, for his proclamation as Emperor of France under the title of Napoleon III, which took place on 2 December 1852.—185

220 The *Customs Union* of the German states was set up in 1834 under the aegis of Prussia because of the need to create an all-German market. During the 1848-49 revolution the Customs Union practically ceased to exist, but in 1853 Prussia managed to revive it and it continued to exist up to 1871.
   By the 'Customs Union business' Marx means a conference on the subject which was to be convened in Vienna on 30 October 1852.—186, 195

221 The first part of this letter was first published abridged in *Der Briefwechsel zwischen F. Engels und K. Marx,* Bd. 1, Stuttgart, 1913 and dated 'beginning of September 1852'. The part dealing with the statistics from factory inspector Horner was first published in Marx/Engels, *Gesamtausgabe,* Abt. III, Bd. 1, 1929 and Marx and Engels, *Works,* First Russian Edition, Vol. XXI, Moscow, 1929 as a separate document mistakenly dated 11 March 1853.
   The whole letter, with the verified date, 23 September 1852, and Engels' memorandum on the English translation of the first chapter of Marx's *Eighteenth Brumaire of Louis Bonaparte* made by Wilhelm Pieper, was first published in Marx and Engels, *Works,* Second Russian Edition, Vol. 28, Moscow, 1962.—188

222 Engels alludes to the active preparations being made by Bonapartist circles to proclaim an empire in France (see Note 219).—189

223 These figures were also used by Marx in his article 'Pauperism and Free Trade.—The Approaching Commercial Crisis' (see present edition, Vol. 11) written on 12 October 1852 for the *New-York Daily Tribune.*—189

224 *Sturm und Drang (Storm and Stress)*—a literary trend in Germany in the 1780s.—192

[225] Marx received Zerffi's let er at the end of August 1852 and used the facts it contained in the article 'Movements of Mazzini and Kossuth.—League with Louis Napoleon.—Palmerston' (see Note 206).—194

[226] The *Volksverein*—an organisation set up in London on 11 August 1852 in a new attempt to amalgamate various groups of German refugees whose representatives concluded the 'Entwurf des Unionsvertrags' (see Note 197). The agreement was signed by Goegg on behalf of the Revolutionary League in America, and by Kinkel and Willich as members of the managing committee of the so-called German-American revolutionary loan (see notes 173 and 27). The aim of the *Volksverein* was to attract Englishmen as well as German refugees. However, owing to its adventurism and to persisting discord among the petty-bourgeois emigrants, the *Volksverein* was as short-lived as other such emigrant organisations before it.—194

[227] Two religious opposition movements, the so-called *German-Catholicism,* and the Protestant *'free communities',* appeared in the 1840s. They sought to establish an all-German national church and rejected the supremacy of the Pope and many dogmas and rites of the Roman Catholic Church. They expressed the German bourgeoisie's discontent with the reactionary system in Germany and its striving to unify the country politically. In 1850 the German-Catholics merged with the 'free communities'.—194, 267

[228] The reference is to Louis Bonaparte's tour of France (see Note 219). Zerffi's letter to Marx of 22 September 1852 contained, in particular, details about his reception in Lyons.—195

[229] Marx ironically calls Bürgers' manuscript 'Das Wesen des Kommunismus', a pun on Feuerbach's *Das Wesen des Christenthums.*—195

[230] *Honi soit qui mal y pense* (Shame be on him who evil thinks)—the motto of the Order of the Garter instituted by Edward III of England in 1350.—195

[231] In view of the financial difficulties of *The People's Paper* the bourgeois members of its London committee (see Note 192) tried to obtain control over it and to hinder further development of the revolutionary proletarian tendency which Jones was following more and more thanks to Marx's active assistance. On 15 and 21 September Jones' opponents held two Chartist meetings at which they attempted to substantiate their accusations against Jones. However both meetings expressed confidence in Jones and the Executive of the National Charter Association.—195

[232] Harney failed in his attempt to create a 'united national party' in England in the autumn of 1852 in order to campaign for general suffrage at the cost of repudiating the other five points of the People's Charter and the social demands of the Chartists.—196

[233] An allusion to the behaviour of the French philistines during Louis Bonaparte's tour of the country (see Note 219).—196

[234] An abridged translation of this letter was first published in *The Letters of Karl Marx,* selected and translated with explanatory notes and an introduction by Saul K. Padover, Prentice-Hall, Inc., Englewood Cliff, New Jersey, 1979.—198, 298, 438, 445, 453, 500, 526

[235] On Herzen's relations with Herwegh see A. I. Herzen, *My Past and Thoughts,* Part V ['Story of the Family Drama'].—199

236 Marx made use of the facts he learned from Zerffi's letter of 5 September 1852 in writing the article 'Movements of Mazzini and Kossuth.—League with Louis Napoleon.—Palmerston' (see present edition, Vol. 11).—200

237 Engels' letter to Dronke has not been found.—204

238 The reference is to Kinkel's escape from prison (see Note 54).—206

239 Wiss' statement is quoted in Marx's and Engels' *The Great Men of the Exile* (see present edition, Vol. 11, p. 303).—206

240 On Marx's request, Cluss sent to *The Morning Advertiser* on 1 November 1852 his reply to the article 'The German "Lone Star"', in which he criticised the activity of the American Revolutionary League (see Note 173), headed by Goegg, Ruge's supporter. The editors refused to publish it.—207

241 Massol's letter to Marx of 25 July (see Note 215).—207

242 Weydemeyer's article against Heinzen was published in the *New-Yorker Demokrat* on 29 January 1852, that of Cluss, 'Karl Heinzen und der Kommunismus, oder der fahrende Ritter auf der wilden, verwegenden Jagd nach dem Schatten seines lahmen Kleppers', in the same newspaper at the end of June-beginning of July 1852.—207

243 *Pièce Taschereau* (the Taschereau document) was fabricated by the French police after the February 1848 revolution in order to discredit Blanqui. It was published on 31 March 1848 in the bourgeois journal *La Revue rétrospective* edited by Taschereau.—209

244 The *Athenaeum* —the name of the clubs which existed in a number of cities in England, including London and Manchester, and frequented by men of letters and scientists.—209, 233, 241, 293, 554

245 The Congress of the American Revolutionary League (see Note 173) was held in Wheeling, West Virginia, USA, in September 1852.—210, 267

246 The article written by Marx on 12 October 1852 for the *New-York Daily Tribune* was translated by Engels into English and sent by Marx to New York on 15 and 19 October as two articles: 'Pauperism and Free Trade.—The Approaching Commercial Crisis' and 'Political Consequences of the Commercial Excitement' (see present edition, Vol. 11).—210

247 Marx and Engels attacked *The Times* and *The Daily News* for supporting the Prussian reactionaries on the issue of the Cologne Communist Trial (see Note 16) in their 'Public Statement to the Editors of the English Press' written on 28 October 1852 (see present edition, Vol. 11).—210

248 The reference is to the interrogation of Bürgers on 9 and 10 October 1852 during the Cologne Communist Trial.—211

249 An allusion to the article on the political parties in England written by Marx on 16 October 1852. Engels translated it into English and Marx sent it to New York as two articles on 2 and 9 November. The first one was published in the *New-York Daily Tribune* on 29 November under the title 'Political Parties and Prospects', the second on 25 November without any title (see present edition, Vol. 11; the title 'Attempts to Form a New Opposition Party' was supplied by the editors of the present edition).—212

250 The reference is presumably to Cluss' article in the *Baltimore Wecker* in which he mentioned false accusations of spying brought against Mrs Brüningk by Kinkel and Willich (see this volume, p. 152).—214, 574

251 Here Engels refers to the attempt of the police agent Stieber, a witness for the prosecution at the Cologne trial on 18 October 1852, to ascribe to the Communist League participation in the so-called Franco-German plot (see Note 143).—215

252 Haupt, a former member of the Communist League, was arrested at the time of the Cologne Communist Trial and gave false evidence during the investigation. The police released him before the trial and he escaped to Brazil. His evidence, damaging to the accused, was cited in Seckendorf's speech for the prosecution on 3 November 1852.—215

253 The translation into English of Marx's article written on 16 October 1852 (see Note 249).—215

254 For details on the arrest of Kothes and Bermbach see Marx's *Revelations Concerning the Communist Trial in Cologne* (present edition, Vol. 11).—216

255 On Engels' advice (see this volume, pp. 208-09), Marx tried through Weerth to get information from the bookseller Duncker about a certain Eisenmann with whom Bangya had allegedly negotiated the publication of Marx's and Engels' pamphlet, *The Great Men of the Exile.*—216

256 Marx's letter to lawyer Schneider II of 26 October 1852 has not been found.—217

257 Engels' letter to Marx of 26 October 1852 has not been found.—218

258 Engels refers to Marx's letter to Schneider II of 26 October 1852 which contained Stieber's evidence (see Marx's letter to Engels of 26 October 1852). Engels sent two copies of it by messengers to Cologne on 27 October: the original in Marx's hand care of Braubach Bros and a copy care of Johann Philipp Becker. Marx himself sent the third and fourth copies, addressed to Hermann Ebner and Georg Gottlob Jung, from London. This is proved by a list of documents dispatched to Cologne during the Communist Trial drawn up by Engels on about 31 October 1852 (see present edition, Vol. 11).—218

259 At the Cologne trial on 23 October 1852 Stieber presented in evidence against the accused the so-called Original Minute-book of the meetings of the Communist League Central Authority, alleged to have been formed again by Marx in London after the arrests in Cologne. According to Stieber's false evidence, the Minute-book was compiled by Rings and Liebknecht. In reality it was fabricated by the spy Wilhelm Hirsch, exposed by and expelled from the Communist League about 19 February 1852. Because of his expulsion it was decided to change the place and day of the weekly meetings of the London District members of the Communist League. Hirsch did not know about this and continued to date the fabricated minutes Thursday, whereas the meetings were then held on Wednesdays. By sending samples of Hirsch's and later Rings' and Liebknecht's handwriting to Cologne, Engels wanted to provide counsel for the defence with documents which would expose the actual author of the 'Original Minute-book'. Thanks to the material supplied by Marx and Engels the police fabrications were exposed and the 'Original Minute-book' was rejected as evidence for the prosecution (see present edition, Vol. 11).—218, 223

260 The 'Original Minute-book' (see Note 259) presented by Stieber to the jury mentioned letters allegedly written to Marx by Mrs Daniels, the wife of one of the accused. On 25 October 1852, the *Kölnische Zeitung*, No. 273, published a statement made by King's Counsel Müller, father of Mrs Daniels, denying that Mrs Daniels had corresponded with Marx and declaring Stieber's 'Original Minute-book' a 'mystification'.—219, 301

261 The reference is to *Revelations Concerning the Communist Trial in Cologne* (see present edition, Vol. 11). Marx began writing the pamphlet at the end of October 1852, when the trial of the Communist League members was still in progress in Cologne, and completed it in early December. On 6 December a copy of the manuscript was sent to the publisher Schabelitz junior in Switzerland, and on the following day a second copy was dispatched to Cluss in the USA. The pamphlet was published in Basle in January 1853, but almost the whole edition (2,000 copies) was confiscated by the police in March in the Baden frontier village of Weill on the way to Germany. In the USA the work was first published in instalments in the democratic Boston *Neu-England-Zeitung* and at the end of April 1853 it was printed as a separate pamphlet by the same publishers.—220

262 An allusion to the campaign in French government circles for the proclamation of an empire (see Note 219).—221

263 In the list of documents dispatched to Cologne during the Communist Trial this letter of Marx, which has not been found, is dated Monday, 25 October 1852 (see present edition, Vol. 11, p. 590).—222

264 This is presumably a slip of the pen, for in *Revelations Concerning the Communist Trial in Cologne*, Chapter III, 'The Cherval Plot' (present edition, Vol. 11, p. 413), it is said that Cherval was admitted to the League of the Just in 1846, i.e. before it was reorganised into the Communit League in June 1847.—222

265 This material was used by the lawyer Schneider II in his speech at the trial on 4 November 1852 and later by Marx in the pamphlet *Revelations Concerning the Communist Trial in Cologne* (see present edition, Vol. 11, pp. 413, 417 and 418).—222

266 The reference is to Marx's correspondence with Hermann Becker concerning the publication of Marx's works. Negotiations to that effect started in December 1850 and resulted in the publication of the first issue of *Gesammelte Aufsätze von Karl Marx* in Cologne at the end of April 1851. It contained the article 'Comments on the Latest Prussian Censorship Instruction' and part of the first article from 'Proceedings of the Sixth Rhine Province Assembly' written by Marx in 1842 (see present edition, Vol. 1). Publication was discontinued following Becker's arrest.—222

267 Roland Daniels sent his manuscript 'Mikrokosmos. Entwurf einer physiologischen Anthropologie' from Cologne in mid-February 1851 for Marx to review it. In his letter to Daniels of 20 March (it has not been found) Marx expressed his opinion of the manuscript. Daniels' work remained unpublished because of his arrest in June 1851 in connection with the Cologne Communist Trial.—222

268 Marx has in mind the minutes which Hirsch kept in the Workers' Society presided over by Stechan, a refugee from Hanover (see Note 25).—222

269 Stieber's letter to Marx of 26 December 1848, which Marx quotes below.—222

270 Marx's letter to Schneider II of 26 October 1852 (see Note 256).—223

271 This excerpt from Becker's letter to Marx of 27 January 1851 is quoted by Marx in *Revelations Concerning the Communist Trial in Cologne* (see present edition, Vol. 11, p. 452).—224

272 Marx's letter to Bermbach has not been found.—224

273 *Van Diemen's Land*—the name initially given by Europeans to the island of Tasmania, which was a British penal colony up to 1853.—224

274 The reference is to the duel between Barthélemy and the French refugee Cournet about 25 October 1852 in which the latter was killed. Barthélemy was sentenced to two months' imprisonment.—224, 295

275 This letter of Stieber's was used by the lawyer Schneider II in his speech at the trial on 4 November 1852 to expose Stieber's past spying activity; Marx quoted this letter in full in *Revelations Concerning the Communist Trial in Cologne* (see present edition, Vol. 11, pp. 435-36).—226

276 The separatist Central Authority was set up by the Willich-Schapper group after the split in the Communist League in September 1850 (see Note 15).—226

277 This refers to the *Social-Democratic Committee of Support for German Refugees* formed at the German Workers' Educational Society in London on 18 September 1849. The Committee included Karl Marx, Heinrich Bauer, Karl Pfänder, Karl Blind, Anton Füster and Frederick Engels (from 3 December 1849). In mid-September 1850 Marx and Engels withdrew from the Refugee Committee because the majority of its members had come under the influence of the Willich-Schapper group.—227

278 Here Marx ironically writes about Stieber's attempt, in his evidence on 18 October 1852, to reduce the disagreements existing between the supporters of Marx and Engels and the Willich-Schapper group to the question of personal rivalry. He ascribed to Marx an aspiration to become a dictator of Germany after a future revolution and to appoint his associates and friends ministers.—227

279 In this connection see K. Marx, *Revelations Concerning the Communist Trial in Cologne* (present edition, Vol. 11, pp. 422-23). In his speech on 4 November 1852 Schneider II exposed Stieber's falsification of facts connected with the confiscation of Marx's letter to Kothes.—228

280 Engels' letter to von Hontheim of 30 October 1852 has not been found.—231

281 The *Red Catechism (Rother Katechismus für das deutsche Volk)* and the letter accompanying it were written by Moses Hess who supported the Willich-Schapper group. The letter was faked by imitating Marx's handwriting. Marx exposed this forgery in a statement sent to the editor of *The Morning Advertiser* and published in that newspaper on 2 November (see present edition, Vol. 11, pp. 380-81). Schneider II's intention to read this statement of Marx at the trial on 4 November drew a protest from the prosecution, but they were forced to give up the idea of using 'the accompanying letter' against the accused (see also K. Marx, *Revelations Concerning the Communist Trial in Cologne*, present edition, Vol. 11, pp. 443-45).—232

282 On Engels' advice, Marx gave evidence on the points listed above, had it certified and sent to Cologne where it was used at the trial by Schneider II.—232

283 This refers to Dronke's letter to Engels of 30 October 1852 in which he warned against Bangya's suspicious behaviour.—232

284 On 21 October 1852 Duncker wrote to Weerth that there was no publisher by the name of Eisenmann (see Note 255).

  Kothes was arrested because the police had intercepted a letter which Marx sent to his address to be delivered to Bermbach (on this see *Revelations Concerning the Communist Trial in Cologne*, present edition, Vol. 11, pp. 422-24).—232

285 Engels' letter to Strohn of 31 October 1852 has not been found.—234

286 The list of documents drawn up by Engels is published in the present edition, Vol. 11, pp. 590-91.—234

287 The reference is to the accompanying letter to the *Red Catechism* (see Note 281).—236

288 The reference is to a letter of 28 October 1852 composed by Bangya in the name of Charles Collmann, a publisher invented by him, concerning the preparations made for publishing Marx's and Engels' manuscript *The Great Men of the Exile*. The letter was not written on a publishers' notepaper and had no post marks. It contained Bangya's note dated 3 November 1852 asking Marx to acquaint himself with Collmann's letter.—237, 239

289 The reference is to Bürgers' trip from Cologne to Hanover, Hamburg, Berlin, Breslau and Dresden made in May 1851 on an assignment from the Cologne Central Authority. The prosecution tried to present Bürgers' trip and his participation in drawing up the Manifesto of the Cologne Central Authority of the Communist League, and also Nothjung's journey to Leipzig in May 1851 mentioned below, as proof of their involvement in a communist plot.—238

290 The *Crystal Palace* was built of metal and glass for the first world trade and industrial exhibition in London in 1851.—238

291 After the 'Original Minute-book' was exposed at the trial as a forgery (see Note 259), Stieber sent police lieutenant Goldheim to London. On his return Goldheim stated at the trial on 3 November 1852 that the book mentioned was not 'a minute-book', but a 'notebook', and that it was actually sold by H. Liebknecht, alleged to be the compiler of the minutes, to the Prussian agent Fleury and contained notes on communists' secret meetings at Marx's house. Goldheim asserted that he had seen a cash receipt in Liebknecht's own handwriting. He also spoke of a 'top secret meeting' at Marx's on 27 October 1852 in connection with the Cologne trial. On 4 November 1852 lawyer Schneider II proved that this evidence for the prosecution was also false. On this see *Revelations Concerning the Communist Trial in Cologne* (present edition, Vol. 11, pp. 429-35 and 438-39).—240, 242

292 Marx was in Manchester in May-June 1852.—241

293 The meeting in memory of Robert Blum in London on 9 November 1852 was organised by Arnold Ruge and his associates. Speeches were made by Ruge, Tausenau, Ronge and other bourgeois radicals and democrats.—241, 246

294 Marx learned about this from lawyer Schneider II's letter of 1 November 1852.—242

295 On Bangya's provocative role in the matter of publishing Marx's and Engels' pamphlet *The Great Men of the Exile* see Marx's article 'Hirsch's Confessions' (present edition, Vol. 12).

    The second part of the pamphlet (see Note 131) was probably not written, though the last lines of this work contain a definite hint that the account of German petty-bourgeois refugees' activities will be continued. Marx's pamphlet *Herr Vogt*, Chapter XII: 'Appendices', Section 6 'The War between Frogs and Mice' contains material on the activity of petty-bourgeois refugee organisations in 1852 (see present edition, Vol. 17, pp. 313-15).—242

296 Fleury's statement proving the falseness of Goldheim's evidence was not published in the *Kölnische Zeitung*. Counsel for the defence got possession of it after the trial. Marx quoted it in *Revelations Concerning the Communist Trial in Cologne* (see present edition, Vol. 11, p. 442).—243

297 Marx wrote this statement on 21 October 1852; the text has not survived. Marx explains in *Revelations Concerning the Communist Trial in Cologne* why the German newspapers refused to publish it (see present edition, Vol. 11, p. 436).—244

298 Marx gives these facts in *Revelations Concerning the Communist Trial in Cologne* (present edition, Vol. 11, pp. 442 and 451-52). Additional information about Hirsch's contacts with the Prussian police agents Greif and Fleury, and the role of the Prussian Embassy in London during the Cologne trial, is to be found in *Herr Vogt*, 'Appendices', Section 4 'The Communist Trial in Cologne' (see present edition, Vol. 17).—245

299 The reference is to the publication in October 1852 of a lithographed statement of accounts and of a statement by Reichenbach who was the treasurer of the so-called German-American revolutionary loan (see Note 27). Reichenbach refused to be in charge of the funds because the idea of the revolutionary loan did not justify itself. Later Marx quoted extracts from Reichenbach's statement in *Herr Vogt*, 'Appendices', Section 6 'The War between Frogs and Mice' (see present edition, Vol. 17, p. 314).—245, 246, 275, 282, 302

300 On Engels' advice Marx wrote to the Frankfurt journalist Ebner asking him whether it would be possible to publish the pamphlet on the Cologne Communist Trial there (see this volume, pp. 238-39 and Note 122). Marx's letter to Ebner has not been found.—245

301 The '*Friends of Italy*'—an organisation founded in London in May 1851 by the English bourgeois radicals on Mazzini's initiative in order to interest the English public in Italy's national liberation.—246

302 Only the author's copy of this letter has survived in Marx's notebook for 1860 among material relating to his work on *Herr Vogt*.—247

303 Marx sent the German original of the statement to Cluss in America on 18 November 1852. Marx's letter has not been found. The statement dated 18 November 1852 was published in the *New-Yorker Criminal-Zeitung*, No. 39, 10 December 1852. Its text differed from the English version edited by Engels at Marx's request and published in English papers, dated 20 November 1852.—247

304 The appeal to German workers in America was written by Marx on behalf of a committee founded in London to organise aid to the communists accused in Cologne. It was signed by the members of the recently disbanded Communist

League who were resident in London—Karl Marx, Frederick Engels, Wilhelm Wolff, Ferdinand Freiligrath, Ernst Dronke, Wilhelm Liebknecht and other German refugees, and also by Ernest Jones. The appeal was sent to Cluss on 7 December 1852 and published in American German-language newspapers (see present edition, Vol. 11).—247

305 *Little Germany*—a name given ironically by Engels to a district in Manchester where German refugees lived.—249

306 The New York printer withheld copies of Marx's *The Eighteenth Brumaire of Louis Bonaparte* (see this volume, p. 160).—251

307 After the 1830 revolution in France, the opposition movement of the so-called demagogues (see Note 139) became more intense in Germany. This caused new police repressions and arrests and increased emigration, especially after an attempt had been made to effect a coup d'état in Frankfurt am Main on 3 April 1833 with the aim of establishing a republic.—251

308 Marx analysed Disraeli's budget in 'Parliament.—Vote of November 26.—Disraeli's Budget' written on 10 December 1852 (see present edition, Vol. 11).—253

309 The reference is to the so-called Franco-German *plot* (see Note 143) inspired to a great extent by Cherval, an agent of the Prussian and French police. On this see Marx's *Revelations Concerning the Communist Trial in Cologne*, present edition, Vol. 11, pp. 407-20.—255

310 Facts proving Bangya's provocative role in the matter of publishing Marx's and Engels' manuscript *The Great Men of the Exile* were cited by Marx in the article 'Hirsch's Confessions' (see present edition, Vol. 12).—256

311 In a letter to Bangya of 28 October 1852 the fictitious publisher Collmann (see Note 288) expressed readiness, for the authors' reassurance, to place the manuscript at their disposal for 48 hours.—257, 258

312 After the Bonapartist coup d'état of 2 December 1851 intensive preparations were made to proclaim France an empire. On 21 and 22 November 1852 a referendum was held on the issue: on 2 December France was officially proclaimed an empire, and the Prince President Louis Napoleon became Emperor Napoleon III. In the period preceding the proclamation of the empire numerous decrees concerning, among other things, the economy and finance were promulgated. Here Marx has in mind two decrees of 18 November 1852: on the foundation of the Société générale du Crédit mobilier and on the handing over of several railways to the Compagnie du chemin de fer de Lyon à Avignon founded on 8 July 1852 (both decrees were published in *Le Moniteur universel*, No. 325, 20 November 1852). The Crédit mobilier became a big joint-stock bank which acted as intermediary in credit and stockjobbing operations and took part in building railways in France and other European countries.—257, 263

313 Engels went to London in the second half of December 1852 and stayed there until 10 January 1853.—257, 271, 304

314 The original of this letter has not survived. It is quoted in Cluss' letter to Weydemeyer of 6-7 January 1853.
    This letter was published in English in part in K. Marx and F. Engels, *Letters to the Americans. 1848-1895*, International Publishers, New York, 1953.—259

315 On the publication of Marx's *Revelations Concerning the Communist Trial in Cologne* see Note 261.—259

316 A reference to the world trade and industrial exhibition in London (see Note 37).—260

317 In a letter to Marx of 21 November 1852 Cluss expressed doubt whether Massol was right in alleging that Proudhon had taken a revolutionary stand in his new works in contrast to those of the 1840s (Massol's letter of 25 July 1852 was sent to Cluss by Marx for information). Cluss' opinion was shared by Weydemeyer.—260

318 *Free Soilers*—members of a mass radical-democratic party of US farmers in the 1840s and 1850s; it merged with the Republican Party when the latter was formed in 1854.—262

319 *Mormons*—members of a religious sect founded in the USA in the 1830s.—262

320 This presumably refers to Marx's contacts with petty-bourgeois circles of French refugees in London.
    Frères et amis—a form of address used in official documents and public speeches at the time of the French Revolution. Later, royalists used it in referring to republicans.—263

321 The original of this letter has not survived. The text is given according to Cluss' letter to Weydemeyer of 6-7 January 1853.—265

322 Marx's letter to Brüningk has not survived.—265

323 The reference is to the publication of Reichenbach's accounts and statement (see Note 299).—266

324 Marx spoke of these facts in *Revelations Concerning the Communist Trial in Cologne* and 'Hirsch's Confessions' (see present edition, vols. 11 and 12).—267

325 News from Schabelitz (see this volume, p. 264) led Marx to believe that *Revelations Concerning the Communist Trial in Cologne* had already been published in Basle. On how matters stood as regards this publication see Note 261.—270

326 Steps to publish Marx's *The Eighteenth Brumaire of Louis Bonaparte* in Switzerland failed.—270

327 See present edition, Vol. 11, pp. 417-18.—270

328 In the letter mentioned here Dana informed Marx that he would pay £ 1 for each article, but promised double pay for articles on vital problems of current politics.—273

329 The original of Marx's letter has not been found. This fragment is reproduced as quoted in Cluss' letter to Weydemeyer of 17 February 1853.—273

330 '*Communia*'—a colony founded by Weitling's associates in Iowa (USA) in 1849 to put in practice the principles of Weitling's utopian communism. The colony ceased to exist in 1853 owing to inner conflicts and financial difficulties.—275, 450

331 At the beginning of 1853 the German liberal historian Professor Gervinus was brought to trial on a charge of incitement to high treason and an attempted breach of the peace in publishing *Einleitung in die Geschichte des 19. Jahrhunderts,*

a book which reactionary circles considered an apology for the democratic system and a criticism of monarchy.—276

332 The international Peace Congress was convened by the bourgeois pacifist organisation, Peace Society, in Manchester at the end of January 1853. Free Traders were especially active at it. The Congress adopted a number of resolutions against anti-French military propaganda in England and against the increase of armaments.

Cobden's pamphlet is assessed and the Peace Congress described in Marx's article 'Capital Punishment.—Mr. Cobden's Pamphlet.—Regulations of the Bank of England' (see present edition, Vol. 11).—276

333 The reference is to the armed conflict between Turkey and Montenegro which was a vassal possession of the Sultan and sought full independence. In early 1853 Turkish troops invaded Montenegro, but the stance adopted by Russia and pressure from Austria soon compelled the Sultan to withdraw them.—277, 278, 288

334 Marx made this rough note in English on J. G. Mayer's letter of 3 February 1853. Marx used the pseudonym Charles Williams when he sent his letters to Szemere in Paris c/o Mayer.—277

335 A reference to the Milan insurrection started on 6 February 1853 by the followers of the Italian revolutionary Mazzini and supported by Hungarian revolutionary refugees. The aim of the insurgents, who were mostly Italian workers, was to overthrow Austrian rule. The insurrection was badly organised and was soon suppressed. Marx analysed it in a number of articles (see present edition, Vol. 11, pp. 508-09, 513-16, 532 and 535-37).—278, 283, 307

336 *Bellinzona*—an administrative town in the Swiss canton of Tessin (Ticino). In the main cities of this canton, a centre of Italian emigration in the nineteenth century, there were print-shops where the supporters of Italy's national liberation had their literature printed.—278

337 Kossuth, who after the defeat of the Hungarian revolutionary army crossed into territory dependent on Turkey and was interned in the fortress of Vidin (Bulgaria), appealed to the insurgents still in the fortress of Komarom on 2 October 1849 to continue the struggle promising speedy support from Britain. However, the Hungarian insurgents had already accepted Austrian terms of capitulation.—279

338 This letter was published in English for the first time, considerably abridged, in Karl Marx and Friedrich Engels, *Correspondence. 1846-1895. A Selection with Commentary and Notes*, Martin Lawrence Ltd., London, 1934.—280, 344

339 Here Marx refers to a letter from Kossuth to Mayne Reid intended for the press. Mayne Reid published a statement in a number of English newspapers (see, e.g., 'M. M. Kossuth and Mazzini and *The Times*', *The Daily News*, No. 2105, 18 February 1853) asserting on behalf of Kossuth that the latter did not take part in the Milan insurrection (see Note 335) and declaring that the address 'In the Name of the Hungarian Nation.—To the Soldiers Quartered in Italy' circulated over Kossuth's signature during the insurrection was a forgery.—280

340 Marx quotes this statement of Della Rocco in the article 'The Attack on Francis Joseph.—The Milan Riot—British Politics.—Disraeli's Speech.—Napoleon's Will' (see present edition, Vol. 11, p. 515).—281

341 Marx has in mind here the English workers' movement for observance by the manufacturers of the Ten Hours' Bill adopted by Parliament in 1847, for its application to all categories of workers and for the repeal of the 1850 law, which despite the 1847 Bill established a $10^1/_2$-hour working day. Marx analyses this movement in 'Parliamentary Debates.—The Clergy Against Socialism.—Starvation' (see present edition, Vol. 11).—282

342 Marx refers to the speech made by John Russell, leader of the Whig Party and member of the Aberdeen Coalition Government, at the opening of Parliament on 10 February 1853. Marx analysed this speech in 'The Italian Insurrection.— British Politics' (see present edition, Vol. 11).—282

343 A reference to John Aberdeen's Coalition Ministry of 1852-55 (the Cabinet of All the Talents), which consisted of Whigs, Peelites and representatives of the Irish faction. Marx described this Ministry in 'A Superannuated Administration.—Prospects of the Coalition Ministry, &c.' (see present edition, Vol. 11).—284

344 A reference to questions in Parliament in connection with rumours that the reactionary governments of the continental powers, Austria in the first place, intended to demand that the British Government should deport political refugees, Mazzini and Kossuth in particular. On 1 March 1853 Palmerston denied in the House of Commons that such demands had been made and declared that, should they be made, the British Government would categorically reject them. However, on 4 March, Aberdeen, head of the Cabinet, stated in the House of Lords that the government was ready to take proceedings against the refugees.—284

345 In June 1850 the British Parliament debated the Anglo-Greek conflict over the so-called Pacifico incident. The house in Athens of this Portuguese merchant, a British subject, was burnt in 1847 and this served as a pretext for Palmerston to send ships to the Greek coast and present an ultimatum to the Greek Government.—284, 455

346 The *debate on the Address* took place at the opening of Parliament in 1850. The usual procedure of drawing up a reply to the Speech from the Throne was used as a pretext for a comprehensive criticism of Russell's Whig Government, of which Palmerston was a member.—284

347 On 3 March 1853 the radical Hume moved in the House of Commons that all tariffs which were in the slightest degree protectionist should be annulled. Marx expressed his opinion on Hume's motion and on Gladstone's and other Cabinet members' attitude to the question in 'Achievements of the Ministry' (see present edition, Vol. 12).—284

348 *Philhellene*—here non-Greek supporter of Greek independence in 1821-29.— 284

349 Engels revealed the essence of the dispute on the Eastern Question between *The Times* and *The Daily News* and described Urquhart's views in 'The Turkish Question' (see present edition, Vol. 12).—286

350 A reference to the trade agreement concluded between Prussia and Austria on 19 February 1853. Marx analysed it in 'Kossuth and Mazzini.—Intrigues of the Prussian Government.—Austro-Prussian Commercial Treaty.—*The Times* and the Refugees' (see present edition, Vol. 11, pp. 537-38).—286

351 Marx has in mind his articles for the *New-York Daily Tribune*: 1. 'Capital

Punishment.—Mr. Cobden's Pamphlet.—Regulations of the Bank of England' (28 January); 2. 'Defense.—Finances.—Decrease of the Aristocracy.—Politics' (8 February); 3. 'The Italian Insurrection.—British Politics' (11 February); 4. 'The Attack on Francis Joseph.—The Milan Riot.—British Politics.—Disraeli's Speech.—Napoleon's Will' (22 February); 5. 'Parliamentary Debates.—The Clergy Against Socialism.—Starvation' (25 February); 6. article of 1 March with additional information about the attack on Francis Joseph and about Kossuth (presumably not published by the newspaper); 7. 'Forced Emigration.—Kossuth and Mazzini.—The Refugee Question.—Election Bribery in England.—Mr. Cobden' (4 March). The article 'Kossuth and Mazzini.—Intrigues of the Prussian Government.—Austro-Prussian Commercial Treaty.—*The Times* and the Refugees', which Marx planned to send off on 11 March, was presumably written between 12 and 18 March and published on 4 April 1853 (see present edition, Vol. 11).—288

352 A reference to articles by Aurelius Ferenc Pulszky, a Hungarian journalist and supporter of Kossuth. As an émigré in London he contributed to the *New-York Daily Tribune* from 1853 to 1860. He signed his articles 'A. P. C.', presumably an abbreviation for Aurelius Pulszky's Correspondence. Marx did not learn about Pulszky's contribution to the *New-York Daily Tribune* until several years later.—288

353 The *entente cordiale*—an expression used to denote the rapprochement between France and Britain after the July 1830 revolution.

The *Holy Alliance*—an association of European monarchs founded in 1815 to suppress revolutionary movements and preserve feudal monarchies in European countries. The Holy Alliance, in which the main role was played by Russia, Austria and Prussia, was dissolved in the late 1820s, but after the 1830 and 1848-49 revolutions attempts were made to resurrect it.—289

354 In compliance with Marx's request Engels wrote for the *New-York Daily Tribune* between 12 March and early April 1853: 'British Politics.—Disraeli.—The Refugees.—Mazzini in London.—Turkey' (jointly with Marx), 'The Real Issue in Turkey', 'The Turkish Question' and 'What Is to Become of Turkey in Europe?' (see present edition, Vol. 12).—289

355 An allusion to Countess Sophie Hatzfeldt's divorce case. Lassalle was in charge of it from 1846 to 1854 and, after the divorce had been granted by the court in July 1851, tried in particular to secure for the Countess her share of the common property of the former couple.—293, 478

356 Engels used this information in the article for the *New-York Daily Tribune* 'The Real Issue in Turkey' (see present edition, Vol. 12).—295

357 A reference to the *Canada Clergy Reserves* founded in 1791-1840, which consisted of a seventh of the revenue from the sale of lands in Canada and were used chiefly to subsidise the Established and Presbytarian churches. The discontent of other churches with such a distribution of funds compelled the British Parliament to pass a law in 1853 authorising the Canadian legislative bodies to distribute these funds among the different churches according to the proportion of the population professing their respective beliefs. Marx described this Bill and the debate on it in the House of Commons in 'Achievements of the Ministry' (see present edition, Vol. 12).—295

358 This letter is a reply to Cluss' letter of 6 March 1853. The unanswered letters were presumably written on 25 February and 2 March 1853.—298

[359] Marx has in mind the publication of *Revelations Concerning the Communist Trial in Cologne* in the *Neu-England-Zeitung* by Cluss in the USA (see Note 261). For this Cluss used a second copy of the manuscript sent by Marx to New York on 7 December 1852. The newspaper published only three fragments on 6 March, 2 and 28 April 1853.—298

[360] Barthélemy was Willich's second during the latter's duel with Schramm in Ostend in September 1850. See Marx's *The Knight of the Noble Consciousness* (present edition, Vol. 12, pp. 492-95).—299

[361] Cluss' letter to Marx of 24 March 1853.—301

[362] A reference to a no-longer-existing letter to Bangya which Marx presumably wrote in Manchester during the period from the end of May to the second half of June 1852 while he and Engels were working on *The Great Men of the Exile.*—301

[363] An allusion to Harvey Birch, the main character in Fenimore Cooper's novel *The Spy.*—301

[364] Hirsch asserted in his confessions that the documents of the Willich-Schapper group had been stolen not by Reuter, as was pointed out by Marx and Engels, but by Fleury (see, in particular, present edition, Vol. 11, pp. 390 and 406, and this volume, pp. 226-27).—302

[365] On the publication of *Revelations Concerning the Communist Trial in Cologne* in the *Neu-England-Zeitung,* see notes 261 and 359.—302

[366] Engels' letter to Marx of 8 April 1853 has not been found.—303

[367] Jomini's best known works on the Napoleonic wars are: *Histoire critique et militaire des guerres de la Révolution de 1792 à 1801,* t. 1-15, Paris, 1819-24; *Vie politique et militaire de Napoléon, racontée par lui-même au tribunal de César, d'Alexandre et de Frédéric,* t. 1-4, Paris, 1827. The first edition of Clausewitz's works, *Hinterlassene Werke über Krieg und Kriegführung,* was published in ten volumes in Berlin in 1832-37. The Napoleonic wars were dealt with in works in volumes 5-8.—305

[368] In February 1846, when an attempt was made to start a revolt in the Polish lands to secure the national liberation of Poland and the insurgents managed to win a temporary victory in Cracow, the Galician peasants also rose in revolt. The oppressed Ukrainian peasants hated the Polish szlachta, and the Austrian authorities succeeded in several places in turning the rebellious peasants against the Polish insurgents. After the suppression of the Cracow revolt, the Galician peasants were also crushed.—306

[369] A reference to the Russell Whig Cabinet (July 1846-February 1852), the Derby Tory Cabinet which replaced it (and was in power till December 1852) and the Aberdeen Coalition Cabinet (see Note 343).—306

[370] In the early 1850s the struggle between Prussia and Austria for supremacy in Germany again became acute: in particular, Austria, with the support of Russia, hampered Prussia's attempts to restore the Customs Union (see Note 220). After the coup d'état in France in December 1851 a new war threatened Europe because Bonapartist circles wished to restore the frontiers of the First Empire. In connection with this Austria made certain concessions when negotiating a trade agreement with Prussia (see Note 350).—307

371 The spring campaign of 1849 in Northern Italy began after Austria and Piedmont resumed hostilities on 12 March. At the decisive battle of *Novara* on 22-23 March 1849 the Austrian army under Radetzky defeated the Piedmontese troops. As a result Austrian rule was restored in Northern Italy.—310

372 The *Világos affair*—the capitulation of the main forces of the Hungarian revolutionary army under Görgey to Paskievich's troops on 13 August 1849.—310

373 The Hungarian revolutionary army relieved Komarom on 22 April 1849 (see Note 134).—310

374 In the spring of 1849 Hungarian troops under Bem marched to the Banat, a district in the Serbian Voivodina, then part of Hungary.

In speaking of the manoeuvre before Hermannstadt (Sibiu), Engels has in mind the successful operations of Bem's troops during the campaign in Transylvania in February-March 1849. During the general advance of the Russian troops in summer 1849 Bem returned to Transylvania, again marched to Hermannstadt, drove out the Russian garrison but, faced by superior forces of the Russian and Austrian armies, was compelled to retreat.—311

375 The extract from this letter is printed as quoted by Cluss in a letter to Weydemeyer of 3 May 1853. It was published in English for the first time abridged in K. Marx and F. Engels, *Letters to Americans. 1848-1895*, International Publishers, New York, 1953.—312

376 The reference is to a series of articles by Pieper published under the general heading 'A Critical History of French Socialism' in *The People's Paper*, Nos. 31-33, 4, 11 and 18 December 1852. Weydemeyer and Cluss planned to publish these articles in *Die Reform*, but Pieper did not finish the series.—312

377 Here Marx has in mind Pieper's material difficulties. On 18 April 1853 Pieper applied to Engels for help, as he could not receive money due to him for private lessons. On receipt of Pieper's letter Engels propably wrote to Marx between 19 and 23 April 1853 inquiring about Pieper's situation. Engels' letter has not been found.—314

378 Marx received Engels' article on Switzerland on 26 April 1853 and dispatched it with his own article to New York on 29 April 1853. The editors published the material on Switzerland as two articles. The first article, including Marx's material, was entitled 'The Rocket Affair.—The Swiss Insurrection' and was published on 14 May 1853; the second article appeared on 17 May 1853 under the heading 'Political Position of the Swiss Republic'; the date of its dispatch from London—1 May 1853—was arbitrarily supplied by the editors (see present edition, Vol. 12). The newspaper published both articles over Marx's name, though the first was written by Marx and Engels, and the second by Engels.—314, 319, 321

379 Marx's letter to Strohn is not extant.—315

380 In April 1853 as a pretext for reprisals against political refugees, the British authorities accused the proprietor of a rocket manufactory in Rotherhithe, in London, of a conspiracy with Kossuth which Marx ironically calls '*Kossuth's gunpowder plot*' by analogy with the Catholic gunpowder plot against James I in England in 1605. In March 1853 the Prussian police arrested several liberal and radical bourgeois leaders in Berlin in an effort to trump up a new conspiracy case. These government and police actions are described in Marx's

articles 'The Berlin Conspiracy', 'The Berlin Conspiracy.—London Police.—
Mazzini.—Radetzky' and Marx's and Engels' article 'The Rocket Affair.—The
Swiss Insurrection' (see present edition, Vol. 12).—316

[381] Marx presumably refers to his letters to Cluss of 25 March and 17 April 1853
(see this volume, pp. 298-300 and 312-14) and one of about 10 April 1853
which is not extant. As emerges from Cluss' letter to Marx of 28 April 1853,
Marx dealt in it with the publication in America of *Revelations Concerning the
Communist Trial in Cologne* as a separate book.—317

[382] An allusion to the past of Henri Savoye, professor of German at Louis-le-
Grand college in 1841-48 and the author of several works on Germany and the
German language.—317

[383] An abridged translation of this letter was published for the first time as an
editorial note to Engels' letter to Marx of 3 December 1851 in Karl Marx and
Friedrich Engels, *Correspondence. 1846-1895*. A Selection with Commentary and
Notes, Martin Lawrence Ltd., London, 1934.—319

[384] This money was collected in America in compliance with the appeal of Marx,
Engels and their associates to help the Communist League members accused in
Cologne and their families.—323

[385] On 21 May 1853 Jones published in *The People's Paper* an appeal to organise
workers' meetings in favour of the People's Charter. At the time Marx wrote
several articles for the *New-York Daily Tribune* on the revival of the Chartist
movement (see present edition, Vol. 12).—325

[386] Marx stayed with Engels in Manchester from 30 April to 19 May and returned
to London on 20 May 1853.—325, 335

[387] An abridged translation of this letter was published for the first time in Karl
Marx and Friedrich Engels, *Correspondence. 1846-1895*, London, 1934. It was
erroneously dated 'about 18 May 1853'. In later English publications the date
of the letter was verified (see Marx and Engels, *Selected Correspondence*, Progress
Publishers, Moscow, 1965).—325

[388] Willich slanderously represented his duel with Schramm in September 1850
(see Note 360) as an attempt by Marx and Engels to get rid of him by having
him killed. Marx refuted this slander in his pamphlet *The Knight of the Noble
Consciousness* (see present edition, Vol. 12, pp. 492-95).—326

[389] *Die Reform* was the organ of the American Workers' Association consisting
mostly of German emigrant workers. Though officially its editor was the
petty-bourgeois democrat Kellner, the newspaper's tendency was determined to
a great extent by Weydemeyer, who became the newspaper's actual editor in
the summer of 1853. Under his influence the paper retained its commitment to
the working class for some time. It often reprinted Marx's and Engels' articles
from the *New-York Daily Tribune*. Marx persuaded his associates (Eccarius,
Pieper and Dronke) to co-operate with *Die Reform*, which regularly published
articles and reports by Cluss and Weydemeyer, some based on material from
Marx's letters. Towards the end of its existence (1854), the petty-bourgeois
influence of its editor-in-chief, Kellner, became dominant.—326

[390] Marx and Engels talked about this during Marx's visit to Manchester from 30
April to 19 May 1853.—326

391 The *Edda*—a collection of Scandinavian mythological and heroic sagas and lays; two versions dating back to the thirteenth century are extant.—328

392 In a statement made shortly after the publication of the final instalment of Marx's *Revelations Concerning the Communist Trial in Cologne* in the *Neu-England-Zeitung*, No. 59, 22 April 1853, Willich threatened the imminent exposure of Marx in that newspaper, and the disclosure of facts he had not hitherto wished to make public. However, he only carried out his threat six months later by publishing a slanderous article, 'Doctor Karl Marx und seine "Enthüllungen"', in the *Belletristisches Journal und New-Yorker Criminal-Zeitung*, Nos. 33 and 34, 28 October and 4 November 1853. Marx replied with *The Knight of the Noble Consciousness* (see present edition, Vol. 12).—330

393 Marx's letter to Dana has not been found.—332

394 A reference to efforts to find a job in Manchester or Liverpool for Wilhelm Wolff, who had lost his last teaching possibilities with Reichenbach's departure to the USA.—334

395 In his statement 'An die Redaktion der *New-Yorker Criminal-Zeitung*' of 2 May 1853 published in the newspaper on 13 May, Willich called Cluss Marx's agent.—336

396 A reference to a unit formed by Willich in November 1848 in Besançon (France) out of German émigré workers and artisans. The practices and morals of this unit were satirically described by Marx and Engels in *The Great Men of the Exile* (see present edition, Vol. 11, pp. 312-15).—336

397 The ideas expressed by Engels here were used by Marx in 'The British Rule in India' (see present edition, Vol. 12).—339

398 *Tartary*—a name given in the nineteenth century to a part of Turkestan in Central Asia.—339

399 Engels refers to Weitling's lost work 'Allgemeine Denk- und Sprachlehre nebst Grundzügen einer Universal-Sprache der Menschheit', written in the first half of the 1840s.—341

400 In 1853, with the active support of the Polish democratic refugees, Alexander Herzen founded the Free Russian Press in London to evade tsarist censorhip. Pointing to this aspect of Herzen's activity, Lenin wrote in his article 'In Memory of Herzen' that he 'was the first to raise the great banner of struggle by addressing his *free Russian word* to the masses' (V. I. Lenin, *Collected Works*, Vol. 18, p. 31). Nikolai Ogarev, another prominent figure among the Russian revolutionary democrats, also took part in the management of the Free Russian Press. Besides a large number of books, pamphlets and leaflets, the Free Russian Press published the periodicals Полярная звезда (The Polar Star) and Колоколъ (The Bell), which played a great part in developing the revolutionary and democratic movement in Russia. In April 1865 the Free Russian Press was moved to Geneva, where it continued functioning up to August 1867.—345

401 A reference to Cluss' letter to Marx of 29 May 1853.—345

402 Marx lived in Chelsea (4 Anderson Street, London, S.W. 3) from August 1849 to April 1850.—345

403 The facts mentioned here were described in greater detail by Marx in a letter to Cluss also written on 14 June 1853 (see Note 407).—345

404 A reference to H. Ch. Carey, *The Slave Trade, Domestic and Foreign: why it exists, and how it may be extinguished,* Philadelphia, 1853. A quotation from Marx's 'Elections.—Financial Clouds.—The Duchess of Sutherland and Slavery' is given on pp. 203-04 of that book.—345

405 The *laws of Manu* (Mānava Dharma—Çāstra)—an ancient Indian collection of instructions defining the duties of each Hindu according to the dogmas of Brahminism. Indian tradition has it that these laws were drafted by Manu, the mythical father of the people, approximately between the second century B.C. and the first century A.D.—348

406 Only an extract of this letter has survived as quoted by Cluss in his letter to Weydemeyer of 28 June 1853. Part of it was published in English for the first time in K. Marx and F. Engels, *Letters to Americans. 1848-1895,* International Publishers, New York, 1953.—348

407 Further Cluss gives the substance of Marx's letter in his own words: 'About the money business Marx says: He has never accepted any financial support; as for the case trumpeted forth by Willich, it was roughly as follows: Marx, it is said, had rented a house in Chelsea (London) as a subtenant, paid his monthly rent regularly, often at the price of great privation. Then the actual owner of the house suddenly turns up and seizes on Marx, as the *sublessor* has paid nothing for a year. English law authorises this procedure. Marx cannot pay, a broker is installed in the house, etc. Marx in a very unfortunate position.—He is a member of the Refugee Relief Committee. The moneys are paid out weekly to individual refugees. The total sum, however, which is provided for the greater part by *our* friends in Europe, is lying idle, and so Marx is "saved", by being granted the necessary sum on condition that he pays it back in fixed instalments when it is required for other refugees—those, it appears, who are alone entitled to relief. This he did conscientiously, and paid back everything, partly out of his own earnings and partly out of money he got from his family. *C'est tout* [That's all].

'I have no lack of material to spin this out; on the contrary, there is an abundance of it. The same applies to the sacrifices he made for the *Neue Rheinische Zeitung,* when the bourgeoisie fell away after the June Revolution [proletarian uprising in Paris in 1848], and the democratic petty bourgeoisie after the state of siege was introduced in Cologne. That's quite something. Marx says he spent about 7,000 talers for the *N. Rh. Z.* ... He says, too, that I can and *should* make use of all the material he gives me, without however involving him in this business as a witness. *Reform*: Marx says *I* am right. He says half Germany will come to New York for the industrial exhibition, and as we have no other publication in this city, we should simply *take no notice* of the stupidities of the *Hornisse* gentlemen [the editor of the *Reform* Gottlieb Kellner and its London correspondent Heinrich Heise published *Die Hornisse* in Cassel in 1848-50] and prudently steer our own course. As is well known, Talleyrand always called to his statesmen: "Avant tout, pas de zèle, pas de zèle!" ["Above all, not too much zeal, not too much zeal!"].'—348

408 A twenty-five thousand-strong political demonstration was organised by the Chartists in Halifax on 26 June 1853 on the occasion of the funeral of Benjamin Ruston, an old Chartist worker. Marx wrote about this demonstration in the article 'Russian Policy Against Turkey.—Chartism' (see present edition, Vol. 12).—350

409 Presumably the reference is to Marx's letter to Cluss sent off about 14 June 1853 (see this volume, pp. 348-50).—351

410 Marx stayed in Manchester from 30 April to 19 May 1853.—351

411 Charles Anderson Dana's letter to Mrs Marx of 1 July 1853.—354

412 Marx analysed this debate and Bright's speech in the article 'The Turkish War Question.—The *New-York Tribune* in the House of Commons.—The Government of India' (see present edition, Vol. 12).—355

413 In April 1851 Abraham Jacobi was awarded the degree of Doctor of Medicine for his dissertation 'Cogitationes de vita rerum naturalium' at Bonn University.—355

414 In a campaign for a revival of the mass movement, leaders of the revolutionary Chartists headed by Jones organised mass meetings all over the country in June and July 1853. Most important were the meeting in Blackstone-Edge (19 June), the meeting and demonstration in Halifax on 26 June (see Note 408), and meetings in Oldham (27 June), Newcastle (3 July) and Mount Sorrel (10 July).—355

415 Engels was in London at the end of July and beginning of August 1853 on the occasion of his mother's visit to England (see this volume, p. 350).—356

416 This is a covering note to Marx's article 'Michael Bakunin' written for *The Morning Advertiser* and published on 2 September 1853 datelined 30 August (see present edition, Vol. 12). It is extant as a copy in Mrs Marx's hand. The signature and address are in Marx's own writing.—358

417 As Cluss' letter to Marx of 23-24 October 1853 and Pieper's letter to Jacobi of 3 September 1853 show, references for Abraham Jacobi, who intended to leave for the USA, were sent to America in early September 1853. But there is no mention of this in Marx's extant letters to Cluss and Weydemeyer and excerpts from them.—359

418 Bakunin wrote to George Sand on 9 July, and in her letter to Marx of 20 July George Sand refuted the calumnious rumours about Bakunin.—360

419 Marx's statement, a draft of which is quoted below, was not published by *The Morning Advertiser*. In view of this Marx put it in *The People's Paper*, No. 71, 10 September 1853 (see present edition, Vol. 12). The texts of the published statement and the draft are not identical.—362, 364

420 The *laws on suspects*—the decree passed by the French Convention on 17 September 1793 and other measures of the Jacobin revolutionary government which declared all persons suspect and subject to arrest who in any way supported the overthrown monarchy, including all former aristocrats and royal officials who had not testified their loyalty to the revolution. These laws were drawn up in such a way that even people not involved in counter-revolutionary activity could be placed in the category of 'suspects'.—363

421 Engels' reply to Marx's letter of 3 September 1853 containing a request for his comments on Marx's draft statement to *The Morning Advertiser* (see Note 419) has not been found.—363

422 A reference to Wilhelm Wolff's impending departure for Manchester. He lived there from the first half of September 1853 to the end of his life in 1864.—364

[423] Marx refers here to the articles on Russian foreign policy, in particular with respect to Turkey, in *The Morning Advertiser* (e.g. of 6 and 7 September 1853, etc.) and in the *New-York Daily Tribune*. Those in *The Morning Advertiser* were written by Karl Blind and those in the *Tribune* by Adam Gurowski.—365

[424] In a letter of 31 July 1853 sent to Ferdinand Freiligrath who passed it on to Marx on 18 August, the Communist League member Carl Wilhelm Klein reported on the formation of a new Communist League community in Philadelphia, where he was living in emigration at the time. He asked the Communist League members in London to help him establish contacts with the communities in Germany and to send in articles for *Gradaus,* a German refugees' newspaper close to the Working Men's Association in Philadelphia at the time. Simultaneously, Marx received from Cluss and Weydemeyer, in reply to his inquiry, information about Klein's own unseemly conduct in Philadelphia. Taking into account Klein's influence among the Solingen workers, Marx recommended that Cluss should maintain contact with him. Marx's reply to Klein's letter has not been found.—365, 367

[425] An extract from this letter is extant as quoted by Cluss in his letter to Weydemeyer of 3 October 1853.—366

[426] Presumably an allusion to the fact that Poesche used the article 'Geld' in *Meyer's Conversations-Lexicon* (Vol. 12, Hildburghausen, Amsterdam, Paris and Philadelphia, 1848, pp. 285-91) as a source for his article.—367

[427] The article 'The Western Powers and Turkey.—Imminent Economic Crisis.—Railway Construction in India' was written jointly by Marx and Engels on 19-20 September 1853.—368, 370

[428] The *knife and fork question*—words, which came to symbolise the Chartists' social programme, pronounced by an English priest and Chartist, J. R. Stephens, at a meeting in 1838. See Engels, *The Condition of the Working-Class in England* (present edition, Vol. 4, p. 519).—372, 377

[429] Presumably Marx mentioned his intention to write articles on these subjects in a no longer extant letter to Engels written between 17 and 28 September 1853.—374

[430] Marx's 'The War Question.—Financial Matters.—Strikes' (dated 7 October 1853) suggests that Engels sent in the promised material and Marx worked it up for this article (see present edition, Vol. 12, pp. 409-15).—374, 376

[431] In September 1853 the Preston manufacturers responded with a lockout to one of the biggest strikes by English workers in the 1850s. The strike was started by the weavers and spinners of mills in and around Preston who demanded a ten per cent wage rise; they were supported by workers in other trades. The lockout lasted until February 1854, but the strike continued after that date. To break the strike the Manufacturers' Association started bringing workers to Preston from Ireland and from English workhouses. In March 1854 the leaders of the strike were arrested, and as funds were low the workers were compelled to return to work. The strike ended in May 1854 (see K. Marx, 'Panic on the London Stock Exchange.—Strikes', present edition, Vol. 12).—374, 376, 513

[432] Textile mill workers and some 5,000 miners went on strike in Wigan (see K. Marx, 'Panic on the London Stock Exchange.—Strikes', present edition, Vol. 12).—376

433 Marx carried out his plans in February and March 1854 by writing 'Russian
Diplomacy.—The Blue Book on the Eastern Question—Montenegro' and
'Declaration of War.—On the History of the Eastern Question' (see present
edition, vols. 12 and 13). He wrote two articles on Denmark (21 October and 4
November 1853): 'Arrest of Delescluze.—Denmark.—Austria.—*The Times* on
the Prospects of War Against Russia' and 'Persian Expedition in Afghanistan
and Russian Expedition in Central Asia.—Denmark.—The Fighting on the
Danube and in Asia.—Wigan Colliers' (see present edition, Vol. 12).—376

434 Only part of this letter is extant.—377

435 At first Wilhelm Wolff intended to emigrate to the USA.—377

436 A reference to the first article in the series *Lord Palmerston* which Marx was
working on from early October to early December 1853 (see present edition,
Vol. 12). The pamphlet *Lord Palmerston* was intended for the *New-York Daily
Tribune*. Simultaneously the articles were published in the Chartist *People's
Paper*, which published eight articles from 22 October to 24 December 1853 as
a single series, each article being preceded by the editorial note: 'Written for
the *New-York Tribune* by Dr. Marx, and communicated by him to us.' The
New-York Daily Tribune published only four articles (their contents corresponded to six articles in *The People's Paper*) as leaders, outwardly unconnected
and with different titles. The sixth and eighth articles of the series were not
published in the *Tribune* at all.

At Marx's request Cluss translated into German the first article published in
the *Tribune*. It was published abridged in New York in the German-language
workers' newspaper *Die Reform*, Nos. 72, 73, 74, 77 and 78, 2, 3, 4, 8 and 9
November 1853. In December 1853 Cluss translated the second and third
articles of the pamphlet from the *Tribune* and the fourth from *The People's
Paper*. The editors of this edition do not have a complete file of *Die Reform* for
1854 at their disposal; it is therefore impossible to say whether the publication
of the German translation was continued.—378

437 On 5 August 1853 the House of Lords rejected the Combination of Workmen
Bill which would have granted limited rights to workers' organisations. In this
context Marx denounced the anti-working-class policy of both the ruling
oligarchy and the liberal and radical bourgeoisie. In the atmosphere of a mass
strike movement, the manufacturers created 'an association for the purpose of
aiding the trade in regulating the excitement among operatives in the
Manchester district' and resolutely opposed the organisation of workers'
associations (see K. Marx, 'The War Question.—British Population and Trade
Returns.—Doings of Parliament', present edition, Vol. 12). Marx thought it
necessary to draw the workers' attention to the fact that the bourgeoisie was
consolidating its forces; with this aim in view he wanted to provide Jones with
facts before his tour of the strike districts. In an article written on 7 October,
i.e. the day after his meeting with Jones, Marx wrote: 'The London press, it
appears, was anxious to withhold the fact from the eyes of the world, that the
Factory Lords were systematically arraying their class against the class of Labor,
and that the successive steps taken by them, instead of being the spontaneous
result of circumstances, are the premeditated effects of a deep-laid conspiracy
of an organized Anti-Labor League!" (see present edition, Vol. 12, p. 412).

To help the strikers a group of Chartists headed by Jones suggested the
setting up of a coordinating workers' organisation, The Mass Movement, which

was to unite Chartists, members of co-operative associations, trade unionists and unorganised workers (see Note 498).—378

438 In this letter Marx continues to set forth for his associates in America certain propositions of the economic theory he was then elaborating (see Note 45). At the time of writing this letter Marx had received from Cluss his article 'Das "beste Blatt der Union" und seine "besten Männer" und Nationalökonomen' published in the New York workers' newspaper *Die Reform* in September 1853, for which Cluss had made use of Marx's earlier letters. (For the text of this article and its analysis see present edition, Vol. 12, pp. 623-32.) The question of rent was among the problems raised in the article. These notes by Marx are directly related to this subject and to the critique he began earlier of the American vulgar economist H. Ch. Carey.—378, 387

439 Presumably Marx continued this letter the next day, 6 October 1853.—383

440 On Tuesday, 18 October 1853, Marx dispatched to New York 'The Turkish Manifesto.—France's Economic Position'. Engels may have taken part in writing it.—388

441 This letter was known earlier only from a copy of it in Cluss' letter to Weydemeyer of 2 November 1853 and partly as rendered by Cluss in his letter to Weydemeyer of 4 November 1853. The extract published in Marx and Engels, *Works*, Second Russian Edition, Vol. 28, and Marx und Engels, *Werke*, Bd. 28, included part of Cluss' text by mistake (the last paragraph).—390

442 As the editors did not regularly send copies of the *New-York Daily Tribune* to him, Marx asked Cluss and Weydemeyer to send him the issues containing his articles. Cluss was compelled to copy out the article 'Revolution in China and in Europe' because he could not buy the newspaper in time.

Marx's letter (presumably of August 1853) containing a request for this article has not been found.—390

443 Cluss corrected the misprints when this article from Marx's *Lord Palmerston* was published in *Die Reform.*—390

444 The Turko-Egyptian fleet was destroyed by combined Russian, English and French squadrons at *Navarino* (Greece) on 20 October 1827.—394

445 In October 1853 Weydemeyer became editor-in-chief of *Die Reform*. As Cluss wrote to Marx on 23-24 October 1853, Weydemeyer was compelled 'to write almost the whole newspaper himself'. In view of this Cluss requested Marx to get his associates to contribute to the newspaper.—396

446 Only an extract from this letter is extant as quoted by Cluss in his letter to Weydemeyer of 7 December 1853.—397

447 Eccarius' articles on the economic and political situation in France were published in *The People's Paper* from September 1852 to May 1853.—397

448 Marx's letter to Jones has not been found.—397

449 Here Marx replies to Cluss' letter of 23-24 October 1853 in which Cluss wrote about the difficulties he had encountered in publishing the translation of Marx's first article from *Lord Palmerston* (see Note 436) in *Die Reform*. The *Tribune* published Marx's work anonymously, as leading articles, so *Die Reform* prefaced its publication with an editorial note: 'The interest aroused by Palmerston's name at the present time has induced us to print this rendering

from the *Tribune*. This essay reveals a more than average knowledge of British affairs by the author, and though it bears no signature, it is easy to tell who the author is.'—398

450 A few lines below Cluss writes: 'Marx added some notes on Urquhart because Jones, in a paper I am to receive, characterises him in a tactless way as an ally of the Russians [Jones' article 'A Russian Movement in England', *The People's Paper*, No. 80, 12 November 1853]. Marx writes [this letter is not extant] that he gave Jones a dressing down for this. I have made up a short article out of the "Urquhartiade"'. Marx's article, 'David Urquhart', was published by Cluss unsigned in *Die Reform*, No. 112, 19 December 1853 (see present edition, Vol. 12).—398

451 Engels' letters to Marx of October-December 1853 have not been found.—399

452 Engels arrived in London at the end of December 1853.—400

453 A reference to Dronke's letter to Engels written from Switzerland at the end of July or the beginning of August 1850. An extract from it was quoted by Marx in *The Knight of the Noble Consciousness* (see present edition, Vol. 12, p. 486).—401

454 On 23 November 1853 Engels wrote a special letter—a statement against Willich, which Marx included in *The Knight of the Noble Consciousness* (see present edition, Vol. 12, pp. 489-93).—401

455 Steffen's letter of 22 November 1853, Miskowsky's letter of 24 November 1853, and Kossuth's certificate of 12 November 1853 concerning Miskowsky were included in Marx's *The Knight of the Noble Consciousness* (see present edition, Vol. 12, pp. 504-05 and 494-95).—401

456 Here and below the reference is to the meetings organised by the Polish refugees in London on Monday and Tuesday, 28 and 29 November 1853, to mark the anniversary of the Polish insurrection of 1830-31.—401

457 Presumably Marx refers to Engels' letter which was written on about 14 December 1853 and is not extant.—403

458 A reference to the London Convention of 15 July 1840 on support for the Turkish Sultan against the Egyptian Pasha Mohammed Ali and to the London Convention of 13 July 1841 which laid down that in peacetime the Straits would be closed to warships of all powers.—404, 432

459 Marx did not realise his plan to continue publishing the series of articles on Palmerston in the *New-York Daily Tribune*. The last article dispatched to New York and recorded in his notebook on 6 December 1853 was not published in that newspaper. In *The People's Paper* it appeared as the eighth in the series 'Lord Palmerston' and ended with the words 'To be continued'.—404

460 Marx agreed to J. C. Juta's proposal to contribute to the newspaper *Zuid Afrikaan* published in English and Dutch. Of the three articles sent by Marx *The Zuid Afrikaan* published only one—'The War in the East' (see present edition, Vol. 12).—405.

461 Engels went to London for Christmas 1853 and left for Manchester on 1 January 1854.—406

462 A reference to the war of Napoleonic France against Spain in 1808-14 which ended in France's defeat.—406

463 Marx refers to Charles Dana's letter to Mrs Marx of 16 December 1853 in which he presumably wrote about Engels' article 'The War on the Danube' published in the *New-York Daily Tribune* on 16 December as a leader. A week earlier, on 7 December, Dana had published another article by Engels, 'Progress of the Turkish War', also as a leader (see present edition, Vol. 12).—407

464 Dana wrote to Mrs Marx about this on 16 December 1853.—407

465 About 16 December 1853 the London publisher Tucker published anonymously the pamphlet *Palmerston and Russia* in *Tucker's Political Fly-Sheets*, No. 1 (a reprint from the *Glasgow Sentinel*) (see Note 541). The pamphlet reproduced the article of the same title published in the *New-York Daily Tribune* on 4 November 1853, the second in this newspaper's publication of *Lord Palmerston*.

The second edition of *Palmerston and Russia,* referred to here, was issued with Marx's participation in early February 1854. Marx made some amendments and additions on the basis of the *People's Paper* publication. On how the whole series of articles *Lord Palmerston* was written and published see this volume, Note 436, and present edition, Vol. 12.—408, 432

466 Engels analysed the fighting between the Russians and the Turks at *Oltenitza* (4 November 1853) and *Citatea* (6 January 1854) in 'The Progress of the Turkish War', 'The War on the Danube' and 'The Last Battle in Europe' (see present edition, Vol. 12).—408

467 At the battle of *Sinope* between Russian and Turkish naval squadrons on 30 (18) November 1853, during the Crimean war, the Turks were defeated.

After the battle of Sinope, Lord Stratford de Redcliffe, British Ambassador to Constantinople, handed the Sultan a recommendation from the British Government to conclude a three months' armistice with Russia; at the same time he tried to get British squadrons sent immediately to the Black Sea.

The *Vienna Protocol* was signed on 5 December 1853 at the conference of representatives of Britain, France, Prussia and Austria. In this Protocol, as in the subsequent Note of 12 December, the four powers offered to mediate in the conflict between Russia and Turkey. As a basis for negotiations they demanded the evacuation of Moldavia and Wallachia by the Russians, renewal of former treaties between Russia and Turkey, guarantee of Christians' rights by special firmans and a reform of the administrative system in Turkey. In a Note of 31 December 1853 the Turkish Government stated its conditions for peace negotiations with the powers mediating: 1) the preservation and guarantee of Turkish territorial integrity; 2) Russian evacuation of the Danubian Principalities; 3) renewal and observance of the London Convention of 1841 (see Note 458); 4) respect of the Sultan's sovereignty. These conditions were approved by a new Vienna conference of the ambassadors on 13 January 1854 and forwarded to the Russian Government. However, Russia refused to accept the mediation of the powers and agreed to direct negotiations with Turkey. The participants in the Vienna conference rejected Russia's proposals.—408

468 A reference to Palmerston's short resignation of his post as Home Secretary (16-24 December 1853). His resignation was not accepted, however (on this see Marx's article 'Palmerston's Resignation', present edition, Vol. 12).—409

469 31 January 1854 was the day of the opening of the British Parliament.—409

470 A reference to the Note signed by the British, French and Prussian Ambassadors in Constantinople on 12 December 1853 and handed to Turkey on 15 December 1853 (see Note 467).—409

471 An allusion to the wars of Napoleonic France and the liberation struggle of the European peoples against its rule waged up to 1814.—409

472 Engels' letter to Steffen has not been found.—409

473 When Engels was in London (see Note 461) he presumably discussed with Marx his plan to write such a work for the English Press. This plan did not materialise.—409

474 Neither Marx's note to Wilhelm Wolff, nor Wolff's letter to Marx has been found.—410

475 The reference is to the Turkish Government's Note of 31 December 1853 (see Note 467).—410

476 By the original (first) Vienna Note Marx means the draft agreement between Russia and Turkey drawn up by the Austrian Prime Minister Buol and adopted at the conference of the French, British and Prussian Ambassadors in Vienna at the end of July 1853. It obliged the Sultan to observe the terms of the Kuchuk-Kainardji (1774) and the Adrianople (1829) treaties on the rights and privileges of the Orthodox Church in the Ottoman Empire. The Turkish Sultan Abdul Mejid agreed to sign the Note but demanded a number of changes and reservations which the Russian Government found unacceptable.—410

477 Marx alludes ironically to the leading article in *The Times* of 20 January 1854 which stated in particular: 'Nevertheless, to all these considerations the Emperor Nicholas opposes a proud intractable temper, heightened, perhaps, by the religious enthusiasm or hereditary excitability of his family, and stimulated by the enthusiasm of his people, which is mixed with a barbarous contempt for nations whose power they cannot compare with their own.'—410

478 Marx refers to the speeches made by Cobden and Bright at the Manchester Reform meeting on 24 January 1854 and reported in *The Times*, No. 21647, 25 January. The speeches, dealing mainly with the foreign policy problems, were analysed in Marx's and Engels' article 'Fortification of Constantinople.—Denmark's Neutrality.—Composition of British Parliament.—Crop Failure in Europe' (see present edition, Vol. 12).—411

479 Cluss' letter to Marx has not been found.—411

480 Here Marx writes about issue No. II in *Tucker's Political Fly-Sheets* series being prepared for publication on the basis of Marx's *Lord Palmerston* (see Note 465). The pamphlet was printed in February-March 1854 anonymously and entitled *Palmerston, What Has He Done?* It reproduced with slight amendments the text of the fourth (except the first four paragraphs) and the fifth articles of the *People's Paper* publication.—412

481 This offer was made by Dana in a letter to Mrs Marx of 16 December 1853. These plans did not materialise.—412

482 The reference is to the second edition of the pamphlet *Palmerston and Russia* in *Tucker's Political Fly-Sheets* series (see Note 465). In subsequent editions of this series this work was entitled *Palmerston and Poland.*—412

[483] Marx has in mind the articles from his *Lord Palmerston* published in *Die Reform* in Cluss' translation. They corresponded to the second and third articles ('Palmerston and Russia' and 'A Chapter of Modern History') in the *New-York Daily Tribune* and the fourth in *The People's Paper* (see Note 436).—412

[484] Marx wrote about this meeting also in a letter to Ferdinand Lassalle of 1 June 1854 (see this volume, p. 455).

Marx described Urquhart in his article 'David Urquhart' published in *Die Reform* on 19 December 1853 (see present edition, Vol. 12).—412

[485] In a letter to Nicholas I of 29 January 1854, Napoleon III proposed as a condition of preserving peace that Russia should withdraw her troops from the Danubian Principalities. On 14 February 1854 the letter was published officially in *Le Moniteur universel*, No. 45. Nicholas I's reply, containing a refusal to accept Napoleon III's proposal, was sent off on 9 February 1854 and published in *Le Moniteur universel*, No. 64, 5 March 1854.—414

[486] In a letter to Marx of 27 March 1854 J. J. H. Smuts, editor of *The Zuid Afrikaan*, refused to accept any further contributions from Marx, for, he wrote, 'the amount of remuneration claimed by [Marx] for such correspondence, entirely exceeds the means which my establishment allows me to apply to such a purpose'.—414

[487] At Marx's request Engels wrote on 13 March 'Retreat of the Russians from Kalafat' (see present edition, Vol. 13).

The *Greek revolution*—the revolt of the Greek population in Epirus, the mountain regions of Thessaly and other territories still subject to Turkey; Marx assessed these events in the article 'The Greek Insurrection' (see present edition, Vol. 13).—414, 444

[488] Marx has in mind Lassalle's letter of 10 February 1854. Engels' letter to Marx mentioned here has not been found.—417

[489] In 1853, with the growth of a massive strike movement of the British proletariat, a group of Chartists headed by Ernest Jones proposed to create a broad workers' organisation, The Mass Movement, which was to unite trade unions and unorganised workers with the primary aim of coordinating strikes in the various districts of the country. The organisation was to be headed by a regularly convened Labour Parliament consisting of delegates elected at meetings of both unorganised workers and of the trade unions associated with The Mass Movement. The Labour Parliament assembled in Manchester on 6 March 1854 and was in session till 18 March 1854. It discussed and adopted the programme of The Mass Movement and set up an Executive of five members. Marx, elected honorary delegate to the Parliament, sent a letter to it (see present edition, Vol. 13), in which he formulated the primary task of the British labour movement—the necessity to create an independent proletarian mass political party. Marx regarded the convocation of the Labour Parliament as an effort to free the labour movement in Britain from narrow trade union limitations.

The attempt to found The Mass Movement failed because the majority of the trade union leaders did not approve of associating the trade unions with the political struggle and did not support the idea of creating a single mass workers' organisation. By the summer of 1854 the strike movement had abated and this also cut short the participation of broad masses of workers in the movement. After March 1854 the Labour Parliament never met again.

Besides the 'Letter to the Labour Parliament', Marx wrote two more articles on the activity of the Labour Parliament: 'Opening of the Labour Parliament.—English War Budget' and 'The Labor Parliament' (see present edition, Vol. 13).—417

490 Marx's letter to Lassalle has not been found.—417

491 Presumably Lassalle's letter to Marx of 7 March 1854.—418

492 Marx's letter to Engels mentioned here has not been found.—418

493 Lassalle's letters to Marx of 10 February and 7 March 1854.—419

494 *Enos* and *Rodosto*—points on the European coasts of the Aegean Sea and the Sea of Marmara where the British and the French army respectively were to disembark. Marx assessed this plan in the article 'English and French War Plans.—Greek Insurrection.—Spain.—China' (see present edition, Vol. 13).—419

495 Engels' ideas expressed here were partly used by Marx in the article 'Russia and the German Powers.—Corn Prices' (see present edition, Vol. 13).—420

496 Engels sent his manuscript 'The Fortress of Kronstadt' to *The Daily News* on 30 March with a letter in which he offered to contribute to this newspaper as a military observer (see this volume, pp. 423-26).
'The Fortress of Kronstadt' was not published during Engels' lifetime; in the present edition it is included in Vol. 13.—420, 422

497 Marx refers to Lassalle's letter of 7 March 1854 (on it see this volume, p. 419). On Palmerston Lassalle wrote in particular:
'True, Palmerston never deserved—not by a long shot—the totally usurped reputation which he enjoys, and has lately been even more primitive than before; but neither is he a Russian agent, at least not *consciously*. His attitude I can best describe to you in the words he said to a friend of his as early as December: *Je veux la Russie, je ne dis pas ruiner, mais lui donner un soufflet pour toute sa vie!* [I want—I don't say to destroy Russia—but to give it a slap in the face that it would remember for ever!]
'It is a fact that he pressed for war from December, etc., and answered every objection that Russia could not concede this or that with "Tant mieux!" ["All the better!"]? (*F. Lassalle. Nachgelassene Briefe und Schriften* herausgegeben von Gustav Mayer. Band III. Der Briefwechsel zwischen Lassalle und Marx. Stuttgart-Berlin, 1922, S. 73).—422, 431

498 The reference is to the secret correspondence of the British envoy to St. Petersburg, Hamilton Seymour, and the British Foreign Secretary Russell, concerning the negotiations between Seymour and Nicholas I on the Turkish question at the beginning of 1853. This correspondence and other documents pertaining to the pre-history of the Crimean War were published as a Blue Book, *Correspondence Respecting the Rights and Privileges of the Latin and Greek Churches in Turkey.* Presented to Both Houses of Parliament by Command of Her Majesty. Parts V, VI, London, 1854. Marx gave a detailed analysis of these documents in 'The Documents on the Partition of Turkey' and 'The Secret Diplomatic Correspondence' (see present edition, Vol. 13).—422

499 Marx's letter to the editors of the *New-York Daily Tribune* of 27 March has not been found. It may have been sent off to New York on 28 March 1854 with the article 'Declaration of War.—On the History of the Eastern Question'.—422

500 Marx used the information he got from Hammer's book later when writing 'Reorganisation of the British War Administration.—The Austrian Summons.— Britain's Economic Situation.—St. Arnaud' (see present edition, Vol. 13).—423

501 On the outbreak of the Crimean War Engels offered his services as military observer to *The Daily News* and sent the editors his article 'The Fortress of Kronstadt' (see Note 496) on 30 March, and after 3 April 1854, at the request of the editors, the article 'The Russian Army', which was to open a series of articles on the Russian army and navy. The article was set and Engels probably received the proofs on 12 April 1854, with a letter from the editor H. J. Lincoln, who asked Engels about his terms. Engels pinned great hopes on this collaboration, believing that permanent work on the newspaper would enable him to give up his commercial activity and move to London. However, as can be seen from Engels' letter to Marx of 20 April 1854, Lincoln cancelled the previous contract when he discovered Engels' political views. Some of the propositions formulated in the article 'The Russian Army' were elaborated in 'The Military Power of Russia' (see present edition, Vol. 13) and 'The Armies of Europe' (see present edition, Vol. 14) published in the *New-York Daily Tribune* and *Putnam's Monthly.*—423

502 John Watts consented to recommend Engels as chief military correspondent to *The Daily News* in his letter to Engels of 27 March 1854.—424

503 Marx translated into English this description of the Russian landing at Dobrudja and included it in his article sent to the USA on 4 April. The editors published the lesser part of the article as a leader 'The European War' (it included Engels' text) and entitled the larger part 'The War Debate in Parliament' (see present edition, Vol. 13).—427

504 *Wasserpolacken*—a name applied in the seventeenth century to Poles living in Upper Silesia and engaged in floating timber on the Oder; later the name was used for the whole Polish population of Upper Silesia which was under German rule from the mid-eighteenth century.—427

505 Engels has in mind H. J. Lincoln's letter of 1 April 1854.—427

506 Cluss' letter has not been found.—428

507 This refers to the stand taken by Palmerston as Foreign Secretary on the problem of Cracow which, according to the Vienna Treaty of 1815, was considered a free city. In Parliament and the press Palmerston passed himself off as 'a friend of Poland' but in fact betrayed its interests when in 1840 the population of Cracow protested against the unlawful occupation of that city by Austrian troops since February 1836 and when in November 1846, after the suppression of the national liberation uprising in Cracow, Austria, Prussia and Russia signed an agreement on the annexation of Cracow to the Austrian Empire. Marx exposed Palmerston's actions in his pamphlet *Lord Palmerston* (see present edition, Vol. 12, pp. 358-70).—430, 432

508 Marx's reply to Lassalle written between 10 February and 7 March has not been found.—430

509 An allusion to *Lord Palmerston* (see present edition, Vol. 12). Excerpts made by Marx from *Parliamentary (Blue) Books* in March-May 1853 and from *Hansard's Parliamentary Debates* for 1831-48 in July-August and September-November 1853 in connection with this work are extant.—432

510 The *Unkiar-Skelessi treaty* of defensive alliance was concluded by Russia and Turkey on 8 July (26 June) 1833. It provided for mutual aid in the event of war with a third power. A secret article of the treaty freed Turkey from the obligation to give military aid to Russia in return for an undertaking to close the Straits to all foreign men-of-war on Russia's demand.—432, 456

511 The *First Anglo-Afghan war* (1838-42) was launched by Britain with the aim of colonising Afghanistan but ended in Britain's defeat.—432

512 In 1838 the Kingdom of the Two Sicilies granted a French company a concession to extract sulphur in Sicily. In April 1840 the British Government, referring to the treaty of 1816 which forbade Naples to grant other countries commercial privileges infringing British interests, ordered its Mediterranean fleet to open hostilities and compelled Naples to cancel its agreement with the French company.—432

513 Marx refers to the attitude of the Whig Government, in which Palmerston held the post of Foreign Secretary, towards Italy and Hungary during the 1848-49 revolution.—432

514 A reference to Cluss' letter to Marx of 4 April 1854.—433

515 The report of Gorchakov, Commander-in-Chief of the Russian army on the Danube, to Nicholas I was reprinted by *The Times* on 19 April 1854 from a special supplement to the *Journal de Saint-Pétersbourg* of 6 April 1854 and entitled 'The Russian Passage of the Danube'. The same issue of *The ·Times* carried an item 'The Russian Fleet in the Black Sea' reprinted from *Русскiй инвалидъ* (and not from *Сѣверная пчела* as Marx wrote) about military operations on the Caucasian coast.—433

516 Engels refers to H. J. Lincoln's letter of 18 April 1854. Engels' reply has not been found.—435

517 A reference to Pieper's letter to Engels of 12 April 1854.—435

518 The reference is to Herzen's address 'The Free Russian Community to the Russian Soldiers in Poland' printed in the Free Russian Press in London about 25 March 1854 in connection with the outbreak of the Crimean War. Herzen called upon the Russian soldiers 'not to use arms against Poland'. The address was immediately reprinted by a number of English, French, Italian and Polish newspapers, *The Daily News* (No. 2471, 21 April 1854) among them.—437

519 This letter of Marx has not been found.—439

520 An allusion to Marx's articles on India ('The British Rule in India', 'The East India Company.—Its History and Results' and others—see present edition, Vol. 12) written in 1853, when the British Parliament debated the prolongation of the East India Company Charter.—439

521 Engels' letter to Cluss has not been found.—441

522 Kossuth, jointly with Mazzini and Ledru-Rollin, criticised the US Senate in the press refusing to prolong George Sanders' powers as Consul in London. This American public figure and journalist maintained contacts with petty-bourgeois emigrants in London. The American newspapers, *The New-York Herald* and *The New-York Times* in particular, attacked Kossuth for his criticism and accused him of meddling in US domestic affairs. Clippings from the American newspapers were sent to Marx by Cluss in his letter of 4 April 1854. Marx forwarded them to Engels probably in his letter of 22 April.—441

523 A reference to Cluss' letter to Marx of 13 April 1854.—442

524 Weydemeyer, editor of *Die Reform*, received a review of Schimmelpfennig's book *The War Between Turkey and Russia* written jointly by Engels and Heise, when the newspaper ceased publication (Weydemeyer to Engels, 16 May 1854). He sent it on to Cluss who wanted to insert it in some other newspaper, preferably *Der Deutsch-Amerikaner*, a weekly published from March 1854 in Chicago by Eduard Schläger (Cluss to Marx, 25 May 1854). The editors of the present edition have no file of *Der Deutsch-Amerikaner* for that period and the fate of the review is unknown.—443

525 An allusion to Schimmelpfennig's proposal to contribute military articles to *Die Reform*. In a letter to Marx of 13 April 1854 Cluss asked for Marx's advice on this point.—444

526 The reference is to a number of reforms carried out in the Ottoman Empire in the spheres of finance, the army, administration and legislation (known as *tanzimat*) between 1839 and the early 1870s. Their practical implementation met with fierce resistance on the part of feudal reaction, particularly at the first stage, prior to the Sultan's new rescript (*hatti-humayouni*) in 1856.—444

527 Odessa was bombarded by a united Anglo-French squadron on 22 April 1854. For details see Marx's 'The Bombardment of Odessa.—Greece.—Proclamation of Prince Daniel of Montenegro.—Manteuffel's Speech', present edition, Vol. 13.—444, 446, 452

528 Marx refers to the notice published by the Russian Ministry of Finance in a special supplement to Коммерческая газета, Nos. 40 and 41, 6 (18) and 8 (20) April 1854 and reprinted in the *Journal de Saint-Pétersbourg*, No. 377, 8 (20) April 1854. Marx apparently used a report reprinted in *The Times*, No. 21726, 27 April 1854, from the *Journal de Saint-Pétersbourg*.—446

529 In 1838 and 1839 the great powers held negotiations to regulate relations between the Netherlands and Belgium which had seceded from the Kingdom of the Netherlands as a result of the 1830 revolution. Previously England supported Belgium, jointly with France, but this time it sided with Russia, Austria and Prussia who sought to impose on Belgium the peace terms worked out by the great powers. France found itself isolated and was compelled to agree to these terms. Louis Philippe's diplomatic defeat was regarded in France as a serious foreign policy humiliation.

In 1839, when the Turkish-Egyptian conflict over Syria, which had been occupied by the Egyptians in 1833, flared up anew, and France supported the Egyptian Pasha Mohammed Ali, Britain, seeking to prevent a growth of French influence in that area, brought diplomatic pressure to bear on France. On 15 July 1840 a convention was signed in London by Britain, Russia, Prussia, Austria and Turkey promising to support the Sultan of Turkey (see Note 458). Louis Philippe, fearing a conflict with this coalition, made a new concession and refused any further support to Egypt.—447

530 Marx's conspectus of H. H. Parish's *Diplomatic History of the Monarchy of Greece* (London, 1838) made early in May 1854 when he was studying the history of Greece is extant.—447

531 The editors of this edition do not have *La Presse* at their disposal. Marx may have used a reprint of this material in *L'Indépendance belge*, No. 123, 3 May 1854.—447

532 *Whitechapel*—a district in London where many foreign emigrants lived. The fire mentioned in this letter happened in Whitechapel on 29 April 1854.—449, 451

533 Engels lived in Berlin as an army volunteer from September 1841 to about late September 1842.—449

534 Here Marx has in mind the patrons of Stehely's confectionery in Berlin in the 1840s, radical-minded men of letters, students and members of 'The Free' (see Note 535).—449

535 *'The Free'*—a group of Berlin Young Hegelians which came into being in the first half of 1842. Among its principal members were Bruno Bauer, Edgar Bauer, Edward Meyen, Ludwig Buhl and Max Stirner. The system existing in the country was criticised by 'The Free' in an abstract manner, their statements were devoid of real revolutionary content, their ultra-radical form often compromised the democratic movement. Many of 'The Free' renounced radicalism in the following years.

For a criticism of 'The Free' see K. Marx and F. Engels, *The Holy Family, or Critique of Critical Criticism* (present edition, Vol. 4).—449

536 The information on Wiss given in the previous letter was passed on to Cluss by Marx in a letter written probably in the first week of May 1854. Marx's letter has not been found.—450

537 Engels' irony is directed at Willich, who in his article 'Doctor Karl Marx und seine "Enthüllungen"' (*Belletristisches Journal und New-Yorker Criminal-Zeitung*, No. 33, 28 October 1853) wrote that Schramm's second Miskowsky vanished without trace after the duel between Schramm and Willich (see Note 360).—451

538 In a letter of 30 April 1854 Cluss informed Marx, among other things, that *Die Reform* ceased publication.—453

539 This is Marx's reply to Lassalle's letter of 20 May 1854 in which the latter asked for information on the plans of the political emigrants in England in connection with the Crimean War and also for Marx's articles on Palmerston which had been published in London as a separate pamphlet (see notes 465 and 480).—454

540 Marx's letters to Lassalle written in the second half of 1854 have not been found.—454

541 A series of twelve pamphlets under the general title *Tucker's Political Fly-Sheets* was published in London by Urquhart's follower Tucker in 1853 and 1854, exposing Palmerston's foreign policy. The first two issues reproduced some sections of Marx's *Lord Palmerston* (see notes 465 and 480). In 1855 Tucker reprinted the series in one volume.—455, 472

542 On 8 May 1852 Russia, Austria, Britain, France, Prussia, Sweden and Denmark signed the London Protocol on the integrity of the Danish monarchy, confirming the indivisibility of the Danish Crown lands, including the Duchy of Schleswig-Holstein. Among the legitimate claimants to the Danish Crown the London Protocol mentioned the Russian Emperor (as a descendant of Duke Charles Peter Ulrich of Holstein-Gottorp who reigned in Russia as Peter III). He waived his rights in favour of Duke Christian of Glücksburg who was proclaimed successor to King Frederick VII. The London Protocol thus created

a precedent for the Russian Tsar to claim the Danish Crown in the event of the Glücksburg dynasty dying out.—456

543 The *Quadruple Alliance* was concluded in April 1834 between Britain, France, Spain and Portugal. Even at the time the treaty was concluded, conflicts of interests appeared between Britain and France which later aggravated relations between the two countries. This treaty was formally directed against the absolutist 'Northern Powers' (Russia, Prussia and Austria), but in actual fact allowed Britain to strengthen her position in Spain and Portugal under the pretext of rendering military assistance to both governments in their struggle against the pretenders to the throne, Don Carlos in Spain and Dom Miguel in Portugal.—456

544 A reference to the London conventions of 1840 and 1841 (see Note 458).—457

545 *Giovane Italia* (Young Italy)—a secret organisation of Italian bourgeois revolutionaries founded by Mazzini. It existed in 1831-34 and 1839-48, its aim being struggle for the independence and unity of Italy.—458

546 Engels apparently refers to Napier's report published in *The Times*, No. 21758, 3 June 1854. It described the action between an English frigate and steamer and three Russian merchant ships near the fortress of Gustavsvaern on 23 May. Two Russian ships were sunk, the third captured. The report called this 'a very gallant feat of arms'.—460

547 In June 1854 Engels simultaneously made notes from A. Görgei, *Mein Leben und Wirken in Ungarn in den Jahren 1848 und 1849* (Bd. I-II, Leipzig, 1852) and from F. Hellwald von Heller, *Der Winter-Feldzug 1848-1849 in Ungarn* (Wien, 1851) written on Windischgrätz's instructions.—460

548 Engels refers to military reports of the Austrian Command published in the official *Wiener Zeitung* and also in *Der Lloyd, Österreichischer Correspondent, Die Presse* and other Austrian newspapers, mostly over Windischgrätz's signature. Engels used them as his main source when writing articles for the *Neue Rheinische Zeitung* on the course of the 1848-49 revolutionary war in Hungary against the Austrian monarchy (see present edition, vols. 8 and 9).—460

549 The reference is to the demands presented to Chancellor Nesselrode by Austria and Prussia after the signing of the treaty on 20 April 1854 (see present edition, Vol. 13, p. 168) on the immediate evacuation of the Danubian Principalities and other territories occupied by the Russians.—461

550 Marx mentions Colonel Grach here because Engels named him in the article 'The Siege of Silistria' (see present edition, Vol. 13, pp. 240-42).—461

551 An allusion by Ruge to Marx, Engels and their associates in the Communist League.—462

552 Engels' accompanying letter has not been found.—464

553 On Friday, 23 June 1854, the article written by Marx jointly with Engels was sent to New York. The *New-York Daily Tribune* published part of it on 10 July as a leader, 'The Russian Retreat'; the other part, containing details about military operations at Silistria, was added by the editors to Marx's article dispatched earlier (on 16 June) and published on 8 July 1854 also as a leader, 'State of the Russian War' (see present edition, Vol. 13).—464

554 Marx apparently has in mind English Press reports on the move of the Circassian troops to Tiflis (Tbilisi), which began in May, and news about the

activity of the Anglo-French mission under Rear Admiral Edmund Lyons. According to *The Times*, the aim of the latter was to establish contact with the Circassian leaders (primarily with Shamyl) for a joint attack on the Russian towns of Sandjak and Anapa. This aim was attained.

For an appraisal of these events see Engels' 'The War' and Marx's and Engels' 'The Russian Retreat' (present edition, Vol. 13).—464

555 This letter has not been found.—466

556 Sentenced to six-year imprisonment at the Cologne Communist Trial, Burgers and Becker served their terms in Glatz and Weichselmünde.—468

557 Marx refers to the fourth bourgeois revolution in Spain (1854-56) which began with a pronunciamento in Madrid on 28 June 1854. Marx analysed the revolutionary events in Spain in several articles written in 1854 (see present edition, Vol. 13).—469

558 Engels complied with Marx's request and sent (by Tuesday, 1 August) material for their joint article 'That Bore of a War' (see present edition, Vol. 13).—472

559 At the evening sitting of the House of Commons on 24 July 1854 the leader of the House, John Russell, announced that Sevastopol had been destroyed and captured by the Anglo-French squadron. However, replying to a question by Disraeli, leader of the Tory opposition, he was compelled to take his words back. The false claim of the capture of Sevastopol by the Allies was deleted from the text of Russell's speech published in *The Times*.

At the sitting of 25 July 1854 Sidney Herbert, Secretary at War, gave reasons for the unsatisfactory food supply of the British expeditionary army and fleet and did his best to justify the Cabinet and War Administration. The speeches of Russell, Disraeli and Herbert were published in *The Times*, Nos. 21802 and 21803, 25 and 26 July 1854. Marx attended the debates on the war in the House of Commons on 24 and 25 July and described them in detail in 'The War Debates in Parliament' and 'The Policy of Austria.—The War Debates in the House of Commons' (see present edition, Vol. 13).—472

560 The summary of Thierry's book written by Marx in French at that time is extant.—473

561 The *Federal Diet*—the central organ of the German Confederation formed in 1815. It met in Frankfurt am Main and consisted of representatives of the German states. The Federal Diet was a vehicle of the German governments' reactionary policy. It ceased to exist during the 1848-49 revolution, was restored in 1851, and existed till 1866.—475

562 This is presumably an allusion to the Mainz Central Investigation Commission instituted by decision of the Conference of German states in Karlsbad in 1819 for an investigation into the 'tricks of the demagogues' (see notes 139 and 307), i.e. for the struggle against the opposition movement in the German states.—475

563 The *Guelphs*—a political party in Italy formed in the twelfth century, during the period of strife between the popes and the German emperors. Consisting mainly of the upper strata of merchants and artisans in the Italian towns who supported the popes, it bitterly opposed the party of the *Ghibellines*, who supported the emperors. The two parties existed till the fifteenth century.—476

564 See notes 380 and 139, 307.—478

565 The reference is to Marx's part of the article sent to the *New-York Daily Tribune* on 29 August 1854. The article was tampered with by the editors, who published the part concerning Bomarsund (written by Engels) as a leader in issue No. 4182 for 13 September 1854. A few sentences from Marx's text were included in the news review in the same number. News about Kars, mentioned by Marx here, was included as a separate paragraph in Pulszky's article also published in that number (see present edition, Vol. 13, Note 293).—480

566 In connection with the bourgeois revolution which started in Spain in 1854 (see Note 557), Marx made a thorough study of the history of the nineteenth-century Spanish revolutions. The result was a series of articles, *Revolutionary Spain*, written between August and November 1854 (see present edition, Vol. 13).—480

567 Marx apparently has in mind the meeting of his mother, Henriette Marx, and his wife, Jenny, in Trier in July-August 1854.—481

568 In the original *Lebensmittel*, a term used by Marx and Engels as an economic category in a number of works, including *The Condition of the Working-Class in England, Manifesto of the Communist Party* and *Capital.*—481

569 *Zouaves*—French colonial light infantry.
Les singes (the apes)—a derogatory nickname for the generals who supported Napoleon III.
On anti-Bonapartist sentiments in the French army, the disturbances among the Zouaves in the French force at Varna in the summer of 1854, see Engels, 'The Attack on Sevastopol' (present edition, Vol. 13, p. 473).—482

570 Engels' article on the military operations in the Caucasian theatre of war sent in by Tuesday, 19 September 1854 (witness entry in Marx's notebook: 'Dienstag. 19 September') was lost, having been dispatched by the *Arctic* which sank in the Atlantic on 27 September 1854.—483

571 For Tuesday, 26 September 1854, Engels wrote 'The Attack on Sevastopol' (see present edition, Vol. 13).—483

572 Marx's letter to Dana has not been found.—484

573 The siege of Sevastopol by the Anglo-French-Turkish forces lasted from 13 (25) September 1854 to 27 August (8 September) 1855.—484

574 Marx refers to an article in the series *Revolutionary Spain* which was sent to America on 30 September 1854. The *Tribune* editors published it as two articles in Nos. 4220 and 4222 on 27 and 30 October 1854 as articles IV and V in Marx's series.—484

575 Engels' letter of 25 (Monday) or 26 (Tuesday) September 1854, mentioned by Marx, has not been found.—484

576 Marx wrote about Saint-Arnaud in three articles sent to New York on 6, 9 and 16 June 1854 as emerges from entries in Marx's notebook. The first article has not been found in the issues of the *New-York Daily Tribune, New-York Weekly Tribune* and *New-York Semi-Weekly Tribune* available to the editors of the present edition. The material relating to Saint Arnaud in the article of 16 June, 'State of the Russian War', was omitted by the *Tribune* editors, and hence only part of the biographical essay on Saint-Arnaud is extant in the article 'Reorganisation of the British War Administration.—The Austrian Summons.— Britain's Economic Situation.—St. Arnaud' (see present edition, Vol. 13).—484

577 The *Tribune* editors added the following sentence at the end of Marx's article 'Espartero': 'Our readers can judge whether the Spanish Revolution is likely to have any useful result or not.'—485

578 The *Tribune* editors added the following sentence to Article I of Marx's *Revolutionary Spain* (published on 9 September 1854): 'Let us hope that the additions now being made to their annals by the Spanish people may prove neither unworthy nor fruitless of good to themselves and to the world.'—485

579 By 'Baron Nicholson's court' Marx means a club—the Judge and Jury Society—formed by Renton Nicholson in London in 1841. Its visitors staged parody trials presided over by Nicholson himself, who was called Lord Chief Baron.—486

580 This article was probably not written because the entry concerning its dispatch is crossed out in Marx's notebook.—486

581 A reference to the Seven Years' War (1756-63) in which almost all European countries took part.—488

582 In 1763, the English journalist John Wilkes criticised King George III's Speech from the Throne in his newspaper *The North Briton*. He was expelled from the House of Commons and outlawed. After his forced flight to France, Wilkes returned to England in 1768, was elected to Parliament four times but each time his election was declared invalid. He was not admitted to Parliament until his fifth election.
   In connection with 'Wilkes' case' letters published in the London newspaper *The Public Advertiser* from 1768 to 1772 and signed Junius became very popular. The author campaigned for Wilkes' rehabilitation and for democratisation of the political system in Britain. In 1772 Junius' letters were published as a book. It was established later that they had been written by the journalist Philip Francis.—489

583 In February 1792 the coalition of European feudal and absolutist states launched a war against revolutionary France. Britain supported this coalition and after France had been proclaimed a republic on 10 August 1792 and King Louis XVI executed in January 1793, it openly entered the war on the side of the coalition in early 1793.—489

584 The suggestion that Robert Adair, British diplomat and Fox's confidential agent, was sent to St. Petersburg with the aim of upsetting William Pitt's plans was made by G. Tomline in *Memoirs of the Life of the Right Honorable William Pitt*, in 3 Volumes, London, 1821.—489

585 In 1756, at the beginning of the Seven Years' War, Admiral Byng was ordered to lead a squadron to the Mediterranean. The squadron was defeated at the battle of the Minorca on 20 May 1756. The government placed the entire responsibility for this on the admiral, who was brought to England under arrest, sentenced to death and shot in March 1757.—490

586 The reference is to a short period (November-December 1808) during the Peninsular War (see Note 462) when the French forces were led by Napoleon himself.—490

587 In 1833-40 Spain was the scene of the so-called first Carlist war between the reactionary feudal and Catholic forces headed by the pretender to the Spanish throne Don Carlos (brother of Ferdinand VII) and bourgeois-liberal forces

supporting the government of Regent Maria-Cristina. The Carlists were defeated.—490

[588] This letter was published in English for the first time abridged in: K. Marx and F. Engels, *Literature and Art*. Selections from Their Writings, N. Y., 1947, p. 134.—492

[589] The *Congress of Verona* of the Holy Alliance (see Note 353) was held from October to December 1822. It decided in favour of French armed intervention against revolutionary Spain and continuance of Austria's occupation of the Kingdoms of Naples and Sardinia, and condemned the national liberation uprisings of the Greek people against the Turkish yoke.—492

[590] The *Order of St Andrew*, the highest order in the Russian Empire, was introduced by Peter the Great in 1698.—492

[591] The *Laibach Congress* (January-March 1821) of the Holy Alliance openly proclaimed the principle of interference by the countries of the Alliance in the internal affairs of other states in support of feudal and monarchist regimes.—493

[592] The *Bidassoa*—a river in the Western Pyrenees on the border between France and Spain. The allusion is to the Peace of the Pyrenees concluded by France and Spain on Faisans Island on the Bidassoa on 7 November 1659 which helped France seize supremacy in Western Europe from Spain.—494

[593] A system of treaties concluded at the Congress of Vienna (1814-15) as a result of the defeat of Napoleonic France.—495

[594] A reference to the diplomatic manoeuvres of the European powers in connection with the national liberation movement of the Greek people against the Turkish yoke (1821-29).—496

[595] This is presumably an allusion to Chateaubriand's pamphlet *De Buonaparte, des Bourbons, et de la nécessité de se rallier à nos princes légitimes pour le bonheur de la France et celui de l'Europe* published in 1814.
The Spanish branch of the Bourbon dynasty succeeded to the Spanish throne in accordance with the will of the childless Habsburg, King Charles II, in favour of the Duke of Anjou, grandson of Louis XIV and great-great-grandson of Henry IV, who became King Philip V of Spain in 1700.—497

[596] Marx alludes ironically to Chateaubriand's journey to Jerusalem, after which he published his three-volume *Itinéraire de Paris à Jérusalem* in 1811.—497

[597] In a letter of 1 November 1854 Charles Dana proposed that Marx should use for his military articles *The War with Mexico* by R. S. Ripley, a book on the operations of the American army in the war against Mexico in 1846-48. Dana wrote: 'This will gratify the national *amour propre* of our readers, and convince them still more thoroughly that your articles are written in all probability by Gen. Scott' (see also this volume, p. 407).—498

[598] On Tuesday, 21 November, Marx sent an article to New York in the series *Revolutionary Spain*, as indicated in his notebook: 'Dienstag. 21. November. Spain. Intervention.' The article was not published in the *New-York Daily Tribune* and the manuscript has not been found.—498

[599] See Note 234. An extract from this letter was published in English also in Marx and Engels, *On the United States*, Progress Publishers, Moscow, 1979.—501

600 Engels' letter has not been found.—501, 510

601 Marx's letter to Freund has not been found.—502

602 Neither Marx's letter to Lassalle nor Lassalle's reply has been found.—502

603 Marx contributed to the *Neue Oder-Zeitung* during 1855, writing his first article for it on 29 December 1854. Marx's articles were published unsigned, but marked 'X'. As there was practically no workers' press during the years of reaction, Marx's contributing to the *Neue Oder-Zeitung* made it possible to maintain contact with Germany and keep German readers informed on the vital problems of international and domestic politics, the working-class and democratic movement, and economic development in the capitalist countries, primarily Britain and France. Marx regularly sent articles on the operations in the Crimean War, and made frequent use of entire reports by Engels for the *New-York Daily Tribune*, translating them into German; he also sent the *Neue Oder-Zeitung* abridged versions of Engels' articles, with occasional changes and additions. Articles from the *Neue Oder-Zeitung* are published in vols. 13 and 14 of the present edition.—502

604 The reference is to the Welcome and Protest Committee formed by the Chartists, headed by Jones, for Barbès' expected arrival in Britain after he was amnestied, and against Napoleon III's intended visit. Barbès was released from prison on Napoleon III's order of 3 October 1854 in acknowledgment of the chauvinist stand he took when the Crimean War broke out. Marx and Engels censured Barbès' behaviour in the article 'The Sevastopol Hoax.—General News' written on 5-6 October 1854: 'From this moment Barbès has ceased to be one of the revolutionary chiefs of France' (see present edition, Vol. 13, p. 491). On 18 October 1854 the emigrant *L'Homme. Journal de la démocratie universelle*, published in London, carried Barbès' letter of 11 October in which he confirmed his attitude to the war but at the same time declared his hostility to the Bonapartist regime. This statement, however, did not save his political reputation and shortly afterwards he gave up politics.—502

605 At one of the meetings held by the Welcome and Protest Committee in London on 26 and 28 November 1854 Jones said among other things that 'the democracy of Britain did not own the word *foreigner*—it looked on the exiles not as Frenchmen, or Italians, but as men, as brothers... At the same time, it desired to give the forthcoming demonstration a truly national and English character. If exiles were on the committee, it might be said exiles have got up the affair, and that it was not a genuine manifestation of British feeling. Therefore the committee would number only British names though it hoped to gather round itself hearts from every land' (*The People's Paper*, No. 135, 2 December 1854).—503

606 Marx has in mind the national liberation war in Spain against the Napoleonic rule (1808-14).—504

607 The reference is to the last, the third unpublished article of Marx's series *Revolutionary Spain*, sent to New York on 8 December 1854. The manuscript has not been found.—504

608 Marx carried out his plans in the article 'Progress of the War' which he wrote jointly with Engels on 14-15 December 1854.—505

609 Engels planned to write a critique of pan-Slavist ideas. Ever since his removal to Manchester in 1850 Engels had been studying the language, literature and

history of the Slav peoples. As can be judged from Marx' letters to Engels of 16 May and 26 June 1855, Marx negotiated the publication of Engels' pamphlet in Germany (see this volume, pp. 535 and 539). But these plans of Marx and Engels remained unfulfilled.

In April 1855 at Marx's request Engels wrote two articles on this subject under the title 'Germany and Pan-Slavism' (see present edition, Vol. 14, pp. 156-62). They were published in the *Neue Oder-Zeitung* and under changed titles in the *New-York Daily Tribune* (see Note 649).—505, 534, 535, 539

610 Engels spent Christmas in London. Engels' letter written on about 15 December 1854 has not been found.—505

611 Marx refers to the trial of the French Blanquist worker Emmanuel Barthélemy, accused of murdering two Englishmen. The English Press made a great fuss over the trial, which did not succeed in clearing up the motives behind the murder. Barthélemy was sentenced to death and executed on 22 January 1855.—505

612 In compliance with this plan Marx wrote two articles, on 29 December 1854 and 1 January 1855, which were published in the *Neue Oder-Zeitung* on 2 and 4 January 1855 under the general title 'Rückblicke' ('In Retrospect'). This marked the beginning of Marx's collaboration with this newspaper (see Note 603).—507

613 The formation of a Foreign Legion for the purpose of reinforcing the British in the Crimea was envisaged by the Enlistment of Foreigners Bill passed in Parliament on 22 December 1854. The Legion was not formed however owing to protests against the use of foreign mercenaries.—508, 520

614 This letter was published in English for the first time abridged in: K. Marx and F. Engels, *Literature and Art*. Selections from Their Writings, N. Y., 1947, p. 106.—508

615 Marx and Heine met and became friends in Paris at the end of December 1843. Marx supported Heine in his disputes with the radical petty-bourgeois opposition who attacked Heine for his criticism of Ludwig Börne, one of their prominent representatives.—509

616 In reply to attacks in the *Allgemeine Zeitung* in April 1848 Heine stated in the supplement to No. 144 of the same paper, on 23 May 1848, that he was compelled to accept the pension his French friends (the historian Mignet, in particular) succeeded in obtaining for him as he was in great straits owing to the prohibition of his books in Germany.—510

617 In a letter of 7 January 1855 Lassalle asked Marx to list the works containing official statistical data on the changes in England's economic position after the repeal of the Corn Laws in 1846 (see Note 72).—511

618 Marx has in mind his economic notes made from September 1850 to August 1853, when he resumed his economic research (see Note 45).—511, 522

619 In January 1854 Marx wrote the following articles for the *Neue Oder-Zeitung*: 'The Opening of Parliament' (on the 24th), 'Comments on the Cabinet Crisis' (on the 26th) and 'Parliamentary News' (on the 27th). At Marx's request Engels wrote for the *New-York Daily Tribune* the article 'The European War' (about 29 January) (see present edition, Vol. 13).—514

620 The reference is to the Aberdeen Coalition Government (see Note 343) which was defeated in the House of Commons on 29 January. On the basis of the material mentioned here and sent by Marx to Engels with his next letter of 31 January 1855, Engels wrote the article 'The Late British Government' for the *New-York Daily Tribune* on 1 February 1855. The same subject was used by Marx in the articles 'The Defeated Government' and 'Two Crises' for the *Neue Oder-Zeitung* in early February 1855 (see present edition, Vol. 13).—515

621 In April 1853 and from March to May 1854 Marx devoted several articles to Gladstone's financial policy. They were published in the *New-York Daily Tribune*, the *Neue Oder-Zeitung* and *The People's Paper*. The most detailed analysis of Gladstone's budget is given in 'The New Financial Juggle; or Gladstone and the Pennies', 'Achievements of the Ministry', '*L. S. D.*, or Class Budgets, and Who's Relieved by Them', 'Riot at Constantinople.—German Table Moving.—The Budget' (see present edition, Vol. 12), 'British Finances.—The Troubles at Preston', 'British Finances' and others (Vol. 13). It has not been established which articles Marx sent to Engels.—515

622 The *Irish Brigade*—the Irish faction in the British Parliament from the 1830s to the 1850s. With the equilibrium existing between the Tories and the Whigs, the Irish Brigade, alongside the Manchester men (see Note 63), could influence the alignment of forces in Parliament and sometimes decide the fate of the government.—516

623 The reference is to the Franchise Bill. As early as February 1852 Russell made a preliminary statement of his intention to introduce it (see his speech in the House of Commons on 9 February 1852, *The Times*, No. 21034, 10 February 1852); however, it was never debated in Parliament.—516

624 Marx refers to the 'Removal of Some Disabilities of Her Majesty's Jewish Subjects' Bill, introduced by Russell in the House of Commons on 24 February and aimed at admitting Jews to the House. Russell's Bill passed the House of Commons but was rejected by the House of Lords. Marx assessed it in the article 'Parliamentary Debates.—The Clergy Against Socialism.—Starvation' (see present edition, Vol. 11).—516

625 At the sitting of the House of Commons on 31 May 1853 Russell stated that the British Parliament should not sanction a state subsidy to the Catholic Church in Ireland because the Catholic clergy were not sufficiently committed to the English Crown and the Constitution. Russell's speech was published in *The Times*, No. 21443, 1 June 1853.—516

626 These Bills were introduced in Parliament in November 1852. Marx analysed and assessed them in the articles 'The Indian Question.—Irish Tenant Right' (see present edition, Vol. 12) and 'From the Houses of Parliament.—Bulwers' Motion.—The Irish Question' (Vol. 14).—517

627 The *Transportation Bill*, which abolished deportation of criminals to penal colonies, was passed on 12 August 1853. After preliminary detention the transportees were given release certificates granting them the right to reside in Britain under police surveillance, employed as cheap labour for public works. Marx assessed this Bill in 'The War Question.—British Population and Trade Returns.—Doings of Parliament' (see present edition, Vol. 12).—518

628 Marx refers to the proposals on the public debt moved by Gladstone in the House of Commons on 8 April 1853. For details see Marx's articles 'The New Financial Juggle; or Gladstone and the Pennies', 'Achievements of the Ministry',

'Affairs in Holland.—Denmark.—Conversion of the British Debt.—India, Turkey and Russia', 'The Russian Humbug.—Gladstone's Failure.—Sir Charles Wood's East Indian Reforms' (present edition, Vol. 12).

At the sitting of the House of Commons on 28 July 1853 Gladstone moved a resolution on measures for creating a public consolidated fund to pay for shares of the South Sea Company, which in fact meant the failure of the plan for conversion of the public debt (see K. Marx, 'Financial Failure of Government.—Cabs.—Ireland.—The Russian Question', present edition, Vol. 12).—518

629 Here.Marx gives the date of the reception in Constantinople of the news of the battle of Sinope on 30 (18) November 1853 (see Note 467).—518

630 On the Note of the four powers see Note 467; on the Vienna Note see Note 476.—518

631 The reference is to the article 'On the History of the Eastern Question' published in the *Journal de Saint-Pétersbourg*, No. 336, 18 February (2 March) 1854 in connection with John Russell's speech in the House of Commons on 17 February 1854. The article alluded to the collusion of the Russian and British governments in the Turkish question supporting its statement by reference to Seymour's secret correspondence in 1853 and the memorandum of 1844. Marx analysed the position adopted by the two powers in the articles 'The Documents on the Partition of Turkey' and 'The Secret Diplomatic Correspondence' (see present edition, Vol. 13).—519

632 Under a law in force in England since 1662 paupers who changed their place of residence or applied to a parish for alms could be returned to their former place of residence by court decision. On 10 February 1854 a Settlement and Removal Bill was introduced in the House of Commons envisaging prohibition of forced settlement of paupers in England and Wales. The Bill was rejected by Parliament.—520

633 Under a law in force in England since the early eighteenth century newly elected MPs were to take an 'oath of abdication' denying the right of any heirs of James II to the throne; the oath contained expressions of loyalty to Christianity. Refusal to take the oath deprived an MP of the right of active participation in the work of Parliament.—520

634 Engels' article 'The Late British Government' (see present edition, Vol. 13 and also Note 620).—520

635 The reference is to Ferdinand Lassalle's letter to Marx of 27 January containing cuttings from the January issues of the *Düsseldorfer Zeitung* and the *Kölnische Zeitung*, and Roland Daniels' letter of 16 January 1855.—521

636 Marx writes about the traditional banquets of petty-bourgeois emigrants held to mark the anniversary of the February 1848 revolution in France.—521

637 A reference to the German Workers' Educational Society in London (see Note 24).—521

638 A reference to the International Committee set up by representatives of the London Chartist Organising Committee (as the Welcome and Protest Committee was called since February 1855; see Note 604) and also French, German, Polish, Hungarian, Italian and other petty-bourgeois refugees. Jones was its President. At the end of 1855 the International Committee became an

independent organisation; renamed the International Association in 1856, it operated until 1859.—521

639 Judging by extant documents, Herzen did not attend the meeting, but received a written invitation to become a member of the International Committee (see Note 638).—521

640 An allusion to Herzen's view of 'old Europe' and 'young Russia' expounded most clearly in *Du développement des idées révolutionnaires en Russie*, par A. Iscander, Paris, 1851; *La Russie et la vieux Monde. Lettres à W. Linton. Esq.*, par A. Herzen; *Le peuple russe et le socialisme. Lettre à Monsieur J. Michelet, professeur au Collège de France*, par A. Herzen. Seconde édition, 1855, and other works. These publications were used by Marx and Engels.—523

641 This may be a reference to Herzen's reply to Ivan Golovin's slanderous article (see this volume, pp. 523-24): 'Reply to Mr. Golovin. To the Editor of *The Morning Advertiser*', published in *The Morning Advertiser* on 15 February 1855.—525

642 Marx refers to the anonymous pamphlet *De la conduite de la guerre d'Orient. Expédition de Crimée. Mémoire adressé au gouvernement de S. M. l'Empereur Napoléon III par un officier général*, Bruxelles, 1855. Its authorship was ascribed to several persons, Prince Napoleon (Joseph Charles Paul Bonaparte) among them. Marx assessed it in the articles 'On the History of the French Alliance' and 'The Brussels *Mémoire*' and Engels in 'Fate of the Great Adventurer' (see present edition, Vol. 14).—526

643 In January and February 1855 Marx read B. G. Niebuhr's *The History of Rome*, a new edition in three volumes, London; 1847-51, and simultaneously made a summary of it entitled 'Römische Geschichte'.—527

644 *Badinguet*—a nickname given to Napoleon III because in 1846 he escaped from prison in the clothes of the mason Badinguet. In April 1855 Napoleon III made an official visit to England.—534

645 Marx and his wife returned to London from Manchester about 6 May 1855.—535

646 In 1854, in connection with the Crimean War and the exacerbation of the Eastern Question, Bruno Bauer published several pamphlets, among them *De la dictature occidentale*, *Die jetzige Stellung Rußlands* and *Rußland und das Germanenthum*. It has not been established which of these is referred to here.—535

647 Marx may have had in mind his letter to Elsner of 17 April 1855, but he could have written to him after his return from Manchester, i.e. after 6 May 1855.—535

648 Marx has in mind the supporters of the Administrative Reform Association set up in May 1855 on the initiative of liberal circles in the City. Taking advantage of the alarm in the country caused by the plight of the British army in the Crimea, the Association hoped by means of mass rallies and with the Chartists' support to bring pressure to bear on Parliament and win broader access to government posts for members of the commercial and finance bourgeoisie. The Association failed in its strivings and soon ceased to exist. Marx repeatedly wrote about the Association's activity and its relations with the Chartists; see for instance his article 'The Agitation Outside Parliament' (present edition, Vol. 14).—536

[649] Marx considered it essential to publish a critique of pan-Slavist theories in the *New-York Daily Tribune* in order to counteract the influence exerted on American public by the articles and pamphlets of a pan-Slavist contributor to the newspaper, A. Gurowski. The *New-York Daily Tribune* published after heavy editing Engels' two articles on pan-Slavism (see Note 609) under the titles 'The European Struggle' and 'Austria's Weakness' on 5 and 7 May 1855 respectively (see present edition, Vol. 14).—536

[650] Dana's letter to Marx of 1 June 1855.—537

[651] Engels wrote the survey 'The Armies of Europe' (see present edition, Vol. 14) from June to September 1855. He was helped in this work by Marx, who collected material for him on various European armies, the Spanish and the Neapolitan in particular, at the British Museum library. The survey was published unsigned in *Putnam's Monthly* in August, September and December.—537, 540

[652] On 29 June Engels wrote 'From Sevastopol' (see present edition, Vol. 14) about the Allies' unsuccessful storm of Sevastopol on 18(6) June 1855—the fortieth anniversary of Waterloo. The main French attack was directed against Malakhov Hill and the English against the Redan (Third Bastion).—538

[653] In a letter of 13 August 1855 which has not survived, Engels asked Weerth, then in Hamburg, to negotiate with Duncker about his, Engels', pamphlet on pan-Slavism (see Note 609). As emerges from Weerth's reply to Engels of 24 August, his negotiations with Duncker failed.—539

[654] A mass demonstration organised by the Chartists was held in Hyde Park on 24 June 1855, in protest against a series of anti-popular measures adopted by Parliament (in particular, the prohibition of Sunday trading). Marx took part in this demonstration with other German revolutionary democrats and described it in 'Anti-Church Movement.—Demonstration in Hyde Park' (see present edition, Vol. 14).—539

[655] Marx has in mind the police reprisals against the participants in the second mass demonstration held, despite the police prohibition, in Hyde Park on Sunday, 1 July 1855, in protest against Sunday Trading Bill (on the first demonstration see Note 654). Marx describes the events in which he took part in 'Agitation over the Tightening-up of Sunday Observance' (see present edition, Vol. 14).—541

[656] A law prohibiting the sale of spirits had been in force in the State of Maine since 1851.

   Know-nothings—a secret political organisation formed in the USA in 1854 against emigrants; the members of this organisation swore to answer 'I know nothing' to all questions about its activity and aims.—542

[657] A reference to Szeredy's letter to Marx of 15 July 1855 containing a request for assistance in publishing and distributing his novel *Asiatic Chiefs* in Britain and the USA.—543

[658] Marx made this request because he intended to write the pamphlet *Lord John Russell* (see present edition, Vol. 14).—543

[659] Marx's pamphlet *Lord John Russell* was published in the *New-York Daily Tribune* on 28 August 1855 condensed into a single article. The pamphlet was published in full in German in the *Neue Oder-Zeitung* as a series of six articles

which appeared from 28 July to 15 August 1855 (see present edition, Vol. 14).—545

660 On the first *Mémoire* see Note 642; the second *Mémoire—Deuzième mémoire adressé au gouvernement de S. M. l'Empereur Napoléon III sur l'expédition de Crimée et la conduite de la guerre d'Orient, par un officier général*, Genève, mai 1855—was ascribed to the French journalist Tavernier and the Belgian officer, adjutant of the War Minister, T. F. Sterckx. Like the first *Mémoire* it was aimed at justifying the actions of the French Command in the Crimean campaign.—545

661 Marx's letter to Dana has not been found.—546

662 On 15 June 1855 Charles Napier published in *The Morning Advertiser* his letters criticising the administrative system in the British Navy, the lack of talent among commanders, and in particular the criminal irresponsibility of James Graham, First Lord of the Admiralty, which came to light during the military operations of the Anglo-French fleet in the Baltic Sea in 1854 and 1855. *The Times* published Napier's article on 24 August 1855. Marx wrote about Napier's letters and his correspondence with Graham in the articles 'Napier's Letters.—Roebuck's Committee', 'Napier's Letter' and 'Another British Revelation' (see present edition, Vol. 14).—546

663 The information Marx had access to was presumably unreliable. It has not been established what newspaper he meant. Herzen met Engländer in 1849, but he already knew at that time that he was an agent of the French and Austrian police and would have nothing to do with him.—548, 553

664 Here Marx compares his enforced departure for Manchester (see Marx to Moritz Elsner, 11 September 1855, this volume, pp. 550-53) with the evacuation of the Southern Side of Sevastopol by the Russian troops on 28-29 August (8-9 September) 1855.—550

665 This is Marx's reply to Elsner, who wrote in his letter of 4 September 1855 about the financial straits of the *Neue Oder-Zeitung* to which Marx contributed during that year (see notes 603 and 612).—550

666 Elsner's letters of 3 and 7 October 1855 to Marx.—554

667 The reference is to two Prussian Constitutions. The first was imposed by King Frederick William IV simultaneously with the dissolution of the Prussian National Assembly on 5 December 1848. It introduced a two-chamber system. The King retained the right not only to rescind the Chambers' decisions but also to revise certain articles of the Constitution. The further strengthening of the reaction led in April 1849 to the dissolution of the Second Chamber elected on the basis of the 1848 Constitution, to the replacement of universal suffrage with a three-class electoral system based on a high property qualification and to the introduction of a new, still more reactionary Constitution which came into force on 31 January 1850.—554

668 On 10 October 1855 *L'Homme*, the French refugee newspaper printed in Jersey, carried an open letter by a leader of petty-bourgeois democratic emigrants, Felix Pyat, to Queen Victoria in connection with her visit to France in August of that year. Anti-Bonapartist in content, this letter was provocative and adventuristic like all Pyat's utterances. It caused a polemic in the English and emigrant press, and serious fears that the so-called Aliens Bill might again come into force (see Note 75). To curry favour with Napoleon III the

Governor of Jersey expelled several French refugees from the island, Victor Hugo among them.—555, 557

669 Lassalle's letters to Marx of 24 September and October (exact date not established) 1855.—556

670 Marx lived in Paris from the end of October 1843 to 3 February 1845 when, on the demand of the Prussian Government, he was expelled from France and compelled to move to Brussels.—556

671 An allusion to Georg Weerth's former activity as a journalist. During the 1848-49 revolution he wrote essays and feuilletons (in verse and prose) for the *Neue Rheinische Zeitung.*—556

672 Marx's letter to Jones has not been found.—557

673 The reference is to a book by Herzen which came out in London in early October 1855. It included the second and fourth parts of *My Past and Thoughts* and was entitled *My Exile in Siberia* (two volumes, London, 1855). The title was supplied by the publishers, Hurst and Blackett, and on about 17 October Herzen lodged a protest with them against the arbitrary change of the title. Reviews published in *The Leader,* (No. 290, 13 October), *Critic, London Literary Journal* (No. 25537, 15 October), *Atlas* (20 October), *Athenaeum* (No. 1460, 20 October), *The Economist* (10 November) and other papers highly appraised Herzen's book.—558

674 Engels' two articles for the *New-York Daily Tribune* were sent to the USA by the steamer *Asia,* which sailed from Liverpool and reached Halifax on 19 December. The newspaper published the first article as a leader entitled 'The State of the War' on 21 December 1855 and the second also as a leader, 'The War in Asia', on 26 December 1855. Engels' authorship of these articles was established during the preparation of this volume.—559

675 In his letter of 20 November 1855 Dana informed Marx that the *Tribune* editors had agreed to publish two articles by Marx every week and to pay him 10 dollars for each.—559, 560

676 Judging by Dana's letter (see Note 675) Marx proposed to organise the dispatch of articles to the *New-York Daily Tribune* directly from the Crimea probably expecting that the German emigrant O. Mirbach, a former Prussian artillery officer who intended to leave for Constantinople, would be the correspondent.—560

677 The article written by Engels on 12 December 1855 and edited by Marx was sent to the USA by the steamer *Pacific* on 16 December and published in the *New-York Daily Tribune* on 29 December 1855 under the title 'The Asiatic Campaign'. Marx's and Engels' authorship of this article was established during the preparation of this volume.—561

678 A nickname given to Bruno Bauer by Marx and Engels in the first half of the 1840s. The Young Hegelians called their own trend 'critical criticism'. See Marx and Engels, *The Holy Family, or Critique of Critical Criticism* (present edition, Vol. 4).—562

679 Engels stayed in London from about 24 December 1855 to early January 1856.—563

680 The first volume of K. F. Köppen's book appeared in Berlin in 1857 entitled *Die Religion des Buddha und ihre Entstehung*, and the second volume in 1859 entitled *Die Lamaische Hierarchie und Kirche*.—563

681 Possible alterations in Engels' article of 12 December 1855 (see Note 677).—563

682 Marx sought to get his associates, former editors of the *Neue Rheinische Zeitung*, including Weerth, to contribute to Weydemeyer's *Die Revolution* (see Note 2).—567

683 Joseph Weydemeyer left Europe on 1 October 1851. Owing to autumn storms the voyage lasted 38 days and the ship did not reach New York till 7 November 1851.—570

684 This letter was published in English for the first time in Karl Marx and Frederick Engels, *Letters to Americans. 1848-1895*, International Publishers, New York, 1953.—572

685 The reference is to a journal which Becker, Weydemeyer and Bürgers planned to start in the spring of 1851; their plan did not materialise.—575

686 At the sitting of the Cologne jury on 23 October 1852 Stieber presented as evidence a faked 'Minute-book' (see Note 259) which provided the defence with an additional material to expose the false nature of the whole trial.—576

687 Marx and Engels used addresses of several businessmen and trading houses for safe conveyance of the documents to the defence counsel at the Cologne Communist Trial, Schneider II, Esser I and von Hontheim. The list of these addresses is given in Vol. 11 of the present edition, pp. 590-91. See also this volume, p. 218.—578

688 The editors of the present edition do not have the original of this letter at their disposal and it is printed according to a copy in Cluss' letter to Weydemeyer of 28 March 1853.—579

689 An allusion to the fact that financial difficulties prevented Weydemeyer and Cluss from buying up from the printers all the copies of *The Eighteenth Brumaire of Louis Bonaparte* printed in New York.—579

690 Jenny Marx presumably refers to the unsuccessful attempt to publish Marx's and Engels' pamphlet *The Great Men of the Exile*.—580

691 The *American funds*—money raised for the so-called German-American revolutionary loan (see Note 27).—580

692 The excerpt from Cluss' letter to Weydemeyer given here expounds the contents of part of Marx's letter to Cluss, which has not survived. The letter was probably written on about 1 May 1853, when Marx was visiting Manchester.—582

693 The reference is to Cluss' letter to Marx of 10 April 1853.—582

694 Engels planned to publish *Revolution and Counter-Revolution in Germany* in German in *Die Reform*. The last, twentieth, article of this work did not appear in the *New-York Daily Tribune* and was probably not written (see Note 214).—582

695 The excerpt from Cluss' letter to Weydemeyer given here contains an account of Jenny Marx's letter to Cluss of 20 May 1853 which has not survived.—583

696 Marx visited Engels in Manchester from 30 April to 19 May 1853.—583

⁶⁹⁷ This excerpt from Cluss' letter to Weydemeyer gives the contents of part of Marx's letter to Cluss which has not survived. The letter may have been written in February 1853.—584

⁶⁹⁸ Marx's letter to Cluss has not survived.—584

⁶⁹⁹ Jenny Marx presumably asks Engels to return Marx's letter to Jacob Schabelitz which she mentions here. The letter, which has not been found, was written at the end of November 1852. In his reply to Marx of 1 December Schabelitz agreed to accept Marx's terms for the publication of the pamphlet *Revelations Concerning the Communist Trial in Cologne*.—585

⁷⁰⁰ The circumstances of the duel between Schramm and Willich referred to here were distorted by the latter in the slanderous article 'Doctor Karl Marx und seine "Enthüllungen"'. Miskowsky was Schramm's second (see present edition, Vol. 12, pp. 494-95, and also Note 360).—586

⁷⁰¹ Karl and Jenny Marx' letter to Cluss has not survived.—587

⁷⁰² Probably a slip of the pen. The meetings of Polish refugees were held on 28 and 29 November 1853 (see Note 456).—587

NAME INDEX

(1797-1870)—participant in the
Italian national liberation movement.—200

Arena, Antoine (d. 1544)—French
satirist.—356

Aretino, Pietro (1492-1556)—Italian Renaissance author of lampoons against
the Pope and European monarchs.—
126

Ariosto, Lodovico (1474-1533)—Italian
Renaissance poet, author of *L'Orlando furioso.*—390

Arnim, Ludwig Achim (*Joachim*) *von*
(1781-1831)—German   romantic
poet.—440

Arnold, Franz—German democrat, took
part in the 1848-49 revolution in
Germany; after its defeat emigrated
to the USA, became an associate of
Adolph Cluss in the early 1850s,
disseminated Marxism in the
USA.—350

Athenaeus (late 2nd-early 3rd cent.)—
Greek   rhetorician   and   grammarian.—70

Auerbach, Berthold (1812-1882)—
German liberal writer of stories
idealising the life of German peasants, later an apologist for Bismarck.—563

Auerswald, Hans Adolf Erdmann von
(1792-1848)—Prussian   general,
Right-wing deputy to the Frankfurt
National Assembly; killed during
Frankfurt uprising in September
1848.—225

Augustus (*Gaius Julius Caesar Oc-
tavianus*) (63 B.C.-A.D. 14)—Roman
Emperor (27 B.C.-A.D. 14).—527

*Aumale, Henri Eugène Philippe Louis
d'Orléans, duc d'* (1822-1897)—son of
Louis Philippe, King of France; took
part in the conquest of Algeria in the
1840s, Governor General of Algeria
(1847-48); emigrated to England
after the February 1848 revolution.—
17, 200

Aurangzeb, Mohi ud-din Mohammed
(1618-1707)—ruler of the Grand
Mogul Empire in India (1658-
1707).—332

B

Babeuf, François Noël (*Gracchus*) (1760-
1797)—French revolutionary, advocate of utopian egalitarian communism, organiser of the Conspiracy of
Equals.—195

Bach, Alexander, Baron von (1813-
1893)—Austrian statesman, lawyer;
Minister of Justice (1848); Minister of
the Interior (1849-59).—106

*Bacon, Francis, Baron Verulam, Viscount
St. Albans* (1561-1626)—English
philosopher, founder of English
materialism; naturalist, historian and
statesman.—544

Badinguet—see *Napoleon III*

Bakunin, Mikhail Alexandrovich (1814-
1876)—Russian democrat, journalist,
participant in the 1848-49 revolution
in Germany; later ideologist of
Narodism and anarchism; opposed
Marxism in the First International.—
67, 306, 359-63, 373

Balzac, Honoré de (1799-1850)—French
realist novelist.—203

Bamberger, Louis (b. 1821)—German
refugee in London, editor of the
Deutsche Londoner Zeitung (1848-
51).—273, 321, 585

Bamberger, Simon—London banker.—
273, 287, 294, 314, 315, 323,
351

Bandiera brothers, *Attilio* (1810-1844)
and *Emilio* (1819-1844)—officers of
the Austrian Navy; leaders of the
Italian national liberation movement,
members of the Young Italy society;
executed for their attempt to raise a
revolt in Calabria (1844).—56

Bangya, János (1817-1868)—Hungarian
journalist and officer, participant in
the 1848-49 revolution in Hungary;
after its defeat Kossuth's emissary
abroad and at the same time agent-
provocateur; later served in the Turkish army under the name of
Mehemed Bey acting as a Turkish
agent in the Caucasus.—31, 32, 45,
71, 93, 95, 101, 120, 124, 126,
130-32, 200, 208, 214, 232-34, 237-
42, 252, 254, 256, 257, 267-70, 275,

281, 291, 296, 301-04, 312-14, 316, 319, 325, 386, 396, 434, 437, 477, 572

Barbès, Armand (1809-1870)—French revolutionary, leader of secret revolutionary societies during the July monarchy; was active in the 1848 revolution, deputy to the Constituent Assembly; sentenced to life imprisonment for participation in the popular insurrection of 15 May 1848, pardoned in 1854; emigrated to Belgium and abandoned politics.—32, 502, 521

Barnum, Phineas Taylor (1810-1891)— American showman, exhibited various freaks and rarities.—4, 103, 527

Barthélemy, Emmanuel (c. 1820-1855)— French worker, Blanquist, member of secret revolutionary societies during the July monarchy and participant in the June 1848 uprising in Paris; a leader of the Société des Proscrits Démocrates et Socialistes in London; sided with the Willich-Schapper group; executed in 1855 on a criminal charge.—128, 198, 224, 296, 299, 300, 505, 510, 515

Barthold, Friedrich Wilhelm (1799-1858)—German historian.—160

Batthyány, Kasimir, Count of (1807-1854)—Hungarian statesman, liberal aristocrat, Minister of Foreign Affairs in the Hungarian revolutionary government of Szemere (1849); after the suppression of the revolution emigrated to Turkey, and then to France.—26, 31, 45

Batthyány, Lajos, Count of (1806-1849)— Hungarian statesman, liberal aristocrat; Prime Minister of Hungary (March-September 1848); pursued a policy of compromise with the Austrian monarchy; shot after the suppression of the revolution.—70

Bauer, Bruno (1809-1882)—German idealist philosopher, Young Hegelian; author of works on the history of Christianity; radical; national-liberal after 1866.—37, 38, 76, 85-87, 94, 97, 102, 146, 147, 449, 462, 486, 490, 505, 535, 538, 562

Bauer, Edgar (1820-1886)—German journalist, Young Hegelian; emigrated to England after the 1848-49 revolution; Prussian official after the 1861 amnesty; brother of Bruno Bauer.—151, 314, 450, 507, 562

Bauer, Heinrich (1813-c. 1852)— German shoemaker, prominent figure in the German and international working-class movement, a leader of the League of the Just, member of the Central Authority of the Communist League, treasurer of the Social-Democratic Refugee Committee; emigrated to Australia in 1851.—14

Bayard, Pierre Terrail, seigneur de (c. 1475-1524)—French warrior called by his contemporaries the *chevalier sans peur et sans reproche.*—453

Bayer, Joseph August (1821-1864)— Austrian army officer and writer; Chief of Staff of Görgey's army during the 1848-49 revolution in Hungary, taken prisoner when the army capitulated in 1849, sentenced to death and later commuted to imprisonment in a fortress, pardoned in 1850.—310

Beaumarchais, Pierre Augustin Caron de (1732-1799)—French dramatist.—38, 297, 300

Becker, August (1814-1871)—German writer, member of the League of the Just in Switzerland, supporter of Weitling; took part in the 1848-49 revolution in Germany; in 1853 emigrated to the USA, where he contributed to democratic newspapers.—154

Becker, Hermann Heinrich (1820-1885)—German lawyer and journalist, took part in the 1848-49 revolution; editor of the *Westdeutsche Zeitung* (May 1849-July 1850); member of the Communist League from 1850; one of the accused in the Cologne Communist Trial (1852), sentenced to five-year imprisonment; later a national-liberal.—9, 20, 23, 34, 115, 142, 143, 212, 222-24, 242, 245, 262, 468, 499, 570, 575, 577, 580

Becker, Johann Philipp (1809-1886)—
German revolutionary, participant in
the democratic movement of the
1830s-50s and the international
working-class movement; fought as
an officer of the Swiss army in the
war against the Sonderbund; prominent figure in the 1848-49 revolution; commanded the Baden people's
militia during the Baden-Palatinate
uprising of 1849; active member of
the First International; friend and
associate of Marx and Engels.—490

Becker, Max Joseph (d. 1896)—German
engineer, democrat, took part in the
Baden-Palatinate uprising of 1849,
after its defeat emigrated to Switzerland and subsequently to the USA.—
72, 582

Beckmann—Prussian police spy in Paris
in the early 1850s, Paris correspondent of the *Kölnische Zeitung.*—194

Beckmann—Beckmann's wife.—194

Bedeau, Marie Alphonse (1804-1863)—
French general, moderate republican
politician; Vice-President of the Constituent and Legislative Assemblies
during the Second Republic; expelled
from France after the coup d'état of
2 December 1851.—199

Belfield, James—a friend of Marx and
Engels in Manchester.—219

Bellune, duke of—see *Victor, Claude Victor Perrin, duc de Bellune*

Bem, Józef (1795-1850)—Polish general,
prominent figure in the national
liberation movement, took part in
the Polish insurrection of 1830-31
and the revolutionary struggle
in Vienna in 1848; a leader of
the Hungarian revolutionary army
(1848-49); after the defeat of the
revolution emigrated to Turkey.
—311

Benningsen—American clerk in Kossuth's office.—261

Béranger, Pierre Jean de (1780-1857)—
French poet and song writer, author
of political satires; democrat.—497

Bergenroth, Gustav Adolph (1813-
1869)—German historian and journalist; petty-bourgeois democrat, took

part in the 1848-49 revolution; left
Germany in 1850.—563

Bermbach, Adolph (1822-1875)—Cologne
lawyer, democrat, deputy to the
Frankfurt National Assembly;
member of the Communist League;
witness for the defence at the Cologne Communist Trial (1852); corresponded with Marx; subsequently a
liberal.—20, 22, 24, 106, 107, 132,
134, 135, 136, 137, 142-43, 215, 216,
224, 230, 259

Bernard, Martin (1808-1883)—French
revolutionary, democrat, leader of
secret revolutionary societies during
the July monarchy, prominent in the
1848-49 revolution, was sentenced to
exile after the events of 13 June
1849, fled to England in the early
1850s and returned to France after
the 1859 amnesty.—50

Bernardin de Saint-Pierre, Jacques Henri
(1737-1814)—French author, naturalist and traveller.—447

Bernays, Karl Ludwig (1815-1879)—
German radical journalist, member
of the League of the Just, an editor
of *Vorwärts!*, the German refugees'
newspaper published in Paris with
Marx's collaboration; emigrated to
the USA after the 1848-49 revolution.—274

Bernhardt—German democrat, refugee
in the USA, an editor of the New
York *Neue Zeit.*—547

Berni, Francesco (c. 1498-1535)—Italian
Renaissance poet known for his
adaptation of Boiardo's *L'Orlando innamorato.*—131

Bernier, François (1625-1688)—French
physician, traveller and writer.—332-
33, 341

*Berry, Charles Ferdinand de Bourbon, duc
de* (1778-1820)—nephew of Louis
XVIII of France.—496

Bertin, Louis Marie Armand (1801-
1854)—French journalist; Orleanist;
publisher of the *Journal des Débats* in
1841-54.—68, 334

Bianca, von—Cologne patrician; juryman in the Cologne Communist Trial
(1852).—206, 238

uty to the Constituent and Legislative Assemblies during the Second Republic.—171, 261

Borchardt, Louis—German physician, acquaintance of Engels in Manchester.—334, 336, 353, 357, 370, 374, 420, 554, 555

Börnstein, Heinrich (1805-1892)— German democratic journalist, lived in Paris from 1842; edited, with Marx's collaboration, the newspaper Vorwärts! founded by him in 1844; emigrated to the USA in 1849 and edited the Anzeiger des Westens (Chicago).—52, 274

Bourbons—royal dynasty in France (1589-1792, 1814-15, and 1815-30), Spain (1700-1808, 1814-68, 1874-1931, and from 1975), and a number of Italian states.—129, 497

Bourqueney, François Adolphe, comte de (1799-1869)—French diplomat, envoy (1841-44) and ambassador (1844-48) to Constantinople; envoy (1853-56) and ambassador (1856-59) to Vienna.—456

Brunswick (Braunschweig), Karl Wilhelm Ferdinand, Duke of (1721-1792)— Prussian general; commanded (from November 1757) the Prussian and allied forces in the Seven Years' War.—526

Brenner-Guéniard—owner of a fashion-shop in Basle.—287

Brentano, Clemens (1778-1842)— German romantic poet.—440

Bright, John (1811-1889)—English manufacturer and politician, a leader of the Free Traders and co-founder of the Anti-Corn Law League.—56, 111, 129, 132, 355, 411, 520

Brockhaus, Heinrich (1804-1874)— German publisher, owner and head of F.A. Brockhaus Publishing House in Leipzig.—158, 182

Bruat, Armand Joseph (1796-1855)— French admiral, commanded a squadron (1854) and the French Navy (1855) in the Black Sea.—547

Brüggemann, Karl Heinrich (1810-1887)—German liberal journalist and economist; editor-in-chief of the

Kölnische Zeitung (1845-55).—367

Brüningk, A., Baron von—German refugee in London (from 1851), maintained contact with the German petty-bourgeois emigrants through his wife Maria Brüningk.—124, 125, 204, 205, 213, 265, 573, 574

Brüningk, Maria, Baroness von (d. 1853)—A. Brüningk's wife, niece of the Russian Princess Darya Lieven.— 112, 114, 120-21, 124, 135, 152, 204, 205, 265, 274, 282, 297, 300, 313, 573, 574

Brunnow, Philipp Ivanovich, Baron von, from 1871 Count (1797-1875)— Russian diplomat, envoy (1840-54, 1858-60) and ambassador (1860-74) to London.—456, 457

Buchheim—German democrat, refugee in London in the 1850s.—499

Buckup—Bradford merchant.—326, 328, 451, 468

Bülow, Adam Heinrich Dietrich, Baron von (1757-1807)—Prussian army officer and military theoretician.—427

Bürgers, Heinrich (1820-1878)—German radical journalist, contributor to the Rheinische Zeitung (1842-43); member of the Cologne community of the Communist League (1848); an editor of the Neue Rheinische Zeitung; member of the Communist League Central Authority from 1850; sentenced to six years imprisonment at the Cologne Communist Trial (1852).—20, 23, 34, 134, 137, 195, 197, 212, 217, 238, 240, 242, 247, 251, 468, 544, 547, 559, 560, 570

Bürgers, Lene—Heinrich Bürgers' sister.—491

Buridan, Jean (c. 1300-c. 1358)— French logician and nominalist philosopher.—170

Burns, Mary (1821-1863)—Irish working-woman, Frederick Engels' first wife.—443

Bute, John Stuart, Earl of (1713-1792)— British Tory statesman, Prime Minister (1761-63).—488

Butler, James Armar (1827-1854)— British army officer, organised the defence of Silistria (1854).—472

of the Free Traders and co-founder of the Anti-Corn Law League, M.P.—56, 129, 132, 252, 276, 411

Coeurderoy, Ernest (1825-1862)—French journalist, republican, revolutionary; shared anarchist views; took part in the 1848-49 revolution in France; emigrated after its defeat.—135, 136, 138

Coffinières, Antoine Siméon Gabriel (1786-c. 1865)—French lawyer, author of works on civil law.—556

Condé, Louis Joseph de Bourbon, prince de (1736-1818)—French general and politician, took part in the Seven Years' War (1756-1763), commanded the French Lower Rhine army in 1762; during the French Revolution commanded detachments of counter-revolutionary émigrés in the wars against the French Republic.—17, 489

Cooper, James Fenimore (1789-1851)—American novelist.—217, 301

Cornelius, Wilhelm—German radical journalist and businessman, a friend of Marx; refugee in London in the 1850s.—434, 502

Cortés, Hernán (Fernando) (1485-1547)—Spanish conqueror of the Aztec state (Mexico) in 1519-21.—501

Cotta, Johann Georg, Baron von Cottendorf (1796-1863)—German publisher, owner of a big publishing house from 1832.—391

Cournet, Frédéric (1808-1852)—French naval officer, republican, discharged from the Navy for his political views in 1847; took part in the 1848-49 revolution in France; emigrated to London after the coup d'état of 2 December 1851; was killed in a duel with Barthélemy.—224, 299

Csorich (Čorič), Anton, barun od Monte Creto (1795-1864)—Austrian general, Croat by birth, lieutenant-field marshal (from 1849), took part in suppressing the October 1848 uprising in Vienna and in the war against revolutionary Hungary; War Minister in 1850-53.—460

Czartoryski, Adam Jerzy, prince (1770-1861)—Polish magnate; close friend of Emperor Alexander I of Russia; Russian Foreign Minister (1804-06); President of the Polish Government during the insurrection of 1830-31, after its suppression headed the Polish monarchist émigrés in Paris.—45

D

Damm—German democrat; President of the Baden Constituent Assembly in 1849; later emigrated to England.—154-56, 255

Dana, Charles Anderson (1819-1897)—American journalist, follower of Fourier, abolitionist; an editor (1848) and then editor-in-chief (1849-62) of the *New-York Daily Tribune*; an editor of the *New American Cyclopaedia* (1857-63); editor-in-chief of the *New-York Sun* (1868-97).—3, 13, 20, 25, 35, 37, 38, 42, 44, 49, 55, 58, 75-77, 80, 86, 90, 91, 97, 99, 102, 107, 115, 120, 126, 127, 131, 133, 137, 146, 148, 158, 180, 181, 183, 185, 189, 195, 210, 212, 214, 216, 219, 229, 236, 237, 255, 265, 272, 275, 288, 289, 292, 293, 315, 328, 331, 351, 352, 354, 390, 400, 404, 407, 412, 439, 484, 498, 500, 502, 503, 537, 546, 559, 560, 583

Daniels, Amalie (1820-1895)—wife of Roland Daniels.—22, 59, 107, 223, 224, 230, 232, 301, 547, 548, 549, 559

Daniels, Franz Joseph—big wine merchant in Cologne, brother of Roland Daniels.—386

Daniels, Roland (1819-1855)—German physician, member of the Cologne Central Authority of the Communist League from 1850, one of the accused in the Cologne Communist Trial (1852), acquitted; friend of Marx and Engels.—9, 20, 22, 115, 142, 195, 212, 222, 238, 275, 386, 468, 479, 521, 544, 547, 549

Dannenberg, Pyotr Andreyevich (1792-1872)—Russian general, commanded a corps on the Danube and in the

Crimea in 1853-54.—470

Dante Alighieri (1265-1321)—Italian poet.—329

Danton, Georges Jacques (1759-1794)— prominent figure in the French Revolution, leader of the Right-wing Jacobins.—363, 521

Da Ponte, Lorenzo (1749-1838)—wrote librettos for a number of Mozart's operas.—556

Darasz, Albert (1808-1852)—prominent figure in the Polish national liberation movement, took part in the 1830-31 insurrection; a leader of democratic organisations of Polish emigrants; member of the Central Committee of European Democracy.—171, 459

Dasent, Sir George Webbe (1817-1896)— English philologist specialising in Scandinavian languages, journalist; assistant editor of *The Times* (1845-70); had contacts with diplomatic circles.—276

Decker, Karl von (1784-1844)—German general and military historian, took part in wars against Napoleonic France.—535

Delane, John Thaddeus (1817-1879)— English journalist, editor-in-chief of *The Times*.—276

Delane, William Frederick Augustus (d. 1858)—English lawyer, one of the financial directors of *The Times*, father of John Delane.—276

Della Rocco, Heinrico Morozzo—Italian refugee, associate of Mazzini.—280

Dembiński, Henryk (1791-1864)—Polish general and prominent figure in the national liberation movement, participant in the Polish insurrection of 1830-31, a commander in the Hungarian revolutionary army in the 1848-49 revolution, after its defeat emigrated to Turkey and then to France.—311

Demidovs—Russian aristocratic family, owners of minefields and iron and steel works.—411

Demuth, Helene (1820-1890)— housemaid and friend of the Marx family.—181, 364, 465, 537

Denman, Joseph—candidate for Manchester in the 1852 elections to Parliament.—111

Derby, earls of—British aristocratic family, many of them cotton magnates.—411

Derby, Edward Geoffrey Smith Stanley, Earl of (1799-1869)—English statesman, Whig until 1853, later a Tory leader; Prime Minister (1852, 1858-59 and 1866-68).—44, 49, 53-54, 56, 58, 69, 119, 147, 197, 215, 515

Desmoulins, Lucie Simplice Camille Benoist (1760-1794)—French writer, prominent figure in the French Revolution, Right-wing Jacobin, friend of Danton.—363

Deutsch, Simon (1822-1877)—Austrian bibliographer of Hebrew literature, radical, contributed to the Vienna *Der Radikale* in 1848; later emigrated to Paris, had connections with the Prussian police.—126

Diderot, Denis (1713-1784)—French Enlightenment philosopher, atheist; leader of the Encyclopaedists.—134

Diebich-Zabalkansky, Ivan Ivanovich (Diebitsch, Hans Karl Friedrich Anton), Count (1785-1831)—Russian field marshal-general, commander-in-chief (1829) of the Russian army during the Russo-Turkish war of 1828-29 and, from December 1830, of the army which crushed the Polish insurrection of 1830-31.—394

Dietz, Oswald (c. 1824-1864)—German architect; took part in the 1848-49 revolution, emigrated to London; member of the Communist League Central Authority, after the split of the League belonged to the separatist Willich-Schapper group, was a member of its Central Authority; later took part in the American Civil War on the side of the Union.—14, 151, 226, 230, 316, 576

Diezel, Gustav (1827-1864)—German scholar, lawyer.—505

Disraeli, Benjamin, Earl of Beaconsfield (1804-1881)—British statesman and writer; sympathised with the Young England group in the 1840s, later a

Tory leader; Chancellor of the Exchequer (1852, 1858-59, 1866-68), Prime Minister (1868, 1874-80).—61, 132, 197, 253, 265, 276, 295, 472, 483, 516, 517, 519

Dobrovský, Josef (1753-1829)—Czech scholar and public figure, founder of Slav philology; his works contributed to the Bohemian national movement in the first half of the nineteenth century.—563

Domenichi, Lodovico (d. 1564)—Italian poet, author of an adaptation of Boiardo's *L'Orlando innamorato.*—131

Donatus, Aelius (4th cent.)—Roman grammarian.—188

Donizetti, Gaetano (1797-1848)—Italian composer.—199

Douglas, Sir Howard (1776-1861)— British general and military writer, author of works on artillery and fortification.—426

Dralle, Friedrich Wilhelm (b. 1820)— German journalist, democrat, refugee in London in the 1850s.—151, 154, 173, 194

Dronke, Ernst (1822-1891)—German journalist and writer, "true socialist" and, later, member of the Communist League and an editor of the *Neue Rheinische Zeitung* (1848-49); after the 1848-49 revolution emigrated to Switzerland and then to England; supporter of Marx and Engels; subsequently gave up politics.—17, 32, 66, 71, 75, 76, 79, 86, 88-90, 91, 95, 97, 101, 109, 113, 120, 124, 133, 134, 138, 146, 148, 152, 158, 182, 189, 199, 200, 201, 204, 211, 219, 223, 231, 232, 234, 235, 239, 240, 243, 275, 282, 290, 296, 302, 303, 304, 312, 316, 319, 321, 323, 324, 326, 328, 356, 358, 362, 364, 372, 386, 391, 396, 397, 400, 402, 412, 436, 445, 451, 461, 463, 464, 465, 468-69, 473, 478, 480, 482, 500, 528, 534, 537, 542, 545, 560, 561, 574, 583, 584-85, 587, 589

Duchâtel, Charles Marie Tanneguy, comte (1803-1867)—French statesman, Orleanist, Minister of Trade (1834-36), Minister of the Interior (1839 and 1840-February 1848).—52

Dulon, Rudolph (1807-1870)—German pastor, a leader of the Friends of Light movement, which opposed the official church; emigrated to the USA in 1853.—71, 173, 417, 459, 462, 588

Duncker, Alexander (1813-1897)— German publisher.—539

Duncker, Franz Gustav (1822-1888)— German politician and publisher.—216, 232

Dundas, Henry, Viscount Melville (1742-1811)—British statesman, Lord Advocate for Scotland (1775-83), Home Secretary (1791-94), President of the Board of Control for India (1793-1801); Secretary for War (1794-1801), First Lord of the Admiralty (1804-05).—490

Dupin, André Marie Jean Jacques (1783-1865)—French lawyer and politician, Orleanist, deputy to the Constituent Assembly (1848-49) and President of the Legislative Assembly (1849-51), later Bonapartist.—47

Durand—French democrat.—199

Dureau de La Malle, Adolphe Jules César Auguste (1777-1857)—French scholar, philologist and archaeologist.—228

Düsar, Pedro—German democrat, took part in the 1848-49 revolution in Germany, brother-in-law of Gustav Struve.—45

E

Ebner, Hermann—German journalist, secret agent of the Austrian police in the 1840s-50s.—22, 99, 222, 238, 276, 483

Eccarius, Johann Georg (1818-1889)— German tailor, prominent figure in the German and international working-class movement, member of the League of the Just and later of the Communist League; a leader of the German Workers' Educational Society in London; member of the General Council of the First International; took part in the English trade union movement.—26, 40, 107, 117, 120,

democratic journalist; took part in the 1848-49 revolution in Germany, emigrated to France, Paris correspondent of the Augsburg *Allgemeine Zeitung* and *Kölnische Zeitung*; police agent.—178, 185, 194, 206

Hagen, Theodor (1823-1871)—member of the Communist League in Hamburg, publisher of the *Neue Rheinische Zeitung. Politisch-ökonomische Revue.*—581

Hain, August—German refugee in London, member of the Communist League, supported Marx and Engels during the split in the League in 1850.—86, 87

Halil Pasha (d. 1856)—Turkish military leader and statesman, repeatedly held ministerial posts; Capudan Pasha (Naval Minister) in 1854-55.—408

Hammel—member of the Communist League in Magdeburg, belonged to the separatist Willich-Schapper group, opponent of Marx and Engels.—169, 177

Hammer-Purgstall, Joseph, Baron von (1774-1856)—Austrian historian, Orientalist, author of works on Turkish history.—423, 428

Hansen—Cologne worker, member of the Communist League, emigrated to the USA in the early 1850s.—79

Harney, George Julian (1817-1897)—prominent figure in the English labour movement, a leader of the Chartist Left wing, editor of *The Northern Star, Democratic Review, Red Republican* and *Friend of the People*; associate of Marx and Engels; in the early 1850s was close to petty-bourgeois circles and temporarily withdrew from the revolutionary trend in the labour movement.—11, 30, 31, 43, 60-61, 67, 89, 93, 96, 99, 107, 162, 164, 196, 266, 282, 401, 587

Harney, Mary (d. 1853)—wife of George Julian Harney.—282

Harring, Harro Paul (1798-1870)—German radical writer, emigrated in 1828, lived in various countries of Europe and America including the USA.—117

Hatzfeldt, Sophie, Countess of (1805-1881)—friend and supporter of Ferdinand Lassalle.—339, 478

Hatzfeldt-Wildenburg, Edmund, Count of (b. 1798)—husband of Sophie Hatzfeldt.—293

Haupt, Hermann Wilhelm (born c. 1833)—German shop assistant; member of the Communist League; arrested with other Cologne communists, he turned King's evidence and was released before the trial; fled to Brazil (summer 1852).—143, 144, 145, 197, 215

Hauser, Kaspar (1812-1833)—a foundling discovered in Nürnberg in 1828 and placed in the care of the Bavarian state; the story of his origin and tragic death provided the theme for a number of literary works.—36

Hayward, Abraham (1801-1884)—British lawyer and journalist; Tory at the beginning of his career, later Peelite; appointed Secretary of the Poor Law Board in 1854.—519

Hebeler, Bernhard—Prussian consul-general in London in the 1830s-60s.—100, 232

Hecker, Friedrich Franz Karl (1811-1881)—German democrat, a leader of the Baden republican uprising in April 1848, after its defeat emigrated to Switzerland and then to the USA; fought in the American Civil War on the side of the Union.—6, 98

Heckscher, Martin—Frederick Engels' physician, a German resident in Manchester.—353

Hegel, Georg Wilhelm Friedrich (1770-1831)—German philosopher.—45, 65, 87, 104, 306, 462, 556

Heilberg, Louis (1818-1852)—German journalist; political refugee in Brussels, member of the Brussels Communist Correspondence Committee (1846) and later of the Communist League; took part in the 1848-49 revolution, emigrated to London at the end of 1850.—124

Heine, Heinrich (1797-1856)—German

revolutionary poet.—61, 121, 276, 401, 438, 455, 469, 504, 509, 544, 568, 587

Heinzen, Karl (1809-1850)—German radical journalist, for a short time took part in the Baden-Palatinate uprising of 1849; from 1847 onwards, opponent of Marx; refugee in Switzerland, England and, from the autumn of 1850, in the USA.— 6, 17, 52, 59, 60-62, 65, 94, 117, 141, 146, 161, 173, 185, 208, 263, 273, 308, 319, 351, 367, 391, 394, 395, 396, 417, 421, 423, 462, 542, 574, 575

Heise, Heinrich (1820-1860)—German democratic journalist, an editor of the newspaper Die Hornisse (1848-50); took part in the 1848-49 revolution in Germany, later a refugee in England.—86, 114, 115, 121, 162, 187, 349, 356, 397, 419, 420, 421, 441-45, 451, 454, 463, 469, 471, 478, 479, 543, 583, 587-89

Helmich, Julius—Westphalian publisher and bookseller; 'true socialist'; refugee in the USA in the 1850s.— 118, 161

Henry IV (Henri IV) (1553-1610)— King of France (1589-1610).—475, 497

Hentze, A.—German army officer, member of the Communist League, belonged to the separatist Willich-Schapper group; witness for the prosecution at the Cologne Communist Trial (1852).— 15, 143, 155, 161, 223, 229, 317, 335, 577

Herbert, Sidney, Baron of Lea (1810-1861)—British statesman, Tory and later Peelite; Secretary at War (1845-46 and 1852-55) and Secretary for War (1859-60).— 284, 472, 508

Herstadt—Cologne banker, juryman in the Cologne Communist Trial (1852).— 206, 238

Herweg—German democrat, took part in the 1848-49 revolution in Germany, refugee in London in the 1850s.— 155, 156, 243

Herwegh, Georg Friedrich (1817-1875)— German democratic poet, took part in the 1848-49 revolution, emigrated to Switzerland; subsequently member of the German Social-Democratic Party.— 199, 262

Herzen, Alexander Ivanovich (1812-1870)—Russian revolutionary democrat, materialist philosopher, journalist and writer; left Russia in 1847, from 1852 lived in England where he established the Free Russian Press and published the periodical Polyarnaya Zvezda (Polar Star) and the newspaper Kolokol (The Bell).— 199, 235, 273, 275, 282, 286, 306, 317, 325, 345, 360, 362, 373, 436, 438, 521-25, 527, 537, 548, 553, 558

Hess, Heinrich Hermann Josef, Baron von (1788-1870)—Austrian general, subsequently field marshal; took an active part in crushing the 1848-49 revolution in Italy; commander-in-chief in Hungary, Galicia and the Danubian Principalities in 1854 and 1855.— 546

Hess, Moses (1812-1875)—German radical writer, a leading 'true socialist' in the mid-40s; member of the Communist League, after its split belonged to the separatist Willich-Schapper group, later supported Lassalle.— 89, 90, 192, 232, 236

Hillgärtner, Georg—German democrat, emigrated after the defeat of the 1848-49 revolution.— 152

Hippocrates (c. 460-c. 377 B.C.)—Greek physician, father of medicine.— 344

Hirsch, Wilhelm—Hamburg shop assistant, Prussian police agent in London in the early 1850s.—9, 41, 59, 66, 218, 222-24, 232-34, 240-44, 266, 301-04, 312, 313, 315, 318, 319, 321, 324, 330, 335, 583

Hochstuhl—German democrat, emigrated to the USA in 1852.—66, 72

Hodde, Lucien de la (Delahodde) (1808-1865)—French writer, member of secret revolutionary societies during the Restoration and the July monarchy, police agent.— 52

Hoffstetter, Gustav von (1818-1874)— Swiss army officer and military writer, took part in the war against the Sonderbund (1847), fought in

ism there, fought in the American Civil War on the side of the Union; President of the Medical Academy in New York (1885-89).—20, 212, 351-53, 355, 358, 372, 375, 402, 403, 542, 587

Jacoby, Johann (1805-1877)—German radical journalist and politician, a Left-wing leader in the Prussian National Assembly (1848).—353

Jellachich (Jellačić), Josef, Count (1801-1859)—Austrian general, Ban of Croatia, Dalmatia and Slavonia (1848-59), took part in suppressing the 1848-49 revolution in Hungary and Austria.—460

Jenni, Samuel Friedrich (1809-1849)—Swiss publisher, radical, editor of the comic newspaper *Der Gukkasten* (Berne).—292

Jérôme—see *Bonaparte, Jérôme*

Joest, Karl—Cologne manufacturer, juryman in the Cologne Communist Trial (1852).—206, 559, 561

Johnson, A.—Bank of England clerk, acquaintance of Ferdinand Freiligrath.—32, 37, 43, 131, 146, 147, 152, 227

Joinville, François Ferdinand Philippe Louis Marie, duc d'Orléans, prince de (1818-1900)—French admiral, son of Louis Philippe; emigrated to England after the February 1848 revolution.—129, 200, 222

Jomini, Henri, Baron von (1779-1869)—Swiss-born general in the French and later the Russian army, military theoretician, author of works on strategy and military history.—305

Jones, Ernest Charles (1819-1869)—prominent figure in the English labour movement, proletarian poet and journalist, Left Chartist leader, editor of *The Northern Star, Notes to the People* and *The People's Paper*; friend of Marx and Engels.—3, 11, 15, 30, 37, 38, 42, 43, 56, 59, 60, 67, 70, 72, 75, 77, 89, 93, 96, 99, 107, 117, 136, 140, 150, 162, 175, 195, 207, 260, 266, 276, 319, 325, 350, 355, 357, 369, 371, 378, 389, 394, 397, 399, 401, 417, 482, 483, 502, 521-23, 525, 527, 536, 547, 557, 560, 562

Jones, Jane (d. 1857)—wife of Ernest Jones.—547

Jones, Richard (1790-1855)—English economist.—62

Jones, Sir William (1746-1794)—English Orientalist and lawyer, author of works on Oriental languages and literature.—341

Jordan, Wilhelm (1819-1904)—German author, deputy to the Frankfurt National Assembly (Left wing and later Centre) (1848).—199

Julius, Gustav (1810-1851)—German democratic journalist, 'true socialist'.—236

Jung, Georg Gottlob (1814-1886)—German writer, Young Hegelian, responsible publisher of the *Rheinische Zeitung*, democrat; deputy to the Prussian National Assembly (Left wing) in 1848, later a national-liberal.—207, 223, 581

Junius—see *Francis, Sir Philipp*

Juta, Jaan Carel (b. 1824)—Dutch merchant, brother-in-law of Karl Marx, husband of his sister Louise.—350, 351, 406

Juta, Louise (1821-c. 1865)—Karl Marx's sister, Jaan Carel Juta's wife.—350, 351

K

Kamm, Friedrich (d. 1867)—German brushmaker, democrat, took part in the Baden-Palatinate uprising in 1849, emigrated to Switzerland after the defeat of the revolution, member of the German Workers' Society in Geneva, emigrated to the USA in 1852.—152, 204

Kant, Immanuel (1724-1804)—German philosopher.—412

Karger—German democrat, refugee in the USA in the 1850s, contributor to the German-language newspaper *Pionier*.—433

Kausler, Franz Georg Friedrich von (1794-1848)—German military historian.—159

Kellner, Gottlieb Theodor (1819-1898)—
German democratic journalist, took
part in the democratic movement in
Cassel during the 1848-49 revolution,
publisher of *Die Hornisse* (1848-50);
emigrated to the USA in 1851, editor
of *Die Reform* (1853 54) and publisher of the *Philadelphia Demokrat*
(from 1856).—273, 312, 318, 326,
349, 366, 428, 583

Keogh, William Nicholas (1817-1878)—
Irish lawyer and politician, a leader
of the Irish Brigade in Parliament,
repeatedly held high judicial posts in
Ireland.—516

Khrulev, Stepan Alexandrovich (1807-
1870)—Russian general, army commander on the Danube and in the
Crimea during the Crimean war,
distinguished himself at the defence
of Sevastopol.—470

Kinkel, Gottfried (1815-1882)—German
poet and journalist, democrat; took
part in the Baden-Palatinate uprising
of 1849, sentenced to life imprisonment by a Prussian court, escaped
from prison and emigrated to England
(1850); a leader of petty-bourgeois
refugees in London; opposed Marx
and Engels.—6, 15, 16, 21, 23, 31,
34, 42, 52, 71, 72, 73-74, 77, 80, 92,
94, 95, 98, 100, 107, 114, 118, 119,
121, 125, 136, 138-43, 148-57, 158,
161, 162, 164, 166, 167, 170, 172,
173, 180, 194, 196, 205, 206, 209,
213, 224, 233, 235, 236, 241, 245,
260-62, 265-66, 273, 274, 283, 304,
308, 313-17, 322, 331, 336, 353, 435,
471, 555, 567-69, 573-75

Kinkel, Johanna (née *Mockel*) (1810-
1858)—German writer, wife of
Gottfried Kinkel.—141, 164, 313,
555, 568

Kinski, Countess (née *Zichy*)
(b. 1824)—Austrian noblewoman.—
194

Kirchmann, Julius Hermann von (1802-
1884)—German lawyer, writer and
philosopher; radical; deputy to the
Prussian National Assembly (Left
Centre) in 1848; deputy to the Second Chamber in 1849; later member

of the Progressist Party.—125

Kiss, Miklós (1820-1902)—Hungarian
army officer, democrat, refugee, Kossuth's agent in France and Italy;
maintained contact with Bonapartist
circles.—171, 194, 268

Klapka, Georg (1820-1892)—general,
commanded one of the Hungarian
revolutionary armies in 1848-49,
commandant of the Komorn fortress
(June-September 1849); emigrated in
1849, maintained contact with
Bonapartist circles in the 1850s; returned to Hungary after the amnesty
(1867).—101, 106, 198, 311, 460

Klein, Carl Wilhelm—German worker,
took part in the Elberfeld and Soling-
en uprisings of 1849, member of the
Communist League; emigrated to the
USA (1852), helped to organise
workers' associations there; active in
the working-class movement in Germany in the 1860s and 1870s,
member of the First International.—
365, 367, 390, 391, 398

Klein, Johann Jacob (c. 1818-c. 1896)—
physician in Cologne, member of the
Communist League, one of the accused in the Cologne Communist
Trial (1852), acquitted.—20

Klose, G.—German refugee living in
London, member of the Communist
League, supported Marx during the
split of the League in 1850.—124

Knesebeck, Karl Friedrich, Baron von der
(1768-1848)—Prussian field marshal-
general, took part in the wars against
Napoleon.—538

Köppen, Karl Friedrich (1808-1863)—
German radical journalist and historian; Young Hegelian.—563

Korff, Hermann—Prussian officer;
democrat; discharged from the army
for his political views (1847); responsible publisher of the *Neue Rheinische
Zeitung* (1848-49); later emigrated to
the USA.—118-20, 160

Korn, Philipp—Hungarian bookseller
and writer, commanded the German
Legion of the Hungarian revolutionary army during the 1848-49 revolution; after its defeat emigrated to

Turkey and then to England; returned to Hungary in 1860.—548, 553

Kościelski, Władysław (1818-1895)— Polish democrat, emigrant, general in the Turkish army under the name of Sefer Pasha (1850s).—360, 546

Kościuszko, Tadeusz Andrzej Bonawentura (1746-1817)—prominent figure in the Polish national liberation movement in the 1790s; took part in the American War of Independence in 1776-83; leader of the Polish uprising of 1794.—68

Kossuth, Lajos (1802-1894)—leader of the Hungarian national liberation movement, head of the Hungarian revolutionary government during the 1848-49 revolution; after the defeat of the revolution emigrated first to Turkey and later to England and the USA; sought support among Bonapartist circles in the 1850s.—13, 21, 30-31, 70, 73-74, 101, 106, 128, 131, 141, 150, 151, 153, 158, 170, 171, 194, 197, 212, 237, 246, 261, 267-68, 269, 278-81, 283-84, 290, 291, 294, 299, 302, 304, 310, 316, 318, 356, 401, 441, 448, 504, 586

Kothes, D.—Cologne merchant, democrat; witness for the defence in the Cologne Communist Trial (1852).— 215, 216, 228, 232, 239, 242, 302

Kräusler—Prussian professor, juryman in the Cologne Communist Trial (1852).—207

Kriege, Hermann (1820-1850)—German journalist, 'true socialist', member of the League of the Just; from 1845 to 1848 lived in emigration in New York where he founded and edited the newspaper Der Volks-Tribun; active in democratic organisations during the 1848-49 revolution in Germany; again emigrated to the USA after its defeat.—353

Krogh, Gerhard Christoph von (1785-1860)—Danish general, commander-in-chief of the Danish army (July 1848-April 1849, 1850) in the Schleswig-Holstein war.—452

Küntzel, H.—Prussian army officer,

military engineer, author of a fortification manual.—103

L

Lafayette (La Fayette), Marie Joseph Paul Yves Roch Gilbert Motier, Marquis de (1757-1834)—French general, took part in the American War of Independence and the French Revolution; a leader of the moderate constitutionalists (Feuillants); took part in the July revolution of 1830.—485

La Ferronnays, Auguste Pierre Marie Ferron, comte de (1777-1842)—French politician and diplomat, ambassador to Copenhagen (1817) and St. Petersburg (1819-27), Foreign Minister (1828-29).—495

Lagarde, Augustin Marie Balthazar Charles Pelletier, comte de (b. 1780)— French general and diplomat, ambassador to Madrid (1820-23).—494

Lamennais (La Mennais), Hugues Félicité Robert de (1782-1854)—French priest, writer, ideologist of Christian socialism.—31, 71, 497

Lamoricière, Christophe Léon Louis Juchault de (1806-1865)—French general, moderate republican; suppressed the June uprising of 1848; War Minister in the Cavaignac Government (June-December 1848); deputy to the Legislative and Constituent Assemblies; banished after the coup d'état of 2 December 1851.—200, 482

Lampon—English journalist, contributor to The Times.—277

Lanckoroński, Count—Polish refugee in London, agent of the Russian government.—172, 301

Landolt, Ernestine—see Liebknecht, Ernestine

L'Aspée, Henry de—Wiesbaden police official, emigrated to London in the early 1850s, helped to expose provocative methods used by the Prussian authorities in staging the Cologne Communist Trial (1852).—316

Lassalle, Ferdinand (1825-1864)— German writer and lawyer; prominent figure in the German working-class movement; participant in the democratic movement in the Rhine Province (1848-49); a founder of the General Association of German Workers (1863).—46, 76, 88, 290, 293, 334, 339, 350, 354, 417-18, 419, 422, 430-33, 478, 481, 491, 502, 511, 514, 521, 543, 553, 556, 557, 588

Law, John (1671-1729)—Scottish economist and financier, Director-General of Finance in France (1719-20); notorious for his speculative scheme (issuing of paper money), which ended in a complete failure.— 263

Lawley, Francis Charles (1825-1901)— British journalist, Gladstone's private secretary (1852-54); the Times correspondent in the USA (1854-65).— 518

Ledru-Rollin, Alexandre Auguste (1807-1874)—French journalist and politician, a leader of the petty-bourgeois democrats, editor of La Réforme; Minister of the Interior in the Provisional Government (February-May 1848), deputy to the Constituent and Legislative Assemblies where he headed the Montagne party; emigrated to England after the demonstration of 13 June 1849.—31, 42, 50, 71, 73, 135, 136, 141, 246, 282, 295, 296, 299, 300, 317, 388, 401, 433, 459

Le Flô, Adolphe Emmanuel Charles (1804-1887)—French general, politician and diplomat, representative of the Party of Order, deputy to the Constituent and Legislative Assemblies during the Second Republic.—48

Legendre, Louis (1752-1797)—prominent figure in the French Revolution, a leader of the Right-wing Jacobins, friend of Danton.—521

Lehmann, Albert—German worker residing in London, leading figure in the League of the Just and the German Workers' Educational Society in London, later member of the Communist League, after its split (1850) belonged to the separatist

Willich-Schapper group and its Central Authority.—41-42

Lehon, Charles Amé Joseph, comte de (1792-1868)—Belgian politician and diplomat, envoy to Paris (1831-42), enjoyed protection at the court of the Orleans.—47

Lehon, comtesse—wife of Charles Lehon, lived in Paris in the 1830s-1850s, enjoyed protection at the court of the Orleans.—47

Lehon, Louis Xavier Léopold, comte de (1832-1879)—French politician, Bonapartist, Chef de Bureau of Minister of the Interior Morny (from 2 December 1851), member of the Corps législatif (from 1856), son of Charles Lehon.—47-48

Leibniz, Gottfried Wilhelm, Baron von (1646-1716)—German philosopher and mathematician.—440

Leiden, Kosmos Damian—wine-merchant in Cologne, juryman in the Cologne Communist Trial (1852).—207, 238

Lelewel, Joachim (1786-1861)—Polish historian and revolutionary, took part in the Polish insurrection of 1830-31, a leader of the democratic wing of Polish emigrants in 1847-48.—172, 563

Lenchen—see Demuth, Helene

Leroux, Pierre (1797-1871)—French writer; utopian socialist, representative of Christian socialism; emigrant in England in 1851-52.—71, 73, 74

Leroy, Achille—see Saint-Arnaud, Armand Jacques Achille Leroy de

Lessing, Gotthold Ephraim (1729-1781)—German writer, critic and philosopher of the Enlightenment.— 345

Leven—Cologne merchant, juryman in the Cologne Communist Trial (1852).—207, 238

Lichnowski, Felix Maria, Prince von (1814-1848)—Silesian landowner, Prussian army officer, deputy to the Frankfurt National Assembly (Right wing); killed during the September 1848 uprising in Frankfurt.—225

Liebknecht, Ernestine (d. 1867)—

Wilhelm Liebknecht's first wife.— 485-86 .

Liebknecht, Wilhelm (1826-1900)— prominent figure in the German and international working-class movement, took part in the 1848-49 revolution, member of the Communist League and the First International, one of the founders and leaders of the German Social-Democratic Party; friend and associate of Marx and Engels.—86, 223, 232, 244, 275, 290, 386, 485, 559, 577

Lieven, Darya (Dorothea) Khristoforovna, Princess (1785-1857)—wife of the Russian diplomat Khristofor Andreyevich Lieven; hostess of political salons in London and Paris.—204, 266, 431

Lieven, Khristofor Andreyevich, Prince (1774-1839)—Russian diplomat, envoy to Berlin (1810-12), ambassador to London (1812-34).—431

Lièvre, Eugène—French democrat, supporter of Hermann Kriege in the 1840s, emigrant in the USA in the 1850s.—323, 324, 542

Lincoln, H. J.—editor of The Daily News.—423-26, 427

Lindenau, Bernhard August (1779-1854)—astronomer and statesman in Saxony, moderate liberal; Minister of the Interior (1831-34), Prime Minister (1831-43).—462

Linton, William James (1812-1897)— English engraver, poet and journalist; democrat; republican; publisher of The Leader; sympathised with the Right-wing Chartists, contributed under the pen-name Spartacus to Chartist publications; lived in the USA from 1866.—107

List, Friedrich (1789-1846)—German economist, advocated protectionism.—45, 147

Loch, George—candidate for Manchester in the 1852 elections to Parliament.—111

Lochner, Georg (born c. 1824)— carpenter; active in the German working-class movement, member of the Communist League and later of the General Council of the First International; friend and associate of Marx and Engels.—15, 372

Löhr, Karl—Bavarian army officer, wrote a book on the military art in Ancient Greece and Rome.—160

Louis IX, 'Saint' (1214-1270)—King of France (1226-1270).—497

Louis XV (1710-1774)—King of France (1715-1774).—489

Louis XVIII (Louis le Désiré) (1755-1824)—King of France (1814-15, 1815-24).—492, 494, 496, 497

Louis Napoleon—see Napoleon III

Louis Philippe I (1773-1850)—Duke of Orleans, King of the French (1830-48).—10, 17, 27, 295, 388, 422, 447, 456, 496, 509

Lowe, Robert, Viscount Sherbrooke (1811-1892)—British statesman and journalist, contributor to The Times; Whig and later Liberal; M.P.; Vice-President of the Board of Trade (1855-58).—277

Löwe, Wilhelm (known as Löwe of Calbe, after the Prussian district of Calbe, which he represented in the Frankfurt National Assembly) (1814-1886)—German democratic politician, Vice-President of the Frankfurt National Assembly, adhered to the Left wing; after the defeat of the 1848-49 revolution left Germany, but returned after the amnesty of 1861; sympathised with the progressists.— 80, 92, 96, 150, 154, 224, 274, 300, 370, 547

Löwenthal—Frankfurt am Main publisher in the 1840s and 1850s.—99, 239

Lüders, Alexander Nikolayevich, Count (1790-1874)—Russian general, commanded a corps on the Danube (1853-54) and the Southern army (1855); commander-in-chief of the army in the Crimea (early 1856).— 470

Lüders, Wilhelm—German democratic journalist, contributed to democratic newspapers in the 1840s and 1850s; refugee in London.—5, 6, 567

Lüning, Otto (1818-1868)—German

1880)—British statesman, Tory, Secretary for War and the Colonies (1852), First Lord of the Admiralty (1858-59, 1866-67), Secretary for War (1867-68).—295

Palmerston, Henry John Temple, Viscount (1784-1865)—British statesman, Tory, Whig from 1830, Foreign Secretary (1830-34, 1835-41, 1846-51), Home Secretary (1852-55), Prime Minister (1855-58, 1859-65).—54, 200, 276, 284-85, 295, 373, 378, 385, 387, 390, 392-93, 398, 404, 409-10, 412, 422, 431, 448, 450, 452, 456, 462, 472, 485, 490, 515, 516, 518-20, 523, 525, 555, 586

Pam—see Palmerston, Henry John Temple, Viscount

Parish, Henry Headley—British historian in the first half of the nineteenth century.—455

Paskievich (Paskiewitsch), Ivan Fyodorovich, Prince (1782-1856)—Russian field marshal-general, fought in wars against Napoleonic France; commander-in-chief (from the summer of 1831) of the Tsarist troops who suppressed the Polish insurrection of 1830-31, Lieutenant (governor) of the Kingdom of Poland from 1832; commander-in-chief of the army which crushed the Hungarian revolution (1849), and of the troops on the western and southern borders of Russia (1854), commanded the Russian army on the Danube (April-June 1854).—461

Peel, Sir Robert (1788-1850)—British statesman, moderate Tory, Home Secretary (1822-27, 1828-30), Prime Minister (1834-35, 1841-46), repealed the Corn Laws in 1846.—195, 284, 368, 432

Pélissier, Aimable Jean Jacques (1794-1864)—French general, Marshal from 1855; participated in the conquest of Algeria in the 1830s-early 1850s; commander-in-chief of the French army in the Crimea (May 1855-July 1856).—546

Pellico, Silvio (1789-1854)—Italian writer, arrested in 1820 for his contacts with the Carbonari and sentenced to twenty years imprisonment; released in 1830, published a book describing the hardships of convicts in Austrian prisons (1832); later abandoned politics.—558

Perczel, Mór (1811-1899)—Hungarian general, took part in the 1848-49 revolution in Hungary, after its defeat emigrated to Turkey and in 1851 to England.—32, 311, 572

Persigny, Jean Gilbert Victor Fialin, comte (1808-1872)—French statesman, Bonapartist, deputy to the Legislative Assembly (1849-51), an organiser of the coup d'état of 2 December 1851; Minister of the Interior (1852-54, 1860-63).—17, 21, 27

Peter the Hermit (c. 1050-1115)—French monk and preacher, peasant leader in the First Crusade (1096-99).—59

Petermann, August (1822-1878)—German geographer and cartographer, editor of the periodicals Mittheilungen aus Justus Perthes' Geographischer Anstalt in Gotha (from 1855).—535, 538

Petzler, Johann—German democrat; music teacher; refugee in London in the 1850s.—419

Pfänder, Karl (c. 1818-1876)—prominent figure in the German and international working-class movement; painter; emigrated to London in 1845, member of the League of the Just, of the Communist League Central Authority, and later of the General Council of the First International; friend and associate of Marx and Engels.—14, 28, 43, 72, 95, 126, 463, 538, 589

Piali—see Zerffi, Gustav

Pieper, Wilhelm (born c. 1826-1899)—German philologist and journalist, member of the Communist League; emigrated to London; was close to Marx and Engels in 1850-53.—8, 9, 11, 13, 14, 16, 22, 23, 29, 33, 37, 67, 71, 117, 146, 175, 179, 183, 184, 186-93, 213, 231, 235, 265, 275, 289, 292, 312, 314, 316, 319, 325, 330,

Schapper, Karl (1812-1870)—prominent figure in the German and international working-class movement, a leader of the League of the Just; member of the Central Authority of the Communist League; took part in the revolution of 1848-49 in Germany, a leader of the separatist group after the split in the Communist League in 1850; later a member of the General Council of the First International.—15, 66, 92, 121, 126, 158, 199, 222, 226, 227, 244, 264, 309, 378, 521

Scharnhorst, Gerhard Johann David von (1755-1813)—Prussian general and politician; after the defeat of the Prussian army by Napoleon I in 1806, head of the commission for a reform of the army; War Minister (1807-10) and Chief of Staff (1810-13); took an active part in the liberation war of the German people against Napoleonic rule.—526

Schärttner—wife of August Schärttner.—162

Schärttner, August (1817-1859)—cooper in Hanau, active in the 1848 revolution and the Baden-Palatinate uprising of 1849; emigrated to London; member of the Communist League, after its split in 1850 joined the separatist Willich-Schapper group and became a member of its Central Authority.—103, 151, 154, 169, 173, 244, 316, 318

Schickel, Johann (1827-1909)—shop assistant in Mainz, member of the Communist League; emigrated to the USA in 1849.—18

Schiller, Johann Christoph Friedrich von (1759-1805)—German poet, dramatist, historian and philosopher.—124, 154, 187, 420, 452, 558

Schily, Victor (1810-1875)—German lawyer, democrat, took part in the Baden-Palatinate uprising of 1849; emigrated to France; member of the First International.—92, 122, 151, 154, 162, 164, 186, 195, 434, 446

Schily—brother of Victor Schily.—187

Schimmelpfennig, Alexander (1824-1865)—Prussian army officer, democrat, took part in the Baden-Palatinate uprising of 1849, left Germany after its defeat; belonged to the separatist Willich-Schapper group; took part in the American Civil War on the side of the Union.—73, 92, 114, 125, 135, 151, 154, 204, 213, 224, 266, 297, 300, 313, 427, 433, 436, 439, 441, 443, 444, 558

Schläger, Eduard—German democratic journalist; refugee in the USA in the 1850s-70s; editor of the *Neu-England-Zeitung* and publisher of the *Deutsch-Amerikaner* in the early 1850s; returned to Germany in 1880.—349, 350, 366

Schmidt, Ernst Friedrich Franz (d. 1853)—German clergyman, deputy to the Frankfurt National Assembly (Left wing) in 1848; emigrated to the USA after the 1848-49 revolution; supporter of Kossuth.—52

Schmolze, Karl Heinrich (1823-1859)—German cartoonist and poet, took part in the 1848-49 revolution; emigrated after its defeat.—162, 313

Schnauffer, Karl Heinrich (c. 1823-1854)—German poet and journalist, democrat; took part in the revolutionary movement in Baden in 1848-49, emigrated after the revolution, lived in the USA from 1851, edited the *Baltimore Wecker.*—157, 204, 491, 574

Schneider II, Karl—German lawyer, democrat; President of the Cologne Democratic Society and member of the Rhenish District Committee of Democrats (1848); deputy to the Second Chamber (extreme Left wing) in 1849; counsel for the defence at the Cologne Communist Trial (1852).—195, 217, 221-24, 226, 228, 231, 234-35, 237, 240, 242, 244

Schöler, Caroline—friend of the Marx family.—558

Schramm, Conrad (Konrad) (c. 1822-1858)—prominent figure in the German working-class movement, member of the Communist League, emigrated to London in 1849; responsible publisher of the *Neue*

*Rheinische Zeitung. Politisch-
ökonomische Revue*; friend and associate of Marx and Engels.—6, 112,
115, 158, 274, 299, 325-26, 336, 542,
545, 569

Schramm, Rudolf (1813-1882)—German
journalist, democrat; deputy to the
Prussian National Assembly (Left
wing) in 1848; emigrated to England
after the 1848-49 revolution; opposed Marx; supported Bismarck in
the 1860s; brother of Conrad
Schramm.—115

Schulz (d. 1852)—chief of police in
Cologne, one of the organisers of the
Cologne Communist Trial (1852).—
142, 197, 227, 252

Schunck—owner of a Manchester trading firm.—353

Schunck—wife of Schunck.—353

Schürmann—German lawyer, counsel
for the defence at the Cologne Communist Trial (1852).—234

Schurz, Carl (1829-1906)—German
journalist, democrat; took part in the
Baden-Palatinate uprising of 1849;
emigrated to Switzerland and then to
the USA, subsequently a US statesman.—74, 95, 125, 154, 167, 168,
172, 194, 197, 236

Schütz, Jacob Friedrich (1813-1877)—
German democrat, took part in the
Baden-Palatinate uprising of 1849,
representative of the Baden Provisional Government in Paris; later a
refugee in England, Switzerland and
America.—92, 96, 115

Schwezler von Lecton—widow of an official resident in Frankfurt am Main.—
225, 226

Scott, Winfield (1786-1866)—American
general, commander-in-chief of the
US army (1841-November 1861);
during the war against Mexico (1846-
48), commanded the army that captured Veracruz and Mexico City.—
407, 501, 503

*Seckendorf, August Heinrich Eduard
Friedrich, Baron von* (1807-1885)—
Prussian legal officer, deputy to the
Second Chamber (Centre) in 1849-
51; public prosecutor at the Cologne

Communist Trial (1852).—238

Ségur, Alexandre Joseph Pierre, vicomte de
(1756-1805)—French writer.—208

Seiler, Sebastian (c. 1810-c. 1890)—
German journalist, member of the
Brussels Communist Correspondence
Committee in 1846, member of the
Communist League, took part in the
1848-49 revolution in Germany;
emigrated to London in the early
1850s, moved to the USA in 1856.—
36, 44, 45, 50, 278, 465, 466

Selim Pasha (Zedlinsky)—Turkish general of Polish descent, commanded the
Turkish army on the Danube in
1853-54.—470

Senior, Nassau William (1790-1864)—
English economist, vulgarised Ricardo's theory.—62

Seymour, George Hamilton (1797-
1880)—British diplomat, envoy to
St. Petersburg (1851-54).—422, 519

Shakespeare, William (1564-1616)—
English dramatist and poet.—21,
162, 391, 440, 502, 558

Shamyl (c. 1798-1871)—leader of the
inhabitants of the mountains in
Daghestan and Chechnya against the
local feudal lords and tsarist colonis-
ers in the 1830s-50s.—395, 418, 464,
477

Sidmouth, Henry Addington, Viscount
(1757-1844) — British statesman,
Tory; Prime Minister and Chancellor
of the Exchequer (1801-04); as Home
Secretary (1812-21) took repressive
measures against the working-class
movement.—54

Sigel, Albert (1827-1884)—German
army officer, journalist, petty-
bourgeois democrat, participant in
the 1848-49 revolutionary movement
in Baden; after the defeat of the
revolution emigrated to England, and
in 1853 to the USA; took part in the
Civil War on the side of the Union.—
154, 173

Sigel, Franz (1824-1902)—Baden army
officer, democrat; a military leader of
the Baden-Palatinate uprising of
1849; emigrated to Switzerland, then
to England and, in 1852, to the USA;

the Prussian political police (1850-60); an organiser of and principal witness for the prosecution at the Cologne Communist Trial (1852); jointly with Wermuth wrote the book *Die Communisten-Verschwörungen des neunzehnten Jahrhunderts.*—215, 218, 219, 222, 224-34, 240, 243, 298, 314-16, 318, 319, 321, 396, 577, 580

Stirner, Max (real name *Schmidt, Johann Caspar*) (1806-1856)—German Young Hegelian philosopher, an ideologist of individualism and anarchism.—50, 55, 135, 161, 170, 174, 449

Stirner-Schmidt, Marie Wilhelmine (née *Dähnhardt*) (1818-1902)—Max Stirner's wife.—130, 170

Stopford, Sir Robert (1768-1847)—English admiral, Commander-in-Chief of the British fleet in the Mediterranean (1837-41).—456

Strassoldo, Julius Cäsar, Count (1791-1855)—Austrian general, took part in suppressing the national liberation movement in Italy in 1848-49; commanded a division stationed in Milan (1853); assistant of Radetzky.—281

Stratford de Redcliffe, Stratford Canning, Viscount (1786-1880)—British diplomat, envoy and then ambassador to Constantinople (1810-12, 1825-28, 1841-58).—408

Strauss—German democrat, emigrated to London in the 1850s.—154

Strauss, David Friedrich (1808-1874)—German Young Hegelian philosopher and journalist.—462

Streit, Feodor (1820-1904)—German lawyer, journalist and publisher, took part in the 1848-49 revolution in Germany.—161, 175, 182

Strodtmann, Adolf (1829-1879)—German writer, democrat; took part in the Schleswig-Holstein revolutionary movement (1848), left Germany in 1850; Gottfried Kinkel's biographer.—125

Strohn, Wilhelm—Communist League member; friend of Marx and Engels; refugee resident in Bradford.—88, 124, 132, 233, 236, 237, 245, 251, 255, 315, 321, 325, 328, 356, 386, 400, 542

Struve, Amalie (d. 1862)—participant in the German democratic movement (1848-49); Gustav Struve's wife.—45

Struve, Gustav von (1805-1870)—German journalist, democrat; a leader of the Baden uprisings in April and September 1848 and of the Baden-Palatinate uprising of 1849; emigrated after the defeat of the revolution; a leader of German refugees in England; took part in the American Civil War on the side of the Union; returned to Germany in 1862.—45, 98, 142

Sutherland, Harriet Elisabeth Georgiana Leveson-Gower, Duchess (1806-1868)—big Scottish landowner, Whig.—273, 289

Szemere, Bartholomäus (*Bertalan*) (1812-1869)—Hungarian politician and journalist; Minister of the Interior (1848) and head of the revolutionary government (1849); emigrated after the defeat of the revolution.—31, 32, 45, 65, 71, 73, 77, 93, 95, 99, 101, 105, 106, 131, 133, 134, 174, 212, 237, 267-70, 277, 280, 291, 299, 302, 304, 313, 572

Szeredy—Hungarian refugee in London, author of the book *Asiatic Chiefs.*—543

Szerelmey, Miklós (1803-1875)—Hungarian army officer, military engineer and journalist; took part in the July 1830 revolution in France and the 1848-49 revolution in Hungary; emigrated to England in 1850.—77, 93, 98, 100, 108

Szirmay, Pál, Count (1804-1883)—Hungarian refugee, emissary of Kossuth in Paris in the early 1850s.—268, 269

Sznayde, Franz (1790-1850)—participant in the Polish insurrection of 1830-31, general of the Baden-Palatinate insurgent army in 1849.—138

T

Tacitus (*Publius Cornelius*) (c. 55-

INDEX OF LITERARY AND MYTHOLOGICAL NAMES

Abraham (Bib.).—326

Achates—character in Virgil's *Aeneid,* Aeneas' loyal fellow-traveller, whose name is symbolical of true friendship.—523

Afrasiab—character in old Persian legends, King of the legendary Turin; was repeatedly defeated in wars with Persia.—342

Alcina—character in Ariosto's *L'Orlando furioso.*—390

Bazile—character in Beaumarchais' *Le barbier de Seville.*—297, 300

Birch, Harvey—character in J. F. Cooper's novel *The Spy.*—217

Cerberus (Gr. myth.)—three-headed dog guarding the entrance to Hades; the name came to signify a fierce guard.—150, 266

Christ, Jesus (Bib.).—41, 42, 73, 296

Corydon—shepherd suffering from unrequited love in pastoral poetry.—336

Don Quixote—title character in Cervantes' novel.—493

Faust—title character in Goethe's tragedy.—262, 447

Fridolin—character in Schiller's ballad *Der Gang nach dem Eisenhammer,* a kindly and modest enamoured youth.—452

Goliath (Bib.)—a Philistine giant slain by David during the war between the Philistines and the Israelites.—440

Isegrim—a wolf in Goethe's poem *Reineke Fuchs.*—585

Jason (Gr. myth.)—leader of the Argonauts in quest of the Golden Fleece, which was guarded by a dragon.—45

Jesus (Bib.)—see *Christ, Jesus*

John (Bib.)—one of the Twelve Apostles, Christ's favourite disciple.—284

King Lear—mythological King of Britain, hero of a legend that provided the theme for Shakespeare's tragedy.—162

Kobes I—a philistine, title character in a satirical poem by Heine; also nickname of Jakob Venedey (Kobes means Jakob in a dialect spoken in Cologne, where Venedey was born).—504, 509

Krapülinski (*Crapülinski*)—one of the main characters in Heine's poem *Zwei Ritter,* a spendthrift Polish nobleman (the name comes from the French word *crapule* meaning gluttony, hard drinking and also scoundrel, idler).—276, 438, 568

Lazarus (Bib.).—590

Leporello—Don Giovanni's servant in Mozart's opera *Don Giovanni.*—556

Ligurio—character in Machiavelli's comedy *Mandragola.*—125

Malvolio—character in Shakespeare's comedy *Twelfth Night.*—440

Manu—legendary law-giver of ancient India; the *Laws of Manu* were compiled by Brahmins between the first and fifth centuries.—348

Mary (Bib.).—310

Nemesis (Gr. myth.)—goddess of retributive justice.—402

Nicia—character in Machiavelli's comedy *Mandragola.*—125

Noah (Bib.)—patriarch, said to have survived the Deluge in a wooden ark built on an order from God.—326

INDEX OF QUOTED
AND MENTIONED LITERATURE

WORKS BY KARL MARX AND FREDERICK ENGELS

Marx, Karl

Achievements of the Ministry (present edition, Vol. 12). In: *New-York Daily Tribune*, No. 3753, April 27, 1853.—334

Affairs in Holland.—Denmark.—Conversion of the British Debt.—India, Turkey, and Russia (present edition, Vol. 12). In: *New-York Daily Tribune*, No. 3790, June 9, 1853.—334

[*Arrest of Delescluze.—Denmark.—Austria.—'The Times' on the Prospects of War Against Russia*] (present edition, Vol. 12). In: *New-York Daily Tribune*, No. 3917, November 5, 1853.—376

The Attack on Francis Joseph.—The Milan Riot.—British Politics.—Disraeli's Speech.— Napoleon's Will (present edition, Vol. 11). In: *New-York Daily Tribune*, No. 3710, March 7-8, 1853.—288, 292, 299

[*Attempts to Form a New Opposition Party*] (present edition, Vol. 11). In: *New-York Daily Tribune*, No. 3622, November 25, 1852.—212, 215, 219, 229, 236, 237

Austrian Bankruptcy (present edition, Vol. 13). In: *New-York Daily Tribune*, No. 4033, March 22, 1854.—439

British Finances (present edition, Vol. 13). In: *New-York Daily Tribune*, No. 4086, May 23, 1854.—515

The British Rule in India (present edition, Vol. 12). In: *New-York Daily Tribune*, No. 3804, June 25, 1853.—346

Capital Punishment.—Mr. Cobden's Pamphlet.—Regulations of the Bank of England (present edition, Vol. 11). In: *New-York Daily Tribune*, No. 3695, February 17-18, 1853.—275, 288, 292

The Chartists (present edition, Vol. 11). In: *New-York Daily Tribune*, No. 3543, August 25, 1852.—136, 145-47, 153, 207

The Class Struggles in France, 1848 to 1850 (present edition, Vol. 10)
— Die Klassenkämpfe in Frankreich 1848 bis 1850 (published in 1850 under the

Lord Palmerston (present edition, Vol. 12). In: *The People's Paper*, Nos. 77-81, 84, 85, 86; October 22, 29, November 5, 12, 19, December 10, 17, 24, 1853.—394, 395, 399, 404, 412, 414, 586
— *I. Palmerston; II. Palmerston and Russia; III. A Chapter of Modern History; IV. England and Russia.* In: *New-York Daily Tribune*, Nos. 3902, 3916, 3930, 3973; October 19, November 4, 21, 1853, January 11, 1854.—385, 387, 394, 395, 398, 399, 404, 412, 430-32, 455, 462, 472, 473, 586
— *Palmerston.* In: *Die Reform*, Nr. 72, 73, 74, 77, 78; 2., 3., 4., 8., 9. November 1853.—378, 379, 390, 408
— *Palmerston and Russia.* 1 ed. London, 1853. 2 ed. London, 1854.—455
— *Palmerston and the Treaty of Unkiar Skelessi.* London, 1854.—455

Michael Bakunin. To the Editor of 'The Morning Advertiser' (present edition, Vol. 12). In: *The Morning Advertiser*, No. 19406, September 2, 1853.—360-61, 373

The 'Model Constitutional State' (present edition, Vol. 7)
— *Der 'Konstitutionelle Musterstaat'.* In: *Neue Rheinische Zeitung*, Nr. 123, 22, Oktober 1848.—451

The 'Model State' of Belgium (present edition, Vol. 7)
— *Der 'Musterstaat' Belgien.* In: *Neue Rheinische Zeitung*, Nr. 68, 7. August 1848.—451

Moralising Criticism and Critical Morality. A Contribution to German Cultural History. Contra Karl Heinzen (present edition, Vol. 6)
— *Die moralisierende Kritik und die kritisierende Moral. Beitrag zur deutschen Kulturgeschichte. Gegen Karl Heinzen.* In: *Deutsche-Brüsseler-Zeitung*, Nr. 86, 87, 90, 92, 94; 28., 31. Oktober, 11., 18., 25. November 1847.—65, 395

Movements of Mazzini and Kossuth.—League with Louis Napoleon.—Palmerston (present edition, Vol. 11). In: *New-York Daily Tribune*, No. 3590, October 19, 1852.—237, 261, 268, 302

The New Financial Juggle; or Gladstone and the Pennies (present edition, Vol. 12). In: *The People's Paper*, No. 50, April 16, 1853.—334

[*Panic on the London Stock Exchange.—Strikes*] (present edition, Vol. 12). In: *New-York Daily Tribune*, No. 3900, October 17, 1853.—372, 375-84

Parliament.—Vote of November 26.—Disraeli's Budget (present edition, Vol. 11). In: *New-York Daily Tribune*, No. 3650, December 28, 1852.—265

Parliamentary Debates.—The Clergy Against Socialism.—Starvation (present edition, Vol. 11). In: *New-York Daily Tribune*, No. 3716, March 15, 1853.—288, 292

Pauperism and Free Trade.— The Approaching Commercial Crisis (present edition, Vol. 11). In: *New-York Daily Tribune*, No. 3601, November 1, 1852.—211

[*Persian Expedition in Afghanistan and Russian Expedition in Central Asia.— Denmark.— The Fighting on the Danube and in Asia.— Wigan Colliers*] (present edition, Vol. 12). In: *New-York Daily Tribune*, No. 3928, November 18, 1853.—376

Political Consequences of the Commercial Excitement (present edition, Vol. 11). In: *New-York Daily Tribune*, No. 3602, November 2, 1852.—211-12

Political Movements.—Scarcity of Bread in Europe (present edition, Vol. 12). In: *New-York Daily Tribune*, No. 3886, September 30, 1853.—368

Political Parties and Prospects (present edition, Vol. 11). In: *New-York Daily Tribune*, No. 3625, November 29, 1852.—212, 214, 219, 229

The Poverty of Philosophy. Answer to the 'Philosophy of Poverty' by M. Proudhon (present edition, Vol. 6)
— Misère de la philosophie. Réponse à la philosophie de la misère de M. Proudhon. Paris-Bruxelles, 1847.—261, 381, 392

The Prussian Counter-Revolution and the Prussian Judiciary (present edition, Vol. 8)
— Die preußische Contrerevolution und der preußische Richterstand. In: *Neue Rheinische Zeitung*, Nr. 177, 24. Dezember 1848.—23, 34

[*Reorganisation of the British War Administration.—The Austrian Summons.—Britain's Economic Situation.—St. Arnaud*] (present edition, Vol. 13). In: *New-York Daily Tribune*, No. 4114, June 24, 1854.—484

A Reply to Kossuth's 'Secretary' (present edition, Vol. 11). In: *New-York Daily Tribune*, No. 3656, January 4, 1853.—261, 269

Result of the Elections (present edition, Vol. 11). In: *New-York Daily Tribune*, No. 3558, September 11, 1852.—164, 207

Revelations Concerning the Communist Trial in Cologne (present edition, Vol. 11)
— Enthüllungen über den Kommunisten-Prozeß zu Köln. Basel, 1853.—217, 220, 221, 238, 247-51, 255, 259-60, 264, 267, 270, 272, 273, 275, 282, 287, 292, 296, 297, 299, 324, 386, 396, 558, 579-81, 584
— [Boston, 1853]—259, 260, 267, 273, 299, 317, 326, 328, 334, 339, 350, 354, 386, 558
— In: *Neu-England-Zeitung*, März-April, 1853.—273, 299, 302, 317, 579-81

Revolution in China and in Europe (present edition, Vol. 12). In: *New-York Daily Tribune*, No. 3794, June 14, 1853.—332, 390

Revolutionary Spain (present edition, Vol. 13). In: *New-York Daily Tribune*, Nos. 4179, 4192, 4214, 4220, 4222, 4244, 4250 and 4251; September 9 and 25, October 20, 27 and 30, November 24, December 1 and 2, 1854.—480, 484, 485, 498

Riot at Constantinople.—German Table Moving.—The Budget (present edition, Vol. 12). In: *New-York Daily Tribune*, No. 3761, May 6, 1853.—331, 355

Rise in the Price of Corn.—Cholera.—Strikes.—Sailors' Movement (present edition, Vol. 12). In: *New-York Daily Tribune*, No. 3873, September 15, 1853.—375-76

[*Russian Diplomacy.—The Blue Book on the Eastern Question.—Montenegro*] (present edition, Vol. 12). In: *New-York Daily Tribune*, No. 4013, February 27, 1854.—376

The Russian Humbug.—Gladstone's Failure.—Sir Charles Wood's East Indian Reforms (present edition, Vol. 12). In: *New-York Daily Tribune*, No. 3801, June 22, 1853.—334

Russian Policy Against Turkey.—Chartism (present edition, Vol. 12). In: *New-York Daily Tribune*, No. 3819, July 14, 1853.—375-76

The Russo-Turkish Difficulty.—Ducking and Dodging of the British Cabinet.—Nesselrode's Last Note.—The East India Question (present edition, Vol. 12). In: *New-York Daily Tribune*, No. 3828, July 25, 1853.—390

The Secret Diplomatic Correspondence (present edition, Vol. 13). In: *New-York Daily Tribune*, No. 4050, April 11, 1854.—446, 473

Soap for the People, a Sop for 'The Times'.—The Coalition Budget (present edition, Vol. 12). In: *The People's Paper*, No. 52, April 30, 1853.—517

[*The Spanish Revolution.—Greece and Turkey*] (present edition, Vol. 13). In: *New-York Daily Tribune*, No. 4148, August 4, 1854.—485

Speech on the Question of Free Trade (present edition, Vol. 6)
— Discours sur la question du libre échange, prononcé à l'Association Démocratique de Bruxelles, dans la séance publique du 9 janvier 1848. [Bruxelles, 1848.]—513

To the Editor of 'The People's Paper' (present edition, Vol. 12). In: *The People's Paper*, No. 71, September 10, 1853.—362-64

The Trials at Cologne. To the Editor of 'The Morning Advertiser' (present edition, Vol. 11). In: *The Morning Advertiser*, No. 19145, November 2, 1852.—235

The Trial of the Rhenish District Committee of Democrats (present edition, Vol. 8)
— Prozeß des Kreis-Ausschusses der rheinischen Demokraten. In: *Zwei politische Prozesse*. Verhandelt vor den Februar-Assisen in Köln. Köln, 1849.—65

Turkey and Russia.—Connivance of the Aberdeen Ministry with Russia.—The Budget.—Tax on Newspaper Supplements.—Parliamentary Corruption (present edition, Vol. 12). In: *New-York Daily Tribune*, No. 3814, July 8, 1853.—517

[*The Vienna Note.—The United States and Europe.—Letters from Shumla.—Peel's Bank Act*] (present edition, Vol. 12). In: *New-York Daily Tribune*, No. 3881, September 24, 1853.—368, 585

The War Debate in Parliament (present edition, Vol. 13). In: *New-York Daily Tribune*, No. 4055, April 17, 1854.—446

The War.—Debate in Parliament (present edition, Vol. 13). In: *New-York Daily Tribune*, No. 4126, July 10, 1854.—466

War.—Strikes.—Dearth (present edition, Vol. 12). In: *New-York Daily Tribune*, No. 3925, November 15, 1853.—395

The War Question.—Doings of Parliament.—India (present edition, Vol. 12). In: *New-York Daily Tribune*, No. 3838, August 5, 1853.—366, 390

The War Question.—Financial Matters.—Strikes (present edition, Vol. 12). In: *New-York Daily Tribune*, No. 3904, October 21, 1853.—385

[*The Western Powers and Turkey*] (present edition, Vol. 12). In: *New-York Daily Tribune*, No. 3988, January 28, 1854.—407

[*The Western Powers and Turkey.—Imminent Economic Crisis.—Railway Construction in*

The Siege of Sevastopol (present edition, Vol. 13). In: *New-York Daily Tribune*, No. 4236, November 15, 1854.—491

The Siege of Silistria (present edition, Vol. 13). In: *New-York Daily Tribune*, No. 4115, June 26, 1854.—460, 461

The Struggle in the Crimea (present edition, Vol. 14). In: *New-York Daily Tribune*, No. 4323, February 26, 1855.—522

The Turkish Question (present edition, Vol. 12). In: *New-York Daily Tribune*, No. 3746, April 19, 1853.—444, 583

The Turkish War (present edition, Vol. 13). In: *New-York Daily Tribune*, No. 4080, May 16, 1854.—436

Two Years of a Revolution; 1848 and 1849 (present edition, Vol. 10). In: *The Democratic Review*, April-June, 1850.—61

The War (present edition, Vol. 13). In: *The People's Paper*, No. 108, May 27, 1854.
— The Exploits in the Baltic and Black Seas.—Anglo-French System of Operations. In: *New-York Daily Tribune*, No. 4101, June 9, 1854.—589

The War Comedy (present edition, Vol. 7)
— Die Kriegskomödie. In: *Neue Rheinische Zeitung*, Nr. 5, 5. Juni 1848.—451

The War in Italy and Hungary (present edition, Vol. 9)
— Der Krieg in Italien und Ungarn. In: *Neue Rheinische Zeitung*, Nr. 257, 28. März 1849.—120, 128

The War on the Danube (present edition, Vol. 12). In: *New-York Daily Tribune*, No. 3952, December 16, 1853.—399-400

The War on the Danube (present edition, Vol. 13). In: *New-York Daily Tribune*, No. 4139, July 25, 1854.—466, 467

War Prospects (present edition, Vol. 14). In: *New-York Daily Tribune*, No. 4459, August 4, 1855.—542

What Is to Become of Turkey in Europe? (present edition, Vol. 12). In: *New-York Daily Tribune*, No. 3748, April 21, 1853.—444, 583

Marx, Karl and Engels, Frederick

Address of the Central Authority to the League, March 1850 (present edition, Vol. 10)
— Die Zentralbehörde an den Bund, London, März 1850 (distributed in handwritten copies).—143

Address of the Central Authority to the League, June 1850 (present edition, Vol. 10)
— Die Zentralbehörde an den Bund, London, Juni 1850 (distributed in manuscript copies).—143

[*Appeal for Support of the Men Sentenced in Cologne*] (present edition, Vol. 11). In: *California Staats-Zeitung*, Januar 1853.—247, 259-60, 282

[*Appeal for Support of the Representatives of the Proletariat Sentenced in Cologne, and Their Families*] (present edition, Vol. 11)
— Aufruf zur Unterstützung der in Köln verurteilten Vertreter des Proletariats und ihrer Familien. In: *New-Yorker Criminal-Zeitung*, Nr. 45, 21. Januar 1853.—282, 297

British Politics.—Disraeli.—The Refugees.—Mazzini in London.—Turkey (present edition, Vol. 12). In: *New-York Daily Tribune*, No. 3736, April 7, 1853.—294, 315, 444, 579

Erklärung. London, den 18. November 1852. In: *New-Yorker Criminal-Zeitung*, Nr. 39, 10. Dezember 1852.—247

A Final Declaration on the Late Cologne Trials (present edition, Vol. 11). In: *The Morning Advertiser*, No. 19168, November 29, 1852.—246-47, 260

From Parliament.—From the Theatre of War (present edition, Vol. 13)
— Aus dem Parlamente.—Vom Kriegsschauplatz. In: *Neue Oder-Zeitung*, Nr. 53, 1. Februar 1855.—515

The German Ideology. Critique of Modern German Philosophy According to Its Representatives Feuerbach, B. Bauer and Stirner, and of German Socialism According to Its Prophets (present edition, Vol. 5)
— Die deutsche Ideologie. Kritik der neuesten deutschen Philosophie in ihren Repräsentanten Feuerbach, B. Bauer und Stirner, und des deutschen Sozialismus in seinen verschiedenen Propheten.— 161

Gottfried Kinkel (present edition, Vol. 10). In: *Neue Rheinische Zeitung. Politisch-ökonomische Revue*, Nr. 4, 1850.—139, 149

The Great Men of the Exile (present edition, Vol. 11)
— Die großen Männer des Exils.—92-99, 101, 103, 109, 116, 120, 123-24, 127, 141, 208, 232, 233, 239, 242, 254, 256, 258, 269, 281, 301, 302, 303, 580, 582

The Late British Government (present edition, Vol. 13). In: *New-York Daily Tribune*, No. 4321, February 23, 1855.—515, 520

Manifesto of the Communist Party (present edition, Vol. 6)
— Manifest der Kommunistische Partei. London, 1848.—60, 165, 203, 308

Progress of the War (present edition, Vol. 13). In: *New-York Daily Tribune*, No. 4276, January 1, 1855.—505

[*Public Statement to the Editors of the English Press*] (present edition, Vol. 11). In: *The People's Paper*, No. 26; *The Examiner*, No. 2335; *The Morning Advertiser*, No. 19143; *The Leader*, No. 136; *The Spectator*, No. 1270, October 30, 1852.—224, 231, 243, 247, 578

WORKS BY DIFFERENT AUTHORS

Balzac, H. de. *Le cabinet des antiques.*—203
— *Le père Goriot.*—203

Barthold, F. W. *George von Frundsberg oder das deutsche Kriegshandwerk zur Zeit der Reformation.* Hamburg, 1833.—160

Batthyány, K. *The Hungarian Revolution. To the Editor of 'The Times'.* In: *The Times,* No. 20998, December 30, 1851.—26

Bauer, B. *The Decline of England.* In: *New-York Daily Tribune,* No. 3423, April 7, 1852.—94
— *De la dictature occidentale.* Charlottenbourg, 1854.—486, 490
— *Deutschland und das Russenthum.* Charlottenburg, 1854.—535
— *Die jetzige Stellung Rußlands.* Charlottenburg, 1854.—535
— *The Present Impossibility of War.* In: *New-York Daily Tribune,* No. 3417, March 31, 1852.—85
— *La Russie et l'Angleterre.* Trad. de l'Allemand. Charlottenbourg, 1854.—505-06, 535
— *Die russische Kirche.* Charlottenburg, 1855.—538
— *Rußland und das Germanenthum.* Zweite Abtheilung. *Die deutsche und die orientalische Frage.* Charlottenburg, 1853.—535
— *Der Untergang des Frankfurter Parlaments.* Berlin, 1849.—37, 38, 76

Beaumarchais, P. A. C. *La folle journée, ou le mariage de Figaro.*—38
— *Le barbier de Séville, ou la précaution inutile.*—297, 300

Bell, A. *Reception and Progress of Kossuth in the United States.* In: *The Friend of the People,* No. 2, February 14, 1852.—30

Bernier, F. *Voyages contenant la description des états du Grand Mogol, de l'Indoustan, du Royaume de Cachemire, etc.* Tomes I-II. Paris, 1830.—332-34, 341

Bertin, A. *Paris, 14 mars.* In: *Journal des Débats politiques et littéraires,* 15 mars 1852.—68

Bible—7, 558
The Old Testament
Ecclesiastes—249, 492
Genesis—327
1 Kings—269
2 Samuel—442, 445
The New Testament
Luke—307
Matthew—7

Blesson, L. *Geschichte des Belagerungskrieges oder der offensiven Befestigungen.* Eine Skizze. Berlin, 1835. (The date in the original is inaccurate.)—160

Bode, A. *Notizen, gesammelt auf einer Forstreise durch einen Theil des Europäischen Russlands.* In: *Beiträge zur Kenntnis des Russischen Reiches und der angränzenden Länder Asiens,* Bd. 19, St. Petersburg, 1854.—505

Boiardo, M. M. *Orlando innamorato.*—131

Bonaparte, J. *Mémoires et correspondance politique et militaire du roi Joseph.* Publiés, annotés et mis en ordre par A. du Casse. T. I-III. Paris, 1853-1855.—406

Bright, J. [Speech in the House of Commons on 1 July 1853.] In: *The Times,* No. 21470, July 2, 1853.—355
— [Speech at the meeting in Manchester on 24 January 1854.] In: *The Times,* No. 21647, January 25, 1854.—411

— [Speech in the House of Commons on 29 May 1854.] In: *The Times,* No. 21754, May 30, 1854.—520

[Bürgers, H.] *Die Freisprechung Kinkels.* In: *Westdeutsche Zeitung,* Nr. 107, 5. Mai 1850.—23
— (anon.) *Die Logik in dem Prozesse Kinkels und Genossen.* In: *Westdeutsche Zeitung,* Nr. 102-104, 30. April, 1., 2. Mai 1850.—23

Butler, S. *Hudibras, a Poem Written in the Time of the Civil War.* Vols. 1-3. London, 1757.—334

Ça ira (French revolutionary song. End of the eighteenth century).—555

Calderón de la Barca, P. *El Mágico prodigioso.*—447

Carey, H. Ch. *Essay on the Rate of Wages: with an Examination of the Causes of the Differences in the Condition of the Labouring Population Throughout the World.* Philadelphia-London, 1835.—62, 93, 345
— *The Harmony of Interests: manufacturing and commercial.* Philadelphia, 1851.— 93, 345
— *The Past, the Present, and the Future.* Philadelphia, 1848.—392
— *The Slave Trade, Domestic and Foreign: Why It Exists, and How It May Be Extinguished.* Philadelphia, 1853.—345-46, 387

Carrion-Nisas. *Essai sur l'histoire générale de l'art militaire, de son origine, de ses progrès et de ses révolutions.* Tomes I-II. Paris, 1824.—159

Cervantes Saavedra, M. de. *Vida y hechos del ingenioso hidalgo Don Quixote de la Mancha.*—170, 447, 480

Chambray, G. *Ueber die Veränderungen in der Kriegskunst seit 1700 bis 1815.* Berlin, 1830.—160

Chamisso, A. von. *Peter Schlemihl's wundersame Geschichte.*—457

Chateaubriand, [F. R.] de. *Atala.*—447
— *Congrès de Vérone. Guerre d'Espagne. Négociations. Colonies espagnoles.* Tomes I-II. Bruxelles, 1838.—492-97
— *René.*—447

Chenu, A. *Les Conspirateurs. Les sociétés secrètes. La préfecture de police sous Caussidière. Les corps-francs.* Paris, 1850.—52, 128

Chesney, F. R. *Précis of a Report on the Russian Campaign of 1828 and 1829, drawn up for the information of the Duke of Wellington.* In: *The Portfolio,* No. 26, July 20, 1836.—393
— *The Russo-Turkish Campaigns of 1828 and 1829: with a view of the present state of affairs in the East.* London, 1854.—426

Cicero, M. T. *Oratio pro Sextio.*—89

Cluss, A. *An den Garanten-Congress des deutschen Anleihens in Cincinnati. Washington, Jan. 23.* In: *Turn-Zeitung,* Nr. 6, 1. März 1852.—42, 71, 92
— *An die Redaction der 'N. Yorker Criminal-Zeitung'. Washington, 17 Mai.* In: *Belletristisches Journal und New-Yorker Criminal-Zeitung,* Nr. 10, 20. Mai 1853.—335
— *Das 'beste Blatt der Union' und seine 'besten Männer' und Nationalökonomen.* In: *Die Reform,* Nr. 48, 49, 50, 51; 14., 17., 21., 24. September 1853.—387
— *Karl Heinzen und der Kommunismus, oder der fahrende Ritter auf der wilden, verwegenden Jugd nach dem Schatten seines lahmen Kleppers.* In: *New-Yorker Demokrat,* end of June or beginning of July 1852.—207

— *Die materielle Kritik und der moralisierende Standpunkt.* In: *Turn-Zeitung,* Nr. 13, 1. Oktober 1852.—578
— (anon.) *Our American Correspondence. Washington, September 20, 1852; Washington, September 30, 1852.* In: *The People's Paper,* Nos. 23 and 24; October 9 and 16, 1852.—575
— (anon.) *Der Staat Wiskonsin.* In: *Die Reform,* Nr. 109, 15. Dezember 1853.—586
— (anon.) *White Mountains (Summit-House),* 21 August 1853. In: *Die Reform,* Nr. 44, 31. August 1853.—366

Cobden, R. [Speech at the meeting in Manchester on 24 January 1854.] In: *The Times,* No. 21647, January 25, 1854.—411
— [Speech in the House of Commons on 26 November 1852.] In: *The Times,* No. 21284, November 27, 1852.—253
— *1793 and 1853. In Three Letters.* London, 1853.—276

Cœurderoy, E. *De la révolution dans l'homme et dans la société.* Bruxelles, 1852.—135-36, 138

Cœurderoy, E., Vauthier, O. *La Barrière du Combat qui vient de se livrer entre les citoyens Mazzini, Ledru-Rollin, Louis Blanc, Étienne Cabet, Pierre Leroux, Martin Nadaud, Mallarmet, A. Bianchi (de Lille) et autres hercules du Nord.* Bruxelles, 1852.—135-36, 138

Coffinières, A.-S.-G. *De la Bourse et des spéculations sur les effets publics.* Paris, 1824.—556

Cooper, J. F. *The Spy.*—217, 301

Dante, A. *La Divina commedia.*—329

Decker, C. *Der kleine Krieg, im Geiste der neueren Kriegführung. Oder: Abhandlung über die Verwendung und den Gebrauch aller drei Waffen im kleinen Kriege.* Berlin und Posen, 1844.—535

De la conduite de la guerre d'Orient. Expédition de Crimée. Mémoire adressé au gouvernement de S. M. l'Empereur Napoléon III par un officier général. Bruxelles, février 1855.—526

Della Rocco. *Mazzini's Proclamation.* (To the Editor of *The Daily News.*) In: *The Daily News,* No. 2107, February 21, 1853.—280

Derby, E. [Speech in the House of Lords on 27 February 1852.] In: *The Times,* No. 21050, February 28, 1852.—56

Diderot, D. *Jacques le fataliste et son maître.* Tomes I-III.—134
— *Le Neveu de Rameau, dialogue.*—134

Dietz, O. *An die deutschen Arbeiter-Vereine.* In: *Schweizerische National-Zeitung,* Nr. 5, 7. Januar 1851.—14

Diezel, G. *Rußland, Deutschland und die östliche Frage.* Stuttgart, 1853.—505

Disraeli, B. [Address to His Constituents.] In: *The Times,* No. 21052, March 2, 1852.—61
— [Speech in the House of Commons on 18 February 1853.] In: *The Times,* No. 21356, February 19, 1853.—516
— [Speech in the House of Commons on 24 July.] In: *The Times,* No. 21802, July 25, 1854.—472

Donizetti, G. *Belisario.* Opera. Libretto by S. Cammarano.—199

Douglas, H. *A Treatise on Naval Gunnery.* London, 1820.—426

[Dronke, E.] *Der Besuch.* In: *Neue Oder-Zeitung,* Nr. 183, 20. April 1855 (Mittagblatt).—534

Dronke, E. *Naturgeschichte der Demokratie.* In: *Die Reform,* 12. April 1854.—451

Dulon, R. *Der Tag ist angebrochen!* Zweite Aufl. Bremen, 1852.—71

Dureau de La Malle, A. J. *Économie politique des Romains.* Tomes I-II. Paris, 1840.—228

[Eccarius, J. G.] *Our Paris correspondence.* In: *The People's Paper,* Nos. 21, 39, 40, 41, 44, 45, 49, 50 and 53; September 25, 1852; January 29, February 5 and 12, March 5 and 12, April 9 and 16, May 7, 1853.—397
— (anon.) *A Review of the Literature on the Coup d'État.* In: *The People's Paper,* Nos. 22, 23, 24, 25, 27, 28, 32 and 33; October 2, 9, 16 and 23; November 6 and 13; December 11, 18, 1852.—397

Die Edda.—328

[Engel, J. J.] *Fürstenspiegel.* Berlin, 1798.—307

Evans, G. de Lacy. [Evidence given before the Committee of Inquiry into the Condition of the British Army in the Crimea.] In: *The Times,* Nos. 21994 and 21995, March 6 and 7, 1855.—527

Ewerbeck, H. *L'Allemagne et les Allemands.* Paris, 1851.—45, 58, 87
— (anon.) *Bakunin.* [Report from Paris.] In: *Neue Rheinische Zeitung,* Nr. 36, 6. Juli 1848.—360, 362-63

Flügel, J. G., Sporschil, J. *Vollständiges Englisch-Deutsches und Deutsch-Englisches Wörterbuch.* Th. 1-2. Leipzig, 1830.—289

Forster, Ch. *The Historical Geography of Arabia; or, the patriarchal evidences of revealed religion.* In two volumes. London, 1844.—326
— *The One Primeval Language Traced Experimentally Through Ancient Inscriptions in Alphabetic Characters of Lost Powers from the Four Continents.* Vol. 1-3. London, 1852-1854.—527

Franceson, C. F. *Grammatik der spanischen Sprache nach einem neuen System bearbeitet.* Leipzig, 1822.—364, 386, 584

[Francis, Sir Philip.] *Letters.* In: *The Public Advertiser,* 1768-1772.—489

Freiligrath, F. *An Joseph Weydemeyer.* I. London, den 16. Januar 1852.—8, 16, 22, 35, 107, 118-19, 125, 160, 161, 241, 245, 571
— *An Joseph Weydemeyer.* II. London, 23. Januar 1852.—22, 35, 107, 118-19, 125, 160, 161, 241, 245
— *Trotz alledem!*—115, 129

Fröhlich, R. A. *Kurzgefaßte tabellarisch bearbeitete Anleitung zur schnellen Erlernung der vier slavischen Hauptsprachen.* Wien, 1847.—201, 204

Gibbon, E. *The History of the Decline and Fall of the Roman Empire.* London, 1776-1788.—326

Gladstone, W. E. [Speech in the House of Commons on 8 April 1853.] In: *The Times*, No. 21398, April 9, 1853.—518
— [Speech in the House of Commons on 28 July 1853.] In: *The Times*, No. 21493, July 29, 1853.—519
— [Speech in the House of Commons on 6 March 1854.] In: *The Times*, No. 21682, March 7, 1854.—518

Goethe, J. W. von. *Faust.*—262, 447
— *Reineke Fuchs.*—585

[Golovin, I.] *Europe.—A Single Man.* In: *The Morning Advertiser*, No. 19394, August 19, 1853.—359, 373
— *How to Write History.* (From a Foreign Correspondent.) In: *The Morning Advertiser*, No. 19407, September 3, 1853.—361, 362, 373
— *To the Editor of 'The Morning Advertiser'.* In: *The Morning Advertiser*, February 13, 1855: *February Revolution.*—523-24

Golovin, I., Herzen, A., Worcell, S. *The Russian Agent, Bakunin. To the Editor of 'The Morning Advertiser'.* In: *The Morning Advertiser*, No. 19398, August 24, 1853.—359, 373

Görgei, A. *Mein Leben und Wirken in Ungarn in den Jahren 1848 und 1849.* Bände I-II. Leipzig, 1852.—104, 128, 310, 460

Goldschmidt, M. [*Einige Skizzen aus seiner Reise nach England während der Zeit der großen Ausstellung.*] In: *Kölnische Zeitung*, Nr. 100, 25. April 1852.—95

Graham, J. G. *Sir Charles Napier and Sir James Graham. The Napier and Graham Controversy. Sir James Graham and Sir Charles Napier.* In: *The Times*, Nos. 22149, 22150, 22152 and 22154; September 3, 4, 6 and 8, 1855.—546

[Greeley, H.] *A German View of American 'Democracy'.* In: *New-York Daily Tribune*, No. 3505, July 13, 1852.—146

Greeley, H. *Isms.* In: *New-York Daily Tribune*, No. 3747, April 20, 1853.—346

Grey, H. G. [Speech in the House of Lords on 7 April 1854.] In: *The Times*, No. 21710, April 8, 1854.—519

Grimm, J. *Geschichte der deutschen Sprache.* Leipzig, 1848.—563

Grimm, J., Grimm, W. *Deutsches Wörterbuch.* Bd. 1. Leipzig, 1854.—563

Gülich, G. *Geschichtliche Darstellung des Handels, der Gewerbe und des Ackerbaus der bedeutendsten handeltreibenden Staaten unserer Zeit.* Bd. 3: Die gesammten gewerblichen Zustände in den bedeutendsten Ländern der Erde während der letzten zwölf Jahre. Jena, 1842.—82

Guerard, J. *Encyklopädie der Kriegskunst zu Lande.* Bd. 1-2. Wien, 1833.—159

Hammer, J. *Geschichte des Osmanischen Reiches, grossentheils aus bisher unbenützten Handschriften und Archiven.* Bd. I-X. Pest, 1827-1836.—423, 428

Handbibliothek für Offiziere, oder Populaire Kriegslehre für Eingeweihte und Laien. Bearbeitet und hrsg. von einer Gesellschaft preußischer Offiziere. 1. Band. Berlin, 1828.—160

[Harney, G. J.] [Marginal note to the English translation of the 'Manifesto of the Communist Party' by Marx and Engels.] In: *The Red Republican*, No. 21, November 9, 1850.—60

[Linton, W. J.] (Spartacus). *The Sense of the Country.* In: *The Star of Freedom,* No. 1, May 8, 1852.—107

Löhr, K. A. *Das Kriegswesen der Griechen und Römer.* Erster Bd. Zweite umgearbeitete und stark vermehrte Auflage. Würzburg, 1830.—160

[Löwe.] *An den Graf Nesselrole.* In: *Deutsche Londoner Zeitung,* Nr. 264, 266; 19. April, 3. Mai 1850.—370

Lütgen, A. *Feldzug der Schleswig-Holsteinischen Armee und Marine im Jahre 1850.* Kiel, 1852.—451

MacCulloch, J. R. *A Dictionary, Geographical, Statistical and Historical, of the Various Countries, Places and Principal Natural Objects in the World.* Vol. 1-2. London, 1841.—540

Machiavelli, N. *Mandragola* (Commedia).—125

Malmesbury, J. [Speech in the House of Lords on 31 March 1854.] In: *The Times,* No. 21704, April 1, 1854.—446

[Marx, F.] *The Russian Agent, Bakunin. To the Editor of 'The Morning Advertiser'.* In: *The Morning Advertiser,* No. 19397, August 23, 1853.—359, 363, 373

[Marx, Jenny.] *Der Volksbund für zerschiedene Welten in Poesie. Pfingstfest der Revolution.* In: *Philadelphier Demokrat,* December 1, 1852.—241

Massey, G. *The Engineers, Operative and Co-Operative.* In: *The Friend of the People,* No. 1, February 7, 1852.—30

Mayne Reid—see Reid, Thomas Mayne

Mazzini, J. *Italy, Austria, and the Pope. A Letter to Sir James Graham, Bart.* London, 1845.—101

Meiners, C. *Geschichte des weiblichen Geschlechts.* Theile I-IV. Hannover, 1788-1800.—207

Mieroslawski, L. *Kritische Darstellung des Feldzuges vom Jahre 1831 und hieraus abgeleitete Regeln für Nationalkriege.* Bd. 1. Berlin, 1847-1848.—138

Miller, J. M. *Siegwart. Eine Klostergeschichte.*—74

M[illerbache]r, A. J. [Hrsg.] *Das Kriegswesen der Römer größtentheils nach antiken Denkmalen.* Bd. 1. Prag, 1824.—160

Minutoli, J. *Spanien und seine fortschreitende Entwickelung mit besonderer Berücksichtigung des Jahres 1851.* Berlin, 1852.—540

Mirkhond, Mohammed. *Rauzât-us-safâ.*—341

Moltke, [H. K. B.] von. *Der russisch-türkische Feldzug in der europäischen Türkei 1828 und 1829.* Berlin, 1845.—435

Mozart, W. A. *Don Giovanni.* Opera in two acts. Libretto by Lorenzo da Ponte.—556

[Müller-]Tellering, F. *Vorgeschmack in die künftige deutsche Diktatur von Marx und Engels.* Cöln, 1850.—331, 336

Napier, Ch. [Military reports.] In: *The Times,* No. 21758, June 3, 1854: *The Baltic Fleet.*—458

— *Sir Charles Napier on the Bombardment of Sweaborg. To the Editor of 'The Times'.* In: *The Times*, No. 22141, August 24, 1855.—546
— *Sir Charles Napier and Sir James Graham. The Napier and Graham Controversy. Sir James Graham and Sir Charles Napier.* In: *The Times*, Nos. 22149, 22150, 22152 and 22154; September 3, 4, 6 and 8, 1855.—546

Napier, J. [Speech in the House of Commons on 22 November 1852.] In: *The Times*, No. 21280, November 23, 1852.—517

Napier, W. F. P. *History of the War in the Peninsula and in the South of France, from the Year 1807 to the Year 1814.* Vol. I-VI. London, 1828-1840.—490, 506

Napoleon III. [Speech in the Senate on 22 January 1853 on the occasion of his marriage to Eugénie de Montijo.] In: *Le Moniteur universel*, No. 23, 23 janvier 1853.—276

Newcastle, H. [Speech in the House of Lords on 1 February 1855.] In: *The Times*, No. 21967, February 2, 1855.—520

Ovid (Publius Ovidius Naso). *Tristia.*—199

Palmerston, H. J. [Speeches in the House of Commons]
— 1 June 1829. In: G. H. Francis. *Opinions and Policy of the Right Viscount Palmerston.* London, 1852.—432
— 20 August 1853. In: *The Times*, No. 21513, August 22, 1853.—518
— 6 February 1854. In: *The Times*, No. 21658, February 7, 1854.—519

Parish, H. H. *The Diplomatic History of the Monarchy of Greece, from the Year 1830, Showing the Transfer to Russia of the Mortgage Held by British Capitalists over Its Property and Revenues.* London, 1838.—455

Peel, R. [Speech in the House of Commons on 16 February 1830.] In: G. H. Francis. *Opinions and Policy of the Right Viscount Palmerston.* London, 1852.—432

Pélissier, A. [Report on the battle of the Chernaya. 18 August 1855.] In: *The Times*, No. 22146, August 30, 1855.—546

Petermann, A. [Hrsg.] *Mittheilungen aus Justus Perthes' geographischer Anstalt über wichtige neue Erforschungen auf dem Gesammtgebiete der Geographie.* Gotha, 1855.—535, 538

Pieper, W. *Die Arbeiter Assoziation in England.* In: *Die Reform*, Nr. 41, 42, 44; 20., 21., 31. August 1853.—13, 71
— *A Critical History of French Socialism.* In: *The People's Paper*, Nos. 31, 32 and 33, December 4, 11 and 18, 1852.—312
— *London, 31. Mai.* In: *Die Reform*, Nr. 22, 15. Juni 1853.—377

Plümicke, J. C. *Handbuch für die Königlich Preußischen Artillerie-Offiziere.* Berlin, 1820.—305

Pösche, Th. *Die 'Klassenkämpfer'.* In: *Neu-England-Zeitung*, 3. September 1853.—366, 369

Poesche, Th., Goepp, Ch. *The New Rome. The United States of the World.* New York, 1852.—366

Proudhon, P. J. *La révolution sociale démontrée par le coup d'état du 2 décembre.* Paris, 1852.—135, 166, 182, 207, 261

— *Système des contradictions économiques, ou Philosophie de la misère.* T. I-II. Paris, [1846].—261

[Pulszky, F.] [An article dated 7 September 1854 and signed A. P. C.] In: *New-York Daily Tribune,* No. 4190, September 22, 1854: *The State of Europe.*—485

Pulszky, F., Pulszky, Th. *White, Red, Black Sketches of Society in the United States During the Visit of Their Guest.* In three vols. London, 1853.—299

Pyat, F. *The Arrest of Sergeant Boichot, at Paris, by the French Government.* In: *The Morning Advertiser,* No. 19646, June 9, 1854.—462

Pyat, F., Caussidière, M. et Boichot, J. B. *Lettre au peuple français.* London, 1852.—170

Raffles, Th. S. *The History of Java.* In two vols. London, 1817.—348

[Reeve, E.] *To the Editor of 'The Morning Advertiser'.* In: *The Morning Advertiser,* December 6, 1855.—558

Reid, Thomas Mayne. *To the Editor of 'The Leader'.* In: *The Leader,* No. 152, February 19, 1853.—280
— *To the Editor of 'The Times'.* In: *The Leader,* No. 152, February 19, 1853.—280

Ricardo, D. *On the Principles of Political Economy, and Taxation.* 3 ed. London, 1821.—62

[Richards, A. B.] *The Base and Brutal Times.* In: *The People's Paper,* No. 51, April 23, 1853.—317

Richards, A. B. *Michel Bakounine and His Accuser. To the Editor of 'The Morning Advertiser'.* In: *The Morning Advertiser,* No. 19426, September 26, 1853.—373

Ripley, R. S. *The War with Mexico.* In 2 vols. New York, 1849.—498, 500-01, 503, 506

[Rouland, G.] *Discours de M. le Procureur Général. Le 3 novembre 1855.* In: *Journal des débats politiques et littéraires,* le 5 novembre 1855.—555

Ruge, A. *Michael Bakunin. To the Editor of 'The Morning Advertiser'.* In: *The Morning Advertiser,* No. 19404, August 31, 1853.—360, 373
— *The Public Law of Europe.* In: *New-York Daily Tribune,* No. 3506, July 14, 1852.—145

Russell, J. [Speeches in the House of Commons]
— 31 May 1853. In: *The Times,* No. 21443, June 1, 1853.—516
— 13 February 1854. In: *The Times,* No. 21664, February 14, 1854.—519
— 11 April 1854. In: *The Times,* No. 21713, April 12, 1854.—519
— 24 July 1854. In: *The Times,* No. 21802, July 25, 1854.—472

Sand, George. [Letter to the Editor of the *Neue Rheinische Zeitung.*] In: *Neue Rheinische Zeitung,* Nr. 64, 3. August 1848.—360, 362

Say, J. B. *Cours complet d'économie politique pratique.* Paris, 1840.—162

Schiller, F. von. *An die Freude.*—187
— *Die Bürgschaft.* Ballade. 154, 559
— *Der Gang nach dem Eisenhammer.*—452

— *Das Lied von der Glocke.*—420
— *Die Piccolomini.*—124

Schimmelpfennig, A. *The War between Turkey and Russia. A Military Sketch.* Philadelphia-London, 1854.—436, 439, 441, 443, 444

Ségur, J. A. de. *Les Femmes, leur condition et leur influence dans l'ordre social chez différents peuples anciens et modernes.* Tomes I-III. Paris-Hambourg, 1803.—208

[Seiler, S.] *Kaspar Hauser, der Thronerbe von Badens.* Zürich, 1840.—36

Seymour G. H. to Lord J. Russell. St. Petersburg, 11 January 1853. In: *The Times,* No. 21693, March 20, 1854.—519

Shakespeare, W. *Hamlet.*—21, 502
— *King Lear.*—162
— *Love's Labour's Lost.*—558
— *A Midsummer Night's Dream.*—391
— *Twelfth Night; or, What You Will.*—440

Simon, L. *Movements of the German Political Exiles.* In: *New-York Daily Tribune,* No. 3369, February 4, 1852.—39, 40, 42

Slick, J. B. *To the Editor of 'The Morning Herald'.* In: *The Morning Herald,* No. 22361, January 5, 1854.—406

Smitt, F. *Geschichte des polnischen Aufstandes und Krieges in den Jahren 1830 und 1831.* Theile I-III. Berlin, 1839-1848.—138, 311, 393

Solis, A. de. *Historia de la conquista de Mexico, poblacion y progressos de la America septentrional, conocida por el nombre de Nueva España.* Madrid, 1732.—501, 503

Spinoza, B. *Ethica ordine geometrico demonstrata et in quinque partes distincta.* Amsterdam, 1677.—144

Stenzel, G. A. *Versuch einer Geschichte der Kriegsverfassung Deutschlands vorzüglich im Mittelalter.* Berlin, 1820.—160

Stirner, M. *Der Einzige und sein Eigenthum.* Leipzig, 1845.—135
— *Geschichte der Reaction.* Berlin, 1852.—50, 55

Szemere, B. *Graf Ludwig Batthyány, Arthur Görgei, Ludwig Kossuth. Politische Characterskizzen aus dem Ungarischen Freiheitskriege.* Hamburg, 1853.—70, 77, 95, 101, 105, 131, 133, 134, 212, 237, 267, 302, 304

Szeredy, J. *Asiatic Chiefs.* London, 1855.—543

Tacitus (Publius Cornelius Tacitus). *Annales.*—180

[Tavernier.] *Deuxième mémoire adressé au gouvernement de S. M. l'Empereur Napoléon III sur l'expédition de Crimée et la conduite de la guerre d'Orient par un officier général.* Genève, mai 1855.—545

Tellering—see Müller-Tellering, E.

Terence (Publius Terentius Afer). *Heautontimorumenos.*—403

Thaly, S. *The Fortress of Komárom (Comorn), During the War of Independence in Hungary in 1848-1849.* London, 1852.—159

Thierry, A. *Essai sur l'histoire de la formation et des progrès du tiers état.* 2-éd. T. I-II. Paris, 1853.—473-76

Thiers, L. A. [Speech in the Legislative Assembly on 24 May 1850.] In: *Le Moniteur universel,* No. 145, 25 mai 1850.—171

Thomas, A. L. *Essai sur le caractère, les mœurs et l'esprit des femmes dans les différens siècles.* Paris-Lousanne, 1772.—208

Tucker's Political Fly-Sheets. Nos. I-XII. London, 1853-1854, 1855.—455, 472-73, 536

Unger, J. *Die Ehe in ihrer welthistorischen Entwicklung.* Wien, 1850.—208

Urquhart, D. *How is the War to Be Carried on? To the Editor of 'The Morning Advertiser'.* In: *The Morning Advertiser,* No. 19583, March 28, 1854.—422
— (anon.) *Indeed?* In: *The Morning Advertiser,* No. 19408, September 5, 1853.—364, 373
— *Progress of Russia in the West, North, and South.* 2nd ed. London, 1853.—430
— *The Relative Power of Russia and Great Britain. To the Editor of 'The Morning Advertiser'.* In: *The Morning Advertiser,* No. 19390, August 15, 1853.—357
— *Time in Diplomacy.—The 'European Recognition'. To the Editor of 'The Morning Advertiser'.* In: *The Morning Advertiser,* No. 19388, August 12, 1853.—357
— (anon.) *Turkey and Its Resources: Its Municipal Organization and Free Trade; the state and prospects of English commerce in the East, the new administration of Greece, its revenue and national possessions.* London, 1833.—284
— *War between England and France. To the Editor of 'The Morning Advertiser'.* In: *The Morning Advertiser,* No. 19391, August 16, 1853.—357
— *What Means 'Protection' of the Greek Church? To the Editor of 'The Morning Advertiser'.* In: *The Morning Advertiser,* No. 19387, August 11, 1853.—357
— *What the Governments of England and Turkey Ought Severally to Do. To the Editor of 'The Morning Advertiser'.* In: *The Morning Advertiser,* No. 19566, March 8, 1854.—417

Virgil. *Aeneid.*—394, 523, 555

Voltaire, F. M. A. *Candide.*—449

Vulpius, Ch. A. *Rinaldo Rinaldini.*—296

Wermuth/Stieber, W. *Die Communisten-Verschwörungen des neunzehnten Jahrhunderts.* Theile I-II. Berlin, 1853-1854.—580

Weydemeyer, J. [Article against Heinzen.] In: *New-Yorker Demokrat,* Nr. 311, 29. Januar 1852.—52, 59-60, 94, 207
— *Der 'demokratische' Mouchard.* In: *Belletristisches Journal und New-Yorker Criminal-Zeitung,* Nr. 7, 29. April 1853.—323, 324, 326, 583
— *Nationalökonomische Skizzen.* In: *Die Reform,* April-August 1853.—312, 318, 583
— *Die revolutionäre Agitation unter der Emigration.* In: *Turn-Zeitung,* Nr. 6, 7, 8; 1. März, 1. April, 1. Mai 1852.—93, 94
— *Weiters in der Willich-Hirsch'schen Angelegenheit.* In: *Belletristisches Journal und New-Yorker Criminal-Zeitung,* Nr. 10, 20. Mai 1853.—335

DOCUMENTS

— [Decree of 25 January 1852 on the resignation of the Minister of Finance Fould.] In: *Le Moniteur universel*, No. 26, 26 janvier 1852.—21

Code pénal, ou code des délits et des peines. Cologne, 1810.—134, 230

Correspondence Respecting the Rights and Privileges of the Latin and Greek Churches in Turkey. Presented to Both Houses of Parliament by Command of Her Majesty. London, 1854 [published in several parts].—422, 446, 519

Fifth Report from the Select Committee on the Affairs of the East India Company, 1812.—347

[House of Commons: Accounts and Papers.] Return of Stamps at 1d. issued to each newspaper published in London, Dublin and Edinburgh, Quarterly, 1851 to 1854.—438

The Manifesto of the Cologne Central Authority of the Communist League, December 1, 1850. In: *Dresdner Journal und Anzeiger*, No. 171, 22. Juni; *Kölnische Zeitung*, No. 150, 24. Juni 1851.—238, 251

Napoléon III. [Letter to Nicholas I of 29 January 1854.] In: *Le Moniteur universel*, No. 45, 14 février 1854; *The Times*, No. 21665, February 15, 1854.—414

Nicholas I. [Letter to Napoleon III of 28 January (9 February) 1854.] In: *Le Moniteur universel*, No. 64, 5 mars, 1854; *The Times*, No. 21681, March 6, 1854.—414
— *Manifesto of the Emperor of Russia [April 11 (23)].* In: *The Times*, No. 21732, May 4, 1854.—446

[Notice by the Russian Ministry of Finance. April 1854.] Коммерческая газета, Nos. 40, 41; 6, 8 апреля 1854 г.; *Journal de Saint-Pétersbourg*, No. 337, 8 (20) avril 1854.—446

Sammlung der für Ungarn erlassenen Allerhöchsten Manifeste und Proklamationen, dann der Kundmachungen der Oberbefehlshaber der kaiserlichen Armee in Ungarn. Buda, 1849-1850.—310, 460

Statuten des communistischen Bundes (1 Dezember 1850) (present edition, Vol. 10). In: *Dresdner Journal und Anzeiger*, Nr. 171, 22. Juni 1851.—66

Strafgesetzbuch für die Preußischen Staaten. Vom 14. April 1851. In: *Gesetz-Sammlung für die Königlichen Preußischen Staaten*, Jg. 1851, Nr. 10, Berlin, 1851.—134

[Tolstoi, Y.] *Bericht über die Kriegs-Operationen der Russischen Truppen gegen die Ungarischen Rebellen im Jahre 1849.* Th. 1-3. Berlin, 1851.—437, 439

Traité d'Unkiar-Iskelessi entre la Russie et la Porte Ottomanne, signé à Constantinople le 8 juillet 1833.—432

Victoria, R. *A Proclamation.* March 29, 1854. In: *The Times*, No. 21702, March 30, 1854.—446

ANONYMOUS ARTICLES AND REPORTS
PUBLISHED IN PERIODIC EDITIONS

Allgemeine Zeitung, Nr. 119, 28. April 1848 (Beilage): [Report from Paris of 22 April].—509
— Nr. 56. 25. Februar 1852 (Beilage): *Buchmacherei.*—50, 55
— Nr. 108, 17. April 1852: *Hansestädte. Hamburg, 13. April.*—95
— Nr. 195, 13. Juli 1852: *Der Communisten-Proceß.*—132
— Nr. 255-257, 11.-13. September 1852: *Baden. Die deutsche revolutionäre Propaganda in London und die Revolutionsanleihe.*—194, 196
— Nr. 9, 9. Januar 1855 (Beilage): *Die Assisenverhandlung gegen Barthélemy.*—510
— Nr. 9, 9. Januar 1855: *Ein Beitrag zur Charakteristik der Engländer.*—509
— Nr. 63, 4. März 1855: [*Der Russe Herzen.*]—527
— Nr. 130, 10. Mai 1855: *Großbritannien. London, 6 Mai.*—537

Baltimore Wecker, September 27, 1852: [A. Brüningk's Statement].—214, 574

The Daily News, No. 1790, February 17, 1852: *France. Paris, Sunday, Evening.*—36
— No. 1975, September 20, 1852: *Progress of Cotton Manufactures.*—189-90
— No. 2105, February 18, 1853: *M. M. Kossuth and Mazzini and 'The Times'.*—283, 290
— No. 2115, March 2, 1853: *A Letter from Mazzini.*—290
— No. 2117, March 4, 1853: *A Letter from Kossuth.*—283, 286, 290

The Economist, No. 437, January 10, 1852: *The Spirit of the Annual Trade Circulars. The Year That Is Past.*—57
— No. 491, January 22, 1853: *The Bank of England and the Rate of Discount.*—275
— No. 498, March 12, 1853: *Turkey and Its Value.*—294-95
— No. 528, October 8, 1853: *Foreign Correspondence.*—388
— No. 535, November 26, 1853: *The Labour Parliament.*—401

Frankfurter Oberpostamts-Zeitung, Nr. 338, 22. Dezember 1848: *Frankfurt, 21. Dec. Berichtigung.*—225

Journal de Saint-Pétersbourg, No. 336, 18 février (2 mars) 1854: [On the Eastern Question].—519
— 4ᵐᵉ Série, No. 351, 7 (19) mars 1854 (leader).—446

Journal des Débats politiques et littéraires, 25 août 1854: *Madrid, 20 août.*—479

Karlsruher Zeitung, Nr. 208, 209, 210, 212, 214, 217, 218, 219, 220, 224; 3., 4., 5., 8., 10., 14., 16., 17., 22. September 1852: *Die deutsche revolutionäre Propaganda in London und die Revolutionsanleihe.*—194, 196

Kölnische Zeitung, Nr. 74, 26. März 1852: **Paris, 24. März; ⁺Paris, 24. März.*—75
— Nr. 99, 24. April 1852: *Amtliche Bekanntmachungen.*—89
— Nr. 183, 27. Juli 1852: **Köln, 26. Juli.*—142
— Nr. 262, 14. Oktober 1852: *Assisen-Procedur gegen D. Herm. Becker und Genossen. Anklage wegen hochverräterischen Complottes.*—575
— Nr. 272, 24. Oktober 1852: *Assisen-Procedur gegen D. Herm. Becker und*

Genossen. Anklage wegen hochverrätherischen Complottes.—576-77
— Nr. 273, 25. Oktober 1852: *Erklärung.*—219
— Nr. 283, 4. November 1852: *Assisen-Procedur gegen D. Herm. Becker und Genossen. Anklage wegen hochverrätherischen Complottes.*—215, 240, 243
— 25. November 1854.—504
— 30. August 1855.—547

The Leader, Vol. IV, No. 152, February 19, 1853: *Kossuth and the Milan Revolt.*—280
— Vol. IV, No. 168, June 11, 1853: *Arnold Ruge.*—345
— Vol. IV, No. 168, June 11, 1853: *A Russian Democratic Printing Office in London.*—345
— Vol. V, No. 243, November 18, 1854: *The British Democrats—Louis Napoleon.*—503

Le Moniteur universel, No. 151, 31 mai 1854: [Report from Belgrade of 29 May 1854.]—458

The Morning Advertiser, No. 19122, October 6, 1852: *The German 'Lone Star'.*—207, 210
— No. 19142, October 29, 1852: *Germany. From our own correspondent. Cologne, Oct. 27.*—231
— No. 19603, April 20, 1854: *Mr Urquhart and 'The Globe'. To the Editor of 'The Morning Advertiser'.*—440
— No. 19615, May 4, 1854: *The Black Sea. The Bombardment of Odessa.*—452
— No. 19749, October 7, 1854: *The Incorporated Society of Licensed Victuallers.*—486
— January 29, 1855.—515
— September 1, 1855 (leader).—546
— November 29, 1855: *To the Editor of 'The Morning Advertiser'* [Letter signed 'One who had been deceived'.]—558
— December 6, 1855: *Mr Herzen's Case* [Letter signed 'Deceived'.]—558
— December 6, 1855: *An Editors' Statement.*—558

The Morning Chronicle, No. 26689, July 9, 1852 (leader).—129
— No. 26705, July 28, 1852: *The French Empire.*—*Secret Treaty of the Three Northern Powers.*—143
— No. 27321, July 21, 1854: *Prussia. (From our own correspondent).*—470
— No. 27365, September 7, 1854: *The Battles of Bayazid and Kuruk-Dere.*—482
— No. 27499, February 13, 1855: *Express from Paris.*—524

The Morning Post, No. 24681, January 28, 1853: *London, Friday, Jan. 28. 1853.*—276
— No. 24682, January 29, 1853: *The Peace and Arbitration Conference.*—276
— No. 24712, March 5, 1853: *Manchester Manufactures.—A Grave Fact.*—289

National-Zeitung, Nr. 248, 24. Dezember 1848: *Deutschland. Frankfurt, 21. Dezbr.*—225

Neue Preußische Zeitung, Nr. 148, 20. Dezember 1848: *Berliner Zuschauer.*—226
— Nr. 233, 7. Oktober 1852: *Assisen-Procedur in der Anklage über Hochverrath gegen Dr. Becker und Genossen.*—210

Neue Rheinische Zeitung. Organ der Demokratie, Nr. 64, 3. August 1848: *Französische Republik. Paris, 31. Juli.* [Editorial introductory remarks to George Sand's letter.]—360

— Nr. 115, 13. Oktober 1848: *Deutschland. Berlin, 10. Oktbr.* [Report on Bakunin's Expulsion, 10 October].—360
— Nr. 177, 24. Dezember 1848: *Dr. Stieber.*—225

New-York Daily Tribune, No. 3446, May 4, 1852: *Justice of Prussia.*—107, 115
— No. 3736, April 7, 1853 (leader).—315
— No. 3761, May 6, 1853: *The American Art-Union Investigation.*—331-32
— No. 3771, May 18, 1853: *Slavery and Emancipation; New Publications.*—346

The Observer, September 10, 1854: *The Battles of Bayazid and Kuruk-Dere* [reproduced from *The Morning Chronicle*].—482

La Patrie, No. 19, 19 janvier 1854: [Report from Constantinople of 2 January 1854].—411

The People's Paper, No. 14, August 7, 1852: *Secret Circular by Kossuth. Consequent Sudden Departure of the Latter.*—150
— No. 21, September 25, 1852: *Defeat of Faction.— Triumph of Principle.*—195
— No. 135, December 2, 1854: *Welcome and Protest Committee for the Reception of Barbès in London. Fraternisation of the French Democracy in London.*—502
— No. 145, February 10, 1855: *The Alliance of the Peoples. The International Committee.*—523
— No. 148, March 3, 1855: *Immense Demonstration in St. Martin's Hall.*—525, 527

Die Reform, Nr. 87, 19. November 1853: *Werbungen in New-York.*—402
— Nr. 88, 21. November 1853: *Das Wirken der 'Militär-Kommission'.*—402
— Nr. 91, 24. November 1853: [Report from Newark.]—404

Republik der Arbeiter, Nr. 52, 25. Dezember 1852: *Schlußbemerkung zum Kölner Kommunistenprozeß.*—275

The Times, No. 20955, November 10, 1851 (leader).—106
— No. 21003, January 5, 1852: *State of Trade. Manchester, Jan. 3.*—5
— No. 21052, March 2, 1852: *London, Tuesday, March 2, 1852.*—61
— No. 21094, April 20, 1852: *Commercial Intelligence. New York, April 7.*—82
— No. 21164, July 10, 1852 (leader).—129
— No. 21180, July 29, 1852: *Secret Treaty of the Three Northern Powers.*—143
— No. 21186, August 5, 1852: *The Approaching Election in the United States.*—146
— No. 21227, September 22, 1852: *Cotton Manufactures.*—189-90
— No. 21243, October 11, 1852: *Prussia. From our own correspondent.*—210, 224
— No. 21316, January 4, 1853 (leader).—516
— No. 21348, February 10, 1853: *In the Name of the Hungarian Nation.— To the Soldiers Quartered in Italy (February 1853).*—279, 280, 283, 290
— No. 21349, February 11, 1853 (leader).—516
— No. 21350, February 12, 1853 (leader).—282
— No. 21365, March 2, 1853 (leader).—285
— No. 21369, March 7, 1853 (leader).—285
— No. 21412, April 26, 1853: [Report from a Berlin correspondent of 22 April.]—319
— No. 21647, January 25, 1854: *Krajova, Lesser Wallachia. Jan. 11.*—410
— No. 21700, March 28, 1854: [Report on the cotton market in Manchester.]—422
— No. 21702, March 30, 1854: *France.*—446

INDEX OF PERIODICALS

The Sun—a liberal daily published in London from 1798 to 1876.—7, 25

The Sunday Times—a weekly published in London from 1822; a mouthpiece of the Whigs in the 1850s.—536

Tages-Chronik—a democratic newspaper published in Bremen from 1849 to 1851. It was edited by Rudolph Dulon; from January 1851 it appeared under the title *Bremer Tages-Chronik. Organ der Demokratie.*—173

Telegraph—see *The Daily Telegraph*

The Times—a daily founded in London in 1785 under the title *Daily Universal Register;* appears under the above title from 1 January 1788.—20, 25, 26, 30, 59, 61, 106, 129, 143, 146, 189, 210, 224, 253, 276, 277, 282, 285, 295, 317, 319, 329, 355, 373, 405, 409, 410, 418, 422, 433, 435, 438, 439, 441, 455, 458, 460, 472, 514, 516, 518, 519, 523, 525, 546, 547, 564

Tribune—see *New-York Daily Tribune*

Die Turn-Zeitung. Organ des socialistischen Turnerbundes—a newspaper of German democratic emigrants in the USA; it was published from 1851 to 1861 monthly and later fortnightly, first in New York and from 1 November 1853 in Philadelphia; Cluss and Weydemeyer were among its contributors.—94, 96, 100, 102, 107, 119, 578

Union—see *The Washington Union*

Das Volk—a German-language newspaper published by the petty-bourgeois democrat Karl Heinzen in the USA in the 1850s.—319

Volkshalle—see *Deutsche Volkshalle*

Der Wanderer—a constitutional monarchist daily published in Vienna from 1809 to 1866.—410

The Washington Union—a newspaper of the Democratic Party in the USA published from 1846 to 1858; Wilhelm Pieper contributed to it in 1853 and 1854.—394, 397, 421, 482, 490

Wecker—see *Baltimore Wecker*

The Weekly Press—see *The Press*

Wehr-Zeitung—see *Deutsche Wehr-Zeitung*

Westdeutsche Zeitung—a democratic newspaper published by Hermann Becker in Cologne from 25 May 1849 to 21 July 1850.—34, 570

The Westminster Review—a quarterly published in London from 1824 to 1914.—404

De Zuid-Afrikaan or *The Zuid Afrikaan*—a newspaper published in English and Dutch in Cape Town from 1830 to 1930; Karl Marx contributed to it in 1854.—405, 414

SUBJECT INDEX

GLOSSARY OF GEOGRAPHICAL NAMES[a]

Adrianople	Edirne	Komarom (Comorn).	Komárom and
Akkerman	Belgorod-		Kamarno
	Dnestrovsky		(two towns)
Argish	Argeş	Königsberg	Kaliningrad
Braila	Brăila	Kustendje	Constanţa
Breslau	Wrocław	Matchin	Maçin
Buseo	Buzău	Navarino	Pylos
Calugereni	Călugăreni	Nissa	Niš
Constantinople	Istanbul	Ofen	Buda
Erzerum	Erzurum	Oltenitza	Olteniţa
Fokshani	Fokşani	Rodosto	Tekirdag
Frateshti	Frăteşti	St. Petersburg	Leningrad
Galatz	Galaţi	Shumla	Shumen
Giurgevo	Giurgiu	Tiflis	Tbilisi
Hermannstadt	Sibiu	Tultsha	Tulcea
Isaktsha	Isaccea	Turna	Turnu-Măgurele
Kalarash	Călăraşi	Waitzen	Vác
Kimpina	Câmpina	Yenikale Str.	Straits
Kimpolung	Câmpulung		of Kerch

---

[a] This glossary includes geographical names occurring in Marx's and Engels' letters in the form customary in the press of the time but differing from the national names or from those given on modern maps. The left column gives geographical names as used in the original; the right column gives corresponding names as used on modern maps and in modern literature.